September 1740.

19.

20.

21.

From this day I grew worse, So that I was
let Blood, and the next day took a Purge
However all that would not do, So I Sent
For Dr monger who approvd what had
been done. He orderd me a mixture of
Juice of Oranges Salt of Wormwood and
Hordealed Cinnomon Water with Some Pre-
pard Pearl, which abated my Feaver, but
did no Service to my Cough, which was very
Severe anights, however with care and good
Nursing, it went away in about a Month,
and I recoverd enough to go to Williamsburg
the 21 of October following.

A Page from the Diary, contained in Notebook "A" in the Library of the University of North Carolina.

Another Secret Diary
of
William Byrd of Westover
1739 - 1741

With Letters & Literary Exercises
1696-1726

EDITED BY
MAUDE H. WOODFIN

TRANSLATED AND COLLATED BY
MARION TINLING

1942
THE DIETZ PRESS, INC. • RICHMOND, VIRGINIA

Printed in the United States of America

PREFACE

In the quest for manuscript material for a biography on the three William Byrds of colonial Virginia, an inquiry to Professor J. G. de Roulhac Hamilton of the University of North Carolina in September, 1936, brought from him the reply that the University owned "two note-books of William Byrd the second, written partly in code." On examination of these notebooks at Chapel Hill in March, 1937, it was clear that they included a diary of William Byrd of Westover, Virginia (1674-1744), in a contemporary shorthand, August 10, 1739, through August 30, 1741, and holograph manuscripts of unpublished letters and literary efforts by Byrd.

Attached to the notebooks was the following memorandum made in 1925 by the late George B. Logan, reference librarian of the University of North Carolina:

"The University library has recently come into possession, through purchase of the library of the late Stephen B. Weeks, of two slightly damaged note-books which we have some reason to believe were once the property of Colonel William Byrd of Westover. They contain transcripts of between ninety and a hundred letters written in England between the years 1717 and 1724 to various men and women in London society who are given fanciful names. The only person who can be clearly identified being the Duke of Argyle. In addition to the letters, the note-books contain several poems, a number of excellently done 'characters' in the fashion of the time, and other miscellaneous material.

"The writer of the letters cannot be positively identified with Colonel Byrd, but there are certain correspondences between them and the facts of Colonel Byrd's life as known through printed sources that seem to point to his authorship.

"The notebooks contain also what appears to be a diary written in short-hand, or perhaps cipher, covering most of the years 1739-41. It does not make use of any of the standard English systems of stenography published before that time.

"The two note-books which are supposed to contain copies of

William Byrd's letters we have designated A and B. A is six and three-eights by three and three-quarter inches in size, and about half an inch thick. Only a small fragment of the binding at the top, where it is hinged, remains; it is of dark brown leather, without markings. The paper is thick and of excellent quality and preservation. B is five and three-fourths by three and one-half inches, and about three-eights inch thick. Here too only a small piece of the binding remains at the top, light brown in color with several lines of tooling visible. The paper is thinner, more brittle, and a number of the papers are torn."

On examination the section in code in notebook A was clearly a diary or journal, since entries were made daily, and the entry following September 21, 1740 was written by Byrd in longhand after an illness of a month. This indicated the character of the other entries.

The manuscripts in longhand in these two notebooks constitute a body of hitherto unknown writings of Byrd. They cover the period 1696-1726 and give much new biographical information as well as evidence of a variety of literary efforts, chiefly during the period of his residence in London, for a quarter of a century, before he wrote the History of the Dividing Line, which has to the present, except for letters, been regarded as his first literary venture.

With photostats of several specimen pages from the 1739-1741 diary, various efforts were made by this editor to find the key to the symbols. Through the valuable coöperation of Dr. Elizabeth Smith Friedman, well known for her work in cryptography, these photostats were submitted to Mr. Edward J. Vogel of Chicago.

Mr. Vogel identified the symbols used by Byrd as a system of shorthand based on that published by William Mason in 1707, described as *La Plume Volante (The flying pen); or the art of shorthand improved; being the most swift, regular, and easy method of shorthand writing yet extant. Composed after 40 years practice and improvement of the said art, by the observation of other methods and the intense study of it.* This was the third book published by Mason, the two previous ones having been put out in 1672 and 1682, respectively.

Mr. Vogel agreed to transcribe the Byrd diary for 1739-1741 from the shorthand as soon as the necessary photostats could be secured from the University of North Carolina. Since the Byrd notebooks were in very brittle condition it was dangerous to handle them for photostating and there was some delay.

At this point of development Mr. Louis B. Wright of the Henry E. Huntington Library announced that a shorthand diary of William Byrd for February 6, 1709, through September 29, 1712, had been found in the Brock collection in that library and that the system of shorthand there used had been identified as that of William Mason by Mrs. Marion Tinling of the Huntington Library staff.[1]

Since Mr. Vogel could devote to the transcription of the diary only his leisure hours, aside from his regular duties as a court reporter, he gladly withdrew from the burden he had generously assumed of transcribing the 1739-1741 portion of the diary from the shorthand.

Through the coöperation of Mr. Wright and Professor Hamilton and by aid of a grant from the American Council of Learned Societies, it was possible to arrange for Mrs. Tinling to transcribe the 1739-1741 section of the diary. Professor Hamilton sent to California in the summer of 1939 the Byrd notebooks from the University of North Carolina library. They were repaired and photostated in the Huntington Library. From these photostats the transcription from the shorthand and the collation have been made by Mrs. Tinling.

Publication in the *Richmond News Leader* on March 10, 1939, of a photostat page from the 1739-1741 diary resulted in the announcement by the Virginia Historical Socie-

---

[1]This portion of the diary was published by the Dietz Press of Richmond in September, 1941. Citations to the 1709-1712 section of Byrd's diary are made in this volume from a manuscript copy helpfully provided by Mr. Wright and Mrs. Tinling before publication of the section they edited.

ty that they had discovered in their collection a notebook containing a section of Byrd's diary for December 13, 1717 through May 19, 1721, presented to the Society in 1876. Though the Virginia Historical Society has not yet made provision for the publication of the 1717-1721 portion of the diary, reference to it is made in this volume with the permission of that Society and through a grant-in-aid made to the editor in 1941 by the American Council of Learned Societies for its transcription. This section of the diary has been transcribed from the shorthand by Mrs. Tinling.[1]

Perhaps the first suggestion that William Byrd of Westover kept a diary in cipher is given in the novel *His Great Self* (Philadelphia, 1892), by Marion Harland (Mrs. Edward Payson Terhune, 1830-1922). As Mary Virginia Hawes, daughter of Samuel Pierce and Judith Anna (Smith) Hawes, Marion Harland spent her childhood in Amelia County, Virginia, and moved with her family to Richmond in 1844. She frequently visited at Westover when it was owned by Major Augustus H. Drewry and his wife, Mary Harrison Drewry (1844-1918). As a member of the Harrison family, daughter of William Mortimer Harrison, of Riverside, who was a direct descendant in the line of the several Benjamin Harrisons of Berkeley, kin to and intimately associated with the Byrds at Westover in the time of William Byrd I, II, and III, Mrs. Drewry had heard much of the family traditions passed down from generation to generation of Byrds and Harrisons at Westover, Berkeley, and Brandon, and other James River estates. That Marion Harland was indebted to her hosts at Westover is attested by her dedication of *His Great Self* "To my Friends, Major and Mrs. Drewry, of Westover, in affectionate memory of happy days spent under that ancient roof, and in acknowledgment of valuable assistance received from host and hostess in the collection of material for my chronicle, this volume is dedicated."

In describing the interests of William Byrd II, and his writing of the History of the Dividing Line and other

[1]References to diary entries falling within these dates, of course, refer to this transcription.

tracts, Marion Harland said, "These 'Tracts' were compiled from the diary he never failed to keep when absent from home. His minutes were sometimes jotted down in cipher upon the pommel of his saddle, sometimes pencilled by the glare of the watch fire while his comrades slept upon the bare ground about him, or scribbled in wayside-hostelry and in the finest private mansions Virginia could boast. Every scrap was jealously treasured." (*His Great Self*, p. 17). While this passage contains the degree of error inherent in family tradition, even when preserved by direct descendants on ancestral estates, it has, too, the core of truth often embedded in such traditions. Now it has been proved, by the discovery of the manuscripts of three portions of a shorthand diary, that Byrd kept a daily journal in cipher; but he kept it at Westover, as well as when he was away from home. Of the nine years covered by the known portions of his shorthand diary, some seven years were spent in Virginia at Westover. About fifty years elapsed between Marion Harland's statement that Byrd kept a diary in cipher and the discovery of the manuscripts of portions of that diary.

The diary for 1739-1741 fills more than half of notebook labeled A in the library of the University of North Carolina and follows the other manuscripts in that book which run in date from March 23, 1716/17 to May 26, 1724. The first page of the notebook has some miscellaneous memoranda, evidently jotted down by Byrd in the period during which he was making entries on its blank pages in his journal for 1739-1741.

Since the contents of notebook B are for the most part of an earlier date than those of notebook A, the manuscripts of notebook B are placed first in Part II in this volume.

The longhand manuscripts in the two notebooks of the University of North Carolina are published in this volume in the sequence in which they occur in those notebooks, except that the page of memoranda on the first page of notebook A and several fragments and badly mutilated pages are placed in Appendix I. There are several loose pages in notebook A and pages seem to be missing from the beginning of notebook B.[1]

I wish to acknowledge with appreciation the permission given by the University of North Carolina to publish the two manuscript notebooks of William Byrd; permission given by the Henry E. Huntington Library to publish A Female Creed; and permission given by the Virginia Historical Society to use for reference the Byrd diary for 1717-1726. Through the coöperation of the University of Pennsylvania in an inter-library loan I was able to secure the text of *Tunbrigalia* (London, 1719). Microfilms made for me by the College of Physicians of Philadelphia and the Army Medical Library of the War Department provided the text of the pamphlet *A Discourse concerning the Plague with some Preservatives against it* (London, 1721). I am indebted for helpful co-operation to Professor J. G. de Roulhac Hamilton, Mr. Louis B. Wright, Mr. Hunter D. Farish and the staff of the Department of Research and Record of Colonial Williamsburg, Inc., to Miss Lucy T. Throckmorton and staff of the University of Richmond library, to Mrs. Nancy Sydnor Haley and staff of the library of Randolph-Macon College for Men, to Mr. Earl G. Swem, librarian of William and Mary College, to Mr. Wilmer B. Hall and staff of the Virginia State Library, to Mr. Clayton Torrence and staff of the Virginia Historical Society, to my friend Miss Sallie Wills Holland, to my colleagues Professors Susan M. Lough, May L. Keller, Margaret Ross, Samuel W. Stevenson and Edward G. Peple, and to Mrs. Edna Lane and Mrs. Elizabeth H. Cotten of the staff of the Library of the University of North Carolina.

To the American Council of Learned Societies I am grateful for grants-in-aid in 1940 for the transcription of the 1739-1741 portion of the shorthand diary of William

[1]To complete the study of Byrd's literary efforts in the period before his final return to Virginia in 1726, revealed in these notebooks and in his diary for 1717-1721, extracts from *Tunbrigalia* (London, 1719) are published in Appendix II, *A Discourse Concerning the Plague with some Preservatives against it* (London, 1721) in Appendix III, and A Female Creed in Appendix IV.

Byrd of Westover and in 1941 for the transcription of the 1717-1721 portion.

Through a grant of funds made to the University of Richmond by the Rockefeller Foundation, a leave of absence was granted me for the academic year of 1941-1942 to complete the preparation of this volume for the press and to continue work on the biographical study of the three William Byrds of colonial Virginia and on an edition of their letters. For the opportunity thus afforded I wish to express my appreciation to the Rockefeller Foundation, to Dr. Douglas S. Freeman, president of the Board of Trustees of the University of Richmond, to Dr. Frederick W. Boatwright, president of the University, and to the Board of Trustees of that institution.

MAUDE HOWLETT WOODFIN.

Westhampton College,
University of Richmond,
March 16, 1942.

CONTENTS

PAGE

PREFACE iii

INTRODUCTION xiii

PART I. The Secret Diary of William Byrd of Westover, 1739-1741 1

PART II. Letters and Literary Exercises of William Byrd, 1696-1726 187

APPENDIXES

I. Miscellaneous Notes and Fragments from Notebooks 389

II. Selections from *Tunbrigalia* 397

III. *A Discourse Concerning the Plague* 411

IV. The Female Creed 445

INDEXES

Index to the Diary 477

General Index 485

INTRODUCTION

William Byrd as a diarist at sixty-five and as a man of letters and affairs from twenty-five to fifty will be revealed by the manuscripts here published from his two notebooks in the Library of the University of North Carolina.[1] The diary from August 10, 1739 through August 31, 1741 reflects the social, economic and political scene in Virginia when the colonial aristocracy was at its height, before the challenges offered to that regime by the revolutionary trends eventuating in 1776 were beginning to undermine its power. Little first-hand evidence, of a private character, for this particular span of years in Virginia has been available to the historian. He has been largely dependent on official records and documents for the story of the first half of the eighteenth century. To the student of the colonial history of Virginia this, as well as other known portions of the Byrd Diary, will be invaluable in the pageant it presents of the movement of life in the period 1700-1750, which has been the least-known period in the colonial story. Then the greatest power was held by the aristocracy that had been built on the triple foundation of land, tobacco and slaves. By 1740 that system was at its height and already there were manifest signs that it had in it some forces of its own disruption.

William Byrd, well on the way to his three score years and ten in 1739, was a fair specimen of the Virginia aristocrat, though he did not embody every characteristic and did have some highly distinctive individual traits not found in most Virginia aristocrats of his time. He was a man whose fortune and position had been made by several generations of forbears who had forced the New World to yield them profit from its virgin wealth. His father's kinsmen, Thomas Stegge, Sr. and Jr., had seen and exploited the opportunities for commerce from England with the settlers in the Chesapeake Bay area when the colony was very young and

[1] See Preface.

had made profit from that trade.[1] They had also seen the opportunities in the Indians' developing desires for European chattels and goods and had helped to push along the white man's penetration of the forests as they trekked inland for this Indian market for English wares paid for in the skins of beaver and otter and bear and other animals whose habitats on the inland streams of the upper reaches of Virginia are mutely suggested to the modern motorist as he speeds on the highway over Otter Creek or Wolf Creek or Beaver Creek or Bear Creek. As they traded they found vantage points for bartering and bought land at the falls of the James or on the Appomattox. With the increase in their holdings in the soil of Virginia their interest in its government grew. They served in its law-making body and in its local governing groups. When Thomas Stegge, Jr. died he left his heir, William Byrd, son of his sister Grace Stegge Byrd and John Byrd, goldsmith of London, land and commercial interests as well as social position in the democratic society of Virginia in the seventeenth century before the failure of Bacon's Rebellion.[2] He also left his young and promising nephew those political connections that meant prestige in a royal colony and steady income in an agricultural economy, since he had served as Auditor-General of the Colony of Virginia.[3]

When young William Byrd,[4] recently arrived from England, came into his inheritance from his uncle, with the solid practical judgment characteristic of his private and public

[1]For general sketches of the rôle of the Stegge-Byrd family in Colonial Virginia see *The Writings of "Colonel William Byrd of Westover in Virginia Esqr."*, ed. John Spencer Bassett, (New York, 1901), pp. ix-lxxxviii; *The Secret Diary of William Byrd of Westover, 1709-1712*, ed. by Louis B. Wright and Marion Tinling, Introduction; *Va. Mag.*, XXXV, 221-245, 371-376, XXXVII, 301-314.

[2]For will of Thomas Stegge, Sr., proved July 4, 1652, see *New England Historical and Genealogical Register*, XXXIX, 160-161. For will of Thomas Stegge, Jr., proved May 15, 1671, see *Ibid.*, XXXIX, pp. 161-162.

[3]*Va. Mag.*, VIII, 236.

[4]For the sake of clarity, references in this volume will be made to William Byrd I, 1653-1704; William Byrd II, 1674-1744; William Byrd III, 1728-1777. These dates are taken from the entries written in the Byrd Family Bible by William Byrd III, and owned in the family of the late W. Gordon Harrison. The year 1652 is given frequently as the year of the birth of William Byrd I and is based apparently on the statement on his tombstone that he died in 1704 after he had lived 52 years.

life, he married the gently born and well-bred daughter of Sir Warham Horsmanden. As the young widow of Samuel Filmer, third son of Sir Robert Filmer,[1] she had fled with her cavalier father from the social disorder of the Puritan revolution to a Virginia yet unshackled by social rigidities. Her effort to raise in a new country sons and daughters worthy of their heritage as the descendants of Sir Warham St. Leger, of Ulcomb, Kent,[2] was difficult. The Byrd home with its pack trains as the mule caravans came and went from the Indian trail southwest and negroes newly or at most recently come from African tribal life did not have the environmental influences Mary Horsmanden Byrd wanted for her children. First William and then his sisters were sent from the Byrd home at the falls of the James to their mother's kin in England, along with the hogsheads of tobacco and furs consigned to Micajah Perry in London, who handled the cargo with enough sagacity and honesty to enable William Byrd in Virginia to pay for the education in England of his several children there.

William Byrd I won not only profits but place and power in the colony's affairs. As Receiver-General and Auditor and member of the King's Council his influence steadily spread until with time he was President of the Council. His lands and his slaves, his Indian trade and cargoes of blacks brought from Africa for sale in an expanding labor market, with his official duties and political interests gave him power when he and his associates dared challenge the policies of the Governor whether he were Francis, Baron Howard of Effingham or Francis Nicholson.

Thus William Byrd the father established his inheritance and helped to mold the pattern of government in eighteenth-century Virginia where the twelve men of the Council were the determining influence in the policies of the royal governor and kept in check his personal plans for profit while they helped to evolve a system that fostered their aims and interests in land-holding, in labor questions and in the tobacco trade. When William Byrd the son came back to Vir-

---

[1]*Va. Mag.* XV, 181.

[2]Collins, *Peerage*, 4th ed., vol. 4, p. 504.

ginia in 1705 after his father's death to assume the estates and the position and to play the rôle of men of his class, as a young man of thirty, his tastes—after nearly twenty years' residence in England, and a stay of something like a year on the Continent—were those of a man of letters, and his habits those of the English gentleman of the time of Queen Anne. When Thackeray was seeking to interpret the English humorists of the eighteenth century to the England of the mid-nineteenth century he wrote: "We can't tell—you would not bear to be told the whole truth regarding those men and manners. You could no more suffer in a British drawing-room, under the reign of Queen Victoria, a fine gentleman or fine lady of Queen Anne's time, or hear what they heard and said, than you would receive an ancient Briton."[1] Though Thackeray spoke under the influence of his especially reserved mid-Victorian contemporaries he made clear his point that manners and customs in Queen Anne's time were different from those of Queen Victoria's day. In all that he wrote Byrd gave clear evidence of his youth spent in the England of the late seventeenth and early eighteenth centuries under the restored Stuarts and the early Hanoverians.

Byrd's special mentor and guide in England had been Sir Robert Southwell, for whom he never lost his deep respect and gratitude.[2] He lived at the Middle Temple from 1692 to 1695, when he was called to the bar. It was William Burnaby of the Temple who with "another hand" gave the English public his translation of the Satire of Petronius in 1694.[3] The theatres of London were entertaining an habitual theatrical audience with restoration dramas, that in their license were in a few years to draw from Queen Anne rather stern restrictions[4] suggestive of the Puritan strain that had not been evident in the reigns of

[1]William Makepeace Thackeray, *The English Humourists of the Eighteenth Century* (London, 1904), p. 67.

[2]See Byrd's Character of Southwell, below, p. 206.

[3]*The Satyr of Titus Petronius Arbiter, A Roman Knight, with its Fragments, recover'd at Belgrade, 1688*, made English by Mr. Burnaby of the Middle-Temple, and another Hand (London, 1694).

[4]Jay Barrett Botsford, *English Society in the Eighteenth Century as Influenced from Oversea* (New York, 1924), pp. 201-02.

Charles II and his luckless brother James nor of the monarchs William and Mary, brought to power by a glorious revolution and acquiescent in their subjects' ways so long as they left unthreatened their political status. As a Fellow in the Royal Society Byrd had heard gifted men, and men not so gifted, discuss the mathematics of Newton or the botanical and medical ideas of Sir Hans Sloane or the infinite minutiæ of animal structures and plant forms and many hitherto unexplored and as yet unfathomed mysteries of the world both far and near.

The manuscripts printed in this volume supply many new biographical facts in Byrd's life during the period 1700-1725, especially when read in the evidence afforded by his diary for 1717-1721. It is possible now definitely to state that all Byrd's letters written to people under imaginary names were written to real people. Just as he cloaked his companions in the survey of the Dividing Line under the suggestive names of Steaddy or Firebrand or Meanwell or Humdrum,[1] so he used the names Facetia or Fidelia or Sabina or Charmante for the women to whom he was writing love letters. In this he was following the fashion of his time.

Byrd's choice of names seems to have been dictated by some significant suggestion in the name chosen, though the peculiar appropriateness in some instances is not now apparent. In some cases there was an identity in personal characteristics with the name of the character in classical literature or English drama or poetry. In others there was satirical reference to the frailty or strength, to a vice or virtue of the person thus satirized. This element of humorous satire is the most common reason for his choice. One has only to recall the numerous such instances in the English literature of the late seventeenth and early eighteenth centuries to realize how fully Byrd was a man of his time in this matter.

These manuscripts, studied in their connection with the

---

[1] *William Byrd's Histories of the Dividing Line Betwixt Virginia and North Carolina*, with Introduction and Notes by William K. Boyd (Raleigh, 1929).

letters of Veramour to Facetia (fifteen copies of which were privately printed in 1913 by the late Thomas F. Ryan),[1] reveal the new and interesting story of Byrd's courtship of Lady Elizabeth Cromwell as Facetia in 1703. When the Ryan letters were published Facetia was not identified. But the fact that in the letter of September 11, [1703] Veramour called Facetia "Lady Betty", her connection with Ireland and the internal evidence of the letters of Byrd to Facetia and to Edward Southwell in this volume make it clear that Facetia was Lady Elizabeth Cromwell, the only daughter and heiress of Vere Essex (Cromwell), 4th Earl of Ardglass and Viscount Lecale [I], and Baron Cromwell. She was twenty-nine years old when, about October, 1703, she married Edward Southwell in spite of Byrd's persistent suit.

Lady Elizabeth Cromwell seems to have had something of her father's spirited temperament and was popular with a large circle of friends and kindred. She walked as a peeress, styling herself Baroness Cromwell after the death of her father in 1687, both at the funeral of Queen Mary II and at the coronation of Queen Anne, though it was later proved that the Barony was one in tail male and not one in fee, and hence not heritable by her.[2] She was vivacious and witty and Byrd, as others, found her entertaining and desirable. It had been rumored in London in 1697 that she was going to marry Mr. O'Neal,[3] and Thomas Wentworth, Lord Raby, later the Earl of Strafford, had paid her court.[4] She was a friend of the dramatist Congreve.[5] Facetia lived

---

[1]*William Byrd Esqr. Accounts as Solicitor General of the Colonies & Receiver Of The Tobacco Tax 1688-1704. Letters Writ To Facetia by Veramour &c.* Printed From The Ms. Copy. MCMXIII. While some of the persons mentioned by name are identified by notes by R. T. N., no identification of Facetia is suggested.

[2]For a full discussion of this point and other details see Cokayne, *Complete Peerage* (London, 1913), III, 557 (note *d*), and 559. For further details see below, p. 191, n. 1.

[3]Narcissus Luttrell, *A Brief Historical Relation of State Affairs* (Oxford, 6 vols., 1857), IV, 280, Sept. 28, 1697.

[4]*The Wentworth Papers, 1705-1739,* . . . with a memoir by James J. Cartwright (London, 1883), p. 70.

[5]Letters of Congreve to Joseph Keally, Esq., London, June 26, 1706, and Nov. 9, 1708, *The Complete Works of William Congreve*, ed. Montague Summers (Soho. The Nonesuch Press, MCMXXIII), I, 80, 86.

only a few years after her marriage, a victim to tuberculosis, or consumption, as then called, but she seems to have kept her wit to the end as attested by the letter of Peter Wentworth from London, January 11, 1709 to his brother Lord Raby, then at Berlin, ". . . . I have sent you a copy of the Dutchess of Ormond's letter to Lady Betty Southwell[1] who she thought a dying, and Lady Betty's answer which has been all the talk of the town for several visiting Days, and now there's about a hundred copy's of them, so that in a little time we may see them in print for they print everything."[2]

Lady Wentworth wrote her son on April 1, 1709, "Your old Mrs. is dead and left three lovely boys behynde and a dismall mallancolly husband: its Lady Betty Southwell whoe made a very good wife, and he a fond husband . . ."[3]

Byrd's letters to Facetia and to Edward Southwell show that he enjoyed in London at this period the social group that included the Earl of Orrery and the family of Sir Robert Southwell as well as the life of the theatre and the coffeehouses and the diversions of Bartholomew Fair and the season at Bath and at Tunbridge Wells, the two most popular English spas of this period. His verses On Some Ladys at Tunbridge in 1700[4] and several characters (included in this volume),[5] that seem to have been written about this time, indicate that he was trying his literary abilities at this period and giving evidence of the characteristics of all his writing, a certain sprightliness in a humorous, satirical vein.[6]

Byrd left this London scene and these social contacts behind him when he returned to Virginia on his father's death but again, in the rôle of Veramour he courted as Fidelia the

[1] *I. e.* Lady Elizabeth Cromwell, who as Betty Southwell, is not to be confused with her husband's sister, Betty Southwell.

[2] *The Wentworth Papers,* p. 70.

[3] *Ibid.* p. 70.

[4] See below, p. 248.

[5] See below, p. 206 and p. 208, characters of Sir Robert Southwell, Huband, and others.

[6] For a rather caustic picture of "a strange underworld of letters" in London at the close of the seventeenth century, see *Cambridge History of English Literature,* ed. A. A. Ward and A. R. Waller (New York, 1913), IX, 285.

beautiful Lucy Parke,[1] daughter of Colonel Daniel Parke of spectacular and notorious fame and tragic end.[2]

Veramour's letters to Fidelia are lyrical in tone and have much of the sprightly charm that have made Byrd's reputation as a writer on the basis of his History of the Dividing Line and other tracts.[3] When Lucy Parke married Byrd on May 4, 1706, the news created interest among his friends in England, who had known of his courtship of Lady Elizabeth Cromwell. Helena Le Grand, daughter of Sir Robert Southwell, wrote her cousin John Percival, later the Earl of Egmont, Byrd's friend from his school days in England until his death, in a letter dated London, 17 Jan. 1706/7, "I writ you in my last I think of Mr. Byrd's marriage in Virginia. They say his wife is as handsome as the Dutchess of Bolton,[4] so he may rest satisfy'd for his share."[5]

During most of the ten years of his marriage with Lucy Parke, Byrd lived at Westover, following the exacting life of the owner of several plantations with stores and mills and hundreds of servants and performing the official functions of members of his class as county lieutenant and member of the King's Council and his peculiar position as Receiver-General of Her Majesty's Revenue in Virginia. Daily he kept up his reading in Hebrew and Greek, with French and Latin now and then but with little attention to writing, as far as our evidence goes, except of letters and other matters connected with his business and political interests.[6] This period from 1706 to 1716 seems to have been,

---

[1]See below, pp. 214-20.

[2]For sketches of Daniel Parke, see *Va. Hist. Port.*, pp. 138-141; *Va. Mag.*, xx, 372-376.

[3]*The Westover manuscripts; containing the history of the dividing line betwixt Virginia and North Carolina; A journey to the land of Eden, A.D. 1733; and a progress to the mines, written from 1728 to 1736, and now first published* (Petersburg, 1841). *The Republican*, a newspaper published at Petersburg, Va., had printed in 1822 installments of Byrd's history of the running of the dividing line.

[4]Even the well-known bachelor, Dr. John Radcliffe (see below, p. 253, n. 2) paid court to the beauty of the Duchess of Bolton. (*The Wentworth Papers*, p. 97.)

[5]Egmont Manuscripts in the custody of S. C. Ratcliff, Historical Manuscripts Commission, in the Public Record Office.

[6]This period of Byrd's life is clearly revealed in his Diary, 1709-1712.

with the years just before his death, one of the two least active spans in his mature life as far as writing was concerned. His diary for 1709-1712 and for 1739-1741 help to explain this by showing how demanding were his interests, first in handling the inheritance after his father's death and then in later years in trying to wrest from a less profitable tobacco trade sufficient income to meet the obligations of the scale of living among the James River planters. By 1740 class consciousness had grown and Byrd heard with twinges of jealousy the nicety with which his friend, Secretary John Carter, entertained at his home, Shirley, a little up the river from Westover.[1]

When Alexander Spotswood began as Lieutenant-Governor to seek to make changes in the internal affairs of Virginia he aroused the ire and antagonism of the majority of the Council and especially of Byrd when he proposed changes in the method of collecting and accounting for the royal revenue in Virginia.[2] In 1714 Byrd received permission to leave Virginia the following year to attend to business matters in England incident to the settling of the estate of Daniel Parke, whose affairs were tangled and whose debts, assumed by Byrd in an agreement made with John Custis, gave him an irritating burden over a long period of time.[3] Though there was reality in this reason a stronger urge was Byrd's desire to try to get Spotswood out of the government of Virginia and, if possible, to succeed him himself.[4] Lucy Parke joined her husband in London in

---

[1]Entry for Jan. 8, 1740, Byrd Diary 1739-1741.

[2]This strife between Spotswood and his Council and the Burgesses can be followed in detail in the documents in C. O. 5/1318, in the published collection of Spotswood's letters, in the Letter Book of John Custis (MSS. Library of Congress) but the Byrd Diary of 1717-1721 sheds much new light on the whole matter. This, with the Custis Letter Book, proves that the episode was much more serious than it has been portrayed. For a general summary of the dispute see Leonidas Dodson, *Alexander Spotswood* (Philadelphia, 1932), and Bassett, pp. lv-lxxv.

[3]Byrd Diary, 1717-1721, and Custis Letter Book. For agreement between Byrd and John Custis, see manuscript in New York Historical Society, Custis MSS., and Byrd Title Book in Va. Hist. Soc.

[4]Byrd Diary, 1717-1721; Bassett, p. lxxiii.

the summer of 1716,[1] leaving behind in Virginia her baby daughter Wilhelmina, less than a year old.[2]

After a brief season of pleasure among her husband's friends and the gayeties of London, where she won admiration and attention, Lucy Parke Byrd died of smallpox on November 21, 1716.[3] But Byrd was not ready to go back to Virginia. Though he had settled the most pressing matters of the Parke estate he was still unwilling to return to Virginia at Spotswood's mercy. He sought the governorship of Maryland in vain, and tried several manœuvres apparently designed to oust Spotswood. He had finally to content himself with returning to Virginia to make peace with Spotswood, but with the assurance from friends at court that Spotswood would not be permitted to oust him from his seat and precedence in the Council. Many of the manuscripts included in this volume were written by Byrd during this period of residence in London from 1715-1720.

His older daughter Evelyn joined him in London in September, 1717[4] and in April, 1719 little Wilhelmina was brought over by his friend, Captain Isham Randolph.[5] Byrd had chambers in London off the Strand on or near Worcester Court and his daughters were cared for by people employed as suitable for that purpose, but they did not live with him. He visited them, and took concern for their health and their training, but did not tie himself down with parental responsibilities. He drove about London with a liveried coachman in his own coach and six.

The panorama of his life in London from 1717 to 1720 as disclosed in his diary shows that his two main pursuits were the quest for a wife of fortune and the resolution of his quarrel with Spotswood to his own political security and advancement, if possible.

---

[1]Letter of Micajah and Richard Perry to John Custis, London, Aug. 23, 1716 (MS., Va. Hist. Soc.).

[2]Wilhelmina Byrd was born Nov. 6, 1715.

[3]In the Ludwell papers, Va. Hist. Soc., is a letter of Philip Ludwell, the elder, in England to his son Philip in Virginia, dated May 7, 1714, with this strangely interesting postscript: "If Will Byrd comes to England advise him not to bring his wife people dye strangely of ye small pox."

[4]Bassett, p. lxxvii.

[5]Byrd Diary, Apr. 17, 29, 1719.

His daily regime of early rising, reading of Hebrew and Greek, saying his prayers and spending the morning in drawing lessons with the teacher Eleazar Albin,[1] or in conferences incident to his political affairs, was varied with visits to a wide coterie of friends, especially in the Southwell family connection, with business conferences with the now aging Micajah Perry in Leadenhall Street and with his son Richard and grandsons, Micajah and Philip Perry, and the drinking of tea with the motherly Mrs. Perry.[2] He went to Court often. On May 28, 1718, in his finest clothes he was among those at Kensington in celebration of the King's birthday.[3] On November 19, 1718 he kissed the hand of King George I when he was presented to His Majesty as Agent for Virginia.[3] He talked with the magnetic Henrietta Howard, Countess of Suffolk, lady in waiting to Caroline of Anspach, Princess of Wales and mistress of George, Prince of Wales.[4] He met the maids of the court, Mary Lepel and Margaret Bellenden, whose beauty and charm have been celebrated in the verses of Pope and Gay, Voltaire and Chesterfield.[5]

He went to Will's coffeehouse almost daily and to Ozinda's or to Garraway's frequently. He walked with the fashionable crowd in St. James's Park and joined Horace Walpole the elder for an occasional stroll. He went to services at St. Clement's, or St. James's Chapel or Somerset Chapel, where, he often confessed, he took a nap during the sermon. He took outings on the Thames and visited his friends at their country places, Lord Orrery near Windsor and the Duke of Argyle at Petersham and his Horsmanden kin at Purleigh in Essex. He went to assemblies at the Spanish Ambassador's, or at Petkum's, the Resident of the Duke of Holstein. He often went to the plays at both theatres, Drury Lane and Lincoln's Inn, and was in the

[1]Albin was a well-known teacher of water color drawing in London, and author of illustrated works on natural history (*Dict. Nat. Biog.*).

[2]Byrd Diary, 1717-1721.

[3]*Ibid.*

[4]See *Letters to and from Henrietta, Countess of Suffolk, and her Second Husband, the Hon. George Berkeley, from 1712 to 1767* (London, 1824).

[5]See *Letters of Mary Lepel, Lady Hervey, with A Memoir and Illustrative Notes* (London, 1821).

audience on the opening night of Tom Killigrew's play *Chit-Chat*[1] with Wilks, Booth, Cibber, Mrs. Porter and Mrs. Oldfield in the leading rôles.[2] He saw the French people act before the King and enjoyed them.[3] He saw the dramatist Congreve at his friend Mrs. Fitz Herbert's[4] and met the King's Hanoverian friend, Madame Kielmansegge and her daughter.[5] He went to concerts given by Anastasia Robinson, the popular prima donna who later married the Earl of Peterborough.[6] He played faro or commerce, basset or piquet, and billiards and bowls, and took his winning or losing of a guinea or more with cheerful acquiescence in his luck but it was a rare occasion when he lost as much as five or ten guineas or perhaps twenty at hazard. He was at court when the King played at dice. He took tickets in the lotteries and went to the masquerades as a running footman, or as a grand mogul or in an indiscriminate domino. Or he acted proverbs or danced as the occasion seemed to warrant. For more serious diversion he went to the meetings of the Royal Society in Crane Court and to their dinners at the famous French tavern, Pontack's. The companions in his pleasures were often the Earl of Orrery or Sir Wilfred Lawson or his young cousin Daniel Horsmanden who was later to come to New York, to become, finally, chief justice of that province.[7] Often in this round of social diversions he visited one of several mistresses kept in succession, or picked up a whore on the London streets or in the parks and carried her to a tavern or bagnio or found a woman to his taste at Mrs. Smith's in Queen's Street.[8]

About a year after Lucy Parke's death, Byrd was eager

---

[1]Diary, Feb. 14, 1719.

[2]John Genést, *Some Account of the English Stage* (Bath, 1832), II, 641-42.

[3]Diary, Nov. 26, 1718. Allardyce Nicoll, *A History of Early Eighteenth Century Drama, 1700-1750* (Cambridge, 1925), p. 5.

[4]Diary, Apr. 24, 1719.

[5]Diary, Mar. 28, 1719; Lewis Melville, *Lady Suffolk and her Circle* (Boston, 1924), pp. 7-8.

[6]*The Autobiography and Correspondence of Mrs. Delaney,* Revised from Lady Llanover's Edition and Edited by Sarah Chauncey Woolsey, 2 vols. (Boston, 1879), I, 42-5.

[7]*Dictionary of American Biography.*

[8]Byrd's Diary 1717-1721 is frank in its numerous entries on this aspect of his life.

to marry a rich London heiress. The story of his courtship of Sabina, Mary Smith, daughter of John Smith, Commissioner of the Excise, who lived in Beaufort Buildings, can be followed by his letters to Sabina printed in this volume, supplemented by the information given in his diary for the period of the courtship.[1]

The clandestine correspondence, the use of invisible ink, the subterfuges devised, the connivance and intrigues of Sabina's sister and brother-in-law, Lord and Lady Dunkellen, the meeting of the rival suitors, the intimations of a challenge to a duel—all make the drama true to its eighteenth-century pattern as the middle-aged colonial widower lost the desirable London heiress to his acceptable rival, the son of a rich English knight who had gained his fortune in the luxury trade with the Levant. Byrd used every argument he could muster to induce Sabina's father to consent to her marriage to him. He promised he would live in England, he argued that as the owner of about 43,000 acres in Virginia and 220 slaves and a prodigious "quantity of stock of every kind" with an annual income of £1,500 to £1,800 he was amply able to take care of her.[2] He finally tried to borrow £10,000 from Micajah Perry to settle on her, but the canny old merchant refused to lend more money to Byrd, already in his debt for money he had borrowed to pay off Daniel Parke's creditors. But it was all to no avail. Byrd's chagrin and disappointment were so great at first that he showed no generosity and considerable vindictiveness, seeking to expose Sabina's duplicity, as he saw it, to his favored rival, Sir Edward Des Bouverie. His failure to win Sabina was one of the keen disappointments of his life, but in a few months he had recovered and accepted the situation with characteristically cheerful acquiescence in his fate.

Within the year he was paying court to the widow Pierson whom he had frequently seen at the Spanish Ambassador's and who lived in fashionable Dover Street, near St. James's

[1]See below, p. 298 ff., and p. 298, n. 2. The identification of Sabina as Mary Smith and of her family was made by Mrs. Tinling as she collated the manuscripts in the North Carolina notebooks and transcribed from the shorthand the Diary for 1717-1721.

[2]Byrd's letter to Vigilante, below, p. 321.

Palace.[1] Through the early months of 1719 he visited her several times a week at her home, saw her at court where he paid her compliments and at the plays where he promenaded with her between acts. He asked her to marry him but she refused, giving as her reason that his children were an obstacle.[2] He tried to make her jealous by his attentions to Henrietta Howard,[3] proposed to her again,[4] and was refused again. When she had refused him a third time,[5] he gave up the pursuit and sought diversions at Tunbridge Wells, though even there he called on her.[6] There he threw himself with full zest into the gayeties of that diverting resort and found healing for his wounded pride and disappointment, as he had done in the summer of 1718 after Sabina had married his rival.

In this period, 1717-1719, Byrd frequently noted in his diary that he wrote something. Repeatedly he referred to the book he was writing in 1718 and reading to his friends.[7]

At Tunbridge Wells in August 1718 he indulged in one of the favorite sports of the place and wrote lampoons and verses.[8] During the season of 1719 when he spent much of

---

[1]This courtship is narrated in detail by Byrd in his Diary for 1717-1721 in entries from June 22, 1718 through July 26, 1719.

[2]Diary, Apr. 12, 1719.

[3]Diary, May 8, 1719.

[4]Diary, May 22, 1719.

[5]Diary, July 7, 1719.

[6]Diary, July 26, 1719.

See after, pp. 259-66 for letters to Zenobia, presumably Mrs. Pierson. Evidently Byrd's courtship of Mrs. Pierson was a topic in the gossip at Tunbridge Wells that summer. In *Tunbrigalia* [London, 1719], which includes verses on a number of ladies written by William Byrd under the pseudonym, "Mr. Burrard" (see note below and Appendix II), are some verses *"By Mr.* Say, *Occasioned by some vile Copies reflecting on the Ladies at* Tunbridge-Wells." These verses take up in turn the charms of the ladies complimented by "Mr. Burrard" in his acknowledged verses in the same volume. Mr. Say's verses include these lines in the concluding stanza:

> "In vain who writes in Satyrs keen
> On *Pierson* vents his cancred Spleen,
> And Fox-like swears the grapes are sour,
> Which out of reach he can't devour."

These lines, read in connection with Byrd's letter to Lady G—— (below, p. 259) and his letters to Zenobia, suggest that he was accused of being the author of the lampoon answered by Mr. Say in his verses.

[7]Diary, June 18, 1718. No suggestion as to the subject of this book is given in his diary, 1717-1721.

[8]Diary, Aug. 16, 17, 1718.

the summer there, he frequently mentioned in his diary that he wrote verses (specifically, on August 24, that he wrote verses on four ladies), or verses to ridicule Mrs. B-r-k-s-t's panegyricks, or songs on his friends or for his friends.[1] Some of these verses were printed in *Tunbrigalia: Or Tunbridge Miscellanies, For the Year 1719* (London, 1719) as the work of "Mr. Burrard."[2] They were in complimentary strain on the Duchess of Montague, Lady Hinchinbrook, Lady Percival, Lady Ranelagh, Lady Isabella Scott, Lady Charlotte Scott, Lady Charles Buck and her sister, Miss Cornish, Mrs. Lethullier and Mrs. P—ll (Polhill).

During his stay in Virginia in 1720-1721, alone at Westover, except for his kindred, young John Brayne and Susan Brayne,[3] and "his people," the servants,[4] Byrd continually noted in his diary that he wrote, using here as in the other sections of his journal the laconic phrase that he wrote some English. During this period of solitude at Westover, though few days passed when he did not pay visits, most often to

---

[1]Diary, entries from July 19 through Sept. 7, 1719.

[2]Copies of *Tunbrigalia* are in Harvard College Library and the University of Pennsylvania Library. See Appendix II for Byrd's verses. A number of other verses in this issue of *Tunbrigalia* seem, on the basis of internal evidence, to have come from the pen of William Byrd, but only those on pages 1-11 are definitely attributed to "Mr. Burrard". With the entries in his diary for July 16 through July 27 and August 1 through September 7, 1719, Byrd's daily diversions at Tunbridge can be followed, with evidence to prove that he was "Mr. Burrard" and to support the view that he wrote a number of other verses in the book.

[3]John Brayne (or Braine) was Byrd's nephew whom he had sent over to Virginia from London to become acquainted with his affairs and to learn "all the nicety of planting" (Byrd to John Custis, Oct. 19, 1717, MS., N. Y. Public Library). He was bookkeeper for Byrd in 1719 (Henrico Minute Book, 1719-25, p. 279). He was at Westover on Byrd's return in 1720. Byrd was dissatisfied with his management and habits, and finally offered to pay his passage to England. Though he refused the offer he left Westover (Diary entries from Feb. 14 through June 18, 1720, John Brayne was the son of Byrd's sister Susan who had married John Brayne in England and died there in 1710. William and Susan Brayne, other children of Byrd's sister, arrived at Westover in June, 1710 (Diary, 1709-1712). Susan (Suky) Brayne, when sent away from the home of her uncle, Robert Beverley, returned on March 19, 1721, to Westover where she had lived on her arrival in Virginia. Byrd expressed sorrow at the news on April 18, 1721, of Billy Brayne's death (Diary, 1717-1721).

[4]Byrd brought with him from England several white servants, including Hannah and Annie. Hannah held a responsible post in the domestic regime at Westover. Annie especially found favor in her master's eyes but refused to become his mistress. (Diary, entries from Dec. 10, 1719 through May 18, 1721.)

Lucy Parke's cousin, Elizabeth Burwell Harrison, widow of his friend Benjamin Harrison, on the adjoining plantation of Berkeley, or entertain visitors at Westover, he wrote *A Discourse Concerning the Plague, with Some Preservatives against it,* under the pseudonym "A Lover of Mankind." This work, or his book on the plague, as Byrd referred to it in his diary, was printed in London in 1721 in a forty-page pamphlet or brochure.[1] This is the only work of William Byrd II printed during his life that has been discovered as yet except for his verses included in *Tunbrigalia.*[2] This pamphlet was printed for J. Roberts near the Oxford-Arms in Warwick-Lane. The title page carries this

[1]Reprinted below as Appendix III.

[2]Appendix II. Byrd's brief paper "An Account of a negro Boy that is dappel'd in several Places of his Body with White Spots", was published in *Philosophical Transactions* (London, 1698), XIX, 781. Byrd read this paper on the peculiar case of the negro boy, who had been brought to London from Virginia by Sir Charles Wager, before the Royal Society on November 17, 1697. (Journal of the Royal Society, Nov. 17, 1697.)

When Byrd was preparing to leave England in 1719 he presented to the Duke of Argyle and to his brother Lord Islay, copies of a description of Virginia. (Diary, Nov. 20, 1719.) Just what Byrd referred to is not clear. When John Oldmixon revised *The British Empire in America* (London, 1741), he said in the preface that he was indebted to an account of Virginia "written with a great deal of Spirit and Judgment by a Gentleman of the Province. . . This refers to the History of Virginia which was written by *Col. Bird,* whom the Author knew when he was of the *Temple,* and the Performance answered the just Opinion he had of that Gentleman's Ability and Exactness" (i, x-xi). No mention of indebtedness to Byrd was made in the original edition of Oldmixon's work (London, 1708).

It is a possibility that the description of Virginia Byrd gave his noble friends and the one Oldmixon used were the same and that it was this description written by Byrd that Jenner used as the basis of information for his so-called translation "Eine Kurtze Beschreibung von Virginia." Jenner said he received this true report from the president of the colony and translated it as well as he could from English into German. (*William Byrd's Natural History of Virginia or The Newly Discovered Eden*, edited and translated from a German version by Richmond Croom Beatty and William J. Mulloy [Richmond, 1940], pp. xxiv-xxviii. The fact that Byrd's description of Virginia used by Jenner in *Neu-Gefundenes Eden* makes no mention particularly of the Roanoke River lands, to promote the settlement of which the volume was published in Switzerland in 1737, seems to argue that Byrd's description was written before he surveyed the boundary line between Virginia and North Carolina in 1728. Byrd was so enthusiastic about the Roanoke River lands that he acquired 20,000 acres there and in 1733 wrote *A Journey to the Land of Eden* (Bassett, pp. 281-329). Byrd was keenly concerned about enticing Swiss to settle his Roanoke land. It seems hardly credible that he would have written any description of Virginia after the acquisition of those lands that did not emphasize their desirability.

In his diary for 1717-1721 he repeatedly made reference in 1718 to the book he was writing. Was this the description of Virginia presented to the

motto from Virgil, "Dii talem Terris avertite Pestem." On the title page is a decorative figure of a squirrel nibbling a nut and the end piece shows a North American Indian dancing with tobacco leaves as decoration instead of the usual feathers, both motifs suggesting the Virginia origin of the work.[1]

When Byrd received at Westover a letter from England on February 14, 1721 telling him that the plague had appeared there his thoughts were turned to that subject. He knew well from his personal contacts the dread in England of a return of the plague after their bitter woe in 1665 when it had taken a toll of 100,000 lives. The death of his wife Lucy Parke in London from smallpox in 1716 and his anxiety for his two young daughters, Evelyn and Wilhelmina,[2] whom he had left there on his return to Virginia, gave him special dread of smallpox, the reigning disease, as Lady Wentworth called it.

Byrd wrote his work on the plague between February 14 and March 22, 1721.[3] He read the finished manuscript to

---

Duke of Argyle and Lord Islay, referred to by Oldmixon and used by Jenner in *Neu-Gefundenes Eden*? If so, was it printed in London? Or did Oldmixon see a copy of Jenner's *Neu-Gefundenes Eden*?

[1]Three copies of this pamphlet have been located in the United States. One is in the Library of the College of Physicians in Philadelphia and two in the Army Medical Library of the War Department in Washington. Neither the British Museum nor the Bodleian Library has a copy, according to letters from those institutions in February, 1942. The pamphlet has a page measurement of 4¾" (width) x 7⅝" and was to sell for a shilling.

Byrd does not in his diary give the title under which his work was printed. He merely referred to it as his book on the plague. Nor did he give a suggestion of the pseudonym used, "A Lover of Mankind". The clue that led to the discovery of Byrd's work in printed form came from a statement in John Nichols, *Literary Anecdotes of the Eighteenth Century; comprizing Biographical Memoirs of William Bowyer, F. S. A. and Many of his Learned Friends* . . . . (6 vols., London, 1812), I, 205, that William Bowyer had advertised in 1721 as actually in the press "A Discourse concerning the Plague, with some Preservatives against it; by a Lover of Mankind."

This statement, with the references by Byrd in his diary in 1721 to writing a book on the plague and sending it to Mr. Perry in London, as well as internal evidence in the pamphlet itself, make clear the identification of the work as William Byrd's.

Apparently Bowyer printed the work for sale by J. Roberts. No issue bearing the Bowyer imprint has been located.

[2]Byrd had been particularly alarmed when his daughter Evelyn was thought mistakenly to have smallpox. (Diary, Jan. 5, 8, 9, 1719.) The younger daughter Wilhelmina did have the smallpox in London in 1719 but in a mild form. (July 14, 15, 30, 1719.)

[3]Diary, Feb. 14, 20, 24, Mar. 16, 22, 1721.

his neighbor at Berkeley, Elizabeth Burwell Harrison, and to Colonel Nathaniel Harrison and to the young Huguenot minister Peter Fontaine, when he spent Saturday night at Westover before the Sabbath morning service in the adjacent old Westover church.[1]

He gave the manuscript to a ship captain who came to Westover on April 4 to deliver to his agent and friend Micajah Perry in London. Mr. Perry apparently performed the rôle of literary agent for Byrd with the same success with which he had handled many other affairs for him, for there is no further reference in the diary to the book on the plague. The printed pamphlet with the London imprint of 1721 is mute evidence of Mr. Perry's fidelity to his trust.

In *A Discourse Concerning the Plague with some Preservatives against it*, Byrd traced the history of plagues and pestilences as revelations of the will of God in the affairs of men, citing the Bible to prove his points. He traced the history of plagues as given in classical writers and examined the theories offered for their origin and the practices proposed for their prevention by ancient and modern historians, philosophers and scientists. He gave references to his authorities in footnotes and displayed his wide range of reading and his interest in the history of ideas about health and medicine. Byrd's association with Sir Hans Sloane, Sir Samuel Garth and other medical men of literary interests in London in the meetings of the Royal Society and in the coffeehouses had helped to stimulate his keen interest in health and medicine, apparent in almost every entry in his diary.

But the main thesis in Byrd's discussion of the plague and ways to prevent it was the argument that tobacco used in various forms and in large quantities was the best way to escape the dreaded malady. He argued that since 1665 when Virginia tobacco had been brought into England in ever increasing quantities there had been no recurrence of the horror of that plague year. The consumption of more

[1]Diary, Mar. 22, 26, and Apr. 8, 1721.

and more Virginia tobacco was to be man's salvation from the deadly scourge.

Throughout the pamphlet Byrd maintained the rôle of an Englishman. As the author, however, he betrayed a knowledge of the southern colonies, and Virginia, especially, and of tobacco that was not common in his generation of Englishmen. In the pamphlet Byrd combined two of his major concerns and vital interests, his constant preoccupation with health and medical matters and his continual effort to find a more lucrative market for his tobacco. Byrd knew by his own diminishing returns from his plantations the danger in the continued production of increasing quantities of tobacco and the dependence of an agricultural people on that one crop as a source of revenue. His experiments with hemp and vineyards were signs of his lack of faith in the single crop of tobacco to maintain prosperity in Virginia.

His pamphlet *A Discourse Concerning the Plague* was an excellent promotion device for the increase of sales of Virginia tobacco, for, whatever one may conclude as to the scientific validity of his theories, the reappearance of the plague in Marseilles in 1720 had brought something like a panic of fear in England. Byrd's pamphlet was just one of a surprisingly large number on the plague printed in London and in Dublin in 1721.[1]

On Byrd's arrival in Virginia in February, 1720, he avoided meeting Spotswood until he had received the desired order in council that would make secure his place in the Council of Virginia in spite of the Lieutenant Governor's attitude. But he held conference with his brother-in-law John Custis in Williamsburg and met there the leading men in his faction in the Council. At Green Spring, the home of his kinsman Philip Ludwell, his most redoubtable ally in his struggle against Spotswood, with the exception of Commissary Blair, he and his friends mapped out their strategy in the struggle for control against Spotswood in the light of his report of his experiences in London.

[1]See list in *Bibliotheca Britannica*, ed. by Robert Watt (Edinburgh, 1824), vol. 3, *sub* Plague. A number of these pamphlets are in the collections of the Army Medical Library of the War Department and the Library of the College of Physicians of Philadelphia.

Byrd did not see Spotswood until he had received on April 24 a letter from his friend Edward Southwell enclosing an order of council for his restoration to his place in the King's Council in Virginia.[1] On April 25 he went with some of his friends to the capitol and presented the order of council to Spotswood, who told him he would not have admitted him to the Council without it.[2] There was a stormy scene with recrimination on both sides. When Spotswood and Byrd had given voice to their grievances against each other, the atmosphere cleared and the breach was healed outwardly. Though they met in social and official relations with apparent friendliness there was still an undercurrent of political strife.[3]

Byrd spent considerable time visiting counties where elections for Burgesses were being held in the autumn of 1720. He made plans with his kinsmen and friends in the Council that were not designed for Spotswood's security. He finally defied the Governor who sought to hold up the appropriation for Byrd's salary as agent for the colony in England until Byrd would promise not to concern himself with matters not specifically mentioned in his instructions. When Byrd did return to England in the summer of 1721 along with Commissary Blair,[4] within a year Spotswood was removed under circumstances and influences that have not yet been made fully apparent.[5]

On Byrd's return to London in 1721, he continued his quest for a wife and also his literary pursuits. In vain he sought, first, to persuade Lady Elizabeth Lee, whom he called Charmante, to marry him. This granddaughter of Charles II, who was a widow when Byrd wrote his love letters to her in 1722, married in 1731 the poet, Edward

---

[1]Diary, April 24, 1720.

[2]Diary, April 25, 1720.

[3]Much new light is given on the controversy with Spotswood and the political situation in Virginia by Byrd in his diary through 1720 until its final entry May 18, 1721. (Byrd Diary 1717-1721.) See below, pp. 368-71.

[4]*Board of Trade Journal*, 1718-1722, p. 328. Neither Blair nor Byrd was present at the meetings of the Council after May 6, 1721. (*Ex. Jour.*, vol. III.)

[5]Dodson, *Alexander Spotswood*, pp. 266-276.

Young, best known as the author of *The Complaint; or, Night Thoughts.*[1]

---

[1]Byrd left among his papers a bundle of letters to Charmante, written between October 23 and November 7, 1722, with this endorsement by himself on the package: "These passionate billets were sent to a lady who had more charm than honour, more wit than discretion. In the beginning she gave the writer of them the plainest marks of her favour. He did not hint his passion to her, but spoke it openly and confirmed it with many a tender squeeze of the hand which she suffered with the patience of a martyr; nay, that she might have no doubt of his intention, he put the question to her in the plainest terms, which she seemed to agree to by a modest silence, and by great encouragement for more than a month afterwards. She saw him every day, received his letters, and fed his flame by the gentlest behaviour in the world, till at last, of a sudden, without any provocation on his part, she grew resty, and, in a moment, turned all her smiles into frowns, and all his hopes into despair. Whether this sudden change was caused by private scandal she had received about him, or from pure inconstancy of temper, he can't be sure. The first is not unlikely, because he had a rival that had no hopes of success openly, and therefore it might be necessary to work underground and blow him up by a mine. This suspicion is confirmed a little by the rival's marrying her afterwards, who then was so poor that 'tis likely the good-natured woman might wed him out of charity; especially as at that time he was so unhealthy that he stood more in need of a nurse than a wife. She did not choose him for his beauty and length of chin, tho' possibly she might for those pure morals which recommended him to his Grace of W—r for a companion. But if, after all, she did not marry him for his virtue neither, then it must have been for this worst quality any husband can have—for his wit. That, I own he has a share of, yet so overcharged and encumbered with words that he does more violence to the ear than a ring of bells; for, if he had never so sharp a wit, a wife may be sure the edge of it will be turned against herself mostly" (Constance C. Harrison, "Colonel William Byrd of Westover, Virginia," *The Century Magazine*, XLII, 163-78).

A fragment of a notebook in the Brock Collection in the Huntington Library, in the same handwriting as those in the University of North Carolina (perhaps one of a series, now widely scattered, and in some instances lost), includes the concluding portion of a letter to Charmante, preceding letter numbered 7, which is dated Sept. 22, 1722, and is complete. This is followed by the first portion of letter No. 8, dated Oct. 4, 1722. Four letters from Byrd to Charmante, dated between Oct. 23 and Nov. 7, 1722, were printed in the *Va. Mag.*, XXXV, 383-388.

Charmante was Lady Elizabeth Lee (1693-1741) who in May 1731 married Edward Young (1683-1765). The known facts in the life of Young accord with Byrd's description of the man Charmante married.

Young's close intimacy with the brilliant and dissolute Philip, Duke of Wharton (1698-1731), a generous patron as long as he had any money, is well attested. Young accompanied Wharton to Ireland in 1717 and in 1721 dedicated to the Duke his "Revenge: a Tragedy." Byrd's criticism of the poet's style has since been corroborated by many critics.

Young's poverty in his early years has been noted by his biographers. But in July, 1730, he was presented by his college, All Souls, to the rectory of Welwyn, in Hertfordshire, and in 1731 he married Charmante. (See *Poetical Works of Edward Young*, Aldine ed., 2 vols., I, xxxiv, "Life of Edward Young, by J. Mitford.")

Byrd's thrust at Young's lack of beauty and length of chin seems borne out by the portrait by Joseph Highmore in All Souls College, Oxford, printed as frontispiece in *The Complete Works, Poetry, and Prose, of the Rev. Ed-*

When Charmante would not marry him Byrd turned to Minionet to whom he had been writing Platonic letters on literary themes since May 1722. She was apparently a friend of Charmante but her identity is still a mystery.[1] She, too, seems to have declined to marry the middle-aged widower from an oversea colony.

Byrd was not only concerned with his own love affairs in 1723 but much perturbed over the courtship of his daughter Evelyn, now sixteen years old, by an English nobleman of whose suit he deeply disapproved. His letters to his daughter Evelyn as Amasia[2] and her lover as Erranti[3] give the first historical evidence for the persistent Virginia legend that Evelyn Byrd, beautiful and gifted, never married be-

---

ward Young . . . to which is prefixed a life of the author by John Doran (2 vols., 1854). See also sketches of Young and of Philip, Duke of Wharton, in *Dict. Nat. Biog.*

Lady Elizabeth Lee, i.e. Charmante, was a granddaughter of Charles II and his mistress Barbara Villiers, Countess of Castlemaine, afterwards Duchess of Cleveland, being the fifteenth child (born May 26, 1693) of their daughter, Charlotte Fitzroy, who married, when very young, Sir Edward Henry Lee, 5th bart., of Ditchley Park, near Spelsbury, Oxfordshire. He was created on June 5, 1674, on his marriage (though under 12 years of age) Baron of Spelsbury, Viscount Quarendon, and Earl of Lichfield (*Herald and Genealogist*, ed. John G. Nichols, III; *Dict. Nat. Biog.*, article on George Henry Lee, 3d Earl of Lichfield; Cokayne, *Baronetage*).

She was, when she married Edward Young, the widow of her cousin, Colonel Francis Lee, a descendant of Sir Henry Lee of Queen Elizabeth's court (*Martha Lady Giffard, Her Life and Correspondence*, ed. Julia G. Longe [London, 1911], pp. 295-307), and had three children, a son and two daughters, by her first marriage. She was probably a widow when Byrd asked her to marry him in 1722, for her daughter Elizabeth, who died in 1736, had married (June 18, 1735) Henry Temple, son of Henry Temple, first viscount Palmerston. Temple died in 1740. Lady Elizabeth or Lady Betty, as she was known to her contemporaries, died in January, 1741. The reference in "Night Thoughts" to three deaths occurring "ere thrice yon moon had filled her horn" is thought to refer (with a poet's license) to these bereavements in the family of the author. Lady Elizabeth and Edward Young had one son, Frederick.

Rumors of Byrd's courtship of the young widow had reached Virginia, and John Custis wrote him in 1723, "it is said that you have a keen appetite to a young wider morsell [*sic*] of about 16 years old" (Custis Letter Book).

No portrait of Lady Elizabeth Lee is known to exist nor is it known whether she inherited her mother's "blameless beauty." (See Henry C. Shelley, *The Life and Letters of Edward Young* [London, 1914], pp. 107-9, 174-75, 221-23.)

[1]For Byrd's letters to Minionet from May 22, 1722 through Feb. 1722/23 see below pp. 371-80. The only clue to Minionet's identity is in the reference, in the letter of May 30, 1722, to her reading with ease Oliver Cromwell's cipher. Efforts to unravel the mystery with this thread have proved futile.

[2]See below, p. 381.

[3]See below, p. 383.

cause in her youth her father had forbidden her to marry the man she loved, who, according to the legend, was the Earl of Peterborough.

When Byrd did win the consent of the heiress Maria Taylor, daughter of the late Thomas Taylor of Kensington, to marry him, he took no chances on her mother's disapproval before the wedding but waited to disclose to her on May 26, 1724 the fact of her daughter's marriage to him on May 9, more than two weeks before.[1] If Byrd wrote Maria Taylor such letters as he wrote Facetia or Fidelia, Sabina or Zenobia, Charmante or Minionet, they have not yet come to light. Byrd's letter to her in Greek is the only one among all the known Byrd manuscripts.[2]

In this first quarter of the eighteenth century before his final return to Virginia in 1726 Byrd had tried his hand at the various literary expressions then most common and characteristic of that time. He wrote *vers de societé*, characters, humorous satire, at least one pamphlet on a current theme, love letters of literary pretensions, letters that were character sketches, the epitaph and that well nigh universal expression of his literary contemporaries, translations from the classics. The manuscript notebooks in the University of North Carolina published in this volume give specimens of all these diverse forms, save the pamphlet.

Byrd's verses have no higher merit than the undistinguished volume of such productions that, all critics agree, were great in quantity and slight in quality.[3] They were a form of entertainment enjoyed by London society[4] and flourished especially at Bath and Tunbridge Wells. They took the form of panegyric or satire, and the latter vein was the more congenial to Byrd.[5] There is an element of satire in almost all his known writings. The diversion they and their friends among the pleasure seekers at the spas and in

---

[1]See letter to Medusa, below, p. 386.

[2]See below, p. 386.

[3]For an excellent treatment of the subject, see Richard C. Boys, *English Poetical Miscellanies, 1700-25* (Baltimore, 1939), pp. 22-24.

[4]*Wentworth Papers,* pp. 93, 97, 235; Helen Sard Hughes, *The Gentle Hertford, Her Life and Letters* (New York, 1940), pp. 419-21.

[5]For Byrd's ideas on the panegyric and satire, see his letter to Minionet, below, p. 374.

London found in these personal verses, stressing peculiar traits either of character or of a physical nature, and often unrestrained either as to theme or expression is a manifestation of the spirit of the time that found more valued expression in the personal poems by Gay and Pope and Swift. A mere scanning of the *Tatler* and the *Spectator* will prove Byrd's kinship with the period, for one meets in Addison's and Steele's essays Sempronia, Clarinda, Panthea, Amaryllis, Sabina, Cleora, Monimia—all of whom one also finds among Byrd's feminine correspondents.

The most interesting of the characters by Byrd in these manuscripts[1] is that of himself under the title Inamorato L'Oiseaux.[2] The analysis is rather penetrating and though not all the details he relates about himself coincide with evidence from other sources it is a remarkably frank and fair picture of its author. From the biographical data in it some new slants are given on Byrd's career. It appears to trace his story to about the time of his return to Virginia in 1705 and seems to have been written around 1704, though he sent it to Minionet in a letter of February 21, 1723.[3] His character of Sir Robert Southwell as Cavaliero Sapiente is devoid of satire and has an apparent sincerity of feeling that gives it high merit.[4] It does have the balance and contrast that writers of characters delighted to achieve. In the names given to his characters Byrd showed again his identification with this period in English letters. The use of Italianate names, found both in France and in England, was common with him, as seen in Duke Dulchetti or Cavaliero Bonieri or Count Sufficiento. Byrd was deft in phrasing and his sharply-drawn contrasts in these characters give them a certain sparkling quality that is often arresting. In choosing to make pointed thrusts at some of the sins and weaknesses of his friends, he was again following the trend of

[1]The letters in this volume indicate that he wrote other characters besides those included in the two notebooks here published.

[2]See below, p. 276.

[3]See below, p. 379.

[4]See below, p. 206. Was this one of the three characters sent by Byrd to Lady Elizabeth Cromwell (Facetia) in his letters to her of June 17 and July 3 [1703]? (*Letters Writ to Facetia by Veramour* [privately printed, 1913]).

his time.[1] When the poet and dramatist Congreve went to Tunbridge he wrote his friend Dennis, ". . . I would have you expect no characters from me; for I profess myself an Enemy to Detraction; and who is there, that can justly merit Commendation?"[2]

All Byrd's characters are of the personal variety. They picture an individual and not a type, a particular person and not a class. The subject matter is often characteristic of the age when no subject was forbidden in polite society and when, as the churchman Dean Swift said, "We call a spade a spade."[3] It was an age when the moral derelictions of kings and their courtiers were the entertainment of the town and the wits in the coffeehouses set no restraints on their tongues or their pens.

Byrd also wrote letters that were really "character sketches," a use of epistles that Addison and Steele developed to an acceptable and popular literary form. His letters to Facetia or to Monymia or to Minionet as well as others in this volume were often of this variety. Perhaps the best example is his characterization of his companions on his journey to London in the letter to Lucretia.[4]

In the broad and ribald sketch "The Female Creed,"[5] Byrd gave free rein to his zest for satire and humor. Internal evidence proves it was written about 1725.[6] It was the

---

[1]On the writing of characters, see *The Cambridge History of English Literature,* IV, 383-391; VIII, 71; Charles Whibley, "Characters" in *Blackwood's Magazine* no. MCXXIV (June, 1909), CLXXXV, 757-769; the writings of Swift, Pope, Chesterfield, Addison, Steele; *Memoirs of the Secret Services of John Macky, Esq., During the Reigns of King William, Queen Anne, and King George. Including also, The True Secret History of the Rise, Promotions, &c. of the English and Scots nobility; Officers, Civil, Military, Naval, and other Persons of Distinction, from the Revolution. In their respective characters at large*; drawn up by Mr. Macky, pursuant to the Direction of Her Royal Highness the Princess Sophia (London, 1895).

Byrd's library included the well known volumes of characters by Theophrastus and by La Bruyère (Bassett, pp. 422, 434).

[2]*The Complete Works of Congreve,* ed. Montague Summers (Soho, The Nonesuch Press, 1923), p. 95.

[3]*Some Materials Towards Memoirs of the Reign of King George II,* ed. Romney Sedgwick (3 vols., London, 1931), I, lviii-ix.

[4]See below, p. 286.

[5]Printed as Appendix IV in this volume from a copy evidently made by the same person who copied the letters of Byrd in the so-called Brandon Letter books in the Brock Collection in the Huntington Library.

[6]See Appendix IV, p. 447.

latest of his writings in this English period of which we have knowledge.

Under the disguise of suggestive names Byrd made sport of the foibles of many women whom he knew in London and others whose social position made them known. It is possible to identify the references in some instances and thus to justify the opinion that under the satirically suggestive names Byrd referred to actual people whom his coterie in London would recognize but whose vulnerable points he could thus more pointedly and unrestrainedly satirize for his own entertainment and that of his friends. Many of the names used in "The Female Creed" occur in his letters and verses and apparently with the same personal reference. No person was immune from the barbs of the wits of his time and no personal traits or physical habits or functions were shielded against their thrusts. Its jibes at superstition and taboos are not to be taken so seriously when Byrd's own concern about the import of his dreams and his consultations with old Abram the conjurer in his love affair with Sabina are recalled.[1] While "The Female Creed" may not enhance Byrd's literary fame, it does identify him more fully with the London literary world of the first quarter of the eighteenth century.

With Byrd's final return to Virginia in 1726 the London scene with its literary tastes and emphasis on persons and their manners and morals were left behind. Though he kept his apartments in beautiful and fashionable Lincoln's Inn for several years with the evident thought that he would go back there, at least for long visits,[2] his growing family and his landed interests kept him in Virginia. He never returned to England. He wrote frequent letters to friends and family connections there. They were, in humor and subject, reminiscent of the somewhat ribald character of the things he wrote while fully under the influence of the social life in London or at Bath or at Tunbridge in the time of Queen Anne and King George I.

---

[1]Diary, Feb. 10, Apr. 3, May 1, 1718.

[2]Letter of Byrd to Mr. Spencer, Virginia, May 28, 1729. Ms., Colonial Williamsburg, Inc.

Henceforth in his daily activity and in his writing his horizon was bounded by Virginia and her colonial ways. His writings thus fall into two distinct periods. Until he was over forty years old, in subject, in form and in character, his writings were identified in every way with the literary currents common in the London of that time. He had his place among the wits of the first quarter of the eighteenth century.

Quite different was the literary output in his last thirty years. In the "History of the Dividing Line," "A Journey to the Land of Eden," and "A Progress to the Mines," the so-called Westover manuscripts, on the basis of which he has enjoyed his distinction as a writer, the colonial scene and its natural features and the people as they were incident to the venture in hand were the materials on which his wit and his satire played.[1]

This same vein of satire and humor is to be found in the writings of both periods. His interest in people is apparent in the latter period but personalities are not his main theme. The surveying of a boundary line across natural barriers, such as the Dismal Swamp and unmapped mountains, and journeys to the mines of ex-Governor Spotswood with their pregnant possibilities for prosperous enterprizes and to virgin lands along the Roanoke River, with their promise of bountiful crops and well-nourished settlers, played on his imagination as a writer and his hope as a Virginia planter, who was finding it increasingly difficult to meet the financial demands upon him from the yearly returns on his tobacco hogsheads. It is true his companions inspired satirical characterization sufficiently keen for him to write a "Secret History of the Dividing Line."[2]

There is a distinctly American quality in these writings of the latter half of Byrd's life, in direct contrast to the ex-

---

[1]The Westover manuscripts have been printed in several editions since the first edition in book form was published in Petersburg, Va., in 1841 by E. & J. C. Ruffin, printers. The edition cited most frequently in this volume is *The Writings of "Colonel William Byrd of Westover in Virginia Esqr."*, edited by J. S. Bassett (New York, 1901).

[2]*William Byrd's Histories of the Dividing Line Betwixt Virginia and North Carolina*, with Introduction and Notes by William K. Boyd (Raleigh, N. C., 1929).

clusively English quality in the writings of his earlier years. Further study and time will doubtless argue that his literary work in the Virginia period from 1726 on, with its colonial scene and theme, has greater literary merit than his work in the London period. This fact in itself may justify the conclusion that William Byrd was more American than English in spite of the knowledge of this new body of his writings, written chiefly in England and published in small part in London before his return to Virginia.

Except for his services in 1728 as one of the commissioners surveying the boundary line between Virginia and North Carolina and again in 1736 to survey the boundary between the princely Fairfax proprietary, known as the Northern Neck, and the King's domain in Virginia, Byrd lived, from 1726 to his death on August 26, 1744, the life of a planter at Westover. As a member of the King's Council he went regularly to the colonial capital of Williamsburg. His family grew until there were three daughters and one son, his heir, William Byrd III, children of his second marriage.[1] These children, with his wife, Maria Taylor, who did not forget her English kin yet thoroughly adapted herself to the life in Virginia, and the two daughters of his first marriage, Evelyn and Wilhelmina, formed the family group about him. His daughter Evelyn died in 1737 and was buried in the old Westover churchyard.

Byrd's shorthand diary beginning August [10], 1739 and ending[2] August 31, 1741 gives a day-by-day journalistic account of his activities. It is seldom introspective and never retrospective. The picture in general of the life of a Virginia planter around 1740 and that of William Byrd, as an individual, may be seen in minute and graphic detail.

---

[1]Anne, born in London, Feb. 5, 1725; Maria, born Jan. 16, 17[27]; William, born Sept. 6, 1728; Jane, born Oct. 13, 1729. (Byrd Family Bible.)

When Byrd and his wife came to Virginia in 1726, they left their little daughter Anne with Maria Taylor's sister. On the marriage of this sister to Francis Otway in 1730, Anne joined her parents at Westover. Charles, Earl of Orrery, was godfather to Anne Byrd (Byrd to Charles, Earl of Orrery, Virginia, June 18, 1730, Orrery MSS., Harvard College Library).

[2]The diary skips from Sept. 8, 1739 to Dec. 5, 1739. The pages for this interval seem to be missing from the manuscript note book.

While the diary covers only two years it is suggestive of the life Byrd led at Westover and on the occasions when he attended the Council sessions in Williamsburg from 1726 to 1744. He had an idea once of selling Westover and going to Jamaica when financial obligations were especially perplexing.[1] He put out feelers from time to time for an appointment to a royal post in Virginia that would give the security of a salary, and he continued to entertain the hope that he might be Governor of Virginia even during this long span of Governor Gooch's tactful and lengthy tenure.[2] But Byrd's more strenuous years were behind him and he was the gentleman planter of considerable leisure though heavy responsibilities, enjoying his fast maturing family and his friends. His life at this time was, in a way, an epitome of the colonial aristocracy at this stage of its evolution.

Byrd continued his habit of reading in the early morning from Greek and Hebrew, and at other times of the day from Latin and French and English. He often entertained the clergy at Westover. His partiality for them is not to be explained solely by his religious inclinations but because he enjoyed conversation with well-read men like the Huguenots, Anthony Gavin and Peter Fontaine. When he went to Williamsburg he consorted most commonly with that stalwart champion of an educated clergy, Commissary Blair. He visited frequently at the home of Lady Susannah Randolph, widow of his congenial friend Sir John Randolph, in whose home literary interests had even been superior to interest to the acquisition of lands and the matter of tobacco. His several plantations took many hours of his time but his spare time went chiefly to bookish interests and educated friends. He thus secured a detachment constantly manifested in his comments on men and affairs, in spite of his responsibilities as the owner of thousands and thousands of

[1]Letter of Byrd to Mr. Beckford (Constance Cary Harrison, "Colonel William Byrd of Westover, Virginia," *The Century Magazine*, XLII, 175).

[2]Byrd persistently desired the office of Governor of Virginia. After the death of Hugh Drysdale, deputy to the Earl of Orkney, Byrd wrote to Lord Orrery, to the Duke of Argyle and to Lord Islay to ask them to use their influence for his appointment as Drysdale's successor. (Byrd to Charles, Earl of Orrery, Virginia the 2d: of February 1726/7, Orrery Mss. in Harvard College Library.)

acres,[1] hundreds of slaves, warehouses and stores. The faculty of William and Mary College, men from the English universities, also found ready welcome and congenial talk from the master at Westover.

Ship captains, whether or not they were Virginia born like Edward Randolph, were frequently entertained at Westover. Through them and through the letters they brought, Byrd and his family kept touch with English happenings and with their distant kinsfolk and friends. The ship captains in turn gave Byrd and his friends a change from the rural routine when they entertained them on their ships, riding at anchor in the James and well supplied with brandies or wines, packed away on their far flung voyages, to furnish zest for the long hours of talk on these ships as they waited for their cargoes. While he enjoyed card games and bowls,[2] there was little of the sportsman in him. He seldom went to races and often stayed at home while others in his family took his small stake to risk it for him. Dancing was through his life apparently his favored exercise. Sociable converse, botanical interests, and his well chosen library of some four thousand volumes[3] were his diversions. There was little of the country squire in Byrd, though he had vast domains of land. He employed overseers and seems to have sought men of higher intelligence than have generally been associated with that rôle.[4] Twelfth Night and Whit Monday were the two holidays celebrated at Westover in this period.

Byrd was a helpful and generous neighbor in the rural society where there were many occasions for neighborly assistance. Especially was he called upon in time of sickness. He had read widely in medicine and had among his

---

[1]At his death Byrd owned not less than 179,440 acres. (Bassett, p. lxxxiii.)

[2]He superintended the turfing of a bowling green at Westover (Diary, March 16, 1721).

[3]For catalogue of the Westover library see Bassett, pp. 413-443.

[4]For example, John Banister, son of the botanist and minister John Banister who had been a friend of Byrd's father (Diary, April 11, 22; Aug. 31, Oct. 11, 1720). John Banister III, of "Battersea", son of the John Banister who was overseer for Byrd, played a prominent rôle in Virginia during the Revolution. (Tyler, *Va. Biog.*, vol. 1, p. 179; *Wm. Q. (2)* X, 178; *Va. Mag.* XI, 164, XXXVI, 37.)

London associates some of the most learned doctors. He prescribed for "his people" with what they must have regarded at times as too generous a hand, and shared his medical stores and knowledge with kindred and friends. He tried on them as well as in his own family ideas he had adopted from his reading and his association with Hans Sloane, Samuel Garth, Radcliffe, and George Cheyne, numbered among the leading medical men and the coffeehouse wits in London. Byrd's own household and other families living on rivers and creeks had not yet learned to escape the recurrent summer chills and fever, though they were learning to treat them with the Jesuit's bark, quinine. Byrd's diary reveals much sickness on his own and neighboring plantations in mid-winter and mid-summer.

Morning and evening Byrd noted the fact that he did or did not say his prayers, confessing thus the obligation he felt upon himself for daily devotions. When the Sabbath came he noted that he did or did not go to church, though the times he stayed away were more numerous than the occasions when he went. He was quick to accept good or ill fortune as an act of Providence and to submit to God's will. He was daily conscious of his relation to God and his obligations as a communicant of the church of England. Scant influence of the Puritanism or deism of his time in his thought is revealed. He felt his dreams were significant and was cheered or depressed as he sought their true meaning.[1] He was quick to forgive and unable to nourish a grievance long. He shunned disagreeable scenes and painful decisions where possible. He had a constant willingness to let each day take care of its own concerns and lived very fully in the present.

Aside from its genealogical value, Byrd's diary for 1739-1741 is unique in the picture it presents of the social life and domestic economy on a James River plantation in the

---

[1]Byrd often noted his dreams in his diary, as, for instance when he dreamed the King's daughter was in love with him (Aug. 27, 1720) or when he dreamed he was favored by the King and made Secretary of State and Lord Oxford gave him advice as to the conduct of that office (Diary, Jan. 2, 1721).

mid-eighteenth century.[1] It offers a sharp contrast in many details of daily life to those presented in the earlier sections of his diary. Not all these differences are to be accounted for by the fact that the diarist was sixty-five years old rather than thirty-five or forty-three, though of course that is an element to be considered in the historical picture.

Nor is the very important fact to be overlooked that the diarist had a more stable domestic world with Maria Taylor, his second wife, as mistress at Westover than had been true in the years 1709-1712 when the high-strung, temperamental Lucy Parke was its charming but inefficient mistress, or in 1720-1721 when, as a widower, Byrd himself looked after much of the domestic detail, with the aid of several white maids whom he had brought with him from England on his return to Virginia in 1720.[2] Treatment of the servants at Westover, both the white in more responsible positions and the black in greater numbers, was more humane than in the earlier periods revealed by Byrd's journal for 1709-1712 and 1717-1721. This change was due probably to the two-fold reason that the master and the mistress were older and more self-restrained and that among the negroes an increasing percentage had been born in Virginia, in spite of the large consignments that were brought in steadily from Africa. In this period the *Virginia Gazette* was stressing in its advertisements of sales of negroes that they were "Virginia born."

The provisioning of the James River plantation by the supplies from the lands on Meherrin River and at the falls of the James is an interesting revelation of the system of distribution. The increasing rôle of the Scotch merchants and the suggestion of country stores scattered through the region from James River through the southside suggest a

---

[1]The first half of the eighteenth century has lacked such portrayal. The valuable diaries of Philip Vickers Fithian (*Journal and Letters*, ed. John Rogers Williams, [Princeton, N. J., 1900]), and of Landon Carter, of which only a portion has been printed (*Wm. Q. (1)*, XIII-XXI), give the picture of the generation just before the Revolution.

[2]Cf. letter of Thomas Jones dated Virginia, July 22, 1728 to his wife, Ann Cocke Pratt, then in London, asking her to bring a servant from England to oversee the difficult and inefficient negroes in their home (Jones Papers, Library of Congress).

development in intra-trade in the colony that has been too little studied.

The new sidelights on personalities long familiar in Virginia's story, such as Commissary Blair and Governor Gooch, as well as Major Henry, father of the Revolutionary orator Patrick Henry, will help towards a more complete understanding of the colonial political scene. The town houses of some of the members of the Council, the Governor's Palace and the taverns and coffeehouse made Williamsburg a center of social as well as official life. The Council's rôle is made clearer in occasional details. Byrd's realistic appraisal of the troops in camp ready to go with Spotswood to Carthagena proved the success of the Assembly's plan to rid the colony of undesirable vagrants.[1]

Byrd's life began and ended in the James River region of the colony of Virginia where Englishmen had planted their first permanent settlement in the New World in 1607. With the security of his wealth, won by his forebears from its land and resources, he had gone back to the Mother Country for education and had found the London scene of the early eighteenth century so congenial that he played his rôle there for many years. How fully he was a part of it, the manuscripts here published, and his diary for 1717-1721, yet unpublished, clearly reveal. But his forebears had cast their fortunes in the colony. To the colony he returned and became absorbed in its political, economic and cultural development. In his latter days, as he neared his three score years and ten, he unconsciously betrayed the way of life in the articulate planter class of that society in the day-by-day entries of his shorthand journal that, by a whimsical destiny, has survived for the years 1739-1741. The life of William Byrd from 1674 to 1744 is the most complete expression in the Virginia of 1607 to 1776 of the cultural kinship and yet emerging differentiations between England and the first of her American colonies.

[1]See below, p. 74, n. 1.

ABBREVIATIONS

For works frequently cited in the footnotes, the following abbreviations are used:

Bassett: *The Writings of Colonel William Byrd of Westover*, ed. J. S. Bassett (New York, 1901).

Cal. S. P.: Calendar of Virginia State Papers and Other Manuscripts, 1652-1781, ed. William P. Palmer, (Richmond, 1875).

Diary, 1709-1712: *The Secret Diary of William Byrd of Westover, 1709-1712*, ed. Louis B. Wright and Marion Tinling (Richmond, 1941).

Diary, 1717-1721: William Byrd, Diary, 1717-1721, Shorthand MS in Virginia Historical Society collections.

Ex. Jour.: Executive Journals of the Council of Colonial Virginia, ed. H. R. McIlwaine (Richmond, 1925-30). Also typed copies in the Virginia State Library of the MS journal for 1739-41.

Goodwin: Edward L. Goodwin, *The Colonial Church in Virginia* (Milwaukee, 1927).

Harker: Edith M. Harker, Chart of Shipping in Virginia, 1736-1766, comp. from the *Virginia Gazette*, MS in University of Richmond library.

Hen. *Stat.: The Statutes at Large; being a Collection of all the Laws of Virginia from the First Session of the Legislature in the Year 1619*, by W. W. Hening (Richmond, 1823).

JHB: Journals of the House of Burgesses of Virginia, ed. H. R. McIlwaine (Richmond, 1908-15).

LJC: Legislative Journals of the Council of Colonial Virginia, ed. H. R. McIlwaine (Richmond, 1918-19).

T's.Q.: Tyler's Quarterly Historical and Genealogical Magazine.

Va. Biog.: Encyclopedia of Virginia Biography, ed. L. G. Tyler (New York, 1915).

Va. Gaz.: The Virginia Gazette.

Va. Hist. Port.: Virginia Historical Portraiture, 1585-1834, ed. A. W. Weddell (Richmond, MDCCCCXXX).

Va. Mag.: The Virginia Magazine of History and Biography.

Wm. Q. (1): The William and Mary College Quarterly, 1st Series.

Wm. Q. (2): The William and Mary College Quarterly, 2nd Series.

PART I

The Secret Diary of William Byrd of Westover, 1739-1741

Transcribed from the Shorthand
by
MARION TINLING

TRANSCRIBER'S NOTE

THE system of shorthand used by Byrd was one taught by William Mason to parliamentarians, clergymen, lawyers, and other students in London during the late seventeenth and early eighteenth centuries. Mason published several revisions of his system (which he, in turn, had adapted from an earlier writer), in 1672, 1682, and 1707. The last revision is the one used by Byrd, though, like most shorthand writers, he adapted the system somewhat to his own uses. Unlike Pepys and other shorthand diarists, Byrd wrote everything, even proper names, in shorthand. As the system omits most vowels, these names have had to be identified from a skeleton of consonants. Where identification has been impossible, the skeleton has been left. The manuscripts, both diary and letter book, were very fragile, and the work of transcription was done entirely from a photostat.[1]

---

[1]All words or phrases which have defied translation, either because the shorthand was baffling or because the manuscript was damaged, have been supplied in brackets or given in skeleton form. Spelling of words, including those that have undergone slight changes in phonography (like "sparrowgrass"), is modern. The temptation to guess at names and phrases has been avoided, yet it is inevitable that there are mistakes in transcription, perhaps even anachronisms in vocabulary. The historian is asked to remember that the diary is in shorthand, where a dot can have any of eight or ten meanings (*of, I, a, the, ed, ing,* any vowel, or any of several prefixes), and which is therefore an imperfect medium for exact language.

The Secret Diary of William Byrd of Westover

August, 1739

[10] . . . folly with Caton[1], God forgive me. I received letters from Dr. Tschiffeley,[2] which I liked not. I read Latin till dinner when I ate pork and peas. After dinner I took a nap and read more Latin. In the evening we played bowls and walked. I prayed.

11. I rose about 5, read Hebrew and Greek. I prayed and had tea. I danced. The weather was cold and clear, the wind northwest. I had five stools from Anderson's pills. I read Latin and wrote English till dinner when I ate boiled pork. After dinner I took a nap. The boat came from the Falls,[3] where the sick were better. In the evening we played bowls. I talked with my people[4] and prayed.

---

[1]Probably Caton Brun, daughter of Caton De Wert and Joseph Brun (see entry and note on Mrs. Brun, Aug. 14, 1739).

[2]Dr. Samuel Tschiffeley (Tscheffelie, Shiffley) was a Swiss physician who became one of the early owners of lots in Richmond (*Va. Gaz.* June 2-9, 1738; plat of Richmond, supposedly in 1742, Va. State Archives). He practiced medicine in Byrd's family and was interested in Byrd's plan for the settlement of Swiss and German protestants on the Roanoke river lands (Correspondence of Byrd and Isham Randolph with John Bartram, *Wm. Q. (2)*, VI, 312-15). Tschiffeley petitioned the Council for 20,000 acres of land on some of the main branches of the James, adjoining lands already granted the settlement of Swiss and German protestants, and the patent was granted him on condition of his bringing into the colony within two years one person for each fifty acres or otherwise paying the usual rights for the land. He did not succeed in establishing his colony and his patent lapsed in 1738 (*Ex. Jour.*, IV, 432). At his death Tschiffeley's estate consisted chiefly of a number of lots in the town of Richmond and several slaves (Henrico Deed and Will Book, 1748-1750, p. 127; will proved by his widow Barbara Tscheffelei [*sic*] Feb., 1749).

[3]The uncle, Thomas Stegge, Jr., from whom the diarist's father William Byrd I inherited the property and business and official interests on which the family's position and fortune were firmly based in colonial Virginia, had acquired large landholdings on both sides of James River at the fall line, where Richmond now stands. Stegge had developed the Falls Plantation on the south side of the river (see plat of this plantation in Byrd Title Book, *Va. Mag.*, XLVIII, 32; see also Bassett, pp. xxxiii-v).

[4]By "my people" Byrd meant his slaves at Westover. The phrase was common in Virginia to the end of the slave regime.

12.[1] I rose about 5, read Hebrew and Greek. I prayed and had tea. I danced. The weather was cold and clear, the wind north. A calf came from Hanover,[2] where things go very well, thank God. I cleaned my mouth and read Latin but went not to church. I ate pigeon and bacon. After dinner we ate melon and talked till the evening when we walked. I talked with my people and prayed.

13. I rose about 5, read Hebrew and Greek. I prayed and had tea. I danced. The weather was cold and cloudy, the wind southeast. I read Latin and wrote English till dinner, when I ate pigeon pie. After dinner read more Latin till the evening, when we played bowls for an hour and then walked. I talked with my people, had milk and apples, and prayed.

14. I rose about 4 and prepared to make a visit to Mrs. Brun[3] who was very bad. I prayed and about 5 took

---

[1]The diarist underscored the date of each Sunday, and we have rendered the designation in italic figures.

[2]While the Hanover County court records for this period are missing, the *Vestry Book of St. Paul's Parish, Hanover County, Virginia, 1706-1786*, tr. and ed. by C. G. Chamberlayne (Richmond, 1940) refers from 1723 on repeatedly to the processioning of Byrd's lands in that parish, and particularly names his "Middle Quarter" (p. 103) and his "2 Quarters" (p. 111). Byrd was County Lieutenant for Hanover in 1726 (*Va. Mag.*, V, 144). See note on John Bickerton under Mar. 6, 1740.

[3]This appears to be Mrs. Brun (or Le Brun), a gentlewoman, who seems to have come to Virginia under the influence of Mr. Ochs who was seeking to promote settlement on Byrd's Roanoke river lands. Byrd befriended Mrs. Brun in misfortune, loaned her £52 sterling, supported her with her children and servants for a time and had gone as her security in purchasing a negro (Byrd to Mr. Ochs, Sept. 5, 1740; Byrd to Madame Brun, Dec. 5, 1740, Brock 188, Huntington Library; Byrd to Mr. Campbell of Norfolk, Nov. 3, 1739, *Va. Mag.*, XXXVI, 359).

The following item from the Charles City court record of August, 1741, sheds light on the woman Byrd consistently called Mrs. Brun, but who was always noted in the court records as Caton (possibly a corruption of the French for Kitty) De Wert: "Benja Harris Gent offers a Deed to be proved from Joseph Brun and Caton De Wert to ye sd Harris but Caton Brun & Mary ann Brun witnesses thereto on their oaths declareing they never saw their father & mother the above sd Jos. Brun & Caton De Wert sign seal or acknowledge the sd deed & thereupon ye sd Deed is rejected.

"Benjamin Harris in open Court tenders a deed to be acknowledged to Mrs Caton De Wert for a certain Tract of land sold her by the sd Harris but she refuseing to accept of ye sd acknowledgement therefore the sd Deed is rejected" (Charles City Order Book, 1737-1751, p. 175).

The grand jury presented to the Charles City Court in November, 1741,

Mina[1] and Miss Brun in the chariot and without accident, thank God, arrived there about 9 and found all the family like ghosts. I gave them my best advice. I ate boiled chicken for dinner and about 4 recommended the family to heaven, left Mina there, and returned safe home and found all well, thank God.

15. I rose about 5, read Hebrew and Greek. I prayed and had tea. I danced. It rained till 10 o'clock. Mr. F-k-l-r came from Mrs. Brun's by whom I sent several things necessary for the sick, God give them success. I wrote letters and read Latin till dinner when I ate fish. After dinner I put things in order, read more Latin and played at bowls. At night talked with my people and prayed. The minx[2] was come.

16. I rose about 5, read Hebrew and Greek. I prayed and had coffee. I danced. The weather was cold and

---

Mrs. Caton Brun and Mary Ann Brun for perjury on the information of Benjamin Harris (*ibid.*, p. 185).

At the December, 1741 court Caton and Mary Ann Brun through their attorney produced a *certiorari* obtained by them from the General Court to stay proceedings in the Charles City court until their case could be heard in equity in the General Court and the proceedings were stayed (*ibid.*, p. 192).

At the same session of the court by virtue of a *habeas corpus* from the Secretary's office further proceedings in the case of Benjamin Harris against Caton De Wert were stayed and the suit referred for trial to the General Court (*ibid.*, p. 190).

But at this December court, Harris, having secured a conditional judgment against Caton De Wert in the September court, the judgment was confirmed on writ of Enquiry in damages awarded to be executed at the next court (*ibid.*, pp. 178-93).

Other suits involving Caton De Wert appear in the Charles City records and in December 1742 John Bachurst got an attachment to be satisfied by the sheriff's selling two horses, a cart, and wheel and one side saddle to satisfy the judgment (*ibid.*, pp. 174, 178, 231, 232).

Caton De Wert died before the June court, 1745, and on his request administration on her estate was granted to Benjamin Harris (*ibid.*, pp. 360, 380, 381, 384, 391, 407).

[1]This was Wilhelmina, or Mina as her father commonly called her, Byrd's only surviving daughter by Lucy Parke, his first wife, since the older daughter Evelyn had died in 1737. Mina was born Nov. 6, 1715. She married Thomas Chamberlayne of King William County, son of William Chamberlayne, merchant and justice of New Kent County, and his wife Elizabeth Littlepage (Bassett, p. 447; *Va. Mag.*, XXXVI, 226-27; Hen. *Stat.*, VI, 319). Byrd wrote Mrs. Sherard in England on Sept. 7, 1740, "Your niece my Daughter is much at your devotion. Her name is Wilhelmina & her accomplishments, if a Father can be a judge as great as any Damsel in this part of the World" (*Va. Mag.*, XXXVII, 105).

[2]Obsolete form of mink.

cloudy, the wind southwest. I wrote letters to [. . .], read Latin and went to hear the children[1] perform their lessons till dinner, when I ate broiled veal. After dinner I heard my wife[2] read French, then read more Latin till the evening, when we played billiards and walked. I talked with my people, had milk and apples, and prayed.

17. I rose about 5, read Hebrew and Greek. I prayed and had tea. I danced. The weather was cold and cloudy, with a little rain, the wind southwest. I read Latin and wrote letters to England till dinner when I ate boiled beef. After dinner put things in order and read more Latin. [. . .][3]

18. I rose about 5, read Hebrew and Greek. I prayed and had tea. I danced. The weather was cold and cloudy, the wind southwest. I read Latin and wrote letters to England till dinner when I ate minced veal. After dinner I put matters in order, read more Latin till 5, then played bowls. I talked with my people. Several people sick above, God preserve them. I prayed.

19. I rose about 5, read Hebrew and Greek. I prayed and had coffee. I danced. The weather was warm and clear, the wind southwest. I cleaned my mouth and went to church and heard a good sermon, and the Secretary[4] was there for the first time in 6 months. Nobody dined with us and I ate pigeon and bacon. After dinner put things in order, read Latin and walked. I talked with my people and prayed, but slept ill.

---

[1]The children of Byrd and his second wife Maria Taylor were Anne, fourteen years old, Maria twelve, William eleven, and Jane ten (Bassett, pp. 447-48).

[2]Byrd married as his second wife (the first, Lucy Parke, having died in London in 1716), Maria Taylor, born 1698, eldest daughter and one of the co-heiresses of Thomas Taylor, of Kensington, England on May 7, 1724. She returned with him to Westover in 1726 and lived there for the rest of a long life until her death in 1771. (Record written in Byrd Family Bible by William Byrd III, now owned by W. Gordon Harrison. Printed versions of this record mistake the year 1698 of Maria Taylor's birth for 1678.)

[3]A line of characters at the bottom of the page is illegible.

[4]John Carter, son of Robert ("King") Carter, was secretary of the colony from 1722 until his death in 1744. He inherited Corotoman from his father and gained Shirley by his marriage to Elizabeth Hill in 1723 (*Ex. Jour.*, IV, *passim*; *Va. Mag.*, XXXII, 48; *Wm. Q. (1)*, X, 167, 175; Gov. Gooch to his

20. I rose about 5, read Hebrew and Greek. I prayed and had tea. I danced. The weather was warm and clear, the wind southwest. I took another [new] negro and sent him to Colonel Harrison,[1] read Latin and wrote letters till dinner, when I ate cold lamb. After dinner it rained a little, with wind, so we played at billiards and I visited the sick and found them better, thank God. Mr. G, [a m-r-ch], desired leave and had it. I prayed.

21. I rose about 5, read Hebrew and Greek. I prayed and had coffee. I danced. The weather was warm and clear, the wind southwest. After breakfast Mr. G went away and I read Latin and settled several accounts and walked among my people till dinner, when I ate fried lamb. After dinner put several things in order, read English, and then played bowls with my son.[2] I talked with my people and prayed. I had a little fever.

22. I rose about 5, read Hebrew and Greek. I prayed and had tea. I danced. The weather was very warm and cloudy, the wind southwest. I was better, thank God, but my sick people continued bad, God preserve them. I wrote several letters and read Latin till dinner when I ate pork and peas. After dinner it rained pretty much. I took a nap, read more Latin, and then played billiards. At night I talked with my people and prayed but had a little fever again.

23. I rose about 5, read Hebrew and Greek. I prayed and had tea. I danced. The weather was warm and cloudy, the wind north. My people were still ill; God save them if

---

brother, May 7, 1733, typed copies of originals in possession of Sir Thomas Gooch, England, Colonial Williamsburg, Inc.; *Letters of Robert Carter, 1720-1727*, ed. Louis B. Wright [San Marino, Cal., 1940]).

[1]Benjamin Harrison, owner of the adjoining plantation of Berkeley, and Byrd's close neighbor, served the county of Charles City as a member of the House of Burgesses from 1736 to 1744. He and his two youngest daughters were killed when lightning struck Berkeley, July 12, 1745 (*Va. Mag.*, XXXII, 97, XLI, 164-5). His will was presented in Charles City County court, August 1745, by William Randolph and Miss Betty Harrison. (Charles City Order Book, 1737-1751, p. 376.)

[2]William Byrd III, the only surviving son of the diarist, was born Sept. 6, 1728 at Westover and died Jan. 1, 1777. (For sketch of his career, see *Va. Mag.*, XXXVII, 301-314.)

it be his good pleasure. I read Latin till one, when Captain Spry[1] came but could eat nothing because he was sick. After dinner I was a little out of order myself but visited my sick people again, who were better, thank God. I had a negro girl die. God's will be done.

24. I rose about 5, read Hebrew and Greek. I prayed and had tea. I danced. The weather was cold and cloudy, the wind east. My people were better, thank God. I wrote letters to England and read Latin. I walked to visit my sick who were better, thank God. I ate cold beef and sallet. After dinner it rained and I read more Latin and then played billiards. At night talked with my people and prayed. It rained abundantly in the night.

25. I rose about 5, read Hebrew and Greek. I prayed and had tea. I danced. The weather was cold, with rain, the wind southwest. My sick were better, thank God, but their fever returned about 10, pretty violently. It rained great part of the day. I read Latin and wrote letters till dinner when I ate cold tongue and sallet. After dinner my wife had an indisposition. My son and I played piquet. I talked with my people and prayed.

26. I rose about 5, read Hebrew and Greek. I prayed and had coffee. I danced. The weather was cold and clear, the wind northwest. My sick people were better, thank God. Several sick above. I went not to church but read Latin till the girls came from church. I ate roast veal. After dinner I read more Latin till the evening and then walked to visit my sick who were better, thank God. I talked with my people and prayed.

27. I rose about 5, read Hebrew and Greek. I prayed and had tea. I danced. The weather was cold and clear, the wind north. My sick seemed better, thank God. I read

---

[1]Captain William Spry, master of the snow *Phoenix,* was active in the Virginia trade (Harker); he entered the Upper District of James River, Aug. 3, 1739 with a cargo of sundry European goods from London, and was ready to clear out of James River for Bristol in late November (*Va. Gaz.*, Dec. 7-14, Nov. 16-23, 1739).

Latin and wrote English till one when old Bridges[1] came and dined with us and I ate roast mutton. After dinner we talked and then came Tom Short[2] and I wrote letters to the Governor,[3] then played bowls, talked at night with my people, and prayed. Mina came just to see us.

---

[1]The portrait painter Charles Bridges, accompanied by several of his children, arrived in Williamsburg in 1735, according to a letter of Governor Gooch to his brother, dated May 26, 1735 (copies of Gooch Letters in Colonial Williamsburg, Inc.). Several portraits of members of the family of the diarist have been attributed to Bridges as the artist. William Sawitzky, Advisory Curator of American Art, the New York Historical Society, thinks the portrait of the diarist's wife, Maria Taylor Byrd, is superior to all the other portraits attributed to Bridges and is of the opinion that if it is by Bridges it was painted in England about the time of her marriage to Byrd in 1724. The portrait of Evelyn Byrd, the diarist's daughter, in Mr. Sawitzky's judgment was done after Bridges' arrival in Virginia. He is further of the opinion that the portrait generally credited as that of the diarist's first wife, Lucy Parke Byrd, is actually a portrait of his daughter Wilhelmina who married Thomas Chamberlayne and was painted as a companion piece to that of Evelyn Byrd. In lecture notes on these portraits Mr. Sawitzky has said, "Just as the red Cardinal in the picture of Evelyn Byrd is an American feature, so are the Indian basket and negro boy servant American features in the picture of Wilhelmina, who in 1735 would have been 20 years old, the apparent age of the young woman in the painting. Remember also Col. Byrd's remark: 'He (Bridges) has drawn my children.' "

Professor John M. Phillips of Yale University in 1936 secured from a descendant of Charles Bridges copies of several letters written by another and elderly kinsman of the artist who owned a manuscript written by his grandfather, William Bridges about 1825-30. According to this manuscript, which both Professor Phillips and Mr. Sawitzky recognize as based only on family tradition, Charles Bridges married in London, in 1683, Miss Alice Flower and came to Virginia in 1735 "as a very old man," and that "around 1740 or so he returned to London to die." (The foregoing details are based on a syllabus of a lecture delivered by Professor Sawitzky on Charles Bridges at New York University, and are cited through the kind coöperation of Professor Sawitzky.)

[2]Thomas Short was one of the fifteen able woodsmen chosen to accompany Byrd on the survey of the Virginia-Carolina boundary line (*William Byrd's Histories of the Dividing Line betwixt Virginia and North Carolina*, ed. W. K. Boyd [Raleigh, 1929], p. 29). Short was named inspector at the public warehouse at Maycocks (or Maycox), across the river from Westover, in 1736, again in 1738, and at Munford's in Prince George County in 1739 (*Ex. Jour.*, IV, 382, 431; *Va. Mag.*, XIV, 230, 347).

[3]William Gooch was Lieutenant Governor and Commander in Chief of the Colony and Dominion of Virginia Sept. 11, 1727 to Oct. 15, 1740. He left Virginia then as Colonel and Quarter Master General on the Carthagena expedition and President James Blair served in his place until his return in July 1741 (see entry for July 30, 1741). On his return from the ill-ventured expedition against the Spaniards, Gooch continued in his former post in Virginia until his final return to England, June 20, 1749 (*Va. Hist. Port.*, p. 504). For his career, see Percy Scott Flippin, "William Gooch, Successful Royal Governor of Virginia," *North Carolina Historical Review*, IV, 37-49.

Byrd expressed esteem for Gooch, writing Charles, Earl of Orrery, Feb. 3, 1728, "By great Accident we have a very worthy man to represent Lord Orkney. It is Major Gooch. . ." (Orrery MSS, Harvard College Library.)

28. I rose about 5, and went with my daughter Anne[1] to visit Mrs. Brun and her sick family. I prayed. The weather was very cold, the wind northeast. We got there about 10 and found Mrs. Brun still sick and several of the family. We played piquet till dinner and I ate stewed chicken. After dinner I took leave and we returned home, where we got about 7. I talked with my people and prayed.

29. I rose about 5, read Hebrew and Greek. I prayed and had tea. I danced. The weather was very cool and clear, the wind north. I beat my man Hampton [*or* Hamilton] for lying and other transgressions. I read Latin and wrote letters till dinner when I ate minced veal. After dinner I put things in order and read Latin till the evening when I played bowls and then walked. Tom Short brought word from town that we should have a war and that it was proclaimed in England.[2] John Ravenscroft[3] came with him. I talked with my people and prayed.

30. I rose about 5, read Hebrew and Greek. I prayed and had coffee. I danced. The weather continued cool and clear, the wind north. I had a small looseness. However, I read Latin and wrote letters. I walked to visit my sick people till dinner, when I ate fish. After dinner I put things

---

[1]Anne Byrd was the oldest child by Byrd's second wife, Maria Taylor Byrd. She was born in London on Feb. 5, 1725; she married, in 1742, Charles Carter, son of Robert ("King") Carter, the second of his three wives. She died Sept. 11, 1757. (Bassett, p. 447; *Va. Mag.*, XXXI, 39-48.)

[2]*The Virginia Gazette,* Aug. 24-31, 1739, carried news of the War of Jenkins' Ear proclaimed in England against Spain, and printed the proclamation of Governor Gooch declaring his readiness to issue Commissions of Marque and Reprisal to apprehend, seize, and take the ships, vessels, and goods belonging to the King of Spain, his vassals and subjects. And the *Gazette* voiced the opinion that "there are Men of Spirit as well as Ability in this Colony, who will fit out vessels for that Purpose to the Honour and Interest of themselves and their Country."

[3]Thomas Ravenscroft in 1723 bought Maycox on James River opposite Westover (*Va. Mag.*, XXXVIII, 128; *Wm. Q. (1)*, XVIII, 213-14). John Ravenscroft, as executor of the will of Thomas Ravenscroft, deceased, brought suit before a Charles City court in July, 1738 (*Va. Mag.*, XXII, 433). John Ravenscroft was named a justice for Prince George County at a meeting of the Council, April 27, 1737 (*Ex. Jour.*, IV, 391; Prince George Minute Book, 1737-1740, *passim*; Charles City Order Book, 1737-1751, pp. 9, 49, 96).

Byrd sent a letter to his fellow student at the Temple, Benjamin Lynde, Chief Justice of Massachusetts, by John Ravenscroft (Byrd to Lynde, Feb. 20, 1736, *Va. Mag.*, IX, 241-44).

in order, read Latin till the evening, then played bowls. Mrs. Brun and her family continued sick. I prayed.

31. I rose about 5, read Hebrew and Greek. I prayed and had tea. I danced. The weather was cold and clear, the wind south. The sick were better, thank God, but my looseness continued. I read Latin and settled some accounts till dinner when I ate sturgeon. After dinner we played billiards and then at bowls and then walked, which tired me extremely. I talked with my people and prayed. Several of my people were sick, God preserve them.

September, 1739

1. I rose about 5, read Hebrew and Greek. I prayed and had tea. I danced. The weather was cold and clear, the wind southwest. My people continued sick, God preserve them. I wrote letters and read Latin till dinner, when I ate fish. Mr. Anderson[1] dined with us. After dinner I put things in order, read Latin, and then played bowls and walked. At night talked with my people and prayed.

2. I rose about 5, read Hebrew and Greek. I prayed and had coffee. I danced. The weather was warm and cloudy, the wind southwest. About 11 went to church and had a good sermon. After church the parson,[2] Mr. Cole[3] and Mr.

---

[1]Possibly Charles, son of Rev. Charles Anderson, minister of Westover Parish 1694-1718 (*Wm. Q. (1)*, IV, 127). When Byrd was surveying the Virginia-Carolina boundary he stopped at Charles Anderson's on the west bank of Meherrin River, that the parson, Peter Fontaine, might christen one of Anderson's children (Bassett, p. 91).

Charles Anderson was named in the will of the Rev. Charles Anderson, 1718, but does not appear as executor with his four sisters when the will of Mrs. Frances Anderson, widow of the Rev. Charles Anderson, was presented in court in 1740 (Charles City Order Book, 1737-1751, p. 115). Frances Anderson was awarded an attachment against the estate of Charles Anderson by the Prince George court in May, 1738, and this same month Charles Anderson was named on the grand jury in that county (Prince George Minute Book, 1737-1740, pp. 106, 119). In Charles City county Bridgen Waddill was authorized to attach a horse belonging to Charles Anderson, "who had absconded, so that process could not be had agt him" in satisfaction of a claim of four pounds current money (Charles City Order Book, 1737-1751, April 1741, p. 156).

A case is recorded in the Henrico County court, March, 1740, by David Bell against Charles Anderson, who had left corn to the amount of eighteen barrels and four bushels at his home in Amelia County, and Anderson failing to appear in court, attachment against the corn was adjudged to Bell (Henrico Order Book, 1737-1746, p. 136). Byrd seems to have had difficulties with Anderson during this same period and to have discharged him from his service, though he later asked to be taken back. (See entries for June 24, 25, July 7, 8, 1740; August 3, 4, 1741.) In 1720 Henry Anderson had been overseer for Byrd at the Falls (Diary, 1717-1721).

[2]Peter Fontaine (1691-1757), Huguenot, educated at Dublin University, had the King's Bounty for Virginia in 1716. After serving various parishes he was minister of Westover Parish from 1720 to 1757. He accompanied Byrd as chaplain in the survey of the Virginia-Carolina boundary line in 1728 (Goodwin, p. 269; *Va. Mag.*, XXXII, 228-29; Perry, pp. 270-72; Charles City Records, 1751-57, p. 494; *Histories of the Dividing Line*, ed. Boyd, *passim*).

Fontaine lived in Charles City County between Weyanoke and Swineyards, about two miles north of the James River (Ann Maury, *Memoirs of a Huguenot Family* [New York, 1853], p. 379).

[3]William Cole belonged to a family prominent in Charles City County and

Wendey[1] dined with us and I ate chicken. After dinner we talked and had coffee. In the evening the parson stayed but the others went away. I talked with my people and prayed. It rained pretty much.

3. I rose about 5, read Hebrew and Greek. I prayed and had coffee. I danced. The weather was warm and clear, the wind west. My people continued sick; God preserve them. I made them a visit. The parson played billiards and heard the children till dinner when I ate boiled pork. After dinner he went away. I read more Latin and then played bowls. In the evening I visited the sick again and found them better, thank God.

4. I rose about 5, read Hebrew and Greek. I prayed and had tea. I danced. The weather was warm and clear, the wind southwest. I had a small fever last night but was better, thank God. I was out of order myself and ate nothing but French beans. After dinner I grew worse but played billiards and held up till the evening, then retired and drank a pint of cold water which made me sweat. I talked with my people and prayed.

5. I rose about 5, read Hebrew and Greek. I prayed and had tea. I danced. The weather was cold and cloudy, the wind southwest. My head ached a little but my fever was off and I continued pretty well all day. I read a little Latin till dinner and ate roast mutton. After dinner we played billiards and I walked to visit the sick, who were better, thank God. In the evening it rained pretty much. I talked with my people and prayed.

6. I rose about 5, read Hebrew and Greek. I prayed and

---

lived at Buckland, adjacent to Westover. In 1739 this William Cole was concerned in building a public warehouse at Swineyards, just below Westover. He was cited on several occasions before the Charles City County court for failure to keep the warehouse in repair. (Charles City Order Book, 1737-1751, pp. 90, 180, 396.) His son William Cole sold a portion of Buckland to William Byrd III in 1769 (*Wm. Q. (1)*, V, 179).

[1]Thomas Wendey was a merchant in Charles City County and frequently brought suit in the county court for recovery of debts. He was a witness to the will of Francis Hardyman, August, 1741. He was presented by the grand jury for "profane swearing" in May, 1742. (Charles City Order Book, 1737-1751, *passim.*)

had coffee. I danced. The weather was clear and cold, the wind north. I walked to visit the sick and found them better, thank God, but I had my fit again about 11, went to bed and drank cold water and sweated violently for four hours. My fever continued till 10. I talked with my people and ate two poached eggs. I slept well, thank God.

7. I rose about 5, read Hebrew and Greek. I prayed and had tea. I danced. The weather continued cold and clear, the wind northwest. I began to take the bark.[1] The minx killed more fowls, confound him! I wrote letters and read Latin till dinner. After dinner came Spalding's[2] storekeeper, and the captain of the plank ship and after them Captain Isham Randolph[3] without news. After dinner all went away but Captain Randolph, who played bowls and then played piquet till 10. I talked with my people and prayed. F-k-l-r brought a letter that Mrs. Brun and her family were better, thank God.

8. I rose about 5, and read Hebrew. I prayed and had coffee. I danced. The weather continued cold and clear, the wind east. I wrote a letter by . . .

[The MS here breaks off at the bottom of a page, and the next page begins with the entry for December 5, 1739; apparently a number of leaves are missing.]

---

[1]I.e. quinine. See Wyndham B. Blanton, *Medicine in Virginia in the Eighteenth Century* (Richmond, 1931).

[2]This was probably Alexander Spalding who dealt in the export corn trade and other mercantile enterprises in Williamsburg with John Lidderdale and was also interested with him in land grants. (See entry for June 11, 1740; *Wm. Q. (1)*, V, 135, 244; XVI, 185; *Va. Mag.*, V, 91; XVI, 87.)

[3]Isham Randolph was the third son of Colonel William Randolph of Turkey Island and Mary Isham his wife. In his early manhood he had followed the sea and Byrd had often seen him during his residence in London. (Diary, 1717-1721.) He held important offices, served as agent for Virginia in England, a burgess, a justice, and adjutant general and then lieutenant general of the colony. He lived at Dungeness in Goochland County (*Va. Mag.*, XLV, 81, 383-86, 394; *Wm. Q. (2)*, VI, 304). Byrd called him "an Israelite without Guile" (Byrd to Hanbury, Mar. 20, 1736, *Va. Mag.*, XXXVI, 215).

He had other interests than statecraft, however, for the ship *Anna* of London, James Straghan, captain, entered the Upper District of James River from London and Guinea, June 1, 1739, with 380 negroes consigned to Isham and Richard Randolph (Harker).

December, 1739

5. I rose about 5, read Hebrew and Greek. I prayed and had tea. I danced. The weather was cold and clear, the wind northwest. I wrote several things and walked; then read Latin till dinner, when Phil Johnson came and made proposals about Annie.[1] I ate broiled mutton. After dinner we walked and at night played cards. I talked with my people and prayed.

6. I rose about 6 and read Luke. I prayed and had coffee. I danced. The weather was cold and clear, the wind northwest. Mr. Johnson went away with a gentle denial. I read Latin till dinner when I ate fish. After dinner we walked about the plantation. A man came that walked from Pennsylvania in his way to Carolina. I talked with my people and played piquet and prayed.

7. I rose about 6, read Hebrew and Greek. I prayed and had hominy. I danced. The weather was cold and foggy, the wind north. The m-n [mine?] inspector came from the other side. I walked and read Latin till dinner when I ate fish again. After dinner I put things in order and then walked about the plantation. At night talked with my people, played piquet, and prayed.

8. I rose about 6, read Hebrew and Greek. I prayed and had tea. I danced. The weather was cold and foggy again, the wind north. I wrote several things and read Latin till one, then walked about the plantation till dinner when I ate

---

[1]Byrd's daughter Annie was born in London, Feb. 5, 1725. She was thus not quite fifteen years old and her youth may have been the reason for the gentle denial given this suitor (Bassett, p. 447). She married, in 1742, Charles Carter of Cleve. Philip Johnson married Elizabeth Bray, daughter of Thomas Bray of Littletown, James River, probably in 1743 (*Va. Mag.*, XXXIV, 109). He represented King and Queen County in the House of Burgesses but later moved to James City County and had a house in Williamsburg known now as Bassett Hall. During the years of his residence there he had twenty-nine slaves baptized in Bruton Parish Church (W. A. R. Goodwin, *Bruton Parish Church Restored* [Petersburg, 1907]; Rutherfoord Goodwin, *Williamsburg in Virginia* [Richmond, 1935]). He resigned his commission as county lieutenant of James City because of old age in 1776 (*Va. Mag.*, XXV, 423; *Wm. Q. (1)*, XVI, 196).

broiled beef. After dinner we talked and walked again. Mrs. Parrish[1] came to thank me for curing her husband. I talked with my people and prayed.

9. I rose about 6, read Hebrew and Greek. I prayed and had tea coffee [*sic*]. I danced. The weather was cold and cloudy and threatened snow, the wind north. However, my family went to church; but I read English till dinner, when I ate boiled beef. After dinner I put up my things in order to go to Williamsburg. I walked about the garden,[2] talked to my people, and prayed.

10. I rose about 6, prayed and had chocolate, then recommended my family to the Almighty and went into the chariot about 8. About 10 Colonel Bolling[3] overtook me and came into the chariot and got to Williamsburg about 3. I put myself in order and walked to the Commissary's,[4] where

---

[1]Edward Parrish and William Parrish appear in the records of Charles City County for this period as serving on the grand jury or in connection with road repairs and other functions for the county (Charles City Order Book, 1737-1751, pp. 65, 105, 127, 146, 159, 166). The will of William Parrish was presented at the January court, 1745, by Mary Parrish as executor (*ibid.*, p. 327). The Parrish family had long been connected with Charles City County (see Diary, 1709-1712).

[2]The garden at Westover was described just about the period of this diary by John Bartram, after a visit there, in a letter to Peter Collinson: "Col. Byrd is very prodigalle his [illegible] in new Gates, gravel Walks hedges and cedars finely twined and a little green house with two or three orange trees with fruit on them in short he hath the finest seat in Virginia." (Bartram Papers, f. 21, July 18 [no year given, but probably 1740], Pa. Hist. Soc.; copy in Colonial Williamsburg, Inc.) The diarist was buried in this garden, where his tomb with its eloquent eulogy is preserved (*Va. Mag.*, XXXII, 36-37). See also *Historic Gardens of Virginia*, compiled by the James River Garden Club, ed. Edith Tunis Sale (Richmond [1923]), pp. 47-53.

[3]Colonel Robert Bolling (1682-1749) had a store and a mill on the Appomattox, thus tapping the trade near the site of the later town of Petersburg at the falls of the Appomattox (*Wm. Q. (2)*, XVI, 545-46). He was a justice and surveyor in Prince George County, a vestryman in Bristol Parish, and held a commission in the county militia (Philip Slaughter, *A History of Bristol Parish, Virginia*, 2d ed. [Richmond, 1879], pp. 140-41; *A Memoir of a Portion of the Bolling Family in England and Virginia* [Richmond, 1868]).

Col. Bolling entertained Byrd in November, 1728, on his return from his survey of the dividing line, at his comfortable home within hearing of the falls of the Appomattox River, and again in 1733 on his return from the "Journey to Eden." (Bassett, pp. 252, 326, 329.)

[4]James Blair, Commissary to Virginia for the Bishop of London, founder and president of William and Mary College for fifty years, president of the Council, and Acting Governor while Governor Gooch was absent on the Carthagena expedition, 1740-41, played a dynamic rôle in the affairs of

I ate a mutton chop and talked till 8, and then returned to my lodgings and put my house in order and prayed.[5]

11. I rose about 6 and read nothing because I went soon to breakfast with the Commissary, where I had chocolate, and then waited on the Governor and went with him to church and from thence to the capitol where we had but seven judges. We tried two prisoners[1] and then had a fine dinner at Wetherburn's[2] and I ate boiled turkey. There I

Virginia, to the jealous mistrust of the Governors and often of his fellow Councillors. For Byrd's attitude toward Blair, see his letter to Major Otway, Feb., 1740 (*Va. Mag.*, XXXVII, 28-32). Governor Gooch soon after his arrival in the colony wrote frankly to his brother about Blair, "The Commissary is a very vile old ffellow, but he does not know that I am sensible of it, being still in appearance good ffriends: the best Policy will be to kill him with kindness, but there is no perplexing device within his reach, that he does not throw in my way, purely because He is not my privy Councillor." (Gooch to his brother, Williamsburgh, June 9, 1728, Gooch letters, Colonial Williamsburg, Inc.) But after years of working with Blair, Gooch came to a fairer estimate of his abilities and in reporting Blair's death in his eighty-eighth year in 1743 he wrote this same brother: "If his Belly had been as sound as his Head and Breast, he might have lived many years longer." (May 14, 1743, *loc. cit.*)

[5]Byrd acquired lot No. 24 in Williamsburg from James Shields for £120 as recorded in deed of sale on May 12, 1707 (York County Records. Deeds, Bonds, Vol. II, p. 234). A later deed, Feb. 26, 1749, recorded the sale by James Crosby to Andrew Buchanan and Company of three lots, "on the south side of the Main Street opposite to the Rawley Tavern which said Lots are marked in the Plan of the said City by the Nos. [*not given*] which formerly belonged to the late Colonell William Bird of Charles City County . . ." (*ibid.*, Book V, p. 393). While Byrd seems to have owned property in Williamsburg, it is not clear where he lodged at this period when attending the sessions of the Council.

[1]*The Virginia Gazette*, published in Williamsburg, carried on Dec. 14, 1739, this item: "At the Court of Oyer and Terminer, held here this Week, the Three following Persons were try'd, viz.

Dorothy Ambler, for Felony; convicted, and burnt in the Hand
John Oldham, for Manslaughter; convicted, and burnt in the hand with a cold Iron.
Jonothan Faithful, for Felony: convicted, and received Sentence of Death."

On Jan. 4, 1740, the *Gazette* reported: "This Day about Twelve o'Clock, Jonothan Faithful was brought out of Goal, attended by the Rev. Mr. Hartswell [see entry for Apr. 20, 1740] to the Place of Execution, whom he heartily thank'd for his Care of him during his Confinement. He also express'd his Gratitude to the Governor for giving him so long a Time; confess'd the Fact for which he was to suffer, declar'd he was in Charity with all Mankind, and desir'd others to take Warning by his unhappy Example."

[2]Henry Wetherburn (or Wetherburne), manager of the famous Raleigh Tavern and other taverns in the colonial capital, was a genial host and made his inn a popular resort for the official group in the government. His arrack punch was widely noted in the colony and his table seems to have had an enviable reputation. Some authorities state that Wetherburn conducted the Raleigh Tavern from 1734 to 1749, but the official publication of Colonial

stayed till 8 o'clock and then went home in Mr. Barradall's[1] chariot and prayed.

12. I rose about 6, and read nothing. I prayed and had coffee. The weather was warm and cloudy, the wind southwest. Mr. Booth[2] and Thornton breakfasted with me. About 11 went again to the capitol and sat till 2 and then dined with Mr. Barradall and ate hashed chicken. After dinner we went to Mr. Kemp's[3] funeral and from thence walked with Colonel Grymes[4] to visit Mr. Needler[5] who was sick. Then returned home and prayed.

Williamsburg, Inc., states that the origins of the Raleigh Tavern are not known, though it was built prior to 1742 and for some years was under the management of Henry Wetherburn (*Raleigh Tavern,* Colonial Williamsburg, Inc.). He married first Mary, widow of Henry Bowcock, inn keeper in Williamsburg, secondly, July 11, 1751, Anne Marot Inglis Shields, daughter of Jean Marot, a Huguenot tavern keeper in Williamsburg, and widow of first Mungo Inglis, and second James Shields (*T's Q.,* IV, 30-31; *Wm. Q. (1),* V, 118).

[1]Edward Barradall, one of the best known lawyers in Virginia in his time, represented the legal interests of Lord Fairfax in the colony and was attorney general of the colony of Virginia from 1737 to his death in 1743, as well as judge of the vice-admiralty court. *Virginia Colonial Decisions: The Reports by Sir John Randolph and by Edward Barradall of Decisions of the General Court of Virginia (1730-40, 1768-72),* ed. R. T. Barton [Boston, 1909], I, 243-48; W. A. R. Goodwin, *Historical Sketch of Bruton Church, Williamsburg, Virginia* [Petersburg, Va.], pp. 102-3; Bassett, p. 401; Fairfax Harrison, *Landmarks of Old Prince William* [privately printed, Richmond, 1924], pp. 163-4, 172).

[2]William Thornton and Thomas Booth owned land in the same precinct with John Bickerton and Mills, when marked off for processioning by the vestry of St. Paul's Parish, Hanover County, Sept. 30, 1751 (*Vestry Book of St. Paul's Parish,* p. 316). Since Bickerton's land is known to have adjoined some of Byrd's land in Hanover and Byrd sold land to Mills (see entry for Aug. 4, 1740), the conclusion seems justified that Byrd made a sale of some of his Hanover land to William Thornton and Thomas Booth (see entry for Mar. 6, 1740).

Thomas Booth was elected a vestryman of St. Paul's Parish on Apr. 5, 1743, and took an active part in its affairs (*op. cit.,* p. 170 *et passim*).

[3]Matthew Kemp was clerk of the secretary's office and of James City County court, an alderman of the City of Williamsburg. He had been earlier a justice of the peace and a burgess for Middlesex County (*Va. Gaz.,* Dec. 7-14, 1739, prints his obituary notice; *Wm. Q. (1),* XXI, 95-6).

[4]John Grymes of Brandon, Middlesex County (1691-1748) served in the Virginia House of Burgesses and in 1725 was made a member of the Council. He was auditor general of Virginia for a brief period, and receiver general from 1723 to his death (*Va. Mag.,* XXVII, 404-5; *Wm. Q. (1),* VI, 145-6). He was a commissioner with Byrd on the survey of the boundaries of the Northern Neck in 1736 (Bassett, p. 410).

[5]Benjamin Needler, who had succeeded Sir John Randolph as clerk of the House of Burgesses in 1734, took his oath as clerk of the Council in 1739. Needler came to Virginia from England about 1711 (Sainsbury Abstracts,

13. I rose about 6 and read nothing. I had coffee and prayed. The weather very cold, the wind northwest and blowing violently in the night. However I went to Colonel Bassett's[1] about 10 and Beverley Randolph[2] went with me. We got there by 2 and dined, when I ate boiled chine. After dinner we talked and drank till 9 and then retired, when I prayed and slept well, thank God.

14. I rose about 6 and read nothing. I prayed. The weather was very cold and clear, the wind northwest. I had tea. About 10 we took leave and proceeded to Daniel Custis's[3] where we got about 3 and found him pretty well. There we had turkey and chine. After dinner Major [Dandridge][4] came to us and sat with us till 9, when we retired to our [divans?] and slept well, thank God.

15. I rose about 6, and read nothing, but prayed and had

1706-14, p. 258, Va. State Archives), and gained recognition as an able lawyer (*Ex. Jour.*, III, IV, *passim*; *Va. Gaz.*, Aug. 3-10, Oct. 19-26, 1739; *T's. Q.*, I, 69; *Va. Mag.*, XIV, 26).

[1]William Bassett, of Eltham, New Kent County, son of William Bassett (1670-1723) was chosen a member of the House of Burgesses in 1742 (*Va. Mag.*, IV, 162). His family and the Byrd family at Westover frequently visited each other (Byrd to William Bassett, Apr. 1, 1739, MS, Library of Congress).

[2]Beverley Randolph was the oldest son of William Randolph (2d) of Turkey Island (see entry for Apr. 14, 1740). He was a justice of the peace for Henrico from 1740 and later served in the House of Burgesses (*Va. Mag.*, XXXII, 386-7, XLVII, 50, XLV, 68; *Wm. Q. (1)*, V, 243).

[3]Daniel Parke Custis, son of John Custis and Frances Parke (daughter of Colonel Daniel Parke), was the nephew of Byrd's first wife, Lucy Parke. He was also Byrd's godson, for Byrd with Governor Spotswood and Hannah Ludwell were his godparents. Daniel Custis must have been a striking looking man, for his father wrote a kinswoman in England in 1731, "If Colonel Parke had lived to see my son, he would have seen his own picture to greater perfection than even Sir Godfrey Kneller could draw it." Colonel Custis was referring to the well-known portrait of Colonel Parke in a crimson velvet coat and wearing the miniature of Queen Anne, presented to him by Her Majesty when he brought her, as messenger from the Duke of Marlborough, the glad tidings of victory at Blenheim (G. W. P. Custis, *Recollections and Private Memoirs of Washington*, ed. B. J. Lossing [New York, 1860], pp. 18-22). He had a considerable library, was interested in gardening, and was on intimate and congenial terms with Byrd. (For his courtship of Byrd's daughter Anne see entry for July 19, 1741.) He married Martha Dandridge, who, after his death in 1757, married George Washington. (*Wm. Q. (1)*, V, 35; *Va. Mag.*, XVII, 404-12; *Va. Gaz.*, Aug. 12-19, 1737.)

[4]Probably John Dandridge, a planter of New Kent County, best known as the father of Martha Dandridge who married first Daniel Custis and second George Washington (*Wm. Q. (1)*, V, 33). Born in 1700, he came to Virginia about 1722, acquired land at Hampton and then settled in New Kent County of which he was clerk in 1747. He died Aug. 31, 1756 (*Va. Biog.*, I, 220-21).

tea. The weather continued cold and clear, the wind west. About 10 we took leave and went home where we got about 3 and found my family well, thank God. I ate cold beef. After dinner we discoursed about many things, I talked with my people and prayed and slept well, thank God. We had 18 hogs from Meherrin.[1]

16. I rose about 6, read Hebrew. I prayed and had coffee. I danced. The weather was warm and cloudy with little rain, the wind southwest. I put my matters in order and went not to church. After church came Mr. Wendey and dined with us and I ate sausage and eggs. In the afternoon Bob came from the Falls where he left all well, thank God. In the evening Mr. Wendey departed and I prayed.

17. I rose about 6, read Hebrew and Greek. I prayed and had coffee. I danced. The weather was warm and foggy, the wind southwest. I wrote several letters. Beverley Randolph went away to Colonel Harrison's and I settled some accounts till dinner when I ate roast chine. After dinner the people went over the river to bring the beef and brought four very late. In the evening we walked. I talked with my people and prayed.

18. I rose about 6, read Hebrew and Greek. I prayed and had tea. I danced. The weather was warm and foggy, the wind southwest. I wrote to the Falls and sent the boat. I settled some accounts and wrote letters till dinner when I ate roast mutton. After dinner I put things in order and walked about the plantation. At night Dr. Tschiffeley came. I talked with my people and with the Doctor and prayed. The moon changed upon warm foggy weather.

19. I rose about 6, read Hebrew and Greek. I prayed and had hominy. I danced. The weather continued foggy,

---

[1]An entry in the Byrd Title Book (p. 190) states: "Mr. Byrd having now a large Quantity of Land upon Roanoke River, thought proper to purchase a Plantation upon Meherrin River, that might serve as a convenient Stage or half way House to that distant Territory. He therefore purchased of George Hicks the Plantation where he lived containing 429 acres, which the said Hicks sold to him by Lease and Release" (papers follow, dated Jan. 12, 1729 and acknowledged in Prince George County court, Jan. 13, 1729, and a plat of the land is sketched facing p. 193).

the wind southwest. The Doctor went away and L-n-r returned to Roanoke;[1] God preserve him and all with him. I wrote letters and settled some accounts till dinner, when I ate sausage and eggs and ate too much. After dinner we walked and played billiards. Tom G-r-n-r was better, thank God.

20. I rose about 6, read Hebrew and Greek. I prayed and had tea. I danced. The weather was cold and clear, the wind northwest. I wrote to Mr. Anderson about his accounts. Tom G-r-n-r was still better, thank God. I played billiards and walked till dinner, when I ate pork griskins. After dinner we walked about the plantation. At [night] came Mr. Hall[2] and Mr. Ravenscroft and stayed about an hour. I played piquet and prayed.

21. I rose about 6, read Hebrew and Greek. I prayed and had tea. I danced. The weather was cold and cloudy, the wind west. Tom was still better, thank God. I wrote a letter to Mrs. Anderson[3] in Hanover and read English till dinner when Mr. Anderson came and dined with us and I ate sparerib. After dinner we talked about our accounts and then walked about the plantation. I talked with my people and prayed.

---

[1]After his survey in 1728 of the boundary line between Virginia and North Carolina, Byrd acquired large tracts of land on Roanoke river, including 20,000 acres he bought from the North Carolina commissioners "between Sable Creek running into the south branch of Roanoke river & the Irvin." He called this "The Land of Eden" and one of his best-known literary works is his account of his "Journey to the Land of Eden" in 1733 (Bassett, pp. 279-331; Byrd Title Book, pp. 162-88; see plat of the 20,000 acres in *Histories of the Dividing Line*, ed. Boyd, p. 268). Byrd's plan for settling a colony of Swiss on a grant of 100,000 acres on both sides the south branch of Roanoke river occupied his interest and attention at this period (*Ex. Jour.*, IV, 443; *William Byrd's Natural History of Virginia* or *The Newly Discovered Eden*, ed. and trans. from a German version by Richmond Croom Beatty and William J. Mulloy [Richmond, 1940]).

[2]This was probably John Hall who in 1730 married Anne Bolling, daughter of Colonel Robert and Anne Cocke Bolling (see entry for Dec. 10, 1739, and Mar. 19, 1741). Hall was a justice in Prince George in 1736-39, and owned lands in Surry, Prince George, Brunswick and Amelia (*Wm. Q. (2)*, XVII, 285; Prince George Minute Book, 1737-1740, pp. 106, 310; Charles City Order Book, 1737-1751, pp. 237, 398).

[3]This may have been Mrs. Charity Anderson, who is frequently mentioned as owning land in Hanover near Byrd's lands there when the lands in St. Paul's Parish were processioned (*Vestry Book of St. Paul's Parish*, pp. 292, 299, 302, 309).

22. I rose about 6, read Hebrew and Greek. I prayed and had tea. I danced. The weather continued warm and clear, the wind southwest. We played billiards. I read English and walked and played billiards till dinner, when I ate tongue and udder. Mr. Braxton[1] and his son and young Mary dined with us. After dinner we talked and walked about the plantation. At night I played cards. I talked with my people and prayed.

23. I rose about 6, read Hebrew and Greek. I prayed and had coffee. I danced. The weather was warm and clear, the wind southwest. About 11 we went to church and had a good sermon. After church nobody came home with us and I ate roast goose. After dinner we walked. My wife had a headache. At night I talked with my people and prayed.

24. I rose about 6, read Hebrew and Greek. I prayed and had tea. I danced. The weather was beginning to change and was like to rain, the wind north, but came soon again to southwest. I spoke too crossly to Mrs. B-r-k-l, God forgive me, about things she had brought from Roanoke. I ate goose giblet. After dinner I walked, talked with my people, and prayed.

25. I rose about 6, read Hebrew and Greek. I prayed and had tea. I danced. The weather was cold and clear, the wind southwest but blowing fiercely. I went not to church, but cleaned myself. After church came John Stith[2]

---

[1]This was George Braxton, Jr., who had lost his wife Mary Carter Braxton, daughter of Robert ("King") Carter in 1736 (*Va. Gaz.*, Sept. 15-22, 1736). The son referred to here may have been either Carter Braxton, born in 1736 (*Va. Hist. Port.*, p. 229), who was one of the signers of the Declaration of Independence, or his other son, George Braxton.

George Braxton, Jr., here referred to, was the son of George Braxton, founder of the family fortunes in Virginia, who died in 1748 at the age of 70 (*Va. Mag.*, VI, 433). Just two months before this entry in the diary George Braxton, Sr., had imported in the ship *Prince of Orange*, Japhet Bird, commander, more than two hundred choice slaves who were offered for sale at York and West Point (*Va. Gaz.*, Aug. 3-10, 1739).

[2]John Stith was the son of Mary Randolph and her husband, either John or William Stith (for genealogists of the Stith family are in conflict on this point; see *Va. Mag.*, XLV, 395-6). His elder brother was Rev. William Stith, President of the College of William and Mary (see entry for June 1, 1740). John Stith's wife was Elizabeth Anderson, daughter of Charles Anderson, who was a close friend of the family at Westover during his twenty-four

and his wife, all the Andersons[1] and Mr. Pinkard[2] with John Stith's son and daughter to dinner, and I ate boiled turkey

---

years as minister in Westover parish. John Stith served in the House of Burgesses and later was lieutenant colonel of Charles City County in 1737 (*Wm. Q. (1)*, XXI, 187). He was a member of the Charles City County court and a churchwarden of Westover parish, as well as rendering many other services in county matters (Charles City Order Book, 1737-1751, *passim*). His son, Anderson Stith, married Joanna Bassett, a friend of Byrd's daughters (see entry for Apr. 7, 1740). He qualified to practice law in Charles City County in 1749. He died in 1768 (*Va. Mag.*, XXII, 436; *Wm. Q. (1)*, VI, 125, XXI, 187).

There has been confusion among genealogists of the Stith family as to the daughter or daughters of John Stith and his wife Elizabeth Anderson. Most writers have assigned to him one daughter, Anne, but this diary does not mention her (*Wm. Q. (1)*, VII, 181-82; *Va. Mag.*, XXII, 131-32, 274; XLV, 403). He seems to have had a daughter Mary who was called Molly (see entry for July 20, 1740), and also a daughter Elizabeth, called Betty (see July 22, 1740 and Apr. 5, 1741).

At least the query seems pertinent as to whether this Betty Stith of the diary was the second wife of Booth Armistead, whom some writers have said married Anne Stith, the supposed daughter of John Stith. Booth Armistead had a daughter Betsey, who appears to at least one genealogist to have been the child of a second marriage. The fact that Booth Armistead was an executor with Anderson Stith of John Stith's estate argues a close connection with this branch of the Stith family (*Wm. Q. (1)*, VI, 231).

Mary Stith, who married Buller Herbert, member of a prominent English family (*Wm. Q. (1)*, VIII, 148; *Va. Mag.*, XVIII, 190) and whose daughter Mary Herbert married Colonel Augustine Claiborne has been a source of unfruitful speculation among genealogists of the Claiborne family. They have tended to assume she was the daughter of Drury Stith of Brunswick who died in 1741, but since he is known to have had the three children, Drury, William and Charles, circumstantial evidence connecting this Mary Stith Herbert with the names Buckner and Bathurst, known to have been connected with Drury Stith, has been the chief dependence of this theory. In his Diary, 1717-1721, Byrd made several references to Drury Stith's two daughters (Apr. 14, 1720; March 6, 1721), and on Aug. 18, 1720 he recorded that he went to Captain Drury Stith's for the marriage of his daughter Mary. On August 31, 1720 he notes in his diary that he walked from Major Munford's to Mr. Herbert's who had brought his wife home the day before. Mary Stith Herbert inherited not only large holdings in land in Virginia but from a kinswoman, Mrs. Grammer of England, "a compleat square Block of Buildings in the City of London" (*Wm. Q. (2)*, II, 14-18, especially note 14, pp. 16-17).

[1]This evidently refers to the children of the Rev. Charles Anderson, rector of Westover parish, 1694-1718. He had five children: (*1*) Elizabeth, who married John Stith [see note above], (*2*) Frances, who married Thomas Pinkard in September 1739 (see entry for Jan. 28, 1740), (*3*) Jane, who married Ellyson Armistead in 1740 or 1741 (see entry for July 20, 1740), (*4*) Charlotte, who married Henry Taylor in 1743 (see entry for July 22, 1740), (*5*) Charles, who married ? (see Sept. 1, 1739 entry; *T's. Q.*, VI, 262-63). The will of Mrs. Frances Anderson, relict of Rev. Charles Anderson, was presented in court in February, 1740 by Frances Anderson and John Stith. (Charles City Order Book, 1737-1751, p. 115.)

[2]Thomas Pinkard was the son of Thomas Pinkard, Gentleman, of Christ Church, Lancaster County. His wife was Frances Anderson [see note above]. Thomas Pinkard's will was proved in 1782 (*Wm. Q. (1)*, XII, 263; *(2)*, VIII, 34).

and oysters. After dinner everybody went away but John Stith and his wife. I supped and prayed.

26. I rose about 6 and read nothing. I prayed and had coffee. I danced. The weather was warm and cloudy, the wind west and blowing hard. M-r-t-n told me of several bad things of Mr. Stevens.[1] I wrote a letter to restore Tom L-s-n to his plantation into which Stevens had put his cousin who never had been an overseer. I ate roast goose. After dinner our company went away and I walked. It began to rain in the evening when Mr. Stevens and Harrison the smith came. I talked with my people and prayed.

27. I rose about 6, read Hebrew and Greek. I prayed and had tea. I danced. The weather was cold and cloudy, the wind northeast. I talked with Mr. Stevens about some things I had heard of him and made him weep but we were friends at last. The bad weather kept him and his friend here. I ate roast turkey. After dinner we talked but could not stir out. I talked with my people and prayed.

28. I rose about 6, read Hebrew and Greek. I prayed and had tea. I danced. It continued to snow, the wind northeast. However Mr. Stevens and his friend went off. Mrs. G-r-v ran away from Mrs. Brun and came here and this day came the two Swiss men[2] that lived with her, complaining that they were starved. It snowed till the afternoon. I could not walk but talked with my people and prayed.

29. I rose about 6, read Hebrew and Greek. I prayed

---

[1]Mr. Stevens was probably an overseer in general charge of Byrd's several plantations on both sides of James river in the region of the site of the city of Richmond. He would seem to have been on very friendly terms with Byrd's librarian and secretary, William Procter (Byrd to Procter, Nov. 18, 1740, Bassett, p. 399). There was an Edward Stevens who secured a judgment against James and Robert Clarke and Thomas Twitty in the Charles City county court, July, 1737. (Charles City Order Book, 1737-1751, p. 14.)

[2]Byrd's plan to settle a colony of Swiss on his Roanoke River lands occupied his interest for several years but brought him disappointment in the end (Bassett, pp. 390-94; *William Byrd's Natural History of Virginia*; A. B. Faust, "Swiss Emigration to the American Colonies in the Eighteenth Century," *American Historical Review*, XXII, 21-44; *JHB*, 1727-1734, 1736-1740; *Ex. Jour.*, IV, *passim;* Ex. Jour., Dec. 10, 1740, Va. State Library; *Va. Gaz.*, Jan. 5-12, 1738; *Va. Mag.*, IX, 225-8, 233, XXXVI, 222, 360-61).

and had tea. I danced. The weather was very cold and clear, the wind northwest, and the sun thawed most of the snow. I read old records and abridged them[1] till dinner, when I ate cold souse. After dinner we played billiards and danced because I could not walk. I talked with my people, played piquet, quadrilled, and prayed.

30. I rose about 6, read Hebrew and Greek. I prayed and had coffee. I danced. The weather was cold and clear, the wind north. There called a man for an order for my wheat at the Falls. We went not to church because it was very wet. Mrs. Duke[2] came here to dinner and I ate roast goose. After dinner she returned over the river. I talked with my people and prayed.

31. I rose about 6, read Hebrew and Greek. I prayed and had sack [*or* sage] tea because my head was giddy. The weather was warm and cloudy, with a little rain. I danced. It rained a little all day. I settled some accounts

---

[1]Byrd probably refers here to the Byrd Title Book, into which were copied deeds, plats, wills and other papers connected with the property of his father and himself. The volume is referred to in the will of Mary Willing Byrd as "the green book of records" (*Va. Mag.*, VI, 353). It is now in the possession of the Virginia Historical Society and its publication in instalments was begun in the *Virginia Magazine of History and Biography*, Vol. XLVII, edited and annotated by Mrs. Rebecca Johnston.

[2]Probably Elizabeth Taylor Duke, daughter of Captain John Taylor (see note on Mrs. Greenhill, Jan. 6, 1740), widow of Henry Duke and, it appears, mother of James, John Taylor and Henry Duke (Charles City Order Book, 1737-1751, p. 94 *et passim*). The relationship between the diarist and the Duke family (see Diary, 1709-1712), goes back to Hannah, daughter of Thomas Grendon, merchant of London (*Va. Mag.*, XIV, 207). She married first Thomas Jennings, second William Bird, third William Duke, and fourth William Archer. While the relationship of this William Bird of Martin's Brandon to the father of the diarist is not clear, there was a close family connection, possibly that of uncle (Robert Stewart, "The First William Bird of Charles City County," *Va. Mag.*, XLI, 189-95, XLII, 41-46, 123-28, 247-51). The relationship of William Duke, who died in 1678, to Henry Duke, who took an active part in political life, was a justice of James City County, a burgess and councillor is not proved (*Wm. Q. (1)*, II, 257, XXVI, 286-87, *(2)*, III, 247; *T.'s Q.*, VII, 213; Prince George Minute Book, 1737-1740, p. 311). He was a witness to the will of William Byrd of Westover, father of the diarist, who died in 1704. (See Jane Morris, *The Duke-Symes Family* [Philadelphia, *c.* 1940]; Samuel Gordon Smyth, *A Genealogy of the Duke, Shepherd, Van Metre Family* [Lancaster, Pa., 1909], p. 278.)

till dinner when I ate boiled chine. After dinner I danced because I could not walk. At night talked with my people and played piquet. We killed one of the Roanoke steers. My head was much out of order, for which I took two Scott's pills. I prayed and slept pretty well, thank God.

January, 1740

1. I rose about 6, read Hebrew and Greek. I prayed and had tea. I danced. The weather cleared up and was warm but blowing fiercely at southwest and then northwest. I settled some accounts till dinner when I ate beefsteak. After dinner I put things in order but it was too cold to walk. I talked with my people and played piquet and prayed.

2. I rose about 6, read Hebrew and Greek. I prayed and had tea. I danced. The weather was cold and clear, the wind northwest. My people carted gravel. I settled some accounts and read records till dinner, when I ate venison pasty. In the afternoon we played billiards and then walked a little. In the evening came the sloop for my wheat. I prayed.

3. I rose about 6, read Hebrew and Greek. I prayed and had coffee. I danced. The weather continued very cold, the wind west. We put the wheat on board the sloop. I read English till dinner when I ate roast beef. After dinner we talked and walked, notwithstanding it was very cold. Old Joe[1] died and was buried. I talked with my people and prayed. It was exceedingly cold.

4. I rose about 6, read Hebrew and Greek. I prayed and had hominy. I danced. The weather was very cold and clear, the wind northwest. We began to cut wood in the swamp. I read English and played billiards till dinner when I ate fried venison pasty. After dinner we played at billiards again and walked a little. In the evening played piquet and talked with my people, then retired and prayed.

5. I rose about 6, read Hebrew and Greek. I prayed and had sage [*or* sack] tea. I danced. The weather was still cold and clear, the wind northwest. I wrote a letter and walked, then read English till dinner when Miss Brun came. I ate broiled beef. After dinner we played billiards and

---

[1]Byrd brought a white servant Joe from England in 1720 (Diary, Feb. 20; Mar. 30, 1720; Mar. 3, 4, 1721).

walked a little. At night talked with my people. All well above, thank God. I played piquet and prayed.

6. I rose about 6, [read] Hebrew and Greek. I prayed and had coffee. I danced. The weather continued very cold and clear, the wind north. I went not to church because it was cold, but all the family went besides, and I put my person in order and wrote a letter to the Falls. I ate roast venison and Mrs. Greenhill[1] dined with us and went away. I talked with my people and prayed.

7. I rose about 6, read Hebrew and Greek. I prayed and had tea. I danced. The weather was cold and clear, the wind northwest. My man Bob went to the Falls. I wrote [cheery?] papers for the day and walked till dinner when I ate cold boiled beef. After dinner we played billiards but it was too cold to walk. I talked with my people, drew twelfth cake,[2] gave the people cake and cider, and prayed.

8. I rose about 6, read Hebrew and Greek. I prayed and had hominy. I danced. The weather was cold and clear,

---

[1]Probably Frances Greenhill, who owned land in Prince George and Surry Counties and was granted the right in 1742 to "dispose of her lands, and other estate, by deed or will, notwithstanding her husband, Joseph Greenhill shall happen to be living" (Hen. *Stat.*, V, 216-19; *JHB*, June 23, 1730; *Wm. Q. (1)*, XXII, 58). Her husband had deserted her after two years of marriage and she had not heard from him for twenty years. Her land in Prince George was known as Dutchy Hill.

From internal evidence it appears that Frances Greenhill was one of the four daughters of Captain John Taylor, of Charles City, later Prince George County, who owned Flower de Hundred on the south side of James River (*T.'s Q.*, II, 116) and left it to his daughters, Frances Taylor Greenhill, Elizabeth Taylor Duke (see entry and note, Dec. 30, 1739), Sarah Taylor Hardyman, wife of Francis Hardyman (see entry and note, Apr. 7, 1740), and Henrietta Maria Taylor Hardyman, wife of John Hardyman, of Prince George County.

In 1721 Francis Hardyman and his wife Sarah sold to John Hardyman for £600 English money the house and 150 acres of the plantation known as Flower de Hundred. This part of the land was bounded on the west by the land and tenements of Mrs. Elizabeth Duke, on the east by the land of John Hardyman and on the south by the land called Dutchy Hill, that had lately been occupied by Joseph Greenhill, husband of Frances Taylor Greenhill (Prince George County Deeds, 1713-28, p. 511).

In 1723 Francis and Sarah Hardyman, John and Henrietta Maria Hardyman, Elizabeth Duke and Frances Greenhill sold land on Pigeon Swamp in Surry County, "part of a tract Capt. John Taylor had of Col. Wm. Randolph deceased" (Surry Wills and Deeds, 1715-1730, pp. 491-95).

[2]The celebration of Twelfth Night with revelry of master and servants was an old English custom, and the drinking of cider and the drawing of

the wind still northwest. Mrs. Greenhill came from the Secretary's and told us of their elegant diversions. I read English till dinner and then ate roast beef. After dinner it rained so that I could not walk. At night played cards and talked with my people.

9. I rose about 6, read Hebrew and Greek. I prayed and had coffee. I danced. The weather was cold and cloudy, with little rain, the wind southwest. It rained a little all day so that Mrs. Greenhill could not go. I read Latin till dinner when I ate sheldrake.[1] After dinner we talked and I danced because I could not walk. At night talked with my people, played piquet and prayed. It blew very hard.

10. I rose about 6, read Hebrew and Greek. I prayed and had tea. I danced. The weather was warm and cloudy, but cleared up about 10, the wind west. I played billiards with my son and then read English till one, then Latin till dinner, when I ate roast goose. After dinner we talked and Mrs. Greenhill went over the river and we played billiards and then walked. I talked with my people and prayed.

11. I rose about 6, read Hebrew and Greek. I prayed and had hominy. I danced. The weather was cold and clear, the wind north. I read Latin and played billiards and read records and Latin till dinner, when I ate goose. After dinner we played billiards and then walked about the garden because the ground was damp. I talked with my people, played cards, and prayed.

12. I rose about 6, read Hebrew and Greek. I prayed and had tea. I danced. The weather was cold and cloudy, the wind north, but cleared up about 10. I read Latin and records till dinner when I ate stewed oysters. After dinner played billiards and walked a little. All was well at the

---

twelfth cake were among its most frequent observations. "Twelfth cake—a large cake used at the festivities of Twelfth night, usually frosted and otherwise ornamented, and with a bean or coin, introduced to determine the 'king' or 'queen' of the feast" (*New English Dictionary*). See also *The Book of Days*, ed. R. Chambers (Edinburgh, 1863), I, 55, 61-65.

[1]Sheldrake, usually designating the genus Tadorna of the duck tribe found on the sandy coasts of Europe, North Africa and Asia, was occasionally applied to the North American canvasback. (*New English Dictionary.*)

Falls, thank God. At night talked with my people, played piquet, and prayed.

13. I rose about 6, read Hebrew and Greek. I prayed and had coffee. I danced. The weather was overcast and cold, the wind north. Miss Caton was better and I gave her the bark. I went not to church but sent the children, but nobody beside was there, nor nobody came to dine. I ate roast hare. After dinner we walked. At [night] Robin Mumford[1] came. I talked with my people and prayed.

14. I rose about 6, read Hebrew and Greek. I prayed and had tea. I danced. The weather was cold and clear, the wind southwest. Mr. Mumford went away, the best with a dram of cherry brandy in his belly. I read records and Latin till dinner when I ate boiled beef. After dinner we played billiards and walked. At night talked with my people, played piquet, and prayed. It rained in the night with much wind.

15. I rose about 6, read Hebrew and Greek. I prayed and had hominy. I danced. It snowed this morning, the wind north and then northwest. [Cleared all away.] I wrote English and read Latin till dinner when I ate goose giblet. After dinner we played billiards and walked in the garden. At night talked with my people, played piquet, and prayed.

16. I rose about 6, read Hebrew and Greek. I prayed and had sage tea. I danced. The weather was cold and clear, the wind northwest. I read Latin and wrote records and walked till dinner when I ate smoked beef. After dinner

---

[1]Robert Mumford (spelled thus by Byrd but commonly now Munford) was a member of the vestry of Bristol parish, Prince George County, and a justice of that county. He served in the House of Burgesses where he was reprimanded by the Speaker on Sept. 1, 1736, for "endeavouring to obstruct the Examination of Witnesses, directed by the Authority of this House, upon a Complaint made against your own Election." He was sent as a commissioner in 1740 to the Catawba and Cherokee Indians to inform them of the treaty with the Six Nations made in August, 1740 and to arrange for them to send deputies in 1742 to Albany to meet the sachems of the Six Nations (*Va. Mag.*, XV, 235-36). His wife was Anna Bland. He died in 1745. (*Wm. Q. (2)*, XI, 110; *T.'s Q.*, XII, 88; *Va. Biog.*, I, 296; *JHB*, 1727-34, 1736-40, pp. 282 *et passim.*)

played billiards and walked a little. At night talked with my people, played piquet and prayed. My daughter Molly's[1] birthday; God preserve her.

17. I rose about 6, read Hebrew and Greek. I prayed and had coffee. I danced. The weather was cold and clear, the wind west, but it clouded about 12; however we walked and I read records and Latin till dinner and ate tripe. After dinner we played billiards and walked about the plantation. At night talked with my people, played piquet and prayed. The moon changed with a west wind.

18. I rose about 6, read Hebrew and Greek. I prayed and had hominy. I danced. The weather was cold and cloudy, the wind north. We played billiards, then read records and then Latin till dinner when I ate broiled mutton. After dinner we played billiards again and walked. I committed folly with F-r-b-y, God forgive me. L-n-r brought 11 hogs from Roanoke and 20 came from the Falls. I prayed.

19. I rose about 6, read Hebrew and Greek. I prayed and had tea. I danced. The weather was cold and cloudy, the wind north and threatened snow, which fell in great quantity in the afternoon. I wrote letters and read Latin till dinner and then ate bacon and eggs. After dinner we played billiards but could not walk because it snowed. At night talked with my people and prayed.

20. I rose about 6, read Hebrew and Greek. I prayed

---

[1]Maria Byrd, born Jan. 16, 1727, died in 1745 (*Va. Gaz.*, Dec. 5-12, 1745). Bassett (p. 447), is evidently in error in stating Maria Byrd was born on Jan. 6. She married Landon Carter of Sabine Hall, Sept. 22, 1742. Byrd's account of the sudden wedding is given in the following letter to Daniel Parke Custis, Sept. 23, 1742: "Your kind present of Sorers came in a good Time when we has a vast deal of company. Amongst the rest was Col^o^. Harrison and his fair Family. The reason of their comeing, was upon my Invitation on account of a certain marriage, I hope made in Heaven, that was solemnized no longer ago than yesterday. If you will come before Sunday, you will be time enough to wish the Partys Joy, and eat a Piece of the Bride Cake. Nothing ever fell out more suddenly than this affair, none of us thought any thing about it at ten in the morning, and by Three the Gordian knot was tyed. When you come you may hear more, and see Two happy Persons. I am My Dear cousins Most obedient servant [signed] W Byrd." (Ms. in N. Y. Public Library.)

and had coffee. I danced. The weather was cold and clear, but abundance of snow fell in the night. My people made paths for which I gave them cider. The minx killed 10 hens this night. Nobody could go to church. I ate boiled mutton. After dinner because I could not walk I danced. Bob came from the Falls. I talked with my people and prayed. When I went into bed I found myself a little giddy; God preserve me.

21. I rose about 6, read Hebrew and Greek. I prayed and had sage [*or* sack] tea. I danced. The weather was very cold and clear, the wind north. The three Swiss took a resolution to go away, all three together, but at last the old man was so wise as to stay. My head was out of order. However I wrote letters till dinner, when I ate bacon and fowl. After dinner I read Latin till the evening, then talked with my people, and prayed.

22. I rose about 6, read Hebrew and Greek. I prayed and had milk porridge because I took physic. I danced. The weather was cold and cloudy, the wind north. I sent away L-n-r to Roanoke. We killed hogs again. I wrote letters till dinner and then ate roast fowl. The minx made us another visit. After dinner we played billiards. My purge worked pretty well. My head was better, thank God. I talked with my people. I sent the boat this morning to the Falls. We played piquet and about 8 I retired and prayed.

23. I rose about 6, read Hebrew and Greek. I prayed and had milk porridge. I danced. The weather continued cloudy and cold, the wind north. My head was better, thank God. I read records and Latin till dinner—fowl fricassee. After dinner we played billiards and walked in the garden. At night I talked with my people, played piquet, and prayed.

24. I rose about 6, read Hebrew and Greek. I prayed and had tea. I danced. The weather was cold and clear, the wind northwest. I read English about the diseases of the head till one and then came the Doctor from the Falls and dined here and I ate roast pork. After dinner Mr. Anderson and I settled accounts and we talked till night.

They both went to Mr. Procter's.[1] I played piquet and prayed.

25. I rose about 6, read Hebrew and Greek. I prayed and had hominy. The weather was cold and clear, the wind southwest. The Doctor and Mr. Anderson went away. I read records and Latin till dinner when I ate sparerib. It snowed again a little till the evening, then danced because could not walk. At night talked with my people. Mrs. Byrd had the headache pretty much. I prayed.

26. I rose about 6, read Hebrew and Greek. I prayed and had sage [*or* sack] tea. I danced. The weather was cold and clear, the wind northwest. My son was hurt in the eye with a snowball; God preserve him. I read records and Latin till dinner when I ate pork griskin. After dinner my man Peter ran here from above. I played billiards and danced. I had letters from England, and prayed.

27. I rose about 6, read Hebrew and Greek. I prayed and had tea. I danced. The weather was cold and cloudy, the wind west. I sent Peter up again with Bob. I put myself in order and sent Mr. Procter over the river. The boat came from the Falls, where all were well, thank God. Mr. B-r-n came and Mr. Ravenscroft and Mr. Wendey to dinner and I ate sparerib. After dinner we talked and had coffee. The company went away. In the evening I talked with my people and discoursed my family till 8, then retired and prayed.

28. I rose about 6, read Hebrew and Greek. I prayed and had tea. I danced. The weather was warm and clear, the wind southwest. I settled some accounts and wrote

---

[1]William Procter, a Scotchman, was tutor and librarian for Byrd at Westover (*Va. Mag.*, X, 398-301). He was one of the witnesses who proved Byrd's will when it was presented to the Charles City County court for probate in February, 1745 (Charles City Order Book, 1737-51, p. 339). He was ordained by the Bishop of London in 1745. He served in Nottoway parish, Amelia County, and in Cumberland parish, Lunenburg County (Goodwin, p. 300; G. MacLaren Brydon, *Addendum to Goodwin's List of Colonial Clergy of the Established Church*, [Richmond, 1933], p. 64; Byrd to Proctor, Nov. 18, 1740, *Va. Mag.*, XXXVII, 108). An appraisal of Procter's estate Dec. 7, 1761, lists considerable property in stock, slaves and a rather extensive library, chiefly of religious works. (Will Book, Amelia County, No. XX, 1761-71, p. 34 *et seq.*)

English. Fanny Anderson[1] came and dined with us and I ate boiled mutton. After dinner came Mr. Stevens and Mr. Wood[2] and told me all were well above. I ate two eggs for supper, talked with my people, and retired about 9 and prayed.

29. I rose about 6, read nothing because I talked with Mr. Stevens and was angry with him for selling my negroes before I knew which were to be sold. However, was friends before he went, which was about 11. I wrote a letter till dinner when Dr. Monger[3] came and I ate roast pigeon. After dinner Fanny Anderson and the Doctor went away and I gave Fanny 24 pounds cotton for her and her sisters to encourage housewifery. I talked with my people and prayed.

30. I rose about 6, read Hebrew and Greek. I prayed and had milk porridge because I took physic. I danced. The weather was cold and clear, the wind north. My purge worked 5 times. I read Latin till dinner when I ate boiled chine. After dinner we walked and at night I talked with my people, played piquet and prayed.

---

[1]Probably a daughter of Mr. Anderson, who was employed by Byrd (see note to entry, Sept. 1, 1739).

[2]Possibly James Wood who was a surveyor and had assisted Byrd and his fellow commissioners for the Crown in mapping out the boundaries of the Fairfax Proprietary. Wood and James Thomas, the younger, were especially delegated to make the survey of the Rappahannock. (Bassett, p. 404; F. Harrison, *Landmarks of Old Prince William*, p. 619). He was the clerk of Frederick County from 1743 to 1760 and the founder of the town of Winchester in 1752. There is a tradition that Lord Fairfax used his influence to make Stephensburg the county seat, but that James Wood with a bowl of toddy influenced one of the justices to cast his determining vote in favor of Winchester. According to the story, Lord Fairfax showed his disapproval of the magistrate who thus bartered his vote by never speaking to him again. (Samuel Kercheval, *History of the Valley of Virginia* [2d ed., Woodstock, Va.], pp. 156-57). Wood served as assistant commissary of the Virginia forces in 1754-55. His son, James Wood, was Governor of Virginia, 1796-1799. (John W. Wayland, *History of Shenandoah County, Virginia*, [Strasburg, Va., 1927], p. 668; Byrd to Mr. Wood, Mar. 20, 1740, Brock MSS, 188.)

It is possible that this refers to Thomas Wood who was appointed surveyor of the road from Shockoe Creek to Gilley's Creek in May, 1739. (Henrico Order Book, 1737-1746, p. 76.)

[3]This may have been Joshua Monger, whose will was presented February 1746 at the Charles City County court by Henry Taylor, executor (Charles City Order Book, 1737-1751, p. 393). Power of attorney of John Custis to Micajah Perry, March 22, 1735, was witnessed by Joshua Munger (Custis Letter Book, MS, Library of Congress).

31. I rose about 6, read Hebrew and Greek. I prayed and had tea. I danced. The weather was cold and clear, the wind northwest. I began to take sage [*or* sack] and claret for my head and so did my wife. I read records and Latin till dinner when I ate roast chine. After dinner I walked and danced. I talked with my people, played piquet and prayed. The wind blew hard at northwest and was very cold.

February, 1740

1. I rose about 6, read Hebrew and Greek. I prayed and had sage [*or* sack] tea. I danced. The weather was very cold and clear, the wind northwest. I read records and Latin and wrote letters till dinner when I ate boiled chine. After dinner I put things in order and read Latin, then danced because it was too cold to walk. I talked with my people and prayed.

2. I rose about 6, read Hebrew and Greek. I prayed and had tea. I danced. The weather was cold and clear, the wind northwest. We cut wood in the swamp. I read records and walked till dinner when Mrs. Duke dined with us and I ate sow's head. After dinner Mrs. Duke went away and I danced because I could not walk. Bob came from the Falls. All well, thank God. I prayed.

3. I rose about 6, read Hebrew and Greek. I prayed and had coffee. I danced. The weather continued cold and clear, the wind northwest. My children all went to church but it was too cold for me. I wrote letters and put myself in order. Mr. Cole came to dinner, and Will Hardyman.[1] I ate boiled beef. After dinner Mr. Cole went away and I walked. I talked with my people and prayed.

4. I rose about 6, read Hebrew and Greek. I prayed and had tea. I danced. The weather was cold and clear, the wind north. I walked and wrote records and read Latin till dinner when I ate sparerib. After dinner we walked again about the plantation. At night I talked with my people and played piquet. I slept but indifferently.

5. I rose about 6, read Hebrew and Greek. I prayed and had hominy. I danced. The weather was cold and clear, the wind north. This was my daughter Annie's birthday,

---

[1]This was probably William Hardyman, son of John Hardyman, of Charles City County, and his wife Mary (daughter of Colonel Francis Eppes) and brother of Francis Hardyman, frequently mentioned in this diary. (See *Wm. Q. (1)*, XI, 47; *Va. Mag.*, II, 302; Charles City Order Book, 1737-1751, *passim.*)

God bless her. My children all went to the Secretary's by invitation. I read records and Latin till dinner when young Mr. Cary[1] and Mr. Fraser[2] came and I ate cold beef. After dinner we walked and talked till night when I talked with my people, played cards and supped, and about 10 retired and prayed.

6. I rose about 6, read Hebrew and Greek. I prayed and had coffee. I danced. The weather was cold and clear, the wind north. The gentlemen stayed this day and saw everything. We played cards and walked till dinner when I ate roast rabbit. After dinner we played billiards again and walked. At night played piquet, and supped. We talked till 9 and then retired.

7. I rose about 6, read Hebrew and Greek. I prayed and had coffee. I danced. The weather was warm and clear, the wind west. Parson Fraser went away and left Mr. Cary here. We played billiards and I read records till dinner when I ate boiled chine. After dinner we played billiards again and then walked. At night played piquet. I talked with my people, ate two eggs and prayed.

8. I rose about 6, read Hebrew and Greek. I prayed and had coffee. I danced. The weather was warm and foggy, but cleared up about 10, the wind southeast. I wrote a letter, read Latin, and walked till dinner when I ate cold beef. After dinner we played billiards and then walked about the plantation. At night played piquet. I talked with my people and prayed.

---

[1]Archibald Cary, born in 1721, was the son of Henry Cary and his second wife, Anne Edwards, of Ampthill. He played a prominent role in leadership in Virginia during the Revolution and has been called by his biographer, "the Wheelhorse of the Revolution" (Robert K. Brock, *Archibald Cary of Ampthill* [Richmond, 1937]).

[2]George Fraser went to England from Virginia for ordination and had the King's Bounty for Virginia in 1738 when he became minister in Dale parish, then in Henrico and later in Chesterfield County. It is possible that he served this parish continuously until 1758 (*Va. Mag.*, XXXIII, 51, 57; Goodwin, p. 270). The Rev. George Fraser was among the legatees by the will dated May 31, 1750, of Mrs. Elizabeth Cary, third wife of Henry Cary (*Va. Mag.*, XXXII, 396). The inventory of the estate of George Fraser filed Aug. 9, 1762 showed that he had an estate of over £782, including fifteen slaves, and "cartoons of Raphel" (Will Book, Chesterfield County, No. 1, part 2, p. 366).

9. I rose about 6, read Hebrew and Greek. I prayed and had coffee. I danced. The weather was very warm and clear, the wind southwest. Mr. Cary took leave and I read records and read English till dinner when I ate souse. After dinner played billiards and walked. At night talked with my people and played piquet. The wind came about to northwest and blew very hard. All well at the Falls, thank God.

10. I rose about 6, read Hebrew and Greek. I prayed and had tea. I danced. The weather was cold and cloudy, the wind northeast. I went not to church but my children went. John Ravenscroft and Captain Dunlop[1] came and dined with us and I ate [p-p-t-y]. After dinner we talked and had coffee. The company went away soon and we walked. I wrote to the Falls, talked with my people, and prayed.

11. I rose about 6, read Hebrew and Greek. I prayed and had tea. I danced. The weather was cold and clear, the wind southeast. My man Tom was sick.[2] I read news and wrote records and then walked till dinner when I ate cold beef. After dinner we played billiards and walked. At night killed a beef, talked with my people, played piquet and prayed.

12. I rose about 6, read Hebrew and Greek. I prayed and had hominy. I danced. The weather was warm and clear, the wind southwest. My daughter dreamed a bad dream about Mrs. Harrison.[3] I walked, played billiards,

---

[1]Probably Captain Colin Dunlop, who is frequently mentioned in the Virginia trade on James River with cargoes to and from Glasgow (Harker). He had cleared out of the Upper District of James River on Aug. 4, 1739, in the ship *Molly*, for Glasgow, with a cargo of 514 hhds tobacco, 29,000 staves, and 400 feet of plank (*Va. Gaz.*, Dec. 7-14, 1739).

[2]Byrd, then in England, but planning shortly to sail for Virginia, noted in his Diary, Nov. 25, 1719, that a man from France, named Tom, who had formerly been his servant, wished to accompany him to Virginia.

[3]Anne Carter, daughter of Robert ("King") Carter of Corotoman, married Benjamin Harrison of Berkeley, it is believed, around 1722. She appears to have died sometime before her husband's tragic death by lightning (*Va. Mag.*, XXXII, 97, XLI, 163). See entry and note for Aug. 20, 1739.

The Byrds at Westover and the Harrisons at Berkeley, adjoining plantations, were neighbors and friends for at least three generations in colonial

and read news till dinner, when I ate fried oysters. After dinner we played billiards again and walked about the plantation. I talked with my people, played piquet and prayed. It rained in the night.

13. I rose about 6, read Hebrew and Greek. I prayed and had tea. I danced. The weather was warm and cloudy and rained sometimes, the wind south. I wrote records and then walked and read English till dinner. I ate cold mutton. After dinner came Robin Goode,[1] and Tom Turpin[2] to offer himself to be my overseer at the Falls. I walked, talked with my people, played piquet, and prayed.

14. I rose about 6, read Hebrew and Greek. I prayed and had tea. I danced. The weather was cold and cloudy, the wind north. The men went away and I read records and Latin till dinner when I ate boiled mutton. After dinner I played billiards and walked about the plantation. At night talked with my people, played piquet and prayed. I took two Anderson's pills.

15. I rose about 6, read Hebrew and Greek. I prayed and had milk porridge. I danced. The weather was cold

---

Virginia. There has descended through her mother, Mrs. Mary Willing Harrison McGuire, daughter of the last Benjamin Harrison who owned Berkeley, to Mrs. Susan McGuire Ellett, wife of Tazewell Ellett, of Richmond, a bedspread that is a work of art. It was fashioned by appliquéing, with skillful embroidery patterns from pastel-colored chintz on a cream-cotton background, designs of birds, flowers, and fruits known in Virginia. Family tradition relates that the women of Berkeley and Westover would meet at regular weekly intervals beneath a trysting tree on the boundary between the two estates and work together in sociable converse on this now treasured heirloom. The tradition holds that Evelyn Byrd, the beautiful daughter of the diarist who died unmarried in 1737, had worked on this spread.

[1]On May 5, 1741, Robert Good [*sic*] was appointed inspector at Warwick in Henrico County by the Council during the disability of Thomas Harris, the regular inspector (*Va. Mag.*, XV, 122). In 1736 Byrd sold Robert Goode of Henrico, Planter, 59 acres of land in Henrico County on south side of James River, touching on Stony Creek (Henrico Deeds and Wills, 1725-37, vol. 4, pp. 579-80).

[2]Thomas Turpin (1708-1790), son of Obedience (Branch) Cocke-Trent and her third husband, Thomas Turpin of Henrico County, mentioned frequently in the Diary, 1709-1712, as overseer for Byrd, was a magistrate in Goochland County in 1735 and sheriff of that county in 1741-43, held county offices later in Cumberland County, and his will was recorded in Powhatan County, September 16, 1790. His wife was Mary Jefferson, daughter of Thomas and Mary (Field) Jefferson, of Henrico, later Chesterfield County (Henrico Order Book, 1707-9, p. 156; *Wm. Q. (1)*, XXV, 109-10).

and clear, the wind northwest and blowing fiercely. I read records and read English and walked till dinner when I ate fish, which the weather afforded. After dinner we played billiards and walked about the plantation. At night played piquet and talked with my people. My pills worked four times.

16. I rose about 6, read Hebrew and Greek. I prayed and had tea. I danced. The weather continued cold and clear, the wind northwest. I read English and walked and examined records till dinner when I ate fish again. After dinner we played billiards and walked. All well at the Falls. I talked with my people, played piquet and prayed. I washed my feet.

17. I rose about 6, read Hebrew and Greek. I prayed and had coffee. I danced. The weather continued cold and clear, the wind southeast. About 11 I went to church and had a sermon that nobody understood. After church Billy Hardyman came with us and I ate boiled mutton. After dinner came Mrs. Greenhill. Bob beat his wife again very much for which I rebuked him. I talked with my people and prayed.

18. I rose about 6, read Hebrew and Greek. I prayed and had tea. I danced. The weather was cold and clear, the wind north. I wrote to the Falls, then walked a little in the garden, then wrote records till dinner when I ate boiled mutton. After dinner put things in order and then set Mrs. Greenhill over the river and walked by myself because my wife was indisposed. I talked with my people and prayed.

19. I rose about 6, read Hebrew and Greek. I prayed and had tea. I danced. The weather continued cold and clear, the wind northeast, and fierce. I read records and walked and then read English till dinner. I ate roast beef. After dinner put things in order and walked about the plantation. At night talked with my people, played piquet, and prayed, but got cold some way or other.

20. I rose about 6, read Hebrew and Greek. I prayed and had tea. I danced. The weather was cold and clear,

the wind north. My cold still continued and I coughed a little. I read records and read English till dinner when I ate fish. After dinner put some things in order and then walked about the plantation. At night talked with my people, played piquet and prayed.

21. I rose about 6, read Hebrew and Greek. I prayed and had tea. I danced. The weather was cold and clear, the wind north with a white frost. I played billiards and ran with my son, then wrote records and read English till dinner when I ate cold beef. After dinner put things in order, played billiards and walked about the plantation. At night talked with my people, played piquet and prayed. My son had a cold.

22. I rose about 6, read Hebrew and Greek. I prayed and had tea. I danced. The weather was cold and clear, the wind northeast. My son was better, thank God, but my cold was worse. I read records and wrote English and walked about till dinner when I ate roast turkey. After dinner I played billiards and then walked about the plantation. At night played piquet, talked with my people, and prayed.

23. I rose about 6, read Hebrew and Greek. I prayed and had tea. I danced. The weather was cold and cloudy, the wind northeast, and threatened snow, but it came not. I read records and wrote English till dinner when I ate hashed turkey. After dinner I read news and walked a little. At night read more news, talked with my people, learned my people were sick above—God forgive us our sins. I prayed.

24. I rose about 6, read Hebrew and Greek. I prayed and had coffee. I danced. The weather continued cold and clear, the wind north. Only my daughters went to church, my son having a great cold, God preserve him. About one came Mr. Spalding and a young gentleman belonging to the man-of-war[1] and dined with us, and I ate roast pigeon.

[1]Sir Yelverton Peyton was in command of the *Hector* man-of-war, which arrived in Virginia in the autumn of 1739 after convoying General Oglethorpe to Georgia (*Va. Mag.*, XIV, 345). He guarded Virginia waters during the winter and spring of 1739-40 and convoyed Gov. Gooch and the

After dinner we talked and walked and at night drank a little till 10. I prayed.

25. I rose about 6 and read little but walked with the gentlemen. I prayed and had coffee. I danced. The weather was warm and clear, the wind west. We persuaded the gentlemen to stay this day and we walked and played billiards till dinner when I ate bacon. After dinner we talked and walked and at night the young people danced. I talked with my people and about 9 retired and prayed. Mr. B-r-b-s came.

26. I rose about 6, read Hebrew and Greek. I prayed and had coffee. I danced. The weather was foggy in the morning, the wind north but cleared up and was warm. The gentlemen took leave about 11 and I read news till one when the Secretary and his lady[1] came to dine with us and I ate boiled rabbit. After dinner we drank a [supper?] glass till 5, when they took leave. In the evening I walked and prayed.

27. I rose about 6, read Hebrew and Greek. I prayed and had milk porridge, because I took pills. I danced. The weather continued clear and warm, the wind north. My physic worked five times. I had a cold and so had most of my children. I read English till dinner when I ate hashed turkey. After dinner I played billiards and walked about the plantation. At night talked with my people, played piquet and prayed. Hampton [*or* Hamilton] was sick.

28. I rose about 6, read Hebrew and Greek. I prayed and had tea. I danced. The weather was warm and smoky, the wind east. My cold continued but not bad, thank God. I read records and walked among my people till dinner when I ate cold mutton. After dinner I played billiards and

---

transports sailing for Carthagena in the fall of 1740 a considerable distance on their way (Letter of Blair, Nov. 6, 1740, Gooch Papers, copies in Va. Hist. Soc.).

[1]The wife of Secretary John Carter was Elizabeth Hill, of Shirley, heiress to that and other estates of her family, who had been prominent for at least three generations in Virginia's economic and political life. After the death of John Carter in 1742 she married Bowler Cocke (*Va. Mag.*, III, 156-8, XXXII, 48; *Wm. Q. (1)*, XVI, 386).

walked about the plantation. At night my cold was worse. I talked with my people and prayed.

29. I rose about 6, read Hebrew and Greek. I prayed and had tea. I danced. The weather was warm and smoky, the wind west, but moderate. My cold was worse. However, I read records and wrote English and walked in the garden till dinner when I ate roast mutton. After dinner we played billiards and then walked about the plantation. At night talked with my people and prayed. Hampton [*or* Hamilton] was sick, and Mr. Procter.

March, 1740

1. I rose about 6, read Hebrew and Greek. I prayed and had tea. I danced. The weather was cold and clear, the wind hard at north. My cold was better, thank God. March came in like a lion with a strong wind. I wrote several things till dinner when I ate cold mutton. After dinner played billiards and walked. At night talked with my people, played cards, and prayed.

2. I rose about 6, read Hebrew and Greek. I prayed and had coffee. I danced. The weather was cold and clear, the wind northwest. I went not to church but put things in order. After church nobody came and I ate fish. After dinner I talked and walked and put up my things. At night talked with my people and prayed.

3. I rose about 6 and prayed. I prepared for my journey with my wife to New Kent. I had tea for breakfast. I recommended my family to heaven and went in the chariot to Daniel Custis' but we got not there till 4 because we lost our way. I ate bacon. We talked of divers things till 9 and then retired and prayed.

4. I rose about 6 and prayed. I read nothing but had coffee for breakfast. It had rained in the night and continued to rain this day by fits. However we resolved to go visit my cousin W-n-s [Wilkinson],[1] being but 5 miles. We got there about 12 and she did her best for us in her little house. I ate bacon. Mrs. F-s-t-r came there. In the evening we were as merry as we could and discoursed till 10 and then retired into our [kennel] and prayed.

---

[1]Probably refers to a member of the family of Rebekah Parke, believed to have been the sister of Byrd's first wife's father, Daniel Parke, who married Daniel Wilkinson (see Diary, 1709-1712). The children of Daniel Wilkinson and Rebekah Parke were George Wilkinson, born 1693; John Wilkinson, born 1698, and Francis Wilkinson, born 1703, who married Mary Cary, daughter of Harwood Cary. The children of Daniel Wilkinson seem to have lived in New Kent, and it may have been one of them to whom Byrd refers as he went through New Kent on his way to Hanover (*Wm. Q. (2)*, XI, 256-57; XX, 561).

5. I rose about 6 and said a Psalter prayer. We had coffee. The weather continued cold and cloudy and threatened more rain. However, we took leave about 10 and proceeded on our journey to Hanover and got to Major Henry's[1] about 2 where I executed a warrant of escheat and then ate fowl and bacon. After dinner we played cards till 10 and then retired.

6. I rose about 6 and prayed. I read a little Greek and had tea. The weather was cold and clear, the wind northwest. Mr. [Cole] came here and went with us to court but called at Captain Bickerton's[2] by the way and executed deeds to Mr. Booth and Mr. Thornton. Then went to court and acknowledged them and returned to Captain Bickerton's again to dinner and ate exceedingly fat beef. In the evening we played with very dirty cards till 9 and then retired.

7. I rose about 6 and read Greek. I prayed and had tea. I danced. The weather continued cold and clear, the wind northwest. About 10 we took leave and returned home by the Falls and by the way made a visit to the Doctor at Richmond and found Mr. Cary's[3] chaise on the other side the river and

---

[1]John Henry, father of Patrick Henry of Revolutionary fame, was county surveyor of Hanover, presiding magistrate, and colonel of militia. Samuel Davies described him as a man better acquainted with Horace than the Bible (*Va. Mag.*, XXXIII, 44-5; *Vestry Book of St. Paul's Parish*; William Wirt, *Sketches of the Life and Character of Patrick Henry,* [Philadelphia, 1840], pp. 19-20). He patented much land (*Ex. Jour.*, IV, *passim*).

[2]John Bickerton was named a member of the county court of Hanover in 1737 (*Ex. Jour.*, IV, 391), and in 1743 was elected to the vestry of St. Paul's Church. He married Mary Todd, daughter of Philip Todd, of King and Queen County (*Va. Mag.*, XXIX, 364, 369). Bickerton owned land adjacent to Byrd's holdings in Hanover according to the following item from the *Virginia Gazette*, Sept. 30-Oct. 7, 1737: "We have Advice from Hanover County, That on St. Andrew's Day, being the 30th of November next, there are to be Horse Races, and several other Diversions, for the Entertainment of the Gentlemen and Ladies, at the Old Field, near Capt. John Bickerton's in that county (if permitted by the Hon. William Byrd, Esq., Proprietor of the said Land)." For further account of the St. Andrew's Day festivities see *Va. Gaz.*, Nov. 11-18, Dec. 2-9, 1737.

[3]Henry Cary, like his father Henry Cary before him, was a building contractor. He built the President's House at the College of William and Mary, among other public structures. He lived in Williamsburg, and later during the period of this diary, about seven miles below the site of Richmond, the Cary estate there first being known as Warwick and then as Ampthill. Cary was Byrd's neighbor at his Falls plantation. He died in 1749. (Fairfax Harrison, *The Virginia Carys* [New York, 1919], pp. 85-90, 172-73.)

went there to dinner. By the way I saw a very bad pasture fence of mine. About 3 got to Mr. Cary's and ate salt fish. After dinner played cards till 10 and prayed.

8. I rose about 6 and read Greek. I prayed and had coffee. The weather continued cold and clear, the wind northwest. About 10 we took leave, crossed the river to our chariot and got home about 3 where we found all well, blest be God. I ate fish. After dinner put matters in order, talked with my people, and prayed.

9. I rose about 6, read Greek. I prayed and had coffee. I danced. The weather was cold and clear, the wind southwest. My son only went to church and I read English till dinner when I ate little beside broth. After dinner I walked and wrote letters to the Falls and then walked. At night talked with my people and prayed. L-n-r came from Roanoke.

10. I rose about 6, read Hebrew and Greek. I prayed and had tea. I danced. The weather was warm and cloudy, the wind southwest. I wrote a French letter. The old Italian and S-l-s-t-r-v came with Captain W-n from Roanoke and went to Mrs. Brun's. I ate roast pigeon. After dinner played billiards and walked. Mr. Ravenscroft came and stayed. I prayed.

11. I rose about 6 and read Hebrew and Greek. I prayed and had coffee. I danced. It rained all night and blew exceedingly hard, the wind northeast. Mr. Ravenscroft could not go over the river so we played cards till dinner, and I ate dried beef. After dinner we talked and had tea and then played cards again till 9. I talked with my people and prayed.

12. I rose about 6 and read nothing because of my company. I prayed and had tea. I danced. The weather was extremely cold, the wind hard at northwest. I talked with the old Italian and found C-r-l-y had cheated me. I read news and played cards till dinner. In the afternoon we talked and had tea. In the evening I sent John Ravenscroft over the river. I talked with my people and prayed.

13. I rose about 6 and read nothing because I wrote letters. I prayed and had tea. I danced. The weather was cold and clear. I set the old Italian over the river with his company and read English till dinner when I ate roast pigeon. After dinner I put things in order till the evening. I did not walk because the wind blew cold. I talked with my people and prayed.

14. I rose about 6, read Hebrew and Greek. I prayed and had tea. I danced. The weather was cold and clear, the wind northwest but moderate. My three daughters set out on their journey[1]—God protect them, and bring them back safe. I read English till dinner when I ate boiled pork. After dinner we played billiards and walked. I talked with my people and prayed.

15. I rose about 6, read Hebrew and Greek. I prayed and had tea. I danced. The weather was cold and clear, the wind north. I read English and wrote till one, then walked and put things in order till dinner when I ate dry beef. After dinner we played billiards and then walked about the plantation. At night talked with my people and prayed. All well at the Falls.

16. I rose about 6, read Hebrew and Greek. I prayed and had coffee. I danced. The weather was cold and clear, the wind east. About 11 I went to church and had a poor sermon. After church I invited four women and six men to dinner, and ate fish. After dinner had coffee and walked in the garden. The company all went away. I talked with my company and prayed.

17. I rose about 6, read Hebrew and Greek. I prayed and had tea. I danced. The weather was cold and clear, the wind west. My people went upon the road and I wrote letters and [read] news till dinner when I ate fish. After dinner played billiards and walked about the plantation. All well at Mount Folly,[2] thank God. I talked with my people, wrote a letter, and prayed. I took physic.

---

[1]To visit the daughters of William Bassett at Eltham in New Kent County.

[2]Mount Folly Neck with 900 acres in New Kent County, was one of the Custis plantations that Byrd acquired as part of his wife Lucy Parke's share

18. I rose about 6, read Hebrew and Greek. I prayed and had milk porridge. I danced. The weather was warm and cloudy, the wind north. I wrote English, read news and walked about till dinner when I ate broiled mutton. After dinner we played billiards and then walked about the plantation. At night I talked with my people and prayed. I dreamed[1] the Secretary had a consumption.

19. I rose about 6, read Hebrew and Greek. I prayed and had tea. I danced. The weather was cold and clear, the wind north. I wrote several letters till 12, when Mrs. Beverley Randolph[2] came. We played cards till dinner when I ate fish. After dinner we talked and had coffee till the evening when she returned to Colonel Harrison's. I talked with my people and prayed.

20. I rose about 6, read Hebrew and Greek. I prayed and had coffee. I danced. The weather was cold and clear, the wind north. I sent my little cart to Meherrin with two negroes, God bless them. About one came Captain Dunlop and dined with us and I ate fish. We talked till 6 when he went away, then walked, talked with my people, and prayed.

---

in her father's estate. See the Byrd Title Book, p. 195 *et seq.* for papers concerning Byrd's settlement with John Custis and the matters involved in that settlement between these two sons-in-law of Daniel Parke; and "Schedule containing an account of all the estate real and personal of Daniel Parke, deceased in Virginia, with the values of the negroes personal estate and of the debts, paid and unpaid" [1715], Transcript in the Emmet Collection No. 6077, N. Y. Public Library, copy in Colonial Williamsburg, Inc., Archives.

Mount Folly was early used as a landmark in the land grants in the peninsula between the York and the James, and Mount Folly (or Follie) path in New Kent County was early a familiar way of travel (Nell M. Nugent, *Cavaliers and Pioneers*, Abstracts of Virginia Land Patents and Grants, 1623-1800, [Richmond, 1934], I, 249, 254, 393, 464).

[1]Byrd repeatedly in this and other portions of the diary betrays an inquiring interest in the significance of his dreams, as well as those of others. During his residence in London he consulted Old Abram, a conjuror, about his love affairs (Diary, 1717-1721, entry for Feb. 10, 1718; see also Diary, 1709-1712).

[2]Mrs. Beverley Randolph was a bride of little more than three years, for she had married Beverley Randolph in 1737, according to the following account from the *Virginia Gazette* (Dec. 23-30, 1737): "Yesterday was sennight Mr. Beverley Randolph, eldest son of the Honorable William Randolph, Esq., one of his Majesty's council of this colony, was married to Miss Betty Lightfoot, niece of the Hon. Philip Lightfoot, Esq., an agreeable young lady with a fortune of upwards of 5000 pounds." (*Va. Mag.*, XXXII, 386-7; Hen. *Stat.*, V, 111-4.)

22.[1] I rose about 6, read Hebrew and Greek. I prayed and had tea. I danced. The weather was cold and clear, the wind north. I read and wrote English, then walked till dinner among my people and ate fish. After dinner my man came from Williamsburg but no news. In the afternoon I walked about the plantation. At night talked with my people. A beef came down. I washed my feet and prayed.

23. I rose about 6, read Greek. I prayed and had coffee. I danced. The weather was cold and clear, the wind still north. I went not to church but put myself in order and read Latin. My son brought nobody from church and I ate fish once more. In the afternoon I read English till 5 and then walked about the plantation. At night talked with my people and prayed.

24. I rose about 6, read Hebrew and Greek. I prayed and had tea. I danced. The weather was cold and clear, the wind northwest. My son and I rode to Hilman[2] with my son [*sic*], and then wrote English and read Latin till dinner when I ate fish again but ate too much, God forgive me. After dinner played billiards and walked. We killed a beef. I talked to my people and prayed.

25. I rose about 6, read Hebrew and Greek. I prayed and had tea. I danced. The weather was warm and clear, the wind north. The fire of wood made it smoky. I wrote letters and read Latin till dinner and then ate ox cheek.[3] After dinner we played billiards and then read news and then walked about the plantation. At night Ned returned from Meherrin. I talked with my people and prayed.

26. I rose about 6 and found my head giddy. I read Hebrew and Greek. I prayed and had tea. I danced. The weather was cold and clear, the wind north. About 11 we

[1]There is no entry for the 21st.

[2]Hilman was the name of one of the Byrd plantations (Memorandum on first page of Byrd's notebook A at the University of North Carolina, the contents of which are published in this volume, records that three hogsheads of tobacco were made at Hilman by Capt. Twine in 1739.)

[3]"The cheek of an ox, especially as an article of food." (*New English Dictionary.*)

went to the Secretary's to visit Mrs. Page.[1] The Secretary was gone to the cockfight. We were merry, however, and had roast beef. After dinner we talked and had tea and about 5 took leave and returned home where all were well, thank God.

27. I rose about 6, read Hebrew and Greek. I prayed and had milk porridge because I took pills. I danced. The weather was cold and clear, the wind north and blew fiercely. My physic worked five times. My head was better. I wrote letters till dinner and then ate boiled eggs. After dinner put things in order, played billiards and then walked. At night came Mr. Wood. I prayed.

28. I rose about 6, read Hebrew and Greek. I prayed and had hominy. I danced. The weather was misty and cold, the wind north. This was my birthday.[2] God preserve my head and grant I may not lose my memory and sense. Colonel John Stith and his wife dined here. After running my line with Mr. Wood here came two Germans.[3] I walked with my daughter Jenny[4] because my wife was sick.

29. I rose about 6, read Hebrew and Greek. I prayed

---

[1]This probably refers to Judith Carter, daughter of Robert ("King") Carter and sister of Secretary John Carter. She survived her husband, Mann Page of Rosewell, Gloucester County, who died in 1730. While few facts are known about Judith Carter Page except that she had five sons and two daughters surviving at the time of her husband's death, she evidently outlived him many years. Her grandson, John Page, born in 1744, later Governor of the State of Virginia, said of her in his autobiography, "I was early taught to read and write by the care and attention of my grandmother, one of the most sensible and best informed women I ever knew." (*Va. Hist. Port.*, pp. 154-5.)

[2]Byrd was born in 1674 and was thus sixty-six years old on his birthday.

[3]Among the early purchasers of lots in the town of Richmond which Byrd had laid off with William Mayo at the Falls of the James in 1733 and first advertised in the *Virginia Gazette* April 20-27, 1737, were numerous Germans. (Copy of a plan of the town of Richmond which appears to be taken in the lifetime of William Byrd II with names of the possessors of lots. Copied from a plan of the town of Richmond filed in office of the Supreme Court of Chancery for the Richmond District. Valentine Museum, Richmond.)

[4]Jane Byrd was the diarist's youngest daughter, born Oct. 13, 1729 (Bassett, p. 449). She married John Page of North End, Gloucester County, in 1746 and had, according to the family genealogist, fifteen children (R. C. M. Page, *Genealogy of the Page Family in Virginia*, [N. Y., 1893], pp. 96-8). The portraits of John Page by Wollaston, and his wife Jane by Hesselius are in the possession of the College of William and Mary (*Va. Hist. Port.*, p. 209).

and had coffee. I danced. The weather was warm and cloudy, the wind north. I walked, read Latin and wrote English till dinner when I ate pancakes. After dinner we played billiards and walked about the plantation. People sick at the Falls—God save them. I talked with my people and prayed. I had a small fever.

30. I rose about 6, read Hebrew and Greek. I prayed and had tea. I danced. The weather was cold and misty, the wind southeast. I was bled and wrote letters and found my head better, thank [God]. I read Latin till dinner when I had several gentlemen from church to dinner. I ate asparagus. After dinner we talked and had coffee till the evening when the company took leave and I retired and prayed. I had several letters from England, among which was one from Sir Charles Wager.[1]

31. I rose about 6 and read nothing because I took a vomit which worked me hard. I prayed and had nothing for breakfast. The weather was cold and cloudy, the wind north. I lay down and ate nothing till the evening and then two eggs only. However I was pretty well, thank God. At night took Squire's Elixir which made me slumber only and not sleep. I prayed.

---

[1]Sir Charles Wager (1666-1743), first lord of the admiralty, was one of Byrd's intimate friends whom he had known well in his years of residence in England (Diary, 1717-1721). They kept up a lively correspondence until Wager's death in 1743. On the first sheet in the manuscript notebook containing this diary for 1739-41 is jotted down with some miscellaneous memoranda in Byrd's handwriting this note: "Sr Ch Wager dyd the 29 Decr 1740 [*sic*]." Byrd had a portrait of his friend at Westover (*Va. Mag.*, XXXVI, 39; XXXVIII, 150).

April, 1740

1. I rose about 6 and read Greek. I prayed and had tea. I danced. The weather was cold and cloudy, and threatened rain but none fell but a few drops. I wrote letters and read Latin till dinner when I ate only four eggs. After dinner I played billiards with my wife and walked about the garden. At night retired, talked with my people, and prayed.

2. I rose about 6, read Hebrew and Greek. I prayed and had tea. I danced. The weather was cold and cloudy, still threatening rain. However, I sent to Williamsburg to make my excuse for not going to Council. I was better, thank God, till one and then my fever began to come. However I ate bitter wort. Mr. U-l-t (*or* V-l-t)[1] came to agree his dispute. I talked with my people and took Squire's Elixir and prayed.

3. I rose about 6, read Hebrew and Greek. I prayed and had tea. I danced. The weather was cold and cloudy, the wind southwest. I was a little better, thank God. I played billiards and walked and then read Latin till dinner, when I ate asparagus. After dinner played again at billiards but did not walk because it threatened rain. G-f-r-y returned from Williamsburg with little news. I talked with my people and prayed. It blew hard in the night with thunder and rain in abundance so that our boat got loose.

4. I rose about 6, read Hebrew and Greek. I prayed and had hominy. I danced. The weather continued cloudy, the wind southwest, and blowing much. My son went to church with his master and I read Latin till dinner when Captain Goodman[2] came and told us of his voyage. I ate potato for

---

[1]Possibly James Vaulton, who figures in the records of Henrico County court during this period in connection with administration of estates (Henrico Order Book, 1737-1746, pp. 135, 145, 149, 151, 155).

[2]Thomas Goodman with his sloop *Lucy* from Barbados with 11 hogsheads and 2 tierces of rum entered Upper District of James River, Aug. 3, 1737 (*Va. Gaz.*, Dec. 7-14, 1739). At a meeting of the Council, Oct. 17, 1741, Thomas Goodman, commodore of the two sloops of war fitted out by the

dinner. After dinner we talked but could not walk because the wind blew cold. I missed my fever and prayed.

5. I rose about 6, read Hebrew and Greek. I prayed and had tea. I danced. The weather was cold and cloudy, the wind west. I read English and Latin and walked about the plantation. I then wrote a letter to the Falls till dinner and then ate fish. After dinner I put things in order and then walked. Mr. Banister[1] came but no news. I talked with my people and prayed.

6. I rose about 6 and read nothing because I wrote letters. I prayed and had coffee. I danced. The weather was cold and clear, the wind west. I went not to church nor did anybody come home to dine with us but only Mr. Banister. I ate roast chicken. After dinner we talked, and walked in the evening, then I talked with my people and prayed.

7. I rose about 6 and I read nothing because I wrote to my daughters by the chair which I sent for them to Colonel Bassett's.[2] I prayed and had coffee. I danced, then rode to visit Frank Hardyman[3] who was bad, having had a fit, but

---

government, and captain of the sloop *Ranger,* was censured for neglect of duty and cowardice and an unsatisfactory account of his behavior in retaking the ship belonging to Plymouth. (Ex. Jour., Va. State Library copy, Oct. 17, 1741; see note on William Clack, under Sept. 6, 1740).

[1]This was John Banister, son of the naturalist John Banister. He lived at Westover for some years. (Diary, Apr. 12, Aug. 31, Oct. 11, 1720.) He had charge of some of Byrd's plantations during his absence in England in 1723. Later he was collector of Upper James River district and vestryman of Bristol parish. He accompanied Byrd on his "Journey to Eden" in 1733. He was a member of the Prince George County court in the period of this diary. (Prince George Minute Book, 1737-1740, April 1738, p. 90.) The William Byrds and the John Banisters were close friends and associates for three generations in colonial Virginia (*T's. Q.*, XVIII, 245; *Va. Mag.*, XXXVI, 37; Slaughter, Bristol *Parish,* p. 15; Bassett, pp. 325, 398).

[2]William Bassett and his wife, Elizabeth Churchill, had three daughters: Elizabeth who married Benjamin Harrison, signer of the Declaration of Independence; Joanna who married Anderson Stith (see entry and note for Dec. 25, 1739); and Priscilla, who married Thomas Dawson, younger brother of William Dawson. Both William and Thomas Dawson served as Commissaries of the Bishop of London and Presidents of William and Mary College (*Wm. Q. (1)*, XVI, 124, 217; XXII, 45-7).

[3]Francis Hardyman (Hardiman) was a justice of Charles City County in 1737, though left out of the commission in 1740 (Charles City Order Book, 1737-1751, pp. 3, 114). His will was proved in Charles City court in August, 1741 (see entry for July 25, 1741, for note of his death). He married first, Sarah Taylor, and second, Jane —— (see note on Mrs. Greenhill, Jan. 6, 1740). The Hardyman family settled in Charles City County in the seven-

returned to dinner with Mr. Banister and ate fricasseed chicken. Dr. Tschiffeley dined with us. After dinner we talked and walked. I talked with my people and prayed.

8. I rose about 6, read Hebrew and Greek. I prayed and had coffee. I danced. The weather was warm and clear, the wind southwest. Mr. Banister went over the river last night and the Doctor went this morning about noon. The boat went away to the Falls and I read Latin and walked till dinner when I ate cold bacon. After dinner we played billiards and then walked to meet our girls who came about 6 in good health, thank God. I talked with my people and prayed. I took ginseng tea.[1]

9. I rose about 6, read Hebrew and Greek. I prayed and had tea. I danced. The weather was warm and clear, the wind west. The sheriff of Brunswick[2] came to settle. About 12 came Captain Dunlop and dined with us and Mr. D-n-l [Donald?][3] came with him and I ate roast pigeon. After

---

teenth century. The Byrds and the Hardymans were neighbors and friends for three generations in the colonial period (*Va. Mag.*, XXI, 184-86; *Wm. Q. (1)*, XI, 47-48).

Francis Hardyman kept an ordinary (Charles City Order Book, 1737-1751, pp. 20, 40, 59). He was cited by Benjamin Harris before the court for keeping his ordinary in a disorderly manner, but the case was dismissed. He figured frequently in suits before the county court and was fined in July, 1739 for not going to church though he was sitting on the bench. (*Ibid.*, pp. 80, 93, *et passim.*)

[1]Byrd's letters and other writings frequently voice the faith he had in the powers of ginseng, which was something of a hobby with him. He wrote Sir Hans Sloane, Aug. 20, 1738, "I believe ever since the Tree of Life has been so strongly guarded the Earth has never produced any vegetable so friendly to men as Ginseng." (Sloane MSS, British Museum, XX, 4055, f. 367.)

[2]Lieutenant Colonel Drury Stith, who had piloted Byrd on his "Journey to Eden" to his copper mine (Bassett, pp. 283-5, 320-22) was a large land owner and public official in Brunswick county. He held the position of clerk of the county and county surveyor from the beginning of government in the county until his death sometime between the date of this entry in Byrd's diary and June of this same year. The will of Col. Drury Stith was presented in the Charles City County court in January, 1742 by Susanna Stith and William Stith. (Charles City Order Book, 1737-1751, p. 197.) He was succeeded as surveyor of Brunswick by his son Drury Stith (*Ex. Jour.*, IV, *passim*; *Wm. Q. (1)*, XXI, 186-88; *Va. Mag.*, XV, 238).

[3]Perhaps James Donald, who was attorney for John Luke & Company, merchants of Glasgow, and appeared in cases before the Charles City court (Charles City Order Book, 1737-1751, pp. 88-89). Later the name appears as James Donald & Company (*ibid.*, July 1749, p. 500) or as Robert & James Donald & Co. (*ibid.*, p. 512).

dinner we talked till 5 when the company went away. I talked with my people, read news and prayed.

10. I rose about 6, read Hebrew and Greek. I prayed and had coffee. I danced. The weather was cold and clear, the wind north. We played billiards and walked. I read news and wrote till dinner when I ate fish. After dinner came two Germans to take lots at Richmond[1] and I was kind to them. We walked about the plantation. At night I talked with my people and prayed.

11. I rose about 6, read Hebrew and Greek. I prayed and had tea with hominy. I danced. The weather was cold and clear, the wind southwest. I talked with the Germans and then [they] went away with the gardener up to Richmond. I read news till dinner and then ate bacon and asparagus. After dinner I put things in order and then walked till I was tired and retired about 9, prayed.

12. I rose about 6, read Hebrew and Greek. I prayed and had tea. I danced. The weather was warm and cloudy, the wind southwest. I read news and played billiards but could not walk because it rained. I put up my things till dinner and then ate fish. After dinner played billiards and

---

[1]Byrd's interest in the sale of lots in the recently laid off town of Richmond was strong during this period. The following advertisement in the *Va. Gaz.*, April 15-22, 1737, gives Byrd's plans for the development of the town: "This is to give Notice, That on the North Side of James River, near the Uppermost Landing and a little below the Falls, is lately laid off by Major Mayo, a Town, called Richmond, with Streets 65 Feet wide, in a pleasant and healthy Situation and well supply'd with Springs of good Water. It lies near the Publick Warehouse at Shoccoe's, and in the midst of great Quantities of Grain, and all kind of Provisions. The Lots will be granted in Fee-Simple, on Condition only of building a House in Three Years Time, of 24 by 16 Feet, fronting within 5 Feet of the Street. The Lots to be rated according to the Convenience of their Situation, and to be sold after this April General Court, by me. William Byrd."

The town of Richmond had piqued Byrd's imagination and promised him profit from that recorded moment in October, 1733 when on his return to Westover from "A Journey to Eden" he had with Major William Mayo "laid the foundation of two large Citys. One at Shacco's, to be called Richmond, and the other at the Point of Appamattuck River, to be nam'd Petersburgh" (Bassett, p. 292; Henrico Order Book, 1737-1746).

Byrd had earlier obstructed an effort in 1729 by a "powerful family," evidently the Randolph family, to have a town laid out at the site later developed as Richmond. Byrd feared if the proposed act passed the Assembly he would be forced to accept 20 shillings an acre for 50 acres in the middle

read more news till night, then talked with my people and prayed. It rained and thundered in the night.

13. I rose about 6, read Hebrew and Greek. I prayed and had coffee. I danced. The weather continued wet, the wind north, so that we could not go to church. About one came Mr. Wendey and Captain Harding[1] and dined with me and I ate roast mutton. After dinner we talked till 5 when the company went away and I talked with my people and prayed.

14. I rose about 6 and prepared for my journey to Williamsburg. I prayed and had chocolate. The weather was cold and cloudy, the wind north. However, about 8 I got into the chariot and went to the ferry where I saw Colonel

---

of his land at Shaccoe's where he said he would not sell 50 acres for £5 an acre. In a letter of protest to the London merchant Micajah Perry, who had much influence in British policy towards Virginia, which he wanted laid before the Council of Trade, Byrd challenged the right of the Virginia Assembly, "a little Assembly, the very shaddow of a Parliament," to ravish away tyrannically a man's land. He sketched the plan by which he would lay out a town at the Falls if there were any real occasion for a town. His plan was for lots of half an acre, granted on easy terms, the grant to hold for fifty years, as long as houses, in his judgment, would stand in Virginia, at 20 shillings fine and one shilling per annum rent, so that reversion and inheritance would remain to his family. (Byrd to Perry, May 27, 1729, MS, Colonial Williamsburg, Inc.)

Several petitions from inhabitants of Goochland County for towns to be laid out at Warwick on the south side of James River and near the falls of the James on the north side, between Shackoes [*sic*] and Gilly's Creek, were reported to the Burgesses on June 3, 1730 from the committee of propositions and grievances. The petition for the town at Warwick was rejected, but that for a town at the Falls, the later site of Richmond on Byrd's land, was referred to the next session of the Assembly. (*JHB*, 1727-1734, 1736-1740, p. 70.) No action appears to have been taken on the matter by the next session of the Assembly in 1732. But on Sept. 14, 1734, the proposition from the counties of Henrico and Goochland for settling a town at Warwick on the land of Thomas Howlett on the south side was referred to the next session of the Assembly (*ibid.*, pp. 193, 200). Byrd's opposition to the proposed town on the north bank of the James had evidently been successful and the way was left clear for him to lay out the town of Richmond on his own plan and at his own time.

[1]Captain William Harding, sailing the ship *Duke of Cumberland,* was in Virginia in the spring of 1740 (Letter of Richard Chapman to Mr. Edward Athawes, Pammonky [Pamunkey], May 4, 1740, by the Duke of Cumberland, Capt. Harding. *Wm. Q. (1)*, XXI, 96). Capt. Harding with the *Duke of Cumberland*, "a prime sailor mounted with 16 Guns and well manned," took tobacco on consignment to John Hanbury, merchant in London (*Va. Gaz.,* Jan. 25-Feb. 1, 1740).

Randolph[1] and his brother Ned[2] who gave me several letters from England. About 3, got to Williamsburg and dined with Lady Randolph[3] and then walked to the Governor's and from thence to Mr. Barradall's and from thence walked home, put my house in order and prayed.

15. I rose about 6 and read nothing because several gentlemen came. I prayed and had coffee. I danced. The weather was warm and clear, the wind southwest. I waited on the Governor and about 10 went to court and sat till 3 and then dined with the Governor and ate boiled turkey. After dinner I went to Colonel Grymes's and from thence home where I wrote several things and prayed.

16. I rose about 6 and read Hebrew and Greek. I prayed and had coffee. The weather was cold and clear, the wind northwest. My head was better, thank God. About 9

---

[1]William Randolph (1681-1742) was the oldest of the seven sons of William and Mary Isham Randolph of Turkey Island. He was called "Councillor" Randolph, was clerk of Henrico court, member of the Council, and treasurer of Virginia. He married Elizabeth Beverley, daughter of Colonel Peter Beverley of Gloucester County and sister of Lady Susanna Randolph. They had five children: Beverley, Peter, William, Mary, Elizabeth (see entry for Mar. 19, 1741; *Va. Mag.*, XXXIII, 395-7, XLV, 68).

[2]Edward Randolph, youngest son of William Randolph of Turkey Island, was a sea captain. He married Miss Groves of Bristol, England, and divided his time between England and Virginia. Byrd saw him at intervals during his residence in England (Diary, 1717-1721). He frequently carried out commissions for the family at Westover as well as other Virginians. He was elected agent for Virginia in London by the Burgesses in 1740, to present a petition regarding the importation of salt, but the Council voted against having an agent in the particular matter and the Burgesses revoked their action. Randolph, who had sailed the ship *Williamsburg* and then the *Randolph*, named his ship for Gov. Gooch—not disinterestedly the Governor thought, as he showed in the following passage in a letter to his brother, "for if a Governor is so fortunate as to be beloved, his name-sake will always get her laden" (June 28, 1729; Gooch Letters, Colonial Williamsburg, Inc., 1728-50, *passim*; *Va. Mag.*, XXXVI, 41, XLV, 84, 394; *JHB*, 1727-1740, pp. 441-42; *Wm. Q. (1)*, XXI, 99-100).

[3]Lady Randolph, the widow of Sir John Randolph, was Susanna Beverley, daughter of Peter Beverley of Gloucester County. Sir John Randolph was a close friend of Byrd, who had known him all his life, and esteemed him greatly and lamented his untimely death in 1737 (*Va. Mag.*, III, 205-8, IX, 239-41, XXXVI, 42). Lady Randolph was the mother of John Randolph, King's Attorney at the outbreak of the Revolution, Peyton Randolph, president of the first Continental Congress, Beverley Randolph, and Mary Randolph who married Philip Grymes of "Brandon." (*Va. Mag.*, XXXII, 141, XLV, 85.) Sir John and Lady Randolph lived in what is known as the Randolph-Peachy House in Williamsburg at the corner of Nicholson and England Streets, facing

visited Colonel Spotswood[1] and then went to the capitol where we sat till 3 and then dined with Wetherburn and ate boiled veal. After dinner walked and then retired to my lodging where I read English and put things in order and prayed and slept well, thank God.

17. I rose about 6, read Hebrew and Greek. I prayed and had chocolate with the Commissary. The weather was cold and clear, the wind northwest. About 9 went to the Commissary's and from thence to court and sat with great patience till 3 and then dined with Wetherburn and ate roast chicken. After dinner we talked till 6 and then walked to Lady Randolph's and had tea. Then I walked home and read French till 9 and then prayed.

18. I rose about 6, read Hebrew and Greek. I prayed and had coffee. I danced. The weather was cold and clear, the wind northwest. About 9 went to Council and from thence to court where we sat till 4 and then dined with Wetherburn and ate roast veal. Colonel Spotswood came. After dinner I walked to Mr. Needler's and then home and wrote a letter and read English and prayed.

19. I rose about 6, read Hebrew and Greek. I prayed and had coffee. The weather continued cold and cloudy, the wind north. About 9 went to the capitol and sat in court without the Governor, who took physic, till afternoon, and then went to Mr. Barradall's to dinner and [ate] roast

---

Market Square and in the neighborhood of the Palace (Goodwin, *Williamsburg in Virginia,* pp. 180-81).

"My neighbor Sir J. Randolph is dead, a great loss to this Country, which has no other effect upon me than my concern for the Publick," Governor Gooch wrote to his brother, Mar. 8, 1737 (Gooch Letters, Colonial Williamsburg, Inc.) Lady Randolph enjoyed a wide reputation as a gracious, hospitable and efficient hostess, whose table was counted elegant, generous and open (*Va. Gaz.*, Mar. 4-11, 1737).

[1]Ex-Governor Alexander Spotswood was in Williamsburg in connection with the enlistment and equipment of Virginia troops for the colonial regiment he was organizing for the expedition against Carthagena in the war with Spain. On this expedition Spotswood was to be second in command under Lord Cathcart and colonel of the American regiment, but he died before the troops sailed and Governor Gooch took his place (Leonidas Dodson, *Alexander Spotswood* [Philadelphia, 1932], pp. 302-3; for the death of Spotswood, see the entry for June 14, 1740).

chicken. After dinner I walked and then returned home because it was cold and read English till 9 and then prayed.

20. I rose about 6, read Hebrew and Greek. I prayed and had coffee. I danced. The weather continued very cold and clear, the wind north. I put myself in order and about 11 went to church,[1] where Mr. Hartwell[2] acted his part well. After church dined with the Commissary and ate chicken and bacon. After dinner went to visit Mrs. Grymes[3] and in the evening walked home and read English till 9 and prayed.

21. I rose about 6, read Hebrew and Greek. I prayed and had coffee. I danced. The weather was cold and clear, the wind southwest, but a white frost this morning. About 10 went to court where we sat till 3 and then dined with Wetherburn and ate roast veal. I sold 300 barrels of corn to Captain Hutchings.[4] I walked round the town and went home and read English till 9 and prayed.

22. I rose about 6, read Hebrew and Greek. I prayed

[1]I. e. to Bruton Parish Church.

[2]Richard Hartwell (spelled Hartswell, Hartwol), who came into Virginia in 1739 with only Deacon's orders, was a problem to Commissary Blair who found it difficult to get him a living because of a suspicion of his unwillingness to return to London for ordination as a clergyman (Perry, p. 362; Goodwin, p. 277). But Hartwell gained the public eye through the *Virginia Gazette.* He accompanied to the gallows as spiritual mentor one Jonathan Faithful and was thanked publicly by him, as he went to his execution, for Hartwell's care of him during his imprisonment. (See note under entry for Dec. 12, 1739; *Va. Gaz.*, Dec. 29-Jan. 4, 1739.) And in the *Gazette* appeared lines written by the Rev. Mr. Hartswell on a Voyage to Virginia in the year 1739, inscribed to Sir Yelverton Peyton, Bart., commanding his Majesty's Ship *Hector* (*Va. Gaz.*, Jan. 25-Feb. 1, 1740). Peyton was well known in Virginia and was a friend of Governor Gooch, whom he had visited at the Palace while his ship was laid up in Virginia through the winter (Gooch to his brother, May 25, 1735, Colonial Williamsburg, Inc.).

[3]Lucy Ludwell, eldest daughter of Philip Ludwell of Green Springs, married John Grymes (see entry for Dec. 12, 1739) in 1715. She was the mother of ten children (*Va. Mag.*, XXVII, 404-6, XXXII, 49).

[4]This was probably the "Mr. Hutchins," (Capt. John Hutchings) a merchant of Norfolk, referred to in the Executive Journals of the Council for May 28 and 31, 1740, who was given the commission by the Council to provide 350 tons of shipping to transport the Virginia troops on the Carthagena expedition and to subsist the sailors under certain terms agreed upon. Capt. Hutchings was a leading citizen as well as active merchant. He served as mayor of the borough of Norfolk in 1737, 1743, and 1755, and represented it in the House of Burgesses, 1738-1755. (*Va. Mag.*, XIV, 351-53, XV, 7, 127-28, 379; Thomas J. Wertenbaker, *Norfolk, Historic Southern Port,* [Durham, N. C., 1931], p. 49.)

and had coffee. The weather was warm and clear, the wind southwest. I wrote letters till 9 then went to the capitol and sat there close till 3, then dined with Wetherburn and ate boiled fowl. After dinner walked to the races[1] and then went to the Governor's and stayed till 9 and then walked home and committed uncleanness, God forgive me.

23. I rose about 6 and read nothing because I wrote letters home. I prayed and had coffee. The weather was cold and cloudy, with little rain. About 9 went to the capitol where we sat till 3 and silenced Mr. Mercer.[2] Dined with Wetherburn and ate calf's head. After dinner walked and a [horse] would needs walk all the way with us. I called at Lady Randolph's, walked home, and prayed.

24. I rose about 6, read Hebrew and Greek. I prayed and had coffee. The weather was cold and clear, the wind southwest. I wrote letters till 9 and then went to the capitol where we sat till 3 and then went to dinner with Wetherburn and ate roast veal. After dinner I walked and in the even-

---

[1]There was a mile course at Williamsburg where races were held and especially featured at the time of the Fairs. In three days of races on this course at the December Fair, 1739, when the stakes were varied and valuable, on the third day "Mr. Gooch's Horse, Top" (i. e. son of Governor Gooch) came in first and won a saddle and bridle valued at about 40 shillings (*Va. Gaz.*, Dec. 7-14, 1739).

[2]John Mercer was a well-known lawyer whose quick temper and decided opinions repeatedly brought him into conflict with judicial and legislative bodies in Virginia. He was censured by the House of Burgesses in 1730 and suspended from practicing law in Prince William court for "violent behavior" to the justices in that county. On his petition he was permitted on Nov. 27, 1738, by action of the Council, to practice in his own business and that of his former clients but on Oct. 25, 1739 this permission was withdrawn. This laconic entry in the diary indicates the question was again brought before the Council at this April meeting.

Mercer came to Virginia from Dublin in 1720, and married Catherine Mason. He was guardian for some years of her nephew, George Mason, author of the Virginia Bill of Rights. Any possible calculation of the influence of Mercer on the educational development of George Mason would be a valuable contribution to Virginia history.

Mercer edited an *Abridgement of the Laws of Virginia* (Williamsburg, 1737), with a continuation in 1739 and a second edition (Glasgow, Scotland, 1759). He was interested in the Ohio Company, led Stafford County in its opposition to the Stamp Act, and made strong efforts to develop the town of Marlborough in Stafford. He died in 1768 (*Wm. Q. (1)*, XVII, 86-7; *Va. Mag.*, XIV, 232-35, 346, XXIII, 74-78; *JHB*, 1727-1734, 1736-1740, pp. 66, 71; Helen Hill, *George Mason, Constitutionalist* [Cambridge, 1938], pp. 9, 12, 13, 93).

ing drank tea with Lady Randolph and then walked home and wrote letters till 10 and then prayed.

25. I rose about 6, read Hebrew and Greek. I prayed and had coffee. I danced. The weather was cold and cloudy, the wind north. I wrote letters till 9 and then went to court where we sat till 3, then dined with Wetherburn and ate chicken and asparagus. After dinner Captain Wilcox[1] came to us who was just arrived but no news. I walked and called at Lady Randolph's and then retired.

26. I rose about 6, read Hebrew and Greek. I prayed and had coffee. The weather was warm and cloudy, the wind southwest and gave hope of rain. About 9 went to the capitol and sat there till 2, then dined with Needler and ate chicken and bacon. After dinner Colonel Robinson[2] and I walked round the town and called at Mr. Grymes's and stayed till 9, then walked home and prayed.

27. I rose about 6, read Hebrew and Greek. I prayed and had coffee. The weather was warm and cloudy, the wind southwest. I wrote letters and went to church and Mr. Fry[3] entertained us. After church I dined with Mr. Francis[4]

---

[1]Captain [John] Wilcox was master of the ship *Rappahannock* that traded between London and James River in this period. The *Virginia Gazette* reported his clearing the Upper District of James River, Sept. 2, 1736 for London with a cargo of 345 hogsheads tobacco, 6,800 staves, skins, and sassafras, and his entry into the Upper District of James River from London in Feb. 1737. He is frequently mentioned in letters of Virginia planters and merchants (*Va. Mag.*, III, 224, XXI, 437, XXIII, 166, 172; *Wm. Q. (1)*, III, 234, XI, 59; Harker).

[2]John Robinson (1683-1749) served in the House of Burgesses in the sessions beginning in 1711 and 1714, and was sworn into the Council in 1721. When Governor Gooch departed for England on June 20, 1749, Robinson served as acting Governor of Virginia for several months until his death on Sept. 5 of the same year. Robinson and Byrd had been close associates when they with John Grymes acted in 1736 as commissioners for the Crown in laying out the bounds of the Fairfax proprietary (*Va. Mag.*, XVI, 216-7; *Ex. Jour.*, III, IV, *passim*; Bassett, p. 410; *Va. Hist. Port.*, pp. 504-5).

[3]Probably Joshua Fry, surveyor and professor of mathematics at the College of William and Mary. Commissary Blair, because of failing health, frequently during this period was unable to conduct the services at Bruton Church and a lay reader would entertain the congregation by reading from a book of homiletics prepared for such occasions. Fry is best known for his work with Peter Jefferson in making the "Map of the Inhabited Parts of Virginia" (1751). (For sketch of Fry see the *Dictionary of American Biography.*)

[4]Richard Francis came to Virginia from England, settled in York Town,

and ate fish. After dinner we walked, then called at the Commissary's and then proceeded to the Governor's where we stayed to supper and about 9 walked home and prayed.

28. I rose about 6, read Hebrew and Greek. I prayed and had coffee. I danced. The weather was cloudy and warm, the wind southwest. About 9 went to court, sat there till 3, then dined with Wetherburn and ate roast lamb. After dinner walked and called on Mrs. Bassett[1] and then at Barradall's where I stayed till 9 and walked home, wrote a letter, and prayed. It rained.

29. I rose about 6, read Hebrew and Greek. I prayed and had coffee. The weather was cold and clear, the wind northwest. About 9 we went first to Council and then to court and sat till 3 and then dined with Wetherburn and ate roast lamb. After dinner we walked and then walked [*sic*] and in the evening called at Lady Randolph's, stayed an hour and then walked home and prayed.

30. I rose about 6, read Hebrew and Greek. I prayed and had coffee. I danced. The weather was cold and clear, the wind north. About 9 went to court and sat till 3 and then dined with Wetherburn and ate roast chicken and asparagus. After dinner we walked and then walked to Lady Randolph's, stayed about an hour and then walked home and prayed.

---

and practiced law. Candidates to practice law were often referred to him by the Council for examination. (*Va. Mag.*, X, 412-13, XIV, 227, XVII, 266; *Wm. Q. (1)*, V, 222.)

[1]The wife of Colonel William Bassett, of Eltham in New Kent County, was Elizabeth Churchill, daughter of William Churchill and Elizabeth Armistead. After the death of her first husband she married in 1752 William Dawson, Commissary and president of the College of William and Mary, who survived his wedding only ten days—a matter of congratulatory comment by some, who believed he was fortunate thus quickly to escape the unhappiness marriage with the widow Bassett would have brought him. She lived until 1779. (*Wm. Q. (1)*, VII, 146, 186-7).

May, 1740

1. I rose about 6, read Hebrew and Greek. I prayed and had coffee. The weather was warm and clear, the wind southwest. At 9 went to court and sat close till 3 and ate roast veal with Wetherburn. After dinner we walked to the race but were soon forced to retire for the rain. I walked to the coffeehouse,[1] and from thence home and wrote a letter to Westover. I prayed.

2. I rose about 5, read Hebrew and Greek. I prayed and had coffee. The weather was warm, with rain, the wind southeast. It rained abundantly in the night. About 9 went to the capitol and sat till 3, when we dined at Wetherburn's and entertained the Governor. I ate boiled tongue. After dinner we drank arrack punch till 6 and then walked. About 8 I walked home, read French, and prayed.

3. I rose about 5, read Hebrew and Greek. I prayed and had coffee. I danced. The weather was warm and clear, the wind southwest. I paid my debts and about 9 went to court and pronounced sentence upon the boy. There we sat till one, then went to the coffeehouse and from thence to Mr. Needler's and ate sturgeon. After dinner walked and called on Mr. Grymes, then walked home and prayed.

4. I rose about 5, read Hebrew and Greek. I prayed and had coffee. The weather was cold and cloudy, the wind north. I wrote several things and put myself in order till 11 and then went to church and Mr. Robinson[2] preached a

---

[1]It is uncertain which of the taverns in Williamsburg was known as the Coffeehouse in 1740. The architectural research of Colonial Williamsburg, Inc., ascribes lot 25 and part of lot 26 on Duke of Gloucester Street to a "coffee house." There was a succession of owners conducting a tavern on this site. Jean Marot, a Huguenot emigrant who had served the first William Byrd as secretary at Westover (*Wm. Q. (1)*, V, 117) ran a tavern on this site 1707-17, Sullivan from 1717-38, and James Shields, 1738-45. Byrd refers to a coffeehouse in Williamsburg in his Diary, 1709-1712. It became definitely known as the English coffeehouse in 1751-54 and is so called in later advertisements (Architectural Summary, Colonial Williamsburg, Inc.).

[2]Francis Robinson, clerk, was usher of the Grammar School of the College of William and Mary. He died in 1741 and an inventory and appraisement of his estate were made in August, 1741 (*Wm. Q. (2)*, I, 56-7).

good sermon. After church I walked to the Governor's to dinner and ate Scotch collops. After dinner we had tea, then walked to Lady Randolph's and from thence home and prayed.

5. I rose about 5, read Hebrew and Greek. I prayed and had coffee. The weather was clear and warm, the wind southwest. I sent Tom to the ferry to stop my chariot there. I paid the rest of my debts and went to the capitol and made a full end to the court, then went home and read till 2 and then went to the Commissary's to dinner and ate boiled mutton. After dinner took leave and walked to Lady Randolph's and from thence home and packed up my things, read Latin and prayed.

6. I rose about 5, prayed and had coffee. About 7 Colonel Randolph came in my Lady's chariot and I went with him to the ferry where I found my chariot and went in that as far as Mr. Hardyman's, who continued bad, then took leave of Colonel Randolph and went home and found all well, thank God. I ate roast pigeon. After dinner put my things in order and then walked about the plantation. At night had milk and strawberries and about 9 retired and prayed.

7. I rose about 5, read Hebrew and Greek. I prayed and had tea. I danced. The weather was warm and cloudy, the wind west. I gave physic to several of the people who were sick. I settled several accounts and put things in order till dinner when I ate roast mutton. After dinner I took a nap and then came Mr. Hall and then Colonel Bolling, who stayed all night and supped. I retired about 10 and prayed.

8. I rose about 5, read Hebrew and Greek. I prayed and had coffee. I danced. I showed all to Colonel Bolling, with which he was pleased. About 12 the company went to the race and so did my family and I gave them all money and sent a pistole myself by Mr. Hall who brought back two about 4 o'clock. I ate cold mutton. After dinner we walked and talked till 9 and then I prayed.

9. I rose about 5, read Hebrew and Greek. I prayed

and had hominy. I danced. The weather was cold and clear, the wind northwest. I settled several accounts and put matters in order. Mr. Hall went away over the river and I ate fish. After dinner I took a little nap, then played billiards and walked about the plantation. My sick were better, thank God. I talked with my people and prayed.

10. I rose about 5, read Hebrew and Greek. I prayed and had tea. I danced. The weather was very cold and clear, the wind north. I played billiards and settled several accounts and walked till dinner and then ate fish. After dinner put several things in order. L-n-r and Mr. O. came over the river and told me all was well. We walked and I talked with my people and prayed.

11. I rose about 5, read Greek only because I wrote a letter. I prayed and had tea. I danced. The weather was cold and clear. About 9 went to church and had a good sermon. After church Mr. Burwell,[1] Mann Page,[2] the parson and Colonel Eppes[3] came to dine, and I ate boiled beef. After dinner we talked and had coffee. We walked and only Colonel Eppes went away. I talked with my people and prayed.

---

[1]This was probably Lewis Burwell, son of Nathaniel Burwell and grandson of Robert ("King") Carter of Corotoman. He had been educated at Eton and at Caius College, Cambridge (*Va. Mag.*, XXI, 197). He returned to Virginia in 1733 after the death of his grandfather and at first, though highly thought of by Governor Gooch, was not popular with his fellow Virginians because of his manner and way of life which, wrote Gov. Gooch, they "think too much upon the reserve, and are apt to construe it into Pride, but I think him a clever young man and intend to promote him to military honour, if I find he deserves favour from me" (Gooch to his brother, July 20, 1733, Gooch Letters, Colonial Williamsburg, Inc.). Lewis Burwell married Mary Willis, daughter of Colonel Francis Willis; his daughter Rebecca was the "Belinda" of Thomas Jefferson's college days. He served in the Council from 1744 and was president of the Council and acting governor of Virginia, 1750-51 (*Va. Hist. Port.*, p. 505; *LJC*, II, 933, *et seq.*; *Wm. Q. (2)*, VI, 207; *Va. Mag.*, X, 177).

[2]Mann Page was the son of Mann Page and Judith Carter Page, and father of John Page, Governor of Virginia and life-long friend of Jefferson. He owned vast quantities of land in Virginia and resided at his father's home, Rosewell, reputed the largest dwelling in colonial Virginia (Page, *The Page Family*).

[3]This may have been either Llewellyn Eppes (see entry for May 22, 1741), William Eppes of Longfield in Henrico and then Chesterfield County, or Richard Eppes of Eppington in Chesterfield County (*Va. Mag.*, III, 293-301, IX, 242, XXXIII, 26). While there is much detailed data of the Eppes

12. I rose about 5 and read only Greek. I prayed and had coffee. I danced. The weather continued cold and cloudy, the wind north. The parson went away but the young gentlemen stayed to dinner, till which we played billiards and bowls, and I ate chicken and bacon. After dinner the young gentlemen went away and I walked with them part of the way to Colonel Harrison's. When I returned I found myself hoarse so I took Anderson's pills. Talked with my people and retired. We had a sturgeon from above.

13. I rose about 5, read Hebrew and Greek. I prayed and had milk porridge. I danced. The weather was cold and clear, the wind southwest. My boat went away and the gardener and all his family in it. My physic worked five times and made my hoarseness better, thank God. I ate cold chicken. After dinner we played billiards and walked. I talked with my people and prayed.

14. I rose about 5, read Hebrew and Greek. I prayed and had tea. I danced. The weather was warm and clear, the wind southwest. My hoarseness was better, thank God. I wrote a letter to my friend Banister on the death of his wife,[1] and ate fried pigeon pie. After dinner played billiards, read Latin and walked. L-s-y [Lucy?] was better, thank God. I talked with my people, washed my feet.

15. I rose about 5, read Hebrew and Greek. I prayed and had tea. I danced. The weather was warm and clear, the wind west, but little of it. I wrote English and then read Latin till dinner when I ate cold beef. After dinner played billiards, wrote more English and then walked about the plantation. Talked with my people, ate strawberries and milk, and prayed.

---

family who played a prominent rôle in Charles City, Prince George, Henrico and Chesterfield Counties, there is still less than definite information about the family in its various relationships.

[1]John Banister, son of the botanist John Banister, married Wilmette —— and had issue: (1) Martha, who married Robert Bolling of Bollingbrook, and (2) John of Battersea, Dinwiddie County (Slaughter, *Bristol Parish,* p. 132; *Va. Biog.,* I, 179). Byrd refers to Wilmette Banister when he stopped at her home on Hatcher's Run with her husband on their return from the Journey to Eden (Bassett, p. 325).

16. I rose about 5, read Hebrew and Greek. I prayed and had hominy. I danced. The weather was warm and clear, the wind west. I wrote English again and read Latin till dinner when I ate cold beef. After dinner played billiards and read more Latin till the evening, when walked about the plantation. At night talked with my people, had strawberries and milk, and prayed. I had a cold.

17. I rose about 5, read Hebrew and Greek. I prayed and had tea. I danced. The weather was cold and cloudy, the wind north and threatened rain but very little fell. I wrote letters and read Latin till dinner and then ate bacon and eggs. After dinner played billiards and then read more Latin till the evening. It just rained enough to hinder our walking. I talked with my people, and prayed. The boat came.

18. I rose about 5, read Hebrew and Greek. I prayed and had tea. I danced. The weather continued cloudy but no rain, the wind north. I wrote several letters but my son went to church. I read Latin till one when Captains Dunlop and Wilson[1] came to dinner and I ate fish. After dinner we had tea. They stayed till 6. I talked with my people and prayed.

19. I rose about 5, read Hebrew and Greek. I prayed and had tea. I danced. L-l-n-r went over the river, notwithstanding it threatened rain, the wind still north. It rained some little showers. I read Latin till one and then came Mr. Fontaine[2] and Mr. Ford[3] of the College. I ate roast pigeon.

---

[1]There was a Captain John Wilson sailing the Glasgow ship *Thistle Galley* to James River in 1736 (Harker). In 1737 there was a Captain Thomas Wilson sailing between Madeira and York river with the sloop *Molly* of Virginia (*ibid.*). Governor Gooch used a "Captain Wilson" as agent in matters from Virginia to London. (Gooch to his brother, Aug. 28, 1742; Gooch Letters, Colonial Williamsburg, Inc.)

[2]This was probably Francis Fontaine, brother of Peter Fontaine, minister of Westover Parish. He had the King's Bounty for Virginia in 1720. He served various parishes, especially York-Hampton in York County. He became professor of Oriental Languages in the College of William and Mary in 1729 (Maury, *Memoirs of a Huguenot Family*, pp. 326-7, 334; Goodwin, p. 269).

[3]Probably Edward Ford, a graduate of Corpus Christi College, Oxford, who was appointed master of the Grammar School at the College of William and Mary in 1738. He returned to England in 1742 to take up his Fellowship

After dinner we walked about and in the evening played cards. I talked with my people and prayed.

20. I rose about 5, and put up my things in order to go to the Falls. I prayed and had tea. The weather continued cloudy, the wind southeast. About 9 I took my departure and went to Mr. Cary's and my daughter Maria went part of the way along with me. I got there about one and ate roast pigeon. After dinner we talked and had coffee. Mr. Fraser and his wife were there. I prayed.

21. I rose about 5 and read Greek only. I prayed and had coffee. The weather was still warm and cloudy, the wind southwest. About 10 went with Mr. Stevens to Falling Creek,[1] and then to Kensington[2] and then to the Falls and [settled] Mr. Stevens his [own]. I ate bacon and eggs for dinner. After dinner I examined his accounts, which were hard to understand. About 8 retired, read English, and prayed. It rained in the night.

22. I rose about 5 and read Greek. I prayed and had milk. The weather cloudy and warm. About 9 went over the river and settled several matters at the town and granted several lots till 2 and then returned over the river and had bacon and eggs again. I talked with some people and received money of Mr. Smith[?] for the [fishing place?], and I understood that Mr. D-v-s [or D-m-s] had entered for it, notwithstanding it be contained within my patent. I returned about 7 to Mr. Cary's.

23. I rose about 5 and read Greek. I prayed and had coffee. The weather was warm, the wind southwest. I

---

at Oxford (Goodwin, p. 270; Lyon G. Tyler, *The College of William and Mary in Virginia*, 1693-1907 [Richmond, 1907], p. 34; Gov. Gooch to his brother, Feb. 15, 1742, Gooch Letters, Colonial Williamsburg, Inc.; *Wm. Q. (2)*, XX, 133, 217).

[1]Byrd acquired in 1707 clear title to 5,644 acres on Falling Creek in addition to other tracts of land in that locality that he had inherited from his father (Byrd Title Book, also published in *Va. Mag.*, XLVIII, 222-227; Bassett, pp. xxxiii-v).

[2]This plantation does not appear to be mentioned in the Byrd Title Book though from the context of the diary it seems to have been located on the south side of the James between the Falling Creek land and the Falls plantation. See Diary 1709-1712, entry for Aug. 19, 1709.

agreed to stay this day provided Mrs. Cary[1] would go to Dr. Gay's.[2] In the afternoon we played piquet till dinner when I ate dry beef and peas. After dinner we went in the calash to Dr. Gay's and had coffee and returned before night, talked and about 9 retired and prayed.

24. I rose about 5, read Greek. I prayed and had coffee. The weather was warm and cloudy, the wind southwest. I took leave about 9, went over the river, and was caught in the rain before I met the coach, but was not very wet. I finished my journey in the chariot and got home about 2 and ate shoat. After dinner looked about, talked with my people, put things in order, and prayed.

25. I rose about 5, read Hebrew and Greek. I prayed and had tea. I danced. The weather was cold and clear, the wind southwest. About 11 went to church and heard a good sermon. After church several gentlemen dined with me and I ate roast pigeon. After dinner we had tea, walked in the garden. The company went away in the evening. I talked with my people and prayed.

26. I rose about 5, read Hebrew and Greek. I prayed and had tea. I danced. The weather was cold and clear, the wind west. I wrote letters to England and settled with

---

[1]This was evidently Elizabeth, the third wife of Henry Cary, though records so far have failed to reveal the date of his marriage to her or her maiden name. She had property in her own right and owned a house in Williamsburg. She was living in Williamsburg in 1750. She left the bulk of her property (her will proved in 1751, Chesterfield Co. Will Book, I, 147) to "John Brickenhead, Peruke Maker in Old Street, near St. Luke's Church, London" and this may offer a clue to a family connection and her maiden name (Harrison, *The Virginia Carys*, p. 172). Another theory advanced for the identity of Cary's wife is that she was Elizabeth Russell, possibly the daughter of John Brush (York County Records, Orders, Wills, vol. 16, p. 424; Brock, *Archibald Cary*, p. 145).

[2]Dr. William Gay was a justice of Henrico County in 1737 and in 1741, a major in the county militia in 1743, a sheriff in 1745 and a justice of Chesterfield County on its formation in 1749. (*Va. Mag.*, XXIII, 94; Henrico Order Book, 1737-1746, *passim.*) His wife was Elizabeth, daughter of Major John and Mary Bolling (*Va. Mag.*, XIII, p. ix, XXII, 107). By her will in 1750 Mrs. Elizabeth Cary, third wife of Henry Cary, left £20 sterling to her god-daughter Betty Gay (*ibid.*, XXXII, 396). His will, dated Mar. 1, 1749, left his lands in Cumberland and Chesterfield counties to his wife, Elizabeth Gay who with his friends John Bolling, Archibald Cary and John Fleming, Jr., was named executor. (Chesterfield Will Book, No. 1, pt. 1, p. 25.)

our sheriff,[1] then read English till dinner when I ate fish. After dinner played billiards and then walked about the plantation. At night talked with my people and prayed. I played the fool with Sally, God forgive me.

27. I rose about 5, read Hebrew and Greek. I prayed and had tea. I danced. The weather was cold and clear, the wind north. I wrote letters till 12 when Henry Cary and his wife came with his son and daughter[2] and dined with us and I ate beans and bacon. After dinner we talked and had coffee, and then walked about the plantation. At night played cards and ate cakes. I talked with my people and prayed.

28. I rose about 5, read Hebrew and Greek. I prayed and had coffee. I danced. The weather was still cold and clear, the wind northwest. About 7 the company went away and I wrote letters and read Latin till dinner when I ate roast mutton. After dinner I took a nap and then read more Latin. Afterwards walked about the plantation. At night talked with my people and prayed.

29. I rose about 5, read Hebrew and Greek. I prayed and had milk porridge because I took physic. I danced. The weather clear and cold, the wind north. I wrote several letters and read Latin and walked about till dinner when I ate cold beef and peas. After dinner we played billiards and then I read more Latin. It rained in the evening which prevented our walking but only in the garden. I talked with my people and prayed. The weather cleared up in the night and was very cold.

30. I rose about 5, read Hebrew and Greek. I prayed and had milk porridge because I took physic. The weather was cold and clear, the wind southeast. I wrote letters to

---

[1]John Williams was appointed on June 14, 1739, sheriff of Charles City County for the ensuing year (*Va. Mag.*, XIV, 341). He qualified as sheriff in August, 1739 (*Va. Mag.*, XXII, 434).

[2]The children of Henry Cary by his second wife Anne, daughter of John Edwards of Surry, were Anne, about whom nothing seems known, Archibald (see entry Feb. 5, 1740), Judith, born 1726, who married David Bell in 1744, and Sarah, born 1729, who married Alexander Spiers in 1748 (Harrison, *The Virginia Carys*, pp. 89-90).

England and read Latin till dinner when I ate roast mutton. After dinner I put things in order, played billiards and took a nap and read more Latin and walked about the plantation. I gave a note for corn above.

31. I rose about 5, read Hebrew and Greek. I prayed and had tea. I danced. The weather was cold and clear, the wind northwest. I read Latin and wrote English and put several matters in order till dinner when I ate beans and bacon. After dinner played billiards and then read more Latin till the evening when I learned all was well above, and also more inhabitants were coming to Richmond soon. I walked about the plantation. At night ate the last supper of the year.[1] I talked with my people and prayed.

---

[1]Among Byrd's many peculiar ideas on diet was his plan of eating only fruit or berries or something equally light instead of a regular supper during the summer months. Diet had been a matter of major concern among the leading physicians in London during the early eighteenth century when Byrd mingled much with them at the London coffeehouses. Diet was especially the hobby of Dr. George Cheyne whose book "Cheyne on Health" was in Byrd's Library (Bassett, p. 421; *The Letters of Dr. George Cheyne to the Countess of Huntingdon,* ed. Charles F. Mullett [San Marino, Cal., 1941]).

June, 1740

1. I rose about 5, read Hebrew and Greek. I prayed and had coffee. I danced. The weather continued cold and clear, the wind north. I wrote letters and went not to church but the children went. About 12 came Captain Wilson and gave me bills of lading but would not stay to dinner but Mr. Wendey and John Ravenscroft came and I ate roast chicken. We walked in the evening when the company went away. I talked with my people, had raspberries and milk. A beef came down. I talked with my people and prayed.

2. I rose about 5, read Hebrew and Greek. I prayed and had tea. I danced. The weather was clear and cold, the wind north. Three Germans that came here yesterday went up very well pleased with their reception. I wrote letters to England and read Latin till dinner when I ate beans and bacon. After dinner came Captain Dunlop and had victuals. Then came Mr. Gavin and his wife[1] and had likewise some supper. We walked in the evening. I talked with my people and prayed.

3. I rose about 5, read Hebrew and Greek. I prayed and had coffee. I danced. The weather was cold and cloudy, with some rain but it soon went over. I wrote letters and played piquet till dinner when I ate roast pigeon. After dinner we played bowls and walked. At night played piquet

---

[1]Anthony Gavin, who had the King's Bounty for Virginia in 1735, served first as minister in Henrico parish and then in St. James parish, Goochland County, 1736-1744. On the division of that parish he remained as minister of St. James-Northam parish until his death around 1750. He also preached to the Huguenots of King William parish at Manakin Town in 1736 and from 1739 to 1744. St. James parish, when Gavin, with missionary zeal, took it up, had three churches 23 and 24 miles from the Glebe and in addition 7 places of service in the mountains. He said he went twice a year to preach in 12 places, he reckoned "better than 400 miles backwards and forwards" and that he forded 19 times the Northanna and Southanna rivers (*Va. Mag.*, II, 206; XIII, 76, 175-76, 183-90, 265; XXXII, 212; Goodwin, p. 271; *Papers Relating to the History of the Church in Virginia, 1650-1776*, ed. William Stevens Perry [1870], p. 360.)

The will of Anthony Gavin, dated Feb. 21, 1745, proved Sept. 18, 1750, left his whole estate to his wife, Rachel (*Va. Mag.*, XXII, 315).

again and ordered the beef to be killed. I talked with my people and prayed.

4. I rose about 5, read Hebrew and Greek. I prayed and had coffee. I danced. The weather was cold and cloudy, the wind north. Mr. Gavin went to Williamsburg but left his wife here. We played piquet to entertain her till dinner when I ate roast beef. In the afternoon we had tea and then played bowls and then walked about the plantation. I talked with my people and prayed. This day we sheared the sheep.

5. I rose about 5, read Hebrew and Greek. I prayed and had coffee. I danced. The weather was cold and overcast, the wind west. I sent Captain Hardyman some Hungary water.[1] We played piquet till 12 when Mrs. Beverley[2] came with her child [*or* children] and Mrs. Carter, about one, in our chariot which I sent for her. I ate roast beef for dinner. After dinner we talked and had coffee. In the evening Mrs. Carter returned home in our chariot and we played bowls and walked. At night talked with my people and prayed. It rained in the night.

6. I rose about 5, read Hebrew and Greek. I prayed and had coffee. I danced. The weather was warm and cloudy, the wind south but cleared up about 9. We played piquet and put things in order till dinner when I ate roast beef. After dinner came young Mr. Cary and brought English letters. We played bowls and walked. At night played piquet, talked with my people, and prayed. I took pills.

7. I rose about 5, read Hebrew and Greek. I prayed and had milk porridge to work my physic. The weather was

---

[1]Hungary water, "a spirit of wine fill'd with the more essential part of Rosemary-flowers," named from a queen of Hungary for whom it was prepared first (*New English Dictionary*). It was much prized in illness and was especially advertised in the *Va. Gaz.*, May 15, 1752. (See letter of William Byrd I to Perry and Lane, July 25, 1689, ordering twelve quarts of Hungary water. Letter Book of William Byrd, Mss., Virginia Historical Society.)

[2]Mrs. Beverley, wife of William Beverley of Blandfield, was Elizabeth Bland, daughter of Richard Bland of Jordan's Point, Prince George County. She had four children, Robert, Ursula, who married William Fitzhugh, Elizabeth who married James Mills, and Anne (*Va. Mag.*, III, 269; XXII, 297-301).

warm and cloudy, the wind west. I read news and put up my things to go to Williamsburg. Mr. Gavin and Mr. Cary and his wife all returned from Williamsburg to dinner and I ate roast rabbit. After dinner we talked and played bowls and walked. I talked with my people and prayed.

8. I rose about 5, read nothing because of much business. I prayed and had coffee. I danced. The weather was very warm and cloudy, the wind southwest. I went not to church because I prepared for my journey. After church Mrs. Carter dined with us and Mr. [Donald] and Mr. Ravenscroft, and I ate boiled beef. After dinner we talked and had coffee. Some of the company went away. I talked with my people and prayed.

9. I rose about 3 and prayed. I had coffee and went into the chariot about 4 and had the weather pretty cold and cloudy. About 11 I got to Williamsburg and went to Council, then dined at Wetherburn's and ate some roast pork. Then walked to Lady Randolph's and had tea, and in the evening walked to the Commissary's and discoursed him and then went home, wrote a letter, and prayed.

10. I rose about 5, read Hebrew and Greek. I prayed and had coffee. The weather was warm and clear, the wind southwest. I waited on the Governor, went to court, and sat till 4, then entertained the Governor at Wetherburn's and I ate calf's head. After dinner went to the camp where were about 300 men,[1] such as they were. Then I walked

[1]These men were assembled as part of the contingent of troops Virginia sent under Gov. Gooch to aid the British in their fight against Spain at Carthagena (Flippin, "William Gooch," *North Carolina Historical Review,* IV, 41-2; *Va. Mag.*, XXX, 1-20; Letters of Gooch to his brother, Colonial Williamsburg, Inc.). Gooch wrote his brother, June 4, 1740, "I have gott about 400 men." He embarked his troops the middle of September and sailed through the Capes of Virginia on Oct. 2 with the four companies raised in Virginia and six companies from Philadelphia under the convoy of His Majesty's sloop *Wolfe* (Gooch Papers, Va. Hist. Soc.).

For Byrd's views on the Carthagena expedition see his letter to Major Otway, Feb. 1740 [i. e. 1741], *Va. Mag.*, XXXVII, 28, and his letter to Sir Charles Wager, May 26, 1740 (*ibid.*, XXXVII, 102-04). Byrd's unflattering opinion of the troops in camp is, in part, explained by a bill put through the Assembly of which Edward Barradall (see Dec. 11, 1739 entry), Attorney General and Burgess for the College of William and Mary, was the author. This plan, which the late Fairfax Harrison called a "diabolically ingenious

with Colonel Digges[1] about an hour, then called at Mr. Blair's, went home and prayed.

11. I rose about 5, read Hebrew and Greek. I prayed and had coffee. The weather was cold and cloudy, the wind southwest. I had several visitors and about 10 went to the capitol where we sat till 3, then dined with Wetherburn and ate broiled chicken. After dinner I walked to the coffeehouse and read news, then received some money of Lidderdale,[2] then walked to Lady Randolph's and drank tea and talked with the girls. In the evening walked home, settled some matters and prayed.

12. I rose about 5, read Hebrew and Greek. I prayed and had coffee. The weather was very hot, the wind southwest. I wrote English and settled some accounts till 10, then went to the capitol and sat till 2. I dined with the Governor and ate young goose. After dinner I walked to Lady Randolph's and had tea. Then walked and called on the Commissary with whom I sat till 9, then walked home and prayed.

13. I rose about 5, read Hebrew and Greek. I prayed and had coffee. The weather continued very warm. About

device," called on the county courts to impress men for the military service who followed no lawful calling or employment, excluding any man who had a vote in the election of burgesses or was or should be an indented or bought servant. This narrowed the field of impressment to ex-convicts. This plan of Barradall to drain off the ex-convicts from Virginia filled that colony's quota and provided a precedent for other colonies (Harrison, *Landmarks of Old Prince William*, I, 164, 172).

[1]Cole Digges, of Belfield, York County (1692-1744) was the son of Dudley Digges, and grandson of Edward Digges, Governor of Virginia. He served in the House of Burgesses and was a member of the Council from 1719 to his death. He was county lieutenant of Elizabeth City, Warwick, and York. He married Elizabeth, daughter of Dr. Henry Tower of York County (*Va. Mag.*, IV, 168-9; *Wm. Q. (1)*, I, 144-45; *Ex. Jour.*, III and IV, *passim*).

[2]John Lidderdale was a merchant in Williamsburg in this period. He also had a store in Prince George County. It seems probable that he represented in Virginia the merchant firm of Robert and John Lidderdale of London. He married Elizabeth Robertson, daughter of William Robertson, clerk of the Council on March 2, 1739 (*Va. Gaz.*, Sept. 9-16, Nov. 18-25, 1737, Mar. 2-9, 1739, Mar. 21-28, 1745; *Wm. Q. (1)*, V, 135, XVI, 185; *(2)*, II, 202-3; *Va. Mag.*, V, 91, XVI, 21; see note on Spalding under Sept. 7, 1739 entry). He brought suits for various sums owed him and in association with Spalding in the Charles City and Prince George county courts. (Charles City Order Book, 1737-1751, pp. 331, 361, 419; Prince George Minute Book, 1737-1740, pp. 183, 300, 392.)

9 I visited Charles Carter[1] and then Colonel Grymes, then went to the capitol and sat till 2 and then dined with Wetherburn and ate Scotch collops. Dr. Mollet[2] dined with us. After dinner I walked to Colonel Lightfoot's[3] where several ladies came. About 8 walked home, wrote a letter, and prayed.

14. I rose about 5, read Hebrew and Greek. I prayed and had chocolate. The weather continued very hot. We had news of Colonel Spotswood's death.[4] I breakfasted with the Commissary where we consulted what he as President was to insist upon. About 10 went to the capitol where it was agreed that the Commissary should be President during the Governor's absence, [and] the Governor and Isham Randolph should have the care of the soldiers. Colonel Grymes and I dined with the Commissary and I ate beans

---

[1]Charles Carter of Cleve (1707-1764) was the third son of Robert ("King") Carter of Corotoman. He inherited from his father his lands in King George and Spotsylvania and the tide of settlement in that region made him a very rich man before his death. He played a constant though relatively modest part in the political life of the colony, serving as a justice and county lieutenant and was a burgess for over a quarter of a century. He had served as one of the commissioners for Lord Fairfax in 1736 in surveying the bounds of the Northern Neck. Though Byrd served for the colony on this commission, their opposing alliances seem to have had no effect on their friendliness. He married Byrd's daughter Anne in 1742. (Bassett, p. 402; *Va. Mag.*, XXXI, 39-69; *The Letters of Robert Carter*, pp. 142-3.) Charles Carter was one of the executors of the will of the diarist and took his oath as executor, Nov. 1745. (Charles City Order Book, 1737-1751, p. 387.)

[2]Dr. Mollet was introduced to Byrd by Sir Hans Sloane when he came to Virginia. Byrd wrote Sloane he had done all he could to keep Dr. Mollet in Virginia but "our clymate was too cold, and his constitution too delicate, or else too lazy, to ride much about without which there are no great Earnings to be made for one of the Faculty in this thin-inhabited Country. About a month ago he took his Departure for Jamaica, where he hopes to get more money with less Trouble." (Byrd to Sloane, Apr. 10, 1741, British Museum, Sloane MSS, Vol. XXII, 4057, f. 20; printed in part in *Va. Mag.*, XXXVII, 104, and entire in *Wm. Q. (2)*, I, 199.)

[3]Philip Lightfoot (1689-1748) was a member of the Council of Virginia and one of the richest men in the colony. He was a leading merchant in Yorktown, and at his death owned plantations in seven counties with houses, store houses and lots in Yorktown, Williamsburg and Blandford and more than 180 slaves, "four wheeled and two wheeled Chaise" and a "coach and six horses." (*Va. Mag.*, V, 83; *Wm. Q. (1)*, III, 106.)

[4]Spotswood died on June 7, 1740 at Annapolis on his way north to plan with the other colonial governments for their contingents in his American regiment for the Carthagena expedition (Dodson, p. 303). On Spotswood's death Governor Gooch, who had been named his alternate, made preparations to command the expedition from the colonies. Commissary Blair as the longest in service in the Council, had been concerned for years as to whether in such

and bacon. After dinner we went to Lady Randolph's and about 8 walked home and prayed.

15. I rose about 5, read Hebrew and Greek. I prayed and had coffee. The weather was warm and cloudy, the wind southwest, with thunder. I put myself in order and about 11 went to church and Mr. Stith[1] entertained us with a good sermon. After church I dined with the Commissary again and ate peas. After dinner we had coffee and then I walked to Mr. Needler's, from thence to Mr. Grymes's and then home and prayed.

16. I rose about 5, read Hebrew and Greek. I prayed and had coffee. The weather continued warm, notwithstanding the rain, the wind west. It threatened more rain and thundered at a distance. I went to Mr. Grymes's and visited the ladies, then went to the capitol and sat there till 2 and then dined with Wetherburn and ate fish. After din-

---

a contingency he as a clergyman would follow the custom of becoming President of the Council and thus acting Governor during Gooch's absence. On the death of Colonel Robert Carter in 1732 Blair wrote to the Bishop of London that, as the eldest in the Council by the old standing instruction, he would be appointed President in case of the death or absence out of the colony of the Governor, but that he understood Byrd intended on account of his gown to seek to set aside the instruction and to obtain a "dormant commission for himself in case of a Governor's demise" (Blair to Bishop of London, Aug. 14, 1732, Oct. 11, 1740, *Wm. Q. (2)*, XX, pp. 118-19, 134-35). There is no evidence, now that the contingency Blair had foreseen had come to pass, that Byrd made any effort to hinder the Commissary from becoming President in regular routine. Gooch stated that he paid Blair as acting Governor during his absence from Virginia on the Carthagena expedition "as much of my salary as amounted to what I received as colonel and quarter master general" (Flippin, "William Gooch," *North Carolina Historical Review*, IV, 41).

[1]While family authorities argue William Stith was the son of William Stith and Mary Randolph, he is entered in the register of Queen's College, Oxford, where he received the B. A. degree in 1728 and M.A. in 1730 as the son of "John Stith of the Virgin Islands" (*Wm. Q. (1)*, XXI, 188. See entry for Dec. 25, 1739). He was master of the Grammar School of William and Mary College, chaplain to the House of Burgesses, and in 1738 became rector of the parish of Henrico. In 1752 he was named president of William and Mary College, though opposed by some as anti-Trinitarian and by Governor Dinwiddie as an unorthodox clergyman and a man of turbulent spirit who endeavored to make a party of the lower class of people as enemies of the Governor in his administration. (*Wm. Q. (2)*, XX, 227-236.) He was author of *The History of the First Discovery and Settlement of Virginia* (Williamsburg, 1747). He married Judith Randolph, daughter of Thomas Randolph of Tuckahoe, described in the *Virginia Gazette* (July 21-28, 1738) as "an agreeable Lady, with a very considerable fortune." (*Va. Mag.*, XLV, 70.)

ner walked again to Colonel Grymes's and stayed till 8, then was carried home, because it rained, and prayed.

17. I rose about 5, read Hebrew and Greek. I prayed and had chocolate. The weather continued cloudy and cold, the wind southeast and threatened more rain. About 10 went to the capitol where we sat tall 2 and the Governor prorogued the Assembly. I dined with Wetherburn and ate roast veal. After dinner I walked to Colonel Grymes's and from thence home and read Latin and prayed. Our two captains[1] made a ball but I went not to it.

18. I rose about 5, read Hebrew and Greek. I prayed and had coffee with the Commissary. The weather was cold and cloudy, the wind southeast. I waited on the Governor and wished him a good journey, then went to Lady Randolph's and then to the new doctor's[2] and then went to dine with Needler and ate roast veal. After dinner went to drink with Mr. Barradall and in the evening walked to the camp and from thence walked home and put up my things and ate some cold lamb with Mrs. [Hargrave?] and then retired and prayed.

19. I rose about 5, read nothing. I prayed and had three dishes of chocolate. The weather was cold and cloudy, the wind southwest. About 6 Colonel Randolph called upon me and carried me to the ferry and there my chariot carried me safe home about one and found all well, thank God. I ate cold lamb. After dinner put things in order and walked about. In the evening talked with my people and prayed.

20. I rose about 5, read Hebrew and Greek. I prayed and had coffee. I danced. The weather was very hot and threatened rain, and we had abundance. I unpacked several

---

[1]While the four captains to command the Virginia troops on the Carthagena Expedition were not named in the Council minutes until Aug. 6, it is probable that Byrd is referring here to two of these four men named captains, Lawrence Washington, Charles Walker, Richard Bushrod and James Mercer. (*Va. Mag.*, XV, 6.)

[2]This may refer to Dr. M-r-t, of whom records seem to be lacking, but who accompanied Byrd from Williamsburg to Westover. (See entry for Aug. 7, 1740.)

things till one and then came Captain Bolling[1] with John Ravenscroft and dined with us and I ate broiled lamb. We talked and had tea till the evening when our company went away and I walked in the garden. I prayed and took two pills.

21. I rose about 5, read Hebrew and Greek. I prayed and had tea. I danced. The weather was cloudy and warm and threatened rain, the wind south. I put several things in order and wrote English and read Latin till dinner when I ate fish. After dinner it rained very hard. All the afternoon I read Latin but could not walk; however at night I talked with my people and prayed. All was well above, thank God.

22. I rose about 5, read Hebrew and Greek. I prayed and had coffee. I danced. The weather was clear and [warm], the wind southwest. Captain Bolling and John Ravenscroft came to breakfast and carried my children to church in his [boat]; however I went not but wrote several letters. I ate dried beef for dinner. After dinner we talked and Bolling entertained the children with his tricks and went away in the evening. I talked with my people and prayed.

23. I rose about 5, read Hebrew and Greek. I prayed and had milk and water. The weather was warm and clear, the wind west. We began to cut our wheat and found it good and in good order. I examined Stevens' account and found it very faulty. I read Latin till dinner and ate cold shoat. After dinner took a nap and read more Latin till the evening and then walked among my harvesters. I talked with the people.

24. I rose about 5, read Hebrew and Greek. I prayed

---

[1]Captain Thomas Bolling traded between Virginia and England and is frequently mentioned by the family at Westover in their letters (*Va. Mag.*, XXXVI, 118, 353; XXXVII, 109). He was master of the ship *Harrison* from London for some years (Harker). He was in James River apparently in the ship *Dunkirk* in the autumn of 1740. (See entry for Aug. 11, 1740; *Wm. Q. (1)*, XXI, 97-8.) There has been confusion apparently of Edward Bolling and Thomas Bolling (*Va. Mag.*, XXXVI, 118), but in the lists of ships trading to and from Virginia as noted in the *Virginia Gazette*, 1736-40, only Capt. Thomas Bolling is listed.

and had tea. I danced. The weather was cool and clear, the wind north. I settled more accounts and read more Latin till dinner, when I ate beans and bacon. After dinner I took a nap and read more Latin till the evening when I walked among the harvesters. I talked with my people and prayed. M-r-t-y came full of complaints against Stevens.

25. I rose about 5, read Hebrew and Greek. I prayed and had tea. I danced and washed my feet. The weather was warm and clear, the wind southwest. I settled accounts and read Latin till dinner, when I ate cold shoat. After dinner came Ned Randolph and his son,[1] but brought little news. After dinner we walked and had tea and [got s-n t-r-n]. At night talked with my people and prayed.

26. I rose about 5, read Hebrew and Greek. I prayed and had coffee. I danced. The weather was cool and cloudy, the wind north. We walked about among the reapers and then played piquet and walked till dinner when I ate roast pigeon. After dinner we talked and had coffee, then played bowls and walked. At night I talked with my people and about 9 retired and prayed.

27. I rose about 5, read Hebrew and Greek. I prayed and had coffee; I danced. The weather was cool and cloudy, the wind northwest. I put things in order and about 11 went to the Secretary's, where we found Charles Carter and his wife.[2] Mr. Randolph went with us and I ate pigeon pie. After dinner we drank very good wine and had coffee and about 6 took leave and returned home and found all well but Bob. I prayed.

28. I rose about 5, read Hebrew and Greek. I prayed and had tea. I danced. The weather continued very cool,

[1]Edward Randolph had two sons, Joseph and Edward, either of whom may be referred to here. Joseph died unmarried and Edward is supposed to have married Lucy, daughter of Benjamin Harrison of Berkeley (*Va. Mag.*, XLV, p. 84). See entry for Dec. 17, 1740.

[2]Mary Walker, daughter of Joseph Walker, a merchant at Yorktown, married Charles Carter in 1728. She died in the spring of 1742 and the following Christmas Charles Carter, then 35 years old, married Anne Byrd, the seventeen-year-old daughter of William Byrd. She died in 1757 and five years later he married as his third wife Lucy, daughter of Captain William Taliaferro of Essex County (*Va. Mag.*, XXXI, 40-41, 44).

the wind northwest. My man Bob continued indisposed. I settled some accounts and wrote letters to the Falls, then read Latin till dinner, when I ate roast lamb. After dinner played billiards and then at bowls, then walked and talked with my people and prayed.

29. I rose about 5, read Hebrew and Greek. I prayed and had coffee. I danced. The weather was cool and clear, the wind west. Wrote letters to the Falls. I went not to church nor did anybody come after church. I read Latin till dinner and then ate boiled mutton. After dinner we talked and I wrote a letter to Mrs. Spotswood.[1] I walked, talked with my people, and prayed.

30. I rose about 5, read Hebrew and Greek. I prayed and had tea. I danced. The weather was warm and clear, the wind southwest. We prepared to entertain Colonel Charles Carter and he and the Secretary with their families came about one and after them Tom Bolling[2] and we had a good dinner and I ate roast rabbit. After dinner we talked and had coffee. All went away in the evening. I prayed.

[1]Spotswood had died on June 7 and this was probably a letter of condolence to his widow, who had entertained Byrd at her home in 1732, a visit he recounted with keen enjoyment in "A Progress to the Mines" when he wrote, "Here I arriv'd about three a'clock, and found only Mrs. Spotswood at Home, who received her Old acquaintance with many a gracious Smile" (Bassett, p. 356). Mrs. Spotswood, who was married to the colonial ex-governor in 1724, was Anne Butler Brayne, daughter of Richard and Anne Brayne of St. Margaret's, Westminster (Dodson, *Alerander Spotswood*, p. 299). After Spotswood's death she married Rev. John Thompson (*Va. Mag.*, X, 143-44). Byrd wrote to Sir Charles Wager pressing the claims of Mrs. Spotswood growing out of her husband's efforts in fitting out the Carthagena expedition, which the Duke of Newcastle was asked to present in a petition to the King. (*Va. Mag.*, XXXVII, 106.)

[2]See entry for June 20, 1740 and note on Captain Bolling.

July, 1740

1. I rose about 5, read Hebrew and Greek. I prayed and had coffee. I danced. The weather was warm and cloudy, the wind southwest and threatened rain. I wrote English and settled some accounts and read Latin till dinner, when I ate cold beef. After dinner put things in order but was confined to the house by the rain which fell in plenty. Afterwards walked in the garden, talked with my people, and prayed.

2. I rose about 5, read Hebrew and Greek. I prayed and had tea. I danced. The weather was cool and cloudy, the wind north. It rained again in the night more than in the day. I wrote a letter and read English news till dinner when I ate cold lamb. After dinner took a nap and then read Latin till the evening when we walked about the plantation. At night talked with my people and prayed.

3. I rose about 5, read Hebrew and Greek. I prayed and had coffee. I danced. The weather was cool and cloudy, the wind southeast. Bob went to Meherrin with my little cart. Several gentlemen came, and among them Mr. Dering[1] who came from Mr. Cary's, and dined and I ate bacon and greens. After dinner we talked and played bowls and walked. I talked with my people and prayed.

---

[1]Probably William Dering, who, in 1737, opened his school at William and Mary College to teach dancing "in the newest French manner" to all gentlemen's sons on Fridays and Saturdays once in three weeks (*Va. Gaz.*, Nov. 18-25, 1737; Dec. 26-Jan. 2, 1738; March 21-28, 1745; Oct. 3-10, 1745). He also gave assemblies at the capitol during the time of the meeting of the General Court in Williamsburg. It would appear that he went to the homes of certain gentlemen to instruct their children, girls as well as boys, in dancing (see entry for June 16, 1741). Little is known about this William Dering, but Byrd's friendliness for him, aside from his devotion to dancing, raises the question as to whether he was any connection of Sir Robert Southwell's wife, Elizabeth, daughter of Sir Edward Dering, whom Pepys called "a very pretty woman" (*Va. Mag.*, V, 150).

Byrd's fondness for dancing, evident through the diary, supports Governor Gooch's report to his brother about the social life in Virginia. Gooch wrote to his brother, Thomas Gooch, soon after his arrival in Williamsburg, Dec. 28, 1727; "The Gentm and Ladies are perfectly well bred, not an ill Dancer in my Govmt." (Gooch Letters, Colonial Williamsburg, Inc.)

4. I rose about 5, read Hebrew and Greek. I prayed and had coffee. I danced. It began to rain and continued all day more or less. I read English and played billiards, then read Latin till dinner when I ate dried beef. After dinner we played billiards again and then read more Latin. I walked a little in the garden [and] talked with my people and prayed.

5. I rose about 5, read Hebrew and Greek. I prayed and had tea. I danced. The weather continued cool and cloudy, the wind northeast. Mr. Dering went away. My wife was indisposed with the colic. I wrote English and Latin till dinner when I ate fish. After dinner took a nap, played bowls and walked about the plantation. I talked with my people and prayed. The veal came.

6. I rose about 5, read Hebrew and Greek. I prayed and had coffee. I danced. The weather was still cloudy, the wind east. My wife was better, thank God. I went not to church because the coachman was gone to Meherrin. I wrote letters. After church came Captain Bolling and his doctor. I ate roast veal. After dinner the Captain went away and I walked about the plantation. I talked with my people.

7. I rose about 5, read Hebrew and Greek. I prayed and had tea. I danced. Mrs. Byrd took a vomit and was better. We began to cut the oats. All well at Roanoke, thank God. I wrote English and read Latin till dinner, when I ate roast veal. After dinner took a nap and read more Latin. It rained a moderate shower. Mr. Anderson came. I talked with my people and prayed.

8. I rose about 5, read Hebrew and Greek. I prayed and had tea. I danced. The weather was warm and clear, the wind southwest. I talked with Mr. Anderson who desired to come again into my service. I wrote several letters and read Latin till dinner and ate minced veal. After dinner Anderson went away and I read more Latin, played at bowls. It rained again. I prayed.

9. I rose about 5, read Hebrew and Greek. I prayed and

had tea. The weather was clear and warm, the wind southwest. My physic worked pretty well. I wrote English [till] 12 when Mrs. Pinkard[1] came and dined with us and I ate only pudding. After dinner we talked and had coffee. In the evening played bowls and Mrs. Pinkard went away. I talked with my people and prayed.

10. I rose about 5, read Hebrew and Greek. I prayed and had tea. I danced. The weather was warm and clear, the wind northwest. We planted some of the plants that came last night from the Falls. I wrote letters to England till dinner and ate fish. After dinner Mr. Hall and his wife[2] came. We played bowls. I talked with my people and prayed.

11. I rose about 5, read Hebrew and Greek. I prayed and had coffee. I danced. The weather was cool and clear. We showed the ladies all our rarities while Mr. Hall went across the river to fish. I read English. Captain Talman[3] came and dined here and so did Mr. Cole, and I ate minced meat. After dinner I put things in order, played bowls, talked with my people, and prayed.

12. I rose about 5, read Hebrew and Greek. I prayed and had tea. I danced. The weather was warm and cloudy, the wind north. The company went away this morning. I wrote letters to England and read English till dinner when I ate fricassee of chicken. After dinner took a nap and then

---

[1]Frances Anderson Pinkard, daughter of the Rev. Charles A. Anderson and his wife Frances. She was married to Thomas Pinkard of Lancaster County in September 1739. (*Wm. Q. (1)*, IV, 127; XII, 263; *T's. Q.*, VI, 263.)

[2]This was probably Anne Bolling, daughter of Robert and Anne Cocke Bolling, who married John Hall. See entry for December 20, 1739, and *Va. Mag.*, IV, 330.

[3]Captain [Henry] Talman, who sailed in various ships, the *Vigor*, galley of Bristol, the *Edward and Anne* of Bristol, or the *Nancy*, was frequently referred to in letters of the Byrd family at Westover (Harker; *Va. Mag.*, XXXVIII, 353; *Va. Gaz.*, June 5-12, 1752). In his letter to Mr. Smyth of Sept. 5, 1740, Byrd wrote, "By the recommendation of Captain Talman whose ship rides over against my House I am encouraged to begin a correspondence with you" (Brock 188, Huntington Library). See letters of Maria Taylor Byrd to her son, William Byrd III, March 15, 1757, July 13 and 18, 1760, telling of rumors that Captain Talman had been taken by privateers (MS. collection of Mr. William Byrd of New York).

read more English till the evening when we played bowls. No news from the Falls. I talked with my people, had apples and milk, and prayed.

13. I rose about 5, read Hebrew and Greek. I prayed and had coffee. I danced. The weather was warm and cloudy, the wind north. I went not to church but wrote letters, then read English and Latin till dinner. My daughters went with Miss Beverley[1] to Colonel Harrison's to dinner and I ate roast chicken at home. After dinner Captain Gray[2] and I had tea. In the evening I walked, talked with my people, and prayed.

14. I rose about 5, read Hebrew and Greek. I prayed and had tea. I danced. The weather was cool and clear, the wind north. I wrote letters and then read English till one and then Latin till dinner when I ate bacon. After dinner put things in order and read more Latin till the evening, when we played bowls. At night talked with my people and prayed.

15. I rose about 5, read Hebrew and Greek. I prayed and had tea. I danced. The weather was cool and cloudy, the wind north, but calm. Captain Bolling came with Captain Talman but went aboard soon. I read English and then Latin. The boat went up this morning. I ate fish. After dinner I put things in order, read more English; then played bowls and walked. I talked with my people and prayed.

16. I rose about 5, read Hebrew and Greek. I prayed and had [. . .]. I danced. The weather continued cool and clear, the wind southwest. I read English till 12 when John Stith came and his wife, who played billiards and talked till dinner, when I ate bacon and chicken. After dinner we

[1]William Beverley of Blandfield and his wife had a daughter Elizabeth, born January 15, 1726. She was thus Byrd's great niece. She married James Mills, of Middlesex County, on August 21, 174[3], and after his death Thomas Griffin Peachey in 1783. She died in 1795 (*Wm. Q. (1)*, III, 112, VI, 192; *Va. Mag.*, III, 269, XXII, 297-301).

[2]This was probably Captain Gray who sailed from Glasgow to Virginia and through whom Byrd's librarian Procter sought to communicate with his friends in Scotland (Procter to his brother, Oct. 25, 1740, *Va. Mag.*, X, 299).

talked and had coffee. In the evening it rained so our visitors stayed. I talked with my people and prayed.

17. I rose about 5, read Hebrew and Greek. I prayed and had coffee. I danced. The weather was warm and cloudy, the wind southwest. We played billiards and then I wrote English till dinner when I ate pigeon pudding. After dinner I took a nap and then put things in order till the evening, when we played bowls. Mrs. Graffenried[1] dined with us. I talked with my people and prayed.

18. I rose about 5, read Hebrew and Greek. I prayed and had chocolate. I danced. The weather was warm and clear, the wind northwest. Mrs. Graffenried went across the river about 12 and I read English and Latin till dinner when I ate fish. Mr. Wood came and settled accounts and told me all was well above. We played bowls and walked. I talked with my people and prayed.

19. I rose about 5, read Hebrew and Greek. I prayed and had tea. I danced. The weather was very warm and

---

[1]This was probably Barbara Tempest (née Needham), daughter of Sir Arthur Needham of Wymondsley, Hertfordshire, England, who married in Charleston, S. C., in 1714, Christopher de Graffenried, son of Christopher de Graffenried who founded New Bern, N. C. She had lived in Philadelphia and Maryland and then had moved to Virginia. In 1721 Mrs. De Graffenried taught dancing in the homes of certain Virginia planters, including Col. Nathaniel Harrison and Francis Hardyman (Diary, Jan. 4, 6, Mar. 5, 6, 1721). At one time she and her husband seem to have conducted an inn in Williamsburg, though they seem also to have lived in Prince George County and he acquired land in Brunswick County. Byrd referred to her in a letter to Sir John Randolph, Jan. 21, 1735, "Upon the news of Mr Stags death Madame La Baronne de Graffenriedt is in hopes to succeed to part of his businesss in town and were it not for making my good Lady Jealous (which I would not do for the World)—I would recommend her to your favour. She really takes abundance of pains and teaches well and were you to attaque her virtue in the furious month of May when the sap rises in women they say as well as in vegetables you would find her as chast as Lucretia" (*Va. Mag.*, IX, 239-41).

The *Virginia Gazette*, Apr. 15-22, 1737, carried this notice: "To the Gentlemen and Ladies—That Mrs. Degraffenreidt intends to have a ball, on Tuesday next, being the 26th Instant, and an Assembly on Wednesday the 27th, at her house in Williamsburg; for which, Tickets will be delivered by her at her House, at any Time before the Ball or Assembly begins." (See also *Va. Mag.*, XIV, 243, XXII, 435; *Wm. Q., (1)*, XV, 202-3; *Christopher von Graffenried's Account of the Founding of New Bern*, ed. with an historical introduction and an English translation, (Raleigh, 1920), pp. 96-7; Thomas P. De Graffenried, *History of the De Graffenried Family from 1191 A.D. to 1925* (1925), pp. 149-151); Prince George Minute Book, 1737-1740, pp. 183, 382; Charles City Order Book, 1737-1751, p. 414).

clear, the wind southwest. My daughter Mina rode to Mrs. Stith's. I read English and Latin till dinner when I ate fricassee of chicken. After dinner took a nap, then read more Latin. In the evening played bowls, talked with my people, and prayed. [. . .][1]

20. I rose about 5, read Hebrew and Greek. I prayed and had coffee. I danced. The weather was still warm and clear. All well at the Falls. I went not to church because it was hot. After church came Colonel Eppes,[2] Jenny Anderson,[3] Molly Stith and Captain Gray, and I ate chicken pudding. After dinner we talked and had coffee. It rained in the evening, and I prayed.

21. I rose about 5, read Hebrew and Greek. I prayed and had coffee. I danced. The weather was cool and clear, the wind north. Jenny Anderson and Molly Stith stayed. I read English till dinner when I ate chicken and bacon. After dinner took a nap and then read Latin. In the evening played bowls and walked. The company went away. We killed a beef. I prayed.

22. I rose about 5, read Hebrew and Greek. I prayed and had hominy. I danced. The weather was warm and clear, the wind southwest. I read English. Betty Stith and

---

[1]Several words are illegible.

[2]Col. Littlebury Eppes figures in suits in Charles City court in this period. His will was presented in Charles City court in December, 1743, by Lewellin Eppes, one of the executors. (Charles City Order Book, 1737-1751, pp. 84, 94, 123, 131, 282, 298.) See note on his son Edmund, Sept. 11, 1740. A case in chancery, presumably growing out of the settlement of his estate, by Edmund Eppes against Lewellin Eppes dragged through the Charles City court for many years, still unsettled in 1751 when the existing Order Book for the county comes to an end. Lewellin Eppes and Edmund Eppes, executors of Littlebury Eppes, brought suit against Richard Kennon and David Stokes, executors of Francis Hardyman. This case also was undecided for many years.

[3]Jane Anderson, daughter of the Rev. Charles A. Anderson, married as his second wife Ellyson Armistead, son of Captain Robert Armistead, in 1740 or 1741 (Mrs. A. W. Garber, *The Armistead Family*, [Richmond, 1910] p. 230; *T's. Q.*, VI, 263). Jane Anderson with her sister Charlotte was appointed to keep the ferry from their own landing to Jordan's Point in Prince George County, which her mother Mrs. Frances Anderson had been authorized on her petition to keep in July 1739 provided she kept a "good and substantial Boat sufficient to carry four horses" (Charles City Order Book, 1737-1751, pp. 92, 115).

Charlotte Anderson[1] came about 11. I read English till dinner and then ate roast beef. After dinner I took a nap and had tea, then played bowls and walked. I talked with my people and prayed.

23. I rose about 5, read Hebrew and Greek. I prayed and had tea. I danced. The weather was warm and cloudy, with a little rain that soon blew over. I wrote English and read Latin till dinner, when old Bridges came and dined with us and I ate cold roast beef. After dinner he went away and I read more English. I walked in the evening, talked with my people, and prayed.

24. I rose about 5, read Hebrew and Greek. I prayed and had milk porridge because I took pills. The weather was cool and clear, the wind north. Major Bolling[2] and Will Kennon[3] breakfasted here but went away about [9]. I read English and Latin till dinner when I ate boiled pigeon. After dinner put things in order and read Latin again. In the evening talked with my people and prayed.

25. I rose about 5, read Hebrew and Greek. I prayed and had coffee. I danced. The weather was cool and cloudy. About 9 it rained a little but held up too soon. I read English and Latin till dinner, when I ate fish. After dinner I took a nap and read more English. In the evening played bowls and walked. I talked with my people, had apples and milk, and prayed.

---

[1]Charlotte Anderson, daughter of the Rev. Charles Anderson, married Henry Taylor in 1743 (*T's. Q.*, VI, 262-63).

[2]Probably this was John Bolling, who later after the formation of Chesterfield county in 1749 became commander of the militia in that county and was more commonly known as Col. Bolling. Byrd appears to refer to him both as Major Bolling and as John Bolling (see entry for Sept. 17, 1740).

John Bolling (1700-1757) was the son of Col. John Bolling and Mary Kennon. He had the reputation of being a pleasure loving man who enjoyed fishing and hunting and dancing and good company. In his early years he lived in Goochland and was a burgess from that county in 1728. Later he lived at Cobbs on the Appomattox and represented Henrico county in the Burgesses from 1742 to 1749 and Chesterfield county later. His first wife was Elizabeth Lewis and his second Elizabeth Blair. (*Va. Mag.*, XXII, 215-217; *Wm. Q. (1)*, XVII, 155, *Memoirs of the Bolling Family*, p. 5).

[3]Will Kennon of Conjurer's Neck in the peninsula between Appomattox river and Swift creek, was justice of Henrico County, 1710, and sheriff of that county in 1720, burgess for Henrico, 1736 and 1740 (*Va. Mag.*, V, 90-1; *Ex. Jour.*, IV, *passim*; *Wm. Q. (1)*, XIV, 132-133).

26. I rose about 5, read Hebrew and Greek. I prayed and had hominy. I danced. The weather was cool and clear, the wind southwest. I read English and Latin till dinner, when I ate fish. After dinner I put things in order. Mr. Procter complained of lowness of spirits, for which I gave him ginseng. The gardener was sick. I walked and talked with my people and prayed. All well above.

27. I rose about 5, read Hebrew and Greek. I prayed and had coffee. I danced. The weather was very warm and clear, the wind southwest. I went not to church but read Latin and put myself [in] order. After dinner Colonel Stith and his wife and Mr. Pinkard and his wife and John Ravenscroft dined with us and I ate boiled beef. After dinner we talked and had coffee. They went away in the evening, and I prayed.

28. I rose about 5, read Hebrew and Greek. I prayed and had hominy. I danced. The weather was exceedingly hot and clear, the wind west with signs of rain but none came. I settled several accounts and read English till dinner, when I ate boiled pigeon and bacon. After dinner I put things in order and took a nap. In the evening played bowls. I talked with my people and prayed.

29. I rose about 5, read Hebrew and Greek. I prayed and had hominy. I danced. The weather continued warm and clear, the wind north. I was a little indisposed but settled some accounts and read Latin till dinner when I ate roast veal. After dinner I took a nap and then read Latin till the evening; then played bowls. I talked with my people. The poor gardener was bad. I prayed.

30. I rose about 5, read Hebrew and Greek. I prayed and had tea. I danced. The weather was warm and foggy, the wind still north and very driving. I settled several accounts and gave the bark to the gardener who was very bad. I read Latin till dinner when I ate minced veal. After dinner took a nap and read more Latin till the evening, when we played bowls and walked. I talked with my people and prayed.

31. I rose about 5, read Hebrew and Greek. I prayed and had coffee. I danced. The weather was warm and clear, the wind southwest and very driving. I read Latin and settled several accounts till dinner, when I ate roast veal. After dinner put things in order, read more Latin. In the evening played bowls. At night talked with my people and prayed. There was great want of rain all over the country; God Almighty send us a good shower, the giver of all good things.

August, 1740

1. I rose about 5, read Hebrew and Greek. I prayed and had tea. I danced. The weather was warm and clear, the wind southwest. About 11 came Colonel Dick Randolph[1] and young Beverley Randolph,[2] and Captain Bolling came ashore to them, and persuaded me to go aboard ship with them, and ate pork and peas and had several sorts of wine, and stayed till 7, till when it had rained hard. G-th-r Beverley and Mr. Pinkard were likewise aboard. We left C-l there and returned home. I talked with my people and prayed. It rained abundance this night.

2. I rose about 5 and read nothing because Isham Randolph came last night. I prayed and had coffee. Colonel Dick breakfasted with us, and Captain Bolling, and were also persuaded to stay to dinner when I ate boiled pigeon and bacon. After dinner the company went away and we played bowls. Mr. Procter was sick again. I talked with my people. All well at the Falls, thank God. I prayed.

3. I rose about 5, read Hebrew and wrote a letter. I prayed and had coffee. Captain Bolling and young Beverley breakfasted with us and then went up, and we went to church and had a good sermon. After church nobody came home with us, but Captain Friend[3] came to dinner and I ate boiled beef. After dinner we and [*sic*] walked in the garden. At night talked with my people and prayed.

---

[1]Richard Randolph of Curles was the fifth son of William Randolph of Turkey Island. He was a Burgess and, like his brother William, served as Treasurer of Virginia. He married Jane Bolling, daughter of John and Mary Kennon Bolling of Cobbs. He died at Bath in England (*Ex. Jour.*, IV, 389; *Va. Mag.*, XLV, 83, 394; *Va. Gaz.*, Apr. 6-13, 1749).

[2]This was probably Beverley Randolph of Gloucester County, son of Sir John Randolph. He married in 1742 Agatha Wormeley, daughter of John and Elizabeth Wormeley of Rosegill, Middlesex County. He represented the College of William and Mary in the House of Burgesses in 1748 (*Wm. Q. (1)*, IV, 118, XX, 17; *Va. Mag.*, XXXVI, 386; XLV, 86).

[3]Captain Charles Friend was actively engaged in the Virginia trade, sailing the ship *Loyal Friend* of London or the ship *Gooch* of London to and from York river to London with a typical cargo of 570 hogsheads of tobacco, 8,000 staves, skins and wine (Harker). Governor Gooch thought highly of him and intrusted to him on occasion a present of "a Pott of Sweetmeats" for His Lordship the Bishop of London (*Va. Mag.*, XXX, 54).

4. I rose about 5 and read nothing. I prayed and had milk porridge because I took physic. I danced. The weather was cool, with rain, the wind north. I prepared matters to go tomorrow to Williamsburg. I read news till dinner when I ate boiled beef. After dinner put things in order and read more news till the evening when Major Mayo came.[1] I talked with my people. Mr. Procter was very bad.

5. I rose about 3, prayed, had three dishes of chocolate, recommended my family to God, went into the chariot about 4 and Major Mayo went with me part of the way. I got to the ferry about 9 and to Williamsburg about one and dined with the Commissary and ate stewed veal. After dinner waited on the Governor, stayed about an hour and walked home, a little giddy; God preserve me. I prayed.

6. I rose about 5; was a little disordered in my head. I read Hebrew and Greek. I prayed and had chocolate with the Commissary. From thence went to Colonel Grymes's and then to Council where we named the Captains of our troops.[2] About 3 dined with Wetherburn and ate fish. After dinner went to the camp[3] and saw our officers; then called on the attorney and walked home and prayed.

7. I rose about 4, prayed and had coffee, and about 5 Doctor M-r-t[4] came and went home with me. We got to the ferry about 8 and proceeded home without any accident where we arrived about 2 and found several very sick. I ate

---

[1]Probably Major William Mayo (*c.* 1684-1744), surveyor, who was associated with Byrd in running the boundary line between Virginia and North Carolina and in laying out the towns of Petersburg and Richmond and in surveying the southern boundary of Lord Fairfax's Proprietary, the Northern Neck. Byrd esteemed Major Mayo highly (see sketch in *Dictionary of American Biography*; Bassett, *passim*; Byrd, *Histories of the Dividing Line,* ed. Boyd, p. 318 *et passim*).

[2]The four captains so named were: 1. Lawrence Washington, elder brother of George Washington, who named Mt. Vernon on the Potomac in honor of the English Admiral commanding the fleet in this expedition; 2. Charles Walker; 3. Richard Bushrod; 4. James Mercer, brother of John Mercer of Marlborough (see note for Apr. 23, 1740), who became a major in the English army (*Ex. Jour.*, Aug. 6, 1740; *Va. Mag.*, XV, 6).

[3]Encampment for the Virginia troops waiting to sail on the Carthagena expedition.

[4]See entry for June 18, 1740, and note on "the new doctor."

salt fish for dinner. My son was gone to the race and returned not till dark with Captain Bolling and several others who delivered him safe about 8, thank God. I talked with my people and prayed.

8. I rose about 5, read Hebrew and Greek. I prayed and had coffee. I danced. The weather was warm and clear, the wind southwest. I was a little out of order and put several [things] in order and played billiards till dinner and ate dry beef. After dinner we played cards till the evening and then bowls. At night we killed a beef. I talked with my people and prayed.

9. I rose about 5, read Hebrew and Greek. I prayed and had tea. I danced. Mr. Procter was better. The weather was warm and clear. I read Latin and played piquet till dinner when Captain Bolling came and dined with us. I ate chicken and bacon. After dinner we talked and played again till the evening when we played bowls. I talked with my people and prayed.

10. I rose about 5, read Hebrew and Greek. I prayed and had coffee. I danced. The weather was warm and clear, the wind southwest. All pretty well above, thank God. I wrote letters. About one came Captain Bolling and dined with us and I ate roast veal. After dinner we talked and then took a nap. I read Latin and walked in the evening and visited the sick. I talked with my people and prayed.

11. I rose about 5, read Hebrew and Greek. I prayed and had tea. I danced. The weather was cool and clear, the wind southwest. I played the fool with Sally, God forgive me. I went with the Doctor on board Bolling,[1]

---

[1]This evidently refers to the ship *Dunkirk* of which Captain Bolling was the master and which sailed from James River about this time. The planters of Virginia seem to have made no distinction in referring to a ship or its captain, as would be indicated by these extracts from the letters of Richard Chapman: To Edward Athawes, Williamsburg, Nov. 2, 1740, "The Exemplifications of our Acts of Assembly were Transmitted to the Board of Trade in Captain Bolling"; to George Carter, Esq., of the Inner Temple, Nov. 16, 1740, "The Exemplification is since transmitted along with the Rest to the Lords Commissioners of Trade, in the Dunkirk, Capt. Bolling" (*Wm. Q. (1)*, XXI, 97-8).

where we found Peter Randolph,[1] Lidderdale, and Mr. Hall, and ate pork and peas. In the evening we returned home and found all pretty well, thank God. I took physic.

12. I rose about 5, read Hebrew and Greek. I prayed and had milk porridge. I danced. The weather was very warm and clear, the wind west. I read Latin, played billiards and piquet till dinner, when I ate minced veal. My physic worked four times. After dinner we did nothing but puff and blow for the heat. In the evening we walked about the plantation. I talked with my people and prayed.

13. I rose about 5, read Hebrew and Greek. I prayed and had tea. I danced. The weather was very hot and clear, the wind southwest. I read Latin and played piquet and billiards and read Latin till dinner when I ate roast pigeon. After dinner we played piquet again and I read Latin till the evening when we walked to visit the sick. I talked with my people and prayed.

14. I rose about 5. I read Hebrew and Greek. I prayed and had coffee. I danced. Betty Beverley went away but was searched because she had taken several things. About 12 came Mrs. Carter and Jenny Anderson and dined with us and I ate lamb's head. After dinner we played cards till the evening when Mrs. Carter and Jenny went away and we walked. I talked with my people and prayed.

15. I rose about 5, read Hebrew and Greek. I prayed and had tea. I danced. The weather was cool and clear, the wind east, with signs of rain that followed. We played cards and billiards till dinner when I ate roast chicken. After dinner we played piquet till the evening when we walked about the plantation. At night came Captain Bolling and stayed. I talked with my people and prayed. We killed a beef.

---

[1]Peter Randolph of Chatsworth in Henrico (*c.* 1712-1764) was the second son of "Councillor" William Randolph (see entry for Apr. 14, 1740). He held many important colonial offices, was a justice of Henrico, burgess, Treasurer of the Colony, member of the Council, and Surveyor General of Customs for the Middle District of North America. He married Lucy Bolling, daughter of Colonel Robert Bolling of Prince George County, in 1738 (*Va. Mag.*, XLV, 68; *Wm. Q. (1)*, V, 244).

16. I rose about 5, read Hebrew and Greek. I prayed and had tea. I danced. The weather was warm and cloudy, the wind south. The Doctor went to visit Colonel Harrison. I wrote English and played billiards till dinner when I ate cold chicken. After dinner put things in order and read Latin till the evening when I walked about the plantation. At night talked with my people and prayed.

17. I rose about 5, read Hebrew and Greek. I prayed and had coffee. I danced. The weather was warm and cloudy, the wind southwest and threatened rain but it fell not. I went not to church but wrote letters and cleaned myself. After church came Colonel Stith and his wife who was indisposed. I ate roast beef. After dinner we talked and had coffee. In the evening they went away and I walked in the garden. I talked with my people.

18. I rose about 5, read Hebrew and Greek. I prayed and had tea. I danced. The weather was still warm and cloudy, the wind southwest. I played billiards and read Latin, then played piquet and looked at my people till dinner when I ate boiled chicken. After dinner played again at piquet till the evening, then walked about the plantation. At night talked with my people and prayed. It grew very cool.

19. I rose about 5, read Hebrew and Greek. I prayed and had tea. I danced. The weather was cool and clear, the wind north. We determined to go to the Secretary's to introduce the Doctor and accordingly we went about 12, when the Secretary came home in no good humor, just before dinner, which was a very indifferent one. I ate sturgeon. After dinner we had tea and went home. In the evening I talked with my people and prayed.

20. I rose about 5, read Hebrew and Greek. I prayed and had tea. I danced. The weather was cool and clear, the wind southwest. The Doctor went away to Williamsburg and I wrote English and read Latin till dinner, when I ate roast pigeon. After dinner I put things in order and

read more Latin till the evening when we played bowls and then walked. I talked with my people.

21. I rose about 5, read Hebrew and Greek. I prayed and had coffee. I danced. The weather was cool and cloudy, the wind south and threatened rain and accordingly it rained all day, a gentle rain. I wrote English till dinner, when I ate fish. After dinner wrote more English till the evening when there was no walking because of the continued rain. I talked with my people and prayed. It rained in the night.

22. I rose about 5, read Hebrew and Greek. I prayed and had tea. I danced. The weather was cool and cloudy, with rain, but held up about 6. We played billiards and I wrote my [nieces] and read Latin till dinner when I ate boiled beef. After dinner I took a nap and read more Latin. In the evening walked in the garden. I talked with my people and prayed. I took physic.

23. I rose about 6, read Hebrew and Greek. I prayed and had milk porridge. I danced. The weather was warm and clear, the wind west. I wrote English and played billiards, then read Latin till dinner when I ate ox cheek. My physic worked four times. After dinner put several things in order till the evening; then played bowls and walked. I talked with my people and prayed. It rained.

24. I rose about 6, read Hebrew and Greek. I prayed and had coffee. I danced. The weather was cool and clear, the wind northwest. I went not to church but prepared for my journey to Williamsburg. After church came Mr. Pinkard and his wife, Jenny Anderson, and Mrs. Eppes, and I ate roast veal. After dinner we had coffee. In the evening they went away and I prayed.

25. I rose about 6, read nothing, and had milk porridge and recommended my family to heaven and got into the chariot about 4 [*sic*] and got to Williamsburg about 12, and went to the capitol and dined with the Governor and ate fricasseed chicken. After dinner drank tea with Lady Ran-

dolph, then walked to the camp and then home and wrote a letter to my wife and prayed.

26. I rose about 6, read Hebrew and Greek. I prayed and had chocolate with the Commissary. The weather was cool and clear, the wind southwest. Went to the capitol and [ciphered] there till 2; then dined with Wetherburn and ate fish. After dinner walked to the camp and saw the men exercise; then walked and wrote letters till 10, but my head was not right. I prayed.

27. I rose about 5, read Hebrew and Greek. I prayed and had coffee. The weather was cool and clear, the wind north. About 10 went to the capitol and read the [journal] and walked about till 2; then dined with Mr. Needler and ate sausage and eggs. Then walked to the camp and from thence home and wrote more letters till 10 and prayed.

28. I rose about 5, read Hebrew and Greek. I prayed and had coffee at Mr. Blair's where I stayed till 10 and then drove to the capitol where the Governor put an end to the Assembly and I dined with Wetherburn and ate roast turkey. After dinner we went to take leave of the Governor in a body;[1] then walked to Lady Randolph's, and then to Mr. Barradall's who was sick, and then home where I wrote letters and prayed.

29. I rose about 5, read Hebrew and Greek. I prayed and had chocolate with the Commissary. There was a great fog, the wind southwest. I walked to several places and made several visits and about 2 dined with Lady Randolph and ate chicken pie. After dinner I made more visits and walked with Isham Randolph about the town and then walked home and put up my things. I prayed. It was very warm again.

30. I rose about 5 and prayed. Major Mills[2] and Mr.

[1]The Council on eve of Gooch's departure in command of the American troops in the Carthagena expedition.

[2]This was probably Nicholas Mills who is frequently mentioned in the records of St. Paul's parish, Hanover County (*The Vestry Book of St. Paul's Parish*), and in the county records as Nich Mills Gent. (*Wm. Q. (1)*, XXI,

P-n-y came about 6 and we had coffee. Then went into Lady Randolph's chariot and went to the ferry where we found Mina and proceeded home where we got about one and found all well, thank God, and had shoat for dinner. After dinner it rained and confined us in the house. I played at cards and I retired.

31. I rose about 5 and read nothing. I prayed and had coffee. I danced. The weather was warm and cloudy. I went not to church myself but my visitors did. I wrote letters and put myself in order. After church Mr. Wendey and I ate roast rabbit. After dinner we talked and walked in the evening, when I talked with my people and prayed.

56). His will was written May 6, 1741 and he was certainly dead by 1749 though the exact date of his death is not known (*T's. Q.*, XIV, 237; *Va. Mag.*, XXXI, 324; XXXVIII, 383).

September, 1740

1. I rose about 5, read Hebrew and Greek. I prayed and had coffee. I danced. The weather was warm and cloudy, the wind north. We played billiards and then played cards till dinner when I ate boiled beef. After dinner we talked and played cards till the evening and then walked about the plantation. I packed up my things to go to Hanover. I talked with my people and prayed.

2. I rose about 4 and drank two dishes of chocolate; then recommended my family to heaven and Major Mills and I got into the chariot about sunrise and drove over the Long Bridge[1] to Hanover. By the way we ate cold roast mutton. About 3 we got to Major Henry's and I ate roast chicken. There was the parson,[2] who invited us to dinner next day. I prayed and rose in the night.

3. I rose about 5 and had a looseness and I prayed and had thick milk. It rained a little; however, we rode to see my land and about 3 dined with the parson and I ate roast chicken. After dinner we returned to Major Henry's through the rain, but were not wet. One of my horses was sick. We talked of the land but the Major came to no determination but seemed a little inclined to be the purchaser. My looseness was better, thank God. I prayed.

4. I rose about 5 and prayed. I had tea and about 6 we

---

[1]Long Bridge spanned the Chickahominy river between Charles City and New Kent counties, just east of the point at which the White Oak Swamp stream emptied into the river (A Map of the Inhabited Part of Virginia . . ., Drawn by Joshua Fry and Peter Jefferson in 1751; *Cal. S. P.*, II, 66; *T's. Q.*, VIII, 254). It is frequently mentioned in this period in the records of Charles City and the August court of that county in this year, 1740, had had a report from gentlemen ordered to view the bridge that it was in "a very dangerous condition." The court took action to require the undertakers for keeping the bridge in repair to be prosecuted. (Charles City Order Book, 1737-1751, pp. 41, 140, 280, 386, 441.)

[2]Patrick Henry, who had the King's Bounty in 1732, followed his brother John Henry to Virginia. After earlier charges he became minister of St. Paul's Parish in Hanover county, 1737-1777. He was the uncle of the Revolutionary orator Patrick Henry. (*Vestry Book of St. Paul's Parish*; Goodwin, p. 278.)

took leave and returned home, the weather being cool and cloudy. By the way ate cold chicken and got home about 3 without any accident. The Major came at last to the resolution of buying the land and paying for it in 6 months. I ate roast veal. After dinner walked and talked with my people and prayed.

5. I rose about 5 and read nothing because I drew the writings between the Major and me. I prayed and had coffee. I danced. It rained a little. We executed the compacts and settled the whole matter, and I ate pork and peas. After dinner I wrote letters and put several things in order till the evening when we walked and talked. I gave audience to my people and prayed.

6. I rose about 5 and read nothing because I unpacked some books that came by Clack.[1] The gentlemen went away in my chariot. I put arms into my books.[2] About one came four of the Randolphs to go on board Captain Bolling. I put things in order till dinner and ate pork and peas. After dinner settled some accounts, talked with my people. Isham Randolph and Beverley came.

7. I rose about 5, read Hebrew and Greek. I prayed and had coffee. I danced. The weather was cool and cloudy,

---

[1]William Clack, captain of the ship *Mercury* and later the *Speedwell,* traded between London and the Upper District of James River, bringing in salt or European goods and carrying away a typical cargo of about 400 hogsheads of tobacco, staves, and skins (Harker). See letter of Edward Athawes, merchant in London to John Carter, Esqr., Rappahannock River in Virginia per the *Mercury,* Capt. Clack, Dec. 22, 1738 (*Va. Mag.*, XXIII, 170). Capt. Clack, sailing a ship belonging to Plymouth with a cargo estimated as worth £14,000 was taken by a Spanish privateer, and Thomas Goodman, commodore of the two ships of war and the sloop *Ranger,* was censured for cowardice by the Council of Virginia in failing to take the Spanish privateer (Oct. 17, 1741, Typed copies of MSS, Ex. Jour. of the Council of Virginia, Va. State Library: Letters of Governor Gooch, Sept. 15, 1741, Oct. 12, 1741, Gooch Papers, Va. Hist. Soc.). Captain Clack reported to Gov. Gooch on his return from Bermuda where his captors put him ashore that "the Spaniards used them well."

[2]Books from Byrd's library, now scattered in various libraries and private collections, have his coat of arms as a bookplate in the front of each volume. The bookplate, which is reproduced in *Va. Mag.*, XXXII, 26, bears the motto "Nulla Palescere Culpa" and the identifying line "William Byrd of Westover in Virginia Esquire." See title page of this volume.

the wind southwest. I went not to church but wrote letters. After church Dick Randolph[1] and G-th-r Beverley came ashore with Captain Bolling and dined with us and I ate salt fish. After dinner the company went away and I walked, then talked with my people and prayed.

8. I rose about 5, read Hebrew and Greek. I prayed and had tea. I danced. The weather was cool and rained almost all day, the wind east. I wrote letters to England and read French till dinner and ate fricasseed chicken. After dinner wrote more letters till the evening, when I danced because I could not walk. I talked with my people and prayed. It grew very cool.

9. I rose about 5, read Hebrew and Greek. I prayed and had tea. I danced. It continued to rain moderately, the wind still northwest [*sic*]. I had several persons sick, God save them. It rained in showers all day and I wrote letters till dinner and ate broiled beef. After dinner I read French and danced because could not walk. I talked with my people and prayed.

10. I rose about 5, read Hebrew and Greek. I prayed and had tea. I danced. The weather was cool and cloudy, the wind north and promised to hold up. God send it may without a [. . .]. I wrote letters till one, when Captain Talman came and dined and I ate boiled beef. After dinner the Captain went away and I read French. I walked in the evening, talked with my people, and prayed. It rained.

11. I rose about 5, read Hebrew and Greek. I prayed and had coffee. The weather was warm and cloudy and rained a little, notwithstanding the wind was northwest. I wrote letters till one when Colonel Eppes and his son[2] came

---

[1]This probably was Richard Randolph Jr. (1715-1786) son of Richard Randolph of Curles (see entry for Aug. 1, 1740; and *Va. Mag.*, XLV, 83).

[2]This was probably Edmund Eppes (see entry for March 15, 1741), though Col. Littlebury Eppes may have had other sons. (See entry and note for July 20, 1740.) Edmund Eppes served as captain of a company in 1740, as captain of a troop of horse in 1741 and later as major in the forces of Charles City County. He was a member of the County court, and in 1745 was sheriff of the county. (Charles City Order Book, 1737-1751, pp. 21, 86, 90, 121, 123, 132, 168, 345, 371, 393, 522.) See entry and note for June 7, 1741.

to go aboard Captain Bolling but returned to dinner and I ate pork and peas. After dinner the company went away. I walked in the garden and talked with my man [*or* men].

12. I rose about 5, read Hebrew and Greek. I prayed and had tea. I danced. The weather was cold and cloudy, but the weather cleared up about 9, thank God, the wind northwest. I wrote a long letter to England and walked in the garden till dinner when I ate roast pigeon. After dinner wrote more letters till the evening and walked. We killed a beef. I read French and prayed. I took pills.

13. I rose about 5, read Hebrew and Greek. I prayed and had milk porridge. I danced. The weather was cool and cloudy, the wind north. I wrote letters to England. My purge worked five times. I read English till dinner when I ate fish. After dinner put things in order and read English till the evening when we walked about the plantation. I talked with my people and read English.

14. I rose about 6, read Hebrew and Greek. I prayed and had coffee. I danced. The weather was warm and misty, the wind north. About 11 went to church and received the Sacrament and had a good sermon. After church the parson came to dinner and so did Major and Captain Bolling and John Ravenscroft and I ate fish. The parson and Dr. Monger stayed. I talked with my people and prayed.

15. I rose about 5, read Hebrew and Greek. I prayed and had coffee. I danced. The weather was cool and misty, the wind north. I settled accounts with Captain Talman and wished his [*sic*] a good voyage. I wrote letters and walked till dinner when I ate pork and peas. After dinner I put things in order and walked in the garden. They killed another beef. Read English and prayed.

16. I rose about 5, read Hebrew and Greek. I prayed and had tea. I danced. The weather was cloudy and threatened more rain, the wind north. I wrote letters and

walked about till one when Colonel Bland[1] came with Dr. Monger and dined with us and I ate broiled lamb. After dinner Colonel Bland went aboard with the Doctor and I walked about the plantation. I talked with my people and prayed.

17. I rose about 5, read Hebrew and Greek. I prayed and had tea. I danced. The weather was warm and cloudy, the wind southwest. Captain Talman came to settle accounts and dined with us and I ate roast pigeon. Mrs. Stith dined with us. After dinner I walked and had coffee. In the evening Colonel Dick Randolph, and Beverley, and John Bolling[2] came but would not stay. I walked and talked with my people.

18. I rose about 5, read only Greek. I prayed and had coffee. I danced. The weather was warm and clear, the wind southwest. I wrote letters till 12 when Captain Bolling and Mr. Harris[3] came and dined with us and I ate bacon and peas. After dinner it rained and blew very hard, but held up for the company to go away. I talked with my people and prayed. Dick C-r-n was better.

19. I rose about 5, read Hebrew and Greek. I prayed and had tea. I danced. The weather was very cool and

---

[1]Richard Bland of Jordan's Point, across the river from Westover, was the son of Richard Bland who had been an agent for Byrd in many matters (see Diary, 1709-12, *passim*). He was active in Prince George County local government, a member of the House of Burgesses continuously from 1742 to 1775, and had an important role in the revolutionary bodies in Virginia and in the Continental Congress of 1774. He was author of *A Letter to the Clergy on the Two-penny Act* and of *An Inquiry into the Rights of the British Colonies* (*Va. Mag.*, IX, 357; *Bland Papers,* ed. Campbell, [Petersburg, 1840] I, xiii-xiv, 36-37; James E. Pate, "Richard Bland's *Inquiry into the Rights of the British Colonies,*" *Wm. Q. (2)*, XI, 20-29).

[2]See entry and note on Major Bolling, July 24, 1740.

[3]Probably Benjamin Harris, Gentleman, who was prominent in business matters and in county politics in Charles City County. He served on the Charles City County court before he removed to Henrico County where he was added to the Commission of the Peace for that county at the August court, 1741 (Charles City Order Book, 1737-1751, *passim*; Henrico Order Book, 1737-1746, *passim*). He ordered his removal from Charles City to Henrico to be certified at the June court in Charles City, 1744. Benjamin Harris was listed as the ninth child of Thomas Harris, of Henrico, whose will was proved June, 1730 (*Va. Mag.*, XIII, 273; XIV, 90; XV, 130; XXXIII, 37; XXXVI, 256).

clear, the wind northwest. Dick C-r-n was better, thank God. I had a bad cold myself; however, I wrote letters till dinner and then ate a blue wing. After dinner came Dr. Monger to see C-r-n. We walked and talked. My cold was worse; God preserve me. I retired soon and prayed.

20. I rose about 5, read Hebrew and Greek. I prayed and had coffee. I danced. The weather was cool and clear, the wind north. My cold grew worse. My cold was extremely bad. Mr. Ravenscroft came to see about building our [*or* another] house and dined with us[1] and I ate only rice milk. After dinner we talked till the evening when I retired in good time and took Squire's Elixir and prayed.

21. I rose about 5 and was much out of order. I read only Hebrew. I danced. The weather was warm and clear, the wind southwest. About 9 poor Dick C-r-n died, notwithstanding all the care we could take of him. Captain Clack dined with us and I ate only pudding. I grew worse and began to cough and have a fever. I retired in the afternoon and prayed.

[*This entry in longhand follows*]

From this day I grew worse, so that I was let Blood, and the next day took a Purge However all that woud not do, so I sent for Dr Monger who approvd what had been done. He ordered me a mixture of Juice of Oranges Salt of Wormwood and Hordealed Cinnomon Water with some Prepared Pearl, which abated my Feaver, but did no service to my Cough, which was very severe anights, however with care and good Nursing, it went away in about a Month, and I recovered enough to go to Williamsburg the 21 of October following.

---

[1]John Ravenscroft (see entry and note for Aug. 29, 1739) built a chapel on Jones Hole Creek in Bristol parish in 1729 (Philip Slaughter, *A History of Bristol Parish, Va.* [Richmond, 1879], p. 15).

October, 1740

21. [*First entry for month*] I rose about 6 and prayed. I had two dishes chocolate and about 8 recommended my family to heaven and got into the chariot with my daughter Annie, and went to the ferry where Lady Randolph's chariot met me and we proceeded to town where I sent Annie to Mr. Needler's and I found my landlord and landlady sick. I put my house in order and prayed.

22. I rose about 6 and prayed. I read Hebrew and Greek. I had chocolate at the Commissary's. The weather was cool and cloudy, the wind north. About 10 I went to the capitol where I sat till 12; then went to Mr. Needler's to see my daughter, where I dined and ate boiled chicken. After dinner I called at Lady Randolph's who was from home, and returned to my lodgings.

23. I rose about 6 and read nothing because I wrote several things. I prayed and had chocolate. The weather was cool and cloudy, the wind north. I went to Lady Randolph's and from thence to the Governor's where I waited on the ladies,[1] and went from thence to court and stayed there till 3 and then dined again with all the council and Mr. Needler and ate roast turkey, and returned and prayed.

24. I rose about 6, read Hebrew and Greek. I prayed and had rice milk. I had a fever last night. The weather was cloudy, with rain, the wind northwest. About 10 went to the capitol and sat there till 3, then dined with Wetherburn and ate roast veal. After dinner I walked home and wrote letters and read French till 8, then retired and missed my fever. I prayed.

25. I rose about 6, read Hebrew and Greek. I prayed and had rice milk. The weather was very cold and clear, the wind northwest. About 10 went to court and sat there

[1]I. e. Gooch's wife, Rebecca Stanton Gooch and his daughter-in-law, daughter of James Bowler of Maryland, who, after the death of the Governor's son, married Warner Lewis of Gloucester County (*Va. Mag.*, XI, 73-4).

till 2 and then went to the Governor's where we dined, it being the Governor's birthday. I ate roast turkey and was very merry but returned about 5 and walked home, read Latin, and prayed. I took two pills.

26. I rose about 6, read Hebrew and Greek. I prayed and had rice milk. The weather was cold and clear, the wind northwest. My physic worked four times and very easy. I went not to church but after church dined with the Commissary and ate roast fowl. After dinner we walked to Colonel Custis'[1] and had cider and from thence walked home, wrote letters, and read French and prayed.

27. I rose about 6, read Hebrew and Greek. I prayed and had rice milk. It rained a little, the wind southeast. About 10 went to court and sat till 3 and then dined with Wetherburn and ate fish. After dinner walked to Colonel Grymes's where I found my wife just come to town. However I walked home in good time, read French and prayed.

28. I rose about 6 and read Hebrew. I prayed and had rice milk. The weather continued cloudy, the wind north. My son [. . .] about 10 o'clock at Colonel Grymes's to see my wife and then went to Council and then to court and sat till 2 and then dined with the President with my wife, then went to Lady Randolph's and then home where I read and prayed.

29. I rose about 6, read Hebrew and Greek. I prayed and had rice milk. It rained much in the night and was cloudy, the wind north. Bob Mumford came and stayed half an hour; then I called to see my wife and then went to

---

[1]John Custis, 1678-1749, was closely connected with Byrd in business and family affairs. He married Frances Parke, sister of Byrd's first wife, Lucy Parke. He was a member of the House of Burgesses and then of the Council. See Articles of Agreement between John Custis, Frances his wife, and William Byrd, Feb. 4, 1711, New York Historical Society; Custis Letter Book, 1717-1741, Library of Congress; Hen. *Stat.*, IV, 29; Custis, *Recollections of Washington*, pp. 16-17.

Custis shared Byrd's interest in the flora and fauna of Virginia (Curwen MSS, American Antiquarian Society, copies in Colonial Williamsburg, Inc.; Letters of Peter Collinson to John Custis, Bartram to Collinson, Dec. 25, 1737, Bartram Papers, Vol. I, f. 16, Penn. Hist. Soc., copies in Colonial Williamsburg, Inc.).

court and about 2 dined with Lady Randolph and ate roast turkey. After dinner we had tea and about 5 walked home, and I wrote a letter and prayed.

30. I rose about 6 and read nothing because my daughter came to visit me. The weather was extremely cold, the wind north. About 10 went to court and sat till one and invited company to Wetherburn's and I ate roast venison. After dinner we had a race which I went not to but won 20 shillings. At night ventured to the ball[1] at the capitol where I stayed till 10 and ate three jellies and then went home and prayed. The President entertained well.

31. I rose about 6, read Hebrew and Greek. I prayed and had rice milk. The weather was cold and cloudy, the wind north. I visited my wife at Colonel Grymes's and then went to court, sat till 3, and then dined with Mr. Attorney and ate boiled mutton. After dinner we talked and had tea till the evening when I walked home and wrote letters.

---

[1]This was the fifty-seventh birthday of George II. Commissary Blair, as Governor in Gooch's absence, was conforming to the custom of the Governor's celebrating the King's birthnight with a ball in the colonial capitol. Governor Gooch made lament to his brother at the expense to the Governor of these occasions, declaring the celebration of His Majesty's birthday cost 100 guineas (Feb. 18, 1727, Gooch Letters, Colonial Williamsburg, Inc.). For another contemporary account of such a celebration, see *Va. Gaz.*, Oct. 28-Nov. 4, 1737.

November, 1740

1. I rose about 6, read Hebrew and Greek. I prayed and had coffee with my family, who went out of town about 9. About 10 I went to court where we sat till 2 and then I dined with Mr. Lidderdale and ate roast partridge. After dinner I walked to Mr. Needler's and from thence walked home, wrote letters, and read English. I took two pills. It blew hard.

2. I rose about 6, read Hebrew and Greek. I prayed and had rice milk. The weather was cold and clear, the wind northwest. My physic worked four times. I wrote letters to England and then dined with the Commissary and ate fish. After dinner we talked till 4 and then I walked to Lady Randolph's and then home, where I wrote letters and prayed.

3. I rose about 6, read Hebrew and Greek. I prayed and had rice milk. The weather was clear and cold, the wind north. About 10 I went to Colonel Grymes's and from thence to court where I pronounced sentence upon two women,[1] then went to council and then finished the court, then dined with Wetherburn and ate venison, then went to the Attorney's and stayed till 10.

4. I rose about 6, read Hebrew and Greek. I prayed and had chocolate with the Commissary. The weather was cold and clear, the wind southwest. I went to Colonel Grymes's; from thence to Mr. Needler's and from thence to the Governor's. From thence to Dr. Mollet's and then to Lady Randolph's and then to Mr. Barradall's, where I dined and ate venison. When we had drunk tea I went home.

5. I rose about 6, read nothing but prepared for my

---

[1]The Council on this same day "advised the Presid't to Pardon the Prisoners und'r Condemnation for the reasons mentioned in Court" (*Va. Mag.*, XV, 10). It was discovered that the criminals convicted at this court were indicted by a Grand Jury of whom one was not a freeholder. Because of this violation of the law the court voted to pardon those convicted (*Ex. Jour.*, Nov. 3, 1740, Va. State Library).

journey. I prayed and had coffee. About 9 came Colonel Bassett who went with me in my chariot and my daughter followed us with Mrs. Bassett. We called at [Furnea's][1] for an hour and then proceeded to Colonel Bassett's where I ate turkey and chine. After dinner we talked till 9 and then retired and prayed.

6. I rose about 6 and read English. I prayed and had coffee. The weather was cold, the wind north. About 9 we took leave and returned home after a tedious journey about 4 and found my family well, thank God. I ate potato and milk. I learned my affairs were pretty well. About 8 I retired and prayed.

7. I rose about 6, read nothing because of putting things in order. I prayed and had tea. I danced. The weather was cold and cloudy, the wind east. I wrote several things and walked about the plantation. I ate roast mutton. After dinner put my matters in order till the evening when we talked till 8, when I retired, read English, and prayed.

8. I rose about 6, read Hebrew and Greek. I prayed and had hominy. The weather was wet, the wind north, and it rained abundance in the night and this morning till 9. I wrote English and settled several accounts till dinner, when I ate roast chine. After dinner I put things in order but could not walk because of the cold. In the evening came news from England and that poor John Grymes[2] was dead.

---

[1]This may refer to Stephen Furnea (or Fornea) who kept an ordinary in Blissland parish in New Kent County where the vestry of that parish held meetings 1726-33 (*Vestry Book of Blissland Parish, 1721-1786*, ed. C. G. Chamberlayne [Richmond, 1935], pp. 26, 36, 37, 41).

[2]John Grymes, eldest son of Colonel John Grymes and Lucy Ludwell Grymes, had died June 30, 1740 at the age of twenty-two (*Wm. Q. (1)*, VI, 145). Young John Grymes had studied at Cambridge in 1735 (*Va. Mag.*, XXXIII, 216). When he went to England to study he was occompanied by William Stith (see June 15, 1740 entry). The two young Virginians were commended to his brother Thomas Gooch of Caius College, later the bishop of Norwich, by Governor Gooch in the following letter: "The bearer hereof is eldest son to Col. Grymes Rr. General of this Colony and my particular friend. He comes to Trinity Hall in your University to study the Law (not with design to practice it) whither one Mr. Carter went about two years since, Brother to the Secretary of this Country, who I very earnestly recomended, as I do now this young Gentleman, to your favour and friendship, and if you will now and then countenance these two young sparks by inviting them to dinner with

A Falls boy told me one of my people died in King William;[1] God's will be done. I prayed.

9. I rose about 6, read Hebrew and Greek. I prayed and had coffee. I danced. The weather was very cold and clear, the wind northwest. I clothed my people at home. I went not to church because of the cold, but cleaned myself. Nobody came after church so we had no company. I ate roast chine. After dinner came the overseer at Meherrin where all was well. I talked with my people.

10. I rose about 6, read Hebrew and Greek. I prayed and had tea. I danced. The weather was cold and clear, the wind west. I sent clothes to Meherrin and read English and wrote several things till dinner, when Captain M-l-t-r [?] dined and I ate roast chine again. After dinner the Captain went away and I walked about the plantation. At night talked with my [people], read English and prayed.

11. I rose about 5, read Greek. I prayed and had tea. I danced. The weather was cold and cloudy. I sent Mr. Procter to Hanover about the escheats. I sent clothes to the Falls. I wrote English till dinner when I ate roast duck. After dinner it rained a little so that I could not walk but danced. At night talked with my people, read English, and prayed.

12. I rose about 6, read Hebrew and Greek. I prayed and had tea. I danced. The weather was cold and cloudy, the wind north. I read English and settled several accounts till 1, when two men came from the Falls about settling my land at Roanoke. I ate boiled chine. After dinner I talked with the men and gave them satisfaction. At night talked with my people, wrote letters, and prayed.

---

you, and drinking our healths, and lett me have a paragraph in one of your Letters concerning them to shew their Relations, you will oblige me to a great degree" (July 5, 1735, Gooch Letters, Colonial Williamsburg, Inc.).

[1]In the settlement in 1712 between John Custis and Byrd of the inheritance of their wives, Frances and Lucy Parke from their father Colonel Daniel Parke, Byrd secured in King William County "far up in Freshes of the River Pamunkey" a plantation of 3,805 acres known by the name of Mangohick (Byrd Title Book, p. 243).

13. I rose about 6, read Hebrew and Greek. I prayed and had coffee. I danced. It continued cloudy with small rain, the wind north. The men went away. I settled some accounts and read news till dinner when I ate rice milk. L-n-r brought in 7 steers from Roanoke, where all was well, thank God. A steer came from the Falls. I danced, talked with my people, and prayed.

14. I rose about 6, read Hebrew and Greek. I prayed and had tea. I danced. The weather continued cloudy, the wind north. The steers were brought over the river in good order, thank God. I read English and put things in order till dinner when I ate roast beef. After dinner came two overseers from King William for clothes who told me two of the people were dead. God's will be done. I prayed.

15. I rose about 6, read Hebrew and Greek. I prayed and had tea. I danced. The weather was cold and clear, the wind fresh at west. I read English and wrote several things till dinner when I ate roast beef. After dinner came Mr. [Ward][1] and the Falls boy with several things. I talked with Mr. [Ward]. L-n-r likewise returned from the Falls. I talked with my people and prayed.

16. I rose about 6; read only Greek because I had business with Mr. [Ward]. The weather was cold and clear, the wind north. I went not to church but put everything in order. After church Mr. Pinkard and his wife and Mrs. Stith came to dine with us and I ate roast goose. After dinner we talked and had coffee. All went away in the evening. I talked with my people and prayed.

17. I rose about 6, read Hebrew and Greek. I prayed and had tea. I danced. The weather continued cold and clear, the wind north. Mr. [Ward] and L-n-r went away and I wrote English and walked about the plantation till dinner, when I ate only rice milk. After dinner put several

---

[1]Possibly Benjamin Ward, (see entry June 27, 1741) for whose orphans Joseph Ward as guardian was ordered at the August session of the Henrico Court, 1741, to appear at the next Court and render account of his guardianship (Henrico Order Book, 1737-1746, p. 155).

things in order and then took another walk among my people. We began to kill our beef from Roanoke. I talked with my people and prayed. The wind blew violently in the night.

18. I rose about 6, read Hebrew and Greek. I prayed and had hominy. I danced. The weather was cold and clear, the wind northwest. I wrote English and walked and put things in order till dinner when I ate goose giblets. After dinner put things in order and received some letters from England and a very foolish one from Mr. Procter. I talked with my people and prayed.

19. I rose and read only Greek because I answered Mr. Procter's letter.[1] I prayed and had tea. I danced. The weather was cold with frost. I wrote English and walked among my people till dinner when I ate souse. After dinner put things in order and walked again. We continued to grind our corn and kill our beef. I talked with my people and prayed.

20. I rose about 6, read Hebrew and Greek. I prayed and had coffee. I danced. The weather continued cool, notwithstanding the wind was northwest. I read English and walked about the plantation till dinner when I ate sheldrake. After dinner put things in order and walked again. In the evening we killed another beef from Roanoke. I talked with my people, wrote letters, read English, and prayed.

21. I rose about 6, read Hebrew and Greek. I prayed and had tea. I danced. The weather continued cold and clear, the wind west. I sent to Williamsburg for letters that came by the fleet. I wrote English and walked till dinner. I ate cold beef. After dinner we put things in order and then walked about the plantation and discovered a [hen-house?] built by Jacob, which I ordered to be demolished. I talked with my people.

---

[1]Byrd's reply to Procter is printed in Bassett, p. 399, and in *Va. Mag.*, XXXVII, 108.

22. I rose about 6, read Hebrew and Greek. I prayed and had tea. I danced. The weather was warm and cloudy, the wind southwest. I wrote English and walked about the plantation till dinner, when I ate beefsteak. After dinner I put matters in order and walked again. In the evening G-f-r-y came from Williamsburg and Henry from the Falls, where two children died. God's will be done. I prayed.

23. I rose about 6, read Hebrew and Greek. I prayed and had coffee. I danced. The weather was warm and cloudy, and rained a little, so that nobody went to church. I cleaned myself and put things in order. After church nobody came and I ate roast turkey. After dinner we walked in the garden, though we had a great fog. In the evening I talked with my people, read English, and prayed. It rained.

24. I rose about 6, read Hebrew and Greek. I prayed and had tea. I danced. The weather was cold, the wind violent at southwest, that carried away our new flat, which I sent no one to look for. Mr. Fontaine came and I bought the old church.[1] I ate cold beef for dinner. In the afternoon we walked about the plantation. At night I learned all were well at the Falls. I prayed.

25. I rose about 6, read Hebrew and Greek. I prayed and had coffee. I danced. The weather was cold and cloudy, the wind north. Mr. Fontaine went away and my boat was found, thank God. We began to get the glass out of the old church. I ate boiled beef. After dinner put things in order, then walked about the plantation. At night talked with my people and prayed.

---

[1]The old Westover church was built by Theodorick Bland on James River a quarter of a mile up the bank from Westover (*Wm. Q. (1)*, XV, 47). There has been uncertainty as to when it was abandoned for the "new church" on Herring Creek (see entry with note for Dec. 12, 1740). The latest surviving tomb in the yard of the old church is that of the diarist's beautiful daughter Evelyn who died in 1737 and was buried there with her grandfather and grandmother, William Byrd I and his wife, Mary (for pictures of tombs in Westover churchyard see *Va. Mag.*, XXXII, 36). In her will in 1813 Mary Willing Byrd, widow of William Byrd III, asked "that a reservation of the church land be made when Westover is sold" (*Va. Mag.*. VI, 353).

26. I rose about 6, read Hebrew and Greek. I prayed and had coffee. The master of the New England bark breakfasted here. It rained and blew hard, the wind south. I wrote English and walked about the plantation till dinner when the Captain dined with us and I ate neat's tongue. After dinner the Captain went away and I danced because could not walk, for it rained a little. At night talked with my people, read English, and prayed.

27. I rose about 6, read Hebrew and Greek. I prayed and had milk porridge. I danced. The weather was cold and clear, the wind southwest. I sent over the wagon to Meherrin. My physic worked four times. I had a pain in my hip but walked nevertheless. I ate salt fish. After dinner walked again and danced till the evening when I talked with my people. I read English and prayed.

28. I rose about 6, read Hebrew and Greek. I prayed and had hominy. I danced. The weather was cold and clear, the wind southwest. My hip was better, thank God. I wrote English till one when Colonel Bland and his cousin came to dine with us and I ate beefsteak. After dinner we talked till 4, when the company went away and I walked. I talked with my people and read English and prayed.

29. I rose about 6, read Hebrew and Greek. I prayed and had [pulse?]. I danced. The weather was cold and cloudy, the wind northeast. I had a little cold, the weather changed so often. I wrote several letters and walked till dinner and ate boiled goose. After dinner I walked again. In the evening learned all was well at the Falls, thank God. I talked with my people, read English, and prayed.

30. I rose about 6, read Hebrew and Greek. I prayed and had coffee. I danced. The weather was clear and cold, notwithstanding it rained abundance last night. I wrote a letter, went not to church, but cleaned myself. After church Dr. Monger and Billy Hardyman brought me some letters and dined and I ate salt fish. After dinner we talked. The company stayed all night and I prayed. Mr. Ludwell[1] and Colonel Armistead[2] arrived safe from England.

[1]Philip Ludwell III was son of Philip Ludwell and Hannah Harrison Ludwell. He married Frances, daughter of Charles Grymes, of Richmond County, was a member of the House of Burgesses and sat in the Council from 1752 until 1760. He spent his last years in England and died there on March 25, 1767. He was the last of the male line of the Virginia Ludwells (*Va. Mag.*, IV, 162; *LJC*, II, III, *passim*; *Gentleman's Magazine*, XXXVII, 144).

[2]Colonel Henry Armistead was repeatedly named by Governor Gooch from 1729 on as first in his list of men in Virginia eligible for a seat in the Council (Gooch Papers, Va. Hist. Soc.). But when in 1742 on the recommendation of Gooch, Lewis Burwell, Jr., was appointed to succeed John Carter, because of his repeated preferment of Colonel Armistead, Gooch wrote the Commissioners for Trade and Plantations, in a postscript added Aug. 1 to a letter dated July 31, 1742, "I have not forgott Col° Armstead [*sic*], but he is not the man he was neither in mind nor Circumstances" (Gooch Papers, Va. Hist. Soc.).

Colonel Armistead, who married the Martha Burwell made notable by Governor Nicholson's passionate wooing, was greatly interested in experiments in raising grapes for wine and making Varina tobacco (Byrd to Mr. Collinson, July 18, 1736, *Va. Mag.*, XXXVI, 354). It seems probable that this trip to England referred to by the diarist had some connection with Armistead's efforts to market his Varina tobacco advantageously, though no positive evidence has been found to support such a conclusion (Letter of Gooch, Aug. 26, 1741, Gooch Papers, Va. Hist. Soc.; *Wm. Q.* (1), VI, 165; *Va. Mag.*, XI, 68; Mrs. A. W. Garber, *The Armistead Family*, pp. 48-9).

December, 1740

1. I rose about 6, read Hebrew and Greek. I prayed and had coffee. I danced. The weather was cool and cloudy, the wind north. I wrote English and walked. My cold continued. I put things in order till dinner when I ate rice milk. After dinner came Doctor Mollet but had no news but a good stomach. After dinner we walked and played cards at night till 9. I prayed.

2. I rose about 6, read Hebrew but no Greek but wrote letters [to go] by the boat. I danced. The weather was cold and clear, the wind west. About 10 the Doctor went off and I wrote English and walked till dinner and ate roast beef. After dinner walked again. At night read English. Mrs. Byrd had the headache. I talked with my people, read English and prayed. My cold continued.

3. Rose about 6, read Hebrew and Greek. I prayed and had [pulse?]. I danced. The weather continued cold and clear, the wind west. I wrote several things, walked and read English till dinner when I ate roast turkey. After dinner we walked again. In the evening the people came with the wagon from Meherrin. I walked at night, talked with my people, read English and prayed. My cold continued. God save me.

4. I rose about 6, read Hebrew and Greek. I prayed and had coffee. I danced. The weather was cold and clear, the wind north. About 12 came John Stith and his wife, Mr. Pinkard and his wife, and Betty Stith, and dined. Captain Branch[1] called but stayed not to dinner. I ate salt fish. After dinner it threatened rain so Mr. Pinkard and his wife stayed; the rest went. I prayed.

---

[1]Captain Thomas Branch belonged to the well-known family of that name that owned land for several generations in the part of Henrico County south of James River that in 1749 became Chesterfield County. He was the son of Thomas and Elizabeth Archer Branch. Thomas Branch refused to serve on a commission of the Peace for Henrico County in 1741 (*Va. Mag.*, XV, 130). His will was dated Oct. 30, 1765. (*Wm. Q. (1)*, XXV, 65-6, XXVII, 275.)

5. I rose about 6, read Hebrew and Greek. I prayed and had coffee. I danced. The weather was warm and cloudy, the wind north. I received letters from England from our friends, who were well, thank God. I walked and wrote English till dinner. Mrs. Stith's daughter and Mrs. Pinkard dined with us and I ate roast mutton. After dinner the company went away. I talked with my people and prayed.

6. I rose about 6, read Hebrew and Greek. I prayed and had tea. I danced. The weather was cold and wet, the wind northeast. It rained great part of the day. I wrote English till dinner when I ate rice milk. After dinner we talked because we could not walk. Nobody came from the Falls. At night I talked with my people, read English and prayed. My cold continued.

7. I rose about 6, read Hebrew and Greek. I prayed and had coffee. I danced. The weather was cold and clear, the wind northwest. I went not to church because it was cold. After church came no company but only Billy Hardyman. I ate roast beef. After dinner we talked and walked a little. Dr. Mollet came in the evening and stayed. I talked with my people and prayed.

8. I rose about 5 and prayed. I drank two dishes chocolate. The weather was cold and clear, the wind north. I recommended my family to the Almighty and about 8 went in the chariot as far as the lower church[1] and then proceeded on horseback to Williamsburg, where we got about 3. I dined with the Commissary and ate roast mutton. After dinner we talked [of] all the news till 8, retired and prayed.

9. Rose about 6 and put my house in order. I prayed and breakfasted with the Commissary upon chocolate. Then

---

[1]This refers to Mapsco church, known as "the lower church" in Westover Parish. It was a brick church and stood about seven miles below Charles City courthouse, and on the road to Sandy Point, the home of the Lightfoot family. It was also convenient to the homes along the Chickahominy (*Colonial Churches in the Original Colony of Virginia,* a series of sketches by especially qualified writers, including sketch of Westover Parish by Mrs. Mary Morris Tyler [Richmond, 1908], p. 122).

went to the Governor's and saw Captain Lloyd[1] and Mr. Stanton.[2] About 12 went to the capitol, spoke to the [grand] jury, sat till 3, dined with Wetherburn, invited Captain Lloyd and other gentlemen, and ate roast venison. Sat till 7 and supped with the ladies at the Governor's; retired about 9 and prayed.

10. Rose about 6, prayed and had coffee. About 10 went to Colonel Grymes's and then returned to the Commissary's to council and kept Mr. Gooch in his place and refused the good King's orders;[3] then dined with the Commissary and ate boiled pork. After dinner went to Lady Randolph's and then to Mr. Barradall's where I stayed with Colonel Robinson till 11; then went home and prayed.

---

[1]Captain Lloyd was in command of a British warship in Virginia waters through the winter of 1740-41 (*Ex. Jour.*, Feb. 24, 25, 1741, MSS of typed copies in Virginia State Library. See entries for Feb. 24 and 25, 1741 in diary). The printed version of the *Ex. Jour.* (*Va. Mag.*, XV, 12) gives his name as Lyde.

[2]Robert Stanton was appointed by Governor Gooch clerk of the Council in 1742 (*Va. Mag.*, XV, 387; XVII, 267). He died about September 1743 (Gooch to his brother, Sept. 20, 1743, Colonial Williamsburg, Inc.).

[3]The Council, Oct. 23, 1739, on recommendation of Governor Gooch had appointed his son, William Gooch, as naval officer for York River (*Va. Mag.*, XIV, 345). A warrant from the Crown named Head Lynch, brother of John Lynch, Dean of Canterbury, to the office. He had settled in Caroline County a few years before. The Council, jealous of their prerogatives, resented this appointment by the Crown without consulting them. The action referred to by Byrd in this diary entry is fully sketched in the Executive Journal for the same date, Dec. 10, 1740:

"His Majestys Warrant under his Sign Manual bearing Date at St. James's the 16th Day of January 1739-40 Countersigned by His Grace the Duke of Newcastle His Majesty's Principal Secretary of State, and Directed to the Lieutenant Governor, and in his absence to the Commander-in-Cheif or the President of the Council for the time being, to authorize the Granting Letters Patent under the Great Seal of this Colony, for appointing Head Lynch Esqr. Clerk of the Naval or Navy Office of York River in the Room of William Robertson Esqr. Deceased, was communicated to the Board by Mr. President, and he desiring the advice of the Council thereupon: after Long Debate, the Majority of the Board were of opinion, That as William Gooch the Younger Esqr., soon after Mr Robertson's Death, was appointed by the Lieutenant Governor (with the advice of the Council) Naval Officer of York River, pursuant to an act of Parliament made in the Fifteen Year of the Reign of King Charles the Second; and has given Security to the Commissioners of his Majesty's Customs, to his Majesty's use, and been by them approved of Pursuant to another act made in 7th, 8th years of the Reign of King William the third: and he having been also in like manner appointed Collector of the Virginia Duties, pursuant to Several Acts of Assembly of this Colony and thro constant Usage in the like Cases (of all which they Conceive his Majesty had not been informed) That an Humble Representation of the Case be made

11. I rose about 6, read only Greek. I appointed an overseer for Mount Folly. I prayed and had coffee. The weather was warm, the wind southwest. I went about 12 to Colonel Grymes's, who was gone; then to the coffeehouse, and then dined with Mr. Needler and ate hog's head. After dinner Dr. Mollet and I walked and in the evening I went to Lady Randolph's, played cards till 9, then went home and retired.

12. I rose about 6, prayed and had rice milk. The weather was cold and cloudy, the wind northeast. I rode to the new church[1] and met my chariot and got home about 3 and found my family well, thank God. I ate salt fish. After dinner I put things in order and walked. At night talked with my people and gave them cider, and prayed.

---

to his Majesty and that the granting the Said Letters Patent to the Said Head Lynch be respited until his Majesty Shall be pleased to Signifie his Pleasure concerning the Premises and it is ordered by Consent of the Parties that in the meantime the Profits of the said Office be sequestered." (MS in Va. State Library.)

Protracted debate as to whether a representation should be made to the Crown before a commission was issued resulted, on April 23, 1741, in a tie vote. A warrant from the Crown April 7, 1742, appointed William Gooch, Esquire, naval officer of York River.

For Byrd's views on this matter see his letter to Major Otway, February 1740 [*i.e.*, 1741], in *Va. Mag.*, XXXVII, 30-31. The official evidence is in the Gooch Papers, Va. Hist. Soc., and the Council Journals, for which the unpublished text (Va. State Library) is fuller than that published in *Va. Mag.*, XIV and XV. Gooch's letters to his brother (in Colonial Williamsburg, Inc.) also give his private version of the matter. See also Lynch's letter to the President of the Council, May 2, 1741, *Va. Mag.*, XV, 118.

Lynch was by way of consolation made Deputy Postmaster General, an office which had been suggested to Gooch for his son but without meeting his approval (Harrison, *Landmarks of Old Prince William*, II, 531-32).

[1]This church, known as Westover Church and still standing, in spite of various vicissitudes of war and temporary neglect, was built on Herring Creek, which flows into James River east of Westover. It was built on land owned by Byrd and known as Evelynton and was about two miles from the house of Westover. (*Colonial Churches in the Original Colony of Virginia*, pp. 119-122; Brock, *Colonial Churches*, pp. 68-69.) Evelyn Byrd, daughter of the diarist, was the last member of his family to be buried in the yard of the old Westover church in 1737. The "new church" as it was called in Charles City records, about whose date there has been doubt (see Bassett, p. xxxi, for statement that the old church was moved in 1731), was certainly in use by May, 1738. (Charles City Order Book, 1737-1751, p. 41.) There is a tradition that the church at Westover was moved from its early site a quarter of a mile from the house to the Herring Creek site two miles away because Byrd's second wife grew weary of entertaining most of the congregation for dinner! (See Diary, July 9, 23, Aug. 20, 1710, for Byrd's resolution to refrain from having guests for Sunday dinner, a resolution quickly broken.)

13. I rose about 6, read Hebrew and Greek. I prayed and had tea. I danced. The weather was cold and clear, the wind northwest. I wrote several things and walked till dinner, when I ate tripe. After dinner put things in order and walked. All well at the Falls, thank God. I talked with my people, sat an hour with my children, retired, read English, and prayed.

14. I rose about 6, read Hebrew and Greek. I prayed and had coffee. I danced. The weather began to be very cold, the wind north, so I went not to church but cleaned myself. Molly Stith came home to dine with us and I ate roast duck. After dinner drank tea, then walked a little in the garden. Molly Stith went home. At night talked with my people, read English, and prayed.

15. I rose about 6, read only Greek because I talked with Mr. Wood who came last night. I prayed and had tea. I danced. It was extremely cold, the wind northwest. We cut wood in the swamp. I persuaded Mr. Wood to go to Roanoke. I ate giblets for dinner. I had a letter from Daniel Custis that he was sick, and I answered it. At night I talked with Mr. Wood, spoke with my people and prayed.

16. I rose about 6, read Hebrew and Greek. I prayed and had hominy. I danced. The weather was cold and cloudy, the wind north, and snowed a little. Mr. Wood went away and I wrote several things till dinner when I ate salt fish. After dinner I put things in order but danced instead of walking because it was overcast. At night I talked with my people, read English and prayed. It rained first, then snowed much.

17. I rose about 6, read Hebrew and Greek. I prayed and had tea. I danced. The weather was cold with a snow, the wind northwest. My man Tom continued sick. I wrote English till one when Mr. Ned Randolph[1] came, but brought no news. I ate roast pork. After dinner we talked till the evening, but could not look out, it was so cold. At night we played cards and supped till 11. I prayed.

---

[1]See entry for June 25, 1740 and note on Ned Randolph and his son.

18. I rose about 6 and read nothing. I prayed and had coffee. I danced. The weather was very cold, with snow and a cold wind at west. Mr. Randolph stayed and we played piquet all the morning till dinner when I ate roast goose. After dinner we talked of several matters till the evening when we played again till supper and I ate potato and milk. About 11 we retired and I prayed.

19. I rose about 6, read Hebrew and Greek. I prayed and had hominy. The weather continued very cold and clear, the wind northwest. However, Mr. Randolph went away and I wrote several things till dinner when I ate rice milk. After dinner it grew cloudy and threatened snow but it came not. I danced because I could not walk. At night talked with my people and prayed.

20. I rose about 6, read Hebrew and Greek. I prayed and had tea. I danced. The weather was cold and clear, the wind west and thawed a little. I wrote English and walked in the gallery[1] till dinner when I ate sparerib. After dinner put several things in order. We lost one of the flats. At night came Mr. [Ward]. I talked with my people and prayed. Dreamed my wife was drowned.

21. I rose about 6, but read nothing because talked with Mr. [Ward]. I prayed and had coffee. I danced. The

---

[1]No evidence has come to light on the design of the house the diarist built at Westover to take the place of the less pretentious residence of his father, and even the date of its erection is not established. Byrd refers in a letter dated Dec. 6, 1735, to Mr. Beckford of Jamaica (*Va. Mag.*, IX, 234-5) to a draught he had had made of his seat of Westover and was sending to his correspondent "which perhaps will appear a little rough, but if it should not be found according to Art, it will make amends by being according to truth." This draught has not, so far as is known, survived. Byrd made extensive repairs and changes at Westover during his stay in Virginia in 1720-21 (Diary). On May 28, 1729 he wrote Mr. Spencer, of London, that he intended in a year or two to set about building "a very good house" (MS letter in Colonial Williamsburg, Inc.).

The gallery Byrd refers to in this entry was evidently a porch (see Feb. 7, 1741 entry). According to an item in the *Virginia Gazette*, Jan. 12, 1749, the house at Westover was "burned to the ground, with the loss of all the furniture, clothes, plate, liquore." Tradition has held that the diarist's son rebuilt Westover exactly as it had been before the fire. Certain architectural details suggest the possibility that the item in the *Gazette* was exaggerated, and the fire did only superficial damage. (See Bassett, p. lxxxviii, n. 3.)

weather continued cold and clear and froze extremely. I talked with Mr. [Ward] about my affairs above till 12, when he went away and I sent more people after my boat, God forgive me. I ate mutton for dinner. After dinner I danced because I could not walk, talked with my people, and prayed.

22. I rose about 6, read Hebrew and Greek. I prayed and had tea. I danced. The weather continued extremely cold, the wind still northwest. No news of my people; God preserve them. I read English. About one the people came, thank God, and brought the lost boat home. I examined my [cellars] and found them improved pretty well. I ate minced mutton. After dinner danced because I could not dance [*sic*]. I talked with my people and prayed.

23. I rose about 6, read Hebrew and Greek. I prayed and had hominy. The weather continued extremely cold; the wind blew hard at northwest. Two of my people brought down a beef in the night because it would not drive [*sic*]. I read English and walked in the gallery till dinner when I ate sausage and eggs. After dinner put things in order and danced because could not walk. At night talked with my people and prayed. It froze extremely hard.

24. I rose about 6, read Hebrew and Greek. I prayed and had tea. I danced. The weather was extra cold and clear, the wind still northwest and the river just frozen over. I wrote letters and walked in the gallery till dinner when I ate mutton steak. After dinner I put things in order and danced because I could not walk. At night L-s-n's son brought two turkeys, and some eggs and a goose came from Hanover. I talked with my people and prayed.

25. I rose about 6, read Hebrew and Greek. I prayed and had coffee. I danced. The weather was very cold and cloudy, the wind north and threatened more snow. Nobody went to church except my son because of the cold. I put myself in order. After church came two playfellows for my

son, young Stith[1] and Hardyman.[2] I ate roast turkey. After dinner we talked and I danced. I talked with my people and prayed.

26. I rose about 6, read Hebrew and Greek. I prayed and had hominy. It snowed all last night and rained all day. God [preserve] us from a freeze. I gave G-r-n, Harry, and A-r-g-l a vomit for going off the plantation and staying all night, which did more good than whipping. I ate roast turkey. After dinner it held up and I talked with my people and prayed. I fell down [m-n-s].

27. I rose about 6, read Hebrew and Greek. I prayed and had tea. I danced. The weather was warmer, the wind southwest in the morning but came at noon again to northwest. I settled some accounts and read English till dinner when I ate roast goose. After dinner my son's visitors went home, notwithstanding the snow. I danced for want of walking. I talked with my people and ordered everything to be well fed.

28. I rose about 6, read Hebrew and Greek. I prayed and had coffee. I danced. It snowed again this morning a little, the wind north. I put myself in good repair and walked in the gallery. Tom fell and hurt his back for which he was bled and had a [s-r-q-r]. I ate broiled turkey for dinner and then walked in the gallery. I talked with my people and prayed. Old B-s-n [*or* B-v-n] died; God save his soul.

29. I rose about 6, read Hebrew and Greek. I prayed and had tea. I danced. The weather was cold and cloudy, the wind southwest but thawed little. I read English and walked in the gallery till dinner when I ate salt fish and eggs.

---

[1]*I.e.*, Anderson Stith (see entry for Dec. 25, 1739).

[2]This was probably Littlebury Hardyman (1725-1770), who was just about the age of the diarist's only son (see Mar. 29, July 23, 1741). Like Byrd's son, Littlebury Hardyman later became a keen supporter of the turf and was owner of the three noted race horses, Partner, Mark Anthony, and Pilot, in 1768-69. He shared with his Hardyman forbears not only his love of horses and racing, but like them also served as a justice in Charles City County (Fairfax Harrison, *The Equine F.F.V.'s*, [Richmond, 1928], pp. 74-6, 97, 141-46).

After dinner I danced because I could not walk. It was warmer and threatened rain but none came. I talked with my people and prayed. I slept not well.

30. I rose about 6, read Hebrew and Greek. I prayed and had tea. I danced. The weather was much warmer and cloudy, the wind west and threatened rain, but it came not, though it thawed all day. I read English till dinner when I ate roast turkey. After dinner I put things in order and danced because I could not walk. At night talked with my people, read English, and prayed.

31. I rose about 6, read Hebrew and Greek. I prayed and had tea. I danced. It continued to thaw, the wind northeast. I read English till dinner when I ate pork and peas. After dinner read English and danced because could not walk. I talked with my people and prayed. It snowed.

January, 1741

1. I rose about 6, read Hebrew and Greek. I prayed and had coffee. I danced. The weather was cold and cloudy, and snowed a little again, the wind northeast. I wrote good wishes to all my family on this new year till dinner, when I ate souse. After dinner could do nothing but dance because it snowed. At night I talked with my people and prayed. I read English and slept but indifferently.

2. I rose about 6, read Hebrew and Greek. I prayed and had tea; I danced. The weather was still cloudy and cold, the wind north and still threatening more snow. I wrote English and mended [?] the fire till dinner when I ate boiled pigeon and bacon. After dinner I put things in order and danced because there was no walking. At night I talked with my people and read English and prayed. It snowed again. God save dumb creatures.

3. I rose about 6, read Hebrew and Greek. I prayed and had tea. I danced. It snowed again this morning, the wind north. I ordered drums of wheat to be thrown to the poor birds. I read English till dinner and then ate broiled pigeon. After dinner I put things in order and then danced instead of walking. At night talked with my people, read English and prayed. The weather began to clear up, thank God.

4. I rose about 6, read Hebrew and Greek. I prayed and had coffee. I danced. The weather was cold and clear, the wind west. Nobody had the courage to go to church because of the snow and cold. I put myself in order and read English till dinner, when I ate boiled pork. After dinner I danced because I could not walk. At night talked with my people and heard the children read. I prayed.

5. I rose about 6, read Hebrew and Greek. I prayed and had tea. I danced. The weather was cold and cloudy, the wind southwest and threatening falling weather. About 12 came Beverley Randolph and his wife and Mrs. Pinkard. We played cards till dinner, when I ate boiled tongue. After

dinner we talked, and had tea about 4; then [they] went away and I danced. I talked with my people and prayed. I took pills.

6. I rose about 6, read Hebrew and Greek. I prayed and had rice milk. I danced. The weather was exceedingly cold, the wind north, so that the river was frozen over. My physic worked three times only. I read English till dinner when I ate little more than broth. After dinner came George B-r-k's son about his accounts and then came Henry from the Falls and told me some of my people were dead. God preserve the rest. I prayed.

7. I rose about 6, read Hebrew and Greek. I prayed and had tea. I danced. It was most violently cold and the river frozen over, the wind north. I wrote a letter to the Falls and read English till dinner when I ate roast goose. After dinner came Daniel Custis but could tell us no news but that his father was better.[1] We talked till the evening when he went to the girls and I talked with the people and prayed. It was a little warmer.

8. I rose about 6, read Hebrew and Greek. I prayed and had coffee. I danced. The weather was not so cold but cloudy, the wind southwest, but the river frozen over except some places which the ducks keep open. I ate goose giblets for dinner. My son was indisposed with a looseness; God preserve him. After dinner we talked of many things. I talked with my people. It rained a little. I prayed.

9. I rose about 6, read Hebrew and Greek. I prayed and had coffee. I danced. The weather was cold and cloudy, the wind north and threatened snow. Some ducks froze to death. My son was better, thank God, but still griped. I wrote English till dinner when I ate broiled turkey. After dinner talked till the evening when I talked with my people, read English and prayed. Ned and Bob were sick.

10. I rose about 6, read Hebrew and Greek. I prayed and had tea. I danced. The weather was cold and cloudy

[1]*I.e.* John Custis. See entry with note for Oct. 26, 1740.

and threatened snow. My son continued still out of order with a bloody flux; God preserve him. Mr. Custis went away and I read English till dinner and then ate boiled chine. After dinner I put things in order and danced, because I could not walk. Bob and Ned were sick. I prayed.

11. I rose about 6, read Hebrew and Greek. I prayed and had tea. I danced. It thawed a little and was cloudy, the wind north. My son [was] better, thank God, and so were the other sick people. I read English and put myself in order till dinner and I ate roast beef. After dinner it thawed pretty much. I danced because I could not walk. I talked with my people, read English, and prayed.

12. I rose about 6, read Hebrew and Greek. I prayed and had tea. I danced. It continued to thaw, notwithstanding the wind was north. My son was better, thank God, but my other people were very bad; God preserve them. I wrote English till dinner and ate roast chicken. After dinner I dried the [o-r-n-g] which were wet. I danced. My sick people were better, thank God. I prayed.

13. I rose about 6, read Hebrew and Greek. I prayed and had hominy. I danced. The weather was warm, with rain, the wind south. My sick people were better, thank God. I wrote English and walked in the gallery till dinner, when I ate cold dried beef. After dinner I walked again in the gallery and danced. At night talked with my people and read English and prayed.

14. I rose about 6, read Hebrew and Greek. I prayed and had tea. I danced. The weather was warm and clear, the wind north, but no frost, but the sun dried the air very much. I wrote English till one and then walked till dinner and ate boiled bacon. After dinner the overseer for Meherrin came. We walked again after dinner. My sick people were better, thank God. John Ravenscroft came and stayed till 8. I prayed.

15. I rose about 6, read Hebrew and Greek. I prayed and had coffee. I danced. The weather was cloudy and

cold, the wind northeast. I set the overseer over the river, which began to be open. I wrote English till one when Will Hardyman and Isham O-n-c-l-s [?] came. I ate boiled beef for dinner. After dinner we talked. I danced because I could not walk. I talked with my people and prayed.

16. I rose about 6, read Hebrew and Greek. I prayed and had coffee. I danced. The weather was cold and cloudy, with rain and snow together, but the rain eventually lost. I wrote English. This was my daughter Mary's birthday;[1] God preserve her many happy years. I ate roast turkey. After dinner I put things in order and danced. My sick man was better, thank God. I talked with my people and prayed.

17. I rose about 6, read Hebrew and Greek. I prayed and had coffee. I danced. The weather was cold and cloudy, the wind north. Our visitors went away and I wrote English. I settled accounts with the tailor and walked till dinner when I ate rice milk. After dinner we walked again and made the best of the fine weather. At night I talked with my people and understood several [were] very sick. I prayed.

18. I rose about 6, read Hebrew and Greek. The weather was cold and clear, the wind northwest. I danced. Abundance of ice came down the river with much rubbish. I went not to church but put myself in order. After church came Mr. Pinkard and his wife and dined with us and I ate boiled pigeon, and bacon. After dinner we talked and had coffee. Then the company went away and I prayed.

19. I rose about 6, read Hebrew and Greek. I prayed and had tea. I danced. The weather was cold and clear, the wind west; the river full of ice that came from above, with all the signs of a fresh. God preserve my people. I read English till dinner when I ate boiled pork. After dinner we walked again. At night I talked with my people, read English, and prayed.

---

[1]She was fourteen years old.

20. I rose about 6, read Hebrew and Greek. I prayed and had tea. I danced. The weather was warm and cloudy, with rain, a great fresh in the river. I walked and read English till dinner when I ate cold boiled beef. After dinner I walked in the gallery because it rained a little, and I danced [away?] the evening. I talked with my people, made my children read, and prayed.

21. I rose about 6, read Hebrew and Greek. I prayed and had tea. I danced. The weather was warm and clear, the wind west. More ice came down the river with logs in abundance. My man Tom got drunk and did not what I bade him; so I beat him and he marched off. I ate dried beef. After dinner we walked. I talked with my people, read English and prayed. Bad news from the Falls.

22. I rose about 6, read Hebrew and Greek. I prayed and had coffee. I danced. It snowed and rained, the wind northeast, but held up about noon. I wrote a long letter to the Falls and ate nothing but battered eggs. After dinner I put several things in order and danced because I could not walk. Several were sick; God preserve them. I talked with my people and prayed.

23. I rose about 6, read Hebrew and Greek. I prayed and had tea. I danced. The weather was cold and cloudy, the wind southeast. I wrote a letter to my man Tom to order him home. I had letters from England but no news. I ate roast turkey for dinner. After dinner L-n-r came to the Point[1] with 43 hogs which we brought over. All well at Roanoke, thank God. I prayed.

24. I rose about 6, read Hebrew and Greek. I prayed and had tea. I danced. The weather was cold and clear, the wind northwest. My man Tom returned and promised

[1]Jordan's Point on the south bank of the James was a little to the west of Westover (Fry and Jefferson Map, 1751). Cogan's (or Coggins) Point, also on the south bank of the James, was a little to the east of Westover. In the law of 1702 a ferry was provided for at Cogan's Point and another at Westopher [*sic*] and the fee at both ferries was 1 shilling for a man and 18 pence for man and horse (Hen. *Stat.*, III, 218-19). In 1748 legal provision was made for a ferry from Westover to Maycox, or Coggins Point, and from Maycox to Westover (Hen. *Stat.*, VI, 13).

fair, so took him into favor. I wrote English till dinner when I ate minced turkey. After dinner I walked to visit the sick and found them better. At night talked with my people, read English, and prayed.

25. I rose about 6, read Hebrew and Greek. I prayed and had coffee. I danced. The weather was cold and cloudy, the wind southwest. My sick people were better, thank God. I went not to church but put myself in order. My son brought nobody from church, and I ate broiled pork. After dinner we walked and at night I talked with my people, read English and prayed. I read letters.

26. I rose about 6, read Hebrew and Greek. I prayed and had tea. I danced. It rained this morning, the wind east. However L-n-r went to the Falls. I settled accounts with the bricklayer. We began to kill our hogs. I wrote English till dinner and then ate roast mutton. After dinner I walked in the garden and at night talked with my people, read English, and prayed.

27. I rose about 6, read Hebrew and Greek. I prayed and had tea. I danced. The weather was cold and clear, the wind north. My boat went up to the Falls. I wrote letters till dinner, when I ate broiled pork. After dinner I put things in order and danced because could not walk. At night talked with my people, read English and prayed.

28. I rose about 6, read Hebrew and Greek. I prayed and had tea. I danced. The weather was cold and it rained and froze, the wind northeast. I wrote English and sent my people away to Roanoke. I ate spareribs. After dinner put things in order but could not walk and contented myself with dancing. At night talked with my people and prayed and read some English.

29. I rose about 6, read Hebrew and Greek. I prayed and had coffee. I danced. The weather was cold and clear, with hail and snow. I examined my children's reading, wrote English, and put things in order till dinner when I ate spareribs. After dinner danced because there was no walk-

ing. Several people sick, of whom care was taken. I talked with my people and prayed.

30. I rose about 6, read Hebrew and Greek. I prayed and had hominy. I danced. The weather was cold and clear, the wind west. I wrote English, examined my children's writing till one, when Mr. Dering came and dined with us and I ate roast chine. After dinner our guest went away and I danced instead of walking. Tom G-r-n-r was sick. I prayed.

31. I rose about 6, read Hebrew and Greek. I prayed and had tea. I danced. It snowed again very much, the wind northeast. It continued to snow all day very hard. I wrote English till dinner and ate battered eggs. After dinner I danced instead of walking. My sick people were better, thank God. I talked with my people, read English, and prayed. An exceedingly cold night.

February, 1741

1. I rose about 5, read Hebrew and Greek. I prayed and had coffee. I danced. It was exceedingly cold, the wind north, but came about to the southwest. There was no going to church because of the snow. I put myself in order till dinner and ate salt fish. After dinner we talked till the evening, when I danced because I could not walk. At [night] read English and prayed. It snowed again.

2. I rose about 5, read Hebrew and Greek. I prayed and had tea. I danced. The weather was cold and cloudy, but thawed a little. God grant this cruel weather may pass away for the sake of the poor dumb creatures! I wrote English till dinner when I ate dry beef. After dinner I could do nothing but dance because I could not walk. I read English and prayed.

3. I rose about 6, read Hebrew and some Greek. I prayed, and had tea. I danced. The weather was cold and clear, the wind west. It thawed pretty much. God continue it. I wrote English till dinner, when I ate cold beef. After dinner I wrote more English and danced instead of walking. At night talked with my people, read English and prayed. It froze very hard again.

4. I rose about 6, read Hebrew and Greek. I prayed and had tea. I danced. The weather was very cold and clear, the wind west, and the moon changed upon a southwest wind, thank God. However, it continued very cold. I wrote English till dinner when I ate roast mutton. After dinner I wrote more English and danced because I could not walk. I talked with my people and prayed.

5. I rose about 6, read Hebrew and Greek. I prayed and had coffee. I danced. It froze very hard last night but was clear, the wind northwest. No news yet of my boat; God send the people well. I wrote English till dinner, when I ate dried beef. After dinner I wrote more English and

danced, then talked with my people and prayed. It was exceedingly cold; God be merciful to his creatures.

6. I rose about 6, read Hebrew and Greek. I prayed and had hominy. I danced. The weather was very cold and clear, the wind north. We could do nothing but get wood and sit by the fire they made. I wrote English till dinner when I ate sparerib. After dinner I wrote more English and danced. At night talked with my people and prayed and slept but indifferently. It froze very hard.

7. I rose about 6, read Hebrew and Greek. I prayed and had tea. I danced. The weather continued very cold but clear, the wind north. The snow thawed a little. I wrote English and read news till dinner when I ate boiled mutton. After dinner I walked in the gallery in the sun and then danced. In the evening I heard my children read, retired about 8, and prayed.

8. I rose about 6, read Hebrew and Greek. I prayed and had coffee. I danced. The weather began to abate, only it was cloudy, the wind southeast. I put myself in order and read news till dinner when I ate salt fish. After dinner I wrote English and danced. In the evening it began to hail and snow which turned into rain in the night. I prayed.

9. I rose about 6, read Hebrew and Greek. I prayed and had tea. I danced. The weather was cold and cloudy, with some rain till 9 and then the wind came to northwest but continued to thaw, thank God. I wrote letters and read English till dinner when I ate boiled pork. After dinner we talked and I walked in the gallery and had the pleasure to see it thaw. I prayed.

10. I rose about 6, read Hebrew and Greek. I prayed and had hominy. I danced. The weather was warm and clear, the wind southwest and it continued to thaw, thank God. I wrote letters till one, when Doctor Mollet came to stay over day with us, and I ate dry beef. After dinner we played and I lost. I talked with my people and [prayed].

11. I rose about 6, read Hebrew and Greek. I prayed

and had tea. I danced. I wrote more letters. It continued to thaw, thank God, the wind southwest. We played cards till dinner when I ate roast mutton. After dinner we talked and the Doctor went away. I danced and walked in the gallery. I talked with my people and prayed.

12. I rose about 6, read Hebrew and Greek. I prayed and had coffee. I danced. The weather was cold and clear, the wind north. I wrote letters to England and put things in order till dinner when I ate cold beef. After dinner I wrote more English again and walked in the gallery; then danced and talked with my people, read English, and prayed.

13. I rose about 6, read Hebrew and Greek. I prayed and had hominy. I danced. The weather was cold and cloudy, the wind northeast and threatening snow but none fell. I wrote English till dinner when I ate sparerib. After dinner I wrote letters, danced, talked with my people, read English and prayed. It was exceedingly cold. God preserve his creatures.

14. I rose about 6, read Hebrew and Greek. I prayed and had tea. I danced. The weather was cold and clear, the wind north, but clouded afterwards. I wrote letters till dinner when I ate boiled chine. After dinner it snowed a little and then turned to rain which continued almost all night. I danced, read English, and prayed.

15. I rose about 6, read Hebrew and Greek. I prayed and had coffee. I danced. It continued to rain till 9 and then began to clear up, the wind west, and was warm. Nobody went to church but I [lost a tooth] and put my person in order till dinner and ate salt fish. After dinner read news and walked in the gallery. I talked with my people and prayed.

16. I rose about 6, read Hebrew and Greek. I prayed and had tea. I danced. The weather was cold and clear, the wind northwest. It blew and rained in the night. I wrote letters to England till dinner and then ate sausage and eggs. After dinner we walked to the old church, then I

danced and talked with my people, read English and prayed. It rained and blew hard.

17. I rose about 6, read Hebrew and Greek. I prayed and had tea. I danced. The weather was cold and cloudy, the wind southwest. I wrote letters to England and read news till dinner, when I feasted [*or* fasted] upon rice milk. After dinner we walked and found the ground pretty dry. I danced. At night talked with my people, read English and prayed. It rained again in the night.

18. I rose about 6, read Hebrew and Greek. I prayed and had tea. I danced. The weather was clear and cold, the wind northwest. I wrote letters to England and read news till dinner when I ate cold tongue. After dinner we walked, notwithstanding it blew very hard. In the evening the tailor came and told us there was another fresh above. I talked with my people and prayed.

19. I rose about 6, read Hebrew and Greek. I prayed and had coffee. I danced. The weather continued cold and clear, the wind north. I had a letter full of news from Parks[1] at Williamsburg, which I read, and wrote to the Falls by the [. . .] and ate roast chine. After dinner we walked about the plantation. A messenger from the Falls where I lost a man; God's will be done.

20. I rose about 6, read Hebrew and Greek. I prayed and had tea. I danced. The weather was cold and cloudy, the wind southwest. Marjorie went up again. I wrote to the Falls. About one came Mr. Pinkard and his wife and

---

[1]William Parks was owner and editor of the *Virginia Gazette*, the first newspaper in Virginia, whose publication he began at Williamsburg in 1736. He set up the press in Williamsburg in 1730 and became public printer for Virginia from 1732 to his death in 1750. He also started, as far as is known, the first and only paper mill in colonial Virginia. He was not only printer, journalist, publisher, bookdealer and paper manufacturer, but was also active in affairs of Bruton parish, and alderman of the town of Williamsburg (Lawrence C. Wroth, *William Parks, Printer and Journalist of England and Colonial America* [Richmond, 1926]; Douglas C. McMurtrie, *The Beginnings of Printing in Virginia* [Lexington, Va., 1935]; Rutherfoord Goodwin, *The Williamsburg Paper Mill of William Parks the Printer*, Reprinted for private circulation from the papers of the Bibliographical Society of America, Vol. 31, Part 1, 1937).

I ate roast goose. After dinner came likewise Doctor Mollet. We walked and played cards at night till ten. I retired and prayed.

21. I rose about 6, and read only Greek. I prayed and had coffee. I danced. The weather was warm and clear, the wind northwest. I prepared for my journey to Williamsburg and settled some accounts till dinner and then ate roast turkey. After dinner we talked and had coffee, and then Pinkard and his wife went away and we talked and about 8 retired and I slept pretty well, thank God. All were well at the Falls.

22. I rose about 6, read Hebrew and Greek. I prayed and had coffee. I danced. The weather was cold and clear, the wind southeast. About 8 a boat came down from the Falls but Jacob was left behind sick. I ate roast beef. After dinner put up my things to go to Williamsburg tomorrow. I talked with my people, gave my orders, and prayed.

23. I rose about 5 and prepared for my journey. I drank three dishes chocolate and recommended my family to the Almighty. The weather cold and cloudy, the wind north. About 8 we got into the chariot and got to [. . .] where we got without anything remarkable about 3 and found young Nelson[1] and his family and Betty [. . .] there. I ate dry beef. We talked and were courteously entertained. I prayed.

24. I rose about 6 and prayed; then wrote a short letter to my wife. It rained in the night but held up in the morning and was warm. I had chocolate. The Doctor[2] and I took leave about 8 and went to Williamsburg. I put myself in order and went to the Commissary's about 12 where we had a council and dined there and I ate roast turkey. At

---

[1]This refers to William Nelson, known as President Nelson, eldest son of "Scotch Tom" Nelson of Yorktown (see entry for May 3, 1741). William Nelson married in 1738 Elizabeth (called Betty), only daughter of Nathaniel Burwell and Elizabeth Carter. Their son, Thomas Nelson, who was later to gain fame as signer of the Declaration of Independence, Governor of Virginia, and Major General in the American army, was born December 26, 1738, and was thus something over two years old when referred to by Byrd (Page, *Genealogy of the Page Family*, pp. 160-61; *Va. Mag.*, IX, 355-56, XXXIII, 189; *Wm. Q. (1)*, V, 244).

[2]*I.e.*, Dr. Mollet. See Feb. 20, 1741.

night went to Lady Randolph's till 9, then retired and prayed.

25. I rose about 6 and played the fool with Sarah, God forgive me. However, I prayed and had coffee. About 9 came Mr. Commissary and paid me £100.[1] About 11 went again to the Commissary's to council and persuaded the men of war to stay two months for the ships.[2] Dined at the Governor's and ate Scotch collops. In the evening went home, packed up my things, and prayed.

26. I rose about 5 and prayed. I prepared for my journey, notwithstanding it had snowed in the night, the wind northeast. About 8 Colonel Randolph came and we went together in my chariot as far as the courthouse, where I dropped him. By the way visited poor Frank Hardyman who seemed better, and got home about 5 and found everybody well, thank God. I ate pea soup and about 9 retired.

27. I rose about 6, read Hebrew and Greek. I prayed and had hominy. I danced. The weather was cold and cloudy, the wind north. I put matters in order and read

---

[1]Byrd received a salary as a member of the Council and a fee as a judge of the Court of Oyer and Terminer. This sum, paid to him by Blair, acting Governor, may be connected with these official services.

[2]The action of the Council is more fully recorded in the unpublished records of that group for Feb. 24 and 25, now filed in copies in the Virginia State Library (awaiting publication in the continuation of the series of Executive Journals of the Council) than in the journal as published in *Va. Mag.*, XV, 11-12. On Feb. 24, the unpublished journal states that the Council provided for "a Letter to Sir Yelverton Peyton Captain of his Majesty's Ship the Hector, Desiring him to convoy the Mast Ships from New England hither: which will not only Induce Captain Lloyd to stay for the Ships in the Tobacco Trade, but enable him to Convoy them directly to England be prepared and Laid before the Board toMorrow Morning."

On the following day the President signed letters to both Sir Yelverton Peyton and Captain Lloyd and the journal has this entry: "The Board being informed by Captain Lloyd that Upon their Letter he had determined to defer his Departure From hence till the 20th, of April, Ordered that an Embargo be Laid on all Ships and Vessels bound for Great Britain until the said Twentyeth Day of April, and that the Naval officers do forthwith notifie the Same to the Masters of Ships in their respective Districts to the End they may prepare in due time to join Captain Lloyd in Kiquotan Road in James River; and that the said Officers take care that no Ship or Vessel bound for Great Britain be cleared until Bond be Given as the Law Directs for observing this Embargo."

But while the sailing of the ships was delayed Sir Yelverton Peyton did not go to Piscataway to convoy the two mast ships as the Council desired but offered them a "handsome excuse" on April 29 (*Va. Mag.*, XV, 117).

English till dinner, when I ate boiled chine. After dinner we talked and it blew so cold I could not walk but danced my dance. Mr. Stevens and Mr. Wood came. I talked with my people and prayed.

28. I rose about 6 and read only Greek. I prayed and had tea. I danced. The weather was cold and clear, the wind north. Mr. Stevens brought me £20 to put me into good humor. I settled some accounts till dinner when I ate roast beef. After dinner we walked and in the evening learned all were well at the Falls. At night talked with my people, read English, and prayed, and slept pretty well, thank God.

March, 1741

1. I rose about 6, read Hebrew only. I prayed and had coffee. I danced. Mr. Dering came and brought Mr. Walthoe[1] the lawyer with him to breakfast. This was a hindrance to my morning work. Three of my children went to the church but brought nobody home. I ate salt fish. After dinner it snowed again so that we kept house. Mr. Dering played on the French horn.

2. I rose about 6, read Hebrew and Greek. I prayed and had tea. I danced. The weather was cold and clear, the wind north. Mr. Dering went away but the other gentlemen stayed. I read news till one when Mr. Nelson and wife and sister[2] came with two Misses Harrison[3] and dined here and I ate pigeon pie. In the evening they went away, and I prayed.

3. I rose about 6 and read Hebrew and Greek. I prayed and had hominy. I danced. The weather was cold and cloudy, the wind south. We persuaded Mr. Walthoe to

---

[1]This was probably Nathaniel Walthoe who came to Virginia during Gooch's absence on the Carthagena expedition with Lord Salisbury's recommendation. (Gooch to Lord Salisbury, Aug. 12, 1741, Col. Wmsburg., Inc.). On Sept. 20, 1743 Gooch wrote his brother he had appointed Walthoe clerk of the Council to succeed Robert Stanton. He was clerk of the General Assembly in 1744 and held that office until his death in 1772. He apparently became an intimate friend of the family at Westover, for his portrait was among those at Westover (*Va. Mag.*, XXXVIII, 148). According to family tradition Walthoe offered Byrd a diamond ring for permission to hang his own picture, wearing his cocked hat, among the portraits of noblemen on the walls of Westover and a later chatelaine of Brandon wore the ring. (Mrs. Burton Harrison, "Colonel William Byrd, of Westover, Virginia," *Century Magazine*, XLII, 174.)

[2]William Nelson had two sisters: Mary who married Edmund Berkeley of Barn Elms, Middlesex County, in 1728, and Sarah, a younger half sister, daughter of his father's second wife. It is probable that Byrd refers to this younger sister, since she did not marry Robert Burwell of Isle of Wight County until some years after this entry in the diary (*Va. Mag.*, V, 415, XXXIII, 189).

[3]Elizabeth and Anne Harrison, daughters of Benjamin and Anne Carter Harrison of Berkeley. Elizabeth, often referred to as Betty, married Peyton Randolph, who presided over the Revolutionary bodies in Virginia and the Continental Congress until his death in 1775; and Anne married William Randolph of Wilton, son of Councillor William Randolph (*Va. Mag.*, XLI, 163-5).

stay another day. We played piquet till dinner when I ate minced turkey. After dinner we played piquet again and I won. I talked with my people and prayed. It rained and blew in the night.

4. I rose about 6, read Hebrew and Greek. I prayed and had milk porridge because I took physic. The weather was cold and clear, the wind northwest. Mr. Walthoe went away to Williamsburg, and Mina went to the Secretary's. I read English till dinner when I ate cold pigeon pie. After dinner I read more English and danced because it was cold. I had five stools, and prayed.

5. I rose about 6, read Hebrew and Greek. I prayed and had coffee. I danced. The weather was warm and clear, the wind west. We walked about the plantation and about one came Mr. Hamilton, of Hampton, with Captain Chapman,[1] who dined with us and I ate sausage and eggs. After dinner we walked about the garden. In the evening played piquet till 10.

6. I rose about 6, read Hebrew and Greek. I prayed and had coffee. I danced. The weather was cold and cloudy, the wind west. The gentlemen went to Williamsburg and my family went to the Secretary's and only Mr. Procter and I were left and I ate battered eggs. After dinner it was cold so I danced instead of walking. Our people and I discoursed and I prayed.

7. I rose about 6, read Hebrew and Greek. I prayed and had tea. I danced. The weather was warm and it had rained in the night, the wind southwest. About 12 came Mr. Dering and we walked till dinner when I ate roast pork. After dinner we walked again. I learned from the Falls

---

[1]This may refer to Richard Chapman, who came to Virginia from England and lived at Chericoke on the Pamunkey River in King William County. He and his brother William Chapman were interested in the tobacco trade at this period. He married Jane Johnson, sister of Nicholas Johnson and granddaughter of Colonel Nicholas Meriwether (*Wm. Q. (1)*, VI, 59-60, XXI, 45; Hen. *Stat.*, V, 114-20). Portions of his letter book have been printed (*Wm. Q. (1)*, XXI, 90-100). It is not definitely known when he came to Virginia, but a Richard Chapman was witness to the will of Robert ("King") Carter in 1730 (*Va. Mag.*, VI, 21).

that their fodder was gone. Heaven preserve the stock. At night wrote to the Falls, talked with my people, read English and prayed.

8. I rose about 6, read Hebrew and Greek. I prayed and had coffee. I danced. The weather was cloudy, with rain, the wind northeast, which hindered going to church. I put myself in order and read English till dinner when I ate roast shoat. After dinner we could not stir out because it rained and snowed again. At night I talked with my people and prayed.

9. I rose about 6, read Hebrew and Greek, prayed and had tea. The weather was foggy but cleared up soon, the wind northwest. Mr. Dering and Mrs. Greenhill who came yesterday went away and I wrote English and walked till dinner and then ate broiled turkey. After dinner we walked again about the plantation. I had a cold but let it go on. I prayed.

10. I rose about 6, read Hebrew and Greek. I prayed and had tea. I danced. The weather was cold and cloudy, the wind southwest. I wrote more English and walked a little and read till dinner when I had battered eggs. After dinner we walked about the plantation. At night came Mr. Wood. I talked with my people and prayed. I coughed a little with my cold.

11. I rose about 6, read Hebrew and Greek. I prayed and had tea. I danced. The weather looked dark and threatened rain, the wind southwest. I did all my business with Mr. Wood. I walked till one when Charlotte Anderson and Betty Stith came with Mrs. Greenhill and I ate boiled mutton. After dinner I walked again. At night talked with my people and prayed. Jenny was sick.

12. I rose about 6, read Hebrew and Greek. I prayed and had coffee. I danced. The weather was warm and cloudy, the wind north. Young Jenny was very sick; God preserve her. The ladies stayed all day. I walked till dinner and ate roast mutton. After dinner the company

went away and we walked again. Jenny grew a little better, thank God. I talked with my people and prayed.

13. I rose about 6, read Hebrew and Greek. I prayed and had hominy. I danced. The weather was cold and cloudy with some rain and thunder, the wind southwest. I settled accounts and walked about the plantation till dinner when I ate cold mutton. Jenny was a little better, thank God. I wrote English till the evening and then walked again. At night read English and prayed. My cold continued. It rained.

14. I rose about 6, read Hebrew and Greek. I prayed and had tea. I danced. The weather was clear and warm, the wind southwest. Jenny was a little better, thank God. I read English and walked. About one came Mr. Fontaine to dinner and I ate neat's tongue. After dinner we talked and walked about the plantation. I talked with my people and prayed.

15. I rose about 6, read Hebrew and Greek. I prayed and had coffee. I danced. The weather was cold and clear, the wind north. About 11 I went to church and had a learned sermon. After dinner Mrs. Carter, John Stith and his wife, Colonel Eppes and his son Ned, and Captain Dunlop dined with us and I ate boiled beef. After dinner we talked and had coffee. Most of the company went away but Mrs. Carter, Jenny Anderson, John Stith and his wife stayed. I talked with my people.

16. I rose about 6, read Hebrew and Greek. I prayed and had coffee. I danced. The weather was cold and cloudy, the wind southeast. Beside our company Johnny Ravenscroft[1] and Mr. Miller[2] came to dine with us. We

---

[1]This would appear to refer to John Ravenscroft, son of John Ravenscroft (see entry and note for Aug. 29, 1739), and grandson of Thomas Ravenscroft. He became a physician and married Rebecca Stark, daughter of Dr. William Stark and Anne Bolling (*Wm. Q. (1)*, XVIII, 213-14).

[2]This was probably Hugh Miller, one of the Scotch merchants who helped to build the thriving town of Blandford in Prince George County. He lived at Greencrofts and was a warden of Bristol parish, 1746-47. His wife was Jane, daughter of Robert and Anne Cocke Bolling. (Charles City Order Book, 1737-1751, pp. 140, 198, 199, 442, 549.)

played cards till dinner. I ate roast rabbit. After dinner we talked and had coffee, and our company went away. I talked with my people and prayed.

17. I rose about 6, read Hebrew and Greek. I prayed and had coffee. I danced. The weather was cold and cloudy, the wind north. I sent up the boat with a good wind and about 11 went to visit Beverley Randolph but he was from home so we proceeded to Dick Randolph's, where we found Parson Stith, and I ate tripe. After dinner we took leave and the coach stuck about two miles from home so that we sent for our horses and got well home at last and found all well, thank God.

18. I rose about 6, read Hebrew and Greek. I prayed and had tea. I danced. The weather was warm and cloudy, with rain sometimes, the wind south. Mrs. Harrison sent some fish which we had for dinner. In the afternoon it thundered and blew hard but held up time enough for us to walk in the garden. At night I talked with my people and prayed.

19. I rose about 6, read Hebrew and Greek. I prayed and had tea. I danced. The weather was cold and clear, the wind west. I sent to Meherrin for the tobacco. About 12 came Beverley Randolph's wife, Annie Bolling,[1] Betty Randolph, Molly Randolph, Fanny Davenport,[2] and Will

---

Hugh Miller was instrumental in securing the charter granted to the Blandford, Virginia, Lodge, F. and A. Masons in 1757, of which he was the Master (Slaughter, *Bristol Parish*, pp. 82-3). His will, dated Dec. 1, 1761, proved 1762, after certain bequests, left the residue of his estate to his brothers and sisters-in-law in Virginia, to wit: Peter Randolph, Esq., Alexander Bolling, John Hall, Robert Bolling, Richard Eppes and Elizabeth Banister. (*Va. Mag.*, IV, 329, X, 323-4; *Wm. Q. (1)*, VI, 128.) The friendship of the Westover family with Hugh Miller continued after the death of the diarist. (See letters of Mrs. Maria Taylor Byrd, Nov. 6, 1757, and Mrs. Elizabeth Carter Byrd, Aug. 16, 1759, to William Byrd III, *Va. Mag.*, XXXVII, 247-48.)

[1]Annie Bolling was probably Anne Cocke, wife of Robert Bolling, whom she married in 1706 (see Dec. 10, 1739 entry). She is thought to have been the daughter of Richard Cocke the younger, of Old Man's Creek, Charles City County. She was the mother of eight children, several of whom are mentioned in this diary (*Va. Mag.*, IV, 96, 329-30).

[2]Possibly the daughter of Joseph Davenport, one time town clerk of Williamsburg. In his will, proved in 1761, he mentions among other children, "Frances Anne Wright, now in England" (*Wm. Q. (1)*, V, 271-2, VII, 17).

Randolph[1] to dinner and I ate roast turkey. After dinner they went away. I talked with my people and prayed.

20. I rose about 6, read Hebrew and Greek. I prayed and had hominy. I danced. About 8 Captain [Marrable][2] went away and then it began to snow, the wind northeast, and continued all day. I read English till dinner and ate minced turkey. After dinner read more English and danced because could not walk. At night talked with my people and prayed. It continued to snow.

21. I rose about 6, read Hebrew and Greek. I prayed and had milk porridge, having taken physic. I danced. The weather was cold and the snow deep, the wind north. I wrote several things and read English till dinner when I ate battered eggs. My physic worked four times. After dinner I put things in order and danced because could not walk. At night talked with my people and prayed. A beef came.

22. I rose about 6, read Hebrew and Greek. I prayed and had coffee. I danced. The weather was cold, with a thaw, the wind still north. About 11 came Mr. Dering and Caton with letters from her mother. He brought a *Gazette*[3] without news. I wrote letters till dinner and then ate salt fish. After dinner we walked in the garden and at night told stories. I talked with my people and prayed.

23. I rose about 6, read Hebrew and Greek. I prayed

---

[1]This group of guests, largely from the Randolph clan, appears to have included chiefly the family of William Randolph II, of Turkey Island, known as "Councillor" Randolph. Beverley Randolph, his oldest son, married Miss Lightfoot, of Sandy Point. Molly Randolph was doubtless his daughter Mary, who married John Price. Betty Randolph was probably his daughter Elizabeth who married Col. John Chiswell. William Randolph was apparently his third son William who married Anne Harrison, daughter of Benjamin and Anne Carter Harrison of Berkeley (*Va. Mag.*, XLV, 68-9). He served in the House of Burgesses for Henrico, 1758-1761.

[2]Probably George Marrable, Jr., son of George and Mary Hartwell Marrable of James City County. He was named on the grand jury of Charles City County in May 1739 and was party to suits in the Charles City court, 1739-1748 (Charles City Order Book, 1737-1751, pp. 80, 107, 117, 468; *Wm. Q. (1)*, XVII, 212).

[3]This reference to the [Virginia] *Gazette* is significant as evidence of its publication, for no copy from Feb. 1, 1740 (no. 183) to Mar. 21, 1745 (no. 451) has been located.

and had tea. I danced. It snowed a little but melted as it fell, the wind north. Mr. Dering went away. The snow melted away before dinner. I ate cold tongue and sallet. After dinner we talked and walked; at night came the boat, and we killed a beef. About 9 we parted and I prayed.

24. I rose about 6, read Hebrew and Greek. I prayed and had hominy. I danced. The weather was cold and clear, the wind northwest. Caton went away. I walked and read English till dinner when I ate ox cheek. After dinner I walked again and read more English. At night talked with my people. All well at Mount Folly, thank God. I prayed.

25. I rose about 6, read Hebrew and Greek. I prayed and had tea. I danced. The weather was cold and clear, the wind still northwest. I read English and walked about the plantation till dinner when I ate goose giblets. After dinner I put things in order and read more English, then walked again. At night talked with my people and read English again and prayed.

26. I rose about 6, read Hebrew and Greek. I prayed and had coffee. I danced. The weather was cold and cloudy, the wind northwest and snowed in the morning a little but soon held up. I read English till dinner when I ate cold roast beef. After dinner we walked about the plantation and had more letters from Mrs. Brun. I talked with my people and prayed.

27. I rose about 6, read Hebrew and Greek. I prayed and had tea. I danced. The weather was cold and clear, the wind northwest. I sent my boat with some provisions for Mrs. Brun, of which there was great need, and I wrote English till dinner [. . .] and called at John Stith's, but dined with Mr. Pinkard, and ate salt fish. We returned home about 5 and found all well, thank God. The overseer came from Roanoke where all was well, but wanting corn. I prayed.

28. I rose about 6, read Hebrew only because talked with my overseer and wrote a letter. The weather warm

and clear, the wind west. Many things happened this day to put me out of humor. About one came John Stith and his wife, Mr. Pinkard and his wife, and I ate bacon and pigeon. After dinner we talked and had coffee. In the evening Ned came but without the tobacco which he had left at Appomattox.[1] I talked with my people and prayed.

29. I rose about 6, read Hebrew and Greek. I prayed and had coffee. I danced. The weather was warm and clear, the wind west. I went not to church and I wrote letters till one when Mr. Dering came and after church Mr. Pinkard and his lady and Frank Hardyman's son,[2] and I ate fish. After dinner we had coffee. The company went away except Mr. Dering and I prayed.

30. I rose about 6, read Hebrew and Greek. I prayed and had coffee. I danced. The weather was cloudy and cold, with rain. I scolded at Ned L-v-y for making so little corn. I read English till dinner and then ate roast turkey. After dinner I put things in order, read more English till the evening, when I talked with my people and prayed.

31. I rose about 6, read Hebrew and Greek. I prayed and had coffee. I danced. The weather was cold and cloudy, the wind north. However my little family went to the launching of Colonel Harrison's vessel but were disappointed for it was not launched. We walked till dinner when I ate fish. After dinner we walked again. At night I talked with my people and prayed.

---

[1]Byrd's father had had a store at Appomattox, the site of an Indian settlement that had early developed as a trading post. (See Diary, 1709-12, *passim*; Hen. *Stat.*, III, 470.)

[2]It appears that Frank (Francis) Hardyman had at least four sons. At the December court, 1741, the churchwardens of Westover parish prosecuted Tabitha Chandler for having a bastard child and Francis Hardyman appeared in open court and took upon himself the obligation to pay her fine of fifty shillings or 500 pounds of tobacco. At the same court John Hardyman was appointed guardian to his brother Littlebury Hardyman, orphan of Francis Hardyman, deceased, sons of his first wife, and in January 1742 Jane Hardyman was appointed guardian of her two children James and Martha Hardyman, children of her deceased husband, Francis Hardyman (Charles City Order Book, 1737-1751, pp. 192, 200, 215).

April, 1741

1. Rose about 5, prayed and had chocolate. The weather was cold and clear after a fog, the wind southwest. About 7 my wife and I went to Hanover in the chariot. Nothing happened extraordinary but in 40 miles we got to Major Henry's about 3, but we dined by the way so needed nothing to eat. We found Mr. Fraser there. We talked till 9 and then retired.

2. I rose about 6, read nothing. I prayed and had chocolate with eggs. The weather was fair and cold, the wind southeast. About 10 we went to Hanover court[1] where I acquired the last piece of land in Hanover. We dined with Parson Henry and ate fowl and bacon. After dinner we had tea and then went to Major Henry's, played cards, and about 10 retired and prayed.

3. I rose about 6, prayed and had chocolate. The weather was cold and clear, the wind southwest. About 7, took leave and returned and by the way dined. We called on Colonel Stith, who was pretty well with his [paresis?]. About 6 got home and found all well, thank God, except A-r-g-l. I talked with my people and learned my business was [in] good order, thank God.

4. I rose about 6, read Hebrew and Greek. I prayed and had tea. I danced. The weather was warm and cloudy, the wind west. I wrote English and walked about the plantation till dinner when I ate cold roast beef. After dinner I put things in order and then walked again. At night I talked with my people. All pretty well at the Falls, thank God. I prayed.

---

[1]In 1737 a Commission of the Peace for Hanover County named William Merriwether [*sic*] chairman, and John Chiswell, John Henry, James Skelton, John Bickerton, William Johnson, William Winston, Jr., Charles Barret and Pouncy Anderson to be added to the then acting justices (*Ex. Jour.*, IV, 391). In June 1741 John Henry, James Skelton, John Bickerton, William Winston, Jr., and Charles Barret were added to the quorum and Sylvanus Morris added to the Commission of the Peace for Hanover (*Va. Mag.*, XV, 126).

5. I rose about 6, read Hebrew and Greek and had coffee. I danced. The weather was cold and cloudy, the wind north. Some of my children went to church and I wrote letters. After church came Betty Stith and her brother Anderson, young Ben Harrison[1] and another boy, and dined here. After dinner we had tea and all went away. I talked with my people and prayed. My man A-r-g-l was sick again and I took all the care of him I could; God save him.

6. I rose about 6, read Hebrew and Greek. I prayed and had tea. I danced. The weather was cold and clear, the wind north. A-r-g-l was a little better, thank God. I wrote English till one when Colonel Stith and his wife and Mr. Pinkard and his wife came to dinner, when I ate roast turkey. After dinner we played bowls. The company stayed. I talked with my people and prayed.

7. I rose about 6, read Hebrew and Greek. I prayed and had coffee. The weather was warm and clear, the wind southwest. We played bowls and billiards till 12; then I wrote English till dinner, when I ate roast pigeon. After dinner we played billiards till the evening when the company went away and I walked. A-r-g-l was better, thank God. My people killed a bullock. I prayed. It rained and blew.

8. I rose about 6, read Hebrew and Greek. I prayed and had tea. I danced. The weather was cold and clear, the wind northwest. We played billiards and then walked about the plantation. I wrote letters till dinner when I ate minced turkey. After dinner I took a nap and then wrote more English till the evening and then walked again. At night talked with my people and prayed.

9. I rose about 6, read Hebrew and Greek. I prayed and had coffee. I danced. The weather was warm and clear,

[1]The son of Benjamin and Anne Carter Harrison of Berkeley, who served in the House of Burgesses for forty sessions, was among the signers of the Declaration of Independence, and Governor of Virginia, 1781-1784. At the time of this entry he was about fifteen years old (*Va. Mag.*, XXIII, 299, XLI, 163). When the will of Col. Benjamin Harrison was presented in court, August 1745, William Randolph and Betty Harrison obtained letters of administration during the minority of Benjamin Harrison, son and heir of the deceased (Charles City Order Book, 1737-1751, p. 376).

the wind southwest. My overseer was indisposed, God preserve him. I wrote English and walked about the plantation till dinner when I ate fish. After dinner we walked again and about 5 came Mr. Spalding but had no news. We talked and had supper and sat up till 10 and prayed.

10. I rose about 6, read Hebrew and Greek. I prayed and had coffee. I danced. It rained and thundered in the night but held up this morning. However Mr. Spalding stayed this day and we played at bowls till dinner when I ate fish. After dinner we played bowls again. At night the women got me to quadrille. I talked with my people and prayed. It rained.

11. I rose about 6, read Hebrew only. I prayed and had coffee. I danced. The weather was warm and cloudy, the wind southwest. However Mr. Spalding went away to Williamsburg and I wrote letters till dinner when I ate tongue and sallet. After dinner I put my things up for Williamsburg and walked in the evening. All well at the Falls, thank God. I prayed.

12. I rose about 5, read Hebrew and Greek. I prayed and had coffee. I danced. The weather was cold and cloudy, the wind north. Mr. Dering brought the newspapers, with nothing in them. I went not to church but put myself in order. After church nobody came but Colonel Eppes and I ate cold beef and sallet. John Ravenscroft came. I talked with my people.

13. I rose about 5, read Hebrew and Greek. I prayed. and had milk porridge because I had taken physic. The weather was cloudy and warm, the wind southwest. I sent away the boat with my things to Williamsburg. I wrote English till dinner and then ate battered eggs. After dinner I packed up my things and then walked about the plantation. At night talked with my people and prayed.

14. I rose about 4, prayed and had chocolate. The weather was warm and cloudy, the wind southwest. I and my daughters Mina and Molly got into the chariot about 5

and went to Williamsburg without any accident. I ate some cold roast beef with Mr. Secretary, then walked to Lady Randolph's and had tea, then to the Governor's, and from thence to my lodgings and prayed.

15. I rose about 5, read Hebrew and Greek. I prayed and had chocolate with the Commissary, and about 10 went to visit poor Mrs. Needler[1] who was a melancholy widow. About 11 went to court and sat till 3 and then dined with the rest of the council at the Commissary's and ate Scotch collops. After dinner walked. In the evening called at Mrs. Barradall's[2] and then walked home and prayed.

16. I rose about 5, read Hebrew and Greek. I prayed and had coffee and my daughters breakfasted with me. I danced. The weather was cold and clear, the wind west. About 10 went to the capitol and sat till 3 and then dined with Wetherburn. After dinner walked. Saw Lady Randolph, who was at Mr. Francis', where we played cards till 9, when I walked home and prayed.

17. I rose about 5, read Hebrew and Greek. I prayed and had tea with my daughters at Mr. Grymes's, then [about] 10 walked to several places and then to the capitol where we sat till 3 and then dined with Mr. Gooch and ate pigeon and asparagus. After dinner we drank Burgundy till 8, then walked home, wrote letters till 10 and then prayed.

18. I rose about 5, read Hebrew and Greek. I prayed and had coffee. I danced. The weather was warm and cloudy, the wind southwest. About 10 I went to the capitol

---

[1]Mrs. Needler, the widow of Benjamin Needler (see Dec. 12, 1739 entry), whose death had occurred since Byrd's previous stay in Williamsburg, was Alice, daughter of Gawin Corbin, of Laneville, King and Queen County. Mrs. Needler inherited under her father's will, proved in 1744, his house and four lots in Williamsburg (*Va. Mag.*, XIV, 26, XXIX, 520).

[2]This may refer to Mrs. Barradall, the mother of the Attorney General, Edward Barradall, who, evidence would seem to indicate, was living as late as 1754 (Randolph and Barradall, *Virginia Colonial Decisions*, I, 243); or it may refer to the attorney's wife, Sarah Fitzhugh, daughter of William Fitzhugh, member of the Council, whom he married on Jan. 5, 1736. Barradall died June 19, 1743 and his wife Oct. 7, 1743 (*T's. Q.*, XVI, 44; *Va. Mag.*, XIV, 5).

where we tried two criminals and about 3 dined with Mr. Attorney and I ate roast fowl. After dinner we had coffee, then I walked and called on Mrs. Needler, then walked home and prayed.

19. I rose about 5, read Hebrew and Greek. I prayed and had coffee. I danced. The weather was cold and clear, the wind northwest and blowing pretty hard. Went not to church, being obliged to write letters. I dined with the Commissary and ate roast veal. After dinner I walked, called at Lady Randolph's, who was out, returned to my lodgings and prayed.

20. I rose about 5, read Hebrew and Greek. I prayed and had coffee. I danced. The weather was cold and clear, the wind west. I wrote letters till 10 and then went to the capitol and sat there till 3 and then dined with Wetherburn and ate fish. After dinner we sat till the evening when I walked to Colonel Grymes's, stayed there till 9, then went home and prayed.

21. I rose about 5, read Hebrew and Greek. I prayed and had chocolate with the Commissary. The weather was cold and cloudy, the wind southwest. About 9 went to the capitol and sat till 2, then went to dine with Colonel Bassett and ate roast veal. After dinner we had coffee and it rained abundance and I went home in the Colonel's chariot and prayed.

22. I rose about 5 and read Hebrew and Greek. I prayed and had coffee at home. About 9 went to the capitol and sat till 3 and then dined with Wetherburn and ate roast fowl. Captain Harding gave us some lemons and we made four bowls of punch and sat till 12 o'clock and then I walked home to my lodgings and made a short prayer.

23. I rose about 5, read Hebrew and Greek. I prayed and had coffee. Colonel Beverley[1] breakfasted with me. It

[1]William Beverley, to whom Byrd refers in this formal manner, was his nephew, son of his sister Ursula and the historian Robert Beverley. William Beverley (*c.* 1698-1756) was clerk of Essex County from 1716 to 1745, and served in the House of Burgesses until he was made a member of the Council in 1751. He was one of the commissioners in 1736 representing Lord Fairfax

rained, the wind north. About 10 went to court and sat there till 4, then dined with Wetherburn and ate boiled veal. After dinner I walked a little and about 7 went home and wrote letters till 9 and then prayed and retired.

24. I rose about 5, read Hebrew and Greek. I prayed and breakfasted with my daughters at Colonel Grymes's. The weather continued cold, the wind north. About 10 went to the capitol and sat till 3, then dined with Wetherburn and ate roast veal; then we walked to the College where was a meeting of the Governors. Then sat with Mr. Dawson[1] till 9, went home and prayed. I had bad dreams and thought I should die in a short time, but as for that, God's will be done.

25. I rose about 5, read Hebrew and Greek. I prayed and had chocolate with the Commissary and Colonel Lee,[2] and Colonel Beverley went with me; then we visited Mrs.

---

in the survey of the boundary of the Fairfax proprietary while his uncle William Byrd represented the colony of Virginia. William Beverley acquired numerous tracts of land, one grant, Beverley Manor, including 118,240 acres of desirable land about the present site of Staunton (*Va. Mag.*, III, 269; XXII, 297-301; XXXVI, 27; Bassett, 401-11; *Cal. S. P.*, I, 228).

Beverley's young son John died at Westover where he was at school in November, 1741, and for his death Beverley, ill and inconsolable, blamed the neglect of "y[t] inhuman Lady [Maria Taylor Byrd] at Westover" (*Wm. Q. (1)*, III, 231, 233).

[1]This may refer either to William Dawson, professor of moral philosophy at the College of William and Mary at this period and after James Blair's death President of the College and Commissary for the Bishop of London, or to his younger brother, Thomas Dawson, who was at this date master of the Indian School of the College and later President of the College and Commissary. (See Lyon G. Tyler, *Williamsburg, the Old Colonial Capital* [Richmond, *c.* 1907], pp. 142-6.) Thomas Dawson went to England in May 1740 to be ordained and the date of his return has not been determined (*Va. Biog.*, I, 161).

[2]Thomas Lee (1690-1750), son of Richard Lee and Letitia Corbin, was the founder of the Stratford line of Lees. He was connected with his uncle Edmund Jenings as agent for the Fairfax family in the Northern Neck, in 1732 became a member of the Council, and just before his death was President of the Council and commander in chief of the colony and Dominion of Virginia (deputy to the Earl of Albemarle) September 5, 1749 to Nov. 14, 1750. He was one of the Virginia commissioners to make the Treaty of Lancaster with the Indians of the Six Nations in 1744, and in 1748 was president of the first Ohio Company. He married Hannah, daughter of Phillip Ludwell II (B. J. Hendrick, *The Lees of Virginia* [Boston, 1935], pp. 47-69; *Va. Hist. Port.*, pp. 175-6, 505; Fairfax Harrison, *Virginia Land Grants* [Richmond, 1925], pp. 54, 97, 159).

Fairfax,[1] and went to the capitol and sat till 3; then dined with Wetherburn because nobody invited us and ate fish. After dinner visited Mrs. Needler and then walked home and prayed.

26. I rose about 5, read Hebrew and Greek. I prayed and had coffee. The weather was warm and clear, the wind west. Mr. Beverley came. About 11 went to church and then dined with the President and ate fowl and bacon. After dinner we had coffee and then visited Colonel Custis, and in the evening went to the Governor's and ate supper till 9, and then returned and prayed.

27. I rose about 5, read Hebrew and Greek. I prayed and had coffee. The weather was warm and cloudy, the wind southwest. I wrote two letters till 10, and then went to the capitol where we sat till 4, and then dined with Wetherburn and ate roast beef. After dinner I took a long walk, called at Colonel Grymes's and about 9 walked home, wrote a letter, and prayed.

28. I rose about 5, read Hebrew and Greek. I prayed and had chocolate with the Commissary. The weather was warm and cloudy, the wind southwest. I visited Jimmy Mumford,[2] who was sick, then went to court and sat there till 3, and then dined with Wetherburn and ate fish. After dinner I walked and called at Lady Randolph's and then walked home and prayed.

29. I rose about 5, read Hebrew and Greek. I prayed and had coffee. Miss Caton Brun came and breakfasted with me. About 10 went to council and then to court and

---

[1]Colonel William Fairfax (see May 3, 1741 entry), was married three times, but the Mrs. Fairfax referred to here was Deborah, daughter of Francis Clarke and his wife Deborah Gedney, of Salem, Mass. She was the mother of Bryan Fairfax (1736-1802) and on her death in 1747 Colonel Fairfax sent her son to Salem to his mother's people for his early education (*Va. Mag.*, XVI, 32-3; Harrison, *Virginia Land Grants*, pp. 162-3).

[2]James Mumford was a member of the vestry of Bristol parish, Prince George County, from 1728 to 1744 and was a major of militia. He lived after 1744 in Amelia County. He married Elizabeth, daughter of Robert Bolling. His will was proved Apr. 25, 1754 (*T's. Q.*, III, 174-75). He accompanied Byrd on his journey to the Land of Eden in 1733 and is frequently mentioned in Byrd's account of that journey (Bassett, pp. 281-329).

sat till 3, then dined with Wetherburn and ate fish again. After dinner we walked and then went home and wrote letters till 10 and then prayed. The weather was very cool.

30. I rose about 5, read Hebrew and Greek. I prayed and had tea with Mr. Grymes. The weather was cold and cloudy, the wind southwest. About 9 went to the capitol and sat there till 3, then dined with Wetherburn and ate boiled mutton. After dinner we walked and then had coffee at the Attorney's; then walked home and prayed. The weather was so cold that we kept constant fires.

May, 1741

1. I rose about 5, read Hebrew and Greek. I played the fool with Sarah; God forgive me. The weather cool and clear, the wind north. Several persons came. About 9 I went to court and sat till 3, then dined with Wetherburn and ate boiled veal and bacon. After dinner I walked and called at Lady Randolph's and stayed till 9, then retired and prayed.

2. I rose about 5, read Hebrew and Greek. I prayed and had tea at Colonel Grymes's. The weather was cold and cloudy, the wind north. I sat in court till 11 and then my daughters and I went to York in Mrs. Needler's chariot to young Mr. Nelson's where we dined and I ate roast fowl. After dinner we visited Colonel Lightfoot, where we drank tea. Walked about the town, talked with a man just come from Jamaica, lay at Mr. Nelson's, and prayed.

3. I rose about 8 and prayed. I had chocolate for breakfast. The weather dry, the wind southwest. About 11 walked to church[1] and had a good sermon; dined with Colonel Lightfoot, and ate fish. After dinner we had tea with old Nelson[2] and in the evening we supped at Mr. Ambler's[3] with Colonel Fairfax[4] and his lady, went home about 9 and prayed.

---

[1] *I.e.*, Grace Church (H. T. Brock, *Colonial Churches in Virginia* [Richmond, *c.* 1930], p. 32).

[2] Thomas Nelson, who migrated from England to Virginia and settled at Yorktown around 1700, was a highly successful merchant and became the progenitor of the Nelson family in Virginia. He was popularly known as "Scotch Tom." Born in 1677, he was aged 64 years when Byrd calls him "old Nelson." He died in 1745. (Page, *The Page Family*, pp. 155-56; *Va. Mag.*, XXXIII, 188.)

[3] Richard Ambler, of York, England, settled at York Town, Virginia, in 1716, and became one of the successful merchants of that thriving colonial port town. He left a large estate in slaves and lands at his death in 1766. He married Elizabeth, daughter of Edward Jacquelin (or Jaquelin) of Jamestown (*Va. Mag.*, XXXIII, 187; *Wm. Q. (1)*, XIV, 126-9).

[4] Col. William Fairfax (1691-1757) of Belvoir on the Potomac came to Virginia in 1733 as agent for his uncle, Thomas, sixth Lord Fairfax, in the Fairfax proprietary. He built Belvoir about 1741. He served as a burgess, was appointed to the Council in 1743, and later became President of that body.

4. I rose about 5 and read English and then prayed and had chocolate. It continued dry, the wind west. About 9 we took leave and went in Mr. Nelson's chariot to Williamsburg, and went to the capitol and sat till 3 and then dined with John Blair[1] and I ate chicken pie. After dinner we walked to the Governor's but the ladies were from home. Then to Lady Randolph's where I stayed half an hour, then walked home, wrote a letter, and prayed.

5. I rose about 5 and put up my things. I prayed and had tea with Colonel Grymes. The weather was warm and dry, the wind north. About 9 went to council, then to court where we sat till 2 and made an end of the court, and then [dined] with Wetherburn. The Secretary dined with us and I ate boiled lamb. After dinner walked with my daughters to take leave of Mrs. Needler and then walked and called at Mrs. Barradall's, then walked home and prayed.

6. I rose about 4, prayed, and had coffee. My daughters came about 5 and we went off about 6 and drove to the ferry where Colonel Randolph came up with us and took my daughter Mina to the courthouse where I picked her up and went home and found all pretty well, thank God, but met with great complaint of the gardener. Mr. Berkeley[?] came to take my stores at Shockoe.[2] He stayed and had supper; we talked about his business till 9, and then retired and I prayed.

One of his sons, Reverend Bryan Fairfax, succeeded to the title as eighth Lord Fairfax. (*Va. Mag.*, XXXVI, 32; Harrison, *Landmarks of Old Prince William*, p. 340; Edward D. Neill, *The Fairfaxes of England and America* [Albany, 1868].)

[1]John Blair, son of Dr. Archibald Blair and nephew of Commissary James Blair, was a member of the Council and served as President of his Majesty's Council and commander in chief of the colony and Dominion of Virginia in 1758 in the interim between Governors Dinwiddie and Fauquier and again in 1768 in the interim between Governors Fauquier and Botetourt (*Va. Hist. Port.*, 507-9; for diary of John Blair for 1751-52 kept in an interleaved almanac for 1751, see *Wm. Q. (1)*, VII, 133-53, VIII, 1-17).

[2]Byrd owned land on Shockoe creek, included in the town of Richmond, where a public warehouse had been provided for in the law of 1730 (Hen. *Stat.*, IV, 266). Byrd's reference to his stores at Shockoe indicates that it was a place of trade in other commodities than tobacco in the now developing town. Byrd seems to have had a number of such stores at strategic river points.

7. I rose about 5, read Hebrew and Greek. I prayed and had coffee. I danced. The weather was cold and cloudy, the wind north. Mr. Berkeley went to Williamsburg and I argued the case with the gardener, who was sorry for what he had done. I ate cold mutton. After dinner I went to the store and then walked about the plantation and prayed.

8. I rose about 5, read Hebrew and Greek. I prayed and had tea. I danced. The weather was cold and clear, the wind west. We killed a beef last night which was pretty good. I wrote and put things in order till dinner, when I ate roast pigeon and asparagus. After dinner took a nap, read English, walked about the plantation. I talked with my people and prayed.

9. I rose about 5, read Hebrew and Greek. I prayed and had tea. I danced. The weather warm and clear, the wind west. A man came about land at Roanoke by whom I wrote two letters. I played the fool with Sally, God forgive me. I wrote letters till dinner and ate roast beef. After dinner I slept and wrote English till the evening, walked, talked with my people, and prayed.

10. I rose about 5, read Hebrew and Greek. I prayed and had tea. I danced. The weather was warm and clear, the wind west. I went not to church because it was warm but put myself in order. After church came Colonel Eppes, John Stith and his daughter Mary and Will Hardyman. I ate roast rabbit. After dinner we had coffee. The company went away. I walked and prayed.

11. I rose about 5, read Hebrew and Greek. I prayed and had tea. I danced. The weather was warm and clear, the wind west. I wrote a letter to the Falls and read English till dinner when I ate roast beef. After dinner put several things in order and read Latin. I could not walk because it rained very much, thank God, with some thunder. I talked with my people and prayed.

12. I rose about 5, read Hebrew and Greek. I prayed and had tea. I danced. It continued to rain and had rained

all night, the wind north. I read English and received letters from England. I walked till dinner and ate tripe. After dinner came Miss Caton and Miss R-s. I read more English and walked about the plantation. Annie came home from Mr. Cary's. I prayed.

13. I rose about 5, read Hebrew and Greek. I prayed and had milk porridge. I danced. The weather was cool and clear, the wind northwest. I read English and walked. I read Latin and put things in order till dinner when I ate pea soup. After dinner I put things in order, read Latin and walked about the plantation. My physic worked five times. I talked with my people and prayed.

14. I rose about 5, read Hebrew and Greek. I prayed and [had] coffee. I danced. The weather was exceedingly cold and clear, the wind north. I sent my wagon to Meherrin. My great flat was lost but found again by a man at Swineyards.[1] I wrote English and walked till dinner. I ate roast pigeon. After dinner read more English and walked, talked with my people and prayed.

15. I rose about 5, read Hebrew and Greek. I prayed and had tea. I danced. The weather was cold and clear, the wind southwest. I read English and settled some accounts, then walked and read Latin till dinner when I ate lamb stones. After dinner I read some English letters, then settled some accounts and walked about the plantation. At night talked with my people and prayed.

16. I rose about 5, read Hebrew and Greek. I prayed and had tea. I danced. The weather was cold and cloudy, the wind southwest. I wrote English and read news and walked in the garden till dinner when I ate cold bacon and sallet. After dinner it rained a good shower and then Mr. Page and Mr. Eppes and his sister [came] to visit Billy. I talked with my people and prayed.

---

[1]Swineyards (Swyneards, Swinyards, Swincherd's), just below Westover on the north bank of the James, was early named one of the sites for a public warehouse (Hen. *Stat.*, IV, 266, 382; V, 141-42). For its location see *A Map of the Inhabited part of Virginia*, &c., drawn by Joshua Fry and Peter Jefferson in 1751.

17. I rose about 5, read Hebrew and Greek. I prayed and had coffee. I danced. The weather was cloudy, with rain, the wind southwest; and nobody could go to church, which was a great disappointment to the young folks. I read news and put myself in order till dinner, then ate broth and boiled mutton. After dinner it rained till the evening. I talked with my people and prayed. It rained abundantly.

18. I rose about 5, read Hebrew and Greek. I prayed and had coffee. I danced. The weather cleared up, the wind west. I sent to Williamsburg and began to plant notwithstanding it was a holiday.[1] I walked and read news till dinner when I ate roast mutton. After dinner it rained a little. I read more news and walked in the garden. I talked with my people and prayed.

19. I rose about 5, read Hebrew and Greek. I prayed and had coffee. I danced. The weather was cold and clear, the wind west. My children all went to Colonel Stith's; God preserve them. I wrote letters and walked till dinner when I ate broiled mutton. After dinner I had letters from Williamsburg and read the news. My children returned safe, thank God. I talked with my people and prayed.

20. I rose about 5, read Hebrew and Greek. I prayed and had tea. I danced. The weather was cold and clear, the wind southwest. I read English and walked and then read news till dinner when I ate roast mutton. After dinner I put things in order and then [read] more news till the evening when we walked. At night I talked with my people and with the gardener and prayed.

21. I rose about 5, read Hebrew and Greek. I prayed and had coffee. I danced. The weather was cold and clear, the wind southwest. About 10 I went with my son to visit M-l-s who lay sick at P-n-t-r. We found [him] better and then dined with Colonel Stith and ate roast chicken and

---

[1]This was Whit Sunday since Easter fell in 1741 on March 29 (Lady Hertford to Lady Pomfret, London, March 26, 1741, in Helen S. Hughes, *The Gentle Hertford Her Life and Letters* [N. Y., 1940], p. 147).

returned home in the evening. A great quarrel between my wife and Mina[1] which made me retire.

22. I rose about 5, read Hebrew and Greek. I prayed and had tea. I danced. The weather was cold and cloudy, the wind north. I read news till one when Ned Eppes and young Lewellin Eppes[2] came and dined with us and I ate bacon and green peas. It rained in the afternoon a good deal so the company stayed. I talked with my people and prayed.

23. I rose about 5, but read nothing because of the company. I prayed and had coffee. I danced. The weather was cold and clear, the wind southwest. A ship called B-r-l-n-t-n [Burlington?] came and brought my clothes. We played piquet till dinner when I ate bacon and peas. Mr. Dering and Mr. [Walthoe] came in [pudding?] time. Mr. Eppes went away. I talked with my people and prayed.

24. I rose about 5, read nothing because I wrote letters. I prayed and had coffee. I danced. The weather was warm and clear, the wind southwest. About 11 I went to church and received the Sacrament. After church Colonel Eppes came home with us to dinner and I ate roast pigeon. After dinner we talked and had coffee. The Colonel went away and we walked. I talked with my people and prayed.

25. I rose about 5, read Hebrew and Greek. I prayed and had tea. I danced. The weather was cold and clear,

---

[1]Maria Taylor Byrd and her stepdaughter Mina were not always at peace. However she showed her continued interest in Mina after Byrd's death. She wrote her son, William Byrd III, in a letter undated but before the death in 1760 of her son's first wife, "I think it was in my last that I gave you a Detail of Mina's Deplorable Condition & of my Inviting her Here, & since then I have not heard from her, so whether or not she will come I cant tell." Again on July 18, 1760 she wrote her son: "As to Mina I have never hear'd from her since Christmas was two year. Anderson Stith's wife [see ante 1739, Dec. 25] that lives in her Neighbourhood says she is well & lives extremely so" (MSS in collection of Mr. William Byrd of New York city).

[2]Lewellin Eppes, Junior, Gentleman, was appointed to take the list of tithables in the upper precinct of Charles City county in May, 1743. (Charles City Order Book, 1737-1751, p. 255.) He was named by the Council in a new Commission of the Peace for Charles City on Dec. 15, 1742 (*Va. Mag.*, XVI, 21). Presumably he was the son of Lewellin Eppes, clerk of that county at least as early as 1737.

the wind southwest. I had a letter from Mr. Procter about his going away. A good journey to him. We played piquet till dinner when I ate salt fish. After dinner came Captain Talman who bought goods from me. We played bowls. Mrs. G-n-s came. I prayed.

26. I rose about 5, read Hebrew and Greek. I prayed and had coffee. I danced. The weather was cold and cloudy, the wind north. I wrote several things and walked about till dinner, when I ate roast beef. After dinner I put things in order, played at bowls and walked about. At night we talked and the company played cards. I talked with my people and prayed.

27. I rose about 5, read Hebrew but went into the chariot about 6 and my two daughters with me. I prayed and had two dishes of chocolate. About 11 I got to Mr. Cary's where I dined and ate fricasseed chicken. After dinner we played piquet and I lost. In the evening I played piquet again till 10 when I retired, prayed and slept pretty well, thank God.

28. I rose about 5 and prayed. I wrote English and had coffee. The weather was cold and clear, the wind north. About 9 I rode to the Falls and from thence and [*sic*] over to Richmond and talked with my tenants and dined with Mr. C-l [Coles?][1] and ate bacon and chicken. After dinner came the Doctor[2] and I walked among all the Germans, then returned over the river and retired about 9 and prayed.

29. I rose about 5 and read Greek. I prayed and had milk. The weather was warm and clear. About 8 to Kensington and from thence returned to Mr. Cary's much

---

[1]Byrd acknowledged a deed to a lot in Richmond to John Coles Gent. on June 1, 1741 (Henrico Order Gook, 1737-1746, p. 147). He had sold him other lands in the same vicinity (Henrico Deeds and Wills, 1725-1737, pt. 4, p. 629). John Coles, whose will was proved in Henrico, March 1748, was a merchant at Richmond and gained considerable fortune (*Va. Mag.*, VII, 101-102; XV, 114; Stanard, Henrico Notes, p. 241). On May 1, 1742, Coles presented a petition signed by himself and others for certification to the Henrico court that the town called Richmond be established by an Act of Assembly (Henrico Order Book, 1737-1746, p. 180).

[2]*I.e.*, Dr. Tschiffeley.

fatigued; however we played piquet till dinner when I ate pigeon pie. After dinner we talked and had coffee; then walked about the garden. Mr. Fraser was there. About 9 retired and prayed.

30. I rose about 5, read English. I prayed and had coffee. The wind was southwest and the weather warm. About 8 I took leave and went over the river, but my horse fell in and wet my saddle, which I stayed half an hour to dry; then went home and found Mrs. Brun and her child there. I ate fish. After dinner walked, talked with my people, and prayed.

31. I rose about 5 but read nothing because of my company. I prayed and had coffee. I danced. The weather was warm and clear, wind southwest. I went not to church but did business of kindness to Mrs. Brun. Mrs. Carter, Jenny Anderson and Molly Stith dined with us and I ate fish. After dinner we talked and had coffee. In the evening the company went. I walked, talked, and prayed.

June, 1741

1. I rose about 4, prayed and went with my wife to Henrico court where I granted several lots.[1] We breakfasted with John Bolling and dined with Parson Stith and ate roast goose. After dinner we returned home without any accident and found all well, thank God. I talked with my people and had strawberries and milk. I was much fatigued, retired soon and read my prayers.

2. I rose about 5, read Hebrew and Greek. I prayed and had tea. I danced. The weather was cold and clear, the wind southwest. Two men came to get land at Roanoke and a poor woman came about an escheat. I put several things in order till dinner when I ate bacon and peas. After dinner I talked more with the Roanoke men, walked, talked with my people, and prayed. It rained.

3. I rose about about [*sic*] 5, read Hebrew and Greek. I prayed and had tea. I danced. The weather was cold and cloudy, the wind north, and we planted pretty much, it having rained abundance last night. Caton came and brought three trunks with her. I walked and wrote letters till dinner and then ate fish. After dinner I wrote more letters and walked about the plantation. In the evening several gentlemen came from court and Theo Bland[2] and Bob Mumford stayed all night. I talked with my people and prayed.

---

[1]Byrd acknowledged deeds and his wife Maria relinquished her right of dower in the land to Richard Randolph, Daniel Weisiger, William Randolph, Jr., Gent., John Bolling, Gent., John Pleasant, Richard Levins, John Gringrethe, Joseph Hopkins, John Cumerin, James Cocke, Gent., Jon Coles, Gent. and Samuel Tschiffely (Henrico Order Book, 1737-46, June 1, 1741, p. 146, Virginia State Archives). The earliest known plat of Richmond, supposed to be as of 1742, lists with the lot numbers the above named early owners of lots in the town though the names are spelled differently in several instances.

[2]Theodorick Bland was the son of Richard Bland, of Jordan's Point, and his wife Elizabeth, daughter of the first William Randolph of Turkey Island. He served as clerk of the court of Prince George County, was its representative in the House of Burgesses several times, and in 1758 was appointed by Governor Fauquier its lieutenant. (*Bland Papers*, I, xiii-xv, and I and II, *passim.*) His sister Anne was the wife of Robert Mumford who accompanied him to Westover on this occasion (Letter of William Beverley to Richard Bland, May 11, 1743, *Wm. Q. (1)*, III, 233).

4. I rose about 5 and read Hebrew only, because of the company. I prayed and had coffee. I danced. The weather was cold and clear. We sheared the sheep this morning. About 10 the gentlemen went over the river. I wrote letters till one when Mr. Miller and his wife[1] came with John Ravenscroft, and Captain Talman dined with us and I ate chicken and bacon. After dinner we had coffee and then played bowls. At night played cards. I talked with my people and prayed.

5. I rose about 5, read Greek. I prayed and had coffee. I danced. The weather was cold and clear, the wind southwest. Mr. Miller and his wife stayed. I wrote English and read news till dinner when the Captain and Mr. Ravenscroft came and dined with us and I ate peas and bacon. After dinner we played bowls and then all the company went away. I talked with my people and prayed.

6. I rose about 5, read Hebrew and Greek. I prayed and had tea. I danced. The weather was cold and clear, the wind southwest. I wrote a letter to England and read news and put several things in order till dinner when I ate fish. After dinner came a letter from Mr. [Ward] by which I learned he was very bad; God preserve him. It rained and thundered in the evening much. I prayed.

7. I rose about 5, read nothing, but [sent a boy off] to the Falls. I prayed and had coffee. The weather was warm and cloudy, the wind west. I went not to church but put myself in order. After church came Ned Eppes and his wife[2] and the parson to dinner and I ate chicken and bacon. After dinner we talked and had coffee. In the evening the company went away and I prayed.

8. I rose about 5 in order for to Williamsburg [*sic*], but was forced to stay till 8 to mend the chariot. I had choco-

[1]See note under entry for March 16, 1741.

[2]This was probably Henrietta Maria Hardyman, sister of Francis Hardyman, who was an administratrix of her husband Major Edmund Eppes in 1757 (*Wm. Q. (1)*, XI, 48. This reference states she was appointed guardian of her children in 1775 but that date is an evident error for 1757). See entry and note for Sept. 11, 1740.

late for breakfast, notwithstanding it was very warm. I got to Williamsburg about 4 and ate minced chicken with the Commissary, where I saw Mr. Dinwiddie,[1] the Surveyor General. In the evening went to the Governor's and stayed the evening till 9 and then walked home and prayed.

9. I rose about 5, read Hebrew and Greek. I prayed and had chocolate with the Commissary. We went first to church and then to the capitol, where I stayed till 3 and made a speech to the grand jury and tried one man. We dined with Wetherburn and I ate chicken and bacon. After dinner we drank arrack punch, but I walked home about 9 and got a pain in my hip by lying with the window open.

10. I rose about 5, read Hebrew and Greek. I prayed and had coffee. The weather was warm and clear, the wind southwest. About 10 went to Council, where we sat till 3 and then dined with the Governor's lady[2] and ate roast pigeon. After dinner we talked and drank Burgundy till the evening; then walked to Lady Randolph's and had tea; then walked to Wetherburn's and received some money and bills; then went home, wrote a letter and put up my things and prayed.

---

[1]Robert Dinwiddie, of Germiston, Scotland, was named Surveyor General of Customs of the Southern ports of the Continent of America in 1738. He appears to have fixed his chief residence in Virginia. When he attempted to take his seat in the Council of Virginia, to which like his predecessors he had been named, the Council refused him a seat and sent a remonstrance to the King. Governor Gooch supported the prerogative of the Crown and the Board of Trade in May, 1742, settled the controversy on the side of the Surveyor-General and against the claims of the Council, resisted as new and dangerous.

Dinwiddie served as lieutenant governor of Virginia, 1751-58, when he and the colonial legislature were at odds in important policies, especially in the case of the pistole fee (*Official Records of Robert Dinwiddie, Lieutenant-Governor of the Colony of Virginia*, ed. R. A. Brock [Va. Hist. Soc. Coll., Vol. III, New Series], I, viii-ix). See *Va. Mag.*, XV, 124-6; Gooch to the Commissioners for Trade & Plantations, Nov. 6, 1741, Gooch Papers, Va. Hist. Soc.

[2]The wife of Governor Gooch was Rebecca, daughter of William Stanton, Esq., of Hampton, Middlesex, England. She survived him more than twenty years. On her death in 1775 she willed the College of William and Mary, in remembrance of the education there of her only son, William Gooch, who died in Virginia in 1742, her gilt sacrament cup and a large folio Bible in four volumes (Letter of Gov. Gooch to his brother, Oct. 21, 1742, Colonial Williamsburg, Inc.; *Va. Mag.*, III, 113, XXXII, 142-3; *Wm. Q. (1)*, XXIII, 173-5).

11. I rose about 4 and had boiled milk, and prayed, and about 5 got into the chariot to return home, and without anything remarkable got well home about 2, but called at Mr. Hardyman's and received £5 for my rent. I found all well, thank God, and ate fish for dinner. After dinner I walked and retired very soon, being much tired, and prayed.

12. I rose about 5, read Hebrew and Greek. I prayed and had milk porridge because I took physic. I was better, thank God. I put things in order and read news. I slept a little. My physic worked four times. I ate fish for dinner. After dinner I put things in order and read more news. We walked in the evening. I talked with my people and prayed.

13. I rose about 5, read Hebrew and Greek. I prayed and had tea. I danced. The weather was warm and clear, the wind southwest. I wrote English and read news till dinner, when I ate fish. After dinner I put up my things in order to go to the Falls next day. In the evening I walked, at night talked with my people, and prayed.

14. I rose about 4, prayed, and had chocolate, and about 5 went in Mr. Dering's chair to Mr. Cary's, but met with rain by the way. We got there about 10 but they were gone to church. However, we had coffee. Then I went to the Falls to see poor Mr. [Ward] who was sick. I found him very bad, but to comfort him told him I would be kind to his wife and child [*or* children], which gave him great content. I ate bacon and eggs and talked with Dr. Tschiffely and Dr. Gay about [. . .].

15. I rose about 5, and read Greek only. I prayed and had milk. Mr. [Ward] continued very bad. I stayed with him pretty much though the room was offensive. Mr. [Braxton] came and brought an account of my tobacco at the warehouse. I had fried chicken. I said all I could to comfort Mr. [Ward] and his wife. In the evening played the fool with Marjorie, God forgive me.

16. I rose about 5, prayed, and after recommending Mr. [Ward] to Providence rode to Mr. Cary's and got there

about 6 and had coffee. Several girls danced, it being Dance day.[1] Parson Fraser was there with his wife. I ate salt fish for dinner. In the afternoon Mrs. Gay came and we played piquet and I won 12 bits. In the evening walked and prayed.

17. I rose about 5 and had coffee. I prayed, and about 6 took leave and went away with Mr. Dering in his chair and got home about 11 and found all well, thank God, and Mr. Banister there and just before dinner came Robin Mumford to dinner, and I ate boiled tongue. After dinner we talked and had tea and then Robin Mumford went away and we walked about the plantation. At [night] talked with my people and had milk and raspberries, and about 9 retired and prayed.

18. I rose about 5, read Hebrew and Greek. I prayed and had coffee. I danced. The weather was warm and clear, the wind southwest. I walked to the store and unpacked some things, then wrote several matters concerning my business at the Falls and posted[?] my new books till dinner and ate fish. After dinner took a nap and put things in order till the evening and then walked. I talked with my people, had raspberries and milk, and prayed.

19. I rose about 5 and read only Hebrew. I prayed and had coffee. I danced. The weather was exceedingly warm and clear, the wind north. Mr. Anderson came to offer his service more. Miss Harrison[2] breakfasted with us and then went away, and Mr. P-r-s came to undertake the business at the Falls. I ate bacon and beans. After dinner I continued to write for Mr. P-r-s. It rained abundantly. A beef came. I prayed.

20. I rose about 5, read Hebrew and Greek. I prayed

---

[1]Dance day was a fixed day on which a dancing master—in this instance it appears to be Mr. Dering, since Byrd left with him the next day—would give lessons at one of the plantation homes, and other young people of the neighboring estates would come to share them.

[2]This was probably Elizabeth Harrison, daughter of Benjamin and Anne Carter Harrison of Berkeley, who seems to have been their oldest child, though it could refer to her younger sister Anne. She did not marry Peyton Randolph until after 1745, as she was single when her father's will was probated (*Va. Mag.*, XLI, 163-5).

and had coffee. I danced. The weather was cold and cloudy, the wind southwest. I settled some accounts and read Latin till dinner when abundance of company came from the other side of the river and I ate chicken and bacon. Mr. [Ward] was very bad at the Falls; God preserve him. The company danced in spite of the weather. It rained, and I prayed.

21. I rose about 5, read Hebrew and Greek. I prayed and had coffee. I danced. The weather was warm and cloudy, the wind southwest. A coachful went to church but I stayed at home and read Latin and put myself in order till dinner when I ate roast rabbit. After dinner we talked and had coffee. In the evening the company went away and I walked in the garden and prayed.

22. I rose about 5, read Hebrew and Greek. I prayed and had tea. I danced. The weather was warm and clear, the wind north. About 11 came Mrs. Cary and her daughter. I read English and played piquet till dinner when I ate chicken and bacon. After dinner we talked and had coffee. I won a great pool. In the evening we walked. There was a beef killed. I prayed. The boat went.

23. I rose about 5, read Hebrew and Greek. I prayed and had coffee. I danced. The weather was cold and clear, the wind west. I read English and played piquet all the morning till dinner when I ate boiled pigeon and bacon. After dinner we talked and had coffee. We played again at piquet till the evening when we walked about the plantation. I talked with my people and prayed.

24. I rose about 5, read Hebrew and Greek. I prayed and had coffee. I danced. The weather was warm and clear, the wind southwest. I read English and played piquet till 2 when Mrs. Miller and Mrs. Greenhill came from over the river to dinner and I ate fish. After dinner we talked and had coffee. We walked in the evening and I played the fool with Sally, God forgive me.

25. I rose about 5, read Hebrew and Greek. I prayed

and had coffee. I danced. The weather was warm and clear, the wind southwest. I wrote three letters and read English and played piquet till dinner and ate roast rabbit. After dinner came two men from Roanoke. It rained again in the afternoon. In the evening I walked in the garden, talked with my people, and prayed.

26. I rose about 5, read Hebrew and Greek. I prayed and had coffee. I danced. The weather was very warm and cloudy, the wind west. I read English and played piquet and put things in order till dinner when I ate roast beef. After dinner we talked and had coffee. My tobacco went to the warehouse and all passed. In the evening I walked about the plantation and at night prayed.

27. I rose about 5, read Hebrew and Greek. I prayed and had coffee. I danced. The weather was warm and clear, the wind southwest. The boat came this morning by which I learned Mr. [Ward] died on Tuesday last. We played piquet till dinner. Young Mr. Cary dined with us and I ate boiled beef. After dinner we talked and had coffee. A calf came from the Falls. I talked with my people and prayed.

28. I rose about 5, read Hebrew and Greek. I prayed and had tea. I danced. The weather was warm and clear, the wind west. About 7 Mrs. Cary and her family went away. I read English. Nobody came from church to dinner. I ate roast beef. After dinner I wrote letters and read English till the evening when we walked about the plantation. At [night] talked with my people and prayed.

29. I rose about 5, read Hebrew and Greek. I prayed and had tea. I danced. The weather was cool and cloudy, the wind southeast. My people began to reap and I wrote letters and worked about, read Latin till dinner, when I ate roast chicken which a minx had killed. After dinner I slept and walked to the reapers. In the evening walked about the plantation and prayed. Mr. Wood came.

30. I rose about 5, read Hebrew and Greek. I prayed

and had tea. I danced. The weather was warm and cloudy, the wind southwest. I talked with Mr. Wood who went away and I wrote letters till 12 when Mr. Beverley Randolph came with Mrs. Randolph and dined with us and I ate tripe. After dinner we talked and had coffee, and walked in the evening about the garden. In the night it rained but good part of our wheat was in the house. I prayed.

July, 1741

1. I rose about 5, read Hebrew and Greek. I prayed and had coffee. I danced. It continued to rain by showers all day so our company stayed. We played piquet till dinner when I ate salt fish. After dinner we had coffee and about 5 I sent my chariot with Mrs. Randolph to Colonel Harrison's. I talked with my people and prayed.

2. I rose about 5. I read Hebrew and Greek. I prayed and had tea. I danced. The weather was cold and cloudy, the wind southwest. Betty and Molly Stith breakfasted with us and then went over the river. I wrote English and read Latin till dinner when I ate hashed chicken. After dinner put things in order in the library, read more Latin and walked about the plantation. I talked with my people. It rained again.

3. I rose about 5, read Hebrew and Greek. I prayed and had tea. I danced. The weather was cold and clear, the wind southwest. I read Latin and wrote letters till dinner when Captain Talman came and I ate roast veal. After dinner we talked and played bowls and then walked to the barn where 8 loads of wheat was [*sic*] brought in. In the evening it rained and I retired and prayed.

4. I rose about 5, read Hebrew and Greek. I prayed and had tea. I danced. The weather was warm and cloudy, the wind southwest. I read Latin and French till one when Mr. Dering came and dined with us and I ate fish. After dinner I put things in order. It rained several showers; however we played bowls. My people made an end of the wheat. I prayed.

5. I rose about 5, read Hebrew and Greek. I prayed and had coffee. I danced. I found another thief in my gardener and Bob[?]. I wrote to the Falls, but went not to church but read French. After church came the Secretary and his lady and I ate fish. After dinner we talked and had coffee.

Mr. Ravenscroft came. About 6 the company went away and I prayed.

6. I rose about 5, read Hebrew and Greek. I prayed and had coffee. I danced. The weather was warm and cloudy, the wind southwest. Ned Eppes came to judge my gardener but he humbled himself and I forgave him. We played piquet all the morning till dinner, and I ate roast veal. After dinner we talked and in the evening played bowls. We learned Mr. Corbin[1] had sent our goods.

7. I rose about [...], read Hebrew and Greek. I prayed and had tea. I danced. The weather was warm and clear, the wind west. We got in our oats. I wrote letters and read Latin till dinner when I ate broiled veal. After dinner I put things in order in the library and then wrote English. In the evening we played bowls. Mr. Banister came from Williamsburg but brought no news. He brought me a letter from Mr. Dinwiddie the Surveyor General in answer to one I wrote in Mr. Banister's favor.

8. I rose about 5, read Hebrew and Greek. I prayed and had coffee. I danced. The weather was warm and clear, the wind northwest. Mr. Banister stayed this day; however I gave him some things to write and I read Latin. Captain W-l-s came to dinner and so did Captain Talman, and I ate fish. After dinner we played bowls, notwithstanding it had rained. In the evening came Mr. Hall.

9. I rose about 5, read Hebrew and Greek. I prayed and had tea. I danced. Mr. and Mrs. Hall went away and Mr. Bland and his cousin came and loitered all the morning but went down the river before dinner, when I ate minced veal. After dinner I put several matters in order and played

---

[1]This may have been Thomas Corbin, son of Henry and Alice Corbin, who owned land in Virginia and became a merchant in London. The will of Gawin Corbin, proved in King and Queen County in 1744, mentions his brother, "the late Mr. Thomas Corbin." Thomas Corbin, merchant in London, with Edmund Jenings, Robert Carter, Gawin Corbin, Jr. and Mr. Edwin Thacker were named by Col. Ralph Wormeley to aid and assist his two young sons, whom he named executors in his will, proved in 1701 (See letters of Robert Carter to Thomas Corbin, *Wm. Q. (1)*, XVII, 253-63; *Va. Mag.*, XXXVI, 288-91).

bowls. We made an end of our harvest. I talked with my people and prayed.

10. I rose about 5, read Hebrew and Greek. I prayed and had milk porridge, having taken physic. I danced. The weather was cold and cloudy, with a little rain, the wind northeast. My face was swelled with a toothache. I read Latin and English till dinner when I ate fish. After dinner my tooth grew easier, thank God. I played bowls. We killed a beef for the ship. I prayed.

11. I rose about 5, read Hebrew and Greek. I prayed and had tea. I danced. The weather continued cold and cloudy, with little rain. I wrote letters to England and read Latin and walked to see my people work till dinner when I ate ox cheek. After dinner I learned all were well at the Falls, thank God. My boat returned from Williamsburg without any goods. I talked with my people.

12. I rose about 5, read Hebrew and Greek. I prayed and had coffee. I danced. The weather was cold and clear, the wind north. I gave physic to several sick people and put my person in order and read Latin till after church. Mrs. Miller came and dined here but none beside came. I ate fish. After dinner I took a nap and then walked about the plantation. At night talked with my people and prayed.

13. I rose about 5, read Hebrew and Greek. I prayed and had tea. I danced. The weather was cold and cloudy, the wind southeast. I sent Charles to Colonel Bassett with a letter about my goods. I read Latin and wrote a letter and settled some accounts and about 2 came Mr. Batte[1] from over the river and dined with me, our women being

[1]Possibly Henry Batte, son of Captain Henry Batte, who belonged to the family of that name who had settled on the Appomattox river in the seventeenth century and had taken a leading part in the exploration of southside Virginia (*Va. Biog.*, I, 182; C. W. Alvord and Lee Bidgood, *The First Explorations of the Trans-Alleghany Region by the Virginians, 1650-1674* [Cleveland, 1912]. A public ferry was run from Henry Batte's in the county of Henrico to Alexander Bolling's in the county of Prince George in 1748 (Hen. *Stat.*, VI, 13). William Batte also figures in the Prince George county records for this period as a party to a suit with Henry Batte and as foreman of the Grand Jury (Prince George Minute Book, 1737-1740, p. 107 *et passim*).

gone to the Secretary's. I played the fool with F-r-b-y, God forgive me.

14. I rose about 5, read Hebrew and Greek. I prayed and had tea. I danced. The weather was warm and cloudy, the wind southwest. I read Latin till 12 when Mr. Dering came from above. I was much out of humor with my people who did amiss. I ate tripe for dinner. After dinner put things in order. It rained again, with much thunder and lightning. I could hear nothing of my goods from Colonel Bassett. I talked with my people and prayed. I slept but indifferently.

15. I rose about 5, read Hebrew and Greek. I prayed and had tea. I danced. The weather was warm and cloudy, the wind west. I wrote letters till 12, when Ned Randolph came and we played piquet till dinner when I ate roast rabbit. After dinner we talked and had tea; then we played bowls. At night I talked with my people and prayed.

16. I rose about 5, read Hebrew and Greek. I prayed and had coffee. I danced. The weather was cold and clear, the wind north. I wrote letters and washed my feet and read Latin till dinner when I ate fish. After dinner put things to rights in the library and in the evening we bowled and walked. My wife was indisposed and I gave her two pills. I had apples and milk and prayed.

17. I rose about 5, read Hebrew and Greek. I prayed and had tea. I danced. The weather was warm and clear, the wind southwest. I wrote letters. Mr. B-p-s was very sick. I read Latin and walked about among my people till dinner, when I ate cold chicken. After dinner I took a nap and then played bowls. I talked with my people and prayed.

18. I rose about 5, read Hebrew and Greek. I prayed and had tea. I danced. The weather was warm and cloudy, the wind southwest. I read Latin and settled some accounts till dinner, when I ate salt fish. After dinner put several things in order, read more Latin and then played bowls. At night talked with my people and prayed. All well at the Falls.

19. I rose about 5, read Hebrew and Greek. I prayed and had coffee. I danced. The weather was warm and cloudy, the wind southwest. I put myself in order and about 11 went to church and heard a good sermon. After church Colonel Eppes, Mr. Custis and Mrs. Duke dined with us and I ate roast veal. After dinner we talked and had coffee. Caton returned with her lawyer.[1]

20. I rose about 5, read Hebrew and Greek. I prayed and had tea. I danced. The weather was very hot and clear, the wind southwest. I settled some accounts and read Latin. It was exceedingly hot and several of my people were sick. I ate stewed veal. After dinner I took a nap and in the evening played bowls and walked. I talked with my people, had apples and milk, and prayed.

21. I rose about 5, read Hebrew and Greek. I prayed and had tea. I danced. The weather was very hot, the wind northwest. Mr. Custis stayed and came with design to make love to Annie.[2] I wrote letters and read Latin till dinner when I ate roast veal. After dinner I put things in order till the evening and then played bowls and walked. Mr. B-p-s continued sick. I prayed.

22. I rose about 5, read Hebrew and Greek. I prayed and had tea. I danced. The weather was very hot and clear, the wind west. Mr. Custis went away and Captain Eppes came and we played piquet. I read Latin between whiles till dinner when I ate minced veal. After dinner we played again till the evening and then played bowls. Mr.

---

[1]Caton Brun, the daughter, was evidently making preparations with Byrd's influence for her opposition to Benjamin Harris in the August Charles City court. See entry for August 14, 1739 and note.

[2]See G. W. P. Custis, *Recollections and Private Memoirs of Washington*, ed. B. J. Lossing, pp. 18-19, where Mrs. Lee remarks that Daniel Custis was quite a desirable match. "His cousin, Evelyn Byrd of Westover, was proposed, but though Colonel Custis desired earnestly the connection, he could not be brought to terms; and at length Colonel Byrd, in a very decided letter, in which he tells the wooer how much he regrets his father's impracticability, as he should have preferred him to all others, adds, that he can not trust to such a 'phantome as Colonel Custis's generosity'." The letter of Byrd was among manuscripts at Arlington, whose present whereabouts are not known. Apparently it was not Evelyn but Anne who was being wooed.

Stevens came and the shoemaker. I had apples and milk, and prayed.

23. I rose about 6, no Hebrew and Greek. I prayed and had coffee. I danced. The weather continued cruelly hot, the wind southwest. Stevens could not account and so went away and carried my Mina with him. I read Latin till dinner when Mrs. Duke came and told us Frank Hardyman was dead. I ate roast pigeon. After dinner I put things in order and played bowls. I prayed.

24. I rose about 5, read Hebrew and Greek. I prayed and had coffee. I danced. The weather was warm and cloudy, the wind southwest. I wrote to Colonel Custis and read Latin till dinner when I ate fish. After dinner I settled some accounts till evening when it began to thunder and rain very much. I talked with my people and prayed heartily and slept but indifferently.

25. I rose about 5, read Hebrew and Greek. I prayed and had coffee. I danced. The weather was cool and clear after the rain, the wind west. I settled accounts with Mr. Custis and read English till dinner when I ate roast tongue. We had a beef brought in the cart. After dinner I put several matters in order and learned all was well above. It rained abundantly again. I talked with my people. Mr. Dering came. I prayed.

26. I rose about 5, read Hebrew and Greek. I prayed and had coffee. I danced. The weather was warm and cloudy, the wind north. I went not to church but put myself in order and wrote several letters. After church came John Stith and his wife who dined here, and I ate fish. After dinner came John Ravenscroft, Mr. Miller and his wife and Mrs. Poythress[1] and stayed till the evening, but the rest stayed here.

---

[1]Evidently a member of the Poythress family long prominent in Charles City and Prince George Counties. William Poythress was justice of Prince George, 1738, and William and Francis Poythress were militia officers of Prince George, 1738. In Charles City, July 1741, there was a suit by Robert Poythress and Robert and Thomas Poythress executors of Joshua Poythress vs. Benjamin Harrison (*Va. Mag.*, XXIII, 32; see Diary, 1709-1712).

27. I rose about 5, read Hebrew and Greek. I prayed and had coffee. I danced. The weather was cool and cloudy, the wind north. Mrs. Duke went away at last, but John Stith and his wife stayed. I wrote letters and read Latin till dinner when I ate roast chicken. After dinner we talked and had tea and in the evening played bowls and walked. I talked with my people and prayed.

28. I rose about 5, read Hebrew and Greek. I prayed and had coffee. I danced. The weather was warm and cloudy, the wind southeast. I wrote letters and read Latin. Both my son and daughter Jenny was sick. I read Latin till dinner when I ate roast lamb. After dinner I put things in order when I likewise read French. In the evening I walked about the plantation. At night talked with my people and prayed.

29. I rose about 5, read Hebrew and Greek. I prayed and had tea. I danced. The weather was warm and clear, the wind west. I turned away my fine gardener for being a rogue. I wrote letters and read Latin till dinner when I ate fish. After dinner put things in order and read some of my invoices of goods. In the evening walked; then talked with my people. B-r-b-s was bad again. I prayed.

30. I rose about 5, read Hebrew and Greek. I prayed and had coffee. I danced. The weather was warm and clear, the wind southwest. I wrote letters and learned from Mr. Custis that the Governor was come.[1] I read Latin till dinner and then ate tripe. After dinner came the overseer at the Falls who said all was well. I read French. My children had fever. I talked with my people and prayed.

Joshua Poythress had been quite wealthy, for his administrators gave bond of £5,000 current money when his will was presented in court (Prince George Minute Book, 1737-1740, April 1740, p. 400).

[1]This entry in the diary will clear up the question as to when Gooch returned to Williamsburg from the Carthagena Expedition, since his wounds and illness as a result of that campaign prevented his attending meetings of the Council for several months.

He wrote his brother on Oct. 13, 1741: "The Virginians were mightily rejoyced at my Return Day and Night firing Guns, Bonfires and Illuminations"—and added "the good Commissary kept believing he should never see me again." (Gooch letters, Colonial Williamsburg, Inc.)

31. I rose about 5, read Hebrew and Greek. I prayed and had tea. I danced. The weather continued warm and clear, the wind southwest. This morning I discharged L-v-y from my service. I settled some accounts. Mr. Dering came to dinner and I ate fish. After dinner put things in order and showed Dering my prints.[1] In the evening John Ravenscroft and Mrs. Miller called. I walked a little and prayed.

---

[1]Byrd had acquired a number of prints during his residence in England (see Diary, 1717-1721). His judgment in matters of art was respected by at least as outspoken a critic as his brother-in-law John Custis (Custis to Byrd, April 10, 1723, Custis Letter Book 1717-1741, MS, Library of Congress). Byrd took lessons in drawing from Eleazer Albin, teacher of watercolor drawing, in London (Diary, Dec. 13, 1717, through Oct. 28, 1719; *Dict. Nat. Biog.*, *sub* Albin).

August, 1741

1. I rose about 5, read Hebrew and Greek. I prayed and had coffee. I danced. The weather continued warm and clear, the wind southwest. Mr. Dering went to town. I wrote letters and read Latin. My son had a fever all day; God preserve him. I ate neat's tongue for dinner. In the afternoon came a boy from the Falls where they want rain. In the evening I walked and prayed.

2. I rose about 5, read Hebrew and Greek. I prayed and had tea. I danced. The weather was cold and cloudy, the wind west. My son had a fever all night but was better this morning, thank God. I went not to church but put myself in order till after church when Mrs. Brun came, Mr. Fontaine and Colonel Stith's daughter. I ate roast pigeon. After dinner we talked. It rained and my son continued better, thank God. In the evening I walked, talked with my people at night and prayed.

3. I rose about 5, read Hebrew and Greek. I prayed and had tea. I danced. The weather was cold and cloudy, the wind north. Mr. Fontaine went away and I read news and then read Latin till dinner when Mrs. Greenhill came and I ate fish. After dinner came Mr. Anderson. I looked over some prints and walked. In the evening I talked with my people and prayed.

4. I rose about 5, no Hebrew and Greek because I talked with Mr. Anderson. I prayed and had coffee. I danced. The weather was clear and warm. Mr. Anderson and Mrs. Greenhill went away and I wrote letters and read Latin and walked among my people till dinner when I ate bacon. After dinner came the sheriff[1] to summon me to court as a witness for Mr. Harris.[2] In the evening I walked about the

---

[1]Francis Dancey was appointed by the Council, June 10, 1741, as sheriff of Charles City County, and qualified for that office in August (*Va. Mag.*, XV, 125, XXI, 86). The Dancey family was one of the wealthiest in Charles City County (Charles City Order Book, 1737-1751, p. 519).

[2]*I.e.*, Benjamin Harris (see extract from Charles City Order Book, August, 1741, p. 175, in note on Mrs. Brun, Aug. 14, 1739).

plantation, talked with my people. My children continued indisposed; God preserve them. I prayed.

5. I rose about 5, read Hebrew and Greek. I prayed and had tea. I danced. The weather was warm and cloudy, the wind west. I read Latin and wrote English. Mrs. Brun went away to court and Miss Caton with her. I ate fish. After dinner I looked over some pictures till 4, when it began to blow violently, with rain and hail that ruined my tobacco and did other damage. I talked with my people and prayed.

6. I rose about 5, read Hebrew and Greek. I prayed and had coffee. I danced. The weather was warm and clear, the wind southwest. We took the [water?] out of the new house. I wrote letters and read Latin till dinner when I ate fish. After dinner I put things in order and made the people dry the wheat in the barn. I read English till the evening, walked about the plantation and saw the damage the gust had made. Mr. Wood came. I prayed.

7. I rose about 5, read Hebrew and Greek. I prayed and had tea. I danced. The weather was warm and cloudy, the wind east. I talked with Mr. Wood, who went away, and I read Latin and wrote English till one when Captain Talman, Mr. Miller and his wife came to dine with us and I ate boiled beef. After dinner we played bowls. A man came from Roanoke and told me L-n-r was a rogue. The company went away.

8. I rose about 5, read Hebrew and Greek. I prayed and had milk porridge because I had taken physic. I danced. The weather was warm and clear, the wind west. I read Latin and wrote English. My physic worked four times. I ate minced chicken. After dinner I took a nap and looked over some French prints. In the evening I walked. My daughter Mina came home. I talked with my people and prayed.

9. I rose about 5, read Hebrew and Greek. I prayed and had coffee. I danced. The weather was clear and warm,

the wind west. I went not to church but put my person in order. After church young Mr. Cary came, and Mr. Procter had an ague. I ate fish. After dinner we talked and walked. It rained a pretty shower. I talked with my people and prayed.

10. I rose about 5, read Hebrew and Greek. I prayed and had tea. I danced. The weather was cold and clear, the wind north. I sent my little cart with the carpenter to Mount Folly. Mr. Cary stayed this day. I read Latin till dinner and then ate roast venison. After dinner came Captain W-n from Roanoke with a man to [buy?] land. We played bowls and I prayed.

11. I rose about 5, read Hebrew and Greek. I prayed and had tea. I danced. The weather was cold and clear, the wind west. I read Latin and settled some accounts till one when Mrs. Carter[1] and her daughter came and afterwards Mrs. Greenhill and Mrs. Miller, and I ate salt fish for dinner. In the afternoon we talked and had coffee, then walked. At night came Mr. [Harmer].[2] I prayed.

12. I rose about 5, read Hebrew and Greek. I prayed and had coffee. I danced. The weather was clear and warm, the wind west. My man Henry continued very bad. I settled some accounts and read Latin till dinner when I ate roast rabbit. After dinner I looked over some prints and took a nap. In the evening I walked among the sick, talked with my people, and prayed.

13. I rose about 5, read Hebrew and Greek. I prayed and had coffee. I danced. The weather was warm and

---

[1]This probably refers to Elizabeth Hill Carter, born in 1731, only daughter of Secretary and Mrs. John Carter of Shirley. She married William Byrd III, son of the diarist, Apr. 14, 1748, and died in 1760, her husband within six months marrying Mary Willing of Philadelphia (*Wm. Q. (1)*, XX, 18, *(2)*, XVI, 416; Bassett, 448).

[2]John Harmer was a merchant in Williamsburg, a justice of York and a vestryman of Bruton parish church. He was concerned in the patenting of a large grant of land on Sherrando River with William Randolph, Peter Jefferson and others in 1737. He was Mayor of Williamsburg in 1745 and returned to Great Britain to live about 1746 (*Ex. Jour.*, IV, 369, 402, 419, 433, 435; *Wm. Q. (1)*, III, 180, XXIV, 29; *T's. Q.*, II, 135; *Va. Gaz.*, Nov. 25-Dec. 2, 1737).

clear, the wind west. I played piquet with the ladies and read Latin. My man Henry was very sick and so was Mr. Procter. I ate boiled lamb. After dinner we talked and had tea, then walked. In the evening came Isham Randolph. I talked with my people.

14. I rose about 5, read Hebrew and Greek. I prayed and had coffee. I danced. The weather was warm and cloudy, the wind southwest. I played piquet. About 12 came Mr. P-r-s and told me all was well at the Falls, thank God. My man Henry was better. After dinner Isham Randolph and Mrs. Carter went away and I walked, then talked with my people and prayed.

15. I rose about 5, read Hebrew and Greek. I prayed and had tea. I danced. The weather was cold and cloudy, and threatened rain. My son was sick again; God preserve him. I wrote English and read Latin. It rained a great deal. I ate broiled pigeon. After dinner it continued to rain. Several of my people were sick. It rained all day and all night. I prayed.

16. I rose about 5, read Hebrew and Greek. I prayed and had coffee. I danced. It continued to rain abundantly, the wind north. Nobody went to church and I put myself in order and wrote Latin till dinner when I ate roast chicken. After dinner put things in order. My son was indisposed; God preserve him. In the evening we walked in the garden. I prayed.

17. I rose about 5, read Hebrew and Greek. I prayed and had tea. I danced. The weather was cold and cloudy, the wind north, and rained a little. I wrote English and read Latin. Mr. Procter continued sick but my son was better. I ate roast shoat. After dinner I looked over some pictures and walked in the garden. At night talked with my people and prayed.

18. I rose about 5, read Hebrew and Greek. I prayed and had tea. I danced. The weather was cold and cloudy, the wind east. Miss Caton went home. I wrote English

and read Latin and walked among my people till dinner and ate fish. After dinner I looked over some prints and then more English till the evening. There was a fresh in the river. I walked and talked with my people and prayed.

19. I rose about 5, read Hebrew and Greek. I prayed and had tea. I danced. The weather was warm, with rain, the wind south. Mr. Procter continued sick, God save him. I wrote letters to England and read Latin till dinner when I ate fish. It rained almost all day so that I could walk only in the garden. I talked with my people and prayed.

20. I rose about 5 and read nothing because I wrote letters. I prayed and had coffee. I danced. The weather was warm and cloudy, the wind southwest. About 11 we went to Beverley Randolph's and got there about 1 and found the old Colonel there, and Captain Randolph. I ate stewed lamb. After dinner we talked and played piquet and I lost and retired about 10 and prayed.

21. I rose about 6 and read English till 9. I prayed and had bad coffee. The weather continued warm and cloudy, the wind southwest. Colonel Dick Randolph came and we talked and played piquet till dinner and I won. I ate chicken pie. After dinner we took leave and returned home where several of the servants were sick. I put things in order, ate apples and milk, and prayed.

22. I rose about 5 and read nothing because wrote letters. I prayed and had coffee. I danced. The weather continued warm and cloudy, the wind west. I wrote letters and walked till dinner when I ate roast chicken. After dinner I put things in order and in the evening walked among my people. Our tobacco drowned[?] above; God's will be done. Henry was [b-r-s-t-n of committing sin].

23. I rose about 5, read Hebrew and Greek. I prayed and had tea. I danced. The weather was foggy, the wind southwest. My wife was sick, God preserve her, and several others. I went not to church but put myself in order and read Latin. After church nobody came to dinner but I ate

minced chicken. After dinner came news from Roanoke that L-n-r was run away. I prayed.

24. I rose about 5, read Hebrew and Greek. I prayed and had tea. I danced. The weather was cold and clear, the wind southwest. I settled accounts [with] Talman and gave [him] my letters, as likewise with Captain D-l-t-n who dined with us and I ate broiled pigeon. After dinner came Captain W-l-s likewise to settle accounts and take leave. I walked with my son. We killed a beef. I prayed. Mr. Wood came.

25. I rose about 5, read Hebrew and Greek. I prayed and had tea. I danced. The weather was cold and cloudy, the wind northeast, and threatened rain and some fell. I settled accounts and wrote an escheat till dinner when I ate roast tongue. After dinner I put things in order. My wife was out of order. In the evening I walked about the plantation. I had a cold; God preserve me.

26. I rose about 5, read Hebrew and Greek. I prayed and had tea. I danced. The weather was warm and cloudy, the wind north. My wife still sick and very [humble; Saint Joseph] save her. I read Latin till dinner when I ate only pudding. After dinner came the cooper from Richmond to pay me some money and get other lots. I walked about the plantation. At night I talked with my people, had apples and milk, and prayed. In the night I had a fever which disturbed me much.

27. I rose about 5, read Hebrew and Greek. I prayed and had coffee. I danced. The weather was warm and cloudy, the wind northwest. My wife was better, thank God, I settled several accounts and read Latin till dinner when I ate battered eggs. After dinner I wrote letters to my lawyer and some others at Williamsburg. It rained pretty much; however I walked in the garden and prayed.

28. I rose about 5, read Hebrew and Greek. I prayed and had tea. I danced. The weather continued cloudy, the wind west. I sent Charles to Williamsburg. My wife was

worse; God preserve her. I sent for Monger but he was from home so I ordered her a glyster that did her much good. I ate bacon. After dinner I wrote and read Latin. In the evening Mrs. Byrd was better, thank God, and her purge stopped and she began to take rest. I talked with my people and prayed.

29. I rose about 5, read Hebrew and Greek. I prayed and had tea. I danced. The weather was warm and foggy, the wind west. The boat came from the Falls with several things. My wife slept pretty well and was much better, thank God. Doctor Tschiffeley came to pay me some money. I ate roast chicken. After dinner I talked with the Doctor and so did my wife. I had a fever in the night [severely].

30. I rose about 5, read Hebrew and Greek. I prayed and had tea. I danced. The weather was cold and cloudy, the wind north. The Doctor went away. Only three of my children went to church, and I put myself in order. After church came Captain Ravenscroft to dinner and I ate bacon and French beans. After dinner we talked, then walked, and prayed.

31. I rose about 5, read Hebrew and Greek. I prayed and had tea. I danced. The weather was cold and clear, the wind north. I sent Mr. Procter to Mr. Fraser about an escheat and then wrote letters till dinner when Doctor Monger came and I ate a fish. After dinner we talked of several matters and then the Doctor went away without a fee because he came not in time. I walked in the evening, and at night talked with my people and prayed.

[End of MS.]

To Monymia.

I threaten'd Monymia with a Billet doux in jest, and now I send her one in earnest; and if I prove so punctual in performing what I threaten, imagin how conscientious I shall be in observing what I promise. Put the case I shoud promise Love and constancy to you, and Indifference to every Thing else that wears Peticoats, yett I shoud vow no more than I coud discharge with Inclination. I had once that fond opinion of my own Strength that I defy'd Love and all its Frailtys: but you have convinc'd me me of my Insufficiency. My Reason us'd to protect me against other Womens charms: but you have engag'd my own Guards against my heart, & and the very Reason that us'd to save, has now betray'd me. Your Wit enchants my understanding and your looks inflame my blood, so that Body and Soule I am yours. Thus Monymia your conquest has been compleat, and there's nothing left to finish your Triumph but generosity and compassion. Pray Venus soften your heart, and make you capable of feeling the same passion you inspire. The Impression you have made on my heart makes you always present to my Fancy. Sometimes I imagin you dresst out in all your charms, carrying Fire and love wherever you turn your Eys. Sometimes I figure you muffled up in mask & hoods, when in pity to mankind you vouchsafe to commit a more moderate slaughter. But in my gayest flights of Imagination, I draw you in a pure

A Page from Notebook "B" in the Library of the University of North Carolina.

PART II

Letters and Literary Exercises

1696-1726

BY

WILLIAM BYRD

Letters and Literary Exercises, 1696-1726

Letters

PAGE

[To Edward Southwell? Fragment] 191
To Brillante 192
To the L^{D} Bordelio 194
To Panthea 196
To Facetia 197, 200
To Babbina 197
To Pulcherio 198
To Parthenissa 213
To Fidelia 214, 216, 218
To Don Altiero 220
To Irene 221
To Seignor Fanforoni 223
To Monymia 229, 232, 241
To Blousini 234
To Clarinda 236-41
To Bellamira 242
To Seignor Shrimponi 249
To my Lady C—— 251, 267
To Seignor Punchino 252
To Seignora Incognita 255
To Count Sufficienti 256
To Lady S—— 257
To Lady G—— 259
To Zenobia 261, 263, 264, 266
To Lady M—— 269
To Preciosa 270
To Vaporina 272
To Lucretia 282, 286
To Facetia in the Bath 284
To Dunella 290
To Sabina, Jan. 15, 1717 to May 6, 1718 298
To Veramour, July 1, 1717 to March 11, 1718 . . 301
To Vigilanti 321, 351
To Lord Tippararari 324, 353

PAGE
To Olibari 339
To Chevalier de Booby 356
To Cleora (1719) 361
To Belinda 361
To Cavaliero Bonboni 368
To Duke Dulchetti 368
To Minionet, May 30, 1722 to Feb. 21, 1723 . . 371
To Amasia, July 20, 1723 381
To Erranti, July 20, 1723 383
To Medusa, May 26, 1724 386
[To Maria Taylor] 386

Characters

Rampana 193
Duke Dulchetti. Argyle 203
Count Sufficiento 204
Cavaliero Slovena 205
Cavaliero Sapiente. Southwell 206
Cavaliero Bonini. Huband 208
D[R]. Glysterio 209
Altana 211
Melantha 228
Wasperini. Herbert 274
Inamorato L'Oiseaux 276
Indamira 296

Literary Pieces

A Song 202
The Ephesian Matron 224
Upon a Fart 245
A Translation of . . . Plyny 246
A Poem upon some Ladys at Tunbridge, 1700 . . 248
Epitaph on the Monument of Edward Nott, Esq. . 359

[Fragment of a letter to Edward Southwell(?)][1]

. . . Joy as well as you. I am not much convinc[t] by your hasty Recommendation of Matrimony, because I can hardly thi[nk] a man qualify'd to decide in that matter that is not out of the Fury of the first deceitfull month. I firmly believe you[r] Joys will out-live the common Term of conjugall Happiness, because the Nym[ph] [yo]u have marry'd has variety enough [to] satisfy the inconstancy of any man liveing. She comprehends all the agr[e]able qualitys of her sex and consequen[tly] will give you neither provocation [nor] excuse to go abroad for change. [And] if you'll take a single mans word for [it] you are like to meet with none of [the] cloying every-day sameness that usually gives the men such a surfeit of their [wives] Gresham Colledge[2] rubbs on at the old [. . .] in every thing except the

---

[1]One or more pages of notebook B have been lost; this fragment, which is the first page in the manuscript, is greatly mutilated. Apparently it is part of a letter from Byrd to Edward Southwell soon after the latter's marriage to Lady Elizabeth Cromwell, the Facetia of Byrd's letters, who died in 1709. Cokayne, *Complete Peerage, sub* Cromwell, states that Lady Elizabeth married Southwell Oct. 29, 1704, but the sketch of Southwell in the *Dict. Nat. Biog.* states that the marriage took place in 1703, as is also attested by Luttrell (Oct. 7, 1703), "Mr. Southwell, secretary of state in Ireland, is married to the lady Betty Cromwell, an heiress of 2000l a year." Edward Southwell wrote to Dr. Hans Sloane from Dublin, Nov. 23, 1703, "If matrimony and the sitting of the Parliament had not of late fully employed my time, I had been inexcusable, not to have imparted to you my late happiness in my marriage. I cannot forget the kind part you had in making the first step in this affair, wch is now brought to this happy Issue. Give my [*sic*] leave now to return you all due acknowledgements, & to assure you that you have 2 affectionate friends & servants in my Lady Betty & mee, who gives you her humble service" (Sloane Papers, Brit. Mus., 4039, f. 215). In her last illness, Lady Elizabeth Cromwell Southwell wrote to Hans Sloane, asking his advice and pledging herself not to betray his assistance to her regular physician, Sir Patrick Dunn (Dublin, Sept. 8, 1708, Sloane Papers, 4041, f. 200). This close intimacy of the Southwell family with Sir Hans Sloane helps to explain Byrd's friendship with him (letters of Byrd to Sloane, Sloane Papers, 4041, ff. 151, 202; 4042, f. 143; 4055, ff. 112, 367; 4058, f. 99; 4068, f. 54).

Edward Southwell was the son of Sir Robert Southwell and a friend of Byrd throughout his life. In 1703 he was Secretary of State for Ireland (*Dict. Nat. Biog.*). In his residence in London from 1717-20, Byrd frequently visited Edward Southwell though his second wife, Anne Blathwayt, daughter of William Blathwayt, had died in 1717, a year after her marriage. (Gertrude Ann Jacobsen, *William Blathwayt* [Oxford, 1932]; *A New History of Gloucestershire* [Cirencester, 1779], p. 496.)

[2]The Royal Society, of which Byrd was a member, held its meetings during this period at Gresham College.

disadvantage [it] suffers by your not being there. The [........][1] to sleep in the chair since he went, Blunder[2] do's his part to make it a [better] Dormitory than any Church in Town I wish you well out of the State-Boggs you mention; tis well known that a Prime Minister walks on very slipper[y] ground. You run the common fate o[f] great-men by being ill-spoken of tho I cant think you are like th[em] too in deserving it. I cou'd as soo[n] believe that Mr Asgile[3] will be translated or that that [*sic*] the excellent Face[tia] will not make you happy Adieu

---

TO BRILLANTE

I am as much astonisht at your being cross, as I shou'd have been at your being kind, the high opinion I have of you, make[s] the first surprizeing, as the low one I have of my self, wou'd do the last. For peace sake Madam, why do you put your self into a[ll] this fury. I'm sure you must be a Woman, by the unreasonableness of your resentment, and a marry'd woman, by your useing tho[se] the worst, that love you best. Allowing, that in the Frenzy of my passion for you, I might use a little more briskness than ordinary in my expression, yet it being with good manners, you ought to have imputed it to excess of Inclination, which dont use to create a quarrel betwixt a Lover and his Mistress. However Madam if you be determin'd to wage War upon me,

---

[1]Several lines are torn off the page.

[2]Byrd, who had been elected a member of the Royal Society in 1696, attended a meeting of the Council of the Royal Society on November 24, 1703, and this letter was apparently written shortly after that date (Maude H. Woodfin, "William Byrd and the Royal Society," *Va. Mag.*, XL, 23-35, 111-124).

John, Lord Somers (1651-1716), lord chancellor of England, was elected President of the Society Nov. 30, 1699 and held that office till 1704. He was known for his formality in bearing as well as for his learning, able use of language, judgment and discernment, courtesy and reserve (*Dict. Nat. Biog.*).

[3]John Asgill (1659-1738) whose pamphlet arguing that death was not obligatory upon Christians was burnt in 1703 by the common hangman, on the Order of the Irish House of Commons, became much involved through purchase of the forfeited estates of Lord Kenmare, whose daughter he married. He was expelled from the Irish Parliament and returned to England where he sat in the House of Commons for Bramber in 1705 but was expelled from that body in 1707 (*Dict. Nat. Biog.;* A. Boyer, *The History of Queen Anne* [1735], pp. 79-313).

for have[ing] too much fire, in contradiction to all the maxims of your Sex; I must stand upon my defence, and by my moderation show, tha[t] all my fire spends itself in love and go[od] nature, while yours breaks out into the m[ore] boisterous passions of rage peevishness and Indignation. If there be any Standers by, I submit to [*sic*] it to their judgment, whether your Warmth or mine b[e] more to be condemn'd, tho I had rather you[d] be graciously pleas'd to be determin'd by [. . .] own understanding, that so I may never [. . .] it to reproach you with [. . . .][1] the distinction I have for you, and [. . .] my self for squandering away so much [good] nature, upon a Nymph that has so little.

RAMPANA[2]

Rampana has been beholden to Nature for such materials, as with a moderate improvem[ent] wou'd make her a finisht woman. And if [it] were not for a large mixture of laziness to keep her fine Qualitys under, Envy wou'd ma[ke] her too many enimys of her own sex, and Love too many admirers of ours. Her understandi[ng] is capable of takeing the brightest polish: [but] her industry to improve her Mind, is discourag['d] by too great a dependance on the beautys of her Body. She may have reason perhaps to think, that her face has charms suffici[ent] to leave no Victory for her wit to make; [yet] she shou'd remember at least, that good senc[e] is necessary to maintain her Conquests. Her Eys have fire enough to inflame the coldest Saint: and her virtue force enough to chill the warmest Sinner. Nobody can have more good humour; but she's unwilling to shew it on all occasions, out of a mortal aversion she has of passing for a Fool. However she is complaisant and good-natur'd where she ought to yeild; but as obstinate as the Fatal Sisters where she ought not. She has so much

[1]Several lines are obliterated.

[2]See below, p. 217. Possibly Rampana was Martha Burwell, a cousin of Lucy and Frances Parke, who was courted by Governor Nicholson and Dr. Archibald Blair, and later married to Henry Armistead. In 1705-6 she was about twenty years old.

generosity, that she fancys she cant with a good grace call any thing hers, except her freinds be the better for it. She is so intirely disinterested that tis not so hard a Task, to perswade her to do other people good, as her self. She takes so little pleasure in the female Joy of being seen, that she lys abed til noon for fear of being too Visible. She prudently considers, that early risers come more within the reach of ill accidents, therefore she lys snugg to be out of harms way. She imagins no misfortune will have the confidence to come to bed to her; and she gives the Devil but a slender chance for it any where else. Abed she is sure to do no hurt: but modestly distrusts her power to avoid it when she's up. She is not apt to think much, and yet speaks better without thinking, than other Ladys do with it. However she has this constant benefit from her want of thought [that it . . .] from the Pride that [. . .] her own Excellences wou'd give her. [She . . .] forward to cultivate the Talents nature has bestow'd upon her, for the good-natur'd intention of not out-shineing other women so much as to make em uneasy. She writes enchantingly, but makes a difficulty of showing it, for fear she shou'd grow too vain upon the commendation. She has a spirit invincible to every thing but Reason, and sometimes twill hold out a great while against that. She loves the conversation of those that have sence: but dont renounce the Company of those that have none; because she has the charity to improve them when they're with her, and the pleasure of laughing at 'em when they're gone.

TO THE L^{D} BORDELIO.

Tis with the utmost regret I am oblig'd to acquaint you that I am disappointed of the dearest hopes I had in the world, the hopes of serving under your L^{p}. I promis'd my self the happiness of being in your Regiment where I might find frequent occasion of showing the infinite respect I have for you. It was that respect alone my L^{d} that ingag'd me to alter the whole course of my life upon Terms that had no temptation but the pleasure of being near your L^{p}. yet that was a charm sufficient to reconcile me to the Army wch I confess was always my aversion before you came into it. But now the Muses are to follow the camp and consequently 9 strumpets more than ordinary who can forbear being a souldier. I'm sure I cou'd not were I to pursue my own wishes. It was the excess of Inclination I had to obey your L^{p} that induc'd me [to] accept the offer you did me the honour to make me, before I had consulted my Relations. I ma[de] no question but when I let them know how much it was my desire that it wou'd be likewise theirs: but to my great mortification I have just now had an express from my Uncle[1] by which he commands me upon my obedience and the expectation I have of his future kindness not to go into the army. This bred a struggle betwixt my Duty and my ambition, & you my L^{d} that know the happiness of a good Uncle, will agree that [. . .] ought to comply with the first. The truth of it is, considering how kind mine has been to me already it would be most ungratefull, and consid[ering] how kind he may be to me hereafter it [. . .][2] make me loose my Preferment, [. . .] will not make me loose your favour. I have [not] vanity enough to imagin you will be in the least disappointed by my being thus forct from you. I know your proposal cou'd have no other motive but my Advantage, and since the unlucky situation of my Affairs makes it more for my advantage to let it alone, I hope the same generosity that mov'd your L^{p} to make the offer, will perswade you to

---

[1]Byrd probably referred to his uncle Daniel Horsmanden, brother of his mother, Mary Horsmanden Filmer Byrd, and son of Warham Horsmanden, who had lived in Virginia during the Commonwealth and was a member of the House of Burgesses and of the Council. Daniel Horsmanden, M. A., Magdalen Hall, Oxford, 1679, was rector at Purleigh in Essex. When Byrd went to England as a young boy he was under the care of this uncle for a time (Letter book of William Byrd I, Va. Hist. Soc.; *Va. Mag.*, XV, 314-317; XXIV, 354). Byrd visited this uncle and his family during his residence in England, 1715-1719, and found frequent and congenial companionship in his cousins, the children of Daniel Horsmanden, whom he saw often in London. He was especially fond of young Daniel (1694-1778) who as early as 1731 went to New York and became chief justice of that colony (Diary, 1717-1721; *Dict. Amer. Biog., sub* Horsmanden).

A very different reason for abandoning a military career was given by Byrd in the character he wrote of himself. There he declared the confinement, dependence, and barbarity of that service made him quickly withdraw. See below, p. 277.

[2]Several lines are torn.

forgive my not being able to accept of it. Besides my Lord you have many other freinds more worthy of this distinction and therefore the Interest of the service is another argument for your dispencing with me. If this change proceeded from Levity or any other reason, but indispensible duty, I shou'd not be able to beg your L^p excuse without the last confusion. But my Inclinations continue the same, and I resist [. . .] at the very time that I am oblig'd to refuse [. . .] or else I shou'd not deserve the honour of being

Your faithfull Servant.

TO PANTHEA[1]

I had the honour of your enchanting letter, and I may very justly call it enchanting, because it pleas'd me at the same time, that it refus'd the dearest of my Inclinati[ons] However I confess you are [. . .] mistr[ess] of the Art of pleaseing, and can dress up pain so delicately as to make it agreeable. But stil I cant forgive your ill-nature, tho I must commend your skil in setting it off. How can you give a man that doats on you so much uneasiness, when tis in your power to give him the most ravishing pleasure? I wou'd be glad to know whether this obstinacy of yours proceed from the love of your self, or your aversion to me. If you pretend the first, I must take the liberty Madam to assure you, you are mistaken, because tis not a kindness to ones self, but a cruelty to refuse Joy. But if you use me so unkindly from an aversion to me, then I must confess I cant pretend to so good Reasons to convert you, because tis harder to convince the Inclinations, than the understanding. But madam if an Indian Sincerity, and a heart as constant to you as pride and want of charity are to the precious Prudes,[2] be

---

[1]Though there seems no clue to the identity of Panthea, in using that name Byrd evidently had in mind Panthea, the wife of Abradas of Susa, famous as the most beautiful woman in Asia. Taken captive by Cyrus, she remained true to her husband, arrayed him for battle and when his body was recovered took her own life to be with him in death. (Xenophon, *Cyropædia,* with an English translation by Walter Miller, 2 vols. London, MCMXIV.)

[2]"precious Prudes" is in a different script, possibly another hand.

any arguments with you, then I shall live in hopes that you'll be more tractable to Your Slave.

TO FACETIA

Nobody Madam was ever more asham'd to ask for a favour than I am to ask your Ladp for a debt.[1] Tis a pain to me to demand it of you, for fear I might seem to reproach your not returning it as unaskt as you reciev'd it. Perhaps I had some reason to hope, you wou'd please to take notice of it yourself, after the several times that I have had the honour to see you. But since excess of happiness, which Im glad to see your Ladp enjoy, may make you forget such a Triffle I that am not so happy may be forgiven if I remember it. Especially if I tell you, that Im about purchasing a Post of great advantage to me, that obliges me to call in all the mony I have. Nothing madam but such a necessity as this, shou'd provoke me to speak in a Business wherein you show so much inclination to be silent. I perswade my self however, that the raiseing such a summ now you have so good a cashier, will not incommode You, if I imagin'd it wou'd, Im sure I shou'd abhor putting You either to the Inconvenience of paying the mony, or to the confusion of excuseing it: but wou'd content my self with ye glory of being a very good sufferer by the services I have endeavour'd to do Facetia, which notwithstanding the late turn of your Inclinations is an exceeding pleasure to

Your Slave

TO BABBINA

This is now the 9th day I have been blind wth an excess of Passion for the brightest of all the Fairys your self. Oh unhappy Hero that I am! What a misery t'is, that Puppys shou'd begin to see after that time and Lovers not? Sure the Gods never conferr'd so much perfection, delightfull Madam, within so small a compass. You are an abridgment

---

[1]See Introduction, p. xviii.

of Female excellence, and tho nature has drawn your dear person in little, yet she has drawn your fine qualitys in great. In that Speck of Entity she has inclos'd spirit enough to animate a machine as bulky as Mrs Ireton or the Dutch-woman.[1] With what transport have I beheld that lively spirit ready to fly away wth the clogg of china-mould that composes your delicate body. If the blast breath'd in at your nostrels, or back side after your conception had been never so little stronge[r] you must have been under a necessity of hanging a young Fellow about your alabaster neck, to keep you from being mo[unted] to the upper Regions. Dearest Madam, figure to your self that such an accid[ent] may happen stil in a windy day, and make discreet provision against it, by by [*sic*] joining to your dainty person about ten stone more of wholesome flesh and bloud, which may fix you down securely to the Earth and guard you from the fate which many of your Kindred the Pigmys have suffer'd before you, of being snatcht away by Cranes and Hurricanes. Now I must tell you precious Madam, that I find my self much about the Weight I prescrib'd to you, and if you wou'd have the goodness to use me in the capacity above mention'd I swear to you by my manhood, an oath I use only upon solemn occasions, I wou'd stick as close to you

As twineing Ivy round the bashfull Tree

Adieu

TO PULCHERIO

I dont know whether I had best address my self to you in your natural or dramatic capacity. Perhaps you may not be yet actually anointed King, but you have been proclaim'd both in Town & Country, and have put on Purple too, wch I thought plainly fore-boded Majty. so that you are already as dread a Soveraign as he at St Germain, who wants nothing

[1]The Dutch Woman was known in England for her acrobatic performances at Bartholomew Fair at the end of the seventeenth and early eighteenth centuries (E. B. Chancellor, *The Pleasure Haunts of London* [London, 1925], p. 325; J. P. Malcolm, *Anecdotes of the Manners & Customs of London* [London, 1810], II, 113). See further reference to the Dutchwoman in Byrd's "Female Creed," below, p. 00. For Byrd's account of Bartholomew Fair, see his letter to Facetia, Sept. 11, 1703, *Letters Writ to Facetia by Veramour.*

but the triffleing circumstances of a Kingdom and a Coronation.[1] Notwithstanding all this I beg leave I may treat you in a natural way, that is, as a Ramp[?] and a whoremaster &c which are Qualitys you wont lay aside so soon as Royalty. I have been as splenatick as the Major with much pride, & no mony, ever since you went a stroleing into ye Country. Our Town is almost virtuous for want of the many Ladys of Quality and fine gentlemen that have abandon'd it. Our very whores are grown chast for want of you & the rest of their good Freinds. If fasting wou'd cure the sin of Incontinence I am confident there wou'd be very little strumpetry left, for few of the poor Jades see a beef steak oftener than Dr Garth[2] fumbles with his wife that is once a fortnight. The many ill-smells we have here wou'd make a man fancy himself at Edinburgh, but that he dos not find the same disturbance between his fingers, that he wou'd there. I design to run away from all these Inconveniences: but what will that avail me since I cant run away from the greatest inconvenience of all the want of you. The Count distinguisht by the several Titles of Poetical keeping, & military set out yesterday to visit the 8th wonder of ye Peak[3] his mistress, how long he intends to keep this Lent of conversing with vertuous women I cant so readily inform you. The day before, he inquird very tenderly after the greatest of Comedia[ns] Pulcherio and told me in my ear, that he was gon down into Hampshire on purpose to entertain the

---

[1] *I. e.* James, the Old Pretender who had been proclaimed King of England by Louis XIV in 1701, when his father, James II, died in exile.

[2] Sir Samuel Garth (1661-1718) was a celebrated English physician and poet, whose poem, *The Dispensary,* published in 1699, ridiculed apothecaries and recorded the first effort to establish dispensaries for outdoor patients. He was a member of the Kit-Kat Club and his witty and ribald remarks were much quoted by his contemporaries (*Dict. Nat. Biog.*; J. W. Croker, *The Georgian Era* [London, 1834], III, 256-58).

[3] The Peak refers to the hilly region, chiefly in Derbyshire, where the bleak moors, the heights and the long deep valleys with their small streams give a scenery that is interesting in its variety and its unusual natural features. The so-called seven wonders of the Peak were well known. (See John Britton and E. W. Brayley, *The Beauties of England and Wales* [London, 1802], pp. 441 ff.; William Bray, Sketch of a Tour into Derbyshire, and M. Ferber, Oryctography of Derbyshire, in John Pinkerton, *A General Collection of the Best and Most Interesting Voyages* [Philadelphia, 1810], 336-465, 465-489.)

Queen with a Play upon her arrival at Winchester,[1] and further that the strowlers had confederated against him to petition her Maj^ty^ that he & all his Troop may be prohibited from intrenching upon their undoubted Priviledges. This [I tell] you betimes that you may be prepar'd to counterplot these invidious Competitors. In return for so kind a hint as this, I live in hopes that you'll release me from the rash agrement I made with you. I was perswaded to it in the time of Affliction when vows are commonly made, from which nice Casuists absolve the devout Christian because they seem to be in some sort extorted from him. However my conscience is more delicate & will not suffer me to break a contract tho it was provokt by pain & Physic. I own indeed that the hatred of paying too dear for dirty pleasures dos mightily corroborate my virtue. Let me have your answer to this important business by the first opportunity, for constitution presses me sore, and the tedious abstinence I have had from the dearest of all mortal amuzements adds Curiosity to my Inclination. Adieu

---

TO FACETIA.

I hope Madam this will have the good luck to find your Lad^p^ and your Fellow Travellour safe by a warm fire amongst the wonders of the Peak. I easily imagin how much you are like to contribute to the recovery of Quietissa[2] by your comfortable presence. That is a remedy so pleasant

---

[1]Queen Anne spent seventeen days at Winchester and planned to complete the unfinished palace there for a jointure house to her consort Prince George (Mocky, *Journey through England*, II, 22).

[2]See Byrd to Facetia, July 27, 1703 (?), in which he said "Prudella & Quietessa were on Tuesday last packt up in the stage coach for Derbyshire, & left ye familys of ye Tattles & the Loyters in despair" and again in his letter of August 25, "They write from Derbishire that Prudella has ever since she went down into ye Country, been in a course of Courtship, & is by this time near a worse precipice than any in ye Peak, that of matrimony." (*Letters writ to Facetia by Veramour.*)

Facetia's aunt, Mary, daughter of Thomas Cromwell, Earl of Ardglass, married William Fitz Herbert, of Tissington, member of an ancient Derbyshire family, and had several children. On her death, William Fitz Herbert married Anne, daughter of Richard Breton, of Elmsthorp, Co. Leicester, and widow of John Parker, of London, and died without male issue in 1697 (Burke, *Peerage*). In his diary for 1717-1721, Byrd repeatedly noted that he went to see Mrs. Fitz Herbert in London, usually about supper time, and ate a light

y^{t} if one cou'd secure a large dose of it, twou'd make a misfortune change its name into a Happiness. Tis ten thousand pitys you shou'd go & throw away y^{t} virtue upon Ireland, a country so disagreeable y^{t} even Toads and spiders disdaign to live in it. Tho I must be so just as to allow it one thing to boast of beyond ye greatest advantages of Eng^{d}, which is ye honour of haveing produc'd a person so extraordinary as your Lad^{p}. For that good reason I cou'd forgive that Kingdom any thing, but ye Injury of takeing you from us.

I wont pretend to tell your Lad^{p} who among all your freinds here is the chief mourner for your absence. I will only say the reproach you was pleas'd to let off upon me at my audience of Congé was wrong in every thing but ye principle from which I hope it proceeded. For I protest I had no mirth at that time but what was as superficial as Blouzina's[1] Religion, or as ye wit of y^{r} Favorite Arroganti.[2] I did laugh tis true, but then that was no more a mark of being pleas'd in me, than crying was a sign of grief in my Ld Fiddle Faddle when he lost ye best wife that ever dyd. I cant say ye best y^{t} ever liv'd.

I dont know y^{t} any body has done a very Wise thing or a very foolish one, tho most of the Parl^{t} men are in Town, since I had ye honour of seing you, and God knows nothing but those 2 extreems will entertain. As for moderate matters and ye common occurrances that happen amongst this wicked Generation I wou'd not robb the Coffee-houses and Visiting-days for fear they shou'd be left destitute of conversation.

Since therefore I am not able to furnish your Lad^{p} wth any noveltys from hence, I must intreat you to accept of an account of what I now fancy may be acting in Derbyshire. In ye first place then I imagin, that you and your happy Spouse ly abed and defy the cold til eleven a clock. What

meal with her. It seems probable that Prudella and Quietessa and Mrs. Fitz Herbert were members of the Derbyshire family into which Lady Elizabeth Cromwell's aunt had married.

[1]See below, p. 234.

[2]Byrd used the term Arroganti in his later writings to refer to Alexander Spotswood. Its reference here is not clear, though he used it in this same implication in a letter to Facetia, Sept. 4, 1703 (?), *Letters writ to Facetia.*

passes there is a mystery guarded from mortal inquisition tho not from mortal Envy. at length after much struggle you get up, and pay a Visit of compassion to ye patient Nymph that is confin'd to her chamber. She with a quiet face that nicely represents her mind bears all her misfortunes but the thoughts of your approaching journy. I can but think how much her late disaster has confirm'd the old quarrel she ever had to violent motion. While your Lad^p^ is setting snugg by her over a dish of milk-coffee, methinks I see ye active Prudella walking with a firm tred and a sincere countenance along ye room, despiseing every other fire but what is begot by stirring up the natural heat. Her conversation most certainly is level'd against that mortal sin Indifference in love, and this very moment I see her spreading out her arms with her elbows as bare as Eves backside while she was yet in Innocence, labouring with speech and motion in defence of that warm argument. Here I am maliciously interrupted in the agreable pursuit of my Imagination and have only time to honour my self with the Tytle of
Your most devoted.

A SONG[1]

Sabina with an Angels face,
By Love ordain'd for Joy,
Seems of the Syren's cruel Race,
To Charm and then destroy.

With all the arts of Look and dress,
She fans the fatal fire:
Thro Pride, mistaken oft for Grace,
She bids the Swain expire.

---

[1]These verses appear to have been written in the full tide of Byrd's wounded pride when Sabina, *i. e.* Mary Smith, favored his rival, Sir Edward Des Bouverie (see Introduction, p. xxv, and below, pp. 298 ff.). The choice of Sabina by Byrd as a name for his "dear Miss Smith" may have been inspired by Congreve's lines,

See, see, she wakes, Sabina wakes!
And now the Sun begins to rise;
Less glorious is the Morn that breaks
From his bright Beams, than her fair Eyes.

The God of Love inrag'd to see,
  The Nymph defy his flame;
Pronounc'd this merciless Decree,
  Against the haughty Dame

Let Age with double speed oretake her;
  Let Love the room of Pride supply;
And when the Fellows all forsake her,
  Let her gnaw the sheets & dy.[1]

DUKE DULCHETTI. ARGYLE[2]

Nobody was ever born with finer materialls to build up a great man. He has an infinite Fond of fire & spirit under ye manage of a most excellent understanding. Heaven has blesst him with a competent store of learning, which he has polisht and made usefull by a perfect knowledge of ye world. The university, the Camp, and many forein Countrys have had ye honour to join with Nature to make him a finisht Gentleman. Fortune has likewise lavisht her highest favours

---

[1]The last stanza is written in much larger script.

[2]John Campbell, 2d Duke of Argyle and Duke of Greenwich (1678-1743) was Byrd's patron (Byrd to Custis, London, Jan. 31, 1715/16, quoted in Custis, *Recollections of Washington,* ed. Lossing). He especially helped Byrd in his fight to retain his seat in the Council of Virginia against the opposition of Lieutenant Governor Spotswood after Argyle had himself been restored to royal favor in 1719 by appointment as lord steward of the household. (Byrd notes in his diary, Feb. 6, 1719, that Argyle had received his white staff.) When in 1719, Byrd left for Virginia he presented to the Duke of Argyle a description of Virginia.

There was a rumor in Virginia in 1720 that the Duke of Argyle had been appointed Governor of Virginia in place of the Earl of Orkney and that Byrd had been named as his Lieutenant to succeed Spotswood. Byrd at once discredited the rumor (Diary, Mar. 18, 1720).

Byrd visited the Duke of Argyle both in London and at his country place at Petersham, with especial frequency after Argyle's restoration to royal favor in 1719 (*ibid., passim,* especially Feb. through Nov. 1719). See the sketch of the Duke of Argyle in the *Dict. Nat. Biog.* Byrd's partisan character of his patron was not the universal appraisal of Argyle by his contemporaries. The Duke of Marlborough wrote his Duchess, "I cannot have a worse opinion of anybody than I have of the Duke of Argyle." (Croker, *Georgian Era,* II, 43). Swift, after having dinner with him at the Lord Treasurer's, wrote Stella, "Argyle went off at six and was in very indifferent humour as usual" (*Journal to Stella,* April 11, 1713). See also Hervey's *Memoirs,* ed. Sedgwick, I, 175.

upon him, all which happy accidents concurr to make him admir'd by every mortall but himself. He has so much sweetness in his temper, so much affability in his carriage that Envy her self cant forbear being reconcild to him. He is an enimy to nothing but villany, and that he abhorrs in all its shapes. He has not ye least complaisance for a Rascal however dignify'd or distinguisht: but has always the sincerity to salute him by his proper name. He is a firm freind, & a generous enimy. No man ever manag'd his fortune with more discretion, that had so much justice and generosity. Next to the infamy of wronging others, he abhorrs ye reflection of being wrong'd himself, so that twou'd be difficult to distinguish his Quality by his exactness in paying his debts. And amongst these he reacons every promise he makes, which he performs with so much puncto that he prevents the very demand of it. Notwithstanding he was born in Scotland & bred in France and Italy, yet he has not ye least dissimulation; nay he is even sincere when he makes love, or when he speaks of himself. He always owns his failings more frankly than he dos his virtues, tho perhaps he dont practice them so much. Indeed his military Education has enabled him to get the better of a Modesty, that with moderate wearing wou'd have stuck by him all his Life. But there are severall happy omens, that forebode those youthfull extravagances will shortly give place to ye superior honesty & good sence that shine in all his other actions.

COUNT SUFFICIENTO.[1]

He has some knowledge of books: but none at all either of himself, or the world. He has an infinite fondness for his own person without haveing any Rival but his mother. Tis pity amongst all his studys he has not lookt a little into himself, as well as he has into a great many other triffles. He really has wit: but tis overcharg'd with so much ill nature that it all sowers into railing & Slander. He ridi-

[1]The key to this character, originally written in ink, has been erased and is not decipherable. See Byrd's letter to Count Sufficienti, below, p. 256.

cul[es] every body: but with so little judgment that he commonly is more mercifull to their vices than their virtues. In this satiricall mirth he gives no quarter: but is constantly ready to sacrifice a good freind to an ill Jest. He has no more gratitude than a whore or a Parson because like them he believes every thing a man can do for him, but justly due to his merit. He has as little justice as a Quaker, and in all his accounts is very apt to place the Creditor on his own side. He has no good nature for others, because he lavishes his whole fond of kindness upon that bleak fantome himself. This blind partiality makes him appear in his own eys ye most sufficient Fop alive. Thus he fancys himself handsom in spight of the aversion of all womankind. The common strumpetry have the ingratitude to despise his weakly figure, tho he wasts the greatest part of his time and his slender income upon them. The frequent Disasters he has met with from these way-fareing Ladys, have turn'd his studys towards Physick, & so have improv'd his mind, to make him amends for the impairing of his Body. After he had thus by Physic, & which is stil worse by his own Physic, very near confounded his feeble constitution, it came into his L^{dps} prudent head to go into the army, for which he was as little qualify'd as a man wou'd be for the bar, after he had cought out half his Lungs. He has an unfortunate Itch to Poetry by which he has rym'd away the Reputation which by the help of good freinds he got by publishing of Prose. He shows as unhappy a tast in the choice of his Diversions as he do's judgment in the choice of his business; for his pleasures have always mischief in em, either to himself or to other people; by wch. he has an opportunity of discovering at once the delicacy of his relish, and the sweetness of his temper.

CAVALIERO SLOVENA[1]

He has very bright natural Parts, and by much study knows almost every thing: but the secret of being the better

[1]The key to this character, originally written in, has been erased and is undecipherable. See a reference to this character, below, p. 378.

for what he knows. However these great Talents have been unlucky to him, for he has read himself out of all Virtue, and reason'd himself out of all Religion. He is a prime Refiner of lewdness, which the poor Gentleman alas has more by Art, than nature; more by habit than constitution. He is not in the least nice in his amours: but humbly contents himself with what is most cheap, & most common, not from the fury of his appetite: but from a double complaisance to his purse and his Laziness. But this untimely thrift often leads him into the expence of paying five guineas to a surgeon to cure a mischance which one guinea cautiously laid out wou'd have prevented. And his laziness is as ill requited as his frugality, for to save the pains of a weeks pursuit of a nymph that is safe, he runs into the fatal trouble of takeing ungentle Physic for a month. He's an insupportable humorist and will conform to other people in nothing but their vices. He has not the least constancy to any thing: but dirty linnen, which he commonly wears til it drop from his back, out of a complaisance to those familiar little creatures that inhabit his person. He has so sensible a negligence in his dress, that those that have the happiness to be near him, may not only see, but even smell that he's a Philosopher. By Virtue of which character, betwixt dozeing and thinking, he often retires so deeply into himself that nature must be very importunate before he will satisfy any of her necessitys.

CAVALIERO SAPIENTE SOUTHWELL.[1]

He had the happiness of an early Virtue in spight of the Ignorance of childhood, & the vanity & madness of youth. He had from his cradle an infirm constitution, which how-

[1]In this character of Sir Robert Southwell (1635-1702), Byrd expressed his grateful admiration for the able diplomatist who had superintended his education in England and had been his patron in the Royal Society. See the sketch of Southwell in the *Dict. Nat. Biog.*; Bassett, pp. xli, xlii, xlvii; Maude H. Woodfin, "William Byrd and the Royal Society," *Va. Mag.*, XL, 23-34, 111-24. The epitaph on Byrd's tomb, in the garden at Westover, has these lines: "Being born to one of the amplest fortunes in this country he was sent early to England for his education; where under the care and instruction of

ever was made up to him by a sound & vigorous mind. But for all this, the frequent interruptions of his health had no unkind Influence on the sweetness & serenity of his temper. He had alone the secret of giveing pleasure to others, at the very moment he felt pain himself. While he was young, he was wise enough to instruct the old, and when he came to be old, he was agreable enough to please the young. All that had the honour of his conversation, confesst that he had a peculiar talent of mixing delight with information. Religion appear'd in all her charms when he was practiceing it; he had Zeal without bitterness, Devotion without hypocrisy, and charity without ostentation. His Principles were so firmly riveted that he was able to converse in a corrupt Court above 30 years, without any prejudice to his Integrity. During that whole time, he signalized his fidelity to his Prince without forfeiting his Duty to his country. And tho he was all that while a Courteour, and in eminent stations, yet he improv'd his Virtue and his understanding more abundantly than his Estate. Nobody had ever a more

---

Sir Robert Southwell, and ever favoured with his particular instructions he made a happy proficiency in polite and various learning; by means of the same noble friend he was introduced to the acquaintance of many of the first persons of that age for knowledge, wit, virtue, birth or high station, and particularly attracted a most close and bosom friendship with the learned and illustrious Charles Boyle Earl of Orrery" (see "The Westover Estate," *Harper's Magazine,* XLII, 801-910).

Byrd sent this character to Minionet in a letter of June 27, 1722, and referred to it again in a letter of July 14 (see below).

The following letter of Sir Robert Southwell to Sir Hans Sloane shows something of the close relationship between Southwell and Byrd as a young man. The letter is undated, but there is a letter of Peter Le Neve to Sir John Percival, June 24, 1701, outlining an itinerary through England in detail, and also a letter of September 1701 in which Percival wrote about his summer travels, especially in Scotland, which is possibly the trip Southwell refers to in his letter to Sloane (Hist. MSS Comm.: *Egmont MSS,* II, 196-206, 206-7). Percival, later Earl of Egmont, was born in 1683 and was thus about ten years younger than Byrd. Southwell's letter is addressed "For Dr Slone In Great Russell Street near Southampton House," and follows: "Having had many Tryalls of your Freindshipp and your acquaintance in the World being soe Generall, Lett me request you to think, where I may find a fitt Companion for my Nephew Sr. John Percivale, who is taking a progresse about England. Mr. Bird was of the mind to partake herein, as well for his owne Recreation, as to obleige me. And I had prepar'd Horses and everything for the purpose. And I was extreamly rejoyc'd in my Mind to have him. but by an accident that hath happen'd, Mr. Bird cannot now stirr from the Towne. Wherefore pray range over all your Bead-Rolls, for that your Successe herein will highly obleige Yr most affect friend and Servant Robert Southwell." (Sloane MSS, Brit. Mus. 4061, f. 38.)

powerfull knack of Education, for he knew how to infuse his own bright Qualitys into all that had the happiness of his tuition, and cou'd give Virtue so many graces, as to make it irresistable. He was so great a Master of Perswasion, that he cou'd charm people into their duty, without the harsh methods of discipline & severity. He devoted most of his time and his thoughts to the glorious & generous design of doing good, and was at once the Friend, and favorite of mankind. Whatever he undertook was forecast with so much prudence and sagacity, that he left no room for repentance. He had a mighty fond of knowledge, and was always the wiser and better for what he knew. He was so uncorrupt, so untainted with Vice and folly, that whoever was intimate with him, had the nearest prospect of Innocence, that he can ever meet with out of Paradise.

CAVALIERO BONINI. HUBAND[1]

He is a man of honour in the best sence, and is more tender of injureing others than of being injur'd himself. He possesses all the noble qualitys requisite to Freindship, and has the penetration to distinguish those that best deserve it. He has such a fond of Good nature, that he is never more happy, than when he is takeing pains to make others so. He never says a foolish thing to reflect upon himself, nor a rude thing to reflect upon another: but there's a smile and a gentleness imprinted on his whole behaviour. His

[1]Possibly Sir John Huband, who was evidently well known in the Southwell-Percival family, and therefore probably to Byrd. The following note was written by Sir John Percival on the margin of his manuscript letter to Lady Coverly, July 13, 1708: "She was a lady of great reading and fine conversation, which was altogether with learned men. She lived in the same house with Sir John Huband, but they were not married, that anyone could tell. Being asked about it she said she only offended against the Canons of the Church . . . Whatever the world thought of her she was a woman of great piety and sense." (Hist. MSS Comm., *Egmont MSS,* II, 229.)

Sir John Huband of Ipsley was created a Baronet by Charles II, Feb. 2, 1661. In 1694 Sir John Huband was elected one of the twenty-four directors of the new bank in London (Luttrell, *Brief Relation,* III, 342). He married Jane, daughter of Lord Charles Paulett, of Dowlas, Hants., and died in 1710, leaving two daughters and a son, Sir John Huband, 2d Baron of Ipsley, who married Rhoda, eldest daughter of Sir Thomas Broughton, Bart., of Broughton, co. Stafford (Burke, *Landed Gentry* [1847], I, 600).

Temper is compounded of all the tender Passions; He has love for the Ladys, pity for the distresst, forgiveness for his Enimys, and Charity for every Creature liveing. His Generosity has no other bounds than his Fortune, neither would it stop there, but for fear of intrenching upon Justice. He is mild as the spring, and kindly divides the fault from the Person in every provocation. He is angry at the crime but favorable to the criminal, and never condemns any body, til good nature it self can find no excuse for him. No wonder if all this benignity & softness in his constitution, inspire him with too strong a disposition to the fair sex. Neither is he so narrow-hearted as to love but one, but he has a boundless inclination to all, whose age dont give them a title to his veneration, rather than to his kindness. But he manages this Foible with so much dexterity & precaution that each nymph thinks herself in possession of his whole heart. No woman after she has given up the Ghost can keep a secret more faithfully than he conceals his Intrigues, so that tho tis possible he may have made some Ladys suffer in their Virtue, yet he never made them suffer in their reputation. From whence we may conclude that he takes care of their safety in this world; but leaves it to them to provide for their security in the next.

DR GLYSTERIO.[1]

He is a Colossus in figure, and much more a Wonder of the World than the Colossus at Rhodes. Nature in all her sporting, never form'd so absolute a Rarity, no not in Africa her principal magazine of monsters & Prodigys. Certainly

---

[1]While the key to this character has also been erased from the manuscript, there is evidence strongly suggestive of its reference to the popular and witty physician, Sir Samuel Garth, whose early effort at poetry in *The Dispensary* had no worthy successors. Garth's wit became legendary even before his death, and his humorous sayings were much quoted in London social and literary circles (Alexander Pope to Teresa and Martha Blount [Sept. 13, 1717], Pope's *Works,* IX, 275; Alderman John Barber to Swift, *Works* of Swift, XIX, 159; *Dict. Nat. Biog.*) Byrd noted in his Diary for April 3, 1711, "I read in the *Dispensary* to the ladies till night."

Byrd was using the term glyster in its now obsolete sense, "A contemptuous name for a medical practicioner" (*New Eng. Dict.*).

those wise men the Astrologers, never knew the stars in so whimsical a position, as when they usher'd into being this motly composition. With a very delicate understanding he says more foolish things in a day, than are said in the 4 courts of Westminster hall[1] in a term. He has a vast memory for every thing, but just for vows, promises and good turns. He is an eminent Physician at the Coffee house, a Poet at the colledge, a sloven at court, a Beau in the country, & a mad man every where. He's never so grave as at a Ball, nor so jocose as at a consultation. Nobody can behave himself with more decency at a Bawdy house, or with more lewdness in civil company. He can cure no distemper so well as the spleen: which yet he dont perform by his wit, so much as by premeditated Buffoonry. His invention is eternally in labour for extravagant, out of the way things, which by their novelty make amends for their want of nature. Thus he's a much better Physician for the well, than the sick, because by giveing mirth he may help to preserve that health, which by giveing Physic he wou'd not be able to restore. He is beholden to the Muses and not to Apollo for all his practice: but he's in a fair way to loose it by the same method he got it, by being much a better Poet than a Physician. Tho now he's disabled for that too for no sooner did the D^rs^ mony begin to gingle in his Pocket: but the muses withdrew their inspiration, & conferr'd it on some other penny less favorite that wanted bread; so that now he writes worse verses than prescriptions. He strain'd his Genius so hard with his First Essay, that like a young Courser he run himself off his wind, and has prov'd a Jade ever since. He's a notorious skimmer of the sciences, and cant spare time from his amusements in Vineager Yard,[2] to penetrate beyond the surface and terms of things. He

---

[1] *I. e.,* the Courts of King's Bench, Common Pleas, Chancery, and Exchequer. For a description of Westminster Palace or Hall in the early eighteenth century, see John Macky, *A Journey through England,* Fourth Edition (London, 1724), I, 203-7.

[2] Vinegar Yard was a narrow court leading out of Catherine Street on the south side of Drury Lane Theatre (E. Walford, *Old and New London,* III, 282).

makes huge pretensions of infidelity to his wife: but she's secure enough, for tho his conscience wou'd give him leave to be unjust to her bed, yet she knows by sad experience she may rely upon his constitution. He wou'd seem to have the utmost contempt for mony by his refuseing of fees, & makeing of Balls: but this generosity serves only to pimp for his covetousness; for so both he and Russel[1] come to have more business, and he fills at once both his purse and the Bills of Mortality.

ALTANA—[2]

Altana is none of those surprizeing Beautys, that strike at first sight, and are forgot upon the first absence. No Body can pretend to commend the brighness [*sic*] of her Eys without giveing a very dark account of his own. Corridons heart might be as safe in her Company, as with his Grand mother, til she begins to speak, and then no syren has either more charms or more cruelty. Her wit has force enough to make a man discredit the faithfull testimony of his Eys, and setts off the disadvantages of her Person, as much as a great fortune do's other harmless faces. This covers more failings than charity, it supplys teeth where they were wanting before, and contracts a wide mouth into humane shape and makes a man forget the [unhappy] Inconvenience betoken'd

---

[1]William Russel (d. 1702), was a well-known Baptist pastor, who wrote controversial pamphlets defending his theological ideas. He seems to have practised as a physician from about 1680 and described certain cures he had made in his *De Calculo Vesicæ* (1691). He lived at St. Bartholomew's Close, London. (*Dict. Nat. Biog.*)

[2]The key to this character has been erased and though there are faint traces left it has not been possible to decipher it. References to her pride and display of rank, here, and in The Female Creed, where she is called the Duchess of Altana (see below, p. 468), suggest that Byrd may have had in mind the Duchess of Monmouth, who was, according to Samuel Johnson "remarkable for inflexible perseverance in her demand to be treated as a princess" (Johnson, *Works of English Poets,* X, 427). When the Duchess of Monmouth frequented the court of the Prince of Wales around 1716 Lady Cowper declared "She had all the life and fire of youth, and it was marvellous to see that the many afflictions she had suffered had not touched her wit and good nature, but at

by that enormous feature. There's life & spirit in every thing she says, even when she's talking with her own Husband. She has a knack very different from the rest of her sex, of dressing up a great deal of good sence in very few words, & so can please the understanding, without doing Violence to the Ears. *She talks so engageingly that silence wou'd be a Vice in her, which is counted a good family-Virtue in other Ladys.* But then alas this Wit of hers, like a Lewdness in old men, appears much more powerfully in her words, than her actions. She lets it loose both upon the Present & the absent, and it carrys so terrible an Edge, that it never can touch a Reputation without wounding it. This engages her Lad^{p} in an eternal War with her own sex, as much as her Face dos with ours. She is too well acquainted with her own Ingenuity, and too little with ye rest of her caracter, from whence it happens, that the maddest of her Lovers never fancy'd finer things of her, than she fondly fancys of her self. She seems to have all sorts of sence, but common sence, and if she have that, it is, as some Ladys have husbands, wth a resolution never to be govern'd by it. She had always an intolerable itch to be admir'd, which made her ply all her parts to bewitch some unguarded swain or other into that folly and then she wou'd allow him no quarter. But she has the pain of seing all her lovers survive their passion, & blessing Diana for their deliverance. If she ever did make any man miserable it must be the forlorn wretch that marry'd her, whose golden dreams are now Vanisht, the enchantment is broke, and he finds himself in the arms of a stale Nymph, who can please but one sence, to the mortification of all the rest.

---

upwards of threescore she had both in their full perfection" (*Diary of Mary Countess Cowper* [London, 1864], p. 125).

It is possible, however, that Altana was Katherine Sedley, daughter of James II by Katherine Sedley, Countess of Dorchester. In girlhood she was known as Lady Katharine Darnley and was given by James II the rank of a duke's daughter with a limited right to bear royal arms. She married James, Earl of Anglesea, and later became the third wife of John Sheffield, Duke of Buckingham. Many stories are told of her pride and Horace Walpole declared she was "more mad with pride than any Mercer's wife in Bedlam" (Mrs. Thomson, *Memoirs of the Court and Times of King George the Second* [London], I, 121).

TO PARTHENISSA[1]

Tis a misfortune that almost stops my pulse, not to have found you all this tedious week alone. I sigh enough to blow out all the candles in the room, When I think on this disappointment, which is the more tormenting, because I cant find out whether it has happen'd by my unkind stars, or your unkind contrivance. Your cruel design of going so suddenly into the country, makes me dispair of haveing a private audience, except good nature on your side concur with strong inclination on mine. I intreat you Madam with a foolish look, and an akeing heart, the plainest symptoms of Love, to admit me into your presence. And when You find me in labour with the mighty secret, heaveing and struggleing to bring it forth, dont be so barbarous as to laugh at me. After tis out, pray let your answer be gentle for fear of reduceing me to the difficulty of chooseing which way I will go out of the World; whether by hanging or drowning, by gunpowder or poyson. You may depend upon it as much as upon your being a Woman, that my good Genius unveil'd to you the sincere sentiments of my soul. Neither is what she told you the effect of a sudden whimsical humour, but of an inveterate Inclination. It is built upon a long acquaintance, which in ten years time never laid open one imperfection in you, but Virtues more numerous than Words in other Ladys; then pray imagin how long my passion wou'd last that rests upon so strong a foundation If any swain alive can answer for his future inclinations, you may depend on mine: but for the present (which is all that a Lover can know) every Vein I have is full of love All my thoughts and all my dreams are Love, which is a stock that I believe wou'd run freely without filling as long as I live. In testimony of this weighty truth, I am ready to endow you

---

[1]Parthenissa was the title of a lengthy romance by Roger Boyle, 1st Earl of Orrery (1621-79), the first six volumes of which were published in 1654 and a complete edition, in three volumes, in 1665. No clue suggests the identity of Byrd's Parthenissa in this letter, presumably written before 1705, but it is interesting to note that Lord Chesterfield later used the name Parthenissa in referring to Patty Blount, the friend of Pope (Lord Chesterfield to Lady Suffolk, Bath, Nov. 2, 1734, *The Letters of Philip Dormer Stanhope, Earl of Chesterfield,* ed. J. Bradshaw [London, 1892], II, 743).

with all my Worldly goods, which is a proof that ought to pass in Love as well as hanging and beating out of brains. My stupid pen cant express the tender thoughts I have on this subject, therefore send out your summons for me to appear with a longing look, and a pale countenance before you. If you shou'd be so hard hearted as to refuse a forlorn wretch yet at least twill be an act of grace not to refuse me at 2^d hand. *That wou'd look as if I were unworthy not only of your Consent, but even of your denyal.* However if what I say be uneasy to you, the same respect that makes me offer it now, will make me forbear it for the time to come. For the only thing in the world I wou'd refuse to do to gain your Love, is that which wou'd make me forfeit the honour of y^r freindship. Adieu.

TO FIDELIA[1]

No courteour can gape for preferment with more impatience than I do to hear from my charming Fidelia. I wish I had a Pigeon that wou'd carry Billets doux as well as some of our Gossips both male and female do spitefull storys then shou'd I have some faint amends for your absence. I want to be inform'd of your health which I pray for at least with the same devotion I do for my own.

---

[1]Fidelia was Lucy Parke, younger daughter of Colonel Daniel Parke. This letter and those following were written apparently between Byrd's return to Virginia, August 16, 1705, following the death of his father (*Ex. Jour.*, III, 27) and his marriage to Lucy Parke on May 4, 1706 (Byrd Family Bible). That Byrd called Lucy Parke by the name Fidelia is proved by his passage in his letter to Irene (see p. 217) written from London in 1716 after his wife's death there from smallpox on Nov. 21, 1716: "I have been made happy with several of Irene's letters, and at this time stand in need of most diversion to support me under the melancholy I suffer for my dear Fidelia's absence." (G. W. P. Custis, *Recollections of Washington,* ed. Lossing, p. 30). In Mrs. Robert E. Lee's introduction to her father's recollections (*ibid.*, p. 16) she attributed a letter to Fidelia, signed Veramour, dated Williamsburg, February 4, 1705 [1705/6?], to John Custis, and as written to Frances Parke. But the style is clearly that of Byrd's letters and the names Veramour and Fidelia also argue that the letter was really from Byrd to Lucy Parke, and one of this series, not, for some reason, copied by Byrd into his notebook. It reads: "May angels guard my dearest Fidelia and deliver her safe to my arms at our next meeting; and sure they wont refuse their protection to a creature so pure and charming, that it would be easy for them to mistake her for one of themselves. If you could but believe how entirely you possess the empire of

Therefore Madam if at this distance you have any charity for me show it by takeing all imaginable care of your self. Remember the utmost felicity this Tawdry world can give, without health is as insipid as the addresses of the wooden squire with the silver spurs, which ought to recommend it in spight of all forbidden fruit which was from the beginning very mischievous to your sex. Tis above a month by Loves calendar since I had the happiness to see you; & methinks the sun loiters in his Course, and seems as loath to leave this side of the Globe as I was to leave you.[1] The nights too appear as long as if Jupiter were getting another Hercules, to rid this Country of our monsters. I tumble and toss and wou'd faign sleep, to supply those wants by imagination which you will not let me supply in substance. O how I grutch the time I am oblig'd to bannish my self from Fidelia! but I must not call it liveing When my heart is 40 miles off.[2] It will be stil a fortnight before I shall come to life again, being oblig'd to make a Visit to my Plantations, to reform some disorders there. In the mean while my Fancy will be the only happy part of my being, because that will never leave you; While all the rest of me must mourn your absence. If you have any good nature write to Your

---

my heart, you would easily credit me, when I tell you, that I can neither think nor so much as dream of any other subject than the enchanting Fidelia. You will do me wrong if you suspect that there ever was a man created that loved with more tenderness and sincerity than I do, and I should do you wrong if I could imagine there ever was a nymph that deserved it better than you. Take this for granted, and then fancy how uneasy I am like to be under the unhappiness of your absence. Figure to yourself what tumults there will arise in my blood, what a fluttering of the spirits, what a disorder of the pulse, what passionate wishes, what absence of thought, and what crowding of sighs, and then imageine how unfit I shall be for business; but returning to the dear cause of my uneasiness: O the torture of six months' expectation! If it must be so long and necessity will till then interpose betwixt you and my inclinations, I must submit, though it be as unwillingly as pride submits to superior virtue, or envy to superior success. Pray think of me, and believe that Veramour is entirely and eternally yours. Adieu. I beg you write as soon as you receive this, and commit your letter to the same trusty hand that brings you this."

[1]This suggests that this letter was written around the time of the autumn equinox in 1705.

[2]Jane Ludwell Parke, daughter of Philip Ludwell and wife of Daniel Parke, lived with her two daughters, Frances and Lucy, at the Parke home on Queens Creek during her husband's absence abroad. (Jane Parke to Daniel Parke, July 12, 1705, MS, Va. Hist. Soc). She died in 1708 at Green Spring, the home of her brother Philip Ludwell (Ludwell to John Custis, Nov. (?) 11, 1708, MS, Va. Hist. Soc.).

distressed Veramour[1] who loves you better than any pamper'd Priest can love himself

Adieu

Pray give your Sister[2] as many Kisses as there are lyes told at Court in a year and I will thankfully repay you wth Interest.

TO FIDELIA

How cou'd my dearest Fidelia counterfeit Indifference so perfectly on Sunday last; that even a Lovers eye which is apt to see every thing it hopes for, cou'd not discern ye least symptomes of Inclination? You must either be mistress of very little love or else of very much disguise. If I cou'd believe ye first, I were undone; or if the last, I shou'd be jealous, that ye same disguise that taught you to act indifference might likewise instruct you to act Love. But I have one expedient to make my self easy in this case, which is, to conclude even against the authority of an old saying, that you have at the same time abundance of tenderness & abundance of discretion.

Nothing but a Lovers magnifying fancy can concieve the horrible distress I was in from what you told me on Saturday night. No tender-hearted Widdow was ever in so much pain at the loss of a first husband, or which is stil worse, at the disappointment of a second, as I was at that unexpected story; especially when I mistrusted that you expresst your self with too little concern. And I should have sigh'd away my very soul for excess of grief, had you not reviv'd me with vows that I believe as firm as Truth it self, and which I depend upon as much, as Lustabunda[3] dos on her own

---

[1]Byrd called himself Veramour consistently in his letters to Facetia, Fidelia, Monymia, or Sabina.

[2]Frances Parke was married to John Custis some time after August 25, 1705. Daniel Parke wrote from London on that date to the elder John Custis giving his permission for the marriage (Custis, *Recollections,* p. 16).

[3]Perhaps Frances Parke, whose marriage probably occurred sometime in the autumn of 1705 between the date of the preceding letter to Fidelia and this one. The marriage was unhappy, the epitaph on the tomb of John Custis declaring that he died "Aged 71 Years and Yet Lived But Seven Years, which was the Space of Time he Kept A Bachelor's Home At Arlington" (Custis, *Recollections,* pp. 16-17; for portrait of Frances Parke Custis, who died March 14, 1715, see *Va. Mag.,* XXXVI, 217; also *Va. Hist. Soc. Coll.,* XI, 99).

confidences, or upon the humble spirit of her husband. After you had the goodness to give me that cordial, my bloud began to circulate and my pulse to beat, and I am as much at rest as is possible at this cruel distance from my Inclinations.

The messenger that has the honour of waiting on you with this, is to return on munday next, and I flatter my self that you will make him welcome to me by appointing him the Bearer of one of yours. Pray Dear Fidelia write a volume, with the firm belief, that every word will be as precious to me, as the comfortable Yes is to a patient Lover, after a courtship as tedious as the siege of Troy.

I have sent your charity to Kiquotan;[1] I wont call it mine, because tis oweing to vour Good-nature. Were it possible my Passion for you cou'd be capable of increase, I shou'd love you better for your kindness to the distresst

I have no encouragement to send my tender Complements to Irene[2] & Rampana[3] now because they wou'd not accept of 'em before. But I suppose they refus'd my Kisses, because they were too few, and therefore this time I will be more liberal, and beg leave to present 'em with as many as

---

[1]The Kecoughtan Indians had a village at the entrance from the Atlantic into James River, whose advantage as a site was early recognized by the white settlers. They quickly made a settlement there and called it Kecoughtan, though that name gradually gave place to Hampton, as it is known to-day (M. L. Starkey, *The First Plantation* [Hampton, Va., 1936]). Sailors on ships anchored there were frequently in distress from various causes, and Byrd may refer to some such need; the records of the colony give no account of any major calamity there at this time.

[2]After the death of his wife Byrd wrote a warm friendly letter to Irene, beginning "I have been made happy with several of Irene's letters, and at this time stand in need of most diversion to support me under the melancholy I suffer for my dear Fidelia's absence. I fear you are too busy in copying after the wise women that Solomon describes, to spend much of your time upon *how do ye's.*" (Custis, *Recollections,* pp. 30-31; this letter, including some Parke-Custis-Byrd letters from Arlington have been ascribed by Mrs. Lee to 1716, which is possibly a confusion resulting from the change in calendar; since Lucy Parke Byrd died in London Nov. 21, 1716, it is clear that the news of her death could not have reached Virginia and a response have arrived in London before the end of 1716.) Byrd seems to have been consistent in using the same fictitious name for the same real person and the Irene of the text and of the 1717 letter was doubtless the same person. It is significant that Byrd in the three known portions of the shorthand diary always referred to persons by their own names, even when he was using fictitious names for them simultaneously in his letters and literary efforts.

[3]See character of Rampana, above, p. 193.

they wou'd bestow upon their own Heros, if they might act without that Reserve which Prudery & Custome impose upon the Ladys. If you will deliver this present, I will pay y^u with interest upon Interest.

Adieu.

TO FIDELIA.

What wou'd some Lovers give for this lucky occasion of beginning a Billet doux! The moment I begin to write, I am entertain'd with the cooing of 2 amorous Turtles. Were I capable of understanding their Language, as well as a certain Philosopher[1] did once upon a time, I wou'd be their Interpreter, and tell you a long story of the tender reproaches they make to one another. But tho I know as little of what these Lovers say, as some Translaters do of what their Authors write, yet like them I venture to guess at their meaning. They talk of nothing but the dearest of all subjects Love, and abound with expressions of tenderness to one another. One complains of too much coldness in her mate, and of the huge inequality of their passions. Another is full of reproaches to his Mistress, for discovering too much distinction to his Rival. A Third tells his fears, least the summer shou'd end too soon, and too hastily conclude the intrigue. Another again like an unreasonable Woman that has bin twice marry'd, is continually upbraiding her last Gallant, with the exceeding kindness of her first. With such tender moans as these they spend their happy days, & reconcile all their murmuring Quarrels with cooing, and billing.

I cant forbear envying these innocent Lovers for the blessing they injoy of being always together; while I, poor I must lament the want of my dear, dear Turtle for many days. Pray have the goodness to help me bear this misfortune, by all ye instances of kindness, you can show; by gracious looks, and gracious actions when I am with you, by

[1]Possibly the reference is to Apollonius of Tyana, who, according to Philostratus, learned after the manner of the Arabs to understand the language of birds, who acquired this art by feeding themselves on the heart or the liver of serpents (Philostratus, *The Life of Apollonius of Tyana,* trans. F. C. Conybeare [London, 1910], I, 57).

tender thoughts and tender Letters when I am from you. Such expressions of favour on your side, and a good stock of patience and forbearance on mine, may perhaps enable me to out-live ye uneasiness of our separation.

I had the honour to ly at Irene's Pallace in my passage hither, where I met with a certain Don Quixot who once wou'd have incounter'd any Windmil or Rattle snake to do you service. Neither the delights of black water swamp,[1] nor the charms of 2 succeeding Mistresses, (wch took possession of his heart within a month of each other) have been sufficient to blot you out of his Inclinations. He remember'd you devoutly in his cups, & with up-cast eys toasted you notwithstanding all your frowns, and in spight of the triumphs of a more successfull Rival. Seignour Carotti was graciously pleas'd to call me Cosen p advance, and Peakamira by the help of some violence, made a shift to squeaze out a dark smile upon me.

The Squire that was my last Ambassadour to you is lately come from Glocester in dispair. His sawcy Nymph reciev'd him with negative Looks, and pronounct sentence of everlasting banishment upon him. Alas distressed swain! I wonder in his return home, he did not meet with a convenient Tree to his likeing, to put an end to his misfortunes. But now I think on't, he cant endure hanging, because they say Judas hang'd himself, who was treacherous, and so not

---

[1]Lands along the Blackwater River had not been opened for settlement until after the treaty of 1677 which confined the tributary Indians to definitely surveyed reservations. Very large entries were made for land on the south side of Blackwater River in that part of Charles City County which in 1703 became Prince George, and in 1690 an Order in Council suspended further surveys. The question of taking up the lands along the Blackwater was an issue for the next twenty years or more (Fairfax Harrison, *Virginia Land Grants* [Richmond, 1925], pp. 34-40). Byrd's father had, as auditor, made a report on the grants of land on the south side of Blackwater in 1703 (Sainsbury Transcripts), and in 1707 Colonel Hill appeared before the Board of Trade to testify that there had been no irregular proceedings in taking up and patenting lands in Virginia (*Journal*, Board of Trade, I, 321). But the Board was not satisfied and in June 1707 instructed Colonel Hunter when going to Virginia to succeed the late Governor Nott to submit to the Board a list of all patents signed and pending, with all details of acreage and form of grant and "an exact survey of the number of acres and a plot of all lands on the south side of Blackwater Swamp and Pamunkey Neck (*ibid.*, I, 385). The capture of Hunter en route to Virginia by a French privateer left the matter of Blackwater lands for his successor to deal with.

to be follow'd by a faithfull Lover. Neither can he bear the thoughts of drowning (he is so very nice) because water [. . .] being counted a fickle Element cannot consist with his mighty constancy. What kind of death he intends to choose, is yet a secret: but if he'll vouchsafe to take my advice he shall e'en dye of that distemper that kill'd the Patriarch, old Age.

Neither do I believe that Sr Fragrant Jessamin has succeeded better in that savage Ladys favour, tho it must be confesst, that he bears his distresses with abundance of solid Philosophy, and wears the same insipid satisfaction in his Face, that he us'd to show. Irene cou'd have instructed him to charm his Mistress infallibly; if he cou'd but prevail with her to whisper a secret in his Ear, she wou'd be smitten as sure as she has a nose, from whence Love wou'd mount into the braine, and from thence descend into her heart.

Thus my dear Fidelia I have given you an account of the state of Love amongst other People. I need not tell you how throughly I feel it my self, because I have mention'd it before, and fear least the repetition of it shou'd prove sickly & mawkish to your stomach. However pray do me the justice to believe, that as those people have most honesty, most virtue, & most courage, that say least of it, so I have the most tender passion in the world for you, tho perhaps I dont stuff my letters, with those fond flourishes, with which the common herd of Lovers spoil a great deal of Paper. But I leave my actions to speak for me, which are always the best vouchers in ye world, and which will always convince you, that I am faithfully and intirely your

Veramour.

TO DON ALTIERO.[1]

Since my arrival in this country, I have had the honour to be acquainted with your Daughters, and was infinitely surpriz'd, to find young Ladys so well quallify'd in Virginia.

[1]In the margin is written "ditto below"—*i. e.* the letter to Seignor Fanforoni, p. 223. The two letters are nearly identical. That to Don Altiero may have been and that to Seignor Fanforoni clearly was addressed to Daniel Parke, who in September 1705 was preparing to leave London to take up his duties as Captain

This surprize was soon improv'd into a Passion for the youngest, for whome I have all ye respect & tenderness in the World. However I think it my duty to intreat your approbation, before I proceed to give her the last testimony of my affection. and the young Lady her self, whatever she may determine by your consent, will agree to nothing without it, If you can entertain a favourable opinion of my Person, I dont question, but my fortune may be sufficient to make her happy, especially after it has bin assisted by your Generosity. If you will vouchsafe to approve of this undertaking, I shall endeavour to recommend my self by all the dutifull regards to your self and all the marks of kindness to your Daughter. No body knows better than your self, how impatient Lovers are, & therefore I hope, you will have the goodness to be as speedy as possible in your determination which I passionately beg may be in favour of

Yours.

TO IRENE

I will never pass for a Prophet, if this do not find you, with your head leaning on your elbow, & offering now & then a tender sigh for the absence of your Torismond.[1]

General and Chief Governor of all the Leeward Islands (Luttrell, *Brief Relation,* Sept. 13, 1705). Since in the later letter Byrd calls him "your Excellency," the letter must fall in date between Parke's appointment as Governor and Byrd's marriage (May 4, 1706) to Lucy Parke. "That sparkish gentleman," Colonel Parke, had left his wife and daughters behind when he went to England about 1697. After various political mishaps in France and in England, he served in Marlborough's campaigns, and as his aide-de-camp brought the news, August 1704, of the glorious victory of Blenheim to the Duchess of Marlborough and to Queen Anne. In spite of the rumor in London that the Queen had promised him the governorship of Virginia (Luttrell, Aug. 24, 1704), he was given the appointment to the Leeward Islands. There, on Dec. 10, 1710, he met his death at the hands of an incensed people, outraged by his misrule and libertine ways. For Parke's career, see *Va. Hist. Port.*; *Va. Mag.*, XX, 372-76; Trevelyan, *England under Queen Anne,* I, 391-97; George French, *The History of Col. Parke's Administration* (London, 1717).

Colonel Parke consented to Byrd's marriage to his daughter and in the letter promised to give her £1000 on her marriage. This sum was among Parke's many debts at his death (John Custis to Byrd, 1725, Custis Letter Book, Library of Congress).

[1]Torrismond, son of Sancho, the deposed King, believing himself son of Raymond, is the lover of Leonora, queen of Aragon, in Dryden's *The Spanish Friar.* Torrismond described himself "as a man abandoned o'er To an eternal lethargy of love."

But courage dear Irene, the time is now approaching, when the happy swain will come & cure your expectation. The Sun wont have got far into the Bull,[1] before, like 2 innocent Turtles, you will be cooing & billing on the chaise d'amitié just within your closet. Methinks I see the loveing pair, with folded arms, and balmy Lips, intercepting the soft accents of my dear, & my soule, which wou'd feign force a passage, but in vain. In the heat of this action I fancy I hear poor Irenes murmur at her mate for stopping her breath. While these gentle feats are performing in ye closet, the impatient Rampana's mouth waters in the chamber, & with a stretch, and an amorous yawn, wishes her knight errand crowded up with her in ye other closet. All this I see with ye eyes of Imagination, which like other lyers, now and then speaks truth when it is not its own case. I foresee that I shall be threaten'd with drawing & quartering, for presume-ing to make such odious discoverys: but I comfort my self with the firm resolution, of suffering any thing for the truth, & shall dare to see your face with more intrepidity, than your guilt will suffer you to see mine.

How transported shou'd I be if Irene shou'd get a robust constitution by my advice of plungeing into cold water! For then I shou'd not only have the pleasure of seeing her in perfect health, but likewise have the comfortable conscience of haveing been ye instrument of so great a blessing to ye world. The cold Bath will infallibly make you as much proof ag^st^ catching Cold, as Grace is against Temptation. Twill prevent the attacks both of ague & feaver, and make you as chearful as a mocking-Bird. Twill cure the Head-ach more effectually, than Infidelity dos Love, and give you a ruddiness of complection that will make it dangerous to see you. If these advantages be not sufficient to recommend this cleanly Remedy, I shall begin to think your good sence is fallen into such generous hands, that you choose to do every one good by it rather than your self. But then you must go in fasting, and stay in ye water 2 minutes, and not fail to

[1] *I. e.* Taurus, the second sign of the zodiac in the spring season.

hold your head under, as long as you can, both at going in, and comeing out. If you'll please to endure this, I will be answerable for the consequences. This will do you a hundred times more service, than the spirits, & other slops, which you take, tho they only serve to destroy your constitution.

Pray bestow my kind salutes upon Rampana, & tho the doings she was speaking of at my comeing away, were not extraordinary; yet tell her I wish the right person may present her with those that are. May angels guard y[e] excellent Irene, & make her always happy Adieu.

TO SEIGNOR FANFORONI[1]

Since my arrival in this Country I have had the honour to be acquainted with your Daughters, and was infinitely surpriz'd to find young Ladys with their accomplishments in Virginia. This surprize was soon improv'd into a Passion for the youngest for whom I have all the respect and tenderness in the world. However I think it my duty to intreat your approbation before I proceed to give her the last testimony of my affection. And the Young Lady her self whatever she may determine by your consent will agree to nothing without it. If you can entertain a favourable opinion of my person, I dont question but my fortune may be sufficient to make her happy, especially after it has been assisted by your Bounty. If you shall vouchsafe to approve of this undertakeing I shall indeavour to recommend my self by all the dutifull Regards to your Exc[y] and all the marks of kindness to your Daughter. Nobody knows better than your self how impatient Lovers are, and for that reason I hope youll be as speedy as possible in your determination which I passionately beg may be in favour of

Your &c.

---

[1]See above, p. 220.

THE EPHESIAN MATRON.[1]

At Ephesus there once liv'd a Lady so celebrated for discretion that she was the Envy of her own sex, and the Wonder of ours. Her Conduct was so very nice, that no Beau had vanity enough to fancy her in love with him, nor any Prude malice enough to blast her character. But alas all this mighty Innocence cou'd not guard her from the misfortune of looseing her Husband. This threw her into all the Romantique Excesses of grief. She beat her faithfull breast, & tore her hair after a most outragious manner; and such a floud of tears issu'd from her Eys, that there was no moisture left for any other Evacuation .... No body cou'd disswade her from attending the Herse to y[e] Place where her husband was to be bury'd, neither did she stop there, but descended likewise into y[e] vault, where she spent whole nights & days in weeping over the insensible Remains. She acted this tragical part so long, til she ran the double hazard of her life by grief, and hunger. And all the intreatys of her freinds were insufficient to perswade her back to her house. She continu'd in that dark abode several days to the admiration of all that heard her story.

She had no soule with her but one trusty maid, that had the complaisance to cry & starve with her mistress. It was

---

[1]This translation of the story of the Ephesian Matron from the *Satyricon* of Petronius was made evidently by Byrd. It is a free translation with effort at literary effect (cf. *Petronius,* with an English translation by Michael Heseltine [London, 1916], pp. 228-35). Byrd noted in his diary (1712, Mar. 13 ff. and May 28 ff.) that he was reading Latin in Petronius.

This story was older than the time of Petronius and appeared in varying forms in the literature of different peoples, including the Chinese. It is the accepted specimen of a Milesian tale. Various translations of the Satyricon, which was literature especially congenial to the tastes of Byrd's period (see *The Spectator,* No. 11), were published in 1694, 1708, 1710, 1713, 1714 (*Cambridge Bibl. of Eng. Lit.*, II, 767).

When Lord Hervey, whose memoirs reveal the age in many of its aspects, characterized a speech of Lord Chesterfield of 1737 in the House of Commons he said it was full of wit and genteel satire and in "the most polished, classical style that the Petronius of any time ever wrote" (Hervey, *Memoirs,* ed. Sedgwick, III, 738-9).

See also W. S. Teuffel, *A History of Roman Literature,* trans. W. Wagner (London, 1873), II, 88-92; Evan T. Sage, "The Text Tradition of Petronius," *American Journal of Philology,* I, 21-39.

her business to dress the melancholey Lamp, which by its gloomy flame seem'd to sympathize with the sad occasion. This story was the standing jest of the ill-natur'd Town, and serv'd up in all companys. The Ladys left off talking of ribbans & Reputations, & the fopps of the favours of their mistresses, for this new subject. Some ridicul'd it as an Extravagance, others as an affectation: but the sages and the Prudes blason'd it as a shineing Instance of conjugall affection.

It happen'd luckily about that time that several criminals were executed near the scene where this Tragedy was acting; And a sentinell was set to guard the Bodys from being stole away by their Relations. He was a handsome young fellow with a nose something long and very broad shoulders, that might recommend y[e] rest of his Person to a distressed Widdow. While he was takeing a melancholly turn about midnight, he chanc't to cast his eye towards the Vault, where he spy'd the glimmering light. He instantly directed his steps that way, and with a martial assurance made bold to interrupt the Ladys sorrow, with this tender address. I percieve Madam by this example of mortality that you are some disconsolate Relict, murmuring against Providence for the death of a kind husband. But let a stranger intreat you, to forbear such intemperate sallys of grief, that will injure both your health and your beauty. Alas these tears are thrown away upon an insensible corps, that cannot return your kindness. Such melting sighs wou'd make the liveing happy, but are useless to the dead. E'er long we shall all dye, but in the mean while let us enjoy every Inch of that short span we have to live. A thousand other feeling things he said, with a grace that was irresistable. However she was not so errant a Widdow as to yield to his first attaque: but rav'd on a while with all the marks of distraction. She goar'd her tender skin in a hundred places, & with rolling Eys and dishievell'd hair made him no answer but with shrieks and Lamentations.

This ill success wou'd have discourag'd any one but a man of War, however he wou'd not give ground, but renew'd his attacque with all the Arguments that Love and Pity cou'd furnish. He rais'd her up from the coffin on w[ch] she was prostrate, and wipt the tears gently from her cheaks. His sighs kept exact time with hers and when she call'd on Death to have compassion on her Grief he call'd on her to have pity on his Love. And at last when he cou'd not gain upon her grief, he try'd what impression [he] cou'd make upon her hunger. For which purpose hav[ein]g open'd his snapsack he besought her to take part of his [ho]mely supper, to recruit the spirits she had lost by [her] long fasting. The maid, who was only a mourner for company, began to lick her lips, at that seasonable offer. Her Eys water'd now no more, but her mouth, neither cou'd decency hold her from falling to, before her Mistress. By the strength of that refreshment she join'd forces with the Cavalier to bring the stubborn Widdow to reason. For Heaven's sake, dear Madam, said she dont give your self over to this out-ragious passion. To what purpose will you do your self so much injury, & your departed Lord no good? He is now happy with the immortal Angels, and why shou'd not you endeavour to be so with mortal men? He cannot hear your crys, & if he cou'd, they wou'd do him no service. Tis in vain to struggle with Destiny who is deaf to all our prayers. Remember that a liveing Gallant is better than a dead Husband. One is warm vigorous flesh and bloud, and the other cold, insensible dust & ashes—of no manner of use to a Woman of two and twenty. Why shou'd you be deaf when you are desir'd to live, and why should you be coy when you are courted to be happy?

First the Lady had the patience to hear these remonstrances and afterwards the good nature to be perswaded by them. With abundance of reluctance therefore she yeilded to the importunity of her 2 councellours, and vouchsaf'd to partake of the Repast; and that her comfort might be compleat, she drank 2 or 3 bumpers to the pious memory of the Deceas'd. This hearty chear rais'd the Widdows good humour so high, that the Hero had not half the trouble to perswade her to love, as before he had to perswade her to live. Neither was her honour half so impregnable as her grief: but she surrender'd her heart and her Person at the first summons.

T'was astonishing to see the scene so intirely chang'd, For the melancholly creature that before was ready to expire upon her husbands corps was now expireing in her Lovers arms. nay she carry'd the jest so far, as to give the Gentleman the last testimony of her love upon the very coffin that held the dead Body.

This wonderfull Intrigue continu'd three days til the Warrier had spent all his pay and his Credit upon the most obligeing mistress that ever was. Neither was this all, for he run the hazzard of his life for her dear sake. For it fell out while he was one night snoaring in her arms, the father of one of the Criminals improv'd so happy an occasion, by takeing down his sons body from the Cross and burying it. The maid was the first that discover'd this misfortune, & instantly brought notice of it. The souldier was confounded at the news, and drawing his sword was upon the point of executeing Justice on himself, to be before hand with y[e] court marshal. However he was not so hasty, but in good manners first took leave of his kind Widdow, and conjur'd her to remember him with as much concern at least as she did her husband.

The Poor Lady full of amazement threw her twineing arms about his neck, and with a thousand tender Intreatys besought him to live for her sake, since she had liv'd for his. He seem'd resolv'd at first, but on her request he vouchsaf'd to do himself no harm. When that point was gain'd, the next was to consider what were the properest measures to be taken on so important an occasion. After some debate, the Pious Widdow bethought herself of an Expedient, that wou'd secure her Gallant from danger. Tis but hanging up my dear husbands body, said she, in the room of that which is taken down, and all will be safe again. This prudent advice was approv'd of by y[e] whole Junto, & instantly put in execution, to the everlasting praise of her that gave it.

MELANTHA[1]

Melantha had a delicacy of Person which pleas'd every body, but an awkward tactless Husband. Her Shape was so exact that no Dress cou'd give it the least advantage. Her complexion disgract the brightest coulours of the painter, and appear'd guiltless of all art, by being above it. Her features were gracefully put together, and taken to pieces were full of the neatest proportion. She had so much sweetness, and so much Innocence in her look, that she at the same moment both tempted Vice and forbid it. She had a gayity in her humour, that wou'd shine out thro the most touching misfortunes. There was so much freedome, and yet so much decency in her Carriage, that Envy her self cou'd neither tax her with too much Pride, or too much Liberty. There was a certain Dolce piquante in her Conversation that pleas'd all but Wounded none. With these and a thousand other charms, she enchanted all the men, without the least intention in her, or the least hopes in them. Her Virtue was a Guard invincible, both against the addresses of the most accomplisht Lover, and the provocations of the most ridiculous Husband; The most engageing Cavalier cou'd never corrupt it, nor the spightfullest Prude blast it. But alas! these glorious qualitys were too heavenly to continue long for Earth. Perfection like Lightening only

---

[1]Melantha was Mary, daughter and sole heir of Sir Henry Calverley, Knight, of Ayerholme in the bishopric of Durham and his wife, Mary, daughter of Sir Henry Thompson of Escrick. She married in Westminster Abbey in April 1696, Bennet Sherard, Baron Sherard of Leitrim (1676-1732). (Chester, *Registers of Westminster Abbey,* p. 33.) Her husband succeeded to the peerage in 1699, was created Baron of Harborough in the county of Leicester in 1714 and Viscount Sherard of Stapleford in the County of Leicester and Earl of Harborough in 1718. Lady Sherard died May 20, 1702 and was buried in Leicestershire. Her only child, "Bennet Henry" was born in April, 1702 and died in August 1702 (Cokayne, *Peerage, sub* Harborough; Burke, *Peerage,* under Sherard; Luttrell, V, 178). While in Virginia in 1720 and alone at Westover, Byrd entertained himself by reading over some of Lady Sherard's old letters (Diary, July 23, 1720).

According to Cokayne, Godfrey Kneller painted the portrait of "the Honble Mrs. Sherard," as Mary Calverley Sherard was known before her husband succeeded to the peerage and while he was a member of Parliament from Rutlandshire. There is a mezzotint engraving of Kneller's portrait (J. C. Smith, *British Mezzotinto Portraits* [London, 1884], III, 1219).

dazzles the World for a moment & then shuts in above ye clouds.

When nature did Melantha form
  She cull'd the finest Clay,
And then in Edens limpid Streams
  She wast the Dirt away.

She wrought a figure so divine,
  So fit for Heav'nly fire,
The Cherubs strove with rival zeal
  Which shou'd this shape inspire.

They well foresee the hapless fate
  That shou'd this Birth attend,
Yet for so spotless flesh and bloud
  They cou'd their bliss suspend.

Zakael born of purest Light
  Forsook eternal day,
And darted thro th' etherial space
  To inform the shineing clay

No wonder then if all the charms
  The gazeing world e'er see,
And all the graces of your sex
  Were neatly join'd in Thee

Nor is it strange malignant stars
  Shou'd hasten on your doom,
Divinity is only seen in glimpse
  And flowers fall off in bloom[1]

TO MONYMIA[2]

The character you give of your self shows a great deal of humility which is a shineing Virtue that setts off all the rest. It is as rarely found pure and unaffected in your sex as true

---

[1]Compare these verses with those on Mrs. H—— in *Tunbrigalia* (1719), pp. 67-68, which also may have been written by Byrd.

[2]Monymia was the heroine in the oft-produced tragedy, *The Orphan,* by Thomas Otway. It was very popular with London audiences and Byrd had had ample opportunity to see it. In his *History of Eighteenth Century Litera-*

and sedate courage is among the men. The Picture you have drawn of your self resembles you very much but is as ill a likeness as Major Creed[1] is of his sister, or as good breeding in a Husband is of sincere Love. I am sorry to see it under your hand, that you can remember scandal longer than a sermon; for that shows that you had rather hear those things which make others worse than they are, than that which shou'd make you better. The next stroke is that you prefer the man that Flatters you to him that is sincere. How great a weakness that is good manners forbids me to tell you: but you may find it out by compareing both those qualitys. Flattery ever includes an Untruth, either by giveing to you fine qualitys that you have not, or else by magnifying those you have. The Flatterer has always some base design in view, and intends to make an advantage by the imposition. He must have a mean opinion of your understanding to think he can perswade you to believe, what good sence must need tell you is a cheat. He must fancy you a Vain silly creature, that will instantly swallow the hook, when tis baited with commendation. All these wicked things are imply'd in the notion of Flattery, and therefore ought to render it as detestable to you as the small pox or Leprosy wou'd be to Her that values her self upon the beauty of her Face. But on the other hand sincerity is a generous and noble Virtue, dareing to speak the Truth tho at the hazzard

---

ture (New York, 1920), Edmund Gosse said "Over the character of Monimia probably more tears have been shed than over that of any stage heroine." Left an orphan, she was under the care of Acasto, whose sons Castalio and Polydore loved her. Married to Castalio she was innocently the victim of Polydore. Her tragedy became the synonym for suffering innocence.

There is a possibility that Monymia referred to by Byrd was Sophia, daughter of Emanuel Scrope Howe (see *Dict. Nat. Biog.*; Lewis Melville, *Lady Suffolk and Her Circle* [Boston, 1924], pp. 52-56), who was maid of honor to the Princess of Wales, later Queen Caroline, and whose intrigue with Anthony Lowther and subsequent death in 1726 are frequently mentioned in the society scandal of the period. Sophia Howe was the heroine of Lord Hervey's poem "Monimia to Philocles," (Countess of Suffolk's *Letters,* I, 35-6).

[1]Major Richard Creed, eldest of eleven children of John Creed (see Pepys) and Elizabeth Creed, philanthropist, was killed at Blenheim. He was buried at Tichmarsh church, where a cenotaph was erected to his memory of the same design as that in the south aisle of Westminster Abbey. Through his mother he was related to Dryden and to Pepys. The sister referred to may have been Elizabeth, who married a Mr. Stuart (*Dict. Nat. Biog., sub* Elizabeth and Major Richard Creed).

of looseing ye good opinion of those that hear it. It has no other end but the advantage of the Party to whom tis directed, disclaiming utterly all selfishness and private interest. Now for all this is it possible that the charming Monymia shou'd choose to be flatter'd rather than dealt with uprightly, and rather have to do with a Villain, than a man of honour? I wish you dont discover in your heart too large a share of vanity, because give me leave to tell you, Whoever loves that other people shou'd flatter them, seldom forget to flatter themselves. It is as nice a distinction between Vanity, and pride (of which last you think your self free) as it is between envy and ill-nature, so that if you are tainted with one, it needs abundance of art to clear your self of the other. However tis my opinion that you have too much pride, if you have more than suffices to keep you clean and honest. You artfully endeavour to shift off the imputation of Inconstancy and ill-nature, by saying that you possess as little of those qualitys as you do of Wit. But that fetch will by no means clear you of those imperfections: but is rather a down-right pleading guilty. For all that have the happiness to know you, must grant that you have a great deal of agreable wit, or else theyll show they have very little themselves. And so by a consequence of your own makeing, you must be both ill natur'd and inconstant. Thus Monymia you are not like to be a gainer by that modesty, by the help of which you get two ill qualitys by disclaiming one. I am sorry to find by your own confession that you are so narrow hearted as to be capable of entertaining a Freindship with no more than one person. Freindship is a discreet considerate passion grounded upon reason, and is only a warm esteem of any person that is master of certain good qualitys that hit your own humour. Now that esteem may be for several as well as for one because several may happen to possess such qualitys. But I suppose when Monymia speaks of Freindship she modestly means that high-flown boisterous freindship which in plainer English is call'd Love. That I must feelingly confess, like Empire will admit of no rival or division. Our Facultys are too much limited to support 2 extreem passions at the same time, and as the

World gos very few can come up to one in a due exaltation. It requires a great many good qualitys to be truly and generously in love, and a fool is no more capable of it, than he is of metaphysics or algebra. The Bulk of those that think themselves in love are lightheaded, and mistake a symptome of the vapours for the noblest passion of human nature. Or else possibly they may be fir'd with foul inclinations, and coulour them with the reputable name of Love, as others call cowardice caution, and covetousness frugality. It is above the flight of a vulgar soul to love rightly and sensibly as I fancy Monymia can, by her declareing she can love but one; How happy is that one whome the Stars have appointed for her? And cou'd I find out any fine qualitys in him that might justify the prudence of your choice, I cou'd wish with all my soule that it might be

Veramour.

TO THE SAME.

You show your self to be a Philosopher in your purpose to prefer the quiet of your mind to all the empty pleasures of the Body. Put that noble purpose in execution and you cant fail of being happy after the most exalted manner. Improve that thought to the utmost, and never admit of a fancy much less an action that may give your mind the least disturbance. All corporeal pleasures are low and brutal, and commonly end in loathing weariness and repentance. Of this opinion was a famous Orator of old, who in spight of his gravity fell in love with an illustrious Harlot call'd Laiis.[1] But she wou'd not admit of his addresses, but on the terms of Twenty Tallents. This extravagant demand restor'd the man to his wits, and made him reply that he wou'd by no means buy Repentance so dear. No Monymia Those are the true pleasures, that leave no sting behind, as the pleasures of sence generally do, which carry a painted

[1]Demosthenes, the great Athenian orator, was among the lovers of Lais from Hyccara, in Sicily, brought to Corinth as a captive. Lais is said also to have been the mistress of Aristippus, the philosopher, and Diogenes the Cynic (Athenæus, *The Deipnosophists,* with an Eng. trans. bv C. B. Gulick [Cambridge, Mass., 1937], VI, 173).

beauty in their faces: while their backsides are full of deformity. They have a luscious sweetness in the mouth, but are gall and poison to the stomach. Our mouths must first be out of tast, like girles that have the green sickness before we can be pleas'd with such trash. But the perfecting our natures, the conquering our weakness, & triumphing over all the glittering Pageantry of the World, are the pleasures that leave a flavour behind them as charming as the very enjoyment; Tho I must confess, to have a relish for these things requires a good Tast and a sound understanding. Children are pleas'd with Bawbles, Fools with Vice, Women with fine Cloaths, and only people of sence with Virtue. This last must therefore be the truest pleasure because tis chose by the Wisest people, and carrys all the marks of happiness along with it. But as this is the highest and most soveraign good, so it requires and deserves the greatest industry to attain it, which is the true reason it has so few Followers. People are discourag'd by the difficulty rather than doubt of its excellence, while at the same time they take more pains in a dirty Intrigue than wou'd suffise to advance them very far in Virtue. However I hope Virtue appears to Monymia in all its charms, and fires her soule with a resolution superior to all the difficultys in her way. How harmonious wou'd an unpolluted soule appear when set in so beautifull a Body! But I cant forbear suspecting that the Vanity which commonly gos along with a fine face, and the treacherous thoughts of being admir'd have a little infected her. Give me leave to tell you these are powerfull adversarys to a compleat Virtue. It is not enough to guard your self from actions y^{t} are criminal: but you must keep your mind, the Divine part of you from all contagion. There are many reasons of convenience and discretion that may protect a Woman from ill actions, nay very often one vice may keep them from committing another, as pride defends some Ladys honour more than their principles. But such terms are too low for our being Virtuous, we shou'd keep from Vice out of a pure affection to Virtue. We ought to be good not out of convenience but duty. We must preserve our minds untainted as well as our bodys, nay we shou'd be more carefull of that, as being infinitely of the greater Value. Whenever that comes to take infection, we are disarm'd of our true defence, and if we dont proceed to action, tis more our good luck than our good Principles. Let me conjure you then my dearest Monymia to abhor every thing that may sully the beauty of your mind. Look upon all commendation from the men as snares lay'd for your Virtue, and remember that the songs of the Syrens were no other than artfull flattery suited to the Fancy of those that hear'd it. And if good manners sometimes will oblige you to hear such dangerous musique, yet let good sence preserve you from being pleas'd with it. Adieu

---

TO BLOUSINI[1]

Pardon me Madam for the liberty I take to disturb you upon a day wherein you seem to have dedicated your self to better things. It is an Interruption to be forgiven that draws a Lady's thoughts from the Dead to the liveing. It will not be long before you will converse altogether with the Dead, and therefore in the mean time let us leave the shades to converse with one another. Tis true you were beholden to both your Husbands, to one for your Estate, and to the other for your quality, but your kind returns to them while they liv'd, intirely balanc't those obligations. Then they were the better for your tenderness: but now that they are

---

[1]Blousini (or Blouzina) seems to have been Lady Howard of Effingham, widow of Francis Howard, Esq., of Great Brookham, in Surrey, fifth Baron Howard, of Effingham, who was Governor of Virginia, resident in the Colony, September 1687 to the spring of 1689, and non-resident acting through his deputy Francis Nicholson until Sept. 20, 1692. She was the second wife of the colonial Governor, who married her in 1690 and left her a widow in 1695. She was Susan, daughter of Sir Henry Felton, Bart., of Playford, in Suffolk, and widow of Philip Harbord, of Stanninghall, Norfolk. She died Dec. 11, 1726 (Burke, *Peerage*). Byrd's punning reference to her is not clear in a letter to Facetia, July 27, 1703(?), when he wrote that London was deserted and "there is hardly any Impertinence or scandal left amongst us; and there would be none at all, if Blouzina would take her Somer-six horses to go out of town." (*Letters writ to Facetia by Veramour,* p. 12.)

In a letter to Mrs. Armiger, a friend in England, written in 1728 or 1729 (mutilated MS, owned by Colonial Williamsburg, Inc.), Byrd, who had evi-

6 foot under ground, all your grief is thrown away upon them. Besides the Ephesian matron has given the world so ill an impression of the extravagant grief of Widdows, that right or wrong they will have it to be counterfeit. Besides Madam ill nature makes people ask how it came to pass, that you cou'd marry a second Husband, before you had worn out your sorrow for the first? And again if that sorrow was washt away, to what purpose did you keep Fast one day of the week in memory of his death? Tis reacon'd a sort of cuckolding a second husband, to think too affectionately of the first, which you must needs have done, while you devoted one day out of seaven to his pious memory. It lookt like giveing onely your Body to my Lord E— and reserving your mind for M^r H— as long as you continu'd to remember him wth so much passion. This must have been an Infidelity to one of 'em at least, and indeed I think to both since you gave your heart intirely to neither. But now His Lordship has likewise departed this life, you have set apart another day of the week to lament his death. So that whoever has the honour to succeed him in your affections must have 2 Rivals. How discourageing this will be to a passionate lover (less than which your constitution abhorrs) I dare not say. Only I believe youll find it hard to get an intire heart for a third part of yours. Pray madam believe all this to be the admonition of a Freind, and not the insinuation of a Lover, and dont imagin that while I squint on your advantage my true sight is levil'd at my own.

Adieu.

---

dently not heard of Lady Effingham's death, wrote: "I want to know whether it be my old Lady Effingham that Mr Darcy has marryd, if it be, he has got the most valuable piece of [an]tiquity I was ever acquainted with. He may depend upon it she'll [. . .] a third day in the week for him, which is the compliment she reli[gi]ously pays her deceast Husbands. Her nativity [. . .] The Stars then foretold she would live til [. . .] and was put into the ground, and then she should [. . .]sting all the seaven days in the week for the de[. . .] Spouses. Had it not been for this Horoscope, I believe [. . .] have ventured upon her myself in the seaventy ninth year [of her] age: But I loved her too well, to let her fast one day in [ev]ery week upon my account."

Byrd's evident dislike for Lady Howard of Effingham may have been a reflection of Virginia political currents, for as Governor her husband had aroused strong opposition among some of the more powerful Virginia families.

TO CLARINDA[1]

Self love is the strongest passion we have, and all our other passions directly center in that. All the romantic love we have for the Ladys, is in order to please our selves, notwithstanding the mighty generosity some Heros pretend to in that Frensy. All our Virtues have this foundation as well as our Vices, tho the first show we love our selves with good sence, while the last show we love our selves with indiscretion. Thus it happens Madam that most people that love themselves, as well as their neighbours do, give into such courses as manifestly tend to their destruction; that is in plain English, they destroy themselves to please themselves. This sounds very odd to common sence: but it happens every day in common practice. A plain Instance of this, amidst a thousand others, is the foolish principle upon which most people marry. They propose happiness to themselves, and yet by an unlucky mistake they take measures that make them unhappy. If they can advance their Fortune by it, they think happiness will as certainly follow, as corruption follows the court or lewdness the Army. They leave Love out of the Articles, without which Marriage can no more give any one happiness than it can Immortality. I confess that mony as much as is sufficient to support us in the way of our Education, may be requir'd to make us easy: but all above that brings at least as much trouble as it dos convenience. Such a superfluity Madam has no power to calm the Tempests of the mind, or to heal the diseases of the Body, but rather increases both. Abundance of mony begets abundance of care, and make us a greater mark for the malicious Thrusts of Fortune. It naturally breeds pride and insolence in our minds, which of all the Vices in the World meet with the greatest mortifications. It multiplys our desires, and consequently multiplys our disappointments. It plunges us into a deal of noise and ceremony, & disarms us of all those peacefull thoughts, that make the very being of true happiness. What with the business and distraction

---

[1] "Clarinda" was substituted for another name which has been blotted out. Since in the body of the letter Byrd referred to his correspondent as Facetia, apparently the letter was first addressed to her.

of a great Estate, our Souls are put out of tune, and all our Inclinations grow dull & earthy. And besides it leads us into endless Excesses, that blast our Virtue, impair our constitution, and shorten our lives. So that upon the whole matter a modest competency (that golden Enough) is all that is requir'd of Fortune for our happiness.

Others madam there are especially of the tender Sex that marry out of an ambition to advance their Quality. A Page and a Coronet have irresistable charms to those mistaken Ladys. What a wretched Tast must it be that can place Happiness in Glittering and Equipage? They are transported with the veneration of the Ignorant, who are apt to admire people for borrow'd feathers. They love dearly to be pointed at in the street with dirty fingers for a guilt coach and half a dozen powder'd slaves behind it. It tickles their vanity to see people get out of the way to give 'em place, not remembering that they wou'd do the same to the Plague, or a Bear broke loose from the stake. What Woman wou'd not give up her person, her Fortune, & her liberty upon such ravishing considerations? How can a Ladys head ach that wears a Coronet, or any sorrow approach her heart, that has the continual comfort of takeing place of all her former acquaintance? These and such as these Madam are the baits that often draw women into the utmost wretchedness. These false lights lead their fancys out of the way of good sence, and make them wander into terrible misfortunes. How many sad examples of this Truth are to be seen every day among the city nymphs, who are made sacrifices either to their Fathers ambition or their own? If they can but marry a Lord their dearest wishes are gratify'd. The Father reacons the summs he has rak't together by Lying, over-reaching, and extortion well bestow'd, if they can make the ungainly Cubb a Countess. And the Daughter thinks her sire gos to the Devil in a good hour, provided she be a woman of Quality by the bargain. Such are the senceless reasonings of Ambition which ever promises wonders and mountains of happiness: but brings forth nothing but disquiet & vexation. When a Woman marrys to advance her Quality, My Lord reacons he has quitted scores by makeing her a Lady; and with good reason, for Pride was all her passion, and that is gratify'd. She did not marry the man but the Lord, nor he the woman but the fortune so that the persons are wholly unconcern'd in this wedding. They are no other than an encumbrance which is always uneasy til it can be quitted. The only good wish His Ld^{p} has for his awkward spouse is that God wou'd take her to himself out of a miserable world: and commonly by his cruel treatment he makes her wish so too What a comfort Facetia is it for a woman to be a Dutches if she must have the pain to see every Drabbella & Fartamira preferr'd in her Husbands Inclinations? What signifys it for her to take place of all other Ladys abroad, if she must give it to her Maids at home? or can she take any pleasure in the respect of other people, while she has the mortification to meet with contempt and nauseating from her Husband?

Adieu.

TO THE SAME

Your Ganemede brought me your Billet this morning, in which you show your self a sturdy champion for the man of Quality. You say a great many good things in their favour, I must confess, but what cause is there so bad, that Wit cant make appear tolerable. I fancy if you pleas'd you cou'd set off a Feaver with so many graces, that one shou'd almost wish for it. An invention so fruitfull as your Lad^{ps} cou'd find arguments to prove Guy Palms[1] a Wit or Lady Betty C—[2] a Beauty: but then both those agreable persons wou'd be more oblig'd to you, than they have been to Nature. It is true there are some few among the nobility that have good sence and good nature: but the Bulk of the upper house must no more have their character from those few, than the Dutch can deserve the character of Well-bred, from the

---

[1]Guy Palmes, son of William Palmes, Esq., was removed as one of the tellers of the Exchequer in 1702 but was allowed a pension of £1000 per annum (Luttrell, III, 376, IV, 315, V, 187).

[2]A possible reference to Lady Betty Cromwell, or Facetia. See Introduction, pp. xviii-xix and above, p. 191, as well as Byrd's denial of her right to be called Venus, below p. 285.

great civility of Monsr D Auerkerk.[1] The Nobility Madam may be divided into 2 sorts, into those those [*sic*] that are made noble themselves, and those that have had their Titles by Inheritance. If we may have the liberty to look into the Heraldry of the first sort, we may find that Ten familys have been innobled by Vice, to one that has been rais'd by Virtue. A little serviceable Villany to the Prince, a base compliance with his inclinations in prejudice of the Country, recommends many to this mark of Royal favour. Some in our age have been made Right Honble for pimping, which is as great a Burlesque upon Quality as an Alderman is upon Knighthood. Some Lawyers are call'd to the upper house for prostituteing the Laws to the Will of their Soveraign, for which they deserve a scaffold rather than a Patent. Some have extended the Prerogative til it crackt, and been made the Kings cousens & councellours for undoing him. Some men of the sword have been made Lords for other mens bravery, when those that had the merit were suffer'd to beg their bread, or dy in a Hospital. Some by Flattering a Prince, bribeing the chief Favorite, or betraying the secrets of their Freinds have been honour'd with supporters. These youll say Madam are distinguishing merits, and ought to recommend the masters of them to the respect of mankind. Tis true the Patent which gives the Title recites some very meritorious action: but a mans character must no more be taken from a Preamble than from a dedication, because both the one & ye other is made by his Flatterers. A Lovers Fancy may as safely be beleiv'd in the drawing his mistresses picture, which makes the nymph an Angel, when she is but an arrant arrant Woman.

Then Madam for those that are born Lords, The World is full of Instances of their Virtue. There's hardly a shopkeeper or a market woman, but can give a feeling testimony of their justice. Most Physicians & Surgeons can witness

---

[1]Henry Nassau, Count and Lord of Auverquerque (1641-1708) accompanied William to England in 1688 as his bodyguard. He rose during William's reign to the rank of general in the English army. King William on his death bed thanked him for his long fidelity. Later, as field marshal in command of the Dutch forces he coöperated with Marlborough in the earlier campaigns of the war of the Spanish Succession (*Dict. Nat. Biog.*).

for their great modesty, and Poets proove their good sence by makeing them believe for truth what all the Town knows to be the rankest Flattery. They are bred up in Pride and ignorance, knowing nothing but that they will be Lords, which is all their Nurses Governours and Tutors teach them. Their Vices are so many Mad^{m} that they are forct to guard themselves against the reproaches of the World by the act of Scandalum Magnatum, As the Catholick Religion keeps her extravagancys from being expos'd, by the Inquisition. This fearfull Penalty upon Truth makes me say no more, but that

I am &c.

TO THE SAME

By your exceeding zeal in defence of Coronets and supporters I gather that you are resolv'd to be related to them. If you shou'd Madam I hope you will be excepted from the general Fate, that follows upon ambitious matches. Indeed you have Charms enough to humble Pride it self, and sence enough to govern a foolish Husband, without letting him percieve your Empire: but then pray be discreet in chooseing your Fool, because some are so unaccountable & out of the common road that no sort of sence can manage them. Tis true sometimes there may happen an Instance of happiness among the wives of men of great quality: but tis as seldom as wit is among the Beaux or humility & hatred of the World among the Clergy. If a Lord commonly do a wife the honour to treat her with good manners before company, he passes for a good husband; but Mad^{m} pray imagin how miserable you will think your self, to be put off with formality instead of fondness, & with outward grimace instead of inward affection. Civility you may expect from every body: but you have a right to every thing that is tender & obligeing from a husband; and less than that will make the vow of marriage more miserable than the vow of chastity. Twere easy Madam to draw the Picture of Happiness in a marriage-state as Poets describe the Elysian Feilds, and a better Author dos Paradise,[1] but there be wondrous few that have the luck to attain it. There must be in the first place a generous disinterested Love on both sides exclusive of all other inclinations. There must be a sort of Heroique Virtue in each, because no Love can subsist long without it be fed by true worth and esteem. There ought to be good sence and a perpetual fund of spirit & invention for the entertainment of one another. There shou'd be an exact harmony of humour, & sympathy of affection. There must be good nature, and an endeavour to prevent each other in all the expressions of kindness and endearment. There must be a magical union of souls, and a constant reciprocation of every thing that is good and tender and obligeing. There must be no other discord but an earnest strife which shou'd please the other most. There ought to be a mutual dedication of the Whole heart, a generous confidence, and a constancy as firm as the foundations of the World, and to make all these fine qualitys agreable there must be good manners to give the best Grace and most engageing turn to every act of kindness and affection. Now Madam if you can hope for all these particulars in any Lord, marry him in the name of happiness. But I am sorry to tell you that Virtue and merit have a certain bashfulness that keep their owners from being great. I have too high an opinion of your good sence to imagin you can marry only for the vanity of walking at the next coronation. None but children & Ideots will value you a jot the more for your quality; and tis a lowness of soul you are not capable of, to be fond of a respect that proceeds from the Ignorance of those that give it, especially when you purchase it at the price of your ease and your happiness. Adieu.

TO MONYMIA.

I threaten'd Monymia with a Billet Doux in jest, and now I send her one in earnest; and if I prove so punctual in performing what I threaten, imagin how conscientious I

[1] *I. e.,* John Milton.

shall be in observing what I promise. Put the case I shou'd promise Love and constancy to you, and Indifference to every Thing else that wears Peticoats, yet I shou'd vow no more than I cou'd discharge with Inclination. I had once that fond opinion of my own strength that I defy'd Love and all its Frailtys: but you have convinc'd me me [*sic*] of my Insufficiency. My reason us'd to protect me against other Womens charms: but you have engag'd my own Guards against my heart, & and [*sic*] the very reason that us'd to save, has now Betray'd me. Your Wit enchants my understanding and your looks inflame my bloud, so that Body and soule I am yours. Thus Monymia your conquest has been compleat, and there's nothing left to finish your Triumph but generosity and compassion. Pray Venus soften your heart, and make you capable of feeling the same passion you inspire. The Impression you have made on my heart makes you always present to my Fancy. Sometimes I imagin you dresst out in all your charms, carrying Fire and love wherever you turn your Eys. Sometimes I figure you muffled up in mask & hoods, when in pity to mankind you vouchsafe to commit a more moderate slaughter. But in my gayest flights of Imagination, I draw you in a pure state of Nature despising all the encumbrance of dress, which may sett off the beauty of other Nymphs, when it only hides yours. Pardon dearest Monymia the rashness of that fancy that presumes to look upon you stark naked: but the Innocence you stil possess, and the Paradise you deserve, make natures Garb the properest for you. And if you shou'd be asham'd off it, God knows whether it might not be an evidence of guilt, as it was in the first Woman. Adieu.

TO BELLAMIRA[1]

Never cou'd Philosopher boast of more Patience that had so much Inclination. I have long'd to be in the number of

[1]William King's *Dialogues of the Dead* (1699), Dialogue VI, "Affectation of the Learned Lady," a dialogue between the unaffected Bellamira and the learned lady Calphurnia, thus characterizes Bellamira in her own words, in response to Calphurnia's question as to how she spent her time, "Why, Madam,

those that are happy in your acquaintance: but my cross-grain'd Destiny to this moment never gave me an opportunity. My Eys have stray'd towards you at church in prejudice of my Devotion, and at my Window in frost and snow I have gaz'd upon you til I have been warmer than any other Fire cou'd make me. Seven times the silver moon has danc't her round, since thwarting Stars have on my passion Frown'd. Perhaps you'll fancy me no very pushing Lover, for not haveing all this while projected some plot or other to bring me acquainted with you. But pray dont impute that forbearance to want of Vigour, which is owing to excess of bashfullness. [. . .][1] But my Impatience has at length got the better of that Enimy to gallant Enterprizes, and tis resolv'd by dint of Billet doux to beg the honour of your acquaintance. Tis pity that a Nymph and a Swain that that [*sic*] are capable of being such a comfort to one another shou'd continue as utter strangers as if the ocian parted them. And yet Venus can witness, we are next neighbours, we see one another every hour of the day, we know one anothers secrets, and stil we are unacquainted. This ought not to be endur'd in so Civil a society as Lincolns Inne,[2] and therefore if you wont admit of a Visit, I swear by Cook upon Little-

---

my own affairs took up some part of my time; music and drawing diverted me now and then: I had sometimes a fancy for work: I now and then went to see a play, when I liked the company I went with better than those I usually found there. I made myself as easy as I could to my acquaintance, and I have still the vanity to think I was not disagreeable to them. And I did not find but if one of us make out in civility what we want in learning, we might pass our time well enough in the world."

Bellamira, a princess whose favor was sought by rival lovers, is the heroine of the play *Bellamira her Dream* by Thomas Killigrew. Byrd would seem to have had in mind the character of Bellamira in King's *Dialogue* rather than in Killigrew's tragi-comedy.

[1]A sentence is crossed out.

[2]Byrd was living at Lincoln's Inn during his residence in England in 1700 (Sainsbury Abstracts, II, 186). He bought the chambers of Sir George Cooke in Lincoln's Inn for £900 and moved into them before he left London in November 1719 to return to Virginia (Diary, Nov. 11, Dec. 8, 1718; July 3, 9, 10, 11, 1719). On his return to England he lived there again and only gave instructions to his agent Mr. Spencer to dispose of these chambers in 1729, though he had returned to Virginia in 1726 and never again went to England (Byrd to Mr. Spencer, Virginia, May 28, 1729, MS, Colonial Williamsburg, Inc.). Though this letter might fall at any period of Byrd's residence in Lincoln's Inn, its inclusion at this point in the notebook suggests some time before Byrd's return to Virginia in 1705.

ton[1] Ill procure an order from the Masters of the Bench, to oblige you to come into Commons, & then you cant hinder me from getting into your Mess. But I hope you wont oblige me to this remedy but generously give me leave to wait upon you. If youll vouchsafe me that Favour, I beseech you let this be the gracious signal of your consent. Precizely at Eleven a clock to morrow morning approach the Window in French Nightcloaths gently reclineing your head upon your Elbow. In one hand hold your bottle of sweet water, and wth the other wave your hankerchief instead of a Flag of peace. Let your Looks be affirmative, and signify by a languishing smile that I may live & be happy. Adieu.

Of the following two poems, the first being upon a Sigh by Mrs Finch,[2] was favorably reciev'd by the Towne, til it was burlesqued by that upon a Fart wch cur'd that Lady of her Itch to Poetry.

UPON A SIGH

Gentlest Air Thou Breath of Lovers,
  Vapour from a secret Fire:
Which by Thee it self discovers,
  E'r yet daring to aspire.

---

[1] *I. e.,* the well-known legal work, Coke upon Littleton. Byrd was admitted to the Middle Temple on April 25, 1692, where he is described in the register as "Son and heir apparent of William Byrd of Cree Church, London, Esq." He was called to the Bar on April 12, 1695 (Letter of H. A. C. Sturgess, Librarian and Keeper of the Records of Middle Temple, dated August 24, 1931). When he returned to Virginia in 1720 he entertained himself on the long and tedious voyage across the Atlantic and prepared for the approaching legal battle against Spotswood by reading Coke upon Littleton (Dec. 12, 1719 to Feb. 7, 1720, Diary).

[2] Byrd's rendering of this poem by Anne, Countess of Winchelsea, (1666-1720), known as Mrs. Finch until her husband, Heneage Finch, succeeded to the title of fourth earl of Winchelsea in 1712, differs in capitalization and spelling and in the last two lines from the text as printed in *The Poems of Anne Countess of Winchelsea,* ed. by Myra Reynolds (Chicago, 1903), p. 138, where it was taken from the folio MS volume of the Countess' poems and entitled *A Sigh.* In this printed text the last two lines read:

Yet e're to their cost they know thee
Ev'ry Nymph may read thee here.

It has been stated frequently that these verses first appeared as The Sigh, anonymously, in Steele's *Miscellany* of 1714 (Reynolds, *op. cit.,* p. lxxxvii),

Softest noat of whisper'd anguish,
Harmony's refinedst part:
Strikeing Whilst Thou seemst to languish,
Full upon the Listeners heart.

Safest Messenger of Passion,
Steeling thro a Crowd of Spys:
Which constrain the outward fashion,
Close the Lips and guard the Eys.

Shapeless Sigh! we ne'er can Show Thee,
Form'd but to assault the Ear:
Yet 'eer to their loss, they know Thee
Every Nymph may read thee there

UPON A FART.[1]

Gentlest Blast of ill concoction,
Reverse of high-ascending Belch:
Th' only stink abhorr'd by Statesmen,
Belov'd and practic'd by the Welch.

---

but they appeared first in *Poems of Affairs of State* (XII, 348) in 1704. (Richard C. Boys, *English Poetical Miscellanies* [Baltimore, 1939], Appendix I, p. 188, no. 1469.) It was reprinted in 1716 in *Poems on Affairs of State,* XIII, 395, and in Dryden and Tonson, *Miscellany Poems,* XIV, 189, as well as in several other miscellanies. The texts of the poem as given by Byrd and by Miss Reynolds have slight variations from the text in Steele's *Poetical Miscellanies* (2d ed., 1727, p. 37).

Byrd's explanation of the withdrawl of the Countess of Winchelsea as a poet (see below, The Female Creed, p. 470), has not been corroborated by other writers. John Middleton Murry, who has said this poem The Sigh should be in every anthology, has made the point that the Countess of Winchelsea, or Ardelia as she was known to her correspondents (including the poet Pope), subscribed to the convention of the day that a woman should be modest about her literary efforts though not in sympathy with such an idea, but that her verses were not in accord with the prevailing fashion for satire and wit and that her reticence may be attributed in part to this fact, which made her seem rather formidable in the society of her time, the age of the Wits. (*Poems by Anne Countess of Winchelsea,* with an introductory essay by John Middleton Murry [London, 1928], pp. 16-18.)

[1]These verses were printed in *Poems on Affairs of State,* 1704 (XII, 441), and in the 1716 edition (XIII, 397); in the Dryden-Tonson *Miscellany* (XIV, 190). No evidence is at hand to prove that Byrd was or was not the author

Softest noat of Inward Gripeing
Sr Reverences finest part,
So fine it needs no pains of Wipeing
Except it prove a Brewers fart.

Swiftest Ease of Cholique pain,
Vapour from a secret stench,
Is rattled out by th'unbred swain,
But whisper'd by the Bashfull wench.

Shapeless Fart! we ne'er can show Thee
But in that merry Female sport
In which by burning blew we know Thee
Th' Amuzement of the Maids at Court.

A TRANSLATION OF THAT DIFFICULT PASSAGE OF PLYNY CONCERNING THE NIGHTINGALE IN THE 10TH BOOK OF HIS NATURAL HISTORY.

In the spring when the Leaves begin to grow thick upon the Trees the Nightingale generally sings fifteen days and nights without intermission. This is an admirable Byrd both for the Compass of her voice which is very much above the proportion of her Body and also for the strength and continuance of her Wind. The more skillfull among these Nightingales have very harmonious strains. Some noats

---

of these lines, though their inclusion in this notebook may indicate that he was. Cf. Matthew Prior, On a Fart Let in the House of Commons (*The Works of the English Poets* [London, 1810], X, 239).

Volume III of *Poems on Affairs of State* (1704) included, according to the title page, poems "written by the greatest Wits of the Age, Viz The Late Duke of Buckingham, Duke of D——re, Late E. of Rochester, Earl of D-t, Lord J-rys, Ld Hal——x, Andrew Marvel, Esq; Col. M-d-t, Mr. St. J-ns, Mr. Hambden, Sir Fleet Shepherd, Mr. Dryden, Mr. St-y, Mr. Pr-r, Dr. G-th, &c. most of which were never before publish'd." The 1716 edition gave the names of the contributors as the late Duke of Buckingham, Duke of Devonshire, Late E. of Rochester, Lord Jefferys, Lord Halifax, Andrew Marvel, Esq; Col. Mordaunt, Mr. St. John, Mr. Hamden, Sir Fleet Shepherd, Mr. Dryden, Mr. Stepney, Mr. Prior, Dr. Garth, &c.

There are slight variations as given in the text in Byrd's notebook and as printed in *Poems on Affairs of State.*

they swell to a surprizeing length, others they divide very artfully, and others they shorten, useing all along very swift and very agreable transitions. One while they run the noats very high and then of a sudden fall them again with great facility. Sometimes you may hear one of em humm a Tune to her self not ventureing to sing it aloud til she has got it perfect. Sometimes she'll sing a Base and sometimes a Treble, now shell run divisions, and then dwell a long time upon one single noat. One time shell take the noat very high at another time very low, & then again she'll use the middle Time. At other times she trills with a sweetness that is very enchanting. In short she has a vast compass with her voice and can take in as many noats as all the Instruments of music put together. Nobody can doubt but the singing of these little Birds is an art, which by cultivateing they bring to a rare perfection. For they have too great a variety of Ayres, and those too different from each other to be the Effect of Instinct, and simple nature. They frequently seem to have a Prize-musique among them in which several of 'em give trial of their skil together: and tis wonderfull to see those that perform the worst, strain their little Pipes til they dye upon the spot, chooseing rather to loose their lives than their Reputation. The young ones will take their lessons with diligent attention, holding their heads on one side and listening til they have got a full notion of ye tune: after which they conn it over, til they are perfect enough to make a publique essay. In the mean time she that takes upon her to be the mistress, wont fail to correct those that are either awkward or negligent, without examining whether the fault be in the Ear or in the want of attention. When Stesichorus was an Infant lying in his Cradle, one of these Nightingales sat upon his head and warbled most melodiously, which was a hopefull Prognostique that he wou'd in time grow to be a Poet of wonderfull sweetness.[1]

---

[1]Byrd's translation of this well-known passage from Pliny is very free and brief, omitting about the latter third of the original chapter. Cf. Pliny, *Natural History,* tr. H. Rackham (Cambridge, 1938), III, Bk. X, Ch. xliii.

A POEM UPON SOME LADYS AT TUNBRIDGE 1700[1]

Lady C.D. Upon the Walks Cornelia moves,
With such a soft engageing Grace:
Her Ayr and easy manner proves
Her high descent from Royal Race

Lady S. Plautinas wit divinely draws,
Our adoration and surprize:
Her charms invite, her Conduct aws,
And wounds like Parthians as she flys.

Mrs W... Cold Phebe's too neglectfull air,
The humble Crowd of Lovers mourn:
Obsequiously her Chains they wear,
And much for Eys & acres burn

Mrs E..k Drusilla warms us with her fire,
Which her too Icey breast denys:
At every smile, some swains expire,
At every frown some Hero dys.

Lady Sm. Foul Madget bursting at such sights,
Confesst her malice and dispair:
The Poplars on the walk she bites,
And with these words she blasts ye Air.

What have not I and Envy done?
Bright looks thro me their bloom forsake:
Whole Familys my Rancour own.
And each grey hair that's left's a snake.

Ease o ye Powers a restless mind,
Some vengeance on these nymphs decree:
Or make their curst Adorers blind,
Or make their features loath'd like mee.

---

[1]See Introduction, p. xxvi, and compare with Byrd's verses on some ladies at Tunbridge in *Tunbrigalia* (1719), Appendix II. This is an early specimen of the type of verse written at Tunbridge Wells, Bath, Epsom and Scarborough, by the "Water Poets," as Richard Steele called them (A. Barbeau, *Life and Letters at Bath in the XVIIIth Century,* [London, 1904], pp. 221-224).

The Naiid Phoce then appears,
Which Goddess guards these healing springs:
Her head above the surface rears,
And bubling in these Accents sings.

Quick to the neighbouring Grove begon,
A bleak & barren Rock you'll find:
Thence throw your crippl'd carcase down,
And ease your self & all mankind.

TO SEIGNOR SHRIMPONI.[1]

I thank you for the favour of your letter, it was a long one and lookt like an Arrear of a long standing. You say so much to assure me that you writ before, that it makes it a great question whether you writ or no. To be so industrious in defending your self from that suspicion Sir looks like relying more upon your Apology than your Innocence. This Matrimony has made you very polite, and instead of changeing you into a Brute (which alas frequently happens) it has transform'd you into a Courteour. Strange metamorphosis, than which Ovid has none more surprizeing! You study'd so many fine things in the flattering days of courtship that you cant leave them off, til the familiarity of Wedlock shall have taught you a coarser stile. Just like my Lord C— that has been so accustomed to military Terms in the army, that he cant forbear useing 'em to the Ladys in his Winter Quarters, or like the Lawyers who are so us'd to the Terms of the Law at the barr, that they cant lay 'em aside in civil

---

[1]Was Shrimponi Byrd's contemporary, Nathaniel Harrison (1677-1727) of "Wakefield," Surry County, who entered the Virginia House of Burgesses from that county in 1699 and was a member of the Assembly of 1700-1702? When the people differed with Governor Francis Nicholson on appropriations to defend the frontiers of New York, Byrd was named agent of Virginia by the Council and Burgesses to present to the Crown an address setting forth their position. When the Board of Trade took exception to the presentation of their address by Byrd in March, 1702, the Council replied that they would use in the future the regular channel through the Governor and not their own agent (Bassett, p. xlvi). According to family tradition, Nathaniel Harrison married Mary Young, widowed daughter of John Cary of Surry County, later of London (*Va. Mag.*, XXXI, 277). His oldest son Nathaniel was born about 1703 (*ibid.*, VI, 233).

company. Tis strange you shou'd fancy nine months a long seige to take a Mistress in, especially when the plunder has made you large amends. To complain of that before marriage under the pangs of Expectation were natural enough: but to lament the length of your courtship after you are in possession of your wishes, looks as if you thought the Game not worth the Candles. But even in that case a Philosopher wou'd not complain for fear of impeaching his own indiscretion: especially since there be other Evils we are a longer time in purchaseing, such as the Gout & the stone which are the purchase of many years, and are almost as great mischiefs as a Wife. If you be the happy man you pretend to be, you ought to think nine months service a small consideration for so inestimable a purchase. In the commonwealth of Love, tis agree'd, that a Woman surprizes a man that consents within the year, and her holding out so long is generally a favour to her Gallant, because for that time tis giveing him a Gracious Reprieve from the galling yoke of Matrimony. I am sorry to find you have no better reasons to prove the great Virtues of your Governour, than by the fullsome Addresses that are made to him. You might as safely take a Ladys Picture from her chambermaid a Lords Character from his Preamble or a Dead mans Reputation from a funeral sermon. The Indians in your neighbourhood can tell you, that they address themselves to the Devil in very civil terms: but tis because they know him to be mischievous, and not because he's good. And for the self same reason the good People of Eng^{d} in their addresses to Oliver Cromwell cry'd him up for a Person of the greatest sanctity that ever was, nay his hopefull son Richard too, by the Addresses in his short reign was commended for his Great Parts and abilitys in governing the State. Far be it from me to contradict the united wisdom of the colony, who have recorded their Governour for so excellent a person: but I will suspend my opinion til they contradict themselves and pull down with their own hands the wooden Idol they have set up. Adieu.

TO MY LADY C——[1]

Now the first choque of your grief is over, I may venture to beseech your Lad^p to give audience to reason. I know Passion will always be heard first, & heard quite out, before twill suffer Philosophy to open its mouth. For this reason People in the first sallys of sorrow and affliction, will recieve no company: but shut themselves up from all their Freinds, and even from good sence it self. Their Fancy paints their misfortune to em in the blackest coulours without any Lights, and every thing appears with an air of misery and desperation. If they look back upon the time past, they are put in mind of Joys they have utterly lost, and if they look forward, tis only to convince themselves those Joys will never return again. Thus the Present time is made insupportable by the melancholly prospect of that which is to come. I doubt not but your Lad^p figures to your self all the glorys of your Daughters Person, which I confess cant be flatter'd with the finest picture Fancy can draw of it. You think of her agreable Wit, which knew how to entertain without the expence of Reputations. You call to mind the charms of her figure, which made other nymphs despair of any conquest in her company. You reflect upon the purity and Innocence of her mind, which disarm'd all the vanity and confidence of her boldest admirours. You remember that delicacy of humour and good-breeding, with which she us'd to enchant the very Envy of those Beautys she eclips'd. All these excellent qualitys you bring back to your mind, to aggravate the loss you have sustain'd. And indeed it were a most unspeakable loss, if your Lad^p shou'd only consider your self, and not your Daughter. But I know your Love to her had more of generosity in it, than to be fond of any advantage of your own in prejudice of her. I have often heard you declare, you cou'd undergo any misfortune to make her happy. If you were sincere when you made that declaration, now is the time for you to show it.

---

[1]Lady C was Mary, daughter of Sir Henry Thompson, of Escrick, and wife of Sir Henry Calverley, of Eryholme in York county. Her daughter, whom Byrd called "Melantha," married Bennet Sherard, later Earl of Harborough, and died in 1702. See above, p. 228.

Do but ballance your own loss, and her gain, and then tell me why you are so much afflicted. Your Lad[p] must own that tho Your Daughter was Mistress of all possible charms: yet by ill health, & a senceless Husband she was very unhappy. It was her hard Fate to be marry'd into a Family that had no tast for perfection. Wit is always a Terror to those that have none. Her beauty was a perpetual reproach to those dowdy Relations that wanted it. and the other brightness of her character did but disparage their False Lights, as a sparkling Diamond dos an awkward Counterfeit. This was an affliction that cut with a double edge, for she dispis'd them, and they hated her. These were circumstances which made her compleatly miserable the short time she liv'd: And cou'd your Lad[p] be so unkind as to wish she had continu'd so? Cou'd you envy such a Daughter the only Remedy that was left for her wretchedness? If you lov'd her, you shou'd rejoice at her deliverance; and if you did not, you have no reason to be sorry at her death. If there be any truth in the agreable accounts we have of Heaven and Paradise, and Elyzium, Her unspotted Innocence has entitled her to a first Row there. There she shines amongst the brightest Stars, and is a Cherub of the foremost order. And is it possible for your Lad[p] out of pure selfishness (as much as you are able) to pull her down from thence, to fix her in the most unhappy condition that ever was? Pray Madam put ingenuously all these questions to your own heart, & comfort your self with the answere which that will give you. ADIEU

TO SEIGNOR PUNCHINO

After a great deal of expectation, I had the pleasure of a Pacquet from my dear Punchino. You need not have made me tarry so long for it, to raise its value, according to that detestable maxim which the Ladys have amongst 'em, That Expectation makes the Blessing dear. How many Faithfull hearts have been broken by this female mistake; & I wish it be not the cause of your Mistresses coldness to you; she dont consider the disadvantage of useing delays to a Gallant of seaven & fourty. I believe while you were favouring me this this [*sic*] Letter, you dreamt you were writeing to your Pastorella, so many sweet things were never said to a Man since Jupiter writ to Ganemede. You Myrtillo's are so us'd to let off douceurs at your Amarillis's,[1] that you cant leave off the infection when you talk to your Freinds; just like the Pedants at the university, that are so accustom'd to ends of Latin, and Punning in their Declamations, that they cant leave them off before a country-congregation. Consider that tho tis pardonable for a man in love to be out of his wits when he talks to his Princess: yet he shou'd quit his flights and his hyperboles upon other occasions, and condescend to use the common sence and common Language of men. News is so scanty at the Bath this year that several Ladys, who are remarquable for fluency of Tongue, have nothing to talk of but the working of their waters. This is so uncommon, that D^r^ R—[2] swears the waters of this place have the blessed virtue of makeing Women silent. If this were true, he ought to have his statue erected for so usefull a discovery, and every marry'd man shou'd contribute towards it. But I'm affraid he has been brib'd by the Town to say this, because if the word of so eminent a Physician can make it pass for Truth, every man will perswade his spouse to come hither. The Duke of B—t & his Dutches[3] have been to

---

[1]For a story of Pastorella and her change from a coquette by the ruse of her aunt Parisatis, see *The Tatler,* No. 9, April 30, 1709. Myrtilus in classical mythology was the son of Hermes and the charioteer of Oenomaus. His treachery gave Pelops the victory in the race, but instead of paying him the agreed bribe Pelops cast him into the sea near Geræstus, in Eubœa. That part of the Aegean sea was thence called the Myrtoan sea (Harper's *Classical Dictionary*). The name Amaryllis was borrowed from the pastorals of Theocritus and Virgil as the name for a pastoral sweetheart, as in the well-known line from Milton's Lycidas, "To sport with Amaryllis in the shade." For the story of Amaryllis and Amyntas, see *The Guardian,* No. 32, April 17, 1713.

[2]John Radcliffe (1650-1714) was a leading physician in London and was famed for his wit. He attended various members of the royal family including William and Mary, and later Queen Anne. He was attacked in a pamphlet, "A letter from a Citizen of Bath to his Excellency Dr. R—— at Tunbridge, 1705," in which he was censured for vilifying the Bath waters and patronizing Tunbridge Wells in spite of the freeman's oath he had taken to aid Bath in any way he could. (*Dict. Nat. Biog.*).

[3]Possibly this referred to Henry Somerset, second Duke of Beaufort (1684-1714) who married on July 7, 1702, Mary, only daughter of Charles Sackville, Earl of Dorset. She died June 18, 1705. The Duke of Beaufort entertained Queen Anne at Badminton in August, 1702. (Burke, *Peerage; Dict. Nat. Biog.*)

show themselves here since their marriage, and W—y says They both do truly make but one body and one soule, because his Grace is all Matter, and his Wife is all Spirit. My noble Ld F—m is lately arriv'd, and by the strength of habit, more than by the force of constitution, has stil an unnatural hankering after Gallantry. In the next place we have Mrs Pal— the Fortune, the Wit, the Prude, & what not? Since Mony has the magical power of produceing every good quality, or at least of hideing every bad one. Just as when a Lady by her fears, or it may be by her pride happens to be chast, she has the general Name of being Virtuous; tho perhaps she is as proud as a Citizen newly made a Countess, as malicious as a shrivell'd Beauty, & as Tarmagent as Xantippe her self, or (to speak more modernly) as my good Lady D—r.[1] Thus a scold, a Gossip, a Backbiter, one irregular in her Figure, and unhappy in her face will be a most accomplisht Person if she have but mony. Gold tho it take the figure of an Ass or a calf will be Worshipt as a God, even by the successors of Aron themselves. It makes the Duke of S—t[2] a Wit, and transforms my dark Lady S—y into an Angel of light. We have no Lampoon yet, but are content to spread scandal by word of mouth. Our Poets drink too much water, which is a great Enimy to the Muses. Besides heres no illustrious folly, no Intrigues of figure for a Poet to work upon wch you'll say is a wonder among so much good company. Adieu.

---

[1]Probably Judith, daughter of Sir Edmund Poley, of Badley, Suffolk, who married Henry Jermyn, first Baron Dover (1636-1708), a gallant of the courts of Charles II and James II, who, after the Restoration, lived quietly at his house near St. James's Park in London or his place at Cheveley. Lady Dover has been described as "un pique provinciable" and as a "lady of a singular good character." Lady Dover died at Cheveley in 1726 (*Dict. Nat. Biog.*).

[2]Charles Seymour, sixth Duke of Somerset, married as his first wife the very wealthy Elizabeth Percy, heiress of the Duke of Northumberland, who was twice widowed before her marriage at the age of sixteen to the Duke of Somerset, whose pride seems to have been as famous as his lack of wit. In spite of the Duke of Somerset's support to Marlborough in the ministerial crisis in 1708, Marlborough rewarded him only with the mastership of the horse, explaining to his wife that he never dreamed of employing so witless a person in anything of consequence. (*Dict. Nat. Biog.;* H. S. Hughes, *The Gentle Hertford* [N. Y., 1940]; *Martha Lady Giffard*, ed. by J. G. Longe [London, 1911].)

TO SEIGNORA INCOGNITA.

The Banter which you sent me by the Penny-post yesterday, made me as merry as it cou'd do the Author. You were delighted with the fancy of my growing extreamly vain upon receiveing a Billet doux from a Lady, and a Fortune; and I was pleas'd with the thoughts of your looking extreemly simple upon the disappointment. All that troubles me in this business is, that you, or any body else shou'd mistake me for one of those Fopps, that interpret not only the civilitys, but even the Ridicule of the Women to be certain proofs of their being in love with them. No madam I am not such a stranger to my self, or so unacquainted with the World, as to believe in miracles, except they be attested by undeniable Evidence; And I think a letter from a Lady to which she has not vouchsaf'd to set her hand, can hardly be accounted such. However Madam I am not so obstinate an Infidel, but if youll give me such proofs as the Nature of the thing requires, I am willing to become a Believer. If you'll please to convince my Eys, and my other sences of the truth of what you tell me, I will believe without reserve. But it is disingenuous in you to apply your self only to my Vanity, wch is so weak as to give Credit to Dreams, and Fancy and even to it self, which is the utmost excess of credulity. This makes you look like an Imposter, who is always carefull to work upon the Passions, and not upon the understanding. Had you thought me Master of that sence, which wou'd justify your haveing a good opinion of me, you shou'd have favour'd me with such arguments as a reasonable man ought to expect in a case of mighty Improbability. I own that sometimes very strange things come to pass in the World, Fools act like Polititians, and men of sence like mad-men; and not only Girles, but men & women have the green sickness, and love nothing so well as Trumpery. All the Passions go by no rule but their own and renounce, the track of common sence intirely. But Love is stil more whimsical and unaccountable than all the rest, because it has Fancy the greatest cheat in nature for its guide. Thus it may happen Madam that you may have so odd a tast as to like me: and since it is possible, it is in your power by good natural arguments to convince me of it, If you'll appoint a Rendevous, where I may have the pleasure of hearing from your mouth the gracious things you mention in your Letter, then I will be converted, and be your Proselite. But that you may suffer no inconvenience by so vast a condescention, I promise you solemnly these two things. First That I will never discover so dear a secret, no not to a mistress tho it were to purchase her consent. And if I do, may the God of Love confound all my Amours with disappointment. In the second place I promise If your Person be half so agreable as your letter, that I will return your Passion with Interest upon Interest, and tho Venus shou'd forbid me to love you to the dreadfull degree of Marriage, yet your exceeding generosity, and your uncommon Fancy will always make me your Freind. In the mean while I wear your Letter in my bosome next my heart, and wish the Author of it there too Adieu.

TO COUNT SUFFICIENTI.[1]

Tis a sad story you tell me my L^{d} that you have taken a hatfull of Pills and Balsom Capivi without measure since I had the honour to see you, and yet your distemper stil continues as violent as ever. Certainly your way-fareing Phillis must have carry'd a terrible sting in her Tail, to leave so much poison behind her, or else your Physician must have taken an improper method with you. Other adventurers of our acquaintance are not so unlucky: but can dispatch a Clap with great safety in 3 weeks, whereas your Lord^{p} has been in strong Pickle these 3 months without relief. I am sorry your respect to the Church, made you choose an Abbot for your D^{r} in this case; it shou'd seem that Venereal cases are a little forrein to his Profession, except he apply'd himself to that study, with a pious design to keep the disasters of his house from being expos'd to a Lay-chyrurgeon. Or else possibly he may have observ'd that these distempers are

[1]See Byrd's character of Count Sufficiento, p. 204.

cur'd too soon in the World to discourage the vice that begets them, and therefore he practices with the charitable intent to make sinners run thro a longer pennance for the good of their souls. Thus my Lord you have no reason to complain of the length of your cure, since tis in order to root out your concupiscence, as well as your disease. I doubt not but now your constitution is humble'd, and while you are under the smart of your distemper, and the greater plague of your physick, you think abundance more justly than you did before. You reflect very seriously upon the vast disproportion there is between 3 months pain and one minutes pleasure. That the short gratification of one sence is very dearly purchas'd at the price of a long mortification of all the rest. Ill lay a wager you can now discourse of the vanity and filthiness of whoreing most pathetically, and muster up a hundred arguments to diswade us thoughtless young Fellows from it. Pray my Lord be pleas'd to take the trouble to set them down in writeing, that so you may not forget them when these afflictions are over. Describe very particularly all the smart you undergo when you converse with y^r^ Pot de Chambre, and all the Loathings and reviling of your stomach, when you swallow half a dozen Pills in a morning. Dont forget the mortification of Water gruel, and soup Maigre, of Balsom, and Injections of Basilicum, Lapis Infernalis, & Diet-drinks. Draw these in plain natural colours (because they need no flourishes to make them more detestable) and when I have the Pleasure to see your Lord^p^ in good health, we will read them over for our edification.

Adieu

TO LADY S——[1]

Were it not for the respect I bear to the Tribe of Levi, I shou'd wish Malino might be put to the Infamy of preaching his own sermons, for disturbing our last conversation. I had promis'd my self mountains of happiness in my Visit to the divine and charming Melantha: but that dear expectation was blasted by the appearance of your Evil Genius. At the

[1]Lady Sherard. See character of Melantha, above, p. 228.

sight of him I found a greater Antipathy in my soul, than Fancirio has to a Cat, or Lotharia to her own Husband. I know he was sent by the Enimy to get Intelligence of your Conduct, and therefore he deserved the civillest treatment due to a Spy, which is to be tosst in a Blanket. One might see him squinting upon you thro the back of the chair with Eys eager for discovery: but I think my Lady Suffolk[1] her self cou'd not act the Prude more discreetly than you did. So that if he make anything of it to your disadvantage it must be owing to his Invention, and not to his discovery. Tho I confess tis a great hardship upon Innocence, to be at the trouble of observing the stiff measures of Prudery, and saveing Appearance, when it has no ill conduct to conceal. That constraint ought be part of the punishment of Those Ladys whose Behaviour, like paint, wont bear being seen in a true Light. A Polite Author of your acquaintance says, Hypocrysy is the homage which [vice pays] to Virtue, and therefore tis an unreasonable [. . .], to make Virtue pay the same homage to herself.[2] When a Lady takes too much liberty with the men in private, tis fit she shou'd undergo the [. . .] of over-acting Virtue in publick; she shou'd pract[ise] stiffness in her looks, in her movement, in her discourse and lace up all her natural Inclinations as straight as Squabbella dos her fat sides, to avoid the censure of an unforgiveing World. But for Innocence to give it self rigorous airs of Discretion, wou'd be as unnatural as it is for Mrs Hammond to paint, whose complection wou'd be more beautifull without it. Besides a Natural & easy freedom is the very character of Innocence, and to affect the

---

[1]Anne, daughter of Robert (Montague), 3d Earl of Manchester, married, as his third wife, James (Howard), Earl of Suffolk, who died in 1689. She survived him for more than thirty years, dying in 1720 (*Dict. Nat. Biog., sub* Earl of Suffolk). She was apparently proverbial in the London of her day as an unusually devoted wife and respectable widow. "Lady Suffolk," wrote A. Stephens to Abigail Harley in 1683, "makes one of the rarest wives that ever I heard of, for her Lord, for the most part, with the gout, and three score and six years old, is confined greatly to his chamber. She never stirs from him and admits very few visits if he be not so well as to see them." (12 Apr. 1683, quoted in Cokayne, *Complete Peerage*).

[2]This quotation is from La Rochefoucauld, a translation of his *L'hypocrisie est un hommage que le vice rend à la vertu* (*Maximes et Oeuvres Diverses,* No. 218 of *Réflexions ou Sentences*).

appearances of Virtue, looks as guilty as it did in Eve to want cloaths to cover her nakedness. Your Godly Relations whose Virtue lys no deeper than their looks, have sufficiently turn'd your stomach against all ridiculous affectation. They are enough to burlesk Prudery out of the World by their awkward way of acting it; The asses Ears thrust themselves always above the Lions skin, and they bray ridiculously when they attempt to roar. For their sakes I hope Melantha will ever abhor artifice and false coulours, as long as she has no blemish to disguise. Let the French Dowdys with their sallow complections put on red: but why shou'd the English nymphs follow them, whome nature has provided wth a better carnation than art can give them. Innocence and a compleat virtue will always be the best guard against the malice of the World, and that Guard you have in Perfection Adieu.

TO LADY G——

I am very much surpriz'd to hear what heinous things are lay'd to my charge, things that never enter'd into my most disappointed thoughts. The malice that invented this accusation had terrible Teeth: but no wit, for it has told the story with so little art, that tis wholly incredible. Had the good natur'd-Author intended to be believ'd he shou'd have wrought up the Plot with some tolerable circumstances of Probability. But instead of that the Venome of the Serpent discovers it self without its subtilty. This happens very favourably for me, at least with one of Your Lad^ps penetration, who Im perswaded will never believe that I have horns grown out of my head, tuskes out of my mouth and claws put out at the end of my fingers without it be prov'd by substancial evidence. You wou'd not take the word of common Fame for so strange an accident, and much less the testimony of an adversary which is commonly more false than Fame. The story that has been told you is altogether as improbable as this, that I shou'd have spoken contemptible things of Zenobia, and given my self ayrs of haveing had that happiness in my power, which I onely had in my

Inclination. There is not a Fiction in ovids Metamorphosis, nor in any of the conversations of Pasquin and Morfario[1] that is more false than this. I were a Monster cou'd I be capable of so ungentlemanly an untruth, and [. . .] first have renounct all pretensions to Honour and good manners. If I might be allow'd to [call witnesses] in my own justification, There be some [. . .] unquestionable Credit that will vouch for [. . .] whenever they heard me mention Zenobia it was with very uncommon marks of respect, which had no fault but by its approaching too near to adoration. Neither was this only in the comfortable days of Hope: but even in the blackest of my dispair. I did never think the Fruit the less beautifull, for being out of my reach, and my Tongue wou'd never have the confidence to rebell against my thoughts, in the dangerous neighbourhood of my Teeth, which would not fail to ressent it. I believe no body can charge me with vanity in the smallest Instances, & therefore it wou'd be strange I shou'd be so in the present Case, where good sence, modesty, Truth, and gratitude wou'd be all in danger. I wou'd put my self upon any trial in this matter, & wou'd not care tho Bealzebub himself were to be summon'd amongst the witnesses, & I'm sure if any appear against me on this occasion, it must be either the Father of Lys himself, or some of his children. There is a certain confidence in Innocence that wou'd make a coward bold, and give Bashfullness it self the courage to brave the most undaunted Impudence. This Innocence supports me Madam under so black an accusation, and makes me hope you will look upon it as the Invention of Spight & ill nature, especially since it comes from People who are not at all remarquable for their Charity. They are ready to believe every Lam-

---

[1]In sixteenth-century Rome a mutilated statue, named Pasquino or Pasquillo, set up by Cardinal Caraffa by his palace near the Piazza Navona, was dressed annually on St. Mark's Day to represent some character of ancient times and was saluted by students of the restored ancient learning in Latin verses, placed on the statue. These salutations to Pasquin gradually became satirical, and the term Pasquinade came to be applied to lampoons, and anonymous articles by authors screened by the name of Pasquin. At the opposite end of the city of Rome, an old statue of Mars, called Marforio, was used by those who would answer attacks posted on Pasquin by posting their replies on Marforio. Affairs of the time and personal differences were thus argued by the "conversations of Pasquin and Marforio." (*New Eng. Dict.*; *Century Dictionary*).

poon to be litterally true, & Every Whisper they credit as an oracle, especially if there be mischief in it. But I depend upon your Lad^{ps} generosity, who never believe any [scandal] but what comes attested by a demonstration.

Adieu

TO ZENOBIA

My Wits were in no small danger by the resolution I had taken to smother the Passion I had for Zenobia. I fancy'd the good old Remedys of Time and absence would cure me, tho Reason & Philosophy had fail'd. I had already taken advice of Seneca Plutarch and Epictetus, I had read over all the Invectives against women, and all the Lampoons upon matrimony. But alas they all toucht my distemper no more than Hellebore dos Folly,[1] and such rules are of no more consequence against Love than Remedys would be against Old Age. T'is a sage thing to preach up patience to a man in a fit of the stone, and discretion to a Lunatique, and very discreet to prescribe good sence to a violent Inclination. But this is really throwing away Wisdom, of which theres so little in this world that I'd have it reserv'd for better purposes. Pray Dont expect that medicines wch never had any effect upon a man in my circumstances shou'd work upon me. Tis the utmost want of charity to deny Remedys that wou'd cure me, and prescribe such as you know will make me worse. What tho Quacks and Prudes & Philosophers have recommended them before you, yet tis the nature of a medicine and not the name that makes it valuable. If Esculapius shou'd tell you that bleeding is very good in a Dropsey and if Dryden in one of his Dedications shou'd declare that my L^{d} S— has Wit or my Lord A—y[2] good

---

[1]Hellebore referred to several plants having poisonous and medicinal properties, especially reputed as specifics for mental disease.

[2]Archibald Campbell, Lord Islay, succeeded his brother, John Campbell (see above, p. 203) as third Duke of Argyle in 1743. He played so important a role in the affairs of Scotland under George II that he was satirically called "the Scotch King." He was, like his brother, out of favor with George I for a season because of his support of the Prince of Wales, but he made his peace with the Crown and later was a steady adherent of the ministry of Sir Robert Walpole. Horace Walpole voiced the general verdict when he said, "Duke

nature yet I suppose you'd believe it n'eer the more for the Authority of the Author that says it. So tho Solomon shou'd hold forth against the follys of Love and shou'd cry up reason & good sence as a specifick against it, yet dont believe him because you see him renounce his own Physick, notwithstanding he had it in more perfection than ever mortal before him. For this reason Madam say no more of manageing a Passion like mine; I might as soon put a curb upon the north wind, and bind the waves of the sea to their good behaviour, as stiffle so outragious an Inclination. And yet after all one smile from you, the magical rehearsing of one single monosyllable will make me easy. And wont you then have the Charity to speak one short word to save me? Don't command me not to come after you into the Country for you may as easily leave your shadow behind you, as me. It is impossible not to follow you tho it shou'd be into Lapland, Nay tho you shou'd take a voyage to Plutos Dominions I wou'd pursue you in spight of Cerberus himself, as some faithfull Lovers have done before me. Thus you are like to be haunted go where you please, and you cant blame me because tis the first principle of all Creatures to follow happiness. And you know tis impossible to act against first principles and so reasonable a Lady can never blame me for doing that which tis impossible to avoid. Pardon me dear Zenobia if my Love appear a little too boistrous; and I have a right to your forgiveness when I assure you tis the consequence of your commands. You charg'd me to stiffle my Passion, which I obey'd with all my might: but tis the property of Love as of all other fire to grow the more Violent by being resisted. Adieu.

Archibald was undoubtedly a dark shrewd man." (Walpole to Sir David Dalrymple, Feb. 10, 1781, Walpole's *Letters,* ed. Cunningham, VIII, 6; *Dict. Nat. Biog.*).

For a highly adverse picture of Lord Islay, see Hervey, *Memoirs,* ed. Sedgwick, I, 296-7. Swift wrote Henrietta Howard, Countess of Suffolk, Aug. 19, 1727, in making puns on her letter to him, "I make nothing of mistaking . . . slily for Ilay" (*Letters of Henrietta, Countess of Suffolk,* I, 265-6).

Byrd was on intimate terms with Lord Islay during his residence in London, 1717-20, and often consulted him in political matters. He presented him with a description of Virginia just before he left London in November, 1719 (Diary, Nov. 20, 1719, and passim from March 1718 through Nov. 1719).

TO THE SAME

Your orders were so positive against my comeing into the Country, that I dare not transgress them. But pray put a just value upon my obedience in this particular, & believe, that while I observe your commands, I rebel against the dearest of my Inclinations. I submit it to your own generosity, whether this Instance of self denyal deserve not to be rewarded by a mercifull Epistle. It is one of the greatest Extravagances of Prudery, that forbids young Ladys to write to the Men, and yet permits em to be Test a test [*sic*] together in a room. If there be any danger for a nymph and a swain to converse with one another, it is near hand, and not at 40 miles distance. And therefore tis ridiculous to imagin there's more indecency in writeing than in talking. Most women indeed have the same reason for not writeing y[t] M[r] Palms has for not being a Be [. . .] Their hand is as difficult to be decypher'd as if some Dutch Mastiff or Munkey had been their Secretary. And their spelling is so irregular that Doctor Wallice[1] wou'd be hard put to it to find out its meaning. From hence it comes, that [writ]ing to the men has been cry'd down as a [sin] by those who cou'd not write without ex[posing] their nonsence, just as some women with [. . .] leggs have pronounc't it indecent to wear Petticoats, for fear of discovering their own [. . .]ty. But you madam have no such reason to th[ink writ]ing a crime, who can do it in perfection. [. . .] even a fault in you to conceal so great a [. . .] All the Graces dance upon your paper, and [. . .] thousand Cupids wanton about your pen [while] you are useing it. These direct your [. . .] while the Muses themselves indite. Who [. . .] bear coveting to read the Effects of so much [. . .]tion. For my part I long for it intirely, [. . .] of you in the name of charity and good [. . .] to write to me by every Post. You have one advantage peculiar to your self, that you need not fear

[1]John Wallis (1616-1703), English mathematician and logician, gained wide fame and considerable fortune by his extraordinary ability in working out difficult cyphers. He deposited in 1653 in the Bodleian Library a collection of some of the letters deciphered by him, with an historical preface, which was published in 1737 by John Davys in his *Essay on the Art of Decyphering* (*Dict. Nat. Biog.*).

my showing your letters. Tho I shou'd have vanity or Infidelity enough to do so treacherous a [thing] yet it wou'd be so far from exposeing a weakness, in you, that it wou'd be proclaiming your perfections. And I shall have one advantage too on my side, which is, that tho you shou'd express your self in terms never so negative, yet I shou'd comfort my self with the belief that your discretion wou'd not suffer you to venture too much kindness in a Letter. Thus madam there is no danger in your doing me so gracious a favour: but in not doing it there may be the hazzard of your giveing an invincible fit of melancholly to him that loves you more

Than Drowning sailor loves the saveing shoar.

Adieu.

TO THE SAME

If you imagin'd how mischievous your silence has been, you wou'd almost think it a vice even in a woman. Every post day I am big with the dear expectation of a letter: but tis to as little purpose, as Lady E— was big last year, when her shape was spoil'd with a Tympany[1] instead of a child. If you were capable of knowing the pain of disappointment, you'd think it an act of ill-nature to occasion it in him that loves you. It is some relief to me to hear you got safe to your journeys end, tho I cou'd never suspect any danger wou'd befall a person of your Innocence. Lady G— let me know that change of air had given you a cold, which I wonder'd at because I fancy'd, that that like good-breeding, was seldom got in the Country. I cant tell whether you remember it or not: but you was in very good company last night, at least your soule was, while your dainty Body was left alone in your bed. I have an officious Demon that tells me every night in my dream where you are, and what you are doing. And particularly last night you were takeing a turn about 12 a clock in Favorita-Park. The Moon lookt

---

[1]Tympany referred to a morbid swelling or tumor. In the Bill of Mortality for 1717, eight persons were reported to have died of Tympany (*Hist. Reg.*, 1717, Diary, p. 52).

Site of the original Thanksgiving in 1619, **Berkeley Plantation** in Charles City Co. graces the banks of the James River.

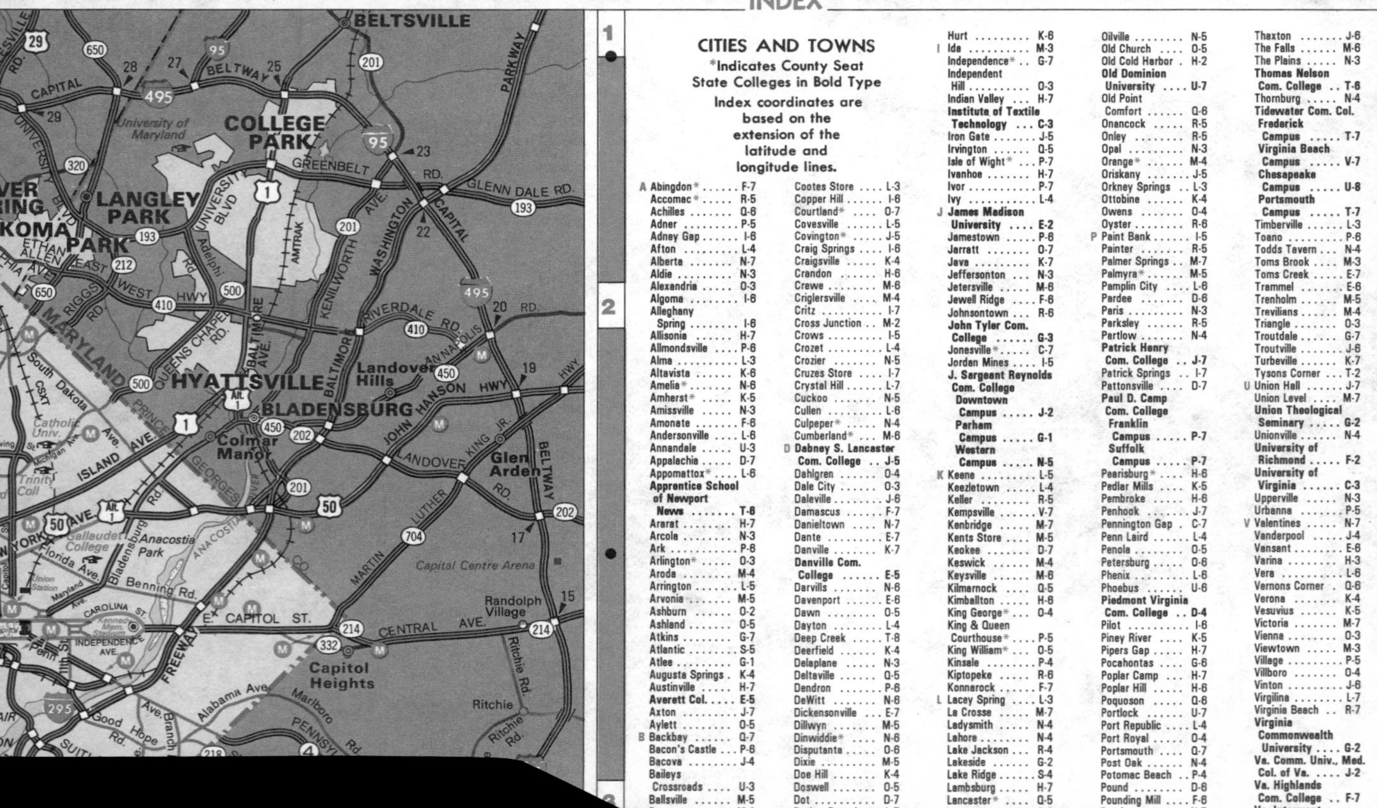

INDEX

CITIES AND TOWNS

*Indicates County Seat
State Colleges in Bold Type
Index coordinates are based on the extension of the latitude and longitude lines.

A
Abingdon* F-7
Accomac* R-5
Achilles Q-6
Adner P-5
Adney Gap I-6
Afton L-4
Alberta N-7
Aldie N-3
Alexandria O-3
Algoma I-6
Alleghany Spring I-6
Allisonia H-7
Allmondsville P-6
Alma L-3
Altavista K-6
Amelia* N-6
Amherst* K-5
Amissville N-3
Amonate F-6
Andersonville L-6
Annandale U-3
Appalachia D-7
Appomattox* L-6
Apprentice School of Newport News T-8
Ararat H-7
Arcola N-3
Ark P-6
Arlington* O-3
Aroda M-4
Arrington L-5
Arvonia M-5
Ashburn O-2
Ashland O-5
Atkins G-7
Atlantic S-5
Atlee G-1
Augusta Springs K-4
Austinville H-7
Averett Col. E-5
Axton J-7
Aylett O-5

B
Backbay Q-7
Bacon's Castle P-6
Bacova J-4
Baileys Crossroads U-3
Ballsville M-5
Banco M-4

Cootes Store L-3
Copper Hill I-6
Courtland* O-7
Covesville L-5
Covington* J-5
Craig Springs I-6
Craigsville K-4
Crandon H-6
Crewe M-6
Criglersville M-4
Critz I-7
Cross Junction M-2
Crows I-5
Crozet L-4
Crozier N-5
Cruzes Store I-7
Crystal Hill L-7
Cuckoo N-5
Cullen L-6
Culpeper* N-4
Cumberland* M-6

D
Dabney S. Lancaster Com. College J-5
Dahlgren O-4
Dale City O-3
Daleville J-6
Damascus F-7
Danieltown N-7
Dante E-7
Danville K-7
Danville Com. College E-5
Darvills N-6
Davenport E-6
Dawn O-5
Dayton L-4
Deep Creek T-8
Deerfield K-4
Delaplane N-3
Deltaville Q-5
Dendron P-6
DeWitt N-6
Dickensonville E-7
Dillwyn M-5
Dinwiddie* N-6
Disputanta O-6
Dixie M-5
Doe Hill K-4
Doswell O-5
Dot D-7
Drakes Branch L-7

Hurt K-6

I
Ida M-3
Independence* G-7
Independent Hill O-3
Indian Valley H-7
Institute of Textile Technology C-3
Iron Gate J-5
Irvington Q-5
Isle of Wight* P-7
Ivanhoe H-7
Ivor P-7
Ivy L-4

J
James Madison University E-2
Jamestown P-6
Jarratt O-7
Java K-7
Jeffersonton N-3
Jetersville M-6
Jewell Ridge F-6
Johnsontown R-6
John Tyler Com. College G-3
Jonesville* C-7
Jordan Mines I-5
J. Sargeant Reynolds Com. College
Downtown Campus J-2
Parham Campus G-1
Western Campus N-5

K
Keene L-5
Keezletown L-4
Keller R-5
Kempsville V-7
Kenbridge M-7
Kents Store M-5
Keokee D-7
Keswick M-4
Keysville M-6
Kilmarnock Q-5
Kimballton H-6
King George* O-4
King & Queen Courthouse* P-5
King William* O-5
Kinsale P-4
Kiptopeke R-6
Konnarock F-7

L
Lacey Spring L-3
La Crosse M-7
Ladysmith N-4
Lahore N-4
Lake Jackson R-4
Lakeside G-2
Lake Ridge S-4
Lambsburg H-7
Lancaster* Q-5
Lanexa P-6

Oilville N-5
Old Church O-5
Old Cold Harbor H-2
Old Dominion University U-7
Old Point Comfort Q-6
Onancock R-5
Onley R-5
Opal N-3
Orange* M-4
Oriskany J-5
Orkney Springs L-3
Ottobine K-4
Owens O-4
Oyster R-6

P
Paint Bank I-5
Painter R-5
Palmer Springs M-7
Palmyra* M-5
Pamplin City L-6
Pardee D-6
Paris N-3
Parksley R-5
Partlow N-4
Patrick Henry Com. College J-7
Patrick Springs I-7
Pattonsville D-7
Paul D. Camp Com. College
Franklin Campus P-7
Suffolk Campus P-7
Pearisburg* H-6
Pedlar Mills K-5
Pembroke H-6
Penhook J-7
Pennington Gap C-7
Penn Laird L-4
Penola O-5
Petersburg O-6
Phenix L-6
Phoebus U-6
Piedmont Virginia Com. College D-4
Pilot I-6
Piney River K-5
Pipers Gap H-7
Pocahontas G-6
Poplar Camp H-7
Poplar Hill H-6
Poquoson Q-6
Portlock U-7
Port Republic L-4
Port Royal O-4
Portsmouth Q-7
Post Oak N-4
Potomac Beach P-4
Pound D-6
Pounding Mill F-6
Powhatan* N-5

Thaxton J-6
The Falls M-6
The Plains N-3
Thomas Nelson Com. College T-6
Thornburg N-4
Tidewater Com. Col.
Frederick Campus T-7
Virginia Beach Campus V-7
Chesapeake Campus U-8
Portsmouth Campus T-7
Timberville L-3
Toano P-6
Todds Tavern N-4
Toms Brook M-3
Toms Creek E-7
Trammel E-6
Trenholm M-5
Trevilians M-4
Triangle O-3
Troutdale G-7
Troutville J-6
Turbeville K-7
Tysons Corner T-2

U
Union Hall J-7
Union Level M-7
Union Theological Seminary G-2
Unionville N-4
University of Richmond F-2
University of Virginia C-3
Upperville N-3
Urbanna P-5

V
Valentines N-7
Vanderpool J-4
Vansant E-6
Varina H-3
Vera L-6
Vernons Corner Q-6
Verona K-4
Vesuvius K-5
Victoria M-7
Vienna O-3
Viewtown M-3
Village P-5
Villboro O-4
Vinton J-6
Virgilina L-7
Virginia Beach R-7
Virginia Commonwealth University G-2
Va. Comm. Univ., Med. Col. of Va. J-2
Va. Highlands Com. College F-7
Va. Intermont College G-5

as bright and gay, as if she intended a new Intrigue with Endymion: and if there be a man in the moon, doubtless he had the same design upon you. You had no sooner enter'd into the Grove of Pines, but instantly you were surrounded with a whole Clan of Fayrys. Pocopunchello their Prince had been marry'd in the morning and at night invited the Principal of his subjects to a Ball, wch he intended to give in that very spot where you see them. They had no sooner spy'd you but his Highness in proper person begg'd the honour of your company. You accepted the invitation, and were posted in a convenient place from whence you might see the whole solemnity. The Bride & Bridegroom were seated upon 2 purple Toadstools, with Canopys of orange leaves over their heads. The stature of the Prince himself, who was taller by the head and shoulders than all the rest, was six Inches & a half without his shoes. The whole company had come that night from the Island of Felicity, mounted upon fleet Zephirs, which travel from Pole to pole in 16 minutes and a second. As soon as they had dismounted, they turn'd their Coursers into the Flower garden to graze upon Jessamin & carnations. Their music was very uncommon, and not a little outlandish. For it was neither better nor worse than a small sow lying all along upon her side, while 7 Piggs play'd upon her Titts most melodiously. The sound came out thro the several Pipes of her snout, Ears and Backside, while at her throat she grunted out a Thorow base with more skil than Segnor Nicola.[1] All this together made a sort of musick like an Organ, tho much finer, from whence without Controversy, came that good old saying of Piggs playing upon Organs.[2] To this Music they

[1]Probably a reference to the Italian opera singer, Nicolini, who was popular in England from 1708 until 1717 when he returned to the Continent. He was noted as an actor as well as a singer (*The Tatler,* No. 115; *The Spectator,* No. 405; John Ashton, *Social Life in the Reign of Queen Anne* [London, 1904], pp. 273-74).

[2]Hogs Norton (or Hoch Norton) was a village whose inhabitants in the seventeenth-century were said to be exceptionally boorish and rustic in their conduct and a proverb ran, "I think thou wast born at Hoggs-Norton, where piggs play upon the Organs" (*Dict. of Eng. Proverbs,* comp. W. G. Smith [Oxford, 1935], p. 190).

daunc't with an agility superior to Monsr Balon,[1] and yet with as much ease as The French Gipseys. You were very much surpriz'd at this novelty, but cou'd not see the end of this solemnity, by this unlucky accident. The Prince kept his Eys constantly upon you, and every moment sigh't with abundance of Tenderness. His Bride observ'd it and instantly reproacht his Infidelity, with a voice so shrill, that it almost burst the Drum of your Ear. And besides that she order'd some of her guard to pinch you without mercy. This was more than sleep cou'd endure, and with excess of pain you wakt. But I believe you remember nothing of it, because Pocopunchello's jealous Bride sprinkled a certain water, made of Poppys & night shade upon your Temples, which made you forget the whole scene, as much as you do what befell you in the state of Preexistence. Adieu.

TO THE SAME

This is the fourth time I have had the confidence to interrupt your contemplation: but I fear that your silence forebodes me no good, because a woman never holds her tongue: but when she's contriveing mischief. The greatest aversion I can perceive in my Temper is to ye displeasing of Zenobia, as you will believe, when to avoid that, I am willing to renounce my most favorite Inclination. Rather than you shou'd be out of humour at my Writeing, I'll deny my troubled mind that offensive way of easing its pain. I'll stiffle my complaints, or at most Ill make them to the winds and the Trees, that are less inexorable than Zenobia. If my Letters displease you, I shall wish I had never learnt to write, as Nero did in the begining of his Reign, when a dead warrant was brought to him to sign. Tis true you have not

[1]Monsieur Balon was a French dancer who was engaged about 1699 by Thomas Betterton, the celebrated English actor, then manager of Lincoln's Inn Fields Theatre, with other French dancers and singers, to entertain the London public. According to Gildon, *A Comparison between the Two Stages* (1702), p. 49, "The Town ran mad to see him [Balon]" (quoted in G. H. Nettleton, *English Drama of the Restoration* [N. Y., 1921], p. 169; see also Montague Summers, *The Playhouse of Pepys* [N. Y., 1935], p. 452; Allardyce Nicoll, *A History of Restoration Drama* [Cambridge, 1928], p. 65, n. 2).

lay'd your commands upon me to forbear writeing, if you had, you had given me an occasion to show my obedience. This wou'd have been some favour, tho like a Coup de Grace, it might have been a killing one. But you have not goodness enough to kill me right out: but chuse rather to buoy me up with a lingering hope that just like the cloaths of those that fall into the water, will certainly help to sinke me at last. However to give you a plain demonstration of my Love, I'll renounce every thing that admits of a paradventure of displeaseing you. Thus Madam Ill prove my Love by my fear of offending you, as Eve prov'd her guilt by runing behind a bush for fear God Almighty shou'd see her naked. If this Billet have the Fate of those I sent before, I will conclude they are unwelcome to you, and will vex you no more by giveing it under my hand that I am &c

---

TO MY LADY C——

What effect it may have upon the passing of your Waters, to recieve a couple of Billets so close upon the heels of one another, I cant determine. If they have the good fortune to please you, no doubt but they will make a quart go off as fast as a gallon wou'd do when You think of Stapleford,[1] or when you talk with Blouzini. That vocal Lady has withdrawn her self out of this Town to go and sweeten her bloud at Tunbridge. I question not but your Lad^{p} will be one of the many sufferers by the exceeding fluency of her Tongue. Youll be provokt to envy those that cant hear without a Trumpet, and to accuse Nature of too much liberality for giveing you five sences when you wou'd have been much easyer with four. The only way you can have to defend your self from this persecution, is to guard your self with some Wit or Beau, on whom she never fails to pour out the stream of her discourse: It is her humour never to talk to a woman if there be a fine Gentleman in Company. For

[1]The chief seat of Bennet Sherard, Lady Calverley's son-in-law, was at Stapleford, three miles from Melton-Mowbray, in Leicester.

this reason pray never appear upon the walks without a Champion to encounter this Medusa, least you run the same fate of poor Niobe, and be turned into stone. Your greatest danger is, least by the outragious volubility of her Tongue she drive all the men from the place. To prevent this Blow, you must lay your commands upon some of the Beaux Esprits, that are now with you to salute her with a foremost place in a Lampoon. And that you may bring this about with the more ease, I will present you with some leads for that purpose. You may please to mention to him her Woolsack-shape, and her vermilion face, that receives its bloom not from paint, but Rattafia.[1] I need not tell you that her tongue is a compleat Cubite & three quarters long, which is so prone to motion, that it wou'd be as mortal to her to stop that, as her Pulse. She had once a feaver, & her Physician told her that talking was very hurtfull to her; Alas Doctor said she, 3 minutes of silence wou'd strangle me. She lys in a mask for her complection, and puts sere cloath upon her knees to supple the skin, and give it the same polish with the rest of her body. Her Devotion at Church is very singular, for she ogles the young fellows dureing the service and casts up her Eys devoutly at publishing the Banes of Matrimony, & the reading of a Proclamation She dresses as gay as a girle of fifteen, that she may have the comfort of seeing something young about her. These are some few strokes of her character, of which the Poet may chuse those he shall judge most mortifying. The next week I intend to come down, & Seignor Honetto will give me the pleasure of his company for as long time as he can spare from his advances to Lord Chancellour. How do's the good, the agreable Melantha? do the Waters show their Healing quality upon her? If they dont may their spring be eternally choakt up, and the detestable Najid hereafter be a close Prisoner in the dark bowells of the Earth. Adieu.

---

[1]A cordial or liqueur flavoured with certain fruits or their kernels (*New Eng. Dict.*). Rattafia was a favorite drink with women in eighteenth century England (J. P. Malcolm, *Anecdotes of the Manners and Customs of London* [London, 1810], I, 170).

TO LADY M——.

Never was Dr Wallice puzzled more to pick out a French Cypher, than I was to read the mystical characters of your Lad^ps letter. There was so much negligence in the Hand, and such a gentiel liberty in the English, that had it not had the honour of your sign manual to it, I shou'd have thought it might have come from one of the nunnerys at Hackney,[1] or else from one of the Ladys Errant of the Towne. However Madam as antique, as Gothick & as grotesk as the hand was, I made shift to decypher it: but nothing cou'd have given me Industry enough to go thro so different a Task, but the Treasure I hopt to find wrapt up in those mysterys. yet How lamentably was I disappointed, when I found your fickle Lad^p in a flame with the German Count that lately ariv'd at Richmond? Instead of discovering some hopes for my self, you convince me that you are intirely another mans. But why in the name of Alecto[2] do you pick me out from all mankind to be your Confident in this amour? Wou'd you have me pimp for my Rival and bring him into the arms of a Lady that I wou'd faign ingross to my self? You tell me he's a man of Quality: but you have no better profe [*sic*] of it than you have of Mr Den—'s[3] wit, that is, his own word for it. All Germans stile themselves counts as soon as they get out of their own country, and I have known several of them y^t have had the humility to equip themselves

[1]Hackney was famous in this period for its boarding schools for girls. When Pepys and his wife visited Hackney Church he recorded in his diary, April 21, 1667, "That which we went chiefly to see was the young ladies of the schools, whereof there is great store, very pretty . . ." Byrd's young sisters, Susan and Ursula, were at school at Hackney, 1688-90. (Letters of William Byrd I, *Va. Mag.*, XXV, 257, XXVI, 132.)

[2]Alecto (She who Rests Not), one of the Greek Erinyes, goddesses of vengeance (Seyffert, *Dictionary of Classical Antiquities, sub* Erinyes).

[3]John Dennis, important critic of the early eighteenth century, though numbered among the wits who frequented Will's coffeehouse, was often the target of ridicule by his contemporaries. He was eccentric, and by 1719 was soured by poverty and literary clashes. Dennis was serious and learned and often flared up in passionate outbursts at the frivolity of Congreve, Purcell and others (R. H. Barker, *Mr. Cibber of Drury Lane* [N. Y., 1939], pp. 118-24). See Congreve's essay on Humour in Comedy, sent to Dennis, July 10, 1695, Edmund Gosse, *Life of Congreve* [London, 1888], pp. 78-82.

in long Lane,[1] and dine in a seller. He has likewise a vast deal of Wit you say, but I wou'd faign know whether you gather it from the bigness of his head, or from the bredth of his shoulders, for your Ladp cant understand any Language he can speak. It may be you make this Inference from the bigness of his nose which amongst the women is a hopefull mark of every good quality. Your Ladp is not particular in your forrein tasts, there are many of that fancy, to prefer the pushing Vigorous stranger to the bashfull Hypocondraique Britton, that is phlegmatick and shrinks from a Ladys Inclination. On the other hand the airy self sufficient Forreigner improves every hint to his own advantage, and even interprets civility & fredome to be stark stareing passion. He is not discourag'd by Frowns nor by the defensive Terms of Pish, and fy, and what do you mean, & whome do you take me to be? These are the bold, whome Fortune favours, and the Ladys (who for whimsicalness and inconstancy out-do Fortune) favour them too. And they have reason, your Ladp will say, because tis a mighty convenience to be ravisht into abundance of pleasure without sinning. From old time it has been the humour of the sex to admire the strength & beauty of the Ravisher, and God forbid you shou'd degenerate from the rest of your kind. There's something monstrous in not being like other women in the disposition of the mind, as well as in the shape of the body. Such an odious singularity wou'd be as much abhorr'd by your Ladp as a nunnery, that has none but old Confessors belonging to it. Adieu.

TO PRECIOSA

You were very sorely affronted at the innocent Declaration which I had the courage to make to you t'other Day. Lord how many squeamish faces, and Ayrs of defyance did you make? How strangely you were surpriz'd, and cou'd hardly forbear starting at the name of love. You lookt as

[1]Long Lane in London reached from Smithfield to Aldersgate Street and "was known for its brokers, its second-hand linen, its upholstery, and its pawnbrokers." (Walter Thornbury, *Old and New London,* II, 363.)

Forbidding as if an impudent Fellow of four-score had mov'd the question. But in spight of all your coldness Madam depend upon it as much as you do upon dying, that you will be glad to love me in the end. You may coulour and knit your dear brows as much as you please, I say it again, you must and shall love me tenderly before you have done. At this place I know you'll pause, and cry what a confident fellow is this? nothing sure was ever so impertinent, & severall other smart things with which your Pride will inspire you. But these are sallys and little Flurts of indignation which will last so short a time, that they'll only serve to prove the fickleness of Your temper. How wofully are you mistaken to fancy that such usage will discourage me? Were you only indifferent, indeed, I shou'd have some reason to fear my address might miscarry: but now I see you nettle'd and angry, I am as sure of you, as if the curtains were drawn about us. When I find a woman capable of my passion, I have the secret to make it what passion I please. And of all the conversions of this kind there's nothing to [*sic*] easy as to turn pride or resentment into love. Nature has half done the work to my hand, for Pride is nothing but a strong love of our selves, and tis only changeing the object and the business is done. The heat is the same, and requires only a different direction. Thus far I may let you into the secret, the rest Ill convince you of by my practice. In the mean time Precious Madam dont have so stiff an opinion of your aversion to me; For Ill let you see that I have skill enough to Foil it tho supported by all your vanity and ill nature. I spare neither Time nor application to win a heart like yours, I abhor an easy conquest, and my love is so heroique as to be inflam'd by difficulty. There are mighty charms in resistance, and the more obstinacy I see in a mistress, the more violent the temptation. I have a constancy that can Follow one & the same scent for seaven years together, without being baulkt. Tho you shou'd never look upon me, but with Frowns, and disdain, yet I shall fancy they become you, by tempering that exceeding sweetness which otherwise might make your charms too luscious. Shou'd you condescend to treat me only with coldness and neglect, I shall follow you with the greater vehemence to warm your Inclinations. Perhaps, for your last shift, you'll play half a score of powerfull Rivals against me: but if you shou'd, Ill make em all dispair of rendering you such faithful such everlasting services, as I shall do. Thus Dear Madam lay what plots you please, I'll infallibly counterplot you, I'll combat your pride with my humility, your aversion with my love, Ill warm your indifference with my flames, and flatter your vanity with artfull commendation, insomuch that youll at last be forct to own your self a mere woman and me

Your Slave.

TO VAPORINA—

Tis very odd advice I am going to give my Dear Vaporina (& which few other people need) to love her self. You can please and charm every thing but your own mind, which seems to be like the troubled sea which cannot rest. You're always upon the Tenterhooks, and that good humour which us'd to enchant all your acquaintance is now quite lost in spleen & vapours. What can be the unlucky cause of so untoward a change? You cant be uneasy in your conscience except it be for letting so many young fellows dye by your Frowns. You cant be in love because there is no heart so cold but your Eys can warm. Your Fortune is plentifull and can give you no handle of complaint. You see no woman so charming as your self, the men adore you in publique, and toast you & sigh for you in private. [Three] & ten of 'em askt me t'other night at ye play who you were. I know an inveterate Woman hater that got a crick in his neck at the Park by turning his head quite round to stare at you. No less than nine Beaux dy'd of consumptions last week & without question two thirds of 'em dy'd for you. All other Beautys have lost their Enbonpoint for the vexation of being eclipst. Envy has cast such a paleness upon their cheaks and sunk their Eys so deep into their heads that their very chambermaids have no more the confidence to tell 'em their handsome. Thus you have all the reason in the world to think your self happy. Nature and Fortune have done all they can towards it, and if you are discontented you are of all creatures the most unreasonable. But I believe those triumphs which please other nimphs have an opposite effect upon you. You are very uneasy at the thoughts of giveing so much pain to the Ladys that envy you. You are disturb'd at the many restless moments which the men endure for your sake. You are distracted with the fears of inspireing 'em wth wicked and impure Inclinations. methinks I overhear you bewailing your self in these moveing terms. Unhappy Wretch that I am! How many Husbands have I caus'd to commit adultry in their hearts? How many young fellows have neglected their Devotion at church to ogle me? How many poor women have by Envy been tempted to slander me and wish me in Hell among ye Furys? How many unlucky swains are now in Bedlam on my account? How many Felons de see have I made by halters & poison? How many have I sent to Flanders to sacrifise themselves to my unfortunate charms? Why was I born or why do I stil live to be the involuntary cause of so much mischeif! Hence Madam I believe proceed those sighs which come so frequently from you. This is the part that pinches you, and makes you unhappy amidst all your advantages. And now I have found out your distemper twill be easy to prescribe a Remedy. And tis the same which a tender hearted Nymph once try'd, who was pretty near in the same circumstances. She scarify'd her sweet Face in several places, and us'd a poisonous ointment which burst her tender skin with blains & scabbs, and swell'd all her features out of knowledge. By this method she put an effectual stop to all the mischeifs occasion'd by her charms, & both men and women might afterwards return to their wits & look upon her with safety. Now if this Receipt be too violent for you, I will tell you one that is more gentle & will have the same success. Lay on white paint, in imitation of some other fine Ladys, every morning for 3 months together, and then leave it off, and Ill ingage you for ever afterwards guiltless of makeing any man uneasy. Adieu.

WASPERINI. HERBERT[1]

Wasperini has the fate to be made of a very valuable mettal, but such as will receive no polish. He has a great deal of wit without the least ornament of Good nature or good manners. He can very easily find out a Fool, and very hardly forbear calling him so. But of all the Fools that divert the World he gives least quarter to the Fool of parts & industry. Those that in spight of nature will be fopps and coxcombs he takes a particular delight in exposeing. He thinks they deserve as little mercy as those women do that will paint a good face til tis very ugly. He has learning enough to see the vanity of it, and to find out that abundance of pendants & virtuosi are not half so wise as they take themselves to be. He has been twice the Tour of France & Italy, and yet is utterly untainted either with complaisance or dissimulation. He detests Flattery so much, and speaks so much unseasonable truth that the Women wou'd never be reconcil'd to him. He was so unhappy in his first rencounter with the fair sex, that he has wag'd war with it ever since. Five hundred strumpets at least have done pennance at the Nunnery of Bridewell[2] for the transgression of one ungenerous Harlot at the Temple. What a chast world shou'd we have if every Justice of Peace had taken as much mercury as Wasperini? He has now so much virtue himself that he can make no allowance for the Frailty of those y^{t} have but little. He has a sourness in his temper

---

[1]The Herbert family either as Barons Herbert of Cherbury or Earls of Pembroke played a prominent part in official and court circles in the early eighteenth century. But the evidence in this character is not conclusive enough to suggest a specific identification.

[2]Bridewell, originally a royal residence, located between Fleet Ditch and Broad Lane, was a prison and house of correction in eighteenth-century London for "idle vagrants, loose and disorderly Servants, Night Walkers, Strumpets, etc." (John Ashton, *Social Life in The Reign of Queen Anne,* pp. 426-29.) Byrd went with Mr. Legrand, the husband of Helena Southwell Legrand, to Bridewell on March 3, 1718, to see the prisoners make pins and the women beat hemp (Diary). Byrd was greatly interested in hemp culture and made repeated experiments in raising it for export. He hoped to find in it a source of revenue to lessen the danger of a one-crop system to the Virginia tobacco growers.

that casts a shade upon his other good qualitys. He is splenitique and uneasy in his own mind, so that tho he worrys other folks, yet he falls foulest upon himself. In this he resembles the pettish Viper which never fails to poison it self when perhaps it but slightly bites its Adversary. A great Estate has not the power to make him happy, but plenty rather supplys fuel to his vapours, and turns all the juices of his Body into melancholly. His quarrel to the women has made him abhor Matrimony: but the froppishness of his constitution makes him an arrant wife to himself. Mirth breaks out as seldome upon his gloomy Face as the winter sun dos in England. When those light intervals are shut in again he looks in as much pain as a splayfooted Beau in pinching shoes. *He is y^r exceeding good freind to day, and tomorrow possibly will be so unacquainted as to crave your name.* His wit like the weapon of a brave man never wounds any one in the back. He gives all mankind fair play, and tells 'em their Faults to their wiskers, that they may parry the thrust as well as they can. He loves a smart Repartee so well that he is not out of humour tho it be pointed ag^st himself. He is very usefull in telling some men bluntly of their faults, which think themself too great for reproof. In this he has no respect of Persons, but dispences his rebukes without favour or distinction. If a Duke wont spare to be a Rascal, he wont spare to call him so, in spight of scandalum magnatum. He never minces nor softens the matter but always draws a villain, and a Fool at full length. His sincerity keeps vice in awe, which else wou'd be apt to grow too rampant. His wit wou'd be admirable if it carry'd a smooth edge, but tis more usefull by being rough, because it increases the Smart. His snarling and flying so feircely at vice gains him the name of Cynick, and his many good qualitys with it, give him the title of the Rough Diamond. All the difference betwixt him and Diogenes is, that he lolls in a coach while the Philosopher liv'd in a Tubb. He knows the convenience of mony and can reconcile good sence to a good Estate, while the other thought wealth and weakness inseperable.

INAMORATO L' OISEAUX[1]

Never did the sun shine upon a Swain who had more combustible matter in his constitution than the unfortunate Inamorato. Love broke out upon him before his Beard, and he cou'd distinguish sexes long before he cou'd the difference betwixt Good & Evil. [. . .][2] *Tis well he had not a Twin-sister as Osyris had, for without doubt like him he wou'd have had an amourette with her in his mothers belly. Love was born to him so long before Reason, that it has ever since slighted its rebukes, as much as old Fopps do the good sence of a young man. However this Frailty has never been without some check, For Diana threw such a Weight of Grace into the opposite scale, that the Ballance has commonly been held very even. And if the Love-scale has happen'd to be carry'd down sometimes, the Counterpoise has not fail'd to mount it up again very suddenly. The struggle between the Senate and the Plebeans in the Roman Commonwealth, or betweext the King and the Parliament in England, was never half so violent as the Civil war between this Hero's Principles and his Inclinations. Sometimes Grace wou'd be uppermost and sometimes Love, neither wou'd yeild and neither cou'd conquer. Like Cesar and Pompey one cou'd not bear an Equal nor t'other a superior.* It must be confesst indeed, His Principles have been sometimes happily supported by the misadventures of his Love, by wch means its own cannon have been turn'd against it self. *This Foible has been an unhappy Clogg to all his Fortunes, and hinder'd him From reaching that Eminence in the World, which his Freinds and his Abilitys might possibly have advanct him to.*

---

[1]In this character of himself, "The Enamored Bird," sent to Minionet in a letter dated Feb. 21, 1722/3 (see below, p. 379), Byrd analyzed himself, for the most part with fidelity to the facts of his life as revealed in his diary, and with considerable insight into his own frailty and strength. It discloses a few hitherto unknown biographical details, especially the military episode. In writing a character of himself he was following a custom of the time, as seen in the well-known character of St. Évremond.

The use of the plural instead of the singular in the French for *bird* was apparently a slip in his copying into this notebook, while the use of *inamorato* suggests the Italian influence in drama and music so prevalent in England at this time.

[2]A sentence is crossed out.

Nature gave him all the Talents in the World for business except Industry, which of all others is the most necessary. This is the spring and life and spirit of all preferment, and makes a man bustle thro all difficulty, and foil all opposition. *Laziness mires a man in the degree in which he was born, and clogs the wheels of the finest qualifications.* Fortune may make a Lazy Fellow great: but he will never make himself so. Diligence gives Wings to ambition by which it soars up to to [*sic*] the highest pitch of advancement. These Wings Inamorato wanted, as he did constancy, which is another ingredient to raise a great Fortune. To What purpose is it for a man to be always upon the wing, if he only fly backward and forward. He must go right out or else he will never go far. He shou'd fix one certain end in his own thoughts, and towards that all his designs, and all his motions shou'd unalterably tend. *But poor Inamorato had too much mercury to fix to one thing. His Brain was too hot to jogg on eternally in the same dull road. He liv'd more by the lively movement of his Passions, than by the cold and unromantick dictates of Reason. This made him wavering in his Resolutions, and inconstant after he had taken them. He wou'd follow a scent with great eagerness for a little while, but then a fresh scent wou'd cross it and carry him as violently another way.* One while the ease with which the Judges loll in their Coaches and doze upon the Bench, tempted him to study the Law: but he was soon taken off by the rapine and mercenariness of that Profession. Then the Gaity of S[t] James's made him fancy to be a Courteour: but the falsness and treachery, the envy and corruption in fashion there quickly made him abandon that pursuit. When this fit was over he was charm'd with the Glory of serving in the army, and thought it a shame for a proper Fellow to live at home in ease, when the Libertys of Europe were in danger: but before he had provided his Equipage, he was discourag'd by the confinement, dependance, & barbarity of that service. *In some frolicks no state appear'd so happy to him as matrimony, the convenience, the tenderness the society of that condition, made him resolve upon his own ruine, and set up for a Wife. He fancy'd it too sullen too splenatique to continue single, and too liable to the inconveniences that attend accidental and promiscuous gallantry. In this humour he'd work himself violently in love with some nymph of good sence, whose Understanding forsooth might keep under all the impertinent starts of a Womans temper. And when he was in love no man ever made so disingageing a figure. Instead of that life and gaity, that freedome and pushing confidence which hits the Ladys, he wou'd look as dismal as if he he [sic] appear'd before his Judge, and not his mistress. Venus and all the Graces wou'd leave him in the lurch in the critical time when they shou'd have assisted him most. When he ought to have had the most fire he had the most flegm, and he was all form and constraint when he shou'd have the most freedome and spirit. He wou'd look like a fool, & talk like a Philosopher, when both his Eys and his Tongue shou'd have sparkled with wit and waggery. He wou'd sigh as rufully as if he sat over a dead freind, and not a live mistress. No wonder this awkward conduct was without success for what woman wou'd venture upon a solemn swain that lookt more like her Confessor than her Gallant, and put her more in mind of a sullen Husband than a sprightly lover? The miscarriage of an honourable amour never disturb'd him so much, but that he wou'd sleep and look much better in his dispair, than he did in the hottest of his Expectation. He was not in half the jeopardy of hanging himself when he lost a mistress, that he was while he was in danger of getting her. While there was hopes he wou'd be assiduous to a fault, not considering that a little neglect in love (like saltpetre in Gunpowder) serves to give force to ye Passion. Whenever his bashfulness gave him leave to declare his mind something wou'd rise in his throat and intercept the untimely Question. A Woman is with more ease deliver'd of a huge boy, than he was of the painfull secret. His Ey-balls wou'd roul with as much gastliness as if he had been strangled. Twas melancholly to see how his heart panted, his spirits flutter'd, his hands trembled, his knees knockt against one another, and the whole machine was in a deplorable confusion. You may guess how ingageing a Declaration must be that was attend-*

ed with so many sorrowfull symptomes. It moved the Nymphs pity at least, if it cou'd not move her inclination. If she cou'd not be kind to a man to whome she had created so much disturbance, yet she cou'd not forbear being civil. Thus whenever Inamorato lost a mistress, he got a freind by way of equivalent, and so Providence made a good Bargain for him when he wou'd have made a wofull one for himself. His Person was agreable enough tho he had a certain cast of pride in his look, which clouded some of the grace of it.[1] Hardly any body likt him that did not know him, and nobody hated him that did. He had almost as many freinds as he had acquaintance and nobody ever fell out with him for any other reason: but because they thought he neglected them.

His conversation was easy, sensible and inoffensive, never bordering either upon profaness, or indecency. He was always tender of the modesty of those that were present, and of the reputation of those that were absent. He was incapable of saying a shocking thing, or of acting an unjust one. He was the never failing freind of ye unfortunate, and good nature was the constantest of all his virtues. He pay'd his Court more to obscure merit, than to corrupt Greatness. *He never cou'd flatter any body, no not himself, which were two invincible bars to all preferment.* He was much readyer to tell people of their faults, than their fine qualitys, because they were already too sensible of these, whereas they were too ignorant of the first. *His soul is so tun'd* to those things that are right, that he is too ready *to be moved at those that are wrong. This makes him passionate, and sorely sensible of Injurys, but he punishes himself more by the resentment than he dos the Party by revenge. If the sun go down upon his wrath twill be sure to rise upon his reconciliation. An Injury never festers or rankles upon his mind: but wasts its self in the First sally of indignation. He is frugal in all Expences upon himself, that he may be generous to the Distresst. He takes more pleasure to supply the wants of others*

[1]This is borne out by the portrait of Byrd, painted in London in 1704 by Godfrey Kneller (reproduced p. 156 in *Va. Hist. Port.;* see p. 160 for an account of its history).

than his own Wantoness. His religion is more in substance than in form, and he is more forward to practice vertue than profess it. He is sincere to an indiscretion himself, and therefore abhors dissimulation in other people. He can sooner be reconcil'd to a professt Enimy than to a pretended Freind. Of all cheats in the world he has least charity for the Holy Cheat, that makes Religion bawd for his Interest and serves the Devil in the Livery of Godliness. His memory is in nothing so punctual as in performing of Promises. He thinks himself as firmly bound by his Word as by his hand & seal, and wou'd be as much asham'd to be put in mind of one, as to be sue'd for the other. He knows the World perfectly well, and thinks himself a citizen of it without the [. . .] distinctions of kindred sect or Country. He has learning without ostentation. By Reading he's acquainted with ages past, and with the present by voyageing & conversation, *He knew how to keep company with Rakes without being infected with their Vices, and had the secret of giveing Virtue so good a grace that Wit it self cou'd not make it ridiculous. He cou'd return from one of the Convents in Drury Lane with as much innocence, as any of the saints from a meeting. He Lov'd to undress wickedness of all its paint, and disguise, that he might loath its deformity.* His discretion never gave him an opportunity to try his courage, for he wou'd never provoke a [. . .] sober man, nor be provokt by a man in drink. *He never interlop't with anothers wife or mistress, but dealt altogether where the Trade was open & free for all Adventurers. If he reflected upon any one t'was by Irony, which a wise man wou'd take for a banter, and a fool for a complement.* His Tongue was so far from embroiling the rest of his Person that upon some occasions it has happily protected it. *He abhors all excesses of strong drink because it wholly removes those Guards that can defend a man from doing & suffering Harm. He's a great freind to temperance, because tis the security of all the other virtues.* It disarms Flesh & bloud of those Tempests wth which it puts out all the lights of Reason. By talking little he is quit of a World of Folly & repentance. His silence proceeds not from want of matter, but from plenty of discretion. He is so great a freind to exactness, that he sometimes allows too little to the frailty of mankind. He wishes every body so perfect, that he overlooks the impossibility of reaching it in this World. He wou'd have men Angells before their time, and wou'd bring down that perfection upon Earth which is the peculiar priviledge of Heaven. This makes him a little too severe upon Faults, which it wou'd not be unjust to forgive. However he wou'd not have Transgressours punisht to procure them pain, but reformation. It proceeds from his hatred of the fault, and not of the offender. *He loves retirement, that while he is acquainted with the world, he may not be a stranger to himself.* Too much company distracts his thoughts, and hinders him from digesting his observations into good sence. It makes a man superficial, penetrateing no deeper than the surface of things. One notice crowds out another, haveing no time to sink into the mind. *A constant hurry of visits & conversation gives a man a habit of inadvertency, which betrays him into faults without measure & without end.* For this reason he commonly reserv'd the morning to himself, and bestow'd the rest upon his business and his freinds.[1] *He often frequented the company of Women, not so much to improve his mind as to polish his behaviour.*[2] There is something in female conversation, that softens the roughness, tames the wildness, & refines the indecency too common amongst the men. *He laid it down as a maxime that without the Ladys, a schollar is a Pedant, a Philosopher a Cynick, all morality is morose, & all behaviour either too Formal or too licentious. He has an excellent talent at keeping a secret, which neither love nor ressentment, Vanity nor lightness can ever draw from him. All the ingenious tortures of the Inquisition cant force him to betray either his Faith, or his Freind.* He always thought Ingratitude the most monstrous of all the vices, because it makes a man

[1]His diary bears out this statement. There were few mornings in the years covered by the known sections of his diary when he did not rise early, read from Greek, or Hebrew or Latin, write and attend to his affairs.

[2]Many of Byrd's correspondents were women. In his diary he showed constantly his desire for feminine society and his pleasure in the company of women of all ages.

unfit for society, which subsists by mutual returns of kindness. *His good-nature is so universal as to extend to all Brute creatures.*[1] *He can not see them ill us'd without the tenderest sentiments of compassion. They are helpless and must submit to all sorts of tyrany while men have some way or other of righting themselves. They have no refuge, no freind, no laws to protect them from injury, but are liable to suffer by the neglect, the wantoness, and cruelty of men. This hard fate he bemoans with a very sensible concern, and the rather, because they have often more merit than their oppressors.*

TO LUCRETIA[2]

Amongst so many packets of Love letters as you every post receive from your admirers, I fear youll have no leisure to allow a slight reading of a tastless epistle from a Relation. I reacon there is to a Tost a certain insipidness in a Kinsmans addresses, which go's on increaseing from a Couzen to a Husband. A stranger of inferior accomplishment hits a womans Tast much better than the finest Gentleman who has the misfortune to be of kin to her. This Madam we find commonly true in practice tho it be not easy to account for so unjust a distinction The reason must doubtless be because that near Relations dont burn so much Incence to their kinswomen and flatter their vanity with so good a grace as strangers do. They are apt to assault them with ill-bred Truths, and to assure them that instead of Goddesses they are no better than frail women. T'is not so great a provocation to a young Lady to uncover her person as t'is to undress her imperfections, because the first, tis possible may make her more agreable, but this will be sure to make her less. However provided youll read my letters and answer them punctually I promise you I will never be so

---

[1]He manifested his thought of them by having grain cast upon the snow at Westover in winter and frequently prayed for protection for the dumb creatures, as he recorded in his diary.

[2]Lucretia, evidently a kinswoman of Byrd, lived in southwest England, a six-day journey by stagecoach from London, by way of Salisbury, (see below, p. 286).

rude as to tell you of one single fault you have. I can safely enter into this engagement Madam because I can discover no shades in your picture but what help to set off and temper the exceeding Lights of it. I can commend you not only with a good grace, but with a good conscience too, and I may the safer do it, because I observe that praise serves only to whet your endeavours after perfection, which serves only to inflame the vanity of other women. Besides I protest your very few follys are so agreable that it needs a world of distinction and a great deal of cynick Philosophy to discover them to be follys. You have the art of makeing those little imperfections so charming, that tis impossible to find fault with them, They are in You what discord is in musique and serve only to make you more enchanting. While the men have their fancy to please, as well as their severer part the Unstanding [*sic*], so long twill be necessary for Women to have a little palatable frailty in order to please irresistably. And were it not for this ingredient in the men, the Empire of Love must sink and young women wou'd have little more charms than their Grandmothers. For Gods sake Madam dont grow too wise therefore nor too perfect for fear of being less agreable. Folly becomes Youth as well as gravity do's grey hairs, and really too much discretion gives a woman an old look, which all the world knows is no advantage to her. If one wou'd inquire nicely into the pretty extravagancys of womens dress and behavior (which very much help to warm the hearts of men) we shou'd be forct to call them follys, and yet how much do they advance the triumphs of the Sex? the same may be said of the bewitching graces of their movement, of their looks, and the enchanting ayres which they contrive to give themselves to the undoing of the Swain that observes them. Let me therefore conjure you dear Couzen til the dreadfull age of 31 (when you know a woma's [*sic*] game is up) to mix 9 grams of folly with one of wisdome, if you have a mind to do remarkable execution. That is the just proportion which Ovid & all the Doctors in the deep science of Love allow to a Woman that wou'd be irresistible. More than this wou'd make you a coquet, and less a Prude, both which characters are detestable. I have the honour to be

Madam

a great admirer of your agreable follys

TO FACETIA IN THE BATH[1]

The Bath had need be prepar'd with all the sweets you mention to correct worse smells, and to protect you from being offended by your own perspiration, just as the elegant M^r^ S—ms lys with his head in a sweet-bag to secure him from the Incence of his own F—ts. How can you or the tawny Nymphs that are with you in the Bath pretend to be Ivory Palaces, when each of you is an eye witness how great a shade nature has cast upon your skins, and how near you approach to the right Feulle-mort complexion? Methinks it shou'd be now too late for Lady Bundle to sweat for a shape, when the market has been so long over for her own wares, and tis time for her to traffique for the pleasure of Mes Demoiselles her Grand daughters. And as for the young Goddesses you mention, were I to act the part of Paris amongst 'em, before I cou'd pretend to pronounce sentence I wou'd not only desire them to put off their cloaths but also to rub off the dirt that hides some part of their beauty. Soap sand and a scrubbing brush might go far in makeing their skins clean: but to make them fair will be as hopeless an experiment as to wash the Negro white. The Learned Dr Burgess[2] hath lately prescrib'd a Bath to the

---

[1]Letters and diaries of the early eighteenth century reveal the habitual casting aside of many of the restraints of modesty at the English spas of the time when conversation had a license, unchecked by the usual niceties observed in the more ordered social intercourse of London and other cities. For a discussion of the type of literary effusion here used by Byrd, see A. Barbeau, *Life and Letters at Bath*, chapters III and IV.

[2]Daniel Burgess was the most prominent nonconformist minister in London in Queen Anne's reign. His meeting house in Carey Street was ruined by the Sacheverell mob and repaired at government expense. He drew large crowds with his style, more oratorical and freer than was the custom among the established clergy, and was widely quoted. Many humorous anecdotes have been printed about his stories. Swift described him in the *Tatler*, No. 66: "There is my friend and merry Companion Daniel. He knows a great deal better than he speaks, and can form a proper discourse as well as any orthodox neighbour" (Ashton, *Social Life*, pp. 350-51; *Dict. Nat. Biog.*).

female saints of his flock to wash the dirt off of their Imaginations; this wou'd be of sovereign use to you & your company, & therefore I wou'd recommend you to him for so usefull a secret. I'm glad Flippante has discover'd the Receipt of stopping the rapidity of a womas [*sic*] tongue by letting her bloud in the back. Tis a kind hint to many a poor Husband in this City to spare no bloud in that part. Poor distressed Psyche that is reduc't so low as to undress at the little statues round about the Bath! how often dos she turn her most shineing parts towards them without makeing the least impression on those wooden Deitys? Sure instead of Cupid which you say is represented by those Figures, it must be Priapus in full vigour, else tis impossible they shou'd work so strongly upon her fancy. But which of the Goddesses is Facetia? She has wit enough to be Minerva, or pride enough to be Juno, and yet I warrant she had rather be addresst by the name of Venus. If the truth were known each of you while you're [naked] fancys her self a Venus surrownded with wanton Cupids patting her upon the Backside. What mistakes dos vanity lead you Damsells into? Since none of you resembles the Queen of Love in any thing but in the liveliness and fury of your Imagination. It wou'd be high-treason to speak such choquing truths to Young Ladys upon firm land but by the statutes of good breeding you know tis allow'd to use liberty of speech upon the water, and if one may be free with any body dresst upon that Element, for a better reason one may be frank with those that are stark naked in it. I had almost forgot to tell you that the Dutch mastiff whome you mention to be of the Party will contrary to the nature of that animal be guilty of infidelity, and discover all your proportions, the scituation of each mole, with all the waggery of your behaviour, and the lively conversation that passes amongst you in that place. I make freindly mention of this to put you upon the requisite precautions, that so whatever innocent extravagances have happen'd may continue a profound secret from our sex, that is apt to draw barbarous consequences from such harmless merriment. I am in ye name of the sweet party here to tell you that none of us need that cleansing which you are obliged to use, to make your selves fit for good company. The Prude you know will take care to keep herself clean, lest her shyness shou'd with reason be construed a fear of being smelt out to be a slut. The Beau without question is neat and clean or else he'll forfeit the bright part of his character, for if he be not that, he is nothing. The Ramp is certainly clean, or else her boistrous motions wou'd be apt to make her unsavory. And lastly for my self I can give it under my hand that I am as sweet as any one can be that perspires 4 Pounds a day, because you know I make vigorous love to a nymph with a Nose truly Roman that smells as quick as a Vulture, tho for very different ends, this to pursue, but she to avoid any thing like carrion.

Adieu.

TO LUCRETIA.

Any one might think the quitting so good conversation, & so agreable a place as Serena punishment enough for a reasonable sinner, without the penance of being packt in a stage-coach for 6 long days together with the most disengageing company in the universe. For my part I thought my sences, thro which my fellow creatures tast so much pleasure, a very great grievance and was almost provokt to envy those who are born deaf and blind. In the first place we had a Country Parson who til this journey never had been out of his own parish since he left the University, which was the year after the Restoration. The man had some learning I must own, but was so impertinent and troublesome with it, that I curst the day that ever his Father sent him to school. His knowledge of the old languages had not made him at all better acquainted with his mother tongue, for in that by the harshness of his voice and the infelicity of his utterance he was almost unintelligible. and for fear he shou'd be too clearly understood by his company he chose to lard his lean English with scraps of Greek & Latin. He attacqut the poor Women according to the rules of Logick, and endeavour'd by a Syllogism to confute the Coachman that the monosyllable Gee was improper to any thing but a carthorse. He knew as little of this world as he did of the next and cou'd talk of nothing that has been done since the time of Domitian. He [. . .] Virginia was an Island lying without Ganges in the East Indies and that it was peopled first by a Colony sent thither by William Rufus. Then to give you a tast of his good breeding, he put out our eys all the way with his broad brimm'd hat which I believe he lay in, for I never see it off dureing the whole Journey. He took care to seat him self on the windward side of the coach that we might all enjoy the perfume of his his [*sic*] Pipe, which never was out of his mouth but only when a Violent Cough came upon him, and then that we might not be loosers by this interruption, his Rheum wou'd fly all about upon our cloaths, and into our faces. His good humour was as remarquable as his good sence, or his good manners. Very many times every day he wou'd reproach a poor Quaker woman, who was one of our fellow-travellers, with her hump back, and told her nature never set such a mark upon any body, but only to signify to the rest of the world that under y[t] deform'd body there lurkt a more deform'd mind. This I thought came with a very ill grace from him who besides the charity one might expect from one in holy orders, had himself the most frightfull face my eyes ever see. He beat a crippled Drawer at one the Inns, who had a wooden leg, because he tread so hard and did not walk on tip-toe: but the poor fellow was even with him and gave him a smart kick on the shins with the wooden leg aforesaid, and then debated with the parson how it was possible for him to tread softly upon a leg that was so hard. Then he was an insupportable sloven and wore his linnen til twas of the same coulour with his coat, tho for that reason I cou'd not be sure he had any on. So that upon the whole matter I think twas very kind to his company to be always smokeing to defend 'em from worse smells. To add to his other perfections he was a stiff virulent Jacobite, and maintained that Kings had a divine Right to put a Curb into the mouths of their subjects and ride [. . .] em as hard as they pleas'd. That God almighty allows to his anointed the undisputed prerogative of trampling upon the necks of his slaves, that he had full power to dispose of their Estates, their Libertys, and their persons as he in his infallible wisdome shou'd think fit, and that it was damnation beyond the power of repentance or purgatory to dispute his sacred will. That if in his mere notion, certain knowledge & absolute authority it shou'd be his Royal pleasure to lye with a subjects Wife or his daughter, it wou'd be High treason against his crown and dignity to oppose it, nay that he ought with all his strength to assist his Maj[y] in case the matron shou'd presume to make resistance. But I have reason to applaud this Principle in the Parson because it helpt us to get rid of him, for at Salisbury the Quaker woman above mention'd went before a magistrate and took her solemn affirmation that the Parson had spoken bitter things against the Government, upon which—not being able to give security for his appearance at the next quarter sessions, he was taken into safe custody, and there we left him full of charity and good intentions towards the People call'd Quakers. But this was but one of our Plagues for we had a certain Female of that sort yclep'd a Prude who disturb'd our small common weath [*sic*] very much. She was a virgin of 33 or thereabouts with a face that wou'd not tempt one 500 Legues from Land. Her features were all stiffen'd with a long habit of squeamish Ayrs, which she had given her self for 14 years together. She had no part of her, free and easy but her tongue which I own, mov'd with a surprizeing facility, and she wou'd take libertys with that tho she laid a strict confinement upon all the rest of her precious person. Most of her Eloquence was level'd at the disorders of her own sex, the licence women took she said was intolerable in a Christian Country, She wonder'd how they cou'd have the confidence to converse with the vile men so freely and even to venture themselves in a room alone with them which she pronounc'd impossible to be done wth safety to their vertue. I askt her whether she cou'd not trust her self alone with the person who set overagainst her in the coach? I warrant her reply'd the parson for she with a great deal of gentleness suffers me to press her knees betwixt mine. This ungallant discovery made a mortal quarrel between those opposites as long as they travel'd together, and nobody triumpht at the parsons disaster so much as this dainty Gentle-woman. She wou'd neither get out or into the coach so much as before the women except they wou'd solemnly promise to shut their Eyes, for said she I shou'd sink into the ground if any body shou'd see my ankle. Ay quoth the Parson the poor woman had the Rickets when she was a Child, and so abhors anyone shou'd see her legs. This you may be sure did not much heal the breach that was formerly between 'em. I askt her what she thought of shewing her Elbows? She told me I had a great deal of assurance to name so obscene a part as that in civil company. I beg'd her pardon for being guilty of so great an indecency, but humbly inquir'd into the reason why so usefull a part as ye Elbow was so much in disgrace with her? She with a disdainfull look reproacht me with Impertinence for repeating things so shocking to a woman of Vertue. You are right madam said her good freind the Parson, for the Elbow is near akin to the knee and all the modest saints of the world know that a womans knee is a hallow'd part and ought to be vail'd from the curiosity of men. Besides said he the skin of the Elbow is shrivel'd and of a darker coulour than the rest of the body, which shews it ought not to be expos'd to the view because tis a deformity. But pray neighbour (continu'd he) what will become of all your shyness at the Resurrection, when you will rise stark naked out of the grave without a Rag to cover your back side, and all the whole universe will be gazeing at you? Sawcy fellow, reply'd she with a look as stern as Alecto, how can you mention such filthy Ideas? I hope the good Angels at that time will find some way to save our modesty, or else I shou'd desire to lye stil in the grave rather than be so confus'd and out of countenance as I shou'd be in such an utter dishabillé. I told her that one so fearfull of the men wou'd do well to live in Spaine Turky or China where the better sort of women were never seen but by their Husbands. Indeed said she I envy the women very much of those Countrys where they are never forced to walk before the men: a womans gate is what she shou'd be very carefull of discovering, because uncharitable inferences may be made from that innocent motion. Now you will be surpriz'd Lucretia when I tell you that this saint of untainted virtue this unsully'd unpolluted nymph had a child by her Uncles coachman, and made this Journey on purpose to meet him at one of the Inns by the way.

TO DUNELLA[1]

I have never writ to you since you quitted this melancholly corner of the world, nevertheless I hope you have not forgot the freindship settled between us when you was here. At that time you may remember, I us'd to unbosome all my greifs to you before I was marry'd, and you must bear with me for doing as much now I am. I have no other freind I can trust with a secret of importance, & therefore without I tell my story to you, I must e'en swallow my sorrows as poor Job us'd to do his spittle.

You may have heard I believe that there is a gentlewoman in my house call'd Incendia.[2] She was forsaken some time

---

[1]This feminine diminutive of Dunn suggests that this letter was written to a kinswoman of the minister Dunn who married Incendia, the subject of this letter.

[2]Incendia was Mrs. [or Miss] J-f-r-y, who was married to Parson Dunn, minister of Hungars Parish, Northampton County, in 1709 (Diary, Sept. 13, 1709). Deserted by her husband, she seems to have lived at Westover in 1711-1712 (Diary), where she was an irritant to both its master and its mistress from time to time, and yet was an intimate confidante of both Lucy Parke Byrd and her sister, Frances Parke Custis. This letter, undated, was apparently written between 1710 and Byrd's return to England in 1715.

Byrd, who quickly forgave personal grievances, was writing to Mrs. Dunn from England in friendly terms, and possibly with satirical humor, after the death of his wife, Lucy Parke. John Custis, his brother-in-law, was much alarmed for fear Byrd would install Mrs. Dunn as mistress at Westover, for he wrote Byrd [1718]: "Mrs. Dun has rec'd a letter from you and has expos't it (I must believe through vanity) to everybody almost: I must tell you y[t] you have not only affronted all yo[r] H[r] relations but y[e] Ladies in y[e] Country in generall: yore writing to Mrs. Dun that you know no woman in Virg[a] so capable of y[e] care & bringing up of yo[r] children as herself: give me leave to bee soe free wth you S[r] as to remove y[e] cursd moat from before y[r] eys y[t] has, to my certain knowledge, most egregiously deceiv'd you after many years; I never thought it proper to undeceive you till now: for certainly if I may compare temporall, wth eternall affairs; Adam himself was not more deceiv'd nor was much y[e] Loss suffered by y[e] first woman y[n] you have bin She says you have beg[d] her to live with you w[n] you come in: sure you are not quite given over to yo[r] own destruction: I am well satisfy'd as long as you keep her; y[e] dearest friends and relations you have will never look wthin your doors; no one has: has [*sic*] more ridiculed railed att and abused you than y[e] woman

ago by her Husband: but she told so fair a story in her own favor, that her freinds cast all the blame upon the man. I cou'd not forbear pittying the matron, especially when I knew she had marry'd a fool whome, she thought she had wit enough to govern. But he was not so much a fool neither but ressented severely her attempting the soveraign. The truth is, she had tolerable good sence, and I thought for that reason she might be an agreable companion for my wife. On this consideration I invited her to my house, & treated her with all the civility due to a Gentlewoman in distress. But she had not been with us long, before I was convinced, that her Husband might have had some provocation to use her as she [*sic*] did. For besides a certain impurity she had upon her almost continually, which was enough to make her loathsome, she had also a thoughtless rash way of Reparté, which a Husband jealous of his authority might think intolerable. I was also confirm'd in that maxime in Oeconomy which informs us, that tis dangerous to admit a woman into your house, who had liv'd very uneasily with her own spouse, for she won't fail to infect any other wife she converses with, with her own humours and infirmitys, and like the Devil, endeavour to bring her to be as unhappy as her self. This I have been so unlucky as to experience in some measure, and if Incendia tarry with us much longer My Wife and I, who us'd to be envy'd for a happy couple, shall very probably come to extremitys. And tis remarquable that every family this Make-bate has liv'd in without her spouse, (who us'd to keep her in some order) hath been unfortunate in this particular. What with seasonable flattery, and humouring all my Wives foibles, and easeing of some of her domestique troubles, she has gain'd so

---

who seems to have such a valued frd; wch abundance will inform you if you desire proof of it: nay she has not spard Mrs Byrd who I am sure was so good a friend to her: I protest solemnly I do not give you this hint out of ye loose prejudices to her, but out of pure friendship to you; and must labor under ye misfortune if you take it otherwise: indeed I was very angry wn I heard she had exposd yor Letter. I wish you may hold in your sane mind as you have signify'd to me in one of yr Lettrs. that is to gett some decayd gentlewon and bring in with you for ye Education of yor children &c. for if Mrs. Dun has ye bringing of ym up, few men yt ever heard of her will venture to marry ym, unless to a very good advantage: I shall say no more on this subject, I hope a word to ye wise is sufficient" (Custis Letter Book).

intire an ascendant over her that she draws her into her Interests even against mine. She has also preacht up a very dangerous doctrine, that in case a Husband dont allow his wife mony enough, she may pick his pocket or plunder his scrutore to do her self justice, of which she is to be her own Judge. I leave it to you Madam whether this be doctrine very conducive to the peace of Familys, and whether those that propagate it don't deserve to be expell'd from all well-govern'd societys in the universe? The following these seditious Rules, and the barefac'd espouseing Incendias practices against me, have bred very unpleasant controversys betwixt me & my Wife, and if some effectual Remedy be not taken in time, I cannot promise for the consequences.

You must know this Gentlewoman carrys on a separate Interest in my Family, [. . .] to keep her self in fine cloaths, to which she has a vast and very unbecomeing inclination. She is homely, middleag'd, & a Parsons cast off wife, and has nothing but what she gets by the opportunity she meets with in my family, and yet she loves to make an appearance as she prettily calls it, and to adorn a Person which by too much gaity only becomes more remarkably disagreable. I consented to her bringing a maid into the family to assist her in her Industrys that she might not employ my servants which I was promis'd she shou'd not do. But not content with this kindness, she has ever since employ'd clandestinely severall of my servants to the neglect of my business, and the breach of her own engagements. And if any of my People dar'd at any time to neglect her affairs, tho it was to do what I had set them about, by her instigation they were chastis'd and threaten'd after a shamefull manner, & were further given to understand, that if they had the impudence to tell me, they shou'd have their tongues cut out. Upon discovering several instances of this unworthy treatment, I must have had a martyrs patience not to have some sharpe expostulations with my Wife concerning them, who has notwithstanding adher'd [. . .]ly to her Confidants interest against her Husband. [. . .] these provocations the most gentle measures I cou'd take was to order positively that none of my servants shou'd ever work in her manufactures.

These orders Incendia was resolv'd to break, but durst not do it openly, [. . .] therefore she thought the only way was to perswade my Wife to threaten all the servants with whips and scorpions, if they ever told me one syllable, tho I shou'd be never so inquisitive about it. And some were in earnest beaten for answering the truth to some questions I put to them. [. . .] You may guess what wars and domestique disputes this created in the family and yet my patience and love of Peace stil forgave it. But behold what a man gets by giveing way to ill usage. My easyness in these points had no other effect but to encourage Incendia to use me worse lately, than ever she had done before. You must understand I have a Weaver in the house, which I keep to weave course cloaths for my servants, and because I was too sensible how ill I had been treated in other cases I charg'd him strictly to weave for nobody without my express orders. However when I was gon abroad Incendia took upon her to command the Weaver to take my cloath out of the loom, and put in a piece of hers, and for that purpose an other of my servants was taken from his work to make her a Beam fit for her purpose. The weaver pleaded his masters orders against what she desir'd, & told her plainly he durst not do it. She with abundance of good grace call'd him a sawcy Rascal for disputeing her commands, and assur'd him she had a great mind to break his head. This did not discharge all her gall, but she came instantly and exasperated my wife against the fellow, notwithstanding her condition made her utterly unfit for such a Ruffle. In short for presumeing to Obey his masters orders, this unhappy servant was not only menaced after a very rugged manner, but had some of his cloaths taken from him. Neither was this all, but when I came home and found fault with the little work, the weaver had done I was told t'was because the fellow had slep't away his time, with a good natur'd Intent to exasperate me against him. The way I came at last to know of this adventure was thus. The Weaver lookt so scared when I came home, that I wonder'd what ail'd him. I askt him several times, as I did the other servants, what had betided him: but not one syllable cou'd I get out of any of 'em, so well they had been disciplin'd to secrecy. Upon this I began to suspect some hard usage, and was resolv'd to fetch it out. I therefore brandisht a good Cudgel over the weavers head protesting I wou'd break his bones, if he did not discover what disturb'd him. When he found himself in this Jeopardy he fell down upon his knees, and told me how he had been us'd for obeying my orders. However to shew what an excess of dissimulation Incendia was mistress of, she pretended to wonder as well as I what had happen'd to the Fellow to make him look so dismall, and with a very grave face said she was confident he had seen a spirit. But Hypocrite as she was, she knew the reason too well and the man might well appear terrify'd in so wretched a circumstance. For he was in danger of beating if he did not follow my orders, and in a fair way of haveing his bones broke if he did. This proceeding had something so unjust to me, and so inhumane to the poor servant that I cou'd contain my self no longer. But because my wife was breeding, and too apt to fly into intolerable passions in favour of her freind Incendia, I concluded the best way wou'd be [. . .] her be quiet, and cooly let her Parasite know, [. . .] I was inform'd of the whole matter. However in justice to the injur'd weaver, I gave it under my hand, that in case she offer'd to discompose my Wife with what I told her, or in case the fellow had any hard word, blow, or other ill usage directly or indirectly on her account, and if he had not immediately his Cloaths restor'd to him, she must pardon me, if I put it out of her power to disturb the peace of my Family any more. I also gave her to understand that for the future none of my servants shou'd without my leave be employ'd, about her affairs, nor punisht for not doing it as some lately have been, or otherwise I shou'd take effectual measures to prevent it. Many are the instances of ill usage which I receive from this Gentlewoman: but I shall mention but one more at present. And that is in relation to her Maid, who it seems is not honest enough to be trusted at large, but is made a close Prisoner in a Room just by mine. In this Jeol she must be duly waited upon by my servants, who must bring up her

Victuals, and carry down her nastiness which is a trouble & anyoance [*sic*] which nobody [. . .] understands the rules of common decency wou'd offer to give a Civil family where they are only upon Courtesy.

Now Dear Madam do you judge, you that pretend to so much Justice, generosity, and good nature your self, whether I am fairly treated in these matters. Is it a handsome return in Incendia for the civility, I show her, to sow Discord & confusion in my Family? or if she hath no regard to me, is it gratitude to my Wife, to put her upon such hazzardous methods, as must with a Husband of spirit and understanding make her wretched? I am very unwilling to come to extremitys: but she may depend upon it, I will be master of my Family in spight of all the weak Politiques practic'd to abuse my good nature. Is it just in her to take my servants from my business, and employ them about hers, expressly against my orders? Is it not the most ungenerous cruelty to whip and threaten servants for their obedience to their master? Is it not introduceing Confusion (the greatest of domestique misfortunes) into a Family, to perswade the mistress to command a servant under severe menaces to do what his master had forbid him to do just before? Certainly that servants condition must be most miserable, who is at so unhappy an incertainty whome to obey. Tell me my Dear freind ought a person with such unsociable qualitys, to be suffer'd in the Family of any man that loves Peace and order, and will assert the soveraignty of his House-hold? I will say no more on this disagreable subject, and have given you this tedious trouble, that you may not be alarm'd, if you hear of any Vigorous measures that I may happen to take, if these unworthy proceedings be not alter'd I shou'd stil be content to continue my Civilitys to Incendia, provided she discontinue those methods that must of necessity root out all confidence betwixt me and my Wife. This heavenly Confide[nce] is the only tye of affection, and when that is bro[ken] farewell Love, farewell Peace, farewell hap-p[iness] T'is impossible to love those we can't trust, and therefore t'is the most absurd thing in nature f[or] a wife to forfeit that sacred fidelity, not only [to] her Husbands Bed, but also to his Interest, [. . .] ment to any freind or flatterer in the Wo[rld]

I am &c

INDAMIRA[1]

Indamira had a most benevolent Soule lodg'd in an agreable Body. There was in her Countenance something so innocent that it gave us a tast how the first of the sex lookt before her Fall. Good-nature had the ascendant in her temper, & spread a sweetness and a grace over all her Features. She had a Cheerfulness in her humour peculiar to a serene and unreproaching Conscience. Her Behavior was easy and engageing in spite of a most retir'd Education. She had that happy turn of good sence that is truly usefull to its owner. It made her triumph over strong Passions, and bind a very voluble tongue to its good behavior. It enabled her to acquit her self with honour in all the various dutys of life. She ador'd the God of Heaven and Earth with an undissembled Piety. She was dutifull and affectionate to none of the most indulgent Parents. Her love to her Husband made even subjection and obedience more pleasant to

---

[1]Indamora, the captive Queen in Dryden's drama *Aureng-Zebe,* is evidently the prototype for Byrd's character so highly praised in this sketch. In the drama of Dryden, Indamora arouses the love of all the men who come under the spell of her eyes, but is faithful under every temptation to Prince Aureng-Zebe to whom she had pledged her faith. Her character is summed up in her lines: "All greatness is in virtue understood;/'Tis only necessary to be good."

It is possible that Indamira was Lucy Burwell, daughter of Lewis Burwell, of Carter's Creek in Gloucester County, Va., and a cousin of Lucy Parke Byrd. She married, Dec. 1, 1704, Edmund Berkeley, who lived before 1713 in Petsworth parish, and then moved to Barn Elms, Middlesex County. He was a member of the Council. Lucy Burwell Berkeley died Dec. 16, 1716 in her thirty-third year. Her husband's will, proved March 3, 1718, mentioned a son Edmund and three daughters, Lucy, Mary, and Sarah. (*Va. Mag.,* XXXV, pp. 34-5).

Byrd frequently mentioned Lucy Berkeley, as "Cousin Berkeley," in his diary, 1709-1712, and on May 3, 1709 described her as "a very pretty, good-humoured woman but seemed to be a little melancholy." Lucy Berkeley and her sisters, Elizabeth, wife of Benjamin Harrison, Martha, wife of Henry Armistead, and Joanna, wife of William Bassett, were of the generation of their cousins, Lucy Parke Byrd and Frances Parke Custis, and the Parke family on Queen's Creek and the Burwell family on Carter's Creek, on opposite sides of the York river, were friendly. This friendship was kept up when the young cousins established homes of their own in Tidewater Virginia.

her than Empire. Her tenderness to her children was intire, but did not amount to an indulgence of their faults. Those of 'em that dy'd before her, she offer'd up with resignation to her maker. In her Intimacys she was delicate, but where she distingusht merit, she was a generous & a faithfull Freind. To those whome Providence had rankt below her, she was full of goodness and condescention. In the neighbourhood where she liv'd, she was a Common Good. She was compassionate to the poor, and cou'd not see an unhappy object without shareing its distress. She made kinder allowances for her neighbours frailtys than her own. When she spake of any bodys faults, twas certainly to themselves, but when she spake of their merit twas to other people. She had a free and generous spirit, which proceeded from the pleasure, not the vanity of obligeing. She had nothing little or narrow in her soul, and was never selfish but in the concerns of Eternity. She dissembled nothing but h[er] own Charitys, which she manag'd with [as] much secrecy as if they had been cri[mes] Her understanding was happely impr[. . .] in the proper accomplishments of her [. . .] Her learning was purely feminine, in [. . .] part of which she excell'd without [. . .]tinence. The improvements of her [. . .] set so easy upon her, that they seem'd to be the bountifull gifts of nature. [. . .] study'd each part of her Province, and [. . .] to be a blessing to her Family. No [. . .] after Pleasure made her neglect to [. . .] her Children, or Superintend her [. . .] She thought it the duty of a Wife [. . .] to make her self agreable, but also [. . .] to her Husband. In all her Expences [. . .] consider'd more his Credit than her own vanity. In her house as well as in her person, there appear'd an elegant sim[. . .]ty, that pleas'd beyond all magnificen[. . .] Every thing about her shew'd much of good tast, and nothing at all of ostentation. [. . .] Minerva her self was not more ingenious in designing, or more dexterous in executeing every curious & usefull worke. Thus good thus engageing was Indamira and was so happy as to dye in the noon of her beauty, and her vertue. Very unlike other Flowers she wither'd not upon her stalk, but was transplanted in full bloom into Paradice. How truly desola[. . .] must the Husband be, that was torn from a consort, & what real Orphans are the ch[. . .]dren that are bereft of such a heavenly Exam[. . .]

While we with Tears for selfish ends
Her hasty fun'ral greiv'd,
The angels that are more her freinds
Were sorry while she liv'd.[1]

TO SABINA.[2] March 23. 171 6/7

The last Masquerade[3] wanted no Creature but th[e] charming Sabina, to make it the most agreable Entertainment in the world. All the Goddesses were there but the Queen of Love, who wou'd have appear'd to disadvantage

---

[1]This concludes the contents of notebook B. The succeeding letter to Sabina begins the contents of Notebook A.

[2]Sabina was Mary, younger daughter of John Smith, Commissioner of Excise, whom Byrd called in a later letter Vigilante (see below, p. 321). She lived in London, apparently, in Beaufort Buildings, on the Strand just west of the Savoy, Beaufort Street running from the Strand to the Thames, next to Worcester Court. (*A new and Exact Plan of the City of London,* 1724.) A contemporary description of this part of London says "Worcester-House, built by a natural Branch of the House of Lancaster, was the Seat of that noble Family for many Ages; but it is now pulled down and built into Tenements, which are called Beaufort-Buildings; the Title of Duke of that Royal Branch, and makes a fine street." (John Macky, *Journey through England,* I, 147.) Thus Byrd could watch Sabina come and go from his window. He had apartments in this immediate neighborhood until he moved in July, 1719 to the chambers of Sir George Cooke in Lincoln's Inn (Diary, July 18, 1719). Mary Smith was 24 years old when Byrd courted her as Sabina, though she claimed to be 20. According to London gossip she was not a favorite with her father (Countess Ferrers to the Honorable Mrs. Shirley, Sept. 24, [1714], in Hist. MSS Comm., *Eleventh Report,* App. IV, pp. 227-28).

The course of Byrd's affair with Sabina can be followed both in his letters and in the portion of his diary from Dec. 1717 until he left England. During the courtship he mentions meeting her at the theater, discussing his affair with a mutual friend, Mrs. B-r-n, and with her sister and brother-in-law, Lord Dunkellen (see below, p. 315), writing to her, and dreaming of her. On July 8, 1718, Sabina married a rival, Sir Edward Des Bouverie. But Byrd continued to mention her, and sometimes to dream of her, after this event. In 1721 Sabina died and was buried at Britford, near Salisbury, in Wiltshire.

[3]An important element of the social life at this period consisted of masquerade balls, such as those introduced by Mr. Heidigger, manager of the Opera House from 1708 to 1734 (William B. Boulton, *The Amusements of London* [London, 1901], I, 91-108. (See below, p. 365).

in any figure but yours. I fear the old Dragon that guards the Golden fruit,[1] wou'd not consent to your tasting so much pleasure abroad, lest you shou'd come to detest your confi[ne]ment at home. However I cant forbear offering you an[o]ther Ticket for the next, which is to be on munday. O that I might have the pleasure of finding you out amongst that new world of whimsical Beings. If I knew nothing of your Dress, I shou'd discover you by meer sympathy tho you were disguiz'd like mother Shi[p]ton.[2] That which is accounted of all the Passions the most blind, wou'd in that single case be the most discerning. I hope I need not wish you Inclination, but power to come, else that fine Place will loose all its charms, and be no better to me than a lonely Desart tho all the Beautys of the Earth be there besides. How shall I know whether my Dearest Sabina will please to accept of my Ticket, If she dos, I beg that this may be the gracious Signal, let her about ten a clock lift up the sash, and look with a consenting smile towards my Appartment. Adieu thou most enchanting of the sex, and may Angels without Envy guard you from every thing that is unfortunate.

Adieu.

This must be plac'd the third.[3]

TO SABINA. Jan. 15. 1717. 1.

The grave People say t'is a weakness to be in love and the Reason they pretend to give, is, because persons in that fanciful circumstance conceive more perfect notions of some dear Nymph than she deserves. This they say is to judge by the Romantick Rules of Imagination, which is the greatest Cheat in the world. I confess that is the unhappy case of

[1] *I. e.,* Sabina's father, John Smith, who steadily opposed Byrd's courtship of his daughter.

[2] The prophecies of Mother Shipton, probably a fictitious character, have been much quoted in England since the middle of the seventeenth century, appearing in various forms in chapbooks.

[3] Though appearing first in the notebook, this is the third of the letters to Sabina in chronology, and Byrd pointed this out in his memorandum. He arranged this correspondence to reveal the full story of his affair with Miss Smith, whose perfidy, as he saw it, he deeply resented.

those swains that are charm'd by the single force of unaided Beauty, which may be able to make a Conquest indeed, but cant preserve it. But where a Woman is agreable as well as beautifull, that is, when besides an enchanting Form, she knows how to entertain you with her humour, when she can soften you with an obligeing Look, and charm you with a gracefull behavior, when her air, her mien, her manner conspire to please and delight you, surely to love such a Woman is just, not only by the allowance of Reason, but from the impossibility of avoiding it. Tell me my Dear Sabina if you cou'd reproach a man for adoreing a Damsel with such irresistable Qualitys, or cou'd you blame the tast of a Hero that shou'd sigh for the sake of the bright Original, of which I shall here trouble you with the Picture? I must beg your permission to call her Sabina, because by that dear name I wou'd understand all that is excellent in the Sex. Sabina then is not so tall as to be masculine, or so low as to be related to the Fairys. She has so easy so regular a shape, that one envys the very girdle that embraces it. The Innocence of her look forbids those desires, which the beauty of her face wou'd otherwise be too apt to kindle. Her Temper is chearfull under the most unnatural confinement. Obedience makes her content to be a Recluse, amidst the Gaity and Pleasures of a vast city. Piety and good Sence makes her submit with Patience to the humours of a peevish & unreasonable Father. He judges so ill as to inferr from his wan[t] of Tast to all Pleasure at fourscore, that she ought to have non[e] at four and Twenty. Like a beautifull Flower he wou'd rather suffer her to wither on the stalk, than be gather'd in bloom, and apply'd to ye faithfull bosome of him that wou'd be ravisht with her Sweetness. Thi[s] is the Picture of the enchanting Nymph, that fills all my thoughts by day, and my Fancy by night. I can paint no Landscape of Happiness without makeing Sabina the Principal Figure. If you know this divine Creature tell her how intirely how eternally I love her, and that I can justify by the strictest rules of good sence, the Passion I have for her.

Adieu.

TO SABINA. Feb. 11. 1717. 2.

The News that you were just going to be marry'd struck a damp into my bloud, and almost threw me into another Feaver. When I consider'd how little the disagreable marmouset deserv'd you, I despis'd him, I hated him; but when I reflected that he was going to take into his detested arms the most engageing Nymph in all this Island of Beauty, I envy'd him with all my soul. But then O the exquisite Joy I conceiv'd at the Report that the match was broke off! It was transporting and penetrated into the very quick of my Heart. I concluded instantly y[t] it must needs have been broke off on Sabina's side, for what Man that has Eys, and Ears, and understanding cou'd reject so charming a Woman on any terms? Were so much Perfection stark naked, and destitute of every advantage of Fortune, I shou'd prefer it to all the glorys of this idle and unsatisfying world. O y[t] my Dear Sabina's Fortune were less, nay she will pardon me if I wish she had none at all, either in present or expectation, y[t] I might give her the best proof in the world with how much passion, and with how little regard to vile Interest I am &c.

TO VERAMOUR. July. 1. 1717.

I receiv'd the letter you sent under the Name of Madam Turnover, and had reason to beleive there was more in the Paper, than was exprest in Black and White. Before that, I had two Billets from you under the like discreet Disguize, and did not doubt but this brought a third of the same tender kind. I therefore went to work in all hast with my Decyphering Elixir, in order to extract your meaning, and bring all that Tenderness to light which I imagin'd you had wrap't in darkness: but to my great Surprize and disappointment, I cou'd not make one syllable of it appear. How much this baulkt my Curiosity, I ought not to tell you; all my Comfort is, that you kindly intended to write me something about your Passion: but made use of so feeble a sort of Liquid, that it cou'd by no means express it. I give you this freindly notice, that you may take more care another time, and not give me the pain of expecting to have a great many fine things said to me, to no manner of Purpose. The Defect was surely in your Tools, for I'm confident of the goodness of mine, which wou'd infallibly have explain'd your Inclinations, had you taken care to signify them properly. And I must reproach you thus far, that had you thought what you wrote to me material for me to know, you had not been so unseasonably negligent on this occasion.

Adieu.

vide Page 1[1]....

TO SABINA July. 2. 1717. 4.

T'is astonishing that my Invisible character shou'd not shew it self upon the application of your Elixir: but I have now taken effectual care to express what I said last in a more intelligible manner. Tis very perverse in the Agreable Sabina to be so shy to an old Acquaintance, for no earthly reason but because I adore her above all Womankind. For this provokeing cause it seems you turn away your head with so sudden a motion whenever I appe[ar] that I fear from being the most faultless figure in the world, you'll come as a punishment for your cruelty to have a wry neck. For Venus sake is love then so heinous a Crime, that it shou'd provoke such forbidding such disdainfull airs? My Dear Sabina need apprehend no danger from her good Genius, which In earnest I am, if wishing her every thing that is agreable, and endeavouring to do her all the service in the world, be a sign of it. No, I swear to you by all the Powers of Love, that tho I had rather possess your Charms, than be soveraign of all the rest of the Sex, Yet I will never be guilty of any thing that I think will offend the dear Nymph, whome I wou'd have to be the happiest, as well as she is the most desireable of Women. Upon this nice Principle I have lately avoided paying my Complements to you, while at the same time my heart glow'd with the most tender Respect.

---

[1] *I. e.,* of Notebook A.

But I can be guilty of that false appearance no longer, for my Body must bow, where my soule adores. If you cou'd look into my heart, you'd beleive that I love you without any mean Regard to your Fortune; I bless my Stars my circumstances are not so low, nor my Avarice so high as to require it. But if Sabina were mistress of no more than the Linnen that covers her agreable person, she wou'd be altogether as enchanting, and I as passionate as now. She may please to remember, that I sigh't for her at a time when her Fortune cou'd be no part of the Temptation. I beseech you dont do that Injustice to your own Charms, as to imagin, I cou'd have any other Reason but them for my Inclination. Alas when a heart is fir'd wth so generous a Flame as mine, twill detest all low considerations. But to give you the plainest argument that my tenderness has no motive but your most engageing Person, I declare, that I wou'd even marry you tho your Geoler shou'd be so hard hearted as to deny his Consent. and then t'is a plain case, you wou'd not be worth one splendid shilling If an act so very heroique be not sufficient to convince you I must pronounce you more unbeleiveing than a free think[er]. I know not what the discerning Sabina may Judge of this offer, but I vow I think in this covetous age, tis a handsome thing to love a Damsel well enough, to marry her with nothing but her good Qualitys. However I wou'd not desire this unless I knew my own Fortune sufficient to make you easy without any addition from yours. as violent as my Passion is for you, I wou'd not ask you to descend in your circumstances below the Post of your Education for my sake: but wou'd be always ready to sacrifice the dearest & most darling of my Inclinations to your happiness. This is true so help me Love, and Heaven.

Adieu.

TO VERAMOUR July 4. 1717.

I must acknowledge the very civil offer which you had the goodness to make me, but can't in conscience accept of it. I thank you nevertheless for your great Generosity, which is all a poor Damsel can do under my Circumstances of Obedience. I need not urge to Veramour the duty of the 5th Commandmant, which by the good leave of Constitution I will religiously observe. Neither ought you to preach up Rebellion against a Parent, in one that I'm confident you wou'd not teach to rebel against a Husband. I don't question but Veramours circumstances are sufficient to recommend him to a good Fortune in a more regular way. When a Man is in condition to go to market fairly, tis surely as unpardonable to steal a Wife, as any other valuable thing. But if you shou'd be averse to proceed in the forms with me, the utmost I can do, is to wish you may have all the happy terms you desire with some Nymph more deserving. However I am so much obliged to you for the over-value you are pleas'd to set upon my qualifications, that I shou'd be ungratefull if I did not wish you happy in marriage as well as in every other concern of life. Adieu.

TO SABINA July 5. 1717. 5.

How short do weak words fall of reaching the sprightly sentiments of the heart! T'is utterly impossible to tell you, how my soul is touch't with the vast obligation of your dear dear Letters. By them you have convinc't me of 2 things for which I must eternally thank you. First that you esteem me a man of honour, by trusting me with your hand writeing; and secondly that you indulge me in the exceeding pleasure of paying my Complements to you. As to the 1st madam you may firmly depend on my Fidelity, for I wou'd sooner tear out my Tongue by the Roots, than suffer it to be guilty of exposeing you. By Eternal Truth I swear, your Writeing is a secret that shall descend with me into the silent Grave. I beseech you therefore my Dear Sabina, continue to repose in me this most endearing Confidence. And may I suffer all the Pains of disappointed Love, if either vanity or levity, negligence or inadvertency tempt me to betray you. Then Madam as to the Indulgence you have been pleas'd to allow my letters, it shall never be abus'd. I will be carefull both to write, and to send them with so much precaution, that no mortal with all the Eys of Argus, and the Ears of Envy, shall ever discover the secret. I trust no Servant to carry my Billets to the Post, but perform that faithfully with my own hand; I only fear that the frequency of their comeing that way may alarm your watchfull Family. I wou'd therefore propose to the lovely Sabina a securer method, of which I shall wait her opinion before I make the least advance towards putting it in practice. Trolly that liv'd with our freind the Prophetess, has been here to desire to wash my Linnen. She told me of her own accord, that she was not without hopes of haveing some business of the same kind from you. Now I know her to be very faithfull, and therefore if you'll give me leave, I will swear her to everlasting secrecy, and trust her to carry my Respects to you: and I beleive the same hand may be the safest way of conveying your Commands to me. I propose this the rather Madam, because I cant conceive how you manage the sending your letters to the Post without confideing in somebody, that may not possibly be so trusty as honest Trolly. However I wont venture to make one single step in this nice affair without your permission, because your good pleasure must govern me more absolutely than a Law. I intreat the Charming Sabina not to beleive, that I was tempting her to violate her duty to her Father, while I was only giveing her an Instance of the intire generosity of my Passion. No by Heaven I wou'd have her faultless as earnestly as I wou'd have her mine; for I cant wish her as happy as an Angel, (which I do from the sincerest of my soul) without wishing her at the same time as innocent. Adieu.

TO SABINA. July 10. 1717.[1]

* *No Husband with tender Ears can ever be more punish't by the outragious Eloquence of His Consort, than I have*

---

[1]This is apparently the first of the letters which Sabina returned to its writer, all of which Byrd has marked in his notebook with an asterisk. The words here italicised Byrd underscored in his copy, apparently with the thrifty intention of repeating the sentences he particularly liked in a later letter, since this one was now wasted.

been by the silence of the agreable Sabina. I have long'd for Her answer with an Impatience, beyond that which one in a burning Feaver longs for drink. Imagin for Gods sake the restlesness, the pain that such a Wretch endures, and then tell me if with all your Good-nature you can give it the swain that loves you. Write therefore I conjure you by all the charms of your dear Person, since I am confident you can trust me. Did you sincerely pray, that good fortune might attend me in all the affairs of Life? if you did, I beseech you don't go about to defeat your own obligeing Wishes. Besides madam I want most earnestly to know, whether you approve of my Proposal about Trolly; or must I interpret your silence for consent. Yet I shou'd be cautious of doing that, because I wou'd not run any Risque of offending Her, whome it shall be the dearest business of my Life to please. I wou'd wander to the end of the World, nay I wou'd wander out of it to oblige you, and can you deny to such a one the comfort now and then of a few enchanting Lines? I intreat you likewise to tell me whether it be impracticable to see you. I wou'd give half an Age of useless life, for the pleasure of conversing half an hour with my Dear Sabina. I have ten thousands things to say to her, and wishes ten thousand times ten thousand to make for her happiness; O that fortune wou'd be so kind as to give me an opportunity of expressing them! If your will were but half so good, as your contrivance is ingenious, you cou'd bring it soon about. Nothing is impossible to so much good sence, as you are Mistress of. *In other things I know you have compassion too, and must it be only wanting towards the man that devotes himself to serve you? Forbid it Love & Gratitude!*

TO VERAMOUR. July 10. 1717.

I am surpriz'd to find you so wretchedly mistaken in the construction which you put upon my innocent letters. I swear by the constancy of my sex, that I meant not to indulge your odious complements to me. T'is strange a woman cant write a civil Epistle to a man, but instantly tis understood by his vanity to be a licence to say soft things to her. Had you taken due heed to the good wishes which I sent you in my last, you wou'd have understood it to be a farewell, and consequently a Prohibition for you to write any more. But since you were so stupid as not to apprehend my Plain meaning in that matter, I am forc't to take this harsher Remedy of returning your last letter unopen'd. Tis true I thought you a man of honour, or I shou'd not have taken upon me the part that so ill becomes a Woman: but instead of answering you my self, I had beseech'd the old Gentleman to do it for me. Sure you think me a very odd Nymph, when you imagin I wou'd carry on a secret correspondence with any Gentleman. That wou'd look as if I intended to dispose of my own person, whereas I'm determin'd to be carry'd to market by my Father. However that you may not hang your self quite, I assure you I have no disrespect for you, tho I dont read your Billet but send it back wth y[e] seal unbroken I am oblig'd to you for your care about the Post, but I was just as cautious as you; in that we jumpt, tho we disagree so widely in other matters. Adieu. and be wise if you can

---

TO SABINA. July 14. 1717. 6.

I'm sorry at my soul I have been so unlucky as to offend the lovely Sabina. The Expression she took so unkindly might I confess seem a little too gallant and unguarded but I protest I meant no more by it but to thank her for suffering me to write to Her. I imagin'd that the receiveing half a dozen tender Billets, and answering some of them not at all unkindly, was a permission for me to write on: but if I had the vanity to misconstrue her meaning I ask ten thousand pardons. I found nothing in either of her Epistles which forbad me that favour, if I had, tho it had mortify'd me never so much, I wou'd have prov'd the greatness of my passion by the extent of my obedience. I love you too sincerely to gratify any pleasure of my own by displeaseing you. But stil I hope, nay I beg and conjure you, if you have any good-nature, to let me write, and if youll vouchsafe me that grace, it shall be under what limitation you please. Had I the honour of waiting upon you, there might be less reason for this petition: but since I must not be so happy as to converse with you any other way, I beg it may be by the Invisible character. How can you accuse me of haveing an ill opinion of you, when you may judge by every thing I say, that I think you the most blameless and most engageing of your sex. You have given me undoubted proof that you think me a man of honour, how can you then suspect me guilty of any dishonourable intent? No I cou'd as soon design my own Destruction as any thing that might bring a stain upon the dear Damsel I love. The private method I had projected of conveying letters, was only to keep you as unsuspected as you are innocent. Whether my charming Sabina shall permit me to write to her or not, I shall eternally continue to adore her, even when time shall have wrinkle'd her fair skin, and drawn up those dear features too near to one another, which now enchant me with their harmonious distance and proportion. Adieu. & be kind if you can.

TO SABINA July 22. 1717.

* *Health wou'd not be more welcome to one that has been long sick,* than a small Billet wou'd be to me from the excellent Sabina. Surely there can be no more crime in writeing to him you can trust, than in speaking. The reason why Prudes are shy of writeing, is because they do it ill: *but nobody expresses better Sence in a more elegant character than you.* No wonder if after giveing me a Tast of your Talent that way I shou'd long to have more of it. *T'is not possible to be content with a little of any thing one likes. Therefore Dearest Sabina write again if you have any Compassion for him that wou'd dye for you, or which is stil more gallant, wou'd live in misery to make you happy.* I conjure you dont fancy this to be a Romantique sally, but the sincerest sentiments of my soul. *All I can doe, all I can say betrays my Inclinations, and all my looks are love. Neither can I scruple to own this, because no passion was ever justi-*

fy'd by so many Heavenly Qualitys. The charms of your Body are beyond every thing but the superior charms of your mind. Who can see the piety you shew to your aged Father without adoreing you? You confine your self from all those pleasures which befit your age and condition for the greater pleasure of obligeing him. You are content to spend your blooming youth in obscurity, to make his age and Infirmitys comfortable to him. You chuse to stew in a close Room to divert him, rather than rove about in the wide world to divert your self. You sweeten all his Peevishness with good humour, and soften his Frowns by your smiles. His years and want of health are to you a full excuse for all his unreasonable humours. There is a most obligeing chearfulness in all your behavior to him, that adds a grace & a loveliness to the most charming of all dutys. O my Dear Sabina who can see this divine Quality in you without concludeing, that a tender Daughter never fails to make a tender wife, especially when he reflects, that this is but one of the many virtues you are mistress of. Adieu & may you be as happy as you are good.

TO SABINA July 24th. 1717 7.

You will not be surpriz'd to hear that your freind Mrs Turnover is in a very sorrowfull condition. The person she loves the most in the world has injoin'd a Pennance upon her very insupportable to our sex, which is silence. This she's resolv'd to undergo, to testify her intire obedience, and indeed tis the highest Instance of it, when the heart is ready to burst, to give it no vent, However with her last words (which us'd to pass for truth) she told this hard-hearted person, that she wou'd in humble silence continue her passion to the end of her Life, and only spend that breath in sighs, which she us'd to spend in offensive words. But alas I fear the dear Creature will not long survive this affliction: but some kind feaver or consumption will quickly put her out of her pain. I pity her with all my soul, and so wou'd you too, if you cou'd but figure to your self an hundredth part of her Chagrin. With tears in her eys she said just before she seal'd up her mouth, that she wish't the lovely Sabina as happy, as she is capable of makeing the swain that loves her. Adieu.

TO SABINA August the 12. 1717. 8.

Notwithstanding the untimely fate of 2 of my Epistles, I will venture to write once again to the charming Sabina, since I have the excuse of designing to divert her. She confines herself so everlastingly at home in pious complement to her Father, that sure she will have the good to forgive me if I shou'd send her some Amuzement. The inclos'd letter from Tunbridge will exercize your decyphering faculty; tis very whimsical, and may help to enliven your solitude. If you'd please to give me leave to write, I wou'd send you all the entertaining things I cou'd get, and carefully avoid every subject that might displease you. It shou'd be the dear business of my life to divert you, and I wou'd forbear giveing you offence as industriously as I wou'd giveing my self pain. Pray Madam be so good as to let me know whether I have your permission to do this, for your soveraign will and pleasure shall direct me in all things. If you shou'd be so hard-hearted as to reject me as a Lover, yet you have no reason to renounce me as a freind, which I vow to you I will be to the last moment of my life, and to the last penny of my fortune. On Thursday I shall go to R——[1] for a week, and if you will allow me the pleasure of writeing, I will send you all the diverting news from thence. In the mean while I wish that Heaven may make you as happy as it has made you agreable, and then I'm sure you'll be the happiest woman in the universe. Adieu.

TO SABINA August the 22d 1717. 9.

The joy I had to see the excellent Sabina again after a long weeks absence, made me almost jump out of the window to tell her how much my soul was delighted. Ever

[1]The word "Richmond" has been filled in here by a second (?) hand.

since I went into the Country I have walkt about like a true Ghost in all the solitary walks I cou'd find, which I endeavour'd to make enchanting by the imaginary presence of the divine Sabina. O that my fancy had been strong enough to deceive me effectually or that those dear Romantick scenes had been real. But alas! I durst not write because you had not sent me your permission, neither had I the confidence to interpret your silence for consent. However the inclos'd verses made upon six fine Ladys at Richmond,[1] will I hope plead my Excuse for this letter. But those Nymphs not being so like painted, as to be certainly distinguish't, there are many more that set up their pretensions to the fine things said in the verses. So that these Epigrams are like to breed as fatal a contention amongst the Richmond Beautys, as the Golden apple did of old amongst the Rival Goddesses. Had Sabina been there the prize wou'd have been confessedly yeilded to her, and the poetry wou'd have been much more sprightly, because the charming subject wou'd have afforded a stronger inspiration. Tomorrow I return to my Hermitage for another week, where I shall indulge that melancholly which Sabina's cruelty has given me. May all the joy that the accomplishment of the most impatient wishes can give, or happiness by surprize bestow, belong eternally to the dearest and most deserving of her sex. Adieu.

TO SABINA. Sep[t] 2. 1717. 10.

The fears I had for my dear Sabina when I heard she was sick can't be conceiv'd by any one who has not lov'd in the tenderest degree. But thanks be to gracious Heaven, that has restor'd her, and afforded me the joy of understanding her recovery. how romantick so ever it may seem to a hard heart, you may beleive me when I protest, that you can suffer nothing which I dont feel with as much agony as you can do, and it wou'd be an ease to me whenever you feel

---

[1]The residence of the Prince and Princess of Wales at Richmond Lodge during the season provided a gay coterie with a social life congenial to Byrd's tastes and habits.

pain, to have it all transferr'd upon my self. I make no difficulty of declareing this because no sympathy was ever built upon more irresistable Reasons. Pray be so good as to let me know whether you are perfectly recover'd, I long to hear and therefore t'will be but charity to satisfy so tender a curiosity. I was in hopes the Country wou'd have diverted my Melancholly, but alas it has increas'd it. I cou'd not for my life call off my thoughts from the dear unkind object that ingrosses my whole heart. Tis some comfort to be near her, and sometimes to have a ravishing glimpse of her thro the window. For my part I had rather have that than converse familiarly with all the other Beautys upon Earth. For fear you shou'd not have seen the answer to the Tunbridge Letter, I send it you inclos'd in hopes it may be some entertainment to you. Adieu my charming Sabina, may you be as happy as an Angel since you are both as good & as beautifull.

TO SABINA Sept 9. 1717

* The Picture of Melantha[1] resembles the charming Sabina so nearly, that I cant deny my self the pleasure of presenting it to her. You have often heard poor Lady Calverley mention her with transport, and I am confident you won't be displeas'd to receive the likeness of one she lov'd so intirely. You will certainly admire those divine Qualitys in another, which modesty keeps you from being sensible of in your self. Melantha is dead, but lives again in Sabina with improvement. That divine Sabina whose heart is more desireable than all the Treasures upon Earth. O happiest of Mortals on whome she shall vouchsafe to bestow that inestimable Blessing! I had rather be that fortunate man than be Emperour of the world, and wou'd sooner chuse a short Life with dear Sabina's Love, than out number the years of Methusalem with all the Beautys of the Seraglio. *But alas*

---

[1]Melantha, or Lady Sherard, daughter of Lady Calverley, died in 1702, a good many years before the date of this letter. The character Byrd mentions is printed above, p. 228. Later, in his letter to Sabina's father, Byrd mentions the opportunities he had had of meeting Sabina at Lady C's—probably the same Lady Calverley here mentioned.

she is silent to all my prayers, nor dare I hope any benefit from her silence, because I fear t'is rather a sign of scorn than consent. O cruel Sabina how can you look with indifference on the Man whose wishes for your happiness, like his love for your person, glow with a never-dying flame! Adieu Adieu Thou charmer of my soule.

TO SABINA October 21. 1717.

* The Return of my last Billet undecypher'd as it was, made me almost distracted. I rav'd I rail'd at my self, at my malignant stars and every Earthly thing but the cruel Sabina whome my Tenderness secur'd from all Reproach. Surely the Present of Melanthas picture ought to have gain'd some Indulgence for the Letter that inclos'd it; but instead of that the harmless Epistle was condemn'd without reading, and the odious writer of it treated with the last contempt. I have nothing to comfort my self withall under so cutting a misfortune, but the certainty that I never did any thing to merit this hard-hearted usage, except loveing you most intirely. I confess if that be a Crime, I am the most profligate criminal in nature: but the charms you are mistress of are more than sufficient to excuse a sin so venial. For Heavens sake what cou'd provoke my dear Sabina to send back my letter, and by that unmercifull act not only pronounce me unworthy of her consent, but even of her denyal. Had she done me the honour to write to me once more, and told me in plain terms that my letters were grown troublesome, from that moment I wou'd have cut off my hands sooner than they shou'd have given her any disturbance. No by all the charms of Sabina I swear, that the strongest Inclination I have, shou'd not tempt me to disobey her, because the self same principle that gives me a passion for my Enchantress, gives me an inviolable desire to please her. If then you have any good nature, any manner of compassion for him that loves you as he loves his soule, I beg for Gods sake you wou'd be so good as to let me see you for one single hour, and Trolly that gives you this, will

tell you how it may be contriv'd without any manner of suspicion or Inconvenience I have something to say that concerns you nearly both to know and to prevent. I have also Proposals to make, which if you cou'd be so gracious as to approve, your generosity shou'd be eternally acknowledg'd by all those tender Returns, with which tis possible for a sincere and constant Lover to make his Mistress happy: *but if to my unspeakable misfortune you shou'd disdain my offer, yet at least you will have this advantage by the audience you give me, that you will from thenceforth rid your self of an offensive Lover, and the Earth soon after of the most miserable Wretch that breaths upon it. I will fly with Eagles wings to that Country where war is hottest, and where death may be courted on the surest terms. There, except destruction be as Coy as you are, I shant fail to put a glorious End both to a slighted passion, and a detested Life. When you hear that I am dead, bestow at least one sigh upon me, and own that twas you I lov'd, and not your Fortune. You may depend upon it, that the last breath I draw shall be a prayer for your happiness. And then let me conjure you my dearest Sabina, not to be surpriz'd, if by a faithfull freind I send you a Present when I am dead, which you were so unkind as to refuse when I was liveing, that is, a faithfull Heart, embalm'd and wrapt up in the 2 first Letters, which you did me the honour to write to me.* Adieu

---

TO SABINA Jany 22. 1718[1]

* If my Dearest Sabina could but figure to her self half the torment I feel, for her haveing sent back my letters, she wou'd never find in her heart to do so cruel a thing: but wou'd condescend to suffer a Passion which she won't return. I have try'd all the Expedients I can to keep my Flame

---

[1]The first mention of Miss Smith in Byrd's diary was on December 22, 1717, when he talked to Mrs. B-r-n of his love and she promised to favor his suit; on the 26th he met Miss Smith at Lincoln's Inn, where he sat next to her at the play; on January 10 he again talked about Sabina with Mrs. B-r-n; on the 22nd he dreamed of Miss Smith, and on the 23rd he mentioned writing to her, evidently referring to this letter.

within bounds, since t'is not possible for Time it self to extinguish it: but it wou'd be as easy to arrest the torrent of female Eloquence, or to bind a Tempest to its good behaviour. If I must not love the enchanting Sabina, Im sure I must not live, and nothing in nature can stop that intire inclination, but what at the same time must stop my Pulse. My Fate therefore Madam is absolutely in your disposal, and either your smiles or Frowns must determine it. I beg most earnestly that you'll be so good as to permit me to make you one Proposal, if you accept it, there can be no pitch of acknowledgment, to which my Gratitude shall not carry me, to make you the happiest of Women: but if you shou'd be so hard-hearted as to refuse me, I must the very short time I have to live be the unhappiest of men. adieu.

TO VERAMOUR Jany 23. 1718[1]

Supposeing this Billet to be as Romantick as all the rest, I did not think it worth a sincere womans while to decypher it. I desire you if I have any Interest in your heart, not to pursue your address in this distant manner: but if you must attaque me, let it be in the forms. A woman is no more to be taken than a Town by randome shot at a distance, but the Trenches must be open'd, and all the approaches must be regular, and rather than abide the last Extremity, tis possible the Garrison may capitulate, especially if terms be offer'd that are honourable. Tis a sad case when a swain is so intolerably dull, that his mistress must prescribe her own method of being taken; however supposeing this blindness to proceed from pure Passion, I will befreind it so far as to tell you, that my Brother[2] is intirely in my Interest: and if you

---

[1]Byrd noted in his diary, Jan. 24, 1718, that he received a letter from dear Miss Smith which forbade him to write but not to hope.

[2]Sabina's only sister, Anne, married first Hugh Parker, Esq., son of Henry Parker of Honington, Warwick, Bart., and was left a widow with seven children. In 1714 she married Michael, Lord Dunkellen, eldest son of the Earl of Clanricarde. On this occasion a bit of gossip about the sisters was written to Mrs. Shirley by the Countess Ferrers: "I forgot to write you a piece of news I heard about a fortnight ago. Lord Dunkellen is going to be married to one Mrs. Parker a widow. She has been so but a year and a half. She has seven children and used to be a coquette with great spirit, but now I

can get into his good graces, he may negociate this important affair betwixt us to both our satisfactions. I expect you'll make the most of this hint, for when a mistress gives her Lover advice, she never forgives him if he dont follow it.

Adieu.

TO SABINA Febr^y ye 24th 171 7/8[1] 11.

Because in matters of nice truth I think I ought to leave off the style of Romance, I must now beg leave to call my dear M^rs S . . . . by her proper name, and tell her nothing but w^t Heaven knows to be the sincere sentiments of my soule. Cou'd the heart of man hold more Love than I felt for you before, the late generous step you have been so good as to make, wou'd increase my Flame beyond all Expression. However madam tho it can't add to the strength of my Passion, yet t'will certainly make it everlasting. And shou'd you hereafter put it into my power, the highest delight of

---

will tell you the good part. She has £800 a year and a house and £25,000 in money. Her father is very rich and very fond of her. He has only one more daughter he does not care for. He is called Portland Smith." (Hist. MSS Comm., *Eleventh Report,* App. IV, pp. 227-9 [quotation modernised].)

Lord and Lady Dunkellen are mentioned frequently in Byrd's diary, and Lord Dunkellen was the go-between when Byrd finally proposed to Sabina's father.

[1] On Feb. 2, 1718, Byrd went to Mrs. B-r-n's hoping to meet Miss Smith, but was disappointed; on the 4th he met her at the play, and again on the 7th, when he led her out. On the 9th he talked of her with Mrs. B-r-n. On the 17th events began to take shape, for Miss Smith sent a message by Lord Dunkellen that a match had been proposed to her but she would not accept until she heard Byrd's proposal, as she felt that she could be happier with him than any man. Walking on air, Byrd went home and wrote a statement of his circumstances for Mr. Smith, which he showed next day to Lord Dunkellen. On the 19th he wrote again (or perhaps rewrote the first letter), and received from Lord Dunkellen instructions from his sister-in-law how to make the proposal in terms best calculated to win his suit. On the 20th he visited his friends the Perrys, and told them about his affair with Miss Smith, and they promised to favor it. On the 22d, at Leveridge's coffeehouse, Lord Dunkellen reported that Mr. Smith would not even look at his proposal, but that Sabina was firm in his favor and would try to bring her father around. Byrd primed Colonel Nicholson and Colonel Blakiston to speak well of him if they were asked, and they promised to do so. On the 23rd Lord Dunkellen told Byrd that he might write again to Sabina if he could do it without arousing the old gentleman's suspicions.

Though not entered at this point in the notebook, it seems obvious that the letters to "Vigilante" and to "Lord Tipparari," *i. e.* Mr. Smith and Lord Dunkellen, printed below, pp. 321 and 324, preceded this letter to Sabina.

my soule will be, to make you the happyest of your sex. How unfortunate it is for so tender a Lover as I am, that your gracious Intentions meet with so much difficulty, however it renders your goodness more heroick, & will inspire me consequently with a higher degree of Gratitude. I conjure you then by all the Transports of mutual Love, to persevere in your generous undertakeing, and tho it shou'd require an Age to bring it about, yet my constancy will be sure to triumph over my Impatience, notwithstanding it be as eager as the warmest inclination can make it. Yet that I may be enabled to bear the delay of my most darling Hopes the more cheerfully, I beg in the mean time that you'll be pleas'd to receive my Letters, and let me have the joy of hearing from you as often as possible. Be so kind my dearest Angel as to inform me of every movement you make, and of the part you wou'd have me act upon all occasions, and you may depend upon my punctual obedience. I percieve to my unspeakable comfort, that you have a soul above the low Thoughts of being set to sale to the highest Bidder; for my part the others may easily bid more mony for you than I, yet I defy any man Liveing to out-bid me in the just Esteem I have of your merit, and in the entire love I have for your charming Person. Were it possible for my Enchantress to know how earnestly I long to see her, she wou'd no longer forbear going to Mrs B . . . .[1] who I am sure wou'd sacredly keep her secret. If I were made acquainted when you'd pay that Visit, I wou'd go there first, and send away my servants, that your spys might take no umbrage at my being there. For Heavens sake agree to this

[1]Mrs. B is probably the Mrs. B-r-n with whom Byrd so frequently discussed his love for Miss Smith. There is some possibility that this was a member of the family of Richard and Anne Brayne of St. Margaret's, Westminster, whose daughter Anne Butler Brayne in 1724 married in England Alexander Spotswood, former Lieutenant Governor of Virginia, and came with him to Virginia in 1730. When Byrd visited the Spotswoods at Germanna in September, 1732, he wrote in his account of the visit: "Here I arrived about three a'clock, and found only Mrs. Spotswood at Home, who received her Old acquaintance with many a gracious smile." ("A Progress to the Mines," Bassett, p. 356.)

In 1714 Spotswood had directed a friend in London to get some Virginia seeds he was sending him from his friend Richard Brayne in Manchester Court, Westminster (Letter dated Virginia, Nov. 26, 1714, C. O. 5/1317, 197).

Rendevous if it be but for once, that I may tell you in the most pathetick terms, how sensible I am of your goodness, and how intirely and eternally I am &c

---

TO VERAMOUR Febr[y] 25. 1718

I got your letter safe tho it was in some Jeopardy of falling into the Enimys hands. That varlet of a Post man pronounc't my name with so loud an Emphasis at the door that I fear'd the old Gentleman wou'd hear it within. Since you are for laying aside all Romance, so will I too, tho really I think I have dealt pretty sincerely with you all along, by which unless you are slow of apprehension indeed, you may guess how I stand affected. But my cautious Father dont think so tolerably of you and your affairs as I do. He says an Estate out of this Island appears to him little better than an Estate in the moon, and for his part he wou'd not give a Bermigham groat for it. He reproved my poor Brother very smartly for offering to propose so chimericall a match for his Daughter, and put the youth to utter silence. I'm sorry to say it, but upon this occation his fear of offending the Father got the better of his forwardness to oblige the Freind. I cant yet bend the inflexible obstinacy of this old Gentleman, who is confirm'd in his opinion of Estates abroad by the perverse notions of some of our well-meaning Kindred. I am sorry for their Ignorance, which is the worse for being invincible, as appears by my not being able to convince them in this particular. For my own part I think an Estate in one country as good as in another, provided it yeild a comfortable Income, and I must pronounce it absurd to transplant your Fortune hither upon my account to loose by it. I am horribly affraid my good Father will close with the first tolerable Proposal that offers, to marry me out of harms way, which according to the present state of my stomach, will be very hard for it to digest. I must make you laugh at my Papa's pleasantry about your Age, he says for my comfort that you and He were both born in the year of our Lord 1650.[1] This he imagin'd would be a home stroke, and ruin all your hopes of succeeding with a Damsel of 20. And he flatters himself that by this slurr he has wiped you clean out of my Inclinations. For fear I may have now said too much, I charge you burn this letter, and dont let so much as your Confessor know that I have writ to you. May I advise you to forget it your self, And I think too twill be for your good to forget the Person that writ it. The first step towards this, will be to return me no manner of answer: but if you must needs reply be sure to make up your Epistle into a square figure, & in a different hand direct it to my Fille de chambre. However that wench must not be privy to the fine things on the Inside, which I expect youll for that reason cloath in the Invisible character. Yet No liveing Creature must know of your writeing after this sort. I cant agree for many Reasons that we shou'd meet at M. B. nor indeed any where else while things remain in this untoward situation. Adieu.

TO SABINA Febr^y 28. 171$\frac{7}{8}$ 12.

I kiss't your dear Letter ten thousand times, and by almost devouring it made your orders about burning unnecessary. But o how cou'd you be so barbarous as to bid me forget you? A wretch upon the Rack cou'd sooner forget the sweet hopes of being easy. When I forget my charming Sabina, the saints above will forget their Bliss, and Heaven will no more remember its darling Attribute of Mercy. You give me pain when you thus injoin me a command impossible to be obey'd: but when you foresee that your Father will dispose of you to another Man, you put me to the Torture, and distress my very soul. Forbid it Love, forbid it Heaven, I wish I had leave to say, forbid it my dearest Mistress! Tell me, I conjure you tell me, wou'd you ever agree to this fatal Resolution? No duty I am sure

---

[1]Byrd was born March 10, 1674. Though Sabina claimed to be 20, Byrd had already mentioned her age as "four and twenty" (Jan. 15, 1717, above). The Funeral book, at the death of John Smith, July 10, 1718, gave his age as 67. (See note on "Vigilante," below, p. 321).

can oblige you to it, for tho I allow that by the Law of God a Daughter may not marry against the consent of her Father, yet by the same Law she has likewise her Negative, and may refuse to marry any man she don't like. There's no point in all Divinity more settled than this, so that I thank God what you fear can't come to pass, except you your self agree to it. I have too good an opinion of your noble nature to suspect, that even the dread of being disinherited will determine you to sell your Inclinations. But if your Father shou'd be so unnatural as to cut you off with one lonely shilling for my sake, I swear by all that is true, by all that is sacred, I will marry you, and love you as tenderly as if you had brought the Dutchess of Somersets fortune. But alas if after all you shou'd be brought to consent to some other match propos'd by your Father, gracious God what wou'd become of me? I shou'd instantly fly away to that country where the voice of war roars loudest, and where a handsome death may be courted on the surest terms. There, except Destruction shou'd disappoint me too, I wou'd not fail to put a glorious end both to a slighted Passion, and a detested life. If in such a case my dear Sabina shou'd hear of my fate do you think she wou'd not bestow one sigh, one pitying tear upon me, and believe that my passion was too generous to be brib'd by any consideration but that of her merit? You might depend upon it, that the last breath I shou'd draw wou'd be an earnest prayer for your happiness. But wou'd it not a little surprize you, to receive with the news of this Tragedy, a present of that faithfull heart after I was dead, which you had been so unkind as to refuse while I was liveing? Imagin now my divine Creature what Distraction the Reality of your marrying another wou'd give me, since I can be so disorder'd with the bare supposition. and if I cou'd not bear another shou'd hand you out of the Playhouse, you may guess how well I shall endure to see a happyer man than my self take you into his arms. I laught indeed at your Papa's Joke about my age, tho if we be cotemporarys he must own at least I have something the better constitution. In that I have the advantage of him at least 40 years, and in time not less I thank God than 30. However he fancy'd he shou'd nick me there, and do my business effectually with his Daughter. I'm sorry that my charmer wont see me at Mrs B—. because I think she might be there both safe and unsuspected: But if not there I beg for Pity sake it may be some where else, if it were no more than once, because I have things of consequence to say to you. I'm perswaded you can confide in me intirely, since you have given me already such generous proofs of your confidence. Pray let me know how far you have let honest Kate into the secret, and how much I may tell your Brother, for I find by your letter I must not tell him all. How stands your sister affected, I wish she prove faithfull? But one single conversation wou'd instruct me in these and many other Inquirys, which makes me again repeat my Prayer, that you wou'd be so good as to agree to it. Adieu my dear dear Sabina may Providence take you into its safest Protection, and inspire you with equal Returns of tenderness for him that is only & everlastingly Your most devoted.

TO VIGILANTE[1]

The opportunity which I had formerly of seeing your fair Daughter at my Lady C, gave me the first Impression I receiv'd of her fine qualitys. But being at that time a marry'd man, I cou'd go no farther than to admire her.

[1]John Smith, of the heraldic family of his name in Lincolnshire, was appointed a commissioner of excise in August, 1698, as Luttrell noted in his diary, where he called him "John Smith, of Beauford Buildings, Esq." Luttrell also noted his re-appointment in June 1700 (IV, 410, 658). He died July 10, 1718, and was buried in Westminster Abbey. The *Historical Register* for 1718 mentioned "July 8th: Mr. Des Bouverie, son of Sir Edward Des Bouverie, marry'd to Mrs. Smyth, daughter of John Smyth, esq., formerly one of the Commissioners of Excise;" and, "July 10: Dy'd John Smyth, Esq., formerly one of the Commissioners of Excise." His will, as of St. Clement Danes, Middlesex, dated 7 July 1718, was proved on the 24th of the same month by his cousin John Smith, Esq., John Orlebar, Esq., one of the Masters in Chancery, and Mr. Conrade de Gols, executors in trust for his two daughters, to whom he left his house in Beaufort Buildings, and all his personalty. (See *The Marriage, Baptismal, and Burial Registers of the Collegiate Church or Abbey of St. Peter, Westminster,* ed. J. L. Chester, 1876, pp. 292-3; also Byrd's diary, July 11, 1718.) Obviously Smith made his will as soon as Sabina had agreed to marry Sir Edward Des Bouverie, and died two days after she had fulfilled her contract.

However haveing since my being disengag'd, lodg'd in your neighbourhood, the frequent sight of her at a distance, has awaken'd in my memory all the Ideas I us'd to have of her Perfections, and kindled them into an intire Respect and Inclination. In this condition I have languisht for some time: but fearing lest the distance of my Estate from hence, might be liable to objection I had not the courage to make a Regular Proposal. However judging it altogether unwarrantable to proceed any other way, I think it my duty to explane my circumstances to you, and humbly intreat your consent. And because affairs of this sort ought above all others to be manag'd with truth and honour, I shall venture to say nothing on this occasion, but what may be fairly consistent with both. According to this good Principle I must beg leave to assure you, that the Estate I have, tho it lye so far off as Virginia, is very considerable. I have there about 43000 acres of Land and 220 Negros at work upon it with a prodigi[ous] quantity of stock of every kind. Some part of this Land is let out to Tenants, and more will be leas't every year. But the usual method of that Country is to seat our own slaves upon it, and send the fruit of their Labour, consisting in Tob° and Naval stores, to England. We can therefore have no certain way of valuing our Estates by the year, but they produce more or less, according as the market happens to be for those Commoditys here. What I can tell you for certain, is, to show how much clear mony my Returns have yeilded the 3 years since I have been over. In the year 1715 they produc'd clear of all charge £1716:5— In the year 1716 they clear'd no more than £1535:14:11. But this year they will yeild more than £1800—as I can prove by the accounts of my merchants in the city that dispose of my Effects, Who are men of great integrity as well as of great substance.[1] This mony comes clear into my

[1] *I. e.,* the firm of Micajah Perry, with whom Byrd's father before him had done business and whose commercial and political influence in the affairs of Virginia was very powerful. Mr. Perry lived at this period in Leadenhall Street, "over against the Affrican Coffee House." The three known portions of Byrd's diary, as well as his letters, show how intimately his personal and business affairs were known to Micajah Perry, who died Oct. 1, 1721, and to his son Richard, who died April 16, 1720, and then to the sons of Richard, Philip and Micajah. See Elizabeth Donnan, "Eighteenth Century English

Pocket after all charges are deducted, which is more than any Estate in England will yeild of £2000 p annum. I cou'd make about £400 a year more of my Returns if I wou'd take the trouble to dispose of them my self. There are besides several other advantages belonging to this kind of Estate, namely y[t] in a few years the value of it will grow to be double what it is at this time, by the increase of the Inhabitants of the Country, and by the great distance from water carriage, all the Land lys that remains now to be taken up. Then I can always make Ten p cent of whatever mony I lay down for the customes of my Tob[o] for prompt Payment. I need not tell you Sir how vastly more advantagious this Estate wou'd be, if I shou'd live upon the place, because I cant harbour the least thought of ever carrying M[rs] S. . . over thither, in case I shou'd be so happy as to marry her. This whole Estate I shou'd be willing to settle upon this marriage, only reserving a liberty of charging it with the summ of £4000 whenever my 2 Daughters[1] shou'd come to marry. I am wholly unacquainted Sir what Fortune you will please to give your Daughter, because my passion for her is too disinterested ever to suffer me to make that Inquiry. But whatever it be, I shall agree to have it settled after what manner you please. For I can assure you without affectation, that Interest is very far from being any motive to this address. As to my Family, which I think shou'd be only mention'd upon these occasions, I am descended from the Family of my name at Broxon in Cheshire where they

---

Merchants: Micajah Perry," *Journal of Economic and Business History,* IV, 70-99; *Notes and Queries,* 8 Ser., VIII (1895), 17; William Purdie Treloar, *A Lord Mayor's Diary, 1906-7, to which is added the Official Diary of Micajah Perry, Lord Mayor, 1738-9* (London, 1920); *Obituary,* comp. Sir William Musgrave, p. 23; Fairfax Harrison, *Virginia Land Grants* (Richmond, 1925), p. 158.

[1]Evelyn, Byrd's older daughter, born July 16, 1707, had joined her father in London in the autumn of 1717. A letter from Byrd to John Custis, Oct. 19, 1717, says: "About 3 weeks ago I troubled you with a letter to let you know that poor Evy was arrived, very safe in Capt. Wray, and is very busy in learning everything that is proper for her." (MS, Emmet Collection, New York Public Library.)

Wilhelmina, the younger daughter, born Nov. 6, 1715, was at this date in Virginia; she joined her father in London in April, 1719, when the little girl made the voyage across the Atlantic in the care of her father's friend, Captain Isham Randolph.

have been seated for more than 20 Generations.[1] Then Sir for my character, you wont expect I shall say any thing of that my self, I must leave it to those that know me best, amongst whome I shall only name my Lord Percevale and Mr Southwell,[2] who are Persons of most unquestionable honour and veracity, & who have been long acquainted with my morals, my Temper, & my Education, and will not deceave you. But you need not confine your inquiry to them, since there are many persons of distinction to whome I have the honour to be perfectly known. To them I submit my character intirely, and am ready when you please to make out all the Facts relateing to my circumstances by undoubted testimony. I own Sir you may marry your Daughter to a better Estate, and to higher Quality: but there is nothing necessary to make her happy, which may not be compasst by my Fortune; especially after it hath been assisted by your generosity. However this I will venture to promise for my self, that if I have the honour to be accepted, the greatest pleasure I shall take in this world, will be to make your daughter happy, and to behave my self in such a manner, as may be most dutifull & most agreable to your self, I humbly recommend my self to your favour, begging that you will be pleas'd to approve my address, which will ever engage me to be with all possible Respect &c.—

TO LORD TIPPARARI.[3]

The Estate I have in Virginia consists in above 43000 acres of Land, about 220 Negros, with a vast stock of every kind upon it. How to value this is difficult, because Land differs greatly in price there, according to the goodness improvement and situation; and so do the Negros according to their Age and qualification. However by the exactest

---

[1]A pedigree was prepared at the Heralds College, London, in 1702 for Byrd. See Bassett, Appendix B.

[2]A discussion of Byrd's close connection with Lord Percival and Edward Southwell may be found above, pp. xviii-xx.

[3]*I. e.,* Lord Dunkellen. This letter, as well as the previous one to Mr. Smith, from the diary entries, apparently should be dated Feb. 18, 1718.

general computation that I am able to make, in case they were to be sold

The Land as t'is built & improv'd may be worth	£20000 . . .
The Negros, many of them being Tradesmen .	7000 . . .
The Stock, and other Personal Estate	6000 . . .
In all . . .	£33000

T'is likewise as hard to reduce the Product of this to any certain yearly value, because that will vary according as the Market happens to be in England for the Commoditys we send over. However I am able to demonstrate to your Lord^p^, that the 3 years I have been over, my Returns from thence have yeilded more than £1500 every year in clear mony, over and above all charges & deductions. The particular Proof of this I am able to make out by such Evidence as will give satisfaction. I shall then also acquaint your Lord^p^ with several other advantages belonging to this Estate, which render it abundantly more valuable. Tho I will not trouble you with the Particulars at this time, but shall be always ready to do it hereafter, whenever you shall command &c.

TO SABINA the 6th of March. 13.

You must needs give me leave to vent my Passion once a week by Billet doux, and God knows t'is pure caution makes me keep that intolerable distance. Were my hand to obey the warm motions of my heart, I shou'd write every hour, every moment. Thus far my Love, all flameing as it is, must yeild to the cold dictates of discretion, and be content to ease it self with sighs and murmurs the rest of the time. But alas why won't my Charmer write in her turn, since her Letters are as welcome to me as Health wou'd be to the sick, or a saveing hand stretch't out to one that is ready to drown. You believe me faithfull to you I am sure, and therefore can never distrust me, and nobody expresses better sence than you in a more elegant character, and therefore you need not distrust your self. Dont wonder that I covet your Letters so passionately, you know too well they're all the comfort I have, and tis impossible to be satisfy'd with a little of any thing one likes. Therefore my dearest Angel write often I conjure you, & when you don't write, be so good as to bestow a tender thought upon me. O why may I not see you? why won't you trust me with that happiness? w^{t} can you apprehend from him whose tenderness & fidelity wou'd make him all obedience? As y^{t} may certainly be without any danger from me, so it might be manag'd without the least suspicion of other People. In the name of good nature how can you refuse this Blessing to the man that wou'd dye for you, and, what is stil more heroick, wou'd live in misery to make you happy? I saw your sister at Petcum's[1] on Munday and found her very obligeing. She told me I was review'd one day last week at Wills Coffee house[2] by your Relation;[3] for Gods sake tell me, what report cou'd he make? She gave me to understand you was at the Play on thursday, when my Evil Genius carry'd me to the other House. I wish to God I had known it, that my Eys might be blesst with the sight of you any where. Heaven grant I may be inform'd when you go again, else all my Industry may miss you between the 2 Houses. I wou'd pray with you every Sunday, if I did not fear it wou'd beget too much suspicion. Lord how hard it is to fetter down Love to the vexatious Rules of Discretion? These dont only oblige me to carry my self with insupportable caution towards your dear self, but also towards your Brother and Sister, who

---

[1]Monsieur Petkum was Resident in England of the Duke of Holstein (*Cal. Treas. Papers, 1714-19*, p. 125; for Dean Swift's reference to a "letter of Petecum, showing the roguery of the Dutch," see his Journal to Stella, in *Works,* ed. Thomas Sheridan, 1803, XXII, 157).

Byrd went often to Petkum's during this period. The entertainment he found there varied from assemblies, playing cards, drinking chocolate, to talking with divers ladies.

[2]Will's coffeehouse, at the corner of Russell Street and Bow Street, Covent Garden, was the rendezvous of Dryden and of later writers in the age of Queen Anne. It was above all the wits' coffeehouse, though it lost its supremacy, at the time of Addison's preëminence, to a new house, Button's, just across the way. Though Byrd visited many London coffeehouses during his residence in England, he was almost daily at Will's.

[3]This may refer to John Orlebar, Master in Chancery, who appears later as a messenger from Sabina to Byrd. See below, p. 339.

hold it not convenient for me to go often to them. Thus I can receive no Intelligence but what you will please to give me, & you may be sure I'm all of a fire to know every thing about you. Tell me therefore my divine Creature in what situation our affair stands, has it yet taken no turn to my advantage? and cant you make some Impression on the curious Person that took the trouble to survey me? Pray answer these importunate Questions, as well as those I had the honour to put to you in my last letter. Adieu my dear Sabina, may you be as happy as Love, and Peace, & health, and the consciousness of haveing done good and generous actions, can make you Adieu.

TO SABINA the 12th of March. 14.

No Husband with tender Ears can ever be more punish't by the outragious Eloquence of his Consort, than I have been lately by my Dear Sabina's silence. I have long'd for her Answers with an impatience beyond that, with which one in a burning feaver longs for drink. Imagin for God's sake the restlessness, the torment that such a wretch indures, and then tell me, if with all your good-nature you can give it the man that adores you. Write therefore, I conjure you by all the charms of your dear Person, and by that act of grace make the tedious time I must languish without you supportable. I'm confident you are convinc't that my Passion for you is sincere & unaffected, because all I can do, all I can say betrays my Inclination, and all my looks are Love. You believe I am faithfull too, and wou'd sooner tear out my own heart all panting from my breast, and expose it to any bodys view, than I cou'd your dear dear Letters. What has my charmer then to fear, or what imaginable Reason can she have who is compassionate to all other Creatures, thus to tortu[re] the Man that devotes himself to serve her? With hands lifted up to Heaven I swear, that I love my Dear Sabina most intirely [. . .] most faithfully, and think my Passion fully justify'd by the engaging Qualitys she is mistress of. The charms of her Body are beyond every thing but the superior charms of her Mind. Who can discern the Piety she shews to her Father without adoreing her. She confines her self from all those Pleasures that befit her Age and condition, for the better pleasure of obligeing him. She is content to spend her blooming youth in obscurity, to make his age and Infirmitys more supportable to him. She chuses to stew in a close Room to divert him, rather than rove about in the wide world to entertain her self. She sweetens all his Peevishness with good humour, and softens his frowns with her smiles. His years and want of health are to her an Excuse in full for all his unaccountable humours. There is a most obligeing cheerfullness in all her behaviour to him, that adds a grace and a loveliness to the most charming of all Dutys. O my dear Enchantress who can perceive this divine Quality in you, without concludeing very naturally that a tender Daughter never fails to make a tender Wife, especially when he reflects that this is but one of the Legion of Vertues you possess? All this I believe in my consience to be true, and therefore no wonder if your Empire over my heart be absolute. No wonder if I spend so many Solitary hours at home, that nothing may draw off my attention from the dear Mistress I love as I do Life, and health, & happiness. No wonder if I breath out so many tender sighs, if I appear with such longing looks, and put my self into so many melancholly Attitudes when I think I am so near, & yet so cruelly confin'd from the enchanting object of all my wishes, all my desires. These Reflections wou'd distract me if in an evening I did not escape from my self, & plunge into what are call'd the Diversions of the Town, which really have no tast for me while you are absent. Judge by all these plain Symptomes the forlorn condition I am in, and imagin how much I shou'd be comforted by your dear letters, and how much I shou'd be charm'd with your inchanting company. Adieu my agreable Sabina may you always be blesst with the compleat enjoyment of what you love, and may you have some sympathy for him who plights you his eternal faith and is with a most intire and everlasting affection &c

TO VERAMOUR.[1] March 11.

I very much wonder upon what grounds you take upon you to conjure me in your letter of the 28th of last month to tell you, whether I shou'd agree to any other match of my Fathers proposeing! I thought I had signify'd my sentiments upon that head in my last, and did not believe I shou'd be at the trouble of any further explanation. You perceive that your fortune cant be made agreable to my Father, without which there can be no hopes of his consent, which I give you my word will intirely govern mine. Your distinction in the duty of a Daughter I look upon as a meer Equivocation, which you must know I think as criminal as right down disobedience. I must therefore assure you in answer to your Question, that as my Resolution is to be obedient, so I can't say how far I may be prevail'd on to marry one propos'd by my Father. As to your enquiry how my Brother and Sister stand affected? I can tell you they will be cautious how they interpose any more with my Papa in your behalf, for my Brother receiv'd a very chocquing Rebuff when he spoke a good word for you in the begining. He was then told truly that he solicited this affair in pure indulgence to my Inclinations out of sinister ends, which was a Reply that carry'd so much injustice to my Lord, that I believe he'll have a care how he burns his fingers any more in this business. As to my other Relations they never countenanc't your proposal, neither are they yet in the least reconcil'd to it, but stil continue their inveteracy. I caution'd you to conceal my letters, because I'm sure my writeing to you in so gentle a manner, is what neither my Brother nor any body else can justify, tho at the same time I think you ought to be convinc't, that I have an intire confidence in your honour. My Hand-maid knows very little of our affair, tho I must tell

---

[1]Byrd noted in his diary for March 12 that he had received a letter from Miss Smith forbidding him to write any more, which gave him much concern. However, Lord Dunkellen wrote him that Sabina would be in the park the next day. Going to the park on the 13th, he saw his lady but dared not speak to her; that night he dreamed pleasantly of her and of her father's death. The next evening, at the Spanish Ambassador's, Lady Dunkellen reported that when another match was proposed Sabina had refused it, saying she could not forget Byrd.

you she's [niley?] suspected, and therefore I will for the future have no more letters directed to her. As she is very innocent, so I shou'd be unwillyng to have her thought guilty, and so come to suffer only for her fidelity to me. But that I may put an end to all the jeolosys & suspicions of my Father, I must desire you if you have the least value in the world for me never to write at all, and by complying with my desire in this particular you will certainly oblige &c

---

TO SABINA the 15th of March[1]

* The last letter I had from my Dear Sabina gave me much pleasure when I receiv'd it, but when I read it very sensible pain. Her forbiding me to write any more went very near my heart, and I had nothing to comfort me, but the hopes this Prohibition proceeded from caution, & not from any displeasure. I cou'd not believe it proceeded from the last without suspecting you to be a little changeable, which I really think you as incapable of, as I am of giveing you just provocation. This thought makes me venture to transgress the letter of your commands, because when I convey an Epistle in a manner impossible to be suspected, I hope I dont transgress your intention. I know your Papa is very watchfull & my Demon tells me, that no longer ago than yesterday he inquir'd if you had not had letters from me? But I can't mention yesterday without bursting out into ten thousand thanks for the generous answer you made your Father, when he propos'd marrying of you before he dy'd. O may Heaven reward your Generosity with the dearest of its blessings, & put it in my power to make you

[1]On the 14th of March Byrd wrote a letter to give to Miss Smith at a concert, but she did not come; however, he met Lady Dunkellen there who told him that Miss Smith had given up hope that their affair could succeed. On the 19th he met Miss Smith in her coach and received a gracious bow; that night he again dreamed of her. Next day he hoped to meet her at the play but she was not there. At the Spanish Ambassador's Lady Dunkellen talked rather enigmatically of his affair with Sabina. On the 22nd, however, he had the pleasure of seeing her at the opera, where he went with Lord Orrery, and submitted with difficulty when he was forbidden to speak to her there. On the 24th, after writing a long letter to Sabina, he was invited to visit Lady Dunkellen, who again encouraged him to write and pursue his suit.

amends by the tenderest acknowledgment! Go on my divine creature in this noble Track, & I doubt not but you may awaken your Fathers nature, and soften him into compassion. I hope a faithfull Lover may be forgiven, if he propose to so disinterested a mistress, the proper methods of working upon her Fathers tenderness. Let a Parent be never so intractable, yet a child may easily find the soft place in his heart, especially when he has so real a fondness as yours has for you. There's nothing needfull for this, but only Prudence to chuse the proper methods, and a little courage to put them in execution. The first I know you are mistress of, and t'is not much above a year that you gave a home instance of the last. For Heavens sake my Dearest Angel rouse up the same generous spirit again, and Ill forfeit my life if you dont succeed in your Wishes. As soon as you find a match propos'd that is like to be accepted, contrive immediately to nip it in the bud, and stifle it in the very Cradle. For if you give your Papa time to make any steps, besides the obstinacy incident to old age, he may think himself perhaps bound in honour to proceed, & by that means you'll have 2 difficultys to encounter instead of one. Therefore in the very Infancy of it throw your self at his feet with gushing tears & intreatys and address to him in terms like these. "I conjure you Sir by all the Bowels of a tender "Parent to have pity on me. If you have any regard for the "Life, any care for the happiness of a Daughter, whose "whole endeavour has been to oblige you, I beg I beseech "you not to force my Inclinations. While you disapprove of "any Person, tho it cost me my life, I will obey you in not "marrying him: but I hope you will never force me to marry "a man, it is not possible for me to love. That wou'd be "sure to make me wretched everlastingly, by involving me "in the blackest Perjury, for how can I vow in the presence "of God to love any man, when I feel in my own heart I can "never do it. I beg of you therefore Sir upon my bended "knees, if you will not be pleas'd to indulge me in marrying "the man I like, that youll permit me at least to mourn away "my Life in solitude, that so I may not make any Body miser- "able but my self. Surely such a Prayer as this will sink deep into your Fathers heart, and turn it towards you tho it were never so inflexible. If you cant take the boldness to say this to him, yet write it, and deliver it upon your knees. Pardon me my divine Creature for useing this freedome with you, for my Demon has acquainted me with so many instances of your compassion for me, that tho my Love can admit of no increase, yet I find my courage greater. This gives me the confidence to propose a safe method of conveying letters to you, that no mortal liveing can ever suspect. If a Line were let down from the window next the Strand of your 2 ꝑ of stairs Room, exactly at 11 a clock at night, when nobody will perceive it, that might reach almost to the Pavement, and lye close to the wall, I wou'd wrap a blank letter without direction in brown paper, being the coulour of the Bricks and fasten it to the end of the Line, and by pulling it give notice when I had done, that it might be drawn up. By this contrivance you may receive letters as often as you please without the least suspicion or Inconvenience. For Gods sake my dear Sabina agree to this, because if you be graciously inclin'd to bring this affair about, twill need the contrivance of us both. Pray let me have your thoughts upon all this matter, and continue your generous sentiments towards him who can never bear to live longer than he has the happiness to be &c.

P.S.

The foregoing letter was writ on Saturday, when I was made to hope that you wou'd be at Mrs Robinsons musick:[1] but being baulkt in that, I durst by no means transgress your commands in sending it by the Post, since you had made my obedience in that particular a Proof of my value for you. But I can assure my dear Sabina, that under this cruel

[1]Anastasia Robinson was a well-known singer in London in the years between 1714 and 1724. She sang leading roles in the operas of the day, such as Händel's *Amadigi* and *Giulio Cesare* and in Buononcini's *Crispo and Griselda.* Some of the biographers of the Earl of Peterborough think he married her secretly sometime between 1722 and 1724 though the marriage was not openly declared until 1735. Anastasia Robinson had a half sister, Margaret, who was also famous as a singer and who married George Arbuthnot, a brother of Dr. Arbuthnot, the wit; another sister, Elizabeth, was also a singer but was too bashful to perform in public. (*Dict. Nat. Biog.;* William Stebbing, *Peterborough* [London, 1890], pp. 197-225.)

Prohibition I have had the most dismal the most melancholly Week that ever I spent since my first creation. And shou'd I live another in that helpless manner, I shou'd be in danger of runing mad. For Gods sake therefore Thou darling of my Soul, if you have any tenderness, any bowels for the man that loves you to utter distraction, say that I may write to you, at least I beg you not to forbid me, that I may have room to interpret your silence for consent. Adieu my dearest Angel may you be all your whole life as happy as you have made me unhappy this last week, and then I'm sure youll be the happyest Woman that ever was born into the world Adieu

---

TO SABINA the 24th of March

I hope my dear Sabina will be so good as to forgive my transgressing her Commands about writeing. The silence I have kept for these last 14 days, is some proof of my obedience especially when she hears I was ready to run distracted for want of giveing my Passion that necessary Vent. Lunacy you know will excuse Violateing the Laws of Heaven, & therefore I hope the apparent danger of it will excuse a smal disobedience to the orders of a Mistress so given to change. Besides I have Necessity to urge in my defence which is in all cases allow'd to be a sufficient Plea. While I can have no other possible way of conveying my sentiments to the Darling of my soule, the not writeing to her might be understood to be a cooling of my Inclination, or giveing over my Pretentions. As to the first I protest to you, that my Life will end with my Love, and my Pulse will stop as soon as my Passion. And for the last, you may depend upon it, I will never abandon my Pretentions til you have given up your self to a Richer, tho you cant to a more ardent & faithfull Lover. I also think my writeing necessary to explain the reason of my not approaching nearer your charming Person at the opera;[1] The not gratifying my own

---

[1]Vanbrugh built in 1705 on the west side of the Haymarket a large house with at least five tiers of boxes known as the Queen's Theatre where Italian opera on its introduction into England was given. Other entertainments, such

desire in that particular was purely to avoid bringing upon the Lady that was with you the suspicion of befreinding my Inclinations; tho at the same time my heart was ready to burst with a longing to speake to you. It has been a great disturbance to me that my dear Sabina shou'd suspect I wou'd teach her to equivocate in her duty to her Father; no, I shou'd be very unwilling to preach up Equivocation to a Father in one that I shou'd wish to be always sincere to a Husband. If you'd please to allow my Letter a cool reading, you'd agree that the doctrine I lay down is justify'd by the Laws of God & man. Nay you wou'd remember too, that a year ago you practiced the very Rules I prescribe, & attested generously your Right of Refusal against the highest ressentment of your Father. You thought it lawfull then or I'm sure you wou'd not have done it; why therefore shou'd it be unlawfull in my case only. But if my dear charmer were but firm in her good disposition towards me, she might wth all the case [*sic*] in the world bring her Father to indulge her Inclinations. Notwithstanding the intractable Airs he is pleas'd to give himself, you know he loves you tenderly, and wou'd in a short time consent to any thing, which he thought necessary for your happiness. Wou'd you but appear melanchollly for one week, and heighten that scene of sorrow with a few seasonable sighs and tears, you'd not fail to melt him into complyance. Such a moveing prospect wou'd sink deep into his soul, & awaken all his tenderness. In the mean time I intreat you my dearest Angel, if you have any bowels for the man that adores you, as soon as ever you find any match propos'd, to nip it in the bud, & stiffle it in the cradle; For shou'd you give your Papa time to make any steps, besides the obstinacy incident to Age, he may think himself bound in honour to proceed, & by that means you will have 2 difficultys to encounter instead of one. *Therefore in the very Infancy of it for Gods sake throw your self at his feet, and with gushing tears intreat him in*

---

as ridottos and assemblies for music and dancing were also held there. Byrd shared with Addision his dislike of Italian opera, declaring his distaste for the "yelping of these forrein Syrens, who charmed with the felonious intent to devour us" (Byrd to Mrs. Armiger, June 25, 1729, MS in Department of Research and Record, Colonial Williamsburg, Inc.).

"terms like these I conjure you Sir by all the tender Regards "of a Parent to take pity on me. If you have any respect "for the life any care for the happiness of your child, I beg "I beseech you not to force my Inclinations. While you dis- "approve of any Person I will not marry him tho it cost me "my life, but on the other side I hope you will never force "me to marry a man I cant love. That wou'd involve me in "the blackest Perjury, for how can I vow in the presence of "the Almighty to love any man when I feel in my own heart "I can never do it. I beg of you therefore my dearest "Father on my bended knees if you wont please to indulge "me in marrying the man I like, that youll permit me at least "to mourn away my life in solitude, that so I mayn't make "any body miserable besides my self. Dont you think my dearest creature that such a prayer as this wou'd touch him to the quick, soften his obstinacy & disarm all his Ressent- ment I think indeed you ought to deel sincerely with him, and not make him believe our affair is at an end when only death can end it. I was told in the City that one Mr Degoals[1] had been enquireing about me & my circumstances, pray tell me if you know such a person? I'm almost distracted to find that in case your Father shou'd propose any other Person, you say you can't tell how far you may be prevail'd on. That declaration makes every part of me tremble & sets my soul a fluttering for Life. Can my dear Sabina so soon forget an Inclination confesst to her Brother, her Father & her God? Cou'd she so easily renounce the man that cou'd not be compleatly wretched, without her acceptance of his passion had helpt to make him so. And think you to be happy with One that is meanly propos'd to your Fortune, while you make another miserable that is sincerely in love with your Person. Flatter not your self my dear Sabina the God of Love has vengeance in store for those that profane his Rights in so mercenary a manner, neither will the pre- tence of obeying a father, that trafficks away his Daughter, in the least expiate the fault. However I have too good an opinion of your honour yr generosity your good nature to

[1]Conrade de Gols was named in John Smith's will an executor in trust for Lady Dunkellen and Mary, Lady Des Bouverie, his two daughters.

believe that you can either be frighten'd or tempted to sell your Inclinations, Read over all the letters you have receiv'd —all you have writ & recollect all your behaviour and then tell me if you can think your self perfectly disingaged remember you own'd your self, nobody cou'd justify your writeing to me, that is, except you intended to carry your generosity further. If you've chang'd y^r mind I must be content to be wretched without reproaching you, but God grant you may not live to reproach your self when you hear of my TRAGEDY however if after all you shou'd give away your heart to a happyer man than my self he must expect to give proof of one good quality besides his Estate.[1] Dont forbid me to write nor dont send back my letters for I am too near distraction to obey either. Adieu my Dearest Angel may you be as happy every moment of your life as you have made me miserable these last 14 days, and then I'm sure youll be the happyest woman that ever was born into the world Adieu.

---

* TO SABINA March 28th

It can be no wonder to my dear Sabina that a heart inflam'd with so strong a passion as mine shou'd be tortur'd with jeolosy. Had she once plighted her faith, my soul wou'd be at rest, but while I remain in this state of incertainty, the fear of looseing what I ardently desire gives me infinite alarm & uneasiness. This makes me suspect that every Creature that enters your doors carrys in some proposal along with him. I fancy him presently to be a Customer, whose Errand is to cheapen my dear Sabina, that is as much above all price as Grace it self, and I hope as impossible to be purchas'd. However methinks I see your Papa ready to deliver you to the highest Bidder, tho he were a

[1]This sentence was evidently disturbing to Sabina, for on the 28th when Byrd met Lady Dunkellen she told him that Miss Smith was out of humor with him for having written her a bullying letter—though the letter was returned to Byrd.

Fool, a Brute, a Devil, or perhaps a compound of all three together. What absurd notions of happiness have most old People, who believe that a womans heart cant ach that is chain'd to a Booby with a great Estate, tho they themselves know many Instances of women made wretched by this very Principle. I own that mony is a very good Ingredient, that is to say—as much as is necessary to live & appear with the best People. But all above that is like Shoes—too big for one, that are more uneasy than if they were less. Tell me my dear Sabina is there any thing requisite to make a reasonable Woman happy that may not be purchas'd by my Fortune? Might she not keep the best company, and have a proper share in every diversion? Wou'd she not have sufficient to satisfy all the wants that a woman of understanding can have? But my misfortune is, that this Fortune lys abroad. That's true, but for Gods sake where's the difference between its lying in Virginia or in Berkshire as long as I receive the Profits of it in London? Nay I have really several advantages that Estates in England want. My Land is not taxt either to King or Poor, which swallows at least a third part of the Rents here. Then mine improves every day more & more, & in a few years will be worth double of what t'is at Present. Besides I can make ten ⅌ cent of mony by paying down the Customes of my yearly Income, while other People are glad to make five. All these advantages consider'd it wou'd be ridiculous to part with this Estate, besides the vast deal of time and difficulty it wou'd require to dispose of it to any tolerable advantage. I wish I had an opportunity to discourse with your Father upon this Subject, or why may I not write to him in very respectfull terms? I fancy he has given some directions to inquire about me, for I find there is not a Merchant in the City tradeing to my Country, but has been askt several questions lately concerning my circumstances. I am perswaded if the charming Sabina wou'd but take the proper method, she might soon find the way to the tender part of her Fathers bosome. When a Parent has a real tenderness for a child, tis very easy to bribe that tenderness a thousand ways. But indeed my dear Enchantress shou'd tell him the whole truth, and cast her self intirely upon his compassion. If your Inclinations continue the same, it is both your duty and your Interest to let him know it without disguize, and he will certainly comply after some little deliberation. When he perceives twill be necessary for your happiness, nature will plead for you. After he's convinc't that your affections are engag'd he'll give way to no new Proposals, and drop those that have been made already. For Gods sake take courage and signalize your constancy on this occasion, and my heart will burn with everlasting gratitude and affection for you. And if the worst shou'd happen that your Papa shou'd alter his will again, as he did last year, & give all away from you, I swear by all my hopes of happiness, that I will marry you, and shall take a pleasure in so lucky an occasion of requiteing your generosity. In the mean time if any Proposal be now afoot, I beg of you not to suffer it to advance too far, but in its Infancy throw your self at your Fathers feet & address him in terms like these "I beseech you Sir by all the tender "Regards of a Parent to take pity on me. If you have any "respect for the life, any care for the happiness of your "child, I beg, I intreat you not to force my Inclinations. As "long as you disapprove of any Person I will not marry him "tho it cost me my life: but on the other side Sir, I hope you "wont force me to marry a man I cant love. Consider the "danger I shou'd incur of being perjur'd, if I shou'd vow in "the presence of the Almighty to love any man, when my "own heart tells me I can never do it. I beg you therefore "my dearest Father if you wont please to indulge my Inclina-"tions, that you'll permit me at least to mourn away my life "in solitude, that I may'nt make any body miserable besides "my self. Dont you think my dearest Angel such a Prayer wou'd touch him to the Quick and soften all his obstinacy. Adieu my dear Sabina may you be whole ages as happy as I shou'd be if I had you panting and consenting in my arms. Adieu.

TO OLIBARI April 1. 1718[1]

The good natur'd way you took yesterday of delivering the worst natur'd message that ever was, makes me resolve to deal ingenuously with you. I was then so surpriz'd and disconcerted at what you told me, that tis no wonder I was out of all condition of returning my answer. Besides there are so many unlucky mistakes happen in delivering of verbal answers, that the surest way will be to send you mine in writeing. I must therefore in the first place return M S— my most humble thanks for discovering a most intire dependence upon my honour. For except she believ'd I had the most of that of any man liveing, she wou'd not have put her self intirely in my power, & afterwards give me all the provocation in the world to expose her. But she has not placed her confidence wrong, because her character as well as her Person shall always be dear to me. Neither wou'd I say any thing to you upon this occasion, except her telling you only a little of our story, made it necessary for me to tell you more for my own justification. Had M[rs] S. not told you her self that she had done me the honour to write several letters to me, the secret shou'd have burst me before I wou'd have discover'd it. However after she has been pleas'd to tell you that those letters were only so many denyals, I think it no infidelity in me, to let you know, that if they were negatives they were really such as plainly imply'd an affirmative. Without question Sir you thought it a great instance of that young Lady's discretion, to send me by so safe a hand my Letter unopen'd; but it will make that discretion seem to come a little too late, when I assure you she had done me the honour to receive and read a great number of em before,

[1]Miss Smith apparently gave up all hope of bringing the affair to a happy conclusion, for Byrd received a call on the 29th from Mr. Orlebar, a Master in Chancery, a messenger from Miss Smith, but as Byrd was out, drinking chocolate with Mrs. Southwell, he missed his caller. Next day when Sabina went out she did not look up at him as was her custom; and on the 30th Mr. Orlebar called and told Byrd that Miss Smith did not care to be troubled by any more letters or addresses. Byrd reports that he said little to him, but when the messenger was gone, the lover gave vent to his unhappiness in weeping. He reported this to Lady Dunkellen who advised him to continue writing. On the 1st of April, therefore, Byrd wrote to Mr. Orlebar the whole story. Afterwards he visited Mrs. B-r-n and told her the story.

writ in the warmest terms that accepted Love cou'd inspire. For Gods sake what can the most partial Friend say in excuse of a Lady that receiv'd Love-letters from a Gentleman til she was so far convinc't of his inclination, as to acknowledge hers for him not only to her Brother, and Father, but at second hand to the Lover himself. Nay to convince you that she went too far to retreat, I can assure you, twas purely by her direction & contrivance that my Lord D— propos'd me to her Father. And even since I was so unfortunate as to have my proposal rejected, she has not only been so good as to receive 5 of my letters full of the most tender Expressions, but has also sent me 2 of hers, in the first of which I was taught how to direct my letters to her, so as they might escape the suspicion of her Father. Nay I believe it can be prov'd under her own hand, that notwithstanding her Papa had rejected my Proposal she wou'd do her Endeavour to work him up to consent to it. That this is all true I dare say she has sincerity enough to own, and supposeing it to be so, I appeal to you Sir, to her Father, or to her own honour and Generosity whether this be not as great encouragement as a Lady can give any man except a positive promise of marriage. For my part all my Partiality for M S can invent no Reason for her sending me this message unless it be that her Generosity may appear the greater in bestowing her heart hereafter upon the man, she had first made to dispair of it. I must therefore beg leave to declare my answer to the message you was pleas'd to bring to me, that as M S has by the plainest Instances of Encouragement made me love her beyond all Recovery, she must excuse me if I continue my Pretensions. as therefore it is not in my power to give over my Passion, so for that reason I cant give over my addresses, and as long as I believe her to be a Woman of honour, justice, & generosity, I can never perswade my self that she is capable of encourageing any Gentleman in this unusual Manner, & disappointing him at last, without any provocation on his part. And this Sir may help to clear up that dark passage of my letter (which may be mistaken for bullying) that whoever has the happiness to marry her must give proof of one good quality besides his Estate. I meant this of his humility, for whoever will marry a woman after he knows that she has encourag'd and disappointed another another [*sic*] Man, must be the humblest Creature alive. This is the deliberate and determin'd Answer of &c.

TO SABINA April 7.[1]

Haveing receiv'd no answer to the Letter I wrote to your Ambassadour extraordinary, wherein I was oblig'd to set forth how much your generous conduct had fixt my Inclinations, & made me unalterably yours, & likewise how impossible it was for me to give over my Pretensions I must interpret this silence to be a confession of what I said, to be just, & a fair permission for me to proceed in my addresses. In the first place therefore I must beg leave to reproach my dear M S, that she shou'd send so cruel a message by a Gentleman that was an utter stranger to me, & lay me under the hard necessity of discovering to him things that I intended to keep eternally lockt up in my Breast. After you had put the seal of honour upon my Lips, why wou'd you break it open with your own hands, and give your Envoy a Commission to tear the dearest of all secrets from my Bosome? Was I not worthy then madam to receive the dreadfull sentence from your own mouth, from that dear mouth that had before own'd some charity for me? or did you scruple to let the same hand forbid me to write any more that no longer than a month before had given me leave to do it and directed me how to do it safely. This Instability in your mind, if I may presume to call it so, racks me to death, & wou'd make any body believe but me, that either your former Conduct was only a Joke, or else what you have acted lately must needs be so. I am ready to offer

[1]Notwithstanding Sabina's decision, Byrd continued to hope; he talked of her with Mrs. Fitz Herbert, dreamed of her, saw her at the Spanish Ambassador's. He went to Old Abram, a conjuror, who gave him hope that Sabina would be kind to him, and was still more encouraged at the news that Sabina had refused Mr. P-t, a gentleman of fortune, because of her inclination to Byrd. On the 7th he wrote to Mr. Perry to borrow £10,000 to settle upon Miss Smith, and then to Sabina.

violence to my self, for fear I may have given you some real provocation; If I have, for Gods sake impute it to the error of my passion which I own is violent enough to act imprudently. If therefore I have been so unhappy as to offend the Darling of my soule, I protest to Heaven it was without my intention, which as long as I live will mean only to please & oblige you. Forgive me then I intreat you, every thing I might write in the hurry of an unguarded Inclination. I can assure you madam whatever I might say in that frenzy, was not design'd to work upon your fear (for then it had indeed been Bullying) but upon your honour, your Justice, your generosity. As well as I love you I wou'd not receive your heart from so mean a Principle as your fear, but only from your pity and generous Inclination. I beg you therefore my divine Creature, by all your hopes of happiness, to receive a dispairing wretch into favour, & I promise I will never offend again, except it be an offence to love you with a most ardent and everlasting affection. Adieu my unkind Enchantress, may you be whole ages as happy as I shou'd be if I had you all panting and consenting in my Arms, and may you stil have some Relentings for &c.

TO SABINA the 17th of April[1]

*Sent back open.

Dos my Dear M S then not so much as know me, nor own him any longer for her Acquaintance that a few weeks ago she was so good as to acknowledge for her Lover? Has she now not even civility for whome she very lately shew'd a good deal of compassion? Alas I am fallen indeed! fallen from the enchanting hopes of being pity'd by the woman I love as I do my own soul, to utter neglect & disregard. Gracious Heaven what can I have done to provoke this

[1]On April 8 Byrd heard that Mr. Perry could not lend him the £10,000; next day he made love to Sabina from his window; on the 11th she would not look up at him when she went out; on the 13th he noted that when he saw her in St. Clement Danes she blushed with love and shame, but would not salute him; on the 16th he noted that both the weather and his understanding were cloudy, for it took him five hours to write a letter to Miss Smith.

dreadfull alteration. I am sure I have neither been inconstant nor unfaithfull to you, no, my heart is wholly & devotedly yours, and if I outlive Methusalem I shall love you tenderly to the last moment. I have writ nothing to you but what was the natural consequence of an intense and lively passion. The Jeolosy of looseing a heart which alone cou'd make me happy might perhaps render me indiscreet: but that was only a proof that my Love was so violent as to be ungovernable, which us'd to be reacon'd no unpardonable provocation. For Gods sake my charming M S forgive me an Imprudence of this Venial kind, & smile again upon the man that adores you. Tis now too late alas to go about to discourage me by this cold and forbidding behaviour, [for the Infection is taken, and taken so strongly, that were I sure to dye, to be distracted, to be undone I wou'd love you on, and my constancy wou'd hold out against all difficulty all discouragement. Tis impossible for me to feel the sting of any other misfortune while I endure the misery of wanting you.][1] That shou'd have been done many months ago and not after the contagion is communicated. Suppose a Person ill of the small Pox shou'd suffer a freind to converse so nearly with him as to give him the distemper, wou'd it not afterwards be a very odd piece of discretion to desire him to keep his distance? Or suppose a good Lady in one of her frolicks shou'd knowingly set fire to her neighbours house, and when tis all over in a flame be so very prudent as to throw cold water upon it to put it out? This is in truth the case of my Love to Dear M S it was suffer'd, it was accepted, it was return'd and inflam'd til it was grown beyond all Remedy, and then it seems tis thought the proper time to begin to slight and discourage it. But God knows it is now too late, for the Infection is taken so strongly, that were I sure to dye, to be distracted, to be undone, I shou'd love you on & feel no other misfortune while I endure the greater misery of wanting you. My dearest Angell may assure her self that as the Passion she has given me is incurable so my Constancy is so great that neither time nor absence, shiness

[1]The words enclosed in brackets are crossed through.

or disdaign neglect or scorn, difficulty or danger can ever discourage it. For let appearances be what they please I have that high opinion of M S good nature as to think that she wou'd not suffer my addresses til I came to love her to distraction without intending to take compassion of me at last. That wou'd be a cruelty she must needs be incapable of, because twou'd be makeing her self guilty of all the wretchedness that will certainly follow upon my disappointment. For Gods sake take pity of me else I am lost for ever, nay twill be my onely Refuge to be lost, for that only can put me out of my insufferable pain. I am very far however from claiming your Pity as a debt, no, I implore it as the highest Instance of grace & generosity, and if ever you be so generous as to marry me, it shall be the business as well as the Pleasure of my whole life to make you the happyest of woman kind. Adieu my Dear M S may you always be happy tho I be miserable, may you laugh while I'm dissolv'd in tears, may you live in uninterrupted Joy, while I hurry on my fate by the deepest Melancholly. Adieu & vouchsafe at least a compassionate look to him you have made the wretchedest of all Gods Creatures.

TO SABINA the 21st of April[1]

There can be no sentence so severe as that which a conscious and repenting offender passes upon himself. If my Dearest M S did but know how much I reproach & condemn my own folly for haveing so barbarously offended her, and indeed how sharply I punish my self for it, she wou'd be more apt to forgive me. I am asham'd and confounded that I shou'd have been so ungratefull as to upbraid you with

[1]On the 18th of April Byrd received back his letter of the day before, but he was sure Miss Smith had read it; and meeting Lord Dunkellen afterward he was told that Sabina had shown the letter to her father. On Sunday at St. Clement's church Sabina would not look at Byrd, and the next day he wrote an unprotesting letter to her.

On the 22d he notes writing two letters, one to Miss Smith and one to her father; perhaps he did not send the one to her father, for it is not in the notebook; the one to Miss Smith he copied fair on the 25th. On the 24th he made a copy of the letter [or letters] to Sabina. This may refer to the copies in the notebook printed here.

your own Generosity, and plead that which was infinitely more goodness than I deserv'd, as an argument for your shewing me stil more. By this ridiculous behaviour I confess I have deserv'd the Just Ressentment you have expresst to me ever since Nothing in nature cou'd discover better sence or a nobler spirit, than my Dear M S has, by treating this Injury in the manner she has done: and tho I have really suffer'd all the torment that a slighted Lover cou'd suffer by it, yet in justice I must needs approve your conduct, and if possible do love you better than I did, both for the good sence and the spirit of it. However Madam tho in truth my fault has been very provokeing, yet I hope there has been nothing worse in it than folly & madness, which are in their own nature not absolutely uppardonable [*sic*]. Besides I can assure you as I hope to be forgiven by Heaven & you, I am most sincerely sorry for my offence, and if you think I have not suffer'd enough already by your Coldness, & the reproaches of my own conscience, I am ready to undergo any further Penance you shall please to lay upon me. And further to shew that my Repentance is compleat, I vow that I will take care never to offend again, but conform my self intirely to your good Pleasure for the time to come. Upon these conditions I humbly beg I may find forgiveness in that good nature & generosity which I have abus'd, especially since by this one fault of mine I give you an occasion of signalizeing half a dozen vertues. I intreat you therefore upon my bended knees, the tears all the while trickleing from my conscious Eys, that you will be so generous as to forgive a penitent Lover his first Fault, who has been so punisht for this that he will never commit a second. Vouchsafe for Gods sake to receive me once more into favour my Dearest my divinest Mrs Smith, and I will own your generosity to the last moment of my Life. Remember nothing is inexorable but Death & the Furys, while God Almighty & all those creatures that approach nearest to his Perfection are easily intreated, where there is any marks of amendment. You madam are exceedingly generous (I have try'd it sufficiently) you are as good natur'd as you can be without folly, I therefore throw my self upon them both, and will not dispair of y[r] Pardon. Tho I have nothing to plead in my Excuse, but that my transgression did not proceed from any intent to offend, but from an apprehension of looseing w[t] I love beyond all things in the world. Besides I protest that the torment I have felt from your just unkindness has been an absolute Purgatory to me, & therefore I hope youll please to think y[t] a sufficient Punishment. For all these reasons be so good madam as to shew me some marks of your being reconcil'd, or I shall run distracted. My Passion is grown to that high pitch, that twill be impossible for me to live much longer under your Displeasure, However let me be never so wretched or never so short-liv'd, I shall be sure to wish that my Dear M S may be always the happyest of all Gods creatures. I am with an affection never to be ended except by death &c

---

TO SABINA April the 25[th][1]

*Come back open.

O that all mankind were as importunate to be reconcil'd to Heaven as I am to my Dear M S, and were as unfeigned in their concern for haveing offended! On this condition they wou'd be sure to be pardon'd even crimes of malice & Infidelity, while Imprudence only, and extravagance of Love in me continue unforgiven. Gracious God how can good-nature be so inexorable, and Good sence so unrelenting! You know, I'm sure you do, that I love you in the tenderest degree, and wou'd suffer any pain, encounter any danger to serve & oblige you: And can you then deny such a one, a compassionate Look, or some other gracious Token of your being in charity with him? I conjure you by all the tenderness of your dear soule, and by all the charms of your enchanting Body, to tell me I have made my Peace, and am restor'd to that degree of favour, which while I was so

[1]On the 26th Byrd received back his letter from Sabina, with a cross one from her. At Will's he heard from Lord Dunkellen that Sir Edward Des Bouverie had been proposed again. On the 27th he saw Sabina, in great confusion, at church, and he spent the afternoon writing to her; next day, after finishing the letter, he felt very melancholy.

happy as to enjoy, I envy'd no monarch on his throne no angel his blissfull seat above. But alas since a Veil has been drawn over your smiles, my bloud has been chill'd, like the air at the great Eclips, when the cheerfull sun was intercepted from the world: but like that too I hope your Pity will soon break out with a new lustre, and revive the heart of him that adores you. I rejoic'd yesterday to see your Father go out again after his tedious confinement. Whatever opinion he may have conceiv'd of me for want of knowing me better, I can assure you no man liveing can have a greater Respect for him than I have. I love him dearly for haveing obliged the world with the most agreable Creature in it. And wou'd he but be so good as to approve of my Addresses to you twou'd prolong his life some years to see his Daughter as happy as all my study, all my Endeavours cou'd make Her. I never had provocation I thank God to murmur at the Fortune Providence has been pleas'd to allot me, til your Father pronounc't it insufficient to recommend me to the honour of his allyance. Then I confess I did repine at its distance because it displeas'd him; tho in truth there is no difference between an Estate in Virginia & in Middlesex as long as I receive the Profits of it in London. I wish he wou'd please to give me leave to explain to him the advantages of this Estate, & I wou'd not doubt but convince a Person of his good understanding that upon the whole matter tis preferable to an Estate in England. O that my Dear M S wou'd interceed with him to grant me this favour, because I do flatter my self, if he were perfectly acquainted with my Character & circumstances he wou'd like me Better. This I can assure both him & you, that the last year my Returns yeilded more than £1800 clear of all charges, and I don't doubt will produce as much this. Now when an Income like this shall be assisted with his Generosity, & manag'd wth common prudence, what is there in this world requisite to make a reasonable Woman happy, that may not be plentifully purchas'd by it. For Gods sake employ your powerfull Interest with him, & I'm confident youll find the way to the tenderest part of his Bosome. I intreat you my Dearest M S, shew this generous Instance of your

Pity and my Heart will burn with everlasting gratitude & affection for you. Adieu my dearest Angel may all the stars in their Courses join their Influence to make you perfectly & unchangeably happy, Adieu

---

TO SABINA April 28

The letter you did me the honour to send me on Saturday rais'd ten thousand tempests in my soule; and well it might when you accus'd me of haveing taken several steps to injure You. The haveing told Mr Oliber so much as I did was wrong I confess, but Ive already let you know my concern upon that head and have humbly ask't your pardon for it. And if you wou'd please to recollect that matter cooly I shou'd hope you'd find nothing so heighnous in it as to deserve an everlasting Ressentment. For Gods sake remember how much you had unbosom'd your self to that Gentleman, how far you had let him into our secret; Remember the cruel message you sent me by him, which was of that import that I cou'd never have justify'd the continuance of my addresses without opening so much of the tender scene to him as I did. In the mean time I was certain this Gentleman wou'd never betray you, because he was a confidant of your own chooseing, as well as your Relation, and since you had trusted him with the secret first, it was both an Example and an Excuse for me to do it afterward. It cou'd therefore be no such unpardonable Infidelity in me to repose a Confidence in one that you thought worthy to trust, neither cou'd it be any Injury to you, because I cou'd never suspect your own Confidant wou'd expose you. If he has not betray'd what I wrote to him, you are not injur'd, and if he has, It is your wrong choice of a freind has deceiv'd me. These madam I own were the motives that induced me to discover to him so much as I did wch you are pleas'd to say was injureing you by premeditation. Now Heaven is my witness I did not intend to injure you at all, tho I confess there was folly in trusting him with so important a secret notwithstanding it was more than probable he wou'd be too tender of your character ever to divulge it. I suppose when you thank God so heartily that it is not in my power to injure your fame, you mean that neither my Honour or Inclination will suffer me to do it. If you mean so you're certainly in the right, because tis impossible for me not to be tender of a womans character when I am so intirely tender of her Person. But madam if you wou'd lay aside your Passion your own good sence wou'd inform you that if I shou'd but nakedly tell the story of our Loves to any one liveing, that knows the difference betwixt Right & wrong, he wou'd condemn you. Nay shou'd I explain the whole matter to your own Father (who is by no means partial to me) he wou'd say you had given me very substancial encouragement. Can you think, if I shou'd shew your letters, especially that of the 25th of February and that which you desir'd my acquaintance in St Andrews Parish in Holbron [*sic*] to give me by way of answer after your Fathers rejecting my Proposals, if I shou'd expose these I say wou'd they not fix a spot upon your character in the judgment of all that have common sence, or the common Principles of Justice? I must therefore conclude madam that in this at least you have stil a good opinion of me, when you can depend upon my honour so far as to put me at defyance tho at the same time you must know that you are intirely in my power. I am cruelly puzzel'd to understand the end of your letter where you are pleas'd to tell me you will take care it shall not be in my power to create any discord where your Papa shall ally you. If you mean by this dark saying to inform me that there is another match propos'd for you which it will not be in my power to break off, I must beg leave to answer that I have the proper arguments in my strong box to perswade any man of Justice & common sence not to marry a Gentlewoman that has proceeded so far with another Gentleman. This madam is plentifully in my power to do if I cou'd be provok't to expose you: but your honour is in too safe hands, and I shall always love you too tenderly to do you the least Injury. You need therefore give your self no trouble in contriveing stratagems to hinder me from doing you that prejudice which I wou'd sooner dye than be guilty of. But if after all the Encouragement you have given me for a year together, if after the Indulgence of your conduct has rais'd my passion to that excess as will cost me dear to remedy, and after you have left such dear Pledges of your kindness in my hands, I say if after giveing me all these hopes of being the happyest man in the world you shall think fit to marry another because he has a greater Estate, I will submit whatever the disappointment cost me. And tho I shou'd certainly be the unhappyest of all mortals under this dreadfull circumstance yet it wou'd not be the least of my concern that you had done a wrong thing, for which I shou'd fear lest providence shou'd in all Justice make you wretched, for haveing made me so. However madam theres one thing I intreat of you before you admit the addresses of another, that you will retire into your closet, and calmly pass over in your mind all that has passt between us, & with attention read over all my letters & your own, When you have done this fall upon your knees and beg of God Almighty to direct your choice so as may be most for your own honour and your own happiness, and then do as he shall put into your heart. Nay I will join my Prayers with yours that if your new choice will make you happyer than I shou'd, that you might marry him. for it will be a very great comfort in my affliction to remember that my Dear Mrs Smith is perfectly happy. I likewise presume to beg one favour more which is, that you will be pleas'd to open the whole scene of our affair to your Father without concealing any one circumstance from his knowledge. In this case I beg you neither to aggravate or extenuate any part of the story but give to every Incident its full force of truth. By this means he will be able to give you his opinion fairly, and his Justice & good sence may help to direct yours. I wou'd have done this myself if I had your permission but I have suffer'd so much displeasure by what I rashly told to Mr Oliber that I wou'd not venture without your leave to make a second discovery. By this you may judge how much I dread your frowns, and with how invincible an affection I am

TO VIGILANTI April the 30th.[1]

To convince you that I have your Daughters Character in my power and to let you see the Indiscretion of your menaces & of her Defyance I here send you a copy of one of those letters she was so good as to write to me since you rejected my Proposals. UT SEQUITUR That this is a true copy the original may prove whenever you please. In this letter you'll perceive a concern that you would not agree to our marriage, a fear that you shou'd by some rash resolution force another match upon her which she might find hard to digest, & a method settled of a fresh correspondence by an invisible character, & directing to her maid so that it might escape your knowledge. By all these kind things I had reason to hope, that she wou'd either marry me notwithstanding your refusal, or else that she intended to work you up into a Consent. I cou'd also produce another of her Epistles in which she desires I may not rest satisfy'd with your answer because she intended to use all her Influence to perswade you. These & many other things I cou'd tell you to perswade you that a Lady cou'd not possibly give a man greater Encouragement Dont this amount to an Engagement to marry me if you wou'd but consent, & to a promise that she wou'd use all her art to perswade you to it? Now Sir you know best whether you have not in all this time offer'd her your leave to marry me, If you have, she has violated her word. And she knows best whether she has us'd her utmost endeavour to obtain your consent, if she has not she has forfeited her Promise. However let this be as it will, she shews abundance of honour, & is strangely consistent with her self, to engage first to marry me if her Father wou'd consent, & to promise to work him up to it, & in 2

[1]On the 29th of April Byrd received a message that Mr. Smith wished to speak to him. After drinking a bottle of champagne to give himself spirit he went to see Mr. Smith, and had a talk with him about the encouragement Sabina had given him; but Mr. Smith remained adamant. On the 30th Byrd wrote to Mr. Smith and showed the letter to Lord Dunkellen.

On May 1st Lord Dunkellen reported that Sabina had cried and had eaten nothing all day. Mrs. B-r-n consulted Old Abram again, who prophesied Byrd's success. On the third, at Daniel Horsmanden's chambers, Byrd wrote another letter to Mr. Smith.

months after this when a better Estate is propos'd, offer to take an oath not to marry me at all tho you shou'd consent never so much. I must be judg'd by you Sir whether this be honour whether this be truth or common justice, if not, why will she break thro all these Vertues, without which a woman is the most abandon'd creature liveing? I must submit it to your good sence how far you must be accessary to these violations if you wont prevent them, & if you perswade her to 'em, how much you must be Principal. Besides I think you will not only do me the greatest injustice in the world, but likewise the Poor Gentleman now in treaty, to marry your Daughter to him under the notion of a woman of honour & truth, when you know at the same time she has all the guilt upon her of haveing encourag'd and disappointed another. To this I may add that both you & the good Lady know that this marriage will not be out of kindness to him, but out of peak to me, which is like to make them both very happy. I pity the the [*sic*] poor Gentleman who is to know nothing of all this, but must be led ignorantly to his fate as an Ox to the slaughter. If there be any avenging Justice in Providence, you may depend upon it, if your Daughter dos marry this man, after all the wrong she has done to me, she will be the wretchedest of women. If you live to see it (as I shall do I'm sure) twill bring your Grey hairs with sorrow to the grave; but if you do not, you must the sooner answer it at the bar of Eternal Justice, for being the author of your Daughters and this Gentlemans misfortunes. Be Judge now your self Sir whether your Daughter's character be not intirely in my hands, & whether it be not in my power, by shewing Sir Edward how prettily his mistress writes, to disappoint this gaudy marriage. However I have been so generous as to give you my word that I will do nothing to hinder this affair, in hopes this handsome behaviour on my part may produce the same on yours. But if it shou'd not, and you shou'd against all the Rules of Justice marry your Daughter to this Gentleman, I shall think my self at full liberty to declare my wrongs aloud to him and all the world, especially since then she will have a Champion whose age & infirmitys will be no excuse for not vindicateing a bad cause.

What the consequences of this may be, I matter not, let them answer it that have been wittingly & designedly the guilty cause. However Sir I thought fit to give you this fair warning in time, lest when you come hereafter to see the just calamitys of your family you might reproach your self for haveing been knowingly the author of 'em. I wish God almighty may direct you & your Daughter to act in this affair in such a manner, as may be most for the honour & happiness of you both. I am with very great Respect &c.

TO VIGILANTI May the 3d

I flatter'd my self that I might before now have receiv'd the honour of your Answer to my letter, which I was the rather encourag'd to hope, from the message you was pleas'd to send me by my servant. After the unjust usage I have had the misfortune to receive from your Daughter, I imagin'd neither you nor she wou'd have been wanting in Civility: but I find I must be ill treated throughout, which is the harder, because t'is expected that the good behaviour shou'd be altogether on the suffering side. Since this is too plainly the case, I shall begin to think that the want of a generosity on one side ought to cancel all obligation to it on the other. I am &c.

TO TIPPERARI[1] May the 6th

I was yesterday surpriz'd to see your Lordp introduce a new Lover to your sister, who about 2 months ago was pleas'd to be the Messenger of her Inclinations to me. This appear'd the more strange, because you had been let into the whole secret of our Amour by the Lady her self, and are a witness both of the Encouragement, and wrong I have

---

[1]Tipperari is, of course, Lord Dunkellen, and this letter seems to have been concocted between Byrd and him, for Byrd notes the following in his diary: on the 5th he met Dunkellen at Leveridge's and was told that the settlement was all arranged and that now was the time to move if he intended; on the 6th he wrote to Lord Dunkellen, and recorded that it worked as they planned. He then wrote a letter to Miss Smith, and later at Will's Lord Dunkellen told him of the distraction the letter had made in the family.

receiv'd. After this I must take the liberty to tell your Lordp, that the carrying Sir Edward to Mrs Smith, was condescending to act a double Part, and careing more for the Interest, than for the honour of your Ladys Family. Besides my Lord I think upon the whole matter, you have not been treated much better than I by this Gentlewoman, because she has made you make the ill figure of being the Minister of her Injustice, & the Tool of her Inconstancy. I can really find out no reason for your Lordp's acting this part, except by endeavouring to marry Mrs Smith to this Gentleman, you intend to be reveng'd for the wrong she has done both to your self and me, for if there be any truth either in fame or Physiognomy, he seems to be perfectly well qualify'd to do justice upon a Lady that has dealt dishonourably by another man. I am &c.

TO SABINA May 6th 1718

I understand by my Demon that the terms are compleatly settled upon which you are to sell both your honour and your happiness, and this day your new Hero is to begin his attaque upon your changeable Inclinations. As to the consequence I wish with all my soul it may be happy for you, tho I never knew any woman act in the character you seem to put on, but came to be substancially miserable. However that I must submit to God Almighty, who knows all the wrong you have done me, and seems to pitch upon Sir Edward in all respects a proper Instrument to avenge it. For my part tho I have it in my power to prevent this marriage and tho I have had all the Provocation in the world to do it yet I cant act so inconsistently as to expose to a stranger the Woman I love, and you shall find I have that sacred regard to my Promise, that I wou'd not break it, tho I were sure by that Violation to recover your affections, which next to truth I value above all things in the world. However madam you must needs think it a most uncommon piece of generosity in me to observe faith towards them that have none, and to treat those persons with honour that seem to have no notion of it themselves. That you dealt very unjustly & very dishonourably by me your own father confesst sufficiently, when he call'd you Jilt & other names of infamy for haveing given me so much encouragement. Now for him after being convinct of this to drive on another match is something so profligate towards you, towards the man that is dealing for you, and towards me y[t] am injur'd, that civility wants a proper name for it. But as for your conduct Madam, tho all the world must condemn you, yet you may plead in your excuse the Violence of the temptation. There is a vast Estate with which a fine Lady cant possibly be miserable. Then your man has so bright an understanding, so sweet so engageing a temper so polite a behaviour, and has a constitution so uninjur'd by excess and disaster that he may well dazzle your Eys and make you forget all the Rules of Truth & Justice. Perhaps you may wonder how I came to make such a Promise to your Father, not to hinder this blessed match when it was so much in my power to do it. For this I had 2 Reasons. 1st because I cou'd not prevent it without exposeing your letters to a stranger, which no provocation shall make me do. and 2[ly] I did firmly believe you had too much honour integrity & truth ever to marry another man after all the Encouragement you had given to me. And if I shou'd be mistaken & you shou'd prove so abandon'd as I [*sic*] do it, I shou'd have the comfort to reflect that it was no great disaster to miss a Damsel that wants those very necessary Vertues. Thus Madam Generosity provokt me to make this Promise and Truth shall make me observe it. However I have stil so good an opinion of you, that you will yet shew your self to be a woman of honour and never consent to a marriage that will brand you with the most infamous of all female characters, and make you wretched beyond all imagination. For Gods sake consider well before you engage too far, and listen to the whispers of your good angel who wou'd faign guard you from those disasters into w[ch] avarice & ressentment are going to lead you. I wish with all my soule you may do that which will be most for your honour and your happiness, for I can assure I have none of that ill natur'd Revenge that will ever make me rejoice in your misfortune tho you will be the guilty cause of a great deal to me. However I forgive you, and may Heaven forgive you too. Tho I cant forbear telling you that in the midst of this dreadfull prospect I must stil hope you will act as a woman of sence & honour and not disappoint the flattering hopes you was pleas'd to give me. May Legions of angels guard you both from doing and suffering ill, and may I live no longer than that I may be a witness and Promoter of your happiness. Adieu.

TO CHEVALIER DE BOOBY May 10th 1718[1]

Sence you did me the honour of a visit the other day I have been beating my Brains to find out who shou'd write those fine Letters which you was pleas'd to shew me. By a certain very gross Expression that I remember in one of 'em I cou'd almost suspect it might come from Mr Smith himself, because it was the very appellation he thought fit to use to his Daughter after I had explain'd to him the Encourage-

---

[1]This letter is written to Sir Edward Des Bouverie, Byrd's successful rival. The "fine letters" mentioned are doubtless the work of Lord Dunkellen, for Byrd noted in his diary on the 7th that Dunkellen showed him the letter he was to write to his rival. On the 8th, Sir Edward visited Byrd, bring Captain W-n with him, and said that he had received a letter from Byrd. This Byrd denied, but he told him the whole story of the perfidy of Sabina. Sir Edward agreed that she had acted wrongly but said that he intended to proceed. On the 9th Byrd wrote a letter to his rival, and on the 10th finished it.

On the 16th, at the Spanish Ambassador's, Byrd was told that Sir Edward Des Bouverie had challenged him, which he declared to be a lie. However, on the 12th he and Daniel Horsemanden had visited a Spaniard that made foils. And on the 19th he heard from Lord Dunkellen that Sir Edward had retained another second to take Captain W-n's place. It is possible that the letter printed below, p. 368, to Cavaliero Bonboni, may be to the second of Sir Edward Des Bouverie and may refer to this incident. No more is mentioned in the diary about a duel.

On June 7 Lord Dunkellen told Byrd that Sabina was to have £1500 laid out upon her wedding clothes. On July 8th Byrd noted simply that Miss Smith was married; and on July 11th that his neighbor Smith had died the night before.

Sir Edward Des Bouverie, who married Sabina, was the eldest son and successor of Sir William Des Bouverie, Knight, an eminent and wealthy Turkey merchant, and his wife Anne, daughter of David Urry. He suceeded to his father's dignities and estate. He represented Shaftesbury in Dorsetshire in the two parliaments of George I and in the first of George II. They had no children, and Lady Des Bouverie died in 1721; Sir Edward survived his wife fifteen years and died at Aix in France on Nov. 21, 1736.

ment she had given me. For my back was no sooner turn'd but he went into the next room, (convinc't as he was of the unfair treatment I had receiv'd,) and with much tenderness and good breeding call'd her Bitch & Jilt. Now the same very injurious Terms appearing in one of those Polite Epistles makes my conjecture not altogether improbable. But whoever might give themselves the trouble to write them I protest to you I did not neither was I privy to the doing of it. Had I thought it proper to acquaint you with my Affair with M[rs] Smith, I wou'd have taken the open handsome way of waiting upon you my self, nor wou'd I for any reason whatsoever have carry'd with me a third Person to be witness to a story so much to that Ladys disadvantage. I can assure you the only reason why I did not go to you was, because I consider'd, that after a Lady has been graciously pleas'd to give a man Encouragement for more than a year together and after frankly declareing her Inclinations, if she think fit to change her mind in favour of a greater Estate, she must have something so wrong in her composition that I am not only easy under the loss of her, but even thank God for the disappointment. Neither indeed wou'd I have taken the trouble to open to you so Extraordinary scene, but that your comeing in so hostile a manner might have made my silence look like fear, which is a suspicion you know a Gentleman ought to avoid by all the methods of truth and Integrity. There is one thing Sir I wou'd beg of you in complement to your mistresses character, which is, that you will be pleas'd not to represent the story differently from what I told it, because as often as I shall hear it told wrong, I must be oblig'd for my own justification to tell it right, which for her sake I shou'd be unwilling to do. And that you may not by any defect of memory be led into a mistake of this kind I must beg leave to recount all the Principal Incidents of our story. M[rs] Smith then did me the honour to hold a Private Correspondence with me for above a year together, without the Privity of her Father, dureing which time she receiv'd about 15 letters from me full of the most passionate expressions, and writ in a character altogether invisible, til her art and industry brought it to light.

In answer to these letters I had the pleasure of about 5 from her, in a style not at all cruel or discourageing. After this, because I was so dull as not to understand several broad hints she had given me to propose my self to her Father, she did me the honour to send my Lord Dunkellen to let me know, that as she had reason to believe I had a great Respect for her, so she cou'd not deny but she had a good opinion of me, & therefore desir'd that I wou'd address my self to her Father. In obedience to her Commands I did make my Proposals, but my Estate lying in another Country it was not agreable to Mr Smith, tho she was so good as to endeavour to perswade him to it by declareing she cou'd be happyer with me than with any body else. How odd soever her fancy might be in this business, she was pleas'd to write to 2 of her Relations to intreat them to interceed with her Father in my behalf. But he continueing averse, order'd her to write to my Lord Dunkellen to give me my answer, which she did indeed in the body of the letter, but in the Envelope she desir'd His Lord^p not to give me that answer because she intended to use all her Interest with her Father to perswade him to it. Thus I was to be trail'd on by the Daughter after the Father had refus'd me, & to confirm me in the hopes of her Favour, she was pleas'd after that to write me a very gracious letter, to let me know how fearfull she was lest her Father shou'd take some rash Resolution to dispose of her to some other Person, which she said she shou'd find hard to digest. She also instructed me at the same time to be sure to write in the Invisible Character, to make up my letters in a square figure, and direct them to her maid, that so they might not fall into the hands of the old Gentleman. According to these kind Instruments I afterwards wrote her 4 or 5 letters conceiv'd in the most tender terms which she was so good as to receive. Thus we continued in very good Intelligence til your Estate came to be propos'd, which made her alter her style, and resolve to sacrifice both her character & Inclination to her Interest. This Sir is a faithfull account of our story, the truth of wch tis too much in my power to prove ever to be disputed, and supposeing it to be so, I must appeal to your cooler thoughts after marriage, whether this Lady has treated me with common honour or common Justice. Her own Father has already condemn'd her by thinking it proper to salute her with the reproachfull terms above mention'd, tho the good man at the same time notwithstanding this confession of his Daughters injustice to me, made no scruple to push on the treaty with you. I was sorry to hear from so good a Judge as your self, that most women now adays treat Gentlemen at this odd rate, but I have too good an opinion of the sex to be of your sentiments in this matter. However I assure you Sir I must own my self much oblig'd to Mrs Smith for being so charitable to me as to cure intirely the wounds of her Eys by the imprudence of her Behaviour in imitation of the Viper that cures by the Vertues of its flesh the dead bite of its teeth. This makes me as easy at least in missing her, as you can be in marrying of her, and I shall esteem it as just a complement to wish me joy upon looseing as to give it you upon gaining so extraordinary a Prize. I am &c.

EPITAPH ON THE MONUMENT OF EDWARD NOTT ESQR GOVERNOUR OF VIRGINIA[1]

Under this marble rest the ashes of His Excellency Edward Nott late Governour of this Colony, who was in his private character a good Christian, and in his Publick a good Governour. He employ'd the authority with which his Soveraign had intrusted him, to do good to the People, and not to insult and oppress them. All the while he held the Government, he remember'd that he was sent by an English

[1]Byrd wrote this epitaph on Colonel Nott at the request of Nathaniel Blakiston, agent for Virginia in England from 1705 until his death (*Ex. Jour.*, IV, 19), and brother-in-law of Nott (Oct. 8, 1718, Diary; Christopher Johnson, "Blakistone Family," *Maryland Historical Magazine*, II, 54-64). As deputy to the Earl of Orkney, Nott was Lieutenant Governor of Virginia from Aug. 15, 1705 until his death on Aug. 23, 1706 (*Va. Hist. Port.*, pp. 449-500; *Va. Mag.*, XIV, 302-3). The Virginia Assembly, May 30, 1718, ordered a marble monument in memory of Nott to be erected in the church-yard at Williamsburg (*LJC*, II, 623). The House of Burgesses entrusted to John Clayton, Attorney General of Virginia, the selection of the monument, not to exceed in cost £60, with such inscription as he thought proper (*JHB*,

Queen, to govern English subjects. Haveing no passion of his own to gratify, but that of doing good, he was content with the limited Authority of his Commission, and stretch't not the Royal Prerogative to make his Power absolute, and his Government arbitrary. He was a Lover of mankind, and bountefull to his Friends, but lost the credit of being generous to his Enimys, by haveing none. By the sanctity of his morals, and by the mildness, prudence, and justice of his administration, he was deservedly esteem'd a Publick Blessing while he liv'd, but when he dy'd his death was lamented as a Publick Calamity. He departed this life the 23[d] day of August 1706 aged years. In gratefull Remembrance of whose many Vertues the General Assembly hath erected this monument.

Whoever thou art that readest the sad tydings of his death, if a Stranger, pity the Country: if a Virginian, thy self.

May 29, 1718, pp. 213-14). For a picture of this monument, see L. G. Tyler, *Williamsburg* (Richmond, 1907), p. 23. The monument, still standing in Bruton Churchyard, bears the following inscription:

[arms]

"Under this Marble Rest ye Ashes
of His Excellency Edward Nott
Late Governor of this Collony who
In his Private character was a good
Christian and in his Public a good
Governor he was A lover of Mankind
And Bountiful to his Friends By ye
Sanctity of his Moralls and ye Mildness
Prudence and justice of his Administra
tion he was Deservedly Esteemed A
Public Blessing while he Lived & when
He Dyed A Public Callamity—he Departed
This Life the 23d Day of August 1706
Aged 49 Years.
In Gratefull Remembrance of who
se many Dutyes the General Assembly
of this Collony have Erected this
Monument."

(*Va. Hist. Soc. Coll.*, XI, 73.)

This inscription is Byrd's composition with the omission of those portions that might be judged to reflect upon the then Governor Spotswood, with whom Byrd was at odds, and of the last lines, perhaps omitted because of limitations of space.

TO CLEORA.[1]

If the way to be well serv'd is to be belov'd by the servant, you'll certainly have your Gardens kept in admirable order. The Grass-plats will be so clean, that you may venture to lye down upon them in your best cloaths. I cant promise that the Flower-garden will appear to you in so much Elegance as it ought, because the bashfull flowers will all shrink & hang their heads, at the presence of something more beautifull than themselves. Perhaps indeed the Rose may increase its lustre by blushing, at the disadvantage it may suffer by the comparison. I shou'd have discover'd more concern at our parting, but that I found my spirits supported by the good Bishop, & by the hopes of recieveing your commands very often. I shall be as impatient as some wives are at the lingering illness of their husbands, til I hear you got well down, therefore be so good as to let me know it by the very first Post. I beg I may always write to you in the stile of a Gardener, that I may have the pleasure of your calling your self *my Mistress*, which tho it have a double meaning, I hope may be understood in the most desirable sence by &c.

TO BELINDA[2]

To express the Tenderness one has for a woman as charming as an Angel, one needs an Angels Tongue. Without that assistance t'is impossible for me to tell my Dear Belinda the sence I have of all her endearing Qualitys. My

[1]On Feb. 9, 1719, Annie Wilkinson, Byrd's laundress and mistress for a time in London, took Byrd to visit her sister, Mrs. B—s, and on Feb. 18 Mrs. B—s came to Byrd's lodgings. He saw her frequently during the next several months, and the affair proceeded apace; but when she asked Byrd for a loan of £50 (April 30, 1719), the relationship was abruptly broken off. The two sisters seem to have been at least temporarily at odds and though Byrd tried to play the role of peacemaker, he definitely dropped both of them. He did pay farewell visits to Mrs. B—s on Oct. 22 and 28 and Nov. 5 and 6 before leaving London to sail to Virginia in December, 1719 (Diary, Feb. 9 through Nov. 6, 1719). Byrd recorded in his diary letters to Mrs. B—s on March 6, 9, 10, 19, 26, April 11 and 13, 1719, as well as on the dates of the letters to Cleora that follow.

[2]See *Tunbrigalia* (London, 1719), pp. 32-33, for some highly uncomplimentary verses "On Belinda" beginning

> "Belinda's bowsy, fat and fair,
> Adorn'd with Collops greasy;

Fancy indeed might paint the Inchanting Picture, but all language must falter at its incapacity of copying it. When I was so happy as to be with my Dear Belinda, my conscious Eys confesst some part of my Passion, tho nothing but Rapture can tell it all. But now that I am absent, my Pen ought to be pluckt from the Pinion of one of Venus's Doves, to express how tenderly I love her. The Quil of a goose can never reach it, but must write things savouring of the animal from which t'was taken. However tho I shou'd say foolish things, yet I hope you'll be so good as to reacon it amongst the symptomes of that passion, that has fated me to be eternally your slave

---

TO CLEORA. March 25.

If my dear Cleora's company that she had from London was agreable, I wish they had been in Paradise when they made her Letter a Post later than she intended: but if they were disagreable, I wish for her sake they had been in Purgatory. Thus you see I am as spitefull as an ancient Virgin to all those that so much as delay the pleasure I take in conversing with you. I'm glad to hear that necessity makes you rise early, tho twou'd be more suitable to your good sence to do a thing out of choice that wou'd so certainly contribute to your health, and good looks, which last at least us'd to be of consideration with the Ladys. It must be pure laziness in you to love your bed that can pretend no other temptation there. Indeed Cleora wou'd make that situation delightfull to him that shou'd be so happy as to be with her there, and were it my case, ye Gods! I shou'd neglect my gardens til they were grown up into a wilderness, before I shou'd once think of getting up. By this licence of Imagination I loose all my wonder at good Methusalem's loveing his bed so intirely. It was certainly you that made him doat on it, for how natural is it to hate the leaveing any

---

These are Perfections not so rare,
Amongst the plump and Easy."

While the authorship of these verses is not indicated the question arises whether Byrd wrote them, since he was the author of several in this volume and these are suggestive of his style and humor.

Place where one has tasted so much Joy. Tis very obligeing in Cleora, to display the pleasures of her habitation in order to inveigle me down, but all other temptations are superfluous, after that very sufficient one of your being there. Tis only adding the streams of a Brook to the ocean which dont seem at all increas'd by 'em; or to use a merrier comparison, such additional arguments are like what a Female sailor did once in the Thames, when the boat ran aground in which she happen'd to be, but all the stream she was able to contribute did not raise the water at all higher. If you wou'd therefore give me an Invitation that I can never resist, tell me that my enchanting Cleora is there, and I shall as naturally obey her call as the needle dos the attraction of the Loadstone, or as the male Turtle dos the cooing of his Mate after Valentines day. However I sincerely think it for your service, to deny my self the pleasure of seeing you, til Fiddle faddle is gone to learn manners & generosity in Holland. In the meantime I conjure you to stay my stomach and sooth my Impatience with writeing much and often, which will be the 2^{d} best amuzement poor Jeremy can have. I wou'd perform your message to Brandivia[1] if I cou'd do it without owning to her that you write to me. I have hitherto been cautious in that point, because I think it high treason against a Mistress to boast of her favours. In the mean time I beg leave to interceed with you in behalf of that unfortunate Damsel. I am ignorant indeed in what manner she has been so unhappy as to offend you, but if her Transgression be not altogether unpardonable, I beg I intreat you to forgive her, always remembering that tis a sister that has offended, & a Lover that interceeds for her. I confess I have been bribed to plead for her, and therefore you must not wonder if I plead very earnestly. You must know she brought me once acquainted with a Nymph I dearly love, one that is charming in her Person, engageing in her humour, and sparkleing in her understanding. I wish with all my soul that Cleora had as strong reasons for granting what I beg, as I have for asking

[1]Apparently a reference to Annie Wilkinson.

it, and then Im sure she'd overlook every provocation on her sister's part, & grant every petition on mine. By this act of grace you will give me the Vanity to hope I have some interest wth you, which let me tell you I had rather have than with any first minister in Christendome. May joy & health, and love & Peace all join their heavenly forces to make Cleora happy, & may she ever entertain some sympathy for &c.

TO CLEORA. April 2. 1719

Your Billets like many other good things the longer they are the better, & my Dear Cleora may as justly make an Apology for being too frequently in her charitys to the distress't, as for writeing too often to me. I honestly intended to tell you on Tuesday how charm'd I was with your last favour: but I was dragg'd out in the morning, & not suffer'd to be my own man all the rest of the day. However my company was not much the better for me, because the Remorse I had for not acknowledging your goodness by the same daylight I receiv'd it, made me as peevish as a looseing Gamester. Some told me I was melanchollly, others that I was in love, and perhaps they were both more in the right than they imagin'd. I take it a little in dudgeon, that you cou'd find no better time to wish for your Gardener, but when you was in company: I had much rather you shou'd long for him when you are all alone, that so he might have the happiness to be in your silent and most retir'd thoughts. When he wishes for his Cleora, he dos it at those times when he cou'd have her intirely to himself, when darkness collects his wandering thoughts, & the Curtains are drawn close about him. *Then poor swain he pants, he sighs, he wishes, then he fondly folds his arms, and fancys his charmer presst within them. But whether am I roveing! you see there's nothing so extravagant and so sawcy as an inflam'd Imagination.* I thought the best way to intitle Brandivia to your forgiveness, was to advise that unhappy nymph to do what you expected from her. She promis'd plentifully that she wou'd write to you by the next Post, which I hope was true, notwithstanding her Genius to Poetry. You discover abundance of good nature, in your kindness to a person that has done so many wrong things to forfeit it: *but my Dear Cleora knows there's nothing shews so much our kindred to the happy Beings above, as benevolence and forgiveness; and as you are like them in many other Instances, I believe you resemble them likewise in this.* This night Mr Heidaker[1] presents us with our last Masquerade, where I shall naturally look for some charming sheepherdess in figure like Cleora, & by a flight of Imagination beleive her to be the self same. Imagin how many passionate, how many tender things I shall whisper to her, while I am under this dear delusion. But alas when she speaks, I shall soon discover a wide difference betwixt her understanding and yours. Then how insipid will she appear upon the comparison, and I shall be apt to treat her with all the coldness and contempt of an Impostor. I shall ramble from one Fair one to another, and finding nothing like the charming Cleora there, shall return early home unsatisfy'd with the tastless diversion. You have an excellent hand at drawing of Pictures, insomuch that I am certain Fiddle Faddle's is like, without ever haveing seen the hopefull Original. All fine pieces may be so distinguisht, in which number I must count every one that is drawn by your Pensil, since what I have already seen of yours appear so masterly to &c.

TO CLEORA. April 7 1719

As obedience is the first vertue an humble servant can shew to his Mistress, I think myself oblig'd immediately to return my dear Cleora a direct answer to her question. You are pleas'd to ask how long it is I have vow'd to undergo the Pennance of your letters? To this I beg leave to

[1] John James Heidigger, commonly called the "Swiss Count," was manager of the Opera house in London from 1708 through 1734. He met with varying success, introduced Ridotti and masquerades at the opera, and in the end amassed a considerable fortune. He was associated with Händel in an operatic partnership at the Haymarket Theatre for some years (Grove's *Dictionary of Music*).

reply in the first place, that your dear letters are so far from being a Pennance to me that they give me more joy than any thing next to your agreable company. And then secondly if they do give me so much joy you may be sure I shall desire to be entertain'd with them as long and as often as you please to bestow them. In matters of happiness we men are no more than Beggars, and they we are told must not be Chusers. The more frequently your favours come, the more reason I shall have to applaud your generosity: *tho I think it a little dangerous to let a Lady know wherein our supream pleasure lys, because then by the rule of Contrarys, she will also understand what will give us the most pain.* This is a piece of knowledge which your sex too often makes an ill natur'd use of, by putting us to the torture whenever their bare suspicion makes 'em fancy we deserve it. But I cant take it into my head that either you will be so hard hearted as to take delight in tormenting me, or I be so undutifull to deserve it at your hand. I think my Dear Cleora reproves me in the wrong place for apprehending that I was not in her retir'd and most tender thoughts. Those fears are no other than ardent wishes that I might be so happy as to entertain you in your solitary moments when the mind makes a free choice of her own Pleasures: Tis I confess some consolation that you'll vouchsafe to think of me sometimes when you are by your self, tho for ought I know it may be as many women think of their Husbands with vexation. One cant forbear you know thinking of the devil Now & then, and disagreable objects will thrust themselves into our thoughts as often as those that are most pleasing, and therefore had you not grutch't me so much satisfaction, you might have told me that You thought of me with pleasure. If my example had any influence, you wou'd not only think of your Gardener but wish for him too even when the Curtains are drawn about you. How can you chide me for those wishes which the love of my dear Cleora inspires. If such be wicked thoughts, I'm sorry nature shou'd have giv'n us inclinations which we are forbid to gratify. This was writeing one law in our minds, and another in our members, one of which must certainly be in vain. I cant blame you for disapproveing of fine things addresst to you in Effigie, because there is danger of your Representatives reaping the advantage of them. But did you desire them to be said to you in proper person you wou'd make a short Errand to Town. Then I wou'd squander all my sweet things upon you and think my store much too small for so many charms. You cou'd appoint no Proxy that wou'd inspire me half so much as the dear Principal, tho I call'd in all the helps of a lively imagination. I try'd this t'other night at the Masquerade, where to say the truth, I met with a Nun shap't like the Queen of love, which brought you full into my thoughts. For your dear sake I squees'd the holy sister's breath almost out of her Body with the Masquerade-Hugg. *By this passionate gripe I shew'd my love to the absent Cleora, and at the same time almost dispatch't her Rival. You can't in conscience disapprove of this behaviour, because it was design'd to gratify 2 of your Passions at once, and a Female must be a little unreasonable that won't be satisfy'd with that.* Methinks Fiddle Faddle is as long resolving to embark for Holland, as if it were to repent, & like that Im affraid too he won't do it at all. Pray make him a a [*sic*] cake for his Voyage, and ship him off the first fair wind, which you wou'd assuredly do if you if you [*sic*] thought him worse than no company at all. *If a swain deserve that sad character especially in the Country he can be fit for nothing but transportation.* But how do I know now that I am not enacting a law against my self, and at the same time, and for the same reason pronouncing sentence upon &c.

TO CLEORA April 14. 1719[1]

I rejoice that I have not at this time so round a summ as £50 of my own to lend you, because 'twill furnish me with an opportunity of being stil more gallant and borrowing it, for the Pleasure of doing my dear Cleora service. I depend

[1]Byrd wrote in his diary for April 13 that he wrote to Mrs. B—s in reply to a letter she had written him asking to borrow £50, and on April 14 that he wrote to Mrs. B—s to refuse the loan.

so implicitly on your good faith to return it at midsummer, that I shall not scruple on the Credit of your word to engage my own for reimbursing my friend at that time. All the objection I have to the doing this, is, that from thenceforth I must not make love to you, lest you suspect that my great readiness to serve you did not proceed from friendship but design, & that I had not so much a desire to supply your wants as to satisfy my own Inclinations. Besides Cleora it wont only make my generosity suspected but also spoil the good grace of yours; for if I might hope to gain your heart after this, it will seem to be purchas't rather than bestow'd. If you'll be so good as to call tomorrow by 12 a clock I will endeavour to procure the mony before that time, which I beg you'll interpret as doing me a pleasure & by no means as receiveing a favour from &c

TO CAVALIERO BONBONI [?][1]

I have been told this afternoon, that you had done me the honour of a challenge, & that I had been so intolerably ill-bred as to refuse you. Whoever was the author of this Report is the Author of a most Vile & Scandalous Lye. But I have too good an opinion of you to suspect you capable of haveing a hand in a story you know to be false. However I shou'd be glad to be satisfy'd of this matter under your own hand, that so at the same time, that I justify my self from so villanous an imputation, I may acquit you from the infamy of haveing invented it. I am &c.

TO DUKE DULCHETTI.[2]

My Lord

The time now draw's near for my Transportation, which makes me repeat my humble Request to your Grace for the letter you was pleas'd to say you wou'd write to Arroganti.

[1] See above, p. 356.

[2] This letter to the Duke of Argyle was probably written Nov. 4, 1719, as on that date Byrd recorded writing to the Duke. Byrd was determined to take with him on his return to Virginia the protection of a letter to Spotswood from

I was so happy as to be in that Gentlemans good graces the 2 first years of his Government, but after that he grew out of humour with me, for reasons which I am very far from being asham'd of, & from thenceforth he endeavour'd to make my Post uneasy to me by introduceing vexatious schemes, which since my Resignation[1] he has thought fit to alter, and return to the old method. After that he was pleas'd to send over to the Junto de Sapienti[2] a heavy charge against me, which they in kindness to him dismisst without hearing. Now my Lord these were sore provocations, but neither they, nor all the bitter things I understand he has been pleas'd to say of me cou'd ever stir me up to attempt his Removal. All that I have done since I came over, has been, to get several hardships remov'd, wch he graciously intended to lay upon that Country; & the success I have had against him in every particular, notwithstanding the strong biass the Junto hath towards Governors, is a proof that I have had Justice on my side. He hath manag'd his matters so politickly, that he has 9 of the council, and a great ma-

---

the Duke, whom he regarded as his patron. On Oct. 24, 1719, Byrd had secured from Argyle a promise to write to the Governor about him, and from then until he secured the letter, at a dinner at Argyle's Nov. 22, just two days before leaving, Byrd made persistent court to the Duke, reminding him on frequent occasions of the desired letter.

On Sept. 13, 1719, Byrd had decided to make a trip to Virginia to look after his affairs. He left London Nov. 24, accompanied by his cousin Daniel Horsmanden and young John Carter; he visited his uncle Rand's family in Sussex, and went aboard ship at Dover on Dec. 9; he arrived in Virginia Feb. 4, 1720, but was confined at Captain Smith's, where he disembarked, until Feb. 8, when he arrived at Colonel Custis's home in Williamsburg; there he saw Colonel Philip Ludwell, Commissary Blair, James Roscow, Frank Lightfoot, Benjamin Harrison, and John Randolph, and later John Clayton. On Feb. 10 he visited Colonel Ludwell, and on Feb. 13 he arrived at Westover in Colonel Hill's coach (Diary).

[1]Byrd sold his place as Receiver General for Virginia to James Roscow for £500. (Byrd to Custis, Oct. 2, 1716, G. W. P. Custis, *Recollections of Washington*, ed. Lossing, p. 29.) Though Roscow's commission of appointment was dated March 26, 1716, he was not admitted to the office by the Council until Jan. 22, 1717 (Bassett, p. lxiii). Byrd apparently did not realize the full sum from the sale of his office for he noted in his diary, Feb. 21, 1721, that he forgave Roscow his bargain.

[2]Byrd probably refers here to the Lords of the Treasury and Spotswood's letter of December 1, 1714 (Spotswood's *Letters*, II, 80-82). The strife between Spotswood and Byrd for domination in Virginia grew in intensity from 1715 until Byrd returned to the colony in 1720, determined to make peace. The dramatic details of this struggle and Byrd's ambitions to succeed Spotswood can be followed fully in the Byrd diary for 1717-21, the MS letterbook of John Custis (Library of Congress), and the documents in C. O. 5/1318.

jority of the commons against him,[1] insomuch that the latter have sent over a publick complaint to His Maj^ty^ of his male administration. But I have stop't it upon full assurance given me here, that the Grievances complain'd of shall be remedy'd. Thus I have proceeded against him in the gentlest manner, and if he will do me justice, he must own me a fair adversary, and that only in those things wherein I judg'd him to be in the wrong. However my Lord the haveing had the presumption to oppose him at all, has given him so hearty a ressentment that I expect no peace unless Your Grace will be so good as to interpose your good offices. As he hath done his utmost to remove me from the Council, so I expect he will continue to do me all the ill turns he can when I come into his Dominions. Amongst the rest I believe he'll leave no stone unturn'd to hinder me from come-

---

In a letter to Sir John Percival, afterwards Earl of Egmont, from Virginia June 22, 1720, Byrd gave this version of the reconciliation with the Lieutenant Governor ". . . for my Senses they are gratifyed very well here, with a very delightful place, and all the liberalities of a charming Clymate, and now this Country is made much more agreable than it was by the intire Reconciliation we have lately brought about betwixt the Governor and the Council. All the people's grievances are redress'd now, neither are any of those hardships to be repeated which I us'd to complain of. I have had so great a share in this happy Revolution, that should I do nothing else while I tarry here, I shou'd think I made a very prosperous voyage, and had some claim to the reward that is promis'd to the Peace-makers. 'Tis really a wonderful change in a very little time, amongst a most divided people to see peace & friendship revive, and all former animosities forgot, as if they had all tasted the waters of forgetfulness. But before the Governor & I cou'd be friends, twas necessary to let out all the sharp humours in a conversation so full of reproaches that 'twas more likely to end in an imediate War than an approaching Peace; yet it took quite another turn, and we were perfect good friends 4 days afterwards. and extended our reconciliation over the whole country, Never was there a more general rejoicing then at this Pacification, and indeed not without reason, for the heat of both Parties was run so high, that all friendship & conversation was quite lost, and it must soon have ended in a general confusion." (From MS Egmont letterbook in the temporary keeping of a member of the Eng. Hist. MSS Comm., P. R. O., and copied in 1930.)

[1]Eight members of the Council, Robert Carter, James Blair, Philip Ludwell, John Smith, John Lewis, William Bassett, Nathaniel Harrison and Edmund Berkeley, had sent to the Board of Trade in the spring of 1717 a representation strongly arguing against Lieutenant Governor Spotswood in their dispute over the courts of oyer and terminer and other questions. Byrd would make the ninth opponent of Spotswood (C. O. 5/1318, pp. 239-243; Dodson, *Alexander Spotswood*, pp. 171-2). The quarrel between Spotswood and the Burgesses finally found articulate circulation in a printed four-page folder entitled *Some Remarkable Proceedings In the Assembly of Virginia Anno 1718*, including the address of the Burgesses to the King and the speech of Spotswood to the Burgesses, Dec. 1, 1718 (Misc. Va. MSS, Photostat, Library of Congress).

ing back so soon as I intend: but to prevent that, I beg your Grace wou'd be pleas'd to tell him, you shall have commands for me next summer & expect me back by that time. This I know will make him cautious of throwing any obstruction in my way which otherwise I am jeolous he will do. I'm confident your Graces Influence over him to be so great, that if you wou'd please to let him know, his assenting to the salary the assembly is willing to give me as Agent,[1] wou'd be agreable to you, I dare say he wou'd do it, without any letter from Mr Secretary Crags[2] which I once intreated your Grace to interceed with him for. And indeed it seems very reasonable, the Assembly of Virginia shou'd have the same liberty of paying an Agent out of their own mony, that the other Plantations have, or else nobody will ever undertake to solicit their Affairs. I have reason to ask a thousand pardons, of your Grace for presumeing to give you so much trouble: but your great generosity gives me the confidence to fly to you on all occasions, and to beg, that whether present or absent you will always allow me the honour to be My Lord &c

---

TO MINIONET May the 30th 1722[3]

I am now going to perform my promise to my charming Minionet with abundance of pleasure, because tis at the same

---

[1]On Byrd's return to Virginia in 1720 when the House of Burgesses again named him as their agent, Spotswood tried to force him to promise, as a condition of approving of the appropriation of £400 that the Assembly had voted Byrd as salary, that he would give his bond to interfere in no matters that fell within the Governor's prerogative. Byrd replied that he would give no such bond if Spotswood should sign a warrant for all the money in the Treasurer's hands, and on another day warmly replied to Spotswood that he would prefer to have his tongue cut out than tied up in his country's service. Spotswood finally agreed in 1722 to the payment of £300 to Byrd. (Diary, Nov. 23, Dec. 19, 20, 21, 23, 1720; Dodson, *Alexander Spotswood,* pp. 266-69.)

[2]James Craggs (1686-1721), appointed one of the principal secretaries of state after Addison's retirement in 1718, had charge of the southern department. Craggs had very loyal friends in Addison, Pope and Tickell, and was popular in the wits' circle. Addison said of him that he never knew a man who had a greater genius for business (*Dict. Nat. Biog.*).

[3]Byrd was in Virginia from Feb. 4, 1720 until after May 18, 1721. He returned to England before Nov. 10, 1721 (*Journal of the Commissioners for Trade and Plantations, 1718-22*, p. 328), remaining there until his final return to Virginia early in 1726. This and the subsequent MSS from this notebook fall in the period of the five years of his last residence in England.

The only clue to the identity of Minionet seems to be the reference to her

time obeying her orders. You will in this Pacquet receive a Picture drawn at full length, so like, that you'll find it out with more ease, than you did Oliver Cromwells Cypher. To encourage you to guess at the Original, I can assure you, you know her better than most Ladys know themselves. If you'd please to apply your self to this way of drawing, you'd certainly out do your Master after a few Tryals. your Genius seems apt for it, & you want nothing but a little Industry to make you shine in this, and many other Productions of the Mind. Cou'd any mortal arrive at Perfection at once it wou'd be the ingenious Minionet, but even she must endeavour to try her wings, if she wou'd learn to fly. Begin therefore Madam with a short sketch, which pray send to me, and in case there shou'd be room for amendment, I will touch it over, admire it, and then blush at my own. Pray be so good as to finish mine, and kindly point out the faults of it. This will help to amuse you in your country Retirement, and vastly improve those Talents, which some people fancy too great all ready for a Woman. Except we sometimes give Flight to our Understandings, they will hover very low, and the Facultys of the soul, like the limbs of the Body, will grow useless without useing. *If your first Essay shou'd not happen to please you, pray remember, there was a time when Dryden was a lame Poet, & Betterton an awkward Actor.* I intreat my Dear Minionet not to distrust her own Abilitys, for Diffidence is a mighty Enimy to great Performances, and both hinders and conceals a world of Perfections. Besides you may venture to trust me with a sight of your attemps that way, because I shall be partial to every thing that comes from so agreable an Author. Nobody will have the pleasure of seeing them but I, and I beg that not above 2 of you may see mine. Thus madam if I can contribute any thing to your Entertainment, you will please to tell me so, otherwise I shall fear I may interrupt your more agreable diversions, which wou'd go very much against the conscience of &c

reading "Oliver Cromwell's Cypher," which, in conjunction with a reference in a letter from Byrd to Mrs. Otway in 1735 (concerning a letter difficult to read, "I wanted Molly Jeffreys to help me decipher it, who is eminently gifted that way"), may imply that Minionet was Molly Jeffreys.

TO MINIONET June the 11. 1722

Your silence makes me apprehend that the agreable Minionet had not the Picture which I had the honour to send her, or which is stil worse, that she did not like it. However I now venture to present her with another, and beg she wou'd please to let me know her thoughts upon it. Tis a very heartless thing, Madam, to endeavour to please, and never to be inform'd whether one dos it or not. If what I mean for your Entertainment is so happy as to meet with success, your being so kind as to let me know it, will double my diligence: but if on the contrary, it shou'd prove disagreable, you shou'd frankly tell me so, that you may be deliver'd from farther Persecution. Thus madam either way tis expedient for you write your mind in this matter, because the self same motive, that makes me endeavour to please you, will make me also cease to plague you, so soon as I am made sensible of it. I wont pretend to say any thing of the Picture, that now kisses your hand, tho' I fear it will not have language enough to speak for it self. I live in hopes of receiveing a better in return, if you will but resolve to go about it. T'will be Ingratitude to Nature for you to disown that she has given you a capacity, *and you will no more be believ'd, than other Ladys wou'd be, if they shou'd disown the faculty of speech.* Pray do justice to your own Talents, & exert them with all your might, with this assurance, that if your Industry bore any proportion to your Genius, my Pictures wou'd be no better than Foils for yours. However tis impossible for me to envy you this or any other superiority, for a very natural Reason, which your Penetration will easily guess. *What a pity tis, that you of all your dear sex, shou'd want a little convenient Vanity, to give you a tolerable opinion of your own Qualifications? If other Females cou'd write but half so well as you can, they wou'd defraud their morning Repose, or their Midnight amuzements for time to practice it, rather than hide an Excellence in which as few of 'em shine as they do in charity for one another.* Adieu my charming Minionet, and be always happy.

TO MINIONET June 16. 1722

At last I have had the pleasure of a letter from the charming Minionet, & so pretty a letter, that it needed not the help of so much Expectation, to make the blessing dear. I shou'd be very sorry to lay any sin to her charge, tho' I think in my Conscience tis little less, to conceal a Talent she possesses in such perfection. *For so much ingenuity not to write, were as ill-natured, as for Beauty to lurk eternally under a Veil, never to bless the Eys, or chear the Heart of any Mortal. Imagin, dear Madam, how barbarous that wou'd be, and how ill Bashfullness wou'd deserve the name of a vertue, that shou'd pretend to cover such charms from being seen. Just so inhumane tis in you, to conceal the Beautys of your pen, with which I am able to say very feelingly, you may write just what you please upon any mans heart.*

You really do Sempronia[1] too much honour, Madam, and I think verily, the sight of her shou'd be so far from makeing you despise your self, *that you might rear up your head with as much secret satisfaction at the sight of that nymph, as when you walk by the side of Pigmelia or Fairyamne in Kensington Garden.*[2] You may much more naturally pretend to be her Rival than mine, and were I the happy Sheepherd, chosen to decide between 2 such Goddesses, my Heart misgives me, that I shou'd certainly give the apple to the agreable Minionet.

The Reason is very plain why most people shou'd be better turn'd for Satyr than Panegyrick, because there is much more Genius necessary to perform the last, than the first. Satyr is much the easyer work of the Understanding, because Nature is always at hand to assist us, when we attempt to sink the character of our neighbour below our own: but to bestow beautys upon others, that may eclips our selves, is so much against the grain, as to be exceedingly

---

[1] In Ben Jonson's drama *Catiline,* Sempronia, who plots with Catiline for the destruction of Rome, is pictured as a less noble and admirable woman than Fulvia, who warns Cicero of the danger to the state.

[2] Kensington Garden was the fabled home of Oberon, King of the Fairies, in Thomas Tickell's poem "Kensington Garden," published anonymously in 1722.

difficult. But I shou'd fancy the Ingenious Minionet an Exception from this Rule for 2 Reasons; first because she wou'd be at a loss for ill nature to point & poison her Satyr withal; & secondly, *because she is us'd to read so many good Qualitys in her own breast, that she has no more to do, than to copy out some of them, & dress them up in her pretty Expression, to make it a very handsome Panegyrick.* However, Madam, since you have a mind to begin with a Picture that has some Deformitys, I here send you one of a very odd Lady: & to be even with me, & to vindicate the honour of your sex, twill be but just in you, to return me the Picture of as odd a man in the same Tast. Since this way is of your own chuseing, Madam, I shall live in hopes of being entertain'd with your performance very soon, & beg you will not torture me with so long an Expectation as you did before. In order therefore to provoke you to a Quick Reply, I can assure you, I had your letter but last night, & to shew my Gratitude, am thanking you for it today. I wish the Enchanting Minionet as much happiness, as she can imagin or desire, & which is stil more, I wish her as happy, as she wou'd make the man, on whome she bestows her heart. I am

---

TO MINIONET June the 27. 1722

While the inchanting Minionet was pleading her Incapacity, to draw the Picture of a swain that is not agreable, she unawares painted one of a nymph that is. And while she was so barbarous as to refuse me the character of another, she gave me the prettyest in the world of her self. Besides there shines this particular Excellence in her Piece, that we are sure tis like, and cant possibly flatter the Dear Original. It has likewise another uncommon beauty in it, that at the same time it was a Panegyrick upon the Painter, it prov'd upon the Comparison a dounright Satyr upon great part of the sex. After this for Heavens sake, How can you fancy the difference betwixt Sempronia & Friskabunda too wide, when there is really a wider, between the charming Minionet, and the Bulk of Woman-kind. Of them I may venture to say with a very free-spoken Poet, Woman! thy name is Frailty: but of her I may pronounce with a sincerity too great for Verse,

> Thou hast no faults, or I no faults can spy,
> Thou art all beauty, or all Blindness I.[1]

You may remember that the Graces and the Furys were both represented in the shape of Women, but if you believe them to be only a Fiction, yet tis made good in too many Instances of real Life. The vast distance between Lucrece and Messalina[2] in ancient story, and between Minionet and Dowdena in the modern, confirm what I say. Light and Darkness, angel and Devil are not more disagreeing than these characters, & yet I am sorry to say, they are all of the same species and the same sex. So that after all, we Painters must not be blam'd for drawing such different Pictures, when the originals themselves are so directly opposite.

I have hitherto only sent my charming Minionet Female characters, but now by way of variety I will present her with one of the Lordly sex.[3] I may venture to assure her that tis a very just one, that she may see there is stil some Excellence left amongst the men; tho' I cant boast that such Instances are more frequent than black swans,[4] or humble clergymen. Pray send your opinion of it very soon, and take your Exceptions very freely where you find it blameable. Without affection I have such a deference for your Judgment, that I shall with Pleasure stand corrected by it; *and let me tell you, we must have a great distinction for that Extraordinary Person, from whose hand correction is pleasant, and that mouth must be charming beyond measure, by which a man wou'd delight to be told of his faults.* For this Reason

---

[1]These lines were addressed by Christopher Codrington to Dr. Samuel Garth on his poem, *The Dispensary,* in 1699. Codrington preceded Byrd's father-in-law, Daniel Parke, as captain general of the Leeward Islands, and had difficulties with the inhabitants of Antigua, as did Parke, who was killed in an uprising there in 1710.

[2]Lucrece, the wife of Tarquinius Collatinus, was the embodiment of the virtues of a Roman matron, (Livy, *History of Rome,* Book I, lvii). Messalina, cousin and third wife of the Emperor Claudius, was the denial of all the virtues of a Roman matron (Tacitus, *The Annals,* Books XI, XII, XIII).

[3]Byrd referred to his character of Sir Robert Southwell, above, p. 206.

[4]Because of his aesthetic interests, Byrd himself has been called the Black Swan (Bassett, p. lxxxviii).

whatever amendments the Engageing Minionet shall please to make to my Performances, they will not fail to be most agreable to me. *May she exceed every creature in happiness, as much as she dos in the Charms both of Body & mind,* and if I might add one wish more, it shou'd be, that she might entertain a tolerable opinion of &c.

TO MINIONET July 14. 1722

No Woman big with child ever long'd more for any thing hard to be got, than I long'd for my charming Minionets letter, and had it not come just as it did, I shou'd have been in danger of miscarrying. I confess by being out of Town I set her the Example of a Weeks silence: but she by the Rules of Female Justice, has paid me double for my omission, and been silent a whole Fortnight. However that she may not plead any such provocation for the future, I shall instantly acknowledge her Favours, & intreat Her to imitate my diligence, as readily as she did my involuntary neglect. I may call it involuntary, *because a Fine, Lady anxious of pleaseing, cou'd as soon intend to neglect her own dear charms, as I cou'd the most agreable of all the Fairy-Race.*
For my part Mad^m^ I durst as well have din'd with the man that eat Fire, as take the same libertys with the lovely sex that you have done, by saying t'is impossible for a Woman to own herself in an Error. How this Maxime may hold in the case of most Females, I must not say, but when you come to apply it to your self, I can only understand it in this sence, that you commit mistakes so very seldome, that the readyest way for you to commit an Error, wou'd be to own your self in one. Then you are unjust to Your own fine Qualitys, when you pronounce the sex so much upon a Level. For my part in this I must take the liberty to differ both from my ingenious correspondent, and the Proverb, and believe Women so very unlike one another, that they are not the same so much as in the dark. Even there I shou'd distinguish the delightfull Minionet from all woman kind, as

long as I had Ears to discern Empty sound from unaffected sence. Thus Madam while you intend to be charitable to your sex, you are cruel to my dear Minionet and I must repeat to you my sincere opinion that she differs from most of 'em as much as an angel of light dos from an angel of Darkness.

However tis by no means peculiar to the women to be so different from one another, for the men are altogether as unlike in every part of their character. This will be evident by compareing this Picture with that of Savienti,[1] both which, whatever imperfections they may have besides, are very like the Originals. If Savienti was a sketch of Perfection, Slovenius[2] will be a full Length of Frailty; and tis well if his monstrous features dont give you a frightfull opinion of all mankind. I wish my lovely Minionet as happy as the full accomplishment of her dearest wishes, cou'd make her, and am most intirely & eternally &c.

TO MINIONET Augst. 2^{d}. 1722.

Madam

I had the mortification to receive my Dear Minionets commands, which tho' expresst with all the gentleness & good sence in the world, were yet very vigorous. They afford me the more pain by being accompany'd with a fear, lest I may have said any thing in my last letter to offend Her. The tast she has already been pleas'd to give me of her Talents, convinces me fully, that the cause of her change blows not from that Quarter, & consequently it must come from some unguarded Expression that escaped me. If that be the unhappy case, I ask you Ten Thousand pardons, and were I but conscious in what particular, I wou'd add the Penalty of self reproach to your displeasure, wch wou'd both hasten & increase my Repentance. For which reason I must intreat the charming Minionet, not to let her silence be so

---

[1] *I. e.*, character of Cavaliero Sapiente (Sir Robert Southwell), above p. 206.
[2] Character of Cavaliero Slovena, p. 205.

determin'd, but that I may stil have the honour of one letter more, to explain sincerely wherein I have had the misfortune to transgress. Otherwise t'wou'd really be a little ungenerous, to banish one who has a very great regard for Her, for reasons that are so mysterious. Let ye Provocation be what ever your suspicions may make it, I will presume to send you one Picture more, to convince you of the sincere sentiments I have of the agreable Minionet, and after that, if it be stil your pleasure that I admire her in silence, I will certainly shew my Regards by my obedience, and always wish you at least as happy as I do &c

---

TO MINIONET[1] Feb^{ry} the 21. 1722/3

When I was last happy in the Conversation of the charming Minionet, I threaten'd her with more of my Pictures, and now that Lent begins to draw near, my being as good as my word may be a seasonable mortification. The first I shall submit to her View, is, of a Gentleman who has the honour to be pretty well known to Her,[2] He also knows her so well as to wish her at least as happy as himself. He really resembles his Picture enough to be a good sort of a man, and gives this certain proof of his fine tast, that he absolutely prefers you to Sempronia, Cornelia,[3] Charmante,

---

[1]It is significant that Byrd did not come to the point of declaring his love to Minionet until this date, after Charmante, Lady Elizabeth Lee, had refused to marry him. See Introduction, p. xxxii.

[2]The picture referred to was apparently Byrd's character of himself as Inamorato L'Oiseaux. See above, p. 276.

[3]In *Tunbrigalia* (London, 1719), p. 16, in verses entitled "The Three Nymphs," by "an Unknown Hand" are these verses:

Cornelia's easy movement fires
'Tis Death to see her dance:
Her Voice resistless Love inspires,
Both with its Sound and Sense.

When first to gain Adonis Love,
Venus in mortal Form appear'd,
Her heavenly Figure to improve,
She dear Cornelia's Shape preferr'd.

and all the brighter ornaments of the sex. He cant with all his modesty be asham'd, to confess a passion so fully justify'd by Reason & good sence. I must own indeed that tis a Princely air to carry on a Courtship thus by Picture, but it has this convenience at least, of hideing the confusion & diffidence of a bashfull Lover. However Madam you will have one advantage very unusual in other addresses, that you will here be able to read the Inside of your admirer before hand, whereas most other Ladys dont find that out til tis too late, and the discovery serves no other Purpose but to inform them, that they are miserable without Remedy. If you cou'd approve of such a Lover, I wou'd be his security you shou'd not find the original exceedingly flatter'd by the Picture. Nay I cou'd Venture to answer yet farther for Him, that he loves you so tenderly, that if you'd but smile upon his Passion, it shou'd be the Endeavour of his whole Life to make you happy. He has a long time felt these tender sentiments, but cou'd never yet muster up Resolution enough to open his Heart to you. He has therefore with much intreaty prevail'd upon me to do it for him, & oh that I were master enough of the gentle art of perswasion, to possess you a little in his favour. Then I shou'd think my self as happy as the very man I was pleading for, which wou'd be the happyest of mortals. May angels guard my Dearest Minionet, and incline her to favour the Intercession of &c.

Upon her fragrant coral Lips
The wanton Loves and Graces play,
Out of her Eyes sly *Cupid* peeps,
And leads our Wishes all astray.

On p. 17, in "the Answer to the Three Nymphs," are these verses:

Cornelia's Movement strongly charms.
Whene'er she deigns to dance,
Her Voice the ravish'd Ear Alarms,
And puts us in a Trance.

But more it can't, for if twas Death
To hear her, or to see,
She'd stop'd long since her Poet's Breath,
And made an end of me.

While both verses are printed anonymously, the greater sprightliness and satirical strain of the "Answer" suggests the possibility that Byrd wrote the reply.

TO AMASIA[1] July 20. 1723.

Considering ye solemn promise you made me, first by word of mouth, & afterwards by letter, that you wou'd not from thence forth have any Converse of Correspondence with the

[1]This letter to Amasia ("the beloved one"), Byrd's older daughter, Evelyn, and the succeeding letter to her suitor, Erranti, give the first authentic evidence for the persistent tradition that Evelyn Byrd died unmarried at the age of thirty because her father would not let her marry the man of her choice (see Introduction, p. xxxiv). Evelyn, born at Westover July 16, 1707, was a frail child. At the age of ten, she joined her father in London, about a year after her mother's death there from smallpox. She was educated in London, though she did not live with her father. He frequently mentions her in his diary for 1717-21: he took her to drive, or to walk in the park, to visit his friends; he often met her at the home of the Perrys; he scolded her when she did not wear gloves, and sent her in his chariot to a ball; he carried her to visit friends to share the excitement of her prize of £25 in a lottery; her illness perturbed him. In school with her was Miss Page, daughter of Byrd's old Virginia friend. When Byrd returned to Virginia in 1719 he left her and her younger sister Wilhelmina in London, but on the voyage was made melancholy by a dream (after drinking punch and eating roasted chestnuts) that he saw her and that that minute she died at three in the morning in London. About a week later, still aboard ship, she appeared to him in his dream with only one hand and since it was the left hand he concluded the dream meant the younger daughter Wilhelmina was alive and the older daughter Evelyn dead.

From the close of the 1721 diary to this letter in 1723 there is no evidence of Evelyn's concerns. Tradition has held that she was presented at court and was greatly admired. Though proof is lacking, the fact seems probable, since her father's diary shows clearly that he moved in court circles, often going to court, and talking with Henrietta Howard, mistress of the Prince of Wales, later George II, friend of Pope, and Swift, and Gay, and Peterborough (see *Letters of Countess of Suffolk,* [London, 1824]). The Duke of Argyle and his equally influential brother, Lord Islay, were his close and interested friends, as well as other court intimates. Descendants of William Byrd treasure a dress and some lace and a fan as mementos of Evelyn Byrd's presentation at court, where tradition holds she made a vivid impression by her beauty and her wit.

After Byrd returned to Virginia in 1726 with his family there is no further light on Evelyn Byrd's life except as reflected in an occasional passage in her father's letters to friends who had known her in England. On Feb. 2, 1727 Byrd wrote to John, Lord Boyle, son of his friend Charles, Earl of Orrery, "My young Gentlewomen like everything in the Country except the Retirement, they can't get the Plays, the Operas, and the Masquerades out of their Heads, much less can they forget their friends. However, the lightness of our Atmosphere helps them to bear all their losses with more Spirit, and that they may amuse themselves the better, they are every Day up to their Elbows in Housewifery, which will qualify them effectually for useful Wives and if they live long enough, for Notable women" (Orrery MSS, Harvard College Library).

About a year later Byrd wrote on Feb. 3, 1728 to Charles, Earl of Orrery, an intimate and congenial friend for nearly thirty years, "One of the most antick Virgins I am acquainted with is my daughter, either our young Fellows are not smart eno' for her, or she seems too smart for them, but in a little Time I hope they will split the Difference" (*Ibid.*).

Evelyn Byrd was buried in the old churchyard at Westover and forty years later her only brother, William Byrd III, directed in his will that his body

Baronet,[1] I am astonisht you have violated that protestation in a most notorious manner. The gracious audience you gave him the morning you left y[e] Towne, & the open conversations you have with him in the Country have been too unguarded, to be deny'd any longer. Tis therefore high time for me to reproach you with breech of duty & breach of faith, & once more to repeat to you, my strict & positive

---

should be "privately buried by the tomb of my sister Evelyn in the old Church Yard." (*Va. Mag.*, XXXVIII, 59). Her epitaph reads in part:

> Here In The Sleep Of Peace
> Reposes The Body
> Of Mrs. Evelyn Byrd,
> Daughter
> Of The Honble William Byrd, Esq.
> The Various and excellent endowments
> of Nature, improved and perfected
> By an accomplished education
> formed her
> For the happiness of her friends
> For the ornament of her country
> . . . .

(Constance Cary Harrison, "Colonel William Byrd," *Century Magazine,* XLII, 170).

The following acrostic, in the fashion of the day, was printed in the *Virginia Gazette,* Nov. 25-Dec. 2, 1737:

> E ver constant to her friend
> V igilant in truth's defense
> E ntertaining to her end
> L ife! brimful of eloquence.
> Y outh in person; age in sense
> N ature gave her store immense.
>
> B ut she's fled and is no more
> Y onder soars in fields of light!
> R obbed of all our little store,
> D eath! oh death! we're ruined quite.

Though it is unsigned, the question naturally arises as to whether her father, who enjoyed verse making, wrote it.

The portrait of Evelyn Byrd now owned by Colonial Williamsburg, Inc., has been ascribed to various artists, but in the opinion of Professor William Sawitzky, Lecturer of Fine Arts, New York University, it was painted by Charles Bridges soon after his arrival in Virginia in 1735. He argues that the appearance of an American wild bird, a red cardinal, perched in a tree in the upper corner of the painting, is further evidence of its having been painted in America (Lecture notes on Charles Bridges by Professor Sawitzky). The portrait has been thus described by a kinswoman of Evelyn Byrd: "She is painted as a shepherdess in a robe of blue-green, in color like Enid's of the 'shoaling sea,' a red-crested bird perched on a brown bough overhead, a straw hat wreathed with morning-glories, in her lap, a knot of the same flowers in her hair, one brown lock escaping upon her shoulder, and a little accrochecoeur upon her brow, her pretty pensive face set on a swanlike throat" (*Cent. Mag.*, XLII, 168).

[1]See following letter to Erranti, and note.

Commands, never more to meet, speak, or write to that Gentleman, or to give him an opportunity to see, speak, or write to You. I also forbid you to enter into any promise or engagement with him of marriage or Inclination. I enjoin you this in the most positive terms, upon the sacred duty you owe a Parent, & upon the blessing you ought to expect upon the Performance of it. And that neither he nor you may be deluded afterwards with Vain hopes of forgiveness, I have put it out of my power, by vowing that I never will. And as to any Expectation, you may fondly entertain of a Fortune from me, you are not to look for one brass farthing, if you provoke me by this fatal instance of disobedience. Nay besides all that, I will avoid the sight of you as of a creature detested. Figure then to your self my Dear Child how wretched you will be with a provokt father, & a disappointed Husband. To whome then will you fly in your distress, when all the world will upbraid you with haveing acted like an Ideot? & your conscience must fly in your face for haveing disobey'd an indulgent Parent. I think my self oblig'd to give you this fair warning, & to point out to you the Rocks upon which you will certainly shipwreck all your happiness in this world, unless you think fit to obey my orders. For God's sake then my dear child, for my sake, & for your own, survey the desperate Precipice you stand upon, & don't rashly cast your self down head long into Ruin. The idle Promises this man makes you will all vanish into smoke, & instead of Love he will slight & abuse you, when he finds his hopes of Fortune disappointed. Then you & your Children (if you shou'd be so miserable as to have any) must be Beggers, & then you may be assur'd all the world will deservedly dispise you, & you will hardly be pity'd so much as by Him who wou'd faign continue &c.

TO ERRANTI[1] July 20th 1723.

I am inform'd upon very good Evidence, that you have for some time taken the trouble to follow Amasia with your

---

[1]Was Erranti the Earl of Peterborough, as tradition, handed down from generation to generation in the Westover-Brandon family, has maintained? Byrd's reference to him as "the Baronet" is the strongest evidence against the

Addresses; that now at last you have play'd the wise part of a Knight Errant, & pursued Her into the Country with a pompous Equipage, that dos Her & your self much honour. What success these worthy steps have met with in the Girle, I know not: but they shall never meet with any in the Father. I fear your circumstances are not flourishing enough to maintain a Wife in much splendour, that has nothing, and just such a Fortune as that my Daughter will prove, if she Ventures to marry without my consent. You are deluded if you believe that any part of my Estate is settled upon Her, or that she has any thing independant of my Pleasure. I confess you have not deserv'd it from me, but I will however stand your Friend so far, as to assure you before hand, that Her Portion will be extreemly small if she bestows her self

---

identification of Peterborough as Erranti, though there is the possibility that the incensed father was speaking disparagingly of Charles Mordaunt, who was at the same time third Earl of Peterborough, first Earl of Monmouth, and Viscount in the Barony of Mordaunt (Burke, *Extinct Peerage*).

Byrd knew Peterborough. He recorded in his diary, Feb. 21, 1719, that he attended Mrs. Robinson's concert (*i. e.* Anastasia Robinson) and sat by Lord Peterborough and had a merry time. The name Erranti could well apply to Peterborough, frequently called the knight errant by his contemporaries, and noted in his day for his traveling from place to place with incredible rapidity. Dean Swift wrote him once, "I remember Lord Oxford's ministry used to tell me that, not knowing where to write to you, they were forced to write at you." (Swift's *Works,* XX, 277.) Swift, who said of Peterborough, "I always loved him well," (Pope's *Works,* VII, 45), gave in verse this picture of Peterborough's wandering habits,

To the Earl of Peterborough Who Commanded
the British Forces in Spain.

Mordaunt fills the trump of fame
The Christian Worlds his deeds proclaim,
And prints are crowded with his name.

In journies he outrides the post
Sits up till midnight with his host,
Talks politicks, and gives the toast.

Knows every prince in Europe's face,
Flies like a squib from place to place
And travels not, but runs a race.

. . . . .

So wonderful his expedition,
When you have not the least suspicion
He's with you like an apparition.

(Swift's *Works,* X, 35).

Peterborough was characterised at the age of fifty by John Macky thus: "He affects Popularity, and loves to preach in Coffee Houses, and publick Places: is an open enemy to Revealed Religion; brave in his Person; hath a good

upon so clandestine a Lover. I have made my Will[1] since I heard of your good intention towards me, & have bequeath'd my Daughter a splendid shilling, if she marrys any man that tempts her to disobedience. After giveing you this friendly warning, I hope you will have discretion enough to leave off so unprofitable a Pursuit, to which no tears on my Daughters part, or Intreatys on yours will ever be able to reconcile &c.

Estate; does not seem Expensive, yet always in Debt, and very poor. A well shaped thin Man, with a very brisk Look." (*Memoirs,* 1895 ed., p. 60). Dean Swift thought this character by Macky for the most part true, though Swift himself humorously called Peterborough, "the ramblingest lying rogue on earth."

There was much about Peterborough to appeal to a young girl of wit and the fact that Anastasia Robinson, the courted and popular prima donna in London, married him secretly about this time, would argue that he still could be a persuasive suitor in spite of his more than threescore years. In fact, when Alexander Pope saw him in 1735 shortly before his death, he said, "No body can be more wasted, no soul can be more alive . . . This is a man that will neither live nor die like any other mortal." (Swift's *Works,* X, 184).

As soldier, courtier, or wit, Peterborough was always brilliant and unpredictable. His lines "To Chloe," beginning "I said to my heart betwixt sleeping and waking," have real lyric beauty. For the best account of his career, that reminds one of fabled heroes, see William Stebbing, *Peterborough* (London, 1890).

As far as time and place are concerned, Erranti could have been the Earl of Peterborough. He was in England in July, 1723 and Pope stayed at Peterborough's house in Bolton street in London during that summer (Pope's *Works,* IX, 426), though Peterborough went to France on a mission in August.

While the fact of Peterborough's secret marriage to Anastasia Robinson is conceded by most students of the period, there is no agreement as to date, the years 1723 or 1724 usually being given. A letter from Arbuthnot to Pope, dated Sept. 1723 by the editors, says Arbuthnot had dined with Peterborough, "spick and span new just come from France," and Mrs. Robinson, and that Peterborough had been busy all that day removing the possessions of the Robinsons. This may refer to Peterborough's installing Anastasia Robinson and her mother and sister in a house near his villa at Parson's Green (Pope's *Works,* VII, 475) and may mark the time of Peterborough's marriage to the singer, which was not publicly owned until another ceremony was performed in 1735.

The tradition that Byrd opposed his daughter's marriage to Peterborough because he was a Catholic is manifestly untrue because, though Peterborough had respect for Anastasia Robinson's Catholic faith, he was not himself a religious man.

These letters to Amasia and to Erranti thus prove the fact that Byrd forbade his daughter Evelyn to marry an English nobleman, but they still leave unproved the identity of that nobleman.

[1]Byrd had made a will on Oct. 8, 1719, before his return to Virginia when he left his two young daughters in London (Diary, Oct. 8, 1719). On May 23, 1711 he noted in his diary, "I began this day to make my will, which I never had done before in my life." No copy of the wills mentioned nor of the will left on his death in 1744 and proved in the Charles City County Court by Mrs. Maria Byrd, one of the executors, in March, 1745 (Charles City Order Book, 1737-1751, p. 339), has yet come to light.

TO MEDUSA[1] May the 26. 1724

I had the honour to marry your Eldest Daughter[2] about a fortnight since, & can assure you it shall be the great business of my life to make her happy. She tells me that she acquainted you with it soon after it happen'd, & begg'd your blessing. I humbly join with her in that Petition, and hope no Instance of Duty will be wanting on our part to deserve it. I am sensible Madam how cruelly I have been misrepresented to you both in my character & circumstances. Tis no unusual thing for men going to be marryed to be painted in malicious Coulours, and so no wonder if I have shared in that common Fate. However I am the less concern'd, because I know those very spitefull storys to be undeserved, and can without much difficulty disprove them. I shou'd think my self very fortunate, madam, if you'd please to let me wait upon you, and shou'd not dispair of quieting the apprehensions you may have of Your Daughters being unhappily marryed; and shou'd be happyer stil if you wou'd give me leave to call my self, what I shall always endeavour to be with the utmost duty and Respect, &c.

[TO MARIA TAYLOR]

τῇ δεσποίνα μαρία ὤȣ εὐπράττειν.

ὅτε μόνην σὲ γλῶσσαν τὴν μητριχὴν γινώσχειν ἐνόμισα, σφόδρα σε ἐφίλησα; ἀλλ' ὁπότε δὴ ϗ Ελλένιχην, τὴν τῶν μȣσῶν γλῶσσην λαλεῖν σὲ χατελάμβανον, ὅλως πέρι σȣ̃ ἐμάνην. Εν τω χαλλει μὲν τὴν Ελήνην, ἐν δε τῇ παίδεια ϗ ἀγχινόια τὴν Σάφφω ἐνίχησας· ȣ̓̃χ ȣ̃ν θαυμάζειν ἄξιον εἰ ὑπο ταυσάυτη τȣ̃ σωματος, ϗ της ψυχης λαμπρότητι ἐπλήχθην ἔπει τὸ τȣ̃ Ἐρωτος φάρμαχον δία τῶν οφθαλμῶν τε ϗ τῶν ὤτων εἰσεδεχόμην. ἔρρωσο.

εἰ ἀντεπιςέλλειν τι ἀξιώσης, Βριτανισὶ ἐπιγραψεῖς.

To M[r] Ornis at Wills Coffee house in Bow street, Covent Garden

---

[1]Medusa was the suggestive but uncomplimentary name Byrd consistently used in referring to his mother-in-law, the wife of Thomas Taylor, of Kensington, England.

[2]*I. e.*, Maria Taylor, born Nov. 10, 1698, whom Byrd married, as his second wife, on May 9, 1724. She died Aug. 28, 1771. (Byrd's Family Bible.)

TRANSLATION: You thought you were in the good graces of Mistress Maria. When I thought you knew only your mother tongue, I was passionately in love with you: but when indeed I learned that you also spoke Greek, the tongue of the Muses, I went completely crazy about you. In beauty you surpassed Helen, in culture of mind and ready wit Sappho: It is not meet therefore to be astonished I was smitten by such grandeur of body and soul when I admitted the poison of Love both through my eyes and my ears. Farewell.

If you deem it to send any reply, you will write it in English. To Mr Ornis[1] at Wills Coffee house in Bow street, Covent Garden.[2]

---

[1] *I. e.* Byrd.

[2] The translation of Byrd's love letter to Maria Taylor was made by Dr. W. A. Harris, emeritus professor of Greek in the University of Richmond.

APPENDIX I

Miscellaneous Notes from the Notebooks

Miscellaneous Notes from the Notebooks

The first page contains memoranda jotted down by Byrd on the first page of Notebook A, a good deal later than the material in the rest of the notebook. The figures on tobacco produced at Westover and his plantation of Hilman are suggestive of the economy of those estates. The note on the death of Wager is patently an error, for Byrd's close friend of many years, Sir Charles Wager, first lord of the admiralty and treasurer of the navy, died May 24, 1743 (*Dict. Nat. Biog.*; Croker, *Georgian Era*, II, 155-56). The list of books may be further identified as: (1) Caradac of Llancarvan, *The History of Wales*, Englished by Humphrey Lloyd, augmented by Dr. Powel, 1584; augmented by W. Wynne, 1697, and 1702; (2) Sir T[homas] H[erbert], *A Relation of Some Yeares Travaile [1627-1630] Into Afrique and the greater Asia*, 1634, 1638, 1639, 1665, and 1677; (3) Francis Hare (1671-1740), Bishop of Chichester, an edition of the Psalms in Hebrew, published 1736, said to have restored the text to its original beauty; (4) John Chamberlayne, *Magnæ Britanniæ Notitia; or, The Present State of Great Britain, with divers Remarks upon the Ancient State thereof* [1716]; (5) Charles Rollin, *The Ancient History of the Egyptians, Carthaginians, Assyrians, Babylonians, Medes and Persians, Macedonians, and Grecians*, 10 vols., 1734-36; 10 vols., 1738-40.

The following sheets are torn and loosely laid in Notebook B. They are apparently scraps of letters to Sabina, and may be compared with those for Feb. 11, 1717, and July 2, 1717, above, pp. 301-2.

Ten hsds of Tob° made at W

by Cap[t] Twine anno 1739

N° 1 gross 1020.			These 7 at Westover
2 gross 1000.			
3 gross 1060.			
4 gross 1120.			
5 gross 1095.			
6 gross 1125.			
7 gross 1140 stem'd			
8 gross 1000			These 3 at Hilman
9 gross 1000			
10 gross 1000			

10560 Gross
1000 Tear

10560 Neat

S[r] Ch. Wager
dyd the 29 Dec[r]
1740

Abbington
Banbury
Carton [?]

Staves 6 foot long one Inch thick four Inch Wide the Heading near 2 Inch thi[k] & 14 Inch Wide of Whiteoak.

D[r] Powels Welsh History writ by Caradoc Abbot of Lancarva[n]

S[r] Thomas Herberts Travels
B[p] of Chichester's Hebrew Salter
Present State of England
Rollins His of the Egyptians Greeks &c.

[TO SABINA]

for what mortal man cou'd reject the charming [...][1]
agreable Sabina on any terms? Were so much [...]
fection stark naked, and destitute of every advantage
of Fortune and Interest, I shou'd prefer it t[...]
all the Glorys of this idle and unsatisfying wo[...]
O that your fortune was less, nay you will b[...]
so good as to pardon me if I wish you had [...]
at all, either in present or expectation, that I [...]
give you the most convincing proof in the [...]
with how much passion, and with how little [...]
gàrd to vile Interest I am &c.

TO SABINA.

Tis very perverse in the agreable Sabina to b[...][2]
shy to an old acquaintance, for no earthly re[...]
but because he adores her above all Woman[...]
For this provokeing cause you turn away y[...]
head with so sudden a motion whenever I [...]
that I fear from being the most faultless [...]
in the world, you'll come as a punishment fo[...]
your cruelty, to have a Wry-neck. For Ven[...]
sake is Love then so heinous a crime, that [...]
shou'd provoke such forbidding, such disdain[...]
airs? My dear Sabina need apprehend no [...]
from her good Genius, which I am in [...]
nest, if wishing her every thing that is agre[...]
endeavouring to do her all the service in the [...]
be a sign of it. No I swear to you by all [...]
Powers of Love, that tho I had rather [...]
charms than be master of all the rest of [...]
yet I will never be guilty of any thing [...]
think will offend the dear nymph [...]
have the happiest, as well [...]
desirable of Women. Up[...]

---

[1]The edge of the page is torn.
[2]The right margin and bottom of the page torn off.

have lately avoided par[. . .]
ing heart you'd believ[. . .]
any Vile regard to Your [. . .]
that my Circumstances are [. . .]
avarice so high as to require it [. . .]
were mistress of no more than the Lin[. . .]
covers her agreable person, she wou'd be [. . .]
as enchanting, and I as passionate as [. . .]
may please to remember that I sigh't for [. . .]
a time when her fortune cou'd be no part[. . .]
temptation. I Beseech you dont do that [. . .]
tice to your own Charms, as to imagin [. . .]
have any other reason but them for my In[. . .]
tion. Alas when a Heart is fir'd with so ge[. . .]
rous a flame as mine, twill detest all [. . .]
considerations. But to give you the highes[. . .]
proof that my tenderness has no motive [. . .]
your engageing person, I declare that I w[. . .]
marry you tho your Father shou'd be so [. . .]
hearted as to deny his Consent, and then tis a[. . .]
plain case you wou'd not be worth one [. . .]
did shilling. If an act so heroick be not s[. . .]
cient to convince you, I must pronounce you
more unbeleiveing than a Free thinker. I
know not what the discerning Sabina may jud[. . .]
of this offer, but I vow I think in this covetous
age tis a handsome thing, to Love a Damsel
well enough to marry her with nothing. Now
I wou'd not desire this, except I knew my own
Fortune sufficient to make you easy, without addition from
yours; as violent as my Passion for you, I wou'd not ask you
to descend in your circumstances below the part of your
Education for my sake: but I wou'd be always ready to sacrifise
the dearest & most darling of my Inclinations to your happiness.
So help me Love and Heaven

APPENDIX II

Selections from *Tunbrigalia* (*1719*)

Selections from *Tunbrigalia*

These verses appear on pages 1-11 of *Tunbrigalia*, and are attributed to "Mr. Burrard." The text and the facsimile title page are taken from the copy of the pamphlet in the library of the University of Pennsylvania. While it is certain that Byrd wrote the verses here quoted, it is probable that others in the volume are also by him. Such a supposition seems justified by various entries in his diary though they do not constitute definite proof. The same women who figure in these verses also are mentioned in other verses in the same edition of *Tunbrigalia*.

Byrd went to Tunbridge Wells July 19, 1719 and returned to London July 26. He made another visit to the Wells August 1 to September 7. His diary gives a detailed account of his stay at the popular spa. He enjoyed the varied social diversions, dances, plays, card games for stakes, raffles, and breakfasts, teas, and dinners with friends, as well as expeditions to the notable places in the vicinity. He was most with his friends the Percivals, the Lyndseys, the Cornish sisters, and his cousins, the Horsmandens. (See Introduction, pp. xxvi-vii.)

He gave much time to the most characteristic pursuit of the resort, writing personal verses in the strain of panegyrics or satires. On occasions he noted in his diary that he spent the whole morning writing verses (Diary, July 19-Sept. 7, 1719).

TUNBRIGALIA:

OR,

Tunbridge Miſcellanies,

For the Year 1719.

Sunt bona, ſunt quædam mediocria, ſunt mala plura
Quæ legis hic ; aliter non fit, Avite, Liber.
Martial.

LONDON:
Printed in the Year M DCC XIX.
(Price One Shilling.)

ON THE
DUTCHESS OF MONTAGUE.
By Mr. Burrard.

In vain *Prometheus* had contriv'd the Plan
Had Heav'n refus'd to animate the Man:
So Fancy forms, . . . but Life must you inspire;
For strong's the Force of your diffusive Fire.
Oh! wert thou added to the heavenly Three,
And *Paris* once again was to decree;
In vain to him the Goddesses would sue,
The Prize in Justice would be due to you.

The Duchess of Montague was Lady Mary Churchill, youngest daughter of the great Duke and Duchess of Marlborough, and wife of John Montague, second Duke. She was very beautiful. Her home, Montague House, known now as the original building of the British Museum, was a famous mansion in the most fashionable life of London at this period. (*Dict. Nat. Biog.*; Hughes, *The Gentle Hertford*, p. 20; *Letters from the Right Honourable Lady Mary Wortley Montague* [1906], p. 225; *Diary of Lady Cowper,* pp. 43-44.)

The Duchess of Montague arrived at Tunbridge Wells on July 21, 1719. On Aug. 5 Byrd attended a private ball where she was present, and on Aug. 7 he played hazard with the Duchess of Montague and Lady Hinchinbrook (see below), and lost thirty shillings (Diary, July 22, Aug. 5, 7, 1719).

On The
Lady Hinchinbrook.

The lab'ring Bee employs her busy Hours,
In gath'ring her Sweets from chosen Flow'rs.
Thus would I have some happy able Muse
In lovely *Hinchinbrook* a Subject chuse.
How inexhaustible's the beauteous Treasure,
Whose Smiles command, and we obey with Pleasure.

Lady Hinchinbroke, (Hinchinbrook) with whom Byrd played at hazard at Tunbridge (Diary, Aug. 7, 1719), was Elizabeth, only daughter of Alexander Popham of Littlecote, Wilts. She married in 1707 Edward Richard Montague, Viscount Hinchinbroke, son of Edward, 3rd Earl of Sandwich and his wife Elizabeth, 2nd daughter of John Wilmot, Earl of Rochester. Lady Hinchinbroke was made one of the ladies of the bedchamber to the Princess of Wales in 1717 (*Hist. Reg.*, 1717, Chronological Diary, p. 9). Her son, John, succeeded his grandfather as 4th Earl of Sandwich. Viscount Hinchinbroke was member of Parliament for Huntingdon from 1713 until his death in 1722. He had a spectacular career. Steele attacked him in the *Tatler* (Nos. 22, 58, 85; see *Camb. Hist. of Eng. Lit.,* IX, 38). He fought a duel with Capt. Campbell in the piazzas of Covent Garden in 1718 (*Hist. Reg.*, 1718, Diary, p. 43). Lady Hinchinbroke married Francis Seymour, Esq., in July, 1728 (*Hist. Reg. 1729.* Chron. Diary, p. 39). Byrd wrote a friend, Mrs. Armiger, in England in 1728, "I am sincerely glad that Lady Hinchin [brook] has bestowed her Charms to so much advantage, tho whoever she has marryed, will have a great disadvantage in comeing after so agreable a man as Lord Hinchinbrook" (MS in Colonial Williamsburg, Inc.).

On the Lady Percival.

Silence were Sin, when, *Percival*, thy Name
Should stand the Monument of lasting Fame.
To speak thy Beauty, tell thy pleasing Air,
With such Perfections as with these compare;
Words were but Wind, for they express no more
Than what the World would say, *They knew before.*
But if good Sense Perfection may define,
Let Conversation shew how great's thy Mind.

Lady Percival was the wife of Byrd's friend of long standing, Sir John Percival, later Earl of Egmont. She was Catherine, elder daughter of Sir Philip Parker à Morley, Baronet, of Erwarton, Suffolk. (*Dict. Nat. Biog.*; Benjamin Rand, *Berkeley and Percival* [Cambridge, 1914], pp. 4-10; Hist. MSS. Comm.: *Egmont Diary*). The Percivals seem to have had a house at Tunbridge Wells, located on Mount Pleasant with grounds and gardens, that later passed into possession of William Gratton (Burr, *Tunbridge Wells,* pp. 104-5).

Lady Percival and her sister were at Tunbridge in August, 1719, and Byrd noted on Aug. 2, that he treated Lady Percival and three daughters of Lord Abercorn at tea and that he walked with Lady Percival and her sister (entries for Aug. 2, 6, 23, 1719, Diary).

On the Lady Ranelagh.

Who good Examples from Discretion draw,
Let 'em look on, and copy *Ranelagh.*
To all Obliging, so sincerely Just,
Her Friendship's equal to the greatest Trust.

Lady Ranelagh (d. 1728) was the widow of Richard Jones, third Viscount and first Earl of Ranelagh (d. 1712), paymaster general of the army for twenty years under Charles II, James II and William III, but expelled from Parliament in 1703, when his accounts were found unsatisfactory in the ruthless party strife of that time (G. M. Trevelyan, *England under Queen Anne,* Vol. I, Blenheim [London, 1930]). Lady Ranelagh was Margaret Cecil, daughter of James Cecil, third Earl of Salisbury, and widow of John, Lord Stawell. The garden and house of the Earl of Ranelagh in Chelsea, known as Ranelagh Gardens, became one of the most popular of the pleasure gardens of London in the mid-eighteenth century (*Hist. Reg.*, 1728, Diary, p. 13; *Dict. Nat. Biog.*, sub Richard Jones; E. Beresford Chancellor, *The XVIIIth Century in London* [London, 1920], pp. 97-108).

On the Lady Isab - - - a Sc - - - - t.

Tho' far unequal to the great Design,
Yet, *Isabella*, shall the Task be mine,
To follow Nature thro' thy lovely Frame,
Compos'd on purpose for the Theme of Fame:
The more we gaze, we find on every View,
Throughout the Masterpiece there's something new.
From ev'ry Look flows some surprizing Grace,
And Affectation here can find no Place;
Just so unite in Harmony no less,
Your Shape, your Mien, and Manner of Address.
Each ruling with such captivating Ease,
As Nature had resolv'd her Work should please.
Against Detraction Conduct's your Defence,
Founded in blushing Modesty and Sense:
So well-bred, courteous, and discreetly free,
You need no Help to speak your Quality.
No wonder this,——since Monmouth's tender Care
So nicely can instruct th' obedient Fair.

Lady Isabella Scott was the daughter of Charles, 3d Lord Cornwallis, and Anne Scott, Duchess of Monmouth and Buccleugh, widow of James, Duke of Monmouth. She died unmarried in 1748. Lady Isabella Scott moved in the circle of the Southwells and Percivals in London (Collins, *Peerage,* sub Cornwallis; *Egmont Diary,* I, 1).

Byrd noted in his diary for July 21, 1719, that he went to the ball at Tunbridge Wells and Lady Isabel Scott, in the phrase of the day "took him out" to dance a French dance with her.

On the
Lady Charlotte Scott.

Here place the Canvas—— Now *Charlotta* sit,
Whilst I your Portraiture attempt to hit.
Apelles left his *Venus* but half done,
And none could finish what he had begun.
Charlotta's Name would make the Genius rise,
In just Proportion to the Enterprize;
But Nature frowns to see me dare aspire,
And poorly spoil what she has left entire:
Confusion is the Lot of such who strive

To innovate on her Prerogative.
Thus I'm perplex'd to trace your easy Way,
And lost in Thought, to make you brisk and gay;
Whilst in your Air, such Sprightliness there flows,
My Colours fail, much more the Hand that draws.

Lady Charlotte Scott was the daughter of James Scott, Earl of Dalkeith, son of the Duke and Duchess of Monmouth, and his wife Lady Henrietta Hyde, daughter of Laurence, Earl of Rochester. She was born April 30, 1697, and died unmarried Aug. 22, 1747 (Burke, *Peerage,* sub Buccleuch).

On THE
Lady Buck and *Mrs.* Cornish.

Engaging *Buck*, yet aweful is thine Air,
At once invites, and dooms us to Despair,
Tho' pleasing, yet forbiddingly severe.
So *Cornish*, by her Smiles and luring Tongue,
Tempts us to love in vain, and be undone.
Thrice happy Wells! where Beauty's in such store,
When could'st thou boast an *Horsmanden*, a *Hoar,*
A *Borrel, Lyndsey, Searle*, and Thousands more?
Subjects like these, when Mortals have to sing,
Invite the Muses to exchange their Spring.

Lady Buck was the wife of Sir Charles Buck, Baronet, of Hamby Grange and the Grove. She was the daughter of Sir Edward Sebright, 3rd Baronet (Cokayne, *Complete Baronetage;* Burke, *Extinct Baronetages; Hist. Reg.,* 1729, Diary, p. 43). Sir Charles Buck and his wife were apparently friends of Byrd's Horsmanden cousins and he visited them in Bow Street in London (Diary, Sept. 9, 1719). While at Tunbridge Wells in August 1719 Byrd saw much of Lady Buck and her sister (see note on Mrs. Hoare, below). On Sept. 3 he entertained Sir Charles Buck and his family at Tunbridge after hearing a play read and they acted proverbs until midnight. In this entry in his Diary Byrd noted that he heard Mr. B-r-r read a play. Could this be a sly reference, quite in keeping with his sense of humor, to a play he had written under the guise of "Mr. Burrard," the disguised spelling of his own name under which these verses he wrote at Tunbridge were published? Byrd dined and supped with Lady Buck, danced French and country dances with her as well, and had her for his partner at a private ball, played at piquet and commerce with her, and lost their entire stake of ten guineas with her at the ace of hearts (Aug. 1 through Sept. 9, 1719, Diary).

The Misses Cornish were apparently granddaughters of Henry Cornish, Sheriff of London, who was tried and executed for treason in 1685 in connection with the Monmouth Rebellion, though the judgment against him was afterwards reversed. Byrd's favorite of the sisters, Sally or Sarah Cornish, was reported in London in 1724 to be much in love with the opera singer, Senesino (Hughes, *The Gentle Hertford,* p. 86). Byrd had played cards with Mrs. Cornish at Tunbridge in the season of 1718, and had seen one of the sisters at his friends', the Lyndseys', in London in November 1718 (Diary, Aug. 26, 27, Nov. 25). He saw much of them during his stay at Tunbridge in August and September, 1719, at dinners and dances, on the Walk and at the amusement houses, and went on an expedition with them to Penshurst, an old mansion famed as the birthplace of Sir Philip Sidney and the home of Dorothy Sidney, wife of the Earl of Sunderland, celebrated in Waller's poems as Sacharissa, and later noted as the seat of the Earl of Leicester. When Byrd went on Nov. 16 to bid Sally Cornish goodbye in London, preparatory to his return to Virginia, she gave him a nutmeg grater to remember her by. (Diary, Aug. 10 through Nov. 19, 1719; *The Wentworth Papers,* pp. 124-25, 280; Thomas B. Burr, *Tunbridge Wells,* pp. 170-87).

Byrd's first cousins, Susanna and Ursula Horsmanden, are frequently mentioned in his diary for 1717-21, both when he visited their home at Purleigh in Essex and at their apartments in London. He seemed to find Susanna (Suky) Horsmanden especially congenial. To which of the sisters he was referring in these verses is not clear.

Sir Charles Buck's sister Mary married Charles Hoar, Esq., of Rushford, in Derbyshire (Burke, *Extinct Baronetages,* sub Buck). In his diary, Byrd noted on August 9 that he went on the Walk at Tunbridge Wells with Lady Buck and her sister, and on August 16, 1719 that he dined at Mrs. Lyndsey's with Lady Buck and her sister and again on August 21, that he had breakfasted with Mrs. Lyndsey and Lady Buck and her sister were there, and on August 31 that he took Lady Buck and her sister to Mr. Horsmanden's to supper, where they ate cold venison pasty and were gay until two in the morning.

William Burrel was appointed Chaplain in Ordinary to George I in 1720 and a Mr. Burrel, one of the messengers of the Chamber to his Majesty, died suddenly on board the Royal Yacht Carolina at Rotterdam in June, 1720. The particular reference here indicated by Byrd is not clear, though probably the lady whose charms he was celebrating belonged to this family attached to the court (*Hist. Reg.* 1720, Diary, pp. 5, 15, 26).

Mr. and Mrs. Lyndsey, who lived in London, were Byrd's close friends during his residence there in 1717-20 as shown in frequent entries in his diary. He visited them often at their home, played cards with them and went with them to plays, masquerades and other social diversions. When he left London to return to Virginia in 1719, in spite of the fact that he had taken her to task for slight indiscretions, Mrs. Lyndsey wept at his departure.

In his stay at Tunbridge Wells in July and August 1719 Byrd saw a great deal of the Lyndseys. He entertained and was entertained by them. He was much out of humor when he was connected with Mrs. Lyndsey in a lampoon. When he returned to London on Sept. 7, he went up in a party with the Lyndseys and the Cornish sisters (July 16 through Sept. 9, Diary).

On Mrs. Lethulier.

See how triumphantly her Beauty blooms,
Commanding Sacrifice by Hecatombs!
Next view the happy Pledge of youthful Years,
Which in such conscious Modesty appears.
The Rosy Blushes peep, and then retire,
Then come again, and tender Love inspire.
Who, when she Dances, can her Movement see,
But's yielding Heart beats Time by Sympathy?

Beauty to her is not deriv'd from Chance,
But Right convey'd by just Inheritance.

The Lethieullier family were an important and wealthy family in London. Sir John Lethieullier, Kt., was succeeded by his son, John Lethieullier, Esq., an eminent Turkey merchant, who died in 1737 at the age of eighty (*Hist. Reg.*, 1737, Diary, p. 63). Christopher Lethieullier, father of the "Lady of Sir Richard Hopkins" died at eighty in 1728 (*Hist. Reg.*, 1728, Diary, p. 51). Christopher Lethieullier who died at Bath in 1736 had been for years a director of the Bank of England (*Hist. Reg.*, 1736, Diary, p. 69). Smart Lethieullier (1701-1760) (see *Dict. Nat. Biog.*) and his brother Charles made valuable collections of antiquities (Nichols, *Literary Anecdotes*, V, 368; *Hist. Reg.*, 1724, Diary, p. 50; 1728, Diary, p. 63; 1733, Diary, p. 13; *The Gentleman's Magazine*, 1739, p. 660). No evidence is at hand to indicate to which of the women of this family Byrd wrote these verses.

On Mrs. P - - - - - - - - ll.

Hear and assist me, all ye powerful Nine,
Assist me on a Subject so divine,
Help me to touch the trembling, conscious Lyre,
And P ——ll's Beauty give the genial Fire;
But endless work —— For Something's still behind
T' increase th' Ideas of the curious Mind.
Let Envy's self, and all the Sex combine,
Through Clouds of Malice P ——ll still shall shine.

Two brothers, David and Charles Polhill (probably connected with the family of Thomas Polhill, of Kent, who married Oliver Cromwell's granddaughter Elizabeth Ireton in 1674) were prominent in official circles in London about this time. David Polhill, to whom a son was born in 1725 and another in 1731, was member of Parliament for Bramber, Sussex, in 1723, was Keeper of Records in the Tower in 1730, and reëlected to Parliament for Rochester in 1731 (*Hist. Reg.*, 1723, Diary, p. 22; 1725, Diary, p. 21; 1730, Diary, p. 60; 1731, Diary, pp. 22, 23). Charles Polhill was among those appointed commissioners of the excise in 1727 and in June of that year he married Mrs. Streatfield of Sevenoaks in the county of Trent (*ibid.*, 1727, Diary, pp. 26, 49). The "Mrs. Polhill" to whom Byrd referredd in these lines is not particularly identified, though he declared she was as pretty as an angel, after he had drunk tea with her and Sally Cornish (Diary, Aug. 26, 1719).

These lines "On Mrs. P - - - - ll" appear anonymously in *Tunbrigalia*, p. 19:

P - - - - lly, wanton, gay and airy,
Wild as Buck, or Midnight Fairy,
Blooming like Rose, and bright as Lilly
So pretty is, and yet so silly;
To Death I fret me at her Folly,
Yet more than Life I love my P——lly.

Did Byrd write these lines also?

In addition to the women to whom he wrote these verses under his pseudonym "Mr. Burrard," the Virginia widower noted in his diary that he played cards, or danced, or took chances on "the Walk" with a number of other ladies whose charms are celebrated in verses ascribed to "Mr. Say" or printed anonymously in *Tunbrigalia*. Among these was Lady Jane Hamilton, whom Byrd sat by at the play and with whom he danced the following evening (Diary, Aug. 13, 14, 1719).

These lines "On Florinda, Or, Mrs. J - - e H - - - n" were printed anonymously in *Tunbrigalia*, pp. 31-32:

FLORINDA's charming, sweet and fair,
Adorn'd with every Grace;
These are Perfections not so rare,
Familiar to her Race.

The Wonder is, that winning Air
Peculiar to the Maid;
That matchless *Something* seated there,
Which baffles all our Aid.

'Tis innocent, yet can ensuare;
Unpractic'd, yet has Wiles;
It knows to conquer without Care,
And to command with Smiles.

It is so easy, you wou'd swear,
Each Nymph might put it on:
But yet so hard, you must declare,
'Tis her's, and her's alone.

APPENDIX III

A Discourse Concerning the Plague (1721)

A Discourse Concerning the Plague

The text and the facsimile title page are here taken from the copy in the Library of the College of Physicians in Philadelphia (see Introduction, pp. xxviii-xxxi).

A Royal Proclamation was published in England in October, 1720, for observing a general fast on December 8, 1720, throughout England and Wales, "for deprecating God's Judgments, and averting the Plague" (*Historical Register*, 1721, Chronological Diary, p. 41).

A

DISCOURSE

Concerning the

PLAGUE,

With ſome

PRESERVATIVES

Againſt it.

By a Lover of Mankind.

Dii talem Terris avertite Peſtem. Virgil.

LONDON:

Printed for J. ROBERTS near the *Oxford-Arms* in *Warwick-lane.* 1721.

1 Shill.

A
DISCOURSE
Concerning the Plague.

There is no question but the disease commonly call'd the Plague, or Pestilence, is more destructive to mankind than any other, and is one of the severest scourges that God Almighty makes use of, to chastize a corrupt and degenerate people: Tho' the Plague certainly is of more general signification than the Pestilence, whether we regard the etymology of the word, or the sense in which 'tis commonly understood, especially in Holy Scripture. We find there the word נגע by us render'd the Plague, is us'd for any considerable stroke, calamity, or distemper, which God is pleas'd to inflict on mankind for their transgressions. [a]For instance, all the dreadful judgments executed upon *Pharaoh*, and his unhappy subjects, are call'd Plagues, tho' none of them, except the destruction of their First-born, seem'd to have had any relation to the Pestilence. [b]So likewise the Leprosy is call'd the Plague in several places. [c]Thus Consumption, Terror, and the burning Ague, as well as Famine and the ravage of Enemies, were all threaten'd under the name of so many Plagues in the Old Testament. Also in the New, [d]that inveterate issue of blood, whereof the woman was heal'd by touching the garment of our Saviour, was term'd a Plague. [e]By the same name other infirmities were call'd, tho' they were nothing akin to the fatal distemper that now goes under that denomination.

Indeed, in some texts 'tis us'd for the Pestilence itself; as when the children of *Israel*, being cloy'd with the bread of Heaven, lusted after flesh in the wilderness, God was pleas'd to indulge their disorderly inclinations with a mighty flight

---

[a] Exod. XI. I. I Sam. IV. 8.
[b] Lev. XIII. 3.
[c] Lev. XXVI. 21.
[d] Marc. V. 29.
[e] Luke VII. 21.

of Quails[f]: but they either eat too greedily of 'em, or else great part of that immense number (which we are told lay round about the camp two cubits thick upon the ground, for several miles together) must have dy'd, and with their stench have corrupted the air, and so brought the Plague amongst the people. [g]So the men, whom *Moses* had detach'd to reconnoitre the land of *Canaan*, all dy'd of the Plague, except *Joshua* and *Caleb*, for terrifying their country-men, and exciting them to murmur against *Moses*. [h]In like manner, when the congregation, after the dismal destruction of *Korah*, and his seditious accomplices, mutiny'd against *Moses* and *Aaron*, the Plague broke out upon them, and destroy'd 14700 Souls. And this sickness might naturally have proceeded from some baleful vapours, that ascended from the bowels of the earth, when it open'd to swallow up these rebellious persons. [i]Thus likewise they lost 24000 more, by another Plague sent by God upon the *Israelites,* for suffering themselves to be seduc'd by the intrigues of the *Moabitish* women, to sacrifice to their idols, and to join themselves to *Baal-peor*.

[k]Indeed that Plague, wherewith God mortify'd the vanity of *David* in numbering the people, is not call'd a Plague, but a Pestilence: and the *Hebrew* word דבר , us'd in this place, is very remarkable, being deriv'd from the root דבר , which signifies to *speak*, *pronounce*, or *decree*, as if this cruel distemper, that sweeps away mankind with a sudden destruction, never happens but by the special sentence and designation of Almighty God. And as other diseases befal us in consequence of our own personal intemperance and disorder, this seems to be sent upon a nation in general, by this particular appointment, to waste and exterminate its inhabitants, for their notorious and crying sins.

Now tho' God be able to do every thing in heaven and in earth, by an immediate act of Omnipotence, yet he is generally pleas'd to work by the ministry of second causes,

---

[f] Num. XI. 33.
[g] Num. XIV. 37.
[h] Num. xvi. 46.
[i] Num. xxv. 9.
[k] 2 Sam. xxiv. 13.

without stepping out of the ordinary track of his Providence. Nevertheless, since natural causes are all subject to his sovereign decrees, how easy is it for his almighty power, to call forth those natural causes, to execute his vengeance upon a depraved and rebellious generation? How easy is it for God to shake the mountains by an earthquake, and out of the clifts thereof make way for contagious damps, that may taint the air with Pestilence? He can, by a strong wind transport numberless insects into our land, which often happens in *Æthiopia*;[l] and from the stench of their corrupted carcasses kindle a Pestilence among us. God is able to withhold the former and the latter rain, or by Blites and Caterpillers to consume the fruits of the earth, [m]so as by Famine to oblige us to feed on such foul and unwholsome things, as naturally beget a Pestilence. Or, which is the more common way of infecting these northern parts of *Europe,* how very easy is it for the divine wisdom so to order it, as that the [n]Infection may be brought by shipping or caravans from some other country. Thus it is frequently transported from Turky and Ægypt, into places that traffick with them. These, and a thousand other ways the providence of God finds out, to introduce a Pestilence into a city or nation, without going out of the order of nature.

However, I am not so arrant a Physician as to conceit, that because the Plague is thus brought upon us in a natural way, that 'tis therefore purely and wholly to be imputed to natural causes. No! God did so frequently menace the *Jews* with this fatal disease, and also make good those menaces by so many dreadful instances, that we should be as great unbelievers as they, if we did not allow, when it befalls a nation, that the hand of God is in it. In that magnificent description, which the prophet [o]*Habakkuk* gave us of the Majesty of God, there's nothing strikes us more, than where he said, *that before him marched the Pestilence;* as if that avenging disease were as inseparable from the terrible Judge

[l] Ludolphi Hist. Æthiop.
[m] Appian. Hist. Rom. 40. Luc. Florus 3.5. Q. Curtius, 9. 10.
[n] Phil. Trans. 165.
[o] Hab. iii. 5.

of Heaven and Earth, as the heathen Poets made the Thunder-bolt from *Jupiter,* to execute his wrath upon his wicked and incorrigible creatures. There is nothing occurs so frequently in the Prophets, as these tremendous expressions. [p]*I will consume them by Pestilence; I will send upon them my Pestilence; I will proclaim a liberty to the Pestilence; and I will plead against them by Pestilence.* These dreadful menaces were directed, indeed, to the *Jewish* nation; but we have great reason to bring them home to ourselves, in case we obstinately persist in our rebellion against God.

The very Heathen seem'd to believe, that this distemper came upon a country by special commission from the Gods, to avenge some enormous crime, or national transgression. We find this by many passages both in the *Greek* and *Roman* Authors; but I shall only instance that remarkable place in the first Iliad of *Homer,* where he tells us, that *Apollo,* to punish the indignity offer'd to one of his Priests by *Agamemnon,* sent a Plague into the *Grecian* camp, which destroy'd abundance of his men.

> [q] Λητοῦς καὶ Διὸς υἱός· ὁ γὰρ βασιλῆϊ χολωθεὶς
> Νοῦσον ἀνὰ στρατὸν ὦρσε κακήν· ὀλέκοντο δὲ λαοί,
> Οὕνεκα τὸν Χρύσην ἠτίμησ' ἀρητῆρα
> Ἀτρείδης.

We may therefore, upon the credit of so general an opinion, venture to believe, without much superstition, that this mortal arrow is shot from the quiver of the Almighty: and then surely the most reasonable remedy we can use against it, will be a sincere repentance and reformation. [r]Our amendment will, like the vigorous achievement of *Phineas,* stay the fury of the Plague, and the same Omnipotence that exerted itself in our punishment, will be as conspicuous in our deliverance.

However, when I recommend an unfeigned repentance and humiliation before God, as the first and greatest preservative against this pernicious distemper, yet I would not be

---

[p] Jer. xiv. 12. Jer. xxxiv. 17. Ex. xxxviii. 22.
[q] Hom. Iliad. lib. I. l. 9.
[r] Num. xxv. 8.

understood thereby to depreciate the application of such natural remedies, as the divine goodness has vouchsafed to reveal to mankind. On the contrary, as God is pleas'd to send this great calamity upon us by natural ways, so it seems agreeable to his wise providence, that we should endeavour both to prevent and cure it by natural applications. But I am humbly of opinion, that in order to induce his infinite goodness, to direct us to these natural remedies, and after that to bless them with success, the most prevailing course we can take, is, heartily to repent of our sins, and reform our corrupt and vicious lives. After this happy step taken, we shall render the business of the Physician more easy, his prescriptions more efficacious, and our constitutions more vigorous to resist and expel the distemper.

Having thus far acted the part of a Divine and a Christian, I will now beg leave to put on the different characters of a Physician and a Naturalist. I will endeavour, out of the most celebrated Authors, to describe this destructive disease, its most frequent causes and symptoms, and after all, conclude with some very proper preservatives, both publick and private, against it.

[s]Of that disease properly call'd the Plague or Pestilence, there seems to be diverse sorts, at least it discovers different symptoms, according to the various causes from whence it proceeds, or according to the several climates or season of the year in which it rages. But those which have happen'd this last Century in *Britain*, and in most other countries of *Europe*, particularly that great Plague in 1665, has been thus describ'd by some eminent Physicians, that were conversant with it.

[t]The Plague is a burning and contagious Feaver, proceeding from an inflammation of the most spirituous parts of the blood, occasion'd by a venemous taint of the air. [u]It most commonly begins with a chilness and shivering, like an Ague, after which succeed violent vomitings, and a most intense feaver. Sometimes too the patient is afflicted with a loose-

[s] Cardan de Subt. 134.
[t] Willis Epit. 592.
[u] Sydenham Obs. Med. 93.

ness, which leaves him not till the hour of his death. From the very beginning the sick person feels an insupportable oppression at his heart, which makes him sigh continually. In this sad condition he languishes, till either nature be enabled to throw off the morbisick matter in Carbuncles, Buboes, or other Impostumes, by the benefit of which (if they can be brought to a kindly maturation) he may recover; or else till the fibers of the blood be broke to pieces by the violence of the conflict, and the frame of it utterly dissolv'd. Then follows a coagulation of the blood; and by its not being able longer to circulate, a mortification, which shews itself in purple spots on sundry parts of the body. These are certain tokens of approaching death, tho' sometimes they are not seen till after the party is dead.

There are some instances too in the beginning, or else in the increase of this fatal disease, that these deadly Tokens break out upon a man in perfect health, and hurry him to his grave, without being preceded by any sensible symptoms of a feaver. This happens thro' the extream subtilty of the contagion, which in an instant coagulates the blood, before nature can raise a feaver in her own defence. So in like manner it frequently falls out, that Buboes and Swellings rise suddenly, without any apparent feaver, or other violent symptom. Thus a man may have the Plague and dye, without perceiving himself to be sick; or on the contrary, without any confinement he may have it and recover, by the benefit of a vigorous and happy constitution. But then this last case rarely happens to any, but persons of remarkable temperance, in whom there are no superfluous humours for the distemper to work upon.

The Plague may break out in any season of the year, when it is brought either by sea or land from some other place. But the most natural time of its beginning is the spring, when people are most inclined to inflammatory diseases. Then as the heat comes on, it spreads its baleful contagion; but abates its fury again as the heat decreases, till the winter happily changes the air into an opposite constitution. Some seeds of the infection may however be left behind, and some few persons may chance to have the

Plague in winter; but then it proves neither so raging nor so frequent. If it should be imported into a new place in winter time, 'tis generally less contagious, and less mortal, being checkt by the nitrous particles, wherewith the air is replete during that season, and by the multitude of fires in every house, which help to correct and subdue the infection; neither in that case does it ever rise to the same dreadful degree of mortality the following spring.

[w]This cruel distemper, is by some Virtuosi, deriv'd originally from *Asia,* as well as the Small-pox: but I conceive the principal reason of that opinion to be, that the Plague is, for the most part, handed from thence into *Europe:* But others think we are altogether as much beholden to *Africa* for it, [x]where infinite swarms of Locusts are often found dead upon the ground; and with the stench of their carcasses, putrify'd by the heat of a perpendicular sun, kindle a Pestilence in the neighbouring countries. Thus much is certain at least, that this disease is no where in the world more frequent than in [y]*Æthiopia* and *Ægypt*; and travellers assure us, that *Grand Cairo* is hardly ever free from it. The truth of it is, the same reason may be given for its being so constantly there, that they give for its being always in the *Turkish* Dominions. Their firm belief of Predestination makes them utterly careless to prevent this dismal distemper; for they will tell you, that if the Plague be writ by fate in their foreheads, all the precautions in the world can't prevent it: nay, they reckon it a kind of impiety, to endeavour to hinder those fatal decrees by our impertinent discretions. For this reason they seldom or never use any rules of prudence, either to prevent or cure their distempers, except only the Small Pox; and in this case they do it rather to save their faces, than their lives; not considering, that one is as subject to fate as the other. They have no professed Physicians, because a true *Turk* will use no doctor but *Mahomet,* nor rely on any sort of physick but the *Alcoran.* [z]Thus the

---

[w] Phil. Trans. 165.
[x] Lud. Hist. Æthiop. i. 13.
[y] Thavenot, par. i.
[z] Sir P. Ricaut. Hist. Turk.

Plague is suffer'd every where in that vast Empire to range at large, without being obstructed either by caution or cure, and from thence 'tis deriv'd to all other Countries that maintain any commerce with them.

But most Christian states, (the *Presbyterians* not excepted, who pretend also to believe in fatality) fansy it may be prevented by care, and therefore employ the requisite precautions. In *England* it us'd formerly to make a visit about once in twenty or thirty years: but since the universal use of Tobacco, it has now been kept off above fifty four years. Without the assistance of this powerful Alexipharmick, it were, humanly speaking, impossible to have warded it off so long, considering the constant and extensive Traffick the *English* have carry'd on to every part of the Levant, and the very little care that has been taken to hinder the Infection. Indeed whenever the Plague does get footing in *Great Britain,* it handles us very severely, as the Small Pox is likewise observed to do: but whether this be owing to our gross feeding, to our excesses, or our climate, the learned must determine.

Some have affirmed that the Plague is utterly unknown in *America,* that 'tis neither original there, nor hath ever been transported thither, by reason of its vast distance from infected countries. I can't conceive upon what this conjecture is founded, except it be, that as the Pox is supposed to be a native of that new world, that alone seems punishment sufficient, without the addition of the Plague. However I very much suspect the truth of this opinion, because we have often heard of distempers there that have been very mortal, and very contagious; insomuch that if they have really not been the Plague, they have been very little better. Besides many parts of *America* are visited by earthquakes, which rending the sides of the mountains, may set at liberty those noxious steams, that engender the Pestilence elsewhere. Other parts of it have been afflicted with Famine, after which often marches the Pestilence in dreadful array. Neither are Locusts wanting, and many other insects, whose mighty armies having laid whole countries waste, at length die themselves of hunger, and infect the air with their corrupted carkasses. Now since *America* does not want the natural causes which in *Asia* produce the Plague, it would be very strange if it miss'd having the fatal effects. But if the new world have not naturally this cruel distemper, yet since it hath furnish'd us with as bad a one of its own growth, 'tis odd enough it never should have received the Plague in requital. However if it be really true, that this cruel scourge be still a stranger there, it must certainly be owing, in a great measure, to the universal use of Tobacco. Most of the southern colonies cultivate this useful Plant, and all in general take it, as well Europeans and Indians, as Negroes; so that there is no complection, no degree of men, but arm themselves with this invincible antidote against the enemy of mankind.

In *Europe* 'tis agreed, that the Plague is for the most part propagated by communication, as when 'tis carry'd from one place to another, either by persons or goods, that bring some taint of the infection along with them. We find by repeated experiences, that in this case the air is really not infected to any great distance, because towns and countries in the neighbourhood of others, where this Plague rages, are saved from the contagion, by prohibiting all commerce and correspondence with them. *Tuscany* was a happy instance of this truth in the year 1656, when it escap'd that terrible Plague, which spread it self over the adjoining States of *Italy,* by the prudent measures taken by the great Duke: and what confirms it still more, is, that in the great Plague, which in 1665, destroy'd so many thousand Souls in this city, there where three entire parishes that continued uninfected to the end.

Supposing then that the Plague comes generally to us by communication, it concerns us very nearly to inquire into such methods of prevention, as may most effectually guard us from being tainted. But the better to pave the way for this inquiry, I shall in the first place mention some directions that have been prescribed and practised by several learned persons, and out of these sum up as many of them as seem most worth our using for this purpose.

[a]In the dreadful Pestilence which visited the City of *Athens,* in the days of *Socrates,* that philosopher recommended temperance as the surest preservative against the infection; and being himself armed with this great virtue, he forbore not to attend upon his sick friends, shewing them the utmost humanity and tenderness in their distress'd condition; yet he never caught the distemper, tho' he daily ministred to them that had it. This certainly was owing to that abstinence, for which he had been ever remarkable. Neither did this divine [b]Philosopher, whom the Oracle had pronounced the wisest of men, enjoy alone the benefit of his own prescription; but those of his Disciples too that excell'd in this virtue, conversed with safety amidst the contagion.

The mighty advantage of temperance in this case, appears not only in single Persons, but likewise in whole Nations. How rarely did the old *Romans* sustain any great damage by the Pestilence in the days of Virtue, when Probity made the Common Wealth flourish, before Luxury was known, while their Consuls and Dictators spent sparingly upon themselves, that they might squander upon their country; when all excess was accounted criminal, and private riches were of no use, but to relieve the poor, and serve the publick. In those happy days, old *Rome* but seldom felt the Plague, and when it did come, it cou'd make but slender execution upon bodies so clean and unpamper'd. We read of no considerable Pestilence among them, till the [c]578th year of the City, when *S. P. Albinus,* and *Q. Mucius Scævola* were Consuls. That happened first among the cattle, which died in so great numbers, that their carcasses putrified before they cou'd be remov'd. This infected the air of consequence, so that the spring following it broke out amongst the people in a terrible manner. Such a multitude of free people were seized with the sickness, that the poor slaves had neither attendance nor burial. Their neglected corps were expos'd in the streets for the Dogs and Vultures to feast upon, which though they assembled in prodigious numbers, cou'd not

---

[a] Diog. in Vita Socratis Aelian 13. 27.
[b] Diog. lib. 2.37.
[c] Tit. Liv. lib 41.26.

Site of the original Thanksgiving in 1619, **Berkeley Plantation** in Charles

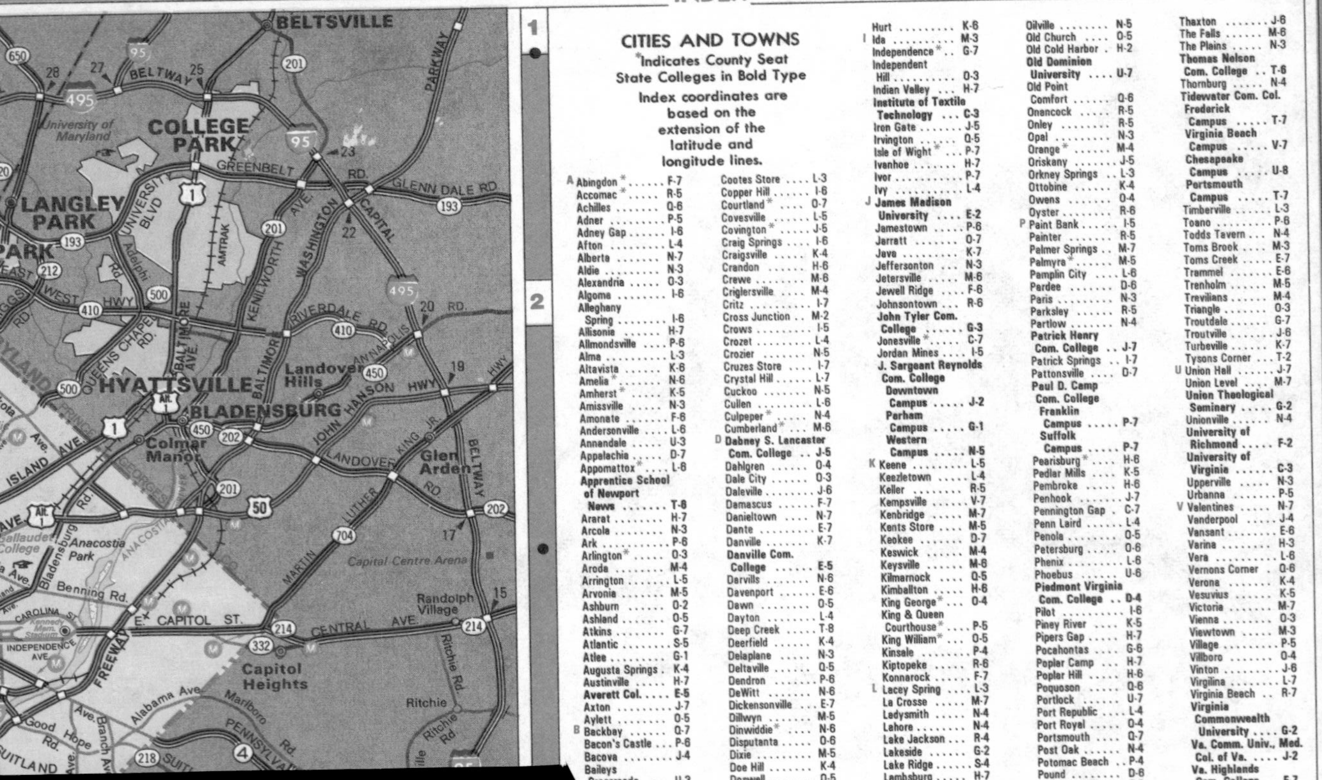

INDEX

CITIES AND TOWNS

*Indicates County Seat
State Colleges in Bold Type

Index coordinates are based on the extension of the latitude and longitude lines.

A Abingdon* F-7
Accomac* R-5
Achilles Q-6
Adner P-5
Adney Gap I-6
Afton L-4
Alberta N-7
Aldie N-3
Alexandria O-3
Algoma I-6
Alleghany Spring I-6
Allisonia H-7
Allmondsville P-6
Alma L-3
Altavista K-6
Amelia* N-6
Amherst* K-5
Amissville N-3
Amonate F-6
Andersonville L-6
Annandale U-3
Appalachia D-7
Appomattox* L-6
Apprentice School of Newport News T-8
Ararat H-7
Arcola N-3
Ark P-6
Arlington* O-3
Aroda M-4
Arrington L-5
Arvonia M-5
Ashburn O-2
Ashland O-5
Atkins G-7
Atlantic S-5
Atlee G-1
Augusta Springs K-4
Austinville H-7
Averett Col. E-5
Axton J-7
Aylett O-5
B Backbay Q-7
Bacon's Castle P-6
Bacova J-4
Baileys Crossroads U-3
Ballsville M-5
Banco M-4

Cootes Store L-3
Copper Hill I-6
Courtland* O-7
Covesville L-5
Covington* J-5
Craig Springs I-6
Craigsville K-4
Crandon H-6
Crewe M-6
Criglersville M-4
Critz I-7
Cross Junction M-2
Crows I-5
Crozet L-4
Crozier N-5
Cruzes Store I-7
Crystal Hill L-7
Cuckoo N-5
Cullen L-6
Culpeper* N-4
Cumberland* M-6
D **Dabney S. Lancaster Com. College** J-5
Dahlgren O-4
Dale City O-3
Daleville J-6
Damascus F-7
Danieltown N-7
Dante E-7
Danville K-7
Danville Com. College E-5
Darvills N-6
Davenport E-6
Dawn O-5
Dayton L-4
Deep Creek T-8
Deerfield K-4
Delaplane N-3
Deltaville Q-5
Dendron P-6
DeWitt N-6
Dickensonville E-7
Dillwyn M-5
Dinwiddie* N-6
Disputanta O-6
Dixie M-5
Doe Hill K-4
Doswell O-5
Dot D-7
Drakes Branch L-7
Dranesville S-2

Hurt K-6
I Ida M-3
Independence* G-7
Independent Hill O-3
Indian Valley H-7
Institute of Textile Technology C-3
Iron Gate J-5
Irvington Q-5
Isle of Wight* P-7
Ivanhoe H-7
Ivor P-7
Ivy L-4
J **James Madison University** E-2
Jamestown P-6
Jarratt O-7
Java K-7
Jeffersonton N-3
Jetersville M-6
Jewell Ridge F-6
Johnsontown R-6
John Tyler Com. College G-3
Jonesville* C-7
Jordan Mines I-5
J. Sargeant Reynolds Com. College
Downtown Campus J-2
Parham Campus G-1
Western Campus N-5
K Keene L-5
Keezletown L-4
Keller R-5
Kempsville V-7
Kenbridge M-7
Kents Store M-5
Keokee D-7
Keswick M-4
Keysville M-6
Kilmarnock Q-5
Kimballton H-6
King George* O-4
King & Queen Courthouse* P-5
King William* O-5
Kinsale P-4
Kiptopeke R-6
Konnarock F-7
L Lacey Spring L-3
La Crosse M-7
Ladysmith N-4
Lahore N-4
Lake Jackson R-4
Lakeside G-2
Lake Ridge S-4
Lambsburg H-7
Lancaster* Q-5
Lanexa P-6
Langley U-2

Oilville N-5
Old Church O-5
Old Cold Harbor H-2
Old Dominion University U-7
Old Point Comfort Q-6
Onancock R-5
Onley R-5
Opal N-3
Orange* M-4
Oriskany J-5
Orkney Springs L-3
Ottobine K-4
Owens O-4
Oyster R-6
P Paint Bank I-5
Painter R-5
Palmer Springs M-7
Palmyra* M-5
Pamplin City L-6
Pardee D-6
Paris N-3
Parksley R-5
Partlow N-4
Patrick Henry Com. College J-7
Patrick Springs I-7
Pattonsville D-7
Paul D. Camp Com. College
Franklin Campus P-7
Suffolk Campus P-7
Pearisburg* H-6
Pedlar Mills K-5
Pembroke H-6
Penhook J-7
Pennington Gap C-7
Penn Laird L-4
Penola O-5
Petersburg O-6
Phenix L-6
Phoebus U-6
Piedmont Virginia Com. College D-4
Pilot I-6
Piney River K-5
Pipers Gap H-7
Pocahontas G-6
Poplar Camp H-7
Poplar Hill H-6
Poquoson Q-6
Portlock U-7
Port Republic L-4
Port Royal O-4
Portsmouth Q-7
Post Oak N-4
Potomac Beach P-4
Pound D-6
Pounding Mill F-6
Powhatan* N-5
Pratts M-4

Thaxton J-6
The Falls M-6
The Plains N-3
Thomas Nelson Com. College T-6
Thornburg N-4
Tidewater Com. Col.
Frederick Campus T-7
Virginia Beach Campus V-7
Chesapeake Campus U-8
Portsmouth Campus T-7
Timberville L-3
Toano P-6
Todds Tavern N-4
Toms Brook M-3
Toms Creek E-7
Trammel E-6
Trenholm M-5
Trevilians M-4
Triangle O-3
Troutdale G-7
Troutville J-6
Turbeville K-7
Tysons Corner T-2
U Union Hall J-7
Union Level M-7
Union Theological Seminary G-2
Unionville N-4
University of Richmond F-2
University of Virginia C-3
Upperville N-3
Urbanna P-5
V Valentines N-7
Vanderpool J-4
Vansant E-6
Varina H-3
Vera L-6
Vernons Corner Q-6
Verona K-4
Vesuvius K-5
Victoria M-7
Vienna O-3
Viewtown M-3
Village P-5
Villboro O-4
Vinton J-6
Virgilina L-7
Virginia Beach R-7
Virginia Commonwealth University G-2
Va. Comm. Univ., Med. Col. of Va. J-2
Va. Highlands Com. College F-7
Va. Intermont College G-5

devour fast enough. This indeed was a dreadful Plague; but it ought to be remembred, that before this time the abstinence of the old *Romans* was grown out of fashion, and luxury was countenanced by the Senate, tho' not by the Laws. One thing at this time was remarkable, that amongst the higher rank none escaped so ill as the priests on this sad occasion, who for that reason were suspected by some prophane persons, to have been higher pamper'd than their fellow citizens. But pampering is so seldom observ'd amongst men of that holy order, that we hope 'twas a malicious aspersion.

The benefit of temperance, both towards the preventing and curing of the Plague, is evident even among the *Turks,* where this distemper seems to be at home in its own proper climate. For notwithstanding their want of precaution, and contempt of physick, yet by the strength of temperance and sobriety, they come off more favourably in the Plague than countries of greater luxury, and more learning; while, for a contrary reason, we *Britons* suffer dreadfully by this disease, having commonly too great a complaisance for our dear bellies.

[d]Amongst the ancient *Greeks,* especially at *Athens,* in the time of the Plague, they us'd to kindle very great fires in every quarter of the town, which they thought purify'd the air. And at the same time private persons (at least the more prudent of them that could afford the expence) kept constant fires in their own houses, to correct the infection. They were wont also, on that dismal occasion, to sprinkle wine upon their doors and windows, imagining that the generous fumes thereof, would prevail over the contagious particles of the air, and render it more salubrious, Tho' the moderns have found vinegar more powerful for that purpose, or at least have fancy'd so.

[e]'Tis the opinion of a modern physician, who had convers'd very much with the Plague, that whoever apprehends himself within reach of the contagion, may in a great measure be preserv'd, if he take care not to swallow his

[d] Thucyd. lib. 2.
[e] D. Dobizensky Phil col. 2.20.

spittle, so long as he continues near those that have the distemper. For he conceives the saliva to be the readiest vehicle to receive the pestilential poison, and carry it down into the stomach, from whence it passes directly into the blood, and works those mortal effects which we see in the Plague. And the better to prevent swallowing the spittle (which in most persons is involuntary action) he advises to chew things of a strong and disagreeable taste, which men naturally spit out, and suffer none of it to go down their throats. But of all strong things he principally recommends Tobacco, which has a quality in it that resists every kind of poison. This preservative he offers us upon his own repeated experience, as well as upon probable and convincing reasons.

[f]Another learned person observing the method taken by unerring nature to expel the venom of the Plague, namely, by carrying it with the circulation of the blood, to the axillary, inguinal, and other glands, where if it stops, and gathers into bubos and imposthumes, and those imposthumes can be brought to suppuration, the patient will be out of danger; but if it open itself a way, and passes along with the natural motion of the blood to the heart, then death follows unavoidably: Observing, I say, the oeconomy of nature, he us'd by way of prevention, to make an incision with a lancet on the right and left side of the groin, and put in a corum; to the end, that by these artificial *sinks,* the poison might find a passage. This caution he practis'd on himself, and several of his friends, when the Pestilence raged at *Prague* in *Bohemia,* in the year 1680. Abundance of purulent matter issued forth at these vents, which guarded such as try'd the experiment, from suffering by the infection, tho' they attended daily those that had it.

This way of driving the venom of the Plague out at these *Common shores,* is countenanc'd by the constant method us'd by the *Turks,* to prevent the sad effects of the Small-pox. However foreign this may seem to our present subject, yet by the good leave of our Physicians, I shall set it down exactly as they perform it.

---

[f] De Alprunus Phil. col. 2.17.

At *Constantinople,* and indeed in the greatest part of the *Turkish* dominions, they stand strangely in fear of the Small-pox on the score of their beauties. Their lives they can trust with fate, but not their faces. To prevent the disfiguring of which, they ingraft this distemper on their children in the following manner. They take a child of any age under ten years old, the younger the better after it can go alone, and find out a person that is sick of a favourable sort. When the pustules are ripe they lance some of them, and receive the matter into a nut-shell, and carry it to the place where the child is. Then with a needle, that hath been dipt into this pocky-poison, they prick the fleshy part of each arm and each thigh, deep enough to fetch blood. In a little time each of these punctures begins to inflame, and rises up into a great boil, which ripens, breaks, and discharges abundance of matter. About the seventh day the symptoms of the Small-pox begin to appear; but great part of the morbisick humour, running out at the four Sinks above mention'd, neither the life nor the beauty of the patient is in any danger. After the child is recover'd, these sores continue open for about twenty days, and intirely cleanse him from all the virulent remains of this disease, which makes every week so terrible a massacre here at *London.*

This notable precaution is practised so universally among the Ottomans, and with such constant success, that 'tis amazing our Physicians, who are in most cases enterprizing enough, have not ventur'd upon it here. But they are particularly cautious of their patient's lives, when they are to introduce any outlandish methods, that may abridge so considerable a branch of their practice. Insomuch that if any publickspirited person should presume to preach it up for the preservation of his fellow citizens, the mob of the faculty would be apt to insult him, and cry out, *Great is the* Apollo *of the* Britons.

A method not very different from this of the Musselmen, is practis'd by the Doctors in the *East Indies,* in all kinds of Feavers. In the very beginning of the distemper they make a drain, by cauterizing some fleshy part of the body. This immediately raises a blister, which they take care to keep running, till the disease is checkt by the plentiful discharge of the febrile matter. This is a very natural method, and promises more success in the beginning of a Feaver, before the strength of the patient is impair'd, than blisters can do, after the distemper has weaken'd nature so much, that she is not in condition to repel that which offends her.

I hope the reader will be so courteous as to forgive this digression, which is by no means a bare curiosity, and give me leave to return to my subject, and mention a very bold experiment undertaken by [g]*Alprunus,* whereby he discover'd, that the pestilential poison surpasses by many degrees all other poisons. But that I may do him exact justice, I will make use of his own words. *Having lanc'd,* said he, *a Plague-boil of Mr. Godfrey Rechel, I collected the virulent matter into a retort, and luting a receiver close to it, I apply'd degrees of fire; at first came over a water, after that a more fat and oyly substance; and last of all a salt ascended into the neck of the retort. The fire being remov'd, and the glasses separated, there issued forth a stink so intolerable, that a thousand old rotten ulcers, with their united stench at Midsummer, could not equal it: and tho' I fancy'd I had sufficiently arm'd all my senses against this subtle venom, by stuffing my ears with cotton, my nose with pessarys, and my mouth with sponges soakt in vinegar and treaks; yet, as if struck with a thunder-bolt, I was instantly seiz'd with a trembling over my whole body. To make short, I gave some of this horribly stinking salt to Monsieur Rechel the right owner, to taste, and then tasted of it myself; and we both agreed, it had an acrimony as great as Aqua Regis.*

Hence no wonder that so many are afflicted in the Plague with violent vomitings, since their stomachs are continually irritated to this expulsion by a poison so exceedingly sharp. No wonder if from the sharpness of this venom agitating the humours, and urging the expulsive faculty, a diarrhoea is often occasion'd, attending the patient till the hour of his death. And no wonder, that from matter so beyond meas-

---

[g] Phil col. 2.17.

ure acrimonious, such piercing pains are felt in bubos, and such burnings in carbuncles.

[h]Another learned author is a great enemy to fear in the time of the Plague, and therefore above all things recommends a perfect composure and intrepidity of mind. He is of opinion, that nothing makes a man so obnoxious to this horrible distemper, as to be afraid of it. *Sancte testor,* says he, *me nullum bucusque vidisse agrum ex Peste, qui non a terrore eam contraxisset.* The reason he gives, is, because it hinders the spirits from exerting themselves, and renders them too languid to repel the infection. Nay, this passion, above all others, according to *Sanctorius*, hinders the perspiration, and by that means multiplys superfluous humours, which serve to increase the putrifaction. For these reasons he intreats and conjures all persons, whose fortune it is to be in the neighbourhood of the Plague, to chear up their drooping spirits, and as they tender their own safety, to inspire themselves with all the courage they possibly can, which will in good earnest be the securest sence against it.

He ascribes all the good suppos'd to be done by Amulets, to the tranquillity the mind gains, by the belief, that there is some very powerful virtue therein. Much the same opinion he has of Treacles, Vinegars, and other Alexipharmacks, whose principal success he conceives owing to the encouragement, with which they inspire the credulous persons that use them. He much approves of chewing such strong things as promote spitting, and hinder it from being swallow'd. He commends the firing of gun-powder, which purifys the air by the explosion, as well as corrects it by its nitrous and sulphureous quality. Bleeding, gentle purging, and other evacuations he allows of before infection, in order to lessen the humours. He applauds the anointing the temples, breast, and wrists, with the oyl of Scorpions, because of its repelling quality: but for that very reason is against anointing the bubos and carbuncles therewith, for fear of driving them in. He recommends nothing so earnestly as those cordials that fortify the heart, and chear the spirits, as being of all others

[h] D. A. Q Rivinus.
[i] De Statica Med. 217.

the most potent preservatives, not only against the Plague, but also against the Small-pox, and all other contagious distempers.

This learned Gentleman seems to have built his notions on the sentiments of *Van-Helmont,* who thought pusillanimity and dejection of mind very pernicious in these malignant cases. Accordingly he was wont to say, that by fortifying his heart with generous wine, and with more generous intrepidity despising all other antidotes, he was able to converse with infected persons in full security; while those who were affrighted and cast down, imbib'd the contagion at all their pores, there being either no spirits at all, or such as were too weak to oppose its entrance.

[k]A young Physician of our own, who would have been a great ornament of the profession, had he not precipitated his own fate, depended too superstitiously on the doctrine of magnanimity. This gentleman, that he might convince the world he was without fear, ran into the opposite extreme of presumption. For in the Plague that happen'd in *England* in the year 1645, he had the courage to visit all ages and degrees of people; and indeed did great service to those poor creatures, whom every other physician, and even their spiritual doctors abandon'd. At this intrepid and good natur'd rate he rush'd every day into the midst of infection, without catching it. Many hundreds receiv'd the benefit of his advice, and he gain'd not only much money from the rich, but many blessings from the poor, for his charitable attendance.

Thus far the call of his profession, as well as the sentiments of humanity, might justify his boldness; but he carry'd both these considerations too far at last, when he was sent for to *Wallingford Castle,* where the Sickness raged terribly. There he found an intimate friend dangerously ill; and having given him a sudorifick with his own hand, that he might raise the sweat the more kindly, he pull'd off his clothes and went to bed to him. To this rash act his friendship transported him, as well as a belief that charity made him invul-

[k] Dr. Sayer.

nerable: But he rose no more from that fatal bed; for taking the distemper immediately he dy'd in that friend's arms he so generously attempted to save, and he that had cur'd many, could not now cure himself.

Neither did this adventurous person wholly depend upon his courage, but the better to keep up that courage, he every morning swallow'd a large draught of generous wine, before he went to infected houses, and constantly repeated the same dose of preservation, after he had finish'd his circuit. With these preservatives he might, perhaps, have continu'd secure, had he approach'd no nearer to danger, than common prudence and self-preservation requir'd.

The famous Dr. *Willis* treats very largely and very learnedly of the Plague, and mentions sundry methods, both publick and private, of preventing it, most of which are very worthy to be put in practice. Nevertheless he seems somewhat superstitious in the belief of the extraordinary power of Amulets; not from the animating hopes they fill the patient withal, but from the effluvia and natural force of the ingredients themselves. His reasoning upon this subject is very philosophical, and rather amuses than convinces: tho' for the rest, his arguments seem to carry a great deal of solidity along with them. However I shall not mention them here, because they will naturally find a place in the Catalogue of Preservatives, with which I shall present the reader by and by: neither shall I blush to own, that I borrow several of them from this experienc'd and celebrated Author, who has deserv'd so well of mankind.

The Physician distinguish'd not only for his learning and diligence, but also for his uncommon sincerity, [1]Dr. *Sydenham,* is very circumstantial and exact in describing the Plague, with its progress, symptoms, and cure; but says hardly anything of the ways of preventing this great evil. He seems rather inclin'd to suspect the efficacy of some of them, if we may judge by the manner wherein he expresses himself upon that head. *As to preservation,* says he, *I know the use of hot antidotes is every where commended, but with*

[1] Obs. Med. 89.

what success has not been yet made out. Indeed it is very probable, that wine drank too freely, and other strong preservatives taken daily at set hours, have hurry'd many into this disease, who might not otherwise have had it. But how great deference soever may be due to this gentleman's opinion, yet 'tis worth observing, that he is after all not so much against the antidote, as against the excess and abuse of it. This certainly all agree would be pernicious, by inflaming the blood and spirits, instead of invigorating them. The truth of it is, no remedy was ever yet found out, not Specificks themselves excepted, but might be very injurious, and even mortal, if taken indiscreetly, or in too great a quantity.

Indeed it would be a very uncomfortable discovery, to find out, that no precaution, no antidote were sufficient to guard us from this unmerciful destroyer. Alas, almost all our hopes lye in preventing a disease so very dangerous and difficult to cure. Its attacks are so sudden, and its progress so rapid, that the venom penetrates like lightning thro' all the passages of life, where it extinguishes our spirits, and curdles our blood into deadly mortifications. This it often surprizes us withal, before nature can have time to raise an ebullition to throw it off. But tho' it should come on more leisurely, and our blood have time to boil into a Feaver, in order to repel this dreadful adversary, yet still the odds will be unequal against us. For if at last our constitutions be not strong enough to drive out the fatal poison, there's but little room for tedious Art to lend her assistance. Because in the first place, this distemper happens, blessed be God, so very seldom in our parts of the world, that few of the faculty have had any experience in it themselves, but must be beholden to their books, and the dark accounts that strangers have given of it. These alas will prove very defective, when we call to mind that the [m]Plague is not altogether the same at one time, and at one place, that it is at another; but will differ according to the various causes from whence it proceeds, or the climate, or perhaps the season in

[m] Cardan de Subt. 134.

which it happens; and what has been found beneficial in one sort, will be hurtful in another.

Moreover by reason of the great mortality of this disease, very few Physicians will venture their precious persons very near those that are sick. For if a Doctor have not natural courage sufficient to look the Plague in the face, 'tis to be fear'd his fortitude will not be much assisted by Faith and Religion: and if the love of mammon can't lead him on to this dangerous charge, I doubt the love of mankind will hardly do it. But tho' some few of the faculty will run the risk of visiting their wretched patients on this occasion, yet that is so very seldom, with so much terror, and at so awful a distance, that 'tis hardly possible they should ever be acquainted with the distemper enough to do any great service. However, supposing the very best, that some worthy sons of *Apollo*, like Dr. *Sayer*, will out of good nature tend upon the sick both duly and faithfully; yet these will prove so very few, and the unhappy patients at the same time so numerous, that many, very many, especially of the poorer sort, must be totally neglected, and the rest but indifferently look'd after. Insomuch that except God be pleased to send them his all-powerful assistance, or unless nature be strong enough to do her own business, they must perish without remedy.

For these reasons, the greatest service, that in this can be done to mankind, is out of the opinions of the best authors, and from the experience of several countries, to collect such methods of preventing this cruel disease, as may be most powerful, by God's assistance, to preserve as many as possible from it. And if I can, by this well meaning essay, but prevent the perishing only of one simple human creature, I shall think my self very happy, and my labour well bestow'd.

But before I prescribe the most probable ways, of preserving private persons, from being infected, I hope it will not be thought improper for me, to hint at such publick precautions, as by the advice of the most experienced Authors, are fit for the Government to take, either when there is only an apparent danger of the Plague, or after 'tis actually begun.

1. In the first place, I would humbly recommend that a general Fast be appointed, to humble our selves, and deprecate the vengeance of an offended God, that his just indignation may be thereby stay'd, and his Pestilence not let loose upon us. Or if that be already broke out, that God may then be prevail'd upon to order the destroying Angel to sheath his dreadful sword, as he was formerly by the seasonable humiliation of [n]*David*, in the threshing floor of *Araunah*. I would also beg that virtue and divine worship might be encourag'd, and profaneness and immorality severely punish'd.

2. That all commerce and correspondence with infected places be forbid under the severest penalties; and that all ships and persons coming from countries suspected, be obliged to a strict Quarantine, without any favour of connivance.

3. That all filthiness promoting putrification be carefully removed from the streets and neighbourhood of the town; That Butchers shambles, Fishmongers, and Poulterers shops, be kept perfectly sweet, and a general cleanliness enjoyed amongst all sorts of people.

4. That the air may be purged, and the venemous particles thereof corrected by great and frequent fires in all parts of the town, at the publick charge. That sulphureous and strong scented things be also burnt in the streets in great quantities, particularly Pitch and Tar, and the stalks of Tobacco. To these I beg leave to add, the frequent firing the great guns round the *Tower*, as well as those in the *Park*, and on the other side of the Water.

5. That no provisions be suffer'd to be sold, or brought into the town, but such as are perfectly sound and wholsome, to be examin'd by Viewers to be sworn for that purpose. That on this occasion the poorest of the people be supply'd at a national expence, to prevent their feeding on tainted or unnatural things.

6. That in case the Plague be already begun, let the utmost caution be us'd to prevent its baleful progress, by

---

[n] 2 Sam. XXIV. 16.

separating those that are infected from the sound, and by causing the corps of the deceas'd to be interr'd very deep in the ground, as soon as may be after they are dead. And that Dogs, Cats, and other Animals, be kept from eating them, which help in some places to propagate the infection.

Thus having premis'd these publick and general rules, to be directed by the Government, I shall next proceed to recommend such other methods of prevention, as may, by the help of God, contribute greatly towards guarding of particular persons, from catching this deadly contagion, if they be duly and diligently observ'd.

1. The first and surest preservative of all will be, a most humble and sincere repentance of our sins, and an unfeigned amendment of life, that God may be thereby mov'd not to pour out the terrors of his fury upon us, nor involve us in the general calamity. When we have made this happy advance, we may hope with confidence for a blessing upon the prudent measures we shall afterwards take for our safety.

2. The next is an exact temperance, sobriety, and moderation in all our enjoyments, which will abate the vicious humours of the body, and make us less dispos'd to receive the sickness; and tho' it should be our fortune to catch the infection, yet our spirits will be more vigorous to encounter and repel it.

3. We must be careful to avoid all violent exercise that may exhaust our spirits and set open our pores, thro' which the subtile venom will find a passage into our bodies. For the same discreet reason, it will be necessary to abstain from immoderate Venery, which renders the pores more lax and spungy, and the spirits more languid.

4. We should do our utmost to be of good courage, and next the Plague itself, avoid being afraid of it. We should keep our spirits chearful and erect, and suffer no fanciful apprehensions to bow down our hearts. A terrify'd and dejected mind will dispose us most unaccountably to suck in the very distemper we are afraid of. But while we are contending with these unmanly fears, we ought cautiously to avoid rushing either thru' vanity or presumption, into the opposite extream of temerity; lest, like Dr. *Sayer*, we pro-

voke our fate, and draw down our own destruction by violence upon our heads.

5. It may be very prudent to open a vein for those who are of a full and florid habit; for by this relief, the blood having a larger field to move in, the circulation may be perform'd with more freedom; and consequently the blood be less liable to infection and coagulation.

6. For such as have been accustomed to excesses, a gentle purge, or a vomit now and then, may be very proper, to remove part of the excrementitious matter, and lessen the gross humours. The best purgative I can recommend for this purpose, is, an infusion of Tobacco in strong Wine, with which anoint the lower part of your bellies; and if you would have the same infusion work by way of emetick, you may then anoint the pit of your stomach with it, till it gives you three or four vomits.

7. By way of alexipharmack, we may twice or thrice every day, when we find our spirits most depress'd, take a moderate glass of Canary, or Palm-wine, in which Virginian Snake-root has been infus'd so long as to make it agreeably bitter. This will have a happy effect, in giving vigour to our spirits to resist the poison and motion of the blood, the better to preserve it from coagulation.

8. As a most necessary and effectual preservative, I earnestly recommend an issue to be made on each side of the groin, which will plentifully drain away the vicious humours; and in case any taint of the Pestilence should find admittance, it will most naturally and safely be cast out at these two common shores.

9. To correct the air, and dissipate the infection, 'twill be of great benefit to make large fires in all the rooms which we most frequent, especially in our bed-chambers, where the fire should be never suffer'd to go out. Because in our sleep, when the pores are most open, the Contagion will meet with the least resistance. And if it might not look a little too frantick, 'twould be very right for us to fire several guns in a day out at our doors and windows, and several pistols in our rooms, carefully confining the smoak, which contains

both a nitre and sulphur, very proper to purge away the pestilential vapour.

10. Instead of all other amulets, and preferable to them all, we shall find a singular virtue against the Plague in fresh, strong, and quick-scented Tobacco. The sprightly effluvia sent forth from this vegetable, after it is rightly cur'd, are by nature peculiarly adapted to encounter and dissipate the pestilential taint, beyond all the antidotes that have been yet discover'd. 'Tis hard to say in what secret manner it performs this powerful operation, but the solution given by Dr. *Willis* and others, of the virtue of those amulets that are made of poisonous things may be apply'd to this case; for Tobacco being itself a poison, the effluvia flowing from it, do, by a similitude of parts, gather to them the little bodies of the pestilential taint, and intirely correct them.

Now that Tobacco is truly a poison, may be prov'd by many experiments. The chymical oyl of it will kill all animals, from a Louse up to an Elephant. The very smoak of it will both purge and vomit; and 'tis so very penetrating, that the infusion will do the same thing, if outwardly apply'd to the stomach and navel. However, like some other poisons, if it be rightly us'd, Tobacco is excellently good in many cases.

Experience teaches us that it will not only heal from fresh wounds of every sort in a little time, [o]but proper preparations of it will likewise cure all kinds of ulcers and old sores in every part of the body. It has been found a specifick in the Itch, and Leprosy, and almost all the distempers of the skin. If we may credit [p]*Julius Palmarius* too, it will cleanse and heal up venereal ulcers with wonderful success; as also the scrophulous sores of the Evil. It will asswage the pain of any part that has been stung with a Nettle, Wasp, or Hornet; and if it be apply'd upon the spot, 'twill cure the bite of a Scorpion, Viper, or mad Dog. In *America* the *Charibbee Indians* constantly apply'd it with success to wounds made with envenom'd Arrows and Darts,

---

[o] Everar. de herb. pan. 35.
[p] De Morb. Contagiosis.

for which purpose they never went to war without it, that they might have their remedy at hand. It is also an excellent vomit for a man, or any other animal that has swallow'd poison, of which the *Spaniards* have often experienc'd the success; by whom also cancers in the breast have been often cur'd with a balsam made of Tobacco.

These are all instances that Tobacco is a powerful resister of poison in every degree: But to bring it still nearer our subject, I have been credibly inform'd, that in the Plague which happen'd about five years ago in the northern parts of *Europe*, nothing was found so effectual in easing the pain of pestilential carbuncles and buboes, and also in curing them, as the juice or powder of this powerful plant.

I think I may with the more confidence extol the singular virtue of Tobacco, in checking the contagion of the Plague, because it has been said by men of observation and integrity, who liv'd in those days, that in the great Plague of 1665, the houses of Tobacco Merchants and Tobacconists, who dealt in large quantities of Tobacco, did wonderfully escape the infection. Nor are those Colonies in *America*, where they plant much Tobacco, ever visited with any distemper like the Pestilence; but if by accident it has happen'd at any time to be carry'd thither by shipping, 'tis presently extinguish'd by the effluvia of this great antidote. An instance of which, as I have been told, fell out in *Virginia*, in the year 1697, when Rear-Admiral Nevil arriv'd there, with a squadron of his Majesty's ships from some of the Islands. They carry'd a very contagious sickness along with them, very like the Plague, of which many of the officers and seamen dy'd, amongst whom was the Admiral himself. His corps, with several others, were carry'd ashore to be bury'd, and many of the sick were landed, in hopes that change of air and fresh provisions might recover them. Yet this disease, tho' very malignant, did not spread at all, but was soon check'd by the wholsome breath of their great *Staple* Tobacco.

It has also been remark'd, that since the use of Tobacco has been so universal in *Great Britain*, that all ranks of people either snuff, chew or smoak, the Plague has not paid us a visit half so often as formerly. For since that terrible one in the year 1665, our Land, blessed be God, has been perfectly free from it, which is now fifty-four years compleat; whereas in the Century preceding that, our ancestors had the Plague no less than five several times, which at a medium was once in twenty years. This is evident from the following Scheme, shewing that this fatal sickness in *England*

	1563		1625
In the years	1594	and also in the years	1645
	1602		1665

Now to what other causes can we reasonably ascribe our escaping this calamity so much longer than we us'd to do? I fear it is not owing to our virtue, which seems by no means to be more conspicuous than that of our ancestors. Nor can it fairly be imputed to our prudence, because no nation, that is not Mahometan, can possibly be more careless. We suffer ships from *Turky*, and from *Alexandria* in *Ægypt,* where the Plague is always more or less, to land their goods and their men without the ceremony of riding Quarantine. We hazard, by this indiscreet proceeding, the health of our people for the benefit of the merchant, which is carrying our notions of trade a little too far. Neither has our cleanliness procur'd us this blessed security, for there never was so little care taken of our Streets, our Night Carts, and Common-shores, as of late years. Nay cleanliness is tax'd by the duty upon soap, and filthiness seems establish'd by a law.

All these matters consider'd, I must own my self at a loss how to account for our having been so long free from infection, unless it be because a vastly greater quantity of Tobacco has of late years been consum'd among us. All degrees of people, the rich as well as the poor, the women as well as the men, do some way or other promote this consumption. Vast magazines of this antidote are distributed into every street, and the Capnometricians of *Crane Court* have computed, that about the ninety-third part of the smoak that covers this great City, must certainly be the smoak of Tobacco. This it is that in probability purges our air, and corrects those noisom damps, that might otherwise beget contagious diseases amongst us. Of this I am the more firmly persuaded for this further reason, because *Great Britain* and *Holland*, which are the two countries in *Europe* that use most Tobacco, have both of them been longest free from the Plague, notwithstanding their commerce with infected places has been greater and at the same time, their precautions much less than of any other nation.

Upon all these considerations I am humbly of opinion, that when there is any danger of a pestilence, we can't more effectually consult our own preservation, than by providing ourselves with a reasonable quantity of fresh, strong scented Tobacco. We shou'd wear it about our clothes, and about our coaches. We should hang bundles of it round our beds, and in the apartments wherein we most converse. If we have an aversion to smoaking, it would be very prudent to burn some leaves of Tobacco in our dining rooms, lest we swallow the infection with our meat. It will also be very useful to take snuff plentifully made of the pure leaf, to secure the passages to our brain. Nor must those only be guarded, but the pass to our stomachs should be also safely defended, by chewing this great *Antipoison* very frequently. This will wonderfully resist the Contagion, and hinder it from descending with our spittle into our stomachs, thro' which lies the high road into our blood. In short, we should, both abroad and at home, by night as well as by day, alone and in company, take care to have our sovereign antidote very near us, an antidote which seems design'd by providence as the strongest natural preservative against this great destroyer.

If these precautions be carefully put in practice, there will be nothing wanting, but humbly to supplicate the divine goodness to send a blessing upon such endeavours for our safety. For in this case, without the assistance of the Almighty, vain alas is the help of man, and all humane knowledge is wretched folly. Let us therefore cast ourselves before his throne, sadly confessing our sins, and deprecating his just vengeance. Let us in the first place intercede for our dear Country, intreating his tender mercy to save those that are already sick, and preserve those that are well from the infection. Then let us, in the spirit of meekness and contrition, pray for ourselves and our families, that it may please God to exempt us from the common Calamity; by no means imputing it to our righteousness that we have thus long escap'd, but steadily believing that unless we amend our lives we are reserv'd for a greater destruction. If we behave ourselves in this lowly and christian manner, we have reason to hope that God will please to be intreated to direct us in the choice of those *Antidotes* that are best, and likewise give them strength and energy to operate vigorously for our preservation.

F I N I S.

APPENDIX IV

The Female Creed (1725?)

The Female Creed

The text of this humorous satire by Byrd is taken from Volume IX of a series of notebooks containing nineteenth-century copies of Byrd's letters and notes (Brock 188), owned by the Huntington Library and printed by their permission. The content, with the use of many of the same subjects and suggestive names used by Byrd in his notebooks in the University of North Carolina (which are in Byrd's handwriting), argue his authorship. It is further attested by the mutilated page of contents in the so-called "Westover Manuscripts," where the first syllable of "Female" has been obliterated by discoloration.[1] The text is here printed as found, without attempt to correct obvious copyist's errors.

Since "the ingenious Jack Sheppard" mentioned (p. 454) was hanged at Tyburn in November, 1724, Byrd clearly wrote this satire after that date. Internal evidence indicates that it was composed before his return to Virginia in 1726. It seems thus to be the last of his known writings in this first period of his literary activity, spanning about the first quarter of the eighteenth century and concerned almost exclusively with the English social scene and characters.

---

[1]The entry "[. . .]male Creed" precedes the entry "History of the Line" in the table of contents of the Westover Manuscripts though the text of this satire is not now included in the bound volume of the MS, now owned by descendants of Byrd. There is a microfilm copy in part including the History of the Line, the Journey to the Land of Eden, and A Progress to the Mines, in the Historical Society of Pennsylvania. The Female Creed was not in the Westover Manuscripts when the volume was described and printed in 1866. See *The History of the Dividing Line and other Tracts from the Papers of William Byrd, of Westover, in Virginia, Esquire*, ed. Thomas H. Wynne (2 vols.; Richmond, 1866), I, xvi-xix.

THE FEMALE CREED.

1. I believe as all good Catholicks ought to do, in Spirits, Demons and Hobgoblins, that like the Prisoners in New-Gate, they are let out of their Hole anights, and suffer'd to play their Pranks at large in the World. That they appear for the most part to Women and children, their Faith and Imagination being exceeding Strong. I believe that these Spectres with their Horns and cloven feet, and with the Hurly-burly they make in the Dead of night, unluckily scare both the maid and her mistress into a Diabetis. Hence it comes to pass that so many Females in all countrys can scarce hold their precious water, haveing been terrify'd in the Nursery with Bul-beggars[1] and Apparitions. This is the case of the unfortunate Dripabunda, who when She fancy'd She saw the Ghost of her deceast Husband, dy'd away for fear the good man was come to life again. From that fatal moment she lost her Retentive faculty, beyond the Relief of Turpentine Pills and Bristol-water, nor can even Dr. Friend,[2] or Apollo himself intirely stop the Leak, but stil whenever she laughs beyond a Simper or a Broad Smile, the liveing Sal-almoniac flows from her. I believe most commonly Spirits delight to haunt old rambleing Houses in the Country, because all sorts of Devils have a passion for Solitude & irregularity. nor do they ever fail to walk in ancient Abbys and Nunnerys, because of the Impurity that was formerly committed therein. In short I believe that all Ghosts hurry back to their dark abode a little before day, because they cant stand the Purity of morning air, Besides every body knows they detest the crowing of a Cock worse than the prayers of a Doctor of

---

[1]Bul is an obsolete word meaning falsehood.

[2]John Freind (1675-1728), eminent physician, classical scholar and politician, played an important role in the medical annals of London and was the author of the *History of Physic.* He wrote two books in defence of the Earl of Peterborough's campaigns in Spain, having accompanied him as physician to the English forces (*Dict. Nat. Biog.*).

Divinity, because it brought St. Peter to the bitter Tears of Repentance.

2. I believe in Fairy, Powks[1] and Robin-good-fellows that they are the diminitive Souls of Dwarfs and Pigmys, full of agility, and like all Dergins[2] exceeding cholerick. That in the days of yore, before the Ladys kept bad hours and every honest man in the Parish was snoaring by the side of his own Wife before nine at night, these dapper Sprights usd to trip it nimbly o're the Green every moonshiny-night, that their movement was as gracefull as their dandy Stature wou'd permit, and withall so very light and alert, that the tender Spires of Grass hardly bent under their feet. I believe these Elfs to shew their love of Cleanliness, wou'd pinch a dirty Slut every night, til her Haunches were as black as a Gammon of Bacon, so that if Drabella or Fustimina had liv'd in those cleanly days, their nether Parts had been nippt to a Jelly. I believe whenever these Whipper-snappers met with a Wench that was gimm and tydy, who had washt her feet, sweppt her house and Scow'rd her Trenchers white, they constantly slid a Silver Penny into her Shoe, to reward her neatness. Did not the nocturnal Revels of our Isle drive away to distant climes these Encouragers of cleanliness, they wou'd surely make Nicena a great Fortune, by dropping into her little Slipper every Night a Five-pound-Piece instead of a Penny, owning by such unusual Generosity, that she is the neatest sweetest creature in the Universe, and capable of pleasing every one of our senses.

3. I believe in Witches, magicians and Sorcerers, that they enter into articles with old Belsebub, which they confirm either by writeing their names, or setting their marks in their own Blood. That by vertue of this contract, they for a while make the poor Devil fetch and carry, or jump over a Stick, as obsequiously as any Scots

[1]Pouk, obsolete form of Puck.

[2]Durgan, or Durgen, in dialect, signifying an undersized person or animal; a dwarf.

member of Parliament, whenever they're pleas'd to wave their Wand or mutter over a few necromantick words. I believe that every Hag, after listing herself in this dark Society, is furnisht with an Imp, which she suckles at a Tet under her left arm. That these small Familiars run on Errands to Lapland, and the High-lands of Scotland, to fetch the Gizzards of solon-Geese, Toads brains and such like lore for Enchantment. I believe that a Crone, who before cou'd hardly crawle upon crutches, can now ride full speed thro' the air on a Broomstick, or Sail over the wide ocean in an Egg-shell as far as New England, to bewitch the saints of that Province.

Indeed I believe that no Conjurour of any kind was ever produced in Ireland because there are no Spiders, Toads or other Poisons in that Kingdome to be mischievous withall. There's a certain ancient Gentlewoman known amongst her neighbours by the name of Mrs. Scare-crow, who when she owes any one a Spite, is sure to overtake them with her Ressentment. Mr. Justice Puzzle haveing threaten'd to indite her Ladyship at the next assises, came off but scurvily, for the very first dark night she whipp't a Kirb into His worships wide mouth and rode him most unmercifully over Hedge and Ditch, til his cloaths were torn to Tatters and his Flesh claw'd off his Bones. and some time after, Miss Giggle makeing merry at the antiquity of her Dress, found her dear person in a most deplorable plight all next day. For the Sorceress sticking a worsted-needle in the Buttocks of an Image, form'd under a proper Constellation, poor Miss was sorely pained in the same noble part for 13 hours together. I believe these Enchantresses can make innocent children vomit up pins by the Dozen, and can roast Piggs by Proxy without bringing them within two Furlongs of the Fire. I believe these Bel-dames can make a Love-powder so very strong, that the proudest Female in Great Britain, even madam Lofty herself, wou'd be humble enough to marry her Foot-man, if she swallow'd but half a scruple of it before she made water in a morning. But what is stranger stil, they know how to tye a magical knot in a Black-ruban and then fix it on a Hat with so irresistable a grace, that no young Woman can forbear running into the arms of him that wears it. They can also plate a young Fellow's forehead over with a Composition as hard as corinthian Brass, that carrys such a charm along with it, that whatever favour he intreats after that, either of a Lady, or a minister of State, tis instantly granted. I believe after all, that Witchcraft thrives abundantly best in cold Climates, such as Lapland, Norway and north Britain, to which refreshing places we may suppose Satan makes as frequent Tripps as he can to cool himself after sweltering in his own Dominions. I must believe too, that Witches receive great power from the Prince of the air, and can sell winds to lewd Sailors to hasten them home to their Harlots and Land ladys, and tho' they often raise storms and Hurricanes ashoar, to blow down churches, and untile Parsonage-houses, yet they raise as few as feassible at sea, for fear of frighting seamen from the oaths and Imprecations, with which they insult Providence in fair weather, to their Prayers.

4. I believe in astrologers, coffee-casters, and Fortune-tellers of every denomination, whether they profess to read the Ladys destiny in their faces, in their palms, or like those of China in their fair posteriors. I believe according as the Planets and Fixt stars happen to be placed in the sky at the Instant of our birth, they forebode what complexion we shall be of, and what is to betide us every year of our lives. I believe my Lady Pilfer cou'd by no means help being light-finger'd, and lifting Fans and china-cups, every time she went to Mother Tomb's, because that Knave Mercury was lord of her ascendant, nor can Furistante well avoid being a vixen and a Termagant, yea and exceeding loud in her Curtain lectures, because she happen'd to be born under Mars, which all the sons of art know to be a boistrous Planet, and since that wanton Huzzy Venus presided at the nativity of poor Miss Frail, how cruel are the Prudes, for allowing no Quarter to that unfortunate

Damsel, because she happen'd to prove more fruitfull than themselves. I believe tho' the Stars hold their heads so high they some times condescend to act the low part of Jonathan Wild,[1] and help People to their gold snuff boxes and Silver Spoons again, that like the Maiden Sisters in St. James' street they kindly bring the Sexes together, and get many a hearty curse for their pains. I firmly believe that casting of Coffee Grounds is a very thriving branch of the Black Art and by the grotesque Figures drawn by Some invisible Painter in the cup, shews the Fortune of the caster pretty plain, but not quite so evidently as the believeing it shews his Folly. I believe from my heart that the Pretender to the crowne of Great Britain has no other hopes of ever putting it on his head, but what the Mistresses of this art inspire him with. I believe if a Bull or a Goat appear in a mans cup, he must needs be a Whore-master, tho' he be a Lord Chancellor or an Arch-Bishop, and if a Bear or a Munky be seen in a Ladys she'll need a vast deal of Grace to keep her honest. If an ass or an owl chance to be there, the happy caster will have a fair Hit to be an alderman, but if the Beast's ears appear longer, or the Bird's countenance graver than ordinary, there are hopes he may come to be a Judge or at lowest a Sergeant at Law. If a ravening wolfe be in the cup, the man may rise in the navy and grow to be a Captain of a man of War, or if he be a Land officer, and good for nothing else, he may live to be a Governour in His Majesty's Plantations.[2] A Dutch mastiff or a Parrot are ill omens

[1]Jonathan Wild (1682?-1725), who posed as an honest merchant and reformer in London but was really a receiver of stolen goods, was hanged at Tyburn, May 24, 1725. He became the hero of many chapbooks (*Dict. Nat. Biog.*; Howard Pyle, "Chapbook Heroes," *Harper's Magazine*, LXXXI, 123-38).

[2]A satirical allusion either to Spotswood (see above, p. xxi), who had served in the English army, rising in rank from ensign to lieutenant colonel, before he was sent to Virginia as Lieut. Governor, deputy to the Earl of Orkney from 1710 to 1722, or to Spotswood's successor, Hugh Drysdale, the incumbent Lieutenant Governor, who was an English major before he was appointed to succeed Spotswood in Virginia (Leonidas Dodson, *Alexander Spotswood* [Philadelphia, 1932], pp. 5, 270; *Va. Hist. Port.*). Byrd would gladly have been in the place of either of these men as the head of the government in Virginia.

in a woman's cup and foretell she'll continue long a pure Virgin and grow as censorious and discreet as Mademoiselle Sky who is so vigorous a Prude she wont suffer a male creature in her house that has not been serv'd like Seresini.[1]

5. I believe as the Turks do, that every man carrys his Fate in his Forehead like 'Squire Limber & has a fair mapp drawn upon his hand of all his adventures in this World. Likewise that Dame Nature has printed on our Rear as in a Almanack what must be-tide us every day in the year. I believe in my conscience we have not a mole markt on our fair skins, but in some measure prognosticates our future Fortune. For example a mole under Madam Tosses[2] left foot betoken'd she wou'd travel much tho' not farther than her vanity and affectation wou'd follow her. A mole under the ingenious Jack Shepherd's[3] left Ear portended he'd come at last, where

[1]Doubtless intended for Senesino, the most famous of the Italian sopranists who were popular in England in this period. He appeared in England first in 1720, having been brought over by Händel. It was Senesino whom the Earl of Peterborough so severely chastised in 1723 at Bath for his affront to Anastasia Robinson, later Peterborough's wife (see letter of John Gay to Swift, Swift's *Works*, XVI, 280; H. S. Hughes, *The Gentle Hertford*, pp. 43, 86, 87; William Stebbing, *Peterborough* [London, 1890], pp. 199-201; article on Senesino in Grove's *Dict. of Music & Musicians*).

[2]A probable reference to Madame Catherine Tofts who sang in opera in London with Nicolini and charmed audiences with the beauty of her voice and the grace of her form though she was ignorant of Italian and chanted her recitatives as Nicolini sang in Italian. She was much discussed in the town because of her foibles and disputes at the opera with her manager. She married Joseph Smith, who went to Venice as consul, and she lived there (in seclusion and mentally unbalanced) until her death. Lady Wentworth gives in her letters the following picture of her life in London: "Mrs. Taufs [*sic*] was on Sunday last at the Duke of Somerset's, where there were about thirty gentlemen, and every kiss was one guinea: some took three, others four, others five at that rate, but none less than one." (Grove's *Dict. of Music*).

The following lines "On Mrs. Tofts" have been generally attributed to Pope:

> So bright is thy beauty, so charming thy song,
> As had drawn both the beasts and their Orpheus along:
> But such is thy av'rice, and such is thy pride,
> That the beasts must have starv'd, and the poet have died."
>
> (Swift's *Works*, XXIV, 40).

[3]John Sheppard (1702-1724), noted robber and criminal who made repeated miraculous escapes from London prisons by his own cunning and audacity, was finally hanged at Tyburn on Nov. 16, 1724, before an audience estimated at 200,000 people. His exploits made him the lucrative hero of the chapmen (*Dict. Nat. Biog.*; Pyle, "Chapbook Heroes").

most Ministers of state deserve to come, to the Gallows. But alas if a Female chance to be markt on either Breast like Miss Tinder or upon either Buttock, like the widdow Touchwood, tis odds but she'll be troubled with a Devil, which nothing but Fasting and Prayer will be able to cast out. I believe in Dogs, Ravens, and Screech-owls, that of all animals they'r the most knowing in Futurity. They can see Death hovering o're a Family as plain as Hogs see the Wind, or maids of Honour Tarts when they burn them. I steadfastly believe when a Curr howls dismally about 2 in the morning that all those who are so unhappy as to hear him will surely dye, tho' the precise time when this is to happen, is not altogether so certain. For tho' the Beast can foretell at least as well as any of the modern Prophets, yet 'tis his misfortune to be but moderately read in Chronology. Indeed they often foretell their own fate to a day, because this prophetick animal howles most when he's near being famisht. Poor Miss Triffle once, when she cou'd not lay her Eyes together for thinking of the Fellows, heard the Turn-spit howle, and gave herself over: however Death passt her by for that time, and compounded for her Flying-Squirrel, so I believe when a Raven flys over any Person's head and croaks precisely 3 times he must infallibly be near his End, especially if he happen to be upon Tiburn Road in a Cart or a Hurdle. The sagacious Bird smells carrion as fragrant as if Kentini was near and with that hoarse note invites his Friends to partake of the Banquet. But in truth this omen is never so infallible as when a Flight of Ravens croaks over an Army drawn up in order of Battle, and just going to engage. Fine Colonel Bounce was really Shockt at it a little before our victory at Ramilies,[1] but attacking the enimy with his usual caution he only fell from his horse before he came within Cannon-shot and escaped. But above all I sincerely believe when the dire Screech owl skreams aloud and flutters about the window of a sick Patient

[1]May 23, 1706.

that Glysterio[1] hath the care of, that the poor soule is not far from his long home. Let him instantly make his Will and Set his House in order, the owl & the Doctor have said it, dye he must as certainly as if the undertaker had done him the civility of a visit.

6. I believe in Dreams, Visions and Impulses, by which Guardian Angels and friendly Demons impart timely notices to us of things to come. In the first place I believe that Dreams like the excessive modesty of Prudes or the overacted Grief of Widdows are to be taken by the contrarys. Just as when Lady Charlot Portly dreamt that an impudent Boar kitten ran up her coats, she was sure to snapp His Grace of Tumbleton and so gratify her dear ambition at the expence of all the tender Passions. So Seignior Tetato dreamt last summer at Tunbridge, that the great Dutch Woman[2] patted him on the Cheak with her Shoulder of Mutton hand, and the next morning the Queen of the Fairys frown'd upon him. However I must believe that those Dreams we have in a morning, when we lye Sprawling on our backs are abundantly the most Significant. It was in one of these morning-slumbers that the agreable Decora fancey'd she saw count Gimcrack rideing Bare-backt upon a colt which galloping up directly to her, cast his feeble Rider plumb into her lap. This dream was too plain to need a Daniel or a Joseph to interpret it. Both her merit and her Destiny conspir'd to make her a Countess, with the charming prospect too, of being soon a Douager. Thus the day had hardly dawned, when Majr. Bluster dreamt that the Devil, dwellt perpetually on his lips, took him up by the chin, with a Promise to shew him London, but disappointed him sore, and shew'd him Tiburn. I believe too, that now and then, when we fall into a Brown study, thinking on nothing or what is next to nothing, the Pleasures of the World, we are on a sudden snatcht up a days Journey towards the moon, we know not how or

[1]See character of Dr. Glysterio, above, p. 209.
[2]See above, p. 198.

which way, where see odd Sights and are let into unaccountable Secrets. Thus Gentelissa one cloudy morning, as she was museing & shakeing her left legg, out of humour she knew not why, & out of order she knew not where, fancy'd on a sudden she saw a smart Fellow in the Equipage of Mercury with Wings fixt to his head and his heels, who in a instant snatcht her up by the foot she was shakeing, and flew away with her to Kingsale.[1] From this vision t'was a plain case her merit was to be rewarded with a miracle, and she wou'd shortly marry both a wit and an Irishman. But Enthusiasts tell us we are most dispos'd to see visions when we are fasting and full of Wind, our souls being then most alert and aptest to ramble out of our Bodys. For this reason we are told the French Prophets us'd to f. . . t in their Raptures and vagarys after a most indecent manner. So the nuns of Drury lane and great Pulteney-street, when the Towne is empty, and tradeing dull, are terrifyd with the vision of Famine stareing them in the face which can betoken nothing better to the poor Jades, but down-right starving. So likewise our Friends the Poets, who sometimes make very slender meals, see the muses dance stark naked. This heavenly Sight inspires them with thoughts too Sublime for any who has meat in his belly, or mony in his Pocket. I believe when we are utterly undisturb'd with passion, sudden Impressions are made on our minds by some invisible power. So Scarrouel while she was a penniless Poets Wife, and consequently kept pretty sharp, had a strong Impulse she shou'd live to carry the Grand Monarch about in Leading-strings and Since the decease of that prodigious Woman, tis said her neice Violetta has had another, that she shall do the same thing by a monarch grander than he. Just so I remem-

[1]Kinsale, located on the southern coast of Ireland, is known in Irish history both for the battle that raged about it in 1601 when Charles Blount, Lord Mountjoy, succeeded in breaking the rebellion of Tyrone by defeating the allied Spanish and Irish, and for the landing there in 1689 of James II in his futile effort to regain his kingdom through the aid of Tyrconnel (Robert Dunlop, *Ireland from the Earliest Times* [1922], pp. 85, 123, 127). The Southwell and Percival families had been closely identified with the history of Kinsale.

ber Philo had an Impression not long ago, that Gloriana wou'd infallibly wed a man with a great nose in his face, and have into the bargain all the advantages, which according to the doctrine of Proportion, are promis'd by that comely Feature.

7. I believe in Death-watches in a wall & Winding-sheets that display themselves in a candle, that they are as certain Fore-runners of Fate, as a Dead warrant, or extream unction. Particularly I believe the Death watch to be a Warning of mortality, given by an Insect which runs before Death, just as they say the Jackal runs before the Lion, to find out his Prey, tho' Sometimes it joggs on before it at a very decent distance. Because you must know, just as many Ticks as the Party hears, so many years she has stil to live. Therefore if any curious Gentlewoman is minded to calculate her own Destiny with exactness, let her count how many of these deadly Sounds she hears. Tis a certain piece of History that Mademoiselle Frizzle was 26 years ago put into so mortal a Fright with one of these Deathwatches, that her very Heart-breakers, that lay upon her Toilet, turn'd as grey as a Gander, yet blessed be God she is stil alive, and strong enough to open her Self a passage to the King with her Elbows, every Drawing-room night let the Throng be never so great, and she may stil receive her pension, and carry that hideous Smile upon her face full 30 years longer, because the fatal Insect tickt 56 times. So a very curious Author affirms, that old Parr[1] in Queen Besses Reign, was scar'd into a Looseness with one of these fancifull Watches, yet he made a shift by eating Sage with his Bread and Butter, and fetching 3 loud Hemms every morning to out-live the omen better than an hundred years. Then I believe the winding-sheets that unfold themselves just beneath the flame of a

[1]Thomas Parr, known as "Old Parr," is said to have lived from 1483 to 1635 and the inscription on his tomb in Westminster Abbey listed the ten princes in whose reigns he is supposed to have lived. John Taylor's *Old, Old, Very Old Man*, a sixpenny pamphlet published in 1635, is the chief source of data on "Old Parr." (*Dict. Nat. Biog.*)

candle, are prodigiously ominous, and foretell the death of her in the company, who has the most Superstition, and wou'd make the devoutest Roman-catholick. But the comfort is, that the decease of that person is rarely very Sudden, because all, because all Southsayers agree, that so great a portion of her life, is yet to come, as there remains of the Candle stil to burn. Thus Her Grace of Dawdledon dicover'd one of these dismall Winding sheets soon after the Restoration, which Scar'd her so heartily that she left off gallantry and false Eybrows for 13 months together, yet to this good day she makes a shift to keep her Corps out of the Grave, and her impatient Grandson out of her Jointure. And the Reason's as plain as the Paint upon her Face, because the Bougie was but just light up, when she beheld this terrifying Spectacle. Indeed had this happen'd after twa's burnt down to the Socket, all the skil of Sr. Charles Scarborough[1] cou'd scarce have sav'd her. This alas was the hard case of the charming Vernelia, while she yet liv'd with her frugal mother just before she was wedded to Priaponi. This delightfull creature descry'd a Winding-sheet in an end of candle after it had been stuck upon a Save-all and to the Regret of mankind dy'd an odd death a few months after. Nor did the Tragedy end there, for the Husband, being made Sensible by the matrons that view'd her, how she came by her end, cut off the enormous cause and bury'd it in the same coffin with Her.

8. I believe that in the High-lands of Scotland, there's an unaccountable Race of Mortals, who have the gift of Second-Sight. These extraordinary Persons comeing into the World, with a Cawl over their Faces, are able to see Spirits as distinctly, as fond mothers see beautys in their own children, or Prudes Blemishes in their neighbours, which nobody else can find out. There's a certain enlighten'd Rabbi tells us, that Balaam's Ass was Second-

[1]Sir Charles Scarburgh, M. D. (1616-1694) was one of the original fellows of the Royal Society and physician to Charles II, James II and Queen Mary. He was also a distinguished mathematician and was fond of natural history (*Dict. Nat. Biog.*).

sighted, & by the help of that extraordinary gift descry'd the Angel in the Highway, when the old Conjurer that was mounted upon Her, cou'd see nothing of the matter, and if the truth were known, I fancy Madam Bundle is endow'd with this noble faculty, because she has ever and anon that frightfull Tweer with her Eyes us'd amongst the Second-Sighted Sisters, when they look for Ghosts, and departed Souls, you must know upon Such occasions, these Gentlewomen are forced to sharpen the Ball of their Eye, just as cats do, when their occupation requires them to see in the dark. Nay what is odder Stil, I verily believe these discerning Females have their Eyes form'd in such a manner, that they are not only able to see Spirits, but can also Spy Thoughts, just as they rise from the Heart, before they get up so high as the Tongue. This they can do more currantly amongst the Ladys, whose delightfull Bosomes are bare, and whose skins are exceeding clear, one of these Sybils told me t'other day in my Ear, that she discover'd thro' Blanchebella's alabaster Breast, a fierce conflict betwixt Prudence and Inclination, whether she shou'd smile on the agreable Colonel or not, but that Prudence, (a prodigious thing among the Fair) wou'd infallibly get the better at last. And tho' she were form'd for love, yet her charms alas like Gripon's Riches, are of no further use than to be gaz'd at. A thousand pitys by G...d! The same penetrating Matron told me that notwithstanding, Miss Olive's complexion be none of the most transparent, yet she cou'd discern Generosity, good nature, sincerity & a thousand other Fine Qualitys quite thro' it.

9. I believe the Itching of Sundry Parts about us, if dilligently attended to, will make notable discoverys of adventures to come. For example, I believe the itching of the nose forebodes plainly, that a woman will be saluted before she go's to bed by Tupeio, who carrys more powder on his Bagg & his thick Shoulders, than Brains in his head, or peradventure the Kiss may come from

some Booby Elder Brother, with whose education his Lady mother had been intrusted. I believe when a young Gentlewoman's Elbow itches, she will shortly steal out of bed from her Sister, like Miss Fondlefellow, & notwithstanding her pretended fear of Spirits, go in quest of a more Significant Bedfellow. I believe for certain if a Wenche's right Eye happens to itch, she'll be cross't in some darling inclination, that will make her weep bitterly. Either that formal old Fellow her Father is positive she shan't go to the Masquerade, or else her Stingy Husband, like Baron Slouch, will refuse to pay a Debt of honour, contracted by her ill fortune last season at the Bath. But were it her left Eye that itcht, matters will happen quite otherwise and she may expect to laugh til Tears of Joy flow from every part, and as it befell Miss Freak, bedew her very heals, nor might this perhaps be any great inconvenience to her, especially if she came from the other Side the Tweed where they say the Ladys never wash their Feet but only on the Eve of St. Andrews day. After this merry omen she'll either hear some clean Double-Entendre, that will tickle her lively Fancy to the quick, or else she may chance to see her discreet Maiden-aunt make a false step, and tumble heels over head, by which her venerable Rump may be unhappily expos'd. But in case a Ladys Backside shou'd itch, let her Summon all her Reason and muster up her whole stock of Patience because something will fall out very soon to provoke her Indignation. Either her Lover, like Squire Sneaksby, will come 2 tedious hours after his assignation, by which the Ducklins prepar'd for his entertainment will be roasted to a cinder, or else her old Servant Blunder will throw a Dish of Coffee & cream upon her cloaths the first day of putting them on, before they have been admir'd at the opera, or the Drawing Room. Or possibly her maid Dandriff may tell her maliciously, that truly madam Viper takes great libertys with Her Lad'ps Person, and particularly had said the night before in a Room full of company, that her Mother us'd to whipp her every Munday morning for not growing faster. Such Personal Reflections will gaul her to the Soul, because you must know, a true fine Lady is more heartily teez'd with Flouts upon her pretty Figure, than upon her Reputation.

10. I believe in Times and Seasons, and critical minutes, that some are strangely lucky and others unaccountably unfortunate. That tis the top of Female Prudence to distinguish nicely in this matter. Particularly I must needs believe, that Childermass-day never fails to be ill bodeing, and a true Believer will undertake nothing upon it, that is not of the last necessity. There's my Lady Poz who laughs at these Serious matters, wou'd venture on this woful day, against the advice of all her She-friends, to Send for the celebrated Dr. Lamb, to cut her Nails and her corns. But she had like to have paid dear for her obstinacy, for the operation gave her Such a gash on the little Toe, that she was forct to live a whole month upon water-gruel to keep it from a mortification. Recommend me to discreet Fartamira, who never pretends to wipe her Backside on Such a day as this, for fear of bedaubing her taper Fingers. I was acquainted with a wise Woman once, who always kept her bed on Childermass day,[1] believing her Self safe in that Snugg Situation, but that precaution fail'd her once very cruelly. For poor Mrs. Straddle, (the Gentlewoman's name) pearching with all her weight upon the Pot, the brittle Utensil flew to pieces, filling the Bed with water of high-perfume, and at the Same time makeing a Wound, which none but a female Surgeon cou'd have the honour to dress. I believe most unfeignedly that Wednsday and Fridays are fatal to all Enterprizes of Spirit, as many a bold Briton finds by monthly Experience. Neither are these only days of Execution, but which is as dreadfull to Protestant Stomachs, they are also days of Fasting. It will always be my opinion that the hapless Galloppante ows the unworthy treatment which she dayly and

---

[1]Childermas Day, or Innocents' Day, celebrated Dec. 28, in commemoration of the slaying of the children in Bethlehem by King Herod's order and considered an unlucky day. (See the *Book of Days,* ed. R. Chambers).

nightly receives from her Husband, to the folly of being marry'd on a Friday. She may hurry about as much as she pleases, to places of diversion, and talk to all the Pretty Fellows when she's there, yet the Dread of going home to her Brute at night, embitters all the Entertainment. Without all question too, that confident varlet Skips owes the miscarriage of his attack upon Wantonessa, to his being Such an Idiot as to undertake it on a Wednsday. Tis true the drawn sword, and the loaded Pistols, were terrible Weapons in the dead of night to a Fine Lady, yet they had not half the force the naked Lover wou'd have carry'd with him at a luckyer time. I believe too, that besides these stated days of ill omen, which all true Believers mark for unfortunate, there are likewise others that are occasionally so to particular Persons. These may certainly be perceiv'd by the lowness of the Pulse, or the sluggishness of the Spirits. When we get up in a morning our heads will feel too heavy for our shoulders and our Hearts too big for our Bosomes. In this lumpish condition when we offer to stir, we dragg our legs after us for all the world like poor Fluxini after the Grand Remede, and what is the strangest part of the story, even our Tongues loose all their female Fluency. It was upon one of these dark days, that the adventurous Elboina[1] lost that round summ at Mother Kemp's, which her fine Necklace and Earrings cou'd but half pay, the other half was discharged by a morgage upon her Honour, at such a Sullen time as this, tis impossible even for Miss Tidy, who dos every thing with a grace, to dress her head to her mind, either the plaits will lye eneaven or the Poke Stand quite ascue, and let her Maid be never so carefull, when she pins up her Gown, she'll unavoidably run a calker into her thrummy Breech. I ever thought Prudentia in the

[1]Probably a misreading by the copyist for Ebonia. See verses to

Ebonia with an Olive Skin
Tempers the Lustre of her Eyes,
Tho' dark without, she's bright within,
So clouds o'er cast the radiant skies.

Tunbrigalia (1719), pp. 14-5.

right, who to correct the infelicity of one of these gloomy days, is so wise as to get out of bed with the wrong-end foremost. Or if thro' inadvertency she neglects that, she takes Refuge in another expedient, and plants her little Foot in the midst of a wholesome Sr. Reverence. Thus by intrenching her Self up to the Chin in good luck, she is able to sustain the choque of Bad with the greater Security. I believe in my conscience, Some happy Persons as soon as they came into the world, had the advantage of being wrappt up in their mothers Smock. That auspicious circumstance alone, is sufficient to set them above the influence of malignant stars, and make every day happy. They do nothing but cut capers, and humm tunes out of the last opera, let the atmosphere be never so heavy, while their less fortunate acquaintance sit in dolefull dumps, jogging along in the Devils trot, and half in the mind to hang themselves up in their own garters. To be sure 'twas such lucky mortals as these, that were the Gainers in the South-sea, that mystery of Iniquity which lifted so many Miscreants into gawdy Equipages, who wou'd ride more becomeing in a Cart, and condemn'd so many hapless Damsels to perpetuall virginity. I believe there's such a happy point of time as a Critical minute, when the most unpromiseing Enterprizes will prosper. This is so very plain a case, that I'm confident if the agreable Dulcimira were to be vigorously attackt in one of these fatal moments, that neither her good understanding, nor her cold constitution wou'd guard her from Surrendering at discretion. So very frail is the strongest female Resolution, at a time when all the humours of the Body flow to the weakest part, and all the passions of the Soul are ripen'd into Love. I believe that the prime Season for Critical minutes, is the merry month of May, because then the Sap rises in the animal as briskly as in the vegetable World. The Hibernian Corporation marrys off more modest Fellows of their nation in this loveing month, than in all the year besides. Against that time those who are destin'd to make their fortunes by the Fair, are taken out of the

Plumping-houses, where by proper operations, and a nourishing Dyet, they are made Fresh & well likeing. After their Persons have by this Regimen gain'd all the Charms they can, the next step is to ransack the Fripperys of Long-lane and Monmouth street for Finery at the best hand, to render them stil more lovely in the Ladys Eyes, and then to make them compleatly irresistable, a Second-hand Chariot is vampt up for these Sons of Fortune, in which they're turn'd loose upon the Sex with this thriveing motto, Loose nothing for want of asking.

11. I believe firmly that our good or bad Fortune may be clearly collocted from the Situation of a Pin upon the Floor. If the head of the pin happen to lye towards a Female, all that she takes in hand that day will certainly prosper. Miss Gimm upon the credit of this good omen, will be sure to give pain before she sleeps, and tho' she put on nothing but the Dowd she lay in, she may depend upon makeing some considerable conquest, so if dear Mademoiselle Alpue will venture her Quarterage that night at my Lady Straffords,[1] she may count upon breaking the Bank and puting Seignor Sonecar, who keeps it, into the vapours. But then I wou'd advise her as a Friend to rely on the Pins head, much rather than her own, and I can assure Miss Longfort, if she can but snatch a Pin off the floor, lying with the head towards her, on a Masquerade day, let her not fail to go thither, tho' she be forct to get out of the Window, or over the Wall, when her good mother is asleep. She may depend upon being hugg'd to her hearts content, by an impudent Rogue of a Runing Footman, who will satisfye all her curiosity, and teach her to make the most of that edifying Diversion. But then alas if the fatal Point of the Pin lye towards a poor Girle, every thing that day will

[1]Thomas Wentworth, Baron Raby and 3d Earl of Strafford (1672-1739) married in 1711 Anne, only daughter and heiress of Sir Henry Johnson, Bradenham, Bucks, who, according to Swift, brought to Lord Strafford a fortune of £60,000 besides the rest of the estate at her father's death. (*Dict. Nat. Biog.*; *The Wentworth Papers* (*1705-1739*); Swift, *Journal to Stella*, Sept. 3, 1711).

fall out wrong, she cannot stoop but she'l squeeze out a f. . . t, or laugh but she'll be-piss her self. The tragical adventure of Madam Pittipat will justify this sad Truth, and convince the stubbornest Infidel. This poor Lady had drest herself as fine as hands cou'd make her, intending to be introduced that night at the Dutchess of Norfolks.[1] But spying a huge Brass pin on her dressing Room floor, pointing directly towards her, her heart Sunk in a instant, & she tore off all her ornaments in a tenth part of the time she had employed in putting them on. And as soon as her surprise wou'd let her Speak, go down this moment, said she to her maid Bodkin, and charge the Porter to let in no creature, for I won't be at home. No sooner were these fatal orders given, but the dear man She desir'd the most in the world to see, was turn'd away from the door. This put her into Such a Rage that she threw her comb-Frey with all its Furniture at Bodkins head, and at the same time wisht the innocent Porter in Purgatory for denying her. The Porter interpreted this Hurricane to be a Countermanding of her first orders, and therefore about an hour after, let in my Lady Larrum who was in mourning for the Second Husband she had fairly talkt to death. Her Ladyship ran nimbly up stairs, to gain the more time for Conversation, and surpriz'd the unfortunate Madam Pitapat dirty and undrest, with no more light in the Room than what the Fire and her Eyes afforded. What confusion to her Self, what Excuses to her Visitor, and what curses to that villian of a Porter, in whose brawny Posteriors the fatal Pin was wisht a thousand times. What a chain of ill-luck was here, one misfortune treading, like Count Marino's Duns, upon the heals of one another. Sure the Tail of a Blazeing Star cou'd not not [*sic*] easily forebode more mischief, than the Tail of this horrid Pin.

---

[1]Thomas, 8th Duke of Norfolk (1683-1732), married in 1709 Mary Maria Winifred Francisca, daughter and sole heir of Sir Nicholas Sherburne, Bart. On his death she married in 1733 Peregrine Widdrington (Burke, *Peerage*). The Duchess of Norfolk moved in the social circle of Edward Southwell and the Earl of Egmont, Byrd's close friends in London (Hist. MSS Comm., *Egmont Diary*).

But I have observed ever Since Nurse Canturbury put it into my head, that this Prognostick never fails, and I shall always pity those Wretches who discover'd a Pin in this mischeivous aspect. I am very sure every step they take that day will be a stumble, and every Relief of the Colick will prove a near Relation of alderman Parsons.[1]

12. I believe that all odd numbers are lucky except the fatal number of 13. Number one is for many reasons esteem'd fortunate, particularly because there is but one Sun in the firmament, to light us out of our beds about noon, and shew us our own dear Faces at our Toilet for 2 hours after. There is likewise no more than one Heart in our fair Bosomes, and but one darling object to fill and inflame that heart. Besides that happy Composition of man and wife, we are told, are no more than one Flesh, and happier stil it wou'l be, if they were also but one mind. Fine Mrs Lurewell Understands the power of this lucky number, and knows she shall give most pain when she wears but one Patch. For this reason she never Sticks on more on a Sunday morning when she gos to church, tho' she have never so many Pimples to conceal. once she put on 2, and not one Fellow lookt upon her dureing the whole Service, except the Parson, while his Flock was engaged about the last Stave of the Psalm. General Swagger is as Scrupulous in his swearing; he believes it very unlucky to swear more than one oath in a minute, which he observes religiously enough while he's fasting and in cold blood, but if a Dun happen to ruffle his temper, or after he has fill'd his Belly, he is too apt to exceed that moderate Rule: tho' after such excess some misfortune or other commonly betides him. Either his plaintiff Spouse will powt, because she has not so smart an Equipage as Mrs. Gawdy, who is no more than a Simple Colonels Lady,

---

[1]Humphrey Parsons (1676?-1741), twice lord mayor of London, was a brewer in Aldgate. He especially enjoyed the favor of Louis XV and had the chief export trade in beer to France, free from import duty. He was elected alderman of Portsoken in March, 1721 (*Dict. Nat. Biog.*).

or else he'll have an ill run at the Groom Porters, for which his tatterd Regiment must suffer in its cloathing.

13. Three likewise ought to be a very fortunate number, because there are precisely so many Graces, and so many meals a day in all Christian countrys. Count Quaff has a profound veneration for this number, and devoutly takes off his 3 Bottles every night in the year. While he keeps within these modest Bounds, he only tells harmless Storys over and over again, and talks of Religion. But if either good wine or good company debauch him farther, his conversation flattens in Bawdy, and he is sure to have a twinge in his Toe next morning. The melancholly Widdow Manlove is fond of number Three to Superstition, especially when tis apply'd to Husbands, and the nightly civilitys which all loveing Husbands ought to pay to their Wives, to preserve the peace of the Family.

14. Then Five is counted happy because we shou'd have just so many Sences, tho' naturallists pretend to say, that those Females of us who have Golden Locks are gifted with six. The Dutchess of Altana has so much faith in this number that she hates to stir abroad with less than 5 Footmen behind her coach.[1] so many she must have with her, tho' she go no where but to the shops, where she is sure to pay for every thing in full proportion to her Equipage. Indeed once upon a Fast-day Her Grace was so humble as to go to church with no more than four. But behold the consequence, the great coach was overturn'd, the foreglass shatter'd all to peices, and the Lady handed in the utmost disorder out of one of the Windows. So that great Oracle of Equity, Count Bribantio had a vast partiality for Five, provided it had three significant cyphers after it. Insomuch that whenever his Eys happen'd to be dazzled with this charming number, especially when it cou'd be made Guineas, his Whigg-Integrity all forsook him in an instant. Under so powerfull a temptation he cou'd not forbear prosti-

[1]See above, p. 211.

tuting the Kings conscience of which he was the unworthy Keeper, and quite forgot that he was the Guardian of the Widdow and the Fatherless.

15. Number Seaven is also counted fortunate because there happen to be so many Planets which influence our Fortunes, and bear the blame of all our Faults. Besides every Seventh day is a Holy day to all the Parish, except the Parson, who is content to be idle all the rest of the Week. There were also seven Wondows [*sic*] of the world, and Seaven champions to destroy monstors, and relieve distressed Damsels. For these Reasons whenever Madam Wool-sack thinks it proper to purge for the benefit of her complexion, she conjures her Apothecary to prepare a Dose that will give her exactly Seaven Stools. Mr. Squirt understands her constitution so nicely, that he can help Her Lad[p] precizely to that wholesome number, provided she will abate something of those Indulgences, with which she pampers her self upon other days. Squire Sparerib has reason to think 7 a happy number, because he repents duly once in Seaven years, of haveing made so many Cuckolds in the city, and so many Cullys at the other end of the Towne. The reason of his Septennial Repentance is plain, he suspects every 7th year to be something of a Climacterick, and consequently to threaten his life. When this sad Revolution comes on, the poor 'Squire is in great agonys, he fasts his Scragged Carcass to a Skeleton, and out-prays a repenting Harlot. If then he stink for fear at the approach of the Smaller Climactericks, he'll surely dye for fear, when the great one stares him in the face. But this number never discovers its vertue so strongly as in the Seventh Son. Others come to Eminence in the Faculty by hard Study and diligent observation, or at least by writeing merry Poems, or by seeming good natur'd and tender of their Patients: but these are taught by Nature & are Doctors born. The Reverend Mr. Arse-smart is one of these Sons of Art, who works wonders among ye Ladys by strokeing them gently with

his hand in some sensible part, by which he dispossesses them of all their distempers. He has most success among those Wives, who have Fumblers for their Husbands, and gains their hearts by prescribeing Bath or Tumbridge [*sic*], where they're sure to meet with more agreable company than they leave at home, and have opportunitys of trying the most effectual Remedy. (Nine is without question an auspicious Number because there are so many Muses, which preside over as many liberal Arts. These harmonious Goddesses warm the Poets Imaginations with many ingenious conceits, and teach them to flatter our vanity most agreably. Tis by the inspiration of the tunefull Nine, that those gentle Sounds of Angel Charms, Heart, Passions, Flames and Sighs are join'd so musically together that no Female can read them without Rapture. Who can doubt the happiness of this Number, who remembers that a child is brought to perfection in nine months, and that a Puppy can see in so many days. Dozini has exactly nine storys which he tells over a pipe with a very good grace, but rather with too much deliberation. He takes a Whiff regularly at every comma, and hauks up the Phlegm at each of the longer pauses. His Jokes might pass well enough at a city-clubb, while they were new, but his acquaintance have now heard them so often that they're forc't to turn the laugh from the story to the Historian. However he is so happy as not to discern the difference, but believing tis the Jest that makes 'em so merry, will be sure to bless them with it again, when they have the good fortune to light into his company. Mrs. Metre,[1] who with great content cou'd hear her Self call'd the British Sappho, wrote a Poem with precizely nine Canto's to be sure in complement to the nine muses. Had she publisht it with that lucky number, it had met with as much applause as the Spectators,[2] which are in nine Volumes, but most

[1] *I. e.* Anne, Countess of Winchelsea. See above, p. 244.

[2] After Addison and Budgell discontinued *The Spectator* in December, 1714 (Vol. 8), William Bond and George Dewell, who appear to have had connection with the Button's Coffeehouse group, revived the *Spectator* with semiweekly numbers from Jan. 3, 1715 to Aug. 1, for 59 numbers, which consti-

unfortunately adding a tenth canto, purely to hook in the elegant description she had made of a Sigh, all the Poem miscarry'd, or the Sigh being handed about fell into the Enimys hands, and was foully burlesqued into a Fart. This put our Sappho into more than a poetical fury, insomuch that she committed the whole Work, foul coppy & all to the merciless flames, the ungratefull Towne, as she modestly express't her self, not being worthy of the Performance.

17. What good Christian can question but Eleven is a fortunate number, when they were just so many Stanch Apostles, which continued faithfull to their Master, and what true Briton but must be fond of the same number, when he remembers that King William & Queen Mary were crown'd the 11th of April, and thereby Secur'd the Libertys of these Kingdomes. Abstemio wisely reasons Temperance the Security of all the other vertues, and therefore tyes himself up to eat no more than just eleven mouthfulls. Once dineing at the polite table of count Eliganti, he ventur'd upon 13, and his passions were so inflam'd that when he went home, he was within a hair's breadth of ravishing his maid. Chatterella almost adores this number because the Tyrany she endur'd from her Lordly Husband expired in eleven years. Dureing that dismal time she enjoy'd no Peace not even in her Slumbers, which were disturb'd with the fancifull

---

tuted the ninth volume in the subsequently published edition of the *Spectator.* The Bodleian Catalogue shows it listed in the Hole Catalogue as follows: "3rd ed. Vol. 9, nos. 636-696 [Hole 8° 911] Lond. 1721." (Walter Graham, *English Literary Periodicals* [New York, 1930], p. 86, and letter of Professor Graham to the editor, dated May 27, 1941). The *Camb. Bibliog. of Eng.* Lit., II, 603, lists the following reprints of *The Spectator:* 7 vols., 1714 (bis); 8 vols., 1718; 8 vols., 1720; 9 vols., 1723 (vol. ix = Bond's continuation); 8 vols., 1724; 16 vols., 1724 (priv. ptd. for the authors).

The rare nine volume edition of the *Spectator* was listed in the library of Byrd (Bassett, p. 423). Peter Jefferson also owned the nine volume set in his library (*Va. Mag.*, X, 391), but it was probably burned when fire destroyed the Jefferson home, Shadwell, on Feb. 1, 1770, for his son Thomas wrote his young friend John Page lamenting the loss in the fire of every paper he had in the world and almost every book (Henry S. Randall, *The Life of Thomas Jefferson,* 1858, I, 58-9). R. S. Crane, and F. B. Kaye, *Census of British Newspapers and Periodicals, 1620-1800* (Chapel Hill, 1927), list no copy of the rare vol. IX in this country.

repitition of the brutal treatment she receiv'd when she was awake. The truth of it is, had she been mistress of that rare gift of Silence, she might have come off better. For when her Husband found himself out-worded by his reproaching consort, (and what man is a match for a Woman at those weapons) he thought himself obliged in order to preserve his authority, to make use of Blows. Thus poor Chatterella's Bones paid dear for the Flippancy of her Tongue, and all the comfort she had amidst so many Stripes, was, that they perfectly cur'd her of the vapours. All her misfortunes were real after that, and by no means hysterick or imaginary.

18. But nothing can be said in favour of that ungracious Number Thirteen, and why it shou'd be so unfriendly too wou'd puzzle even Pythagoras himself, or the great Sr Isaac Newton. A late virtuoso tells us indeed, that of those who dine at good Tables, Death takes every year one out of 13. This I confess is enough to bring that number into disgrace, among men of tast & Spirit, who choose a merry life and a short, but why it shou'd do so with those temperate People, who never make a full meal except it be abroad, I cant unriddle. There's Maj^r^ Thrift who lives by Rule in his own House, and walks round the Park, after dinner to digest a Poacht-Egg, has Such dismal apprehentions of 13 at Table, that he wou'd not be one of the number, tho' he were to eat with my Lord Lavish, and carry off the Plate with which the Side-board is loaded, when he had done, yet the Maj^r^ likes 13 well enough, when he go's to market, and can with much haggleing get so many Sprats to the dozen. My good Lady Junket carrys her destestation [*sic*] of this unlucky number much farther and tho' she loves her gut more than other Females do a coach & six, or Fine Cloaths, yet she once refus'd to tast a Pye, because it had 13 ortolans[1] in it, and this too when Lent was just ended, and there was not a morsel of any think else for Supper. How unfortunate was the Curiosity

[1]A species of bunting, a small bird especially desired for its delicate flavor.

which made her Lad^p inquire how many of those rare Birds were immur'd in the Crust? But certain it is, that the moment her question was answer'd, She lay'd down her Knife & Fork, retir'd from the Table, and pretended she cou'd not eat, tho' her poor Guts croakt all the while at their disappointment.

19. I believe verily who ever blunders and throws down the Salt at Table, will pay for it by some dire misfortune. The Reason's as plain as Miss Primsy's affectation, for in former days salt us'd to make the Feasts of the Gods savory, and has always been usefull to man in seasoning his Soups and his Venison-pastys. It was also made use of heretofore in contracts and covenants, with design to keep them from breaking, just as we use it now to preserve our Beef and our Pork from corrupting. Therefore if it be unlucky to knock down an innocent Robin-red-breast or a swallow, because they do no harm, it must be much more unlucky, to throw down our Salt, that dos so much good. This was sufficiently verify'd in Voracio once at a City Feast, who, as he was reaching in too great a Hurry for a slice of Westphalia,[1] happen'd to over-set one of the dirty Salts (it seems the Lord Mayor's utensils are all of this base metal, for fear his Fellow citizens shou'd pocket them up with the Sweet-meats.) Immediately upon this Disaster, a grave Aldermans Lady, who was indeed old and ugly enough to be a Witch, bad him beware, or Some mischief wou'd betide him. Voracio instead of being thankfull for this sage admonition, only answer'd her Lad^p with a very ingenious Horse-laugh not having time to wast upon idle Repartees. But the omen Soon overtook him, for being incautiously engag'd with a Plate full of Marrow Pudding, one of the Splinters of the Bone stuck so fast in his Throat, that it needed all the skill of the handy Forcipio to pluck it out. Just so Mrs. Hiccup one Sunday in her zeal to help Mr. Cant to a Tit-bit, after preaching his Congregation into a Lethargy, and himself

[1]The famous Westphalia ham.

into Convulsions, had the mishap to Spil the Salt. Tongue cant express the agonys she was in upon this accident. She burst into Such a flood of Tears, that all the other fountains of her body were dry'd up for Six & thirty hours. She beat her breast wrang her hands, and cry'd in mournfull accents, alas Mr. Cant I'm undone. The good man was full of astonishment at this Sudden outcry & stood aghast with his mouth wide open, & his Eyes fixt in his head. But learning at length the cause of this sore affliction, he did all he cou'd to pacify her, but he might sooner have pacify'd the shakeing fit of an ague. There was but one thing in nature cou'd comfort her, and that stood in a corner cup-board of her closet, and had often asswaged her afflictions, when nothing else wou'd. Thither She retir'd for Relief, but swallowing the consolation too greedily, a few Drops went the wrong way, and had infallibly choakt her, had not good Mr. Cant, with great presence of mind set her that moment on her head, and with the end of a Tobacco-pipe, which he always carry'd about him, powerfully blow'd wind into her Tail.

20. In short I believe in the Philosophers-stone, the perpetual motion, the squareing of the circle, the tameing of a Shrew, and what is more incredible than all the rest, I believe in the constancy and Fidelity of Man. Just as my mother and Grandmother did before me, I believe all the dear creature urges about his Passion is punctually true, that his Sighs flow directly from his heart, that his Flames are unfeigned, and his addresses have never the least squint upon my Fortune, but are all fairly meant to my Person. That all the Sweet things that fall from his enchanting lips concerning the Lightening of my Eyes, the Bloom of my complexion, the easiness of my shape, the smartness of my Wit, and the engageing Turn of my Conversation, are Truths as evident as that our sex is vain, and loves to be neatly flatter'd. I believe that dear delightful man will prove as constant to my Charms, as the Tydes are to the Moon, and like them

his love will flow at least twice every Four and Twenty hours. I believe that his oaths, and his vows, and his protestations will be all performed to a tittle, without the least grains of allowance. I believe these Eyes of mine will fix his Wandering heart, tho' til the moment it felt their power, it was more wavering than the Wind, and rather than not change at all, wou'd change for the Worse, like the rovering Fly, which after being cloy'd with hony, wants something Savory, and longs to finish its Repast upon a T. . . d. Nay I believe in my conscience, that tho' my Adorer loves Wine, and wenches, and gameing, more fondly than Pamperoni loves his Gut, yet my superior Prudence and attractions are sufficient to reclaim him, and to reform his wayward Inclinations into a loyal, confin'd, serious, harmless conjugal Love.

O Woman, great is thy Faith!

INDEX TO THE DIARY*

A

Ambler, Richard, **1741**, May 3.
Anderson, Mrs. Charity, **1739**, Dec. 21.
Anderson, Charles, **1739**, Sept. 1, Dec. 20, 21; **1740**, Jan. 24, 25, July 7, 8; **1741**, June 19, Aug. 3. 4.
Anderson, Charlotte, **1740**, July 22; **1741**, Mar. 11, 12.
Anderson, Frances, **1740**, Jan. 28, 29.
—sister of, **1740**, Jan. 29.
Anderson, Henry, **1739**, Sept. 1.
Anderson, Jane, **1740**, July 20, 21, Aug. 14, 24; **1741**, Mar. 15, May 31.
Anderson family, **1739**, Dec. 25.
Anderson's pills, **1739**, Aug. 11.
Appomattox, **1741**, Mar. 28.
Armistead, Col. Henry, **1740**, Nov. 30.
Assembly, **1740**, June 17, Aug. 28.
Attorney, Mr., *see* Barradall.

B

Backurst, John, **1739**, Aug. 14.
Balls, **1740**, June 17, Oct. 30.
Banister, John, **1740**, Apr. 5, 6, 7, 8, May 14 (wife's death); **1741**, June 17, July 7, 8.
Barradall, Edward, **1739**, Dec. 11, 12; **1740**, Apr. 14, 19, 28, June 18, Aug. 6, 28, Oct. 31, Nov. 3, 4, Dec. 10; **1741**, Apr. 18, 30.
Barradall, Mrs., **1741**, Apr. 15, May 5.
Bartram, John, **1739**, Aug. 10.
Bassett, Col. William, **1739**, Dec. 13; **1740**, Apr. 7, Nov. 5; **1741**, Apr. 21, July 13, 14.
—daughters of, **1740**, Apr. 7.
Bassett, Mrs. William (Elizabeth Churchill), **1740**, Apr. 28, Nov. 5.
Batte, Henry, **1741**, July 13.
Berkeley, Mr., **1741**, May 6, 7.
Beverley, Elizabeth, **1740**, July 13, Aug. 14.
Beverley, G-th-r, **1740**, Aug. 1, Sept 7.
Beverley, Col. William, **1740**, Apr. 23, 25, 26.
Beverley, Mrs. William (Elizabeth Bland) and her child, **1740**, June 5.
Bickerton, Capt. John, **1740**, Mar. 6.
Blair, The Rev. James, **1739**, Dec. 10, 11; **1740**, Apr. 17, 20, 27, May 5, June 9, 10, 12, 14 (made Acting Governor), 15, 18, Aug. 5, 6, 26, 28, 29, Oct. 22, 26, 28, 30, Nov. 2, 4, Dec. 8, 9, 10; **1741**, Feb. 24, 25, Apr. 15, 19, 21, 25, 26, 28, June 8, 9.
Blair, John, **1741**, May 4.
Bland, Col. Richard, **1740**, Sept. 16, Nov. 28; **1741**, July 9.
—cousin of, **1740**, Sept. 16; **1741**, July 9.
Bland, Theodorick, **1741**, June 3.
Bolling, Maj. John, **1740**, July 24, Sept. 14, 17; **1741**, June 1.
Bolling, Col. Robert, **1739**, Dec. 10; **1740**, May 7, 8.
Bolling, Mrs. Robert (Anne Cocke), **1741**, Mar. 19.
Bolling, Capt. Thomas, **1740**, June 20, 22, 30, July 6, 15, Aug. 1, 2, 3, 7, 9, 10, 11, 15, Sept. 6, 7, 11, 14, 18.
Books, **1740**, Sept. 6; **1741**, June 18.
Booth, Thomas, **1739**, Dec. 12; **1740**, Mar. 6.
Branch, Capt. Thomas, **1740**, Dec. 4.
Braxton, George, **1739**, Dec. 22; **1741**, June 15.
—son, and young Mary, **1739**, Dec. 22.
Bricklayer, **1741**, Jan. 26.
Bridges, Charles, **1739**, Aug. 27; **1740**, July 23.
Brun (Le Brun), Mrs. Caton De Wert, **1739**, Aug. 10, 14, 15, 28, 30, Sept. 7, Dec. 28; **1740**, Mar. 10; **1741**, Mar. 26, 27, May 30, 31, Aug. 2, 5.
Brun, Miss Caton, **1739**, Aug. 10, 14; **1740**, Jan. 5, 13; **1741**, Mar. 22, 24, Apr. 29, May 12, June 3, July 19, Aug. 15, 18.
Brun, Mary Ann, **1739**, Aug. 14.
Brunswick, **1740**, Apr. 9.
Building, **1740**, Sept. 20.
Burwell, Lewis, **1740**, May 11.
Bushrod, Richard, **1740**, June 17, Aug. 6.

---

*It would be manifestly impossible to index such a work as this detailed journal with any completeness. We have tried to include all names of persons and places, all important biographical and historical events, and the more important subject references.

The reference is to date of entry rather than to the printed page. The diarist used the new-style calendar throughout.

Footnotes are included in the entry to which they are appended.

Unidentified names are indexed in skeleton form as they appear in the Diary.

Byrd, Anne (Nanny), **1739**, Aug. 16, 28, Dec. 5 (proposals); **1740**, Feb. 5 (birthday), Oct. 21, 22, 30, Nov. 5; **1741**, May 12, July 21.
Byrd, Evelyn, **1739**, Aug. 27.
Byrd, Jane (Jenny), **1739**, Aug. 16; **1740**, Mar. 28; **1741**, Mar. 11, 12, 13, 14, July 28.
Byrd, Maria (Molly), **1739**, Aug. 16; **1740**, Jan. 16 (birthday), May 20; **1741**, Jan. 16, Apr. 14, 16, 17, May 2, 5, 6.
Byrd, Wilhelmina (Mina), **1739**, Aug. 14, 27; **1740**, July 19; **1741**, Mar. 4, Apr. 14, 16, 17, May 2, 5, 6, 21, July 23, Aug. 8.
Byrd, William II, visits sick family, **1739**, *Aug.* 14, 28; sends negro to Harrison, 20; loses a slave, 23; ill, *Sept.* 4 ff.; proposals made for daughter, *Dec.* 5, and denied, 6; at Williamsburg, 10-13; attends funeral, 12; visits Col. Bassett, 13; and Daniel Custis, 14; returns home, 15; restores overseer to plantation, 26; scolds Mr. Stevens, 27; abridges old records, 29; celebrates Twelfth Night, **1740**, *Jan.* 7; reads medicine, 24; angry with overseer for selling negroes, 29; journeys to New Kent, *Mar.* 3; visits Daniel Custis, 3, cousin Wilkinson, 4; Major Henry, 5; at Hanover court, 6; returns home, 7, 8; daughters visit at Bassetts', 14; entertains, 16; sends negroes to Meherrin, 20; visits Hilman, 24; prays for health on birthday, 28; excuses self from attending Council, *Apr.* 2; daughters return, 8; sells Richmond lots, 10; in Williamsburg, *Apr.* 14—*May* 6; sells corn, *Apr.* 21; pays debts, *May* 3, 5; doses his people, 7; visits the Falls, 20-23; returns home, 24; visits Williamsburg, *June* 9-19; visits army camp, 10, 18; receives money, 11; visits ship, *Aug.* 1, 11; goes to Williamsburg, 5-7; in Williamsburg, 25-30; sees the camp, 25, 26, 27; takes leave of Governor, 28; goes to Hanover, *Sept.* 1, and sells land there, 4; ill, 21; in Williamsburg, *Oct.* 21; at races, 30; sentences prisoners, *Nov.* 3; goes to Col. Bassett's, 5, and returns home, 6; buys Westover church, 24; takes out windows, 25; at Williamsburg, *Dec.* 8-12; celebrates New Year, **1741**, *Jan.* 1; goes to Williamsburg, 23-26; sends provisions to Mrs. Brun, *Mar.* 27; at Hanover, *Apr.* 1-3; acquires land, 2; at Williamsburg, 14—*May* 1; at York, 2-4; sells goods, 25; visits the Falls and Richmond, 27-30; falls in river, 30; charity to Mrs. Brun, 31; sells land, *June* 1; goes to Williamsburg, 8; tries a man, 9; collects rent, 11; goes to Falls, 14-15; receives goods, *July* 6; reads invoices, 29; summoned to court, *Aug.* 4; goes to Randolphs', 20-21; has fever, 26-29.
Byrd, Mrs. William II (Maria Taylor), **1739**, Aug. 16, 25, 27, Dec. 23; **1740**, Jan. 25, 31, Feb. 18, Mar. 3, 28, Apr. 1, July 5, 6, 7, Aug. 25, Oct. 27, 28, 29, 31, Dec. 2, 20; **1741**, Feb. 24, Apr. 1, May 21, June 1, July 16, Aug. 23, 25, 26, 27, 28, 29.
Byrd, William III, **1739**, Aug. 16, 21, 25; **1740**, Jan. 10, 26, Feb. 21, 22, 24, Mar. 9, 23, 24, Apr. 4, May 18, Aug. 7, Oct. 28, Dec. 25, 27; **1741**, Jan. 8, 9, 10, 11, 12, 25, May 16, 21, July 28, Aug. 1, 2, 15, 16, 17, 24.
B-r-k, George, son of, **1741**, Jan. 6.
B-r-k-l (B-k-r-l), Mrs., **1739**, Dec. 24.
B-r-n, Mr., **1740**, Jan. 27.

C

Carolina, **1739**, Dec. 6.
Carpenter, **1741**, Aug. 10.
Carthagena expedition, **1740**, June 10, 14, Aug. 28 (Governor leaves).
Carter, Col. Charles, **1739**, Aug. 28; **1740**, June 13, 27, 30.
Carter, Mrs. Charles (Mary Walker), **1740**, June 27.
Carter, Elizabeth, **1741**, Aug. 11.
Carter, John (Secretary), **1739**, Aug. 19; **1740**, Jan. 8, Feb. 5, 26, Mar. 18, 26, June 27, 30, Aug. 19; **1741**, Mar. 4, 6, Apr. 14, May 5, July 5, 13.
Carter, Mrs. John (Elizabeth Hill), **1740**, Feb. 26, June 5, 8, Aug. 14; **1741**, Mar. 15, May 31, July 5, Aug. 11, 14.
Cary, Archibald, **1740**, Feb. 5, 7, 9, June 6; **1741**, June 27, Aug. 9, 10.
Cary, Henry, **1740**, Mar. 7, May 20, 22, 27, June 7, July 3; **1741**, May 12, 27, 29, June 14, 16.
Cary, Mrs. Henry (Elizabeth ——),

1740, May 23, 27, June 7; 1741, June 22, 28.
—daughter of, 1740, May 27; 1741, June 22, 28.
—son of, 1740, May 27.
Chamberlayne, Thomas, 1739, Aug. 14.
Chapman, Capt. Richard, 1741, Mar. 5.
Charles City Court, 1739, Aug. 14.
Children, 1739, Aug. 16, Sept. 3; 1740, June 22; 1741, Jan. 4, 29, 30, Feb. 7.
Clack, Capt. William, 1740, Sept. 6, 21.
Coachman, 1740, July 6.
Cockfight, 1740, Mar. 26.
Coffeehouse, 1740, May 1, 3, June 11, Dec. 11.
Cole, Mr. (of Hanover), 1740, Mar. 6.
Cole, William, 1739, Sept. 2; 1740, Feb. 3, July 11.
Cole, *see also* C-l.
Coles, John, 1741, May 28.
Commissary, *see* James Blair.
Cooper, 1741, Aug. 26.
Corbin, Thomas, 1741, July 6.
Corn, 1740, Apr. 21, May 30, Nov. 19; 1741, Mar. 28, 30.
Cotton, 1740, Jan. 29.
Council of State, 1740, Apr. 2, 18 ff., June 9; Commissary made Acting Governor, 14; appoints officers, Aug. 6; keeps Mr. Gooch in place, Dec .10; persuades men-of-war to stay two months, 1741, Feb. 25.
Court, county, 1740, Mar. 6; 1741, Apr. 2, June 3, Aug. 4, 5; *see also under county names.*
Crime, 1740, Nov. 3.
Custis, Daniel, 1739, Dec. 14; 1740, Mar. 3, Dec. 15; 1741, Jan. 7, 10, July 19, 21, 22, 25, 30.
Custis, Col. John, 1740, Oct. 26; 1741, Jan. 7, Apr. 26, July 24.
C-l, 1740, Aug. 1.
C-r-n, Dick, 1740, Sept. 18, 19, 21 (death).

D

Dancey, Francis, 1741, Aug. 4.
Dancing, 1740, Feb. 25, July 3; 1741, Apr. 10, June 16, 20.
Dandridge, Maj. John, 1739, Dec. 14.
Davenport, Frances, 1741, Mar. 19.
Dawson, Mr., 1741, Apr. 24.
Dering, Edward, 1740, July 3, 5; 1741, Jan. 30, Mar. 1, 2, 7, 9, 22, 23, 29, Apr. 12, May 23, June 14, 17, July 4, 14, 25, 31, Aug. 1.
De Wert, *see* Brun.
Diet, rules of, 1740, May 31.
Digges, Col. Cole, 1740, June 10.
Dinwiddie, Robert, 1741, June 8, July 7.
Doctor, *see* Mollet *or* Tschiffeley.
Donald, James, 1740, Apr. 9.
Dreams, 1740, Feb. 12, Mar. 18, Dec. 20; 1741, Apr. 24.
Duke, Mrs., 1739, Dec. 30; 1740, Feb. 2; 1741, July 19, 23, 27.
Dunlop, Capt. Colin, 1740, Feb. 10, Mar. 20, Apr. 9, May 18, June 2; 1741, Mar. 15.
D-l-t-n, Capt., 1741, Aug. 24.
D-n-l, Mr., 1740, Apr. 9, June 8.
D-v-s, Mr., 1740, May 22.

E

England, 1739, Aug. 29; 1740, Nov. 30, Dec. 5.
Eppes, Col., 1740, May 11, July 20, Sept. 11; 1741, Mar. 15, Apr. 12, May 10, 24, July 19.
Eppes, Mr. (and his sister), 1741, May 16.
Eppes, Mrs., 1740, Aug. 24.
Eppes, Capt. Edmund (Ned), 1740, Sept. 11; 1741, Mar. 15, May 22, 23, June 7, July 6, 22.
Eppes, Mrs. Edmund (Henrietta Maria Hardyman), 1741, June 7.
Eppes, Lewellin, Jr., 1741, May 22.

F

Fairfax, Col. William, 1741, May 3.
Fairfax, Mrs. William (Deborah Clarke), 1741, Apr. 25, May 3.
Falling Creek, 1740 May 21.
Falls Plantation, 1739, Aug. 11, Dec. 16, 18, 30; 1740, Jan. 6, 7, 12, 18, 20, 22, 24, 27, Feb. 2, 9, 13, 16, 18, Mar. 7, 9, 15, 29, Apr. 5, 8, May 20, June 28, 29, July 10, 12, 20, Aug. 2, Nov. 8, 11, 12, 13, 15, 22, 24, 29, Dec. 13; 1741, Jan. 6, 7, 21, 22, 26, 27, Feb. 19, 20, 21, 22, 28, Mar. 7, Apr. 4, 11, May 11, 28, June 7, 13, 14, 15, 18, 19, 20, 27, July 5, 11, 18, 30, Aug. 1, 29.
Ferry, 1740, Apr. 14, May 5, 6, June 19, July 20, Aug. 5, 7, 30; 1741, Jan. 23, May 6.
Fishing, 1740, May 22, July 11.
Fontaine, Mr., 1740, Nov. 24, 25; 1741, Mar. 14, Aug. 2, 3.
Fontaine, Francis, 1740, May 19.
Fontaine, The Rev. Peter, 1739, Sept. 2, 3; 1740, May 11, 12, Sept. 14;

1741, June 7.
Ford, Edward, 1740, May 19.
Francis, Richard, 1740, Apr. 27; 1741, Apr. 16.
Fraser, The Rev. George, 1740, Feb. 5-7, May 20; 1741, Apr. 1, May 29, June 16, Aug. 31.
Fraser, Mrs. George, 1740, May 20; 1741, June 16.
Friend, Capt. Charles, 1740, Aug. 3.
Fry, Mr., 1740, Apr. 27.
Furnea (Fornea), Stephen, 1740, Nov. 5.
F-k-l-r, Mr., 1739, Aug. 15, Sept. 7.
F-s-t-r, Mrs., 1740, Mar. 4.

G

Gardener, 1740, Apr. 11, May 13, July 26, 29, 30; 1741, May 6, 7, 20, July 5, 6, 29.
Gavin, The Rev. Anthony, 1740, June 2, 4, 7.
Gavin, Mrs. Anthony (Rachel ——), 1740, June 2, 4.
Gay, Dr. William, 1740, May 23; 1741, June 14.
Gay, Mrs. William (Elizabeth Bolling), 1741, June 16.
General Court, 1739, Dec. 11, 14; 1740, Apr. 15-19, 21-May 5, June 10, Nov. 2, Dec. 9; 1741, Apr. 15, 18, May 5, June 9.
George II, King of England, 1740, Oct. 30, Dec. 10.
German settlers, 1739, Aug. 10; 1740, June 2; 1741, May 28.
Gooch, Col. William, 1739, Aug. 27, Dec. 11; 1740, Apr. 14, 15, 19, 22, 27, May 2, 4, June 10, 12, 14, 17, 18, Aug. 5, 25, 28, Oct. 23, 25, Nov. 4, Dec. 9; 1741, Feb. 25, Apr. 14, 26, May 4, June 8, July 30.
Gooch, Mrs. William (Rebecca Stanton), 1741, June 10.
Gooch, William, 1740, Dec. 10; 1741, Apr. 17.
Goode, Robert, 1740, Feb. 13.
Goodman, Capt. Thomas, 1740, Apr. 4.
Governor, *see* Col. William Gooch.
Graffenried, Mrs. Barbara Needham, 1740, July 17, 18.
Gray, Capt., 1740, July 13, 20.
Greenhill, Mrs. Frances Taylor, 1740, Jan. 6, 8, 9, 10, Feb. 17, 18; 1741, Mar. 9, 11, June 24, Aug. 3, 4, 11.
Grymes, Col. John, 1739, Dec. 12; 1740, Apr. 15, 26, May 3, June 13, 14, 15, 16, 17, Aug. 6, Oct. 27, 28, 31, Nov. 3, 4, Dec. 10, 11; 1741, Apr. 17, 20, 24, 27, 30, May 2, 5.
Grymes, Mrs. John (Lucy Ludwell), 1740, Apr. 20.
Grymes, John, Jr., 1740, Nov. 8 (death).
G, Mr., 1739, Aug. 20, 21.
G-n-s, Mrs., 1741, May 25.
G-r-n-r, Tom, 1739, Dec. 19, 20, 21; 1741, Jan. 30.
G-r-v, Mrs., 1739, Dec. 28.

H

Hall, John, 1739, Dec. 20; 1740, May 7, 8, 9, July 10, 11, Aug. 11; 1741, July 8, 9.
Hall, Mrs. John (Anne Bolling), 1740, July 10; 1741, July 9.
Hampton (or Hamilton), 1739, Aug. 29; 1740, Feb. 27, 29.
Hamilton, Mr., 1741, Mar. 5.
Hanover, 1739, Aug. 12; 1740, Mar. 5-7, Sept. 1-4, Nov. 10, Dec. 24; 1741, Apr. 1.
Hanover Court, 1739, Aug. 12; 1741, Apr. 2.
Harding, Cap. William, 1740, Apr. 13; 1741, Apr. 22.
Hardyman, Capt. Francis, 1740, Apr. 7, May 6, June 5; 1741, Feb. 26, June 11, July 23 (death).
—son of, 1741, Mar. 29.
Hardyman, Littlebury, 1740, Dec. 25, 27.
Hardyman, William, 1740, Feb. 3, 17, Nov. 30, Dec. 7; 1741, Jan. 15, May 10.
Hargrave, Mrs., 1740, June 18.
Harmer, John, 1741, Aug. 11.
Harris, Benjamin, 1739, Aug. 14; 1740, Sept. 18; 1741, Aug. 4.
Harrison, Anne, 1741, Mar. 2.
Harrison, Col. Benjamin, 1739, Aug. 20, Dec. 17; 1740, Mar. 19, May 12, July 13, Aug. 16; 1741, Mar. 31, July 1.
Harrison, Mrs. Benjamin (Anne Carter), 1740, Feb. 12; 1741, Mar. 18.
Harrison, Benjamin, Jr., 1741, Apr. 5.
Harrison, Elizabeth, 1741, Mar. 2, June 19.
Harrison, the smith, 1739, Dec. 26.
Hartwell, The Rev. Richard, 1740, Apr. 20.
Harvesters, 1740, June 23, 24, 26; 1741, June 29.
Henrico Court, 1741, June 1.

Henry, Maj. John, 1740, Mar. 5, Sept. 2, 3; 1741, Apr. 1, 2.
Henry, The Rev. Patrick, 1740, Sept. 2, 3; 1741, Apr. 2.
Hilman, 1740, Mar. 24.
Hutchins, Capt., 1740, Apr. 21.

J

Jamaica, 1741, May 2.
Johnson, Philip, 1739, Dec. 5, 6.

K

Kemp, Matthew, 1739, Dec. 12 (funeral).
Kennon, William, 1740, July 24.
Kensington, 1740, May 21; 1741, May 29.
King William County, 1740, Nov. 8, 14.

L

Land, 1739, Aug. 10; 1740, Mar. 5, 6, Sept. 3-5, Nov. 11, 12; 1741, Apr. 2, May 9, June 1, 2, Aug. 10, 25, 26, 31.
Lawyers, 1741, July 19, Aug. 27; *see* Walthoe.
Lee, Col. Thomas, 1741, Apr. 25.
Lidderdale, John, 1740, June 11, Aug. 11, Nov. 1.
Lightfoot, Col. Philip, 1740, June 13; 1741, May 2, 3.
Lloyd, Capt., 1740, Dec. 9; 1741, Feb. 25.
Long Bridge, 1740, Sept. 2.
Ludwell, Philip, 1740, Nov. 30.
Lynch, Head, 1740, Dec. 10.
L-s-n, Tom, 1739, Dec. 26.
L-v-y, Ned, 1741, Mar. 30, July 31.

M

Mangohick, 1740, Nov. 8.
Mapsco church, 1740, Dec. 8.
Marrable, Capt., 1741, Mar. 20.
Mayo, Maj. William, 1740, Aug. 4, 5.
Medicine, 1739, Aug. 11, Dec. 8, 31; 1740, Jan. 13, 24, 31, Feb. 14, Mar. 31, Apr. 2, 8, May 12, June 5, July 7, 26, 30, Sept. 20, 21; 1741, Aug. 28.
Meherrin, 1739, Dec. 15; 1740, Mar. 20, 25, July 3, 6, Nov. 9, 10, 27, Dec. 3; 1741, Jan. 14, Mar. 19, May 14.
Mercer, James, 1740, June 17, Aug. 6.
Mercer, John, 1740, Apr. 23.
Militia, 1740, June 10, 14, 18, Aug. 6, 25, 26, 27.
Miller, Hugh, 1741, Mar. 16, June 4, 5, July 26, Aug. 7.
Miller, Mrs. Hugh (Jane Bolling), 1741, June 4, 5, 24, July 12, 26, 31, Aug. 7, 11.
Mills, Maj. Nicholas, 1740, Aug. 30, Sept. 2-5.
Minx, 1739, Aug. 15, Sept. 7; 1740, Jan. 20, 22; 1741, June 29.
Mollet, Dr., 1740, June 13, 18, Nov. 4, Dec. 1, 2, 7, 11; 1741, Feb. 10, 11, 20, 24.
Monger, Dr., 1740, Jan. 29, Sept. 14, 16, 19, 21, Nov. 30; 1741, Aug. 28, 31.
Mount Folly, 1740, Mar. 17, Dec. 11; 1741, Mar. 24, Aug. 10.
Mumford, James, 1741, Apr. 28.
Mumford, Robert, 1740, Jan. 13, 14, Oct. 29; 1741, June 3, 17.
Music, 1741, Mar. 1.
M-l-t-r, Capt., 1740, Nov. 10.
M-r-t, Dr., 1740, June 18, Aug. 7, 11, 16, 19, 20.

N

Needler, Benjamin, 1739, Dec. 12; 1740, Apr. 18, 26, May 3, June 15, 18, Aug. 27, Oct. 21, 22, 23, Nov. 1, 4, Dec. 11.
Needler, Mrs. Benjamin (Alice Corbin), 1741, Apr. 15, 18, 25, May 2, 5.
Negroes, 1739, Aug. 23, 1740, Jan. 29, Mar. 20.
Nelson, Miss, 1741, Mar. 2.
Nelson, Thomas, 1741, May 3.
Nelson, William, 1741, Feb. 23, Mar. 2, May 2, 4.
Nelson, Mrs. William (Elizabeth Burwell), 1741, Feb. 23, Mar. 2.
New England, 1740, Nov. 26.
New Kent County, 1740, Mar. 3-7.

O

Oats, 1740, July 7; 1741, July 7.
O-n-c-l-s, Isham, 1741, Jan. 15.

P

Page, Mr., 1741, May 16.
Page, Mrs. Judith Carter, 1740, Mar. 26.
Page, Mann, 1740, May 11.
Parks, William, 1741, Feb. 19.
Parrish, Mrs., 1739, Dec. 8.

Pennsylvania, 1739, Dec. 6.
Peyton, Sir Yelverton, 1740, Feb. 24; 1741, Feb. 25.
Pictures, 1741, July 31, Aug. 3, 5, 8, 12, 17, 18.
Pinkard, Thomas, 1739, Dec. 25; 1740, July 27, Aug. 1, 24, Nov. 16, Dec. 4; 1741, Jan. 18, Feb. 20, 21, Mar. 27, 28, 29, Apr. 6.
Pinkard, Mrs. Thomas (Frances Anderson), 1740, July 9, 27, Aug. 24, Nov. 16, Dec. 4, 5; 1741, Jan. 5, 18, Feb. 20, 21, Mar. 28, 29, Apr. 6.
Portraits, 1739, Aug. 27.
Poythress, Mrs., 1741, July 26.
President, *see* Blair.
Procter, William, 1740, Jan. 24, 27, Feb. 29, July 26, Aug. 2, 4, 9, Nov. 11, 18, 19; 1741, Mar. 6, May 25, Aug. 9, 13, 17, 19, 31.
P-n-y, Mr., 1740, Aug. 30.
P-r-s, Mr., 1741, June 19, Aug. 14.

R

Races, 1740, Mar. 6, Apr. 22, May 1, 8, Aug. 7, Oct. 30.
Randolph, Beverley, 1739, Dec. 13, 17; 1740, Sept. 6; 1741, Jan. 5, Mar. 17, June 30, Aug. 20.
Randolph, Mrs. Beverley (—— Lightfoot), 1740, Mar. 19; 1741, Jan. 5, Mar. 19, June 30, July 1.
Randolph, young Beverley, 1740, Aug. 1, 3, Sept. 17.
Randolph, Edward, 1740, Apr. 14, June 25, 27, Dec. 17, 18, 19; 1741, July 15.
—son of, 1740, June 25.
Randolph, Elizabeth, 1741, Mar. 19.
Randolph, Capt. Isham, 1739, Sept. 7; 1740, June 14, Aug. 2, 29, Sept. 6; 1741, Aug. 13, 14, 20.
Randolph, Mary, 1741, Mar. 19.
Randolph, Peter, 1740, Aug. 11.
Randolph, Col. Richard, 1740, Aug. 1, 2, Sept. 17; 1741, Mar. 17, Aug. 21.
Randolph, Richard, Jr., 1740, Sept. 7.
Randolph, Lady Susanna, 1740, Apr. 14, 17, 23, 24, 25, 29, 30, May 4, 5, 6, June 9, 11, 12, 14, 18, Aug. 25, 28, 29, 30, Oct. 21, 22, 23, 28, 29, Nov. 2, 4, Dec. 10, 11; 1741, Feb. 24, Apr. 14, 16, 19, 28, May 1, 4, June 10.
Randolph, Col. William II, 1740, Apr. 14, May 6, June 19; 1741, Feb. 26, May 6, Aug. 20.
Randolph, William III, 1741, Mar. 19.
Randolph family, 1740, Sept. 6.
Ravenscroft, Capt. John, 1739, Aug. 29, Dec. 20; 1740, Jan. 27, Feb. 10, Mar. 10, 11, 12, June 1, 8, 20, 22, July 27, Sept. 14, 20; 1741, Jan. 14, Apr. 12, June 4, 5, July 5, 26, 31, Aug. 30.
Ravenscroft, John, Jr., 1741, Mar. 16.
Richmond, 1739, Aug. 10; 1740, Mar. 7, Apr. 10, 11, May 22, 31; 1741, May 28, June 1, Aug. 26.
Roanoke, 1739, Aug. 10, Dec. 19, 24, 31; 1740, Jan. 18, Mar. 9, 10, July 7, Nov. 12, 13, 17, 20, Dec. 15; 1741, Jan. 23, 28, Mar. 27, May 9, June 2, 25, Aug. 7, 10, 23.
Robinson, The Rev. Francis, 1740, May 4.
Robinson, Col. John, 1740, Apr. 26, Dec. 10.
R-s, Miss, 1741, May 12.

S

Secretary, *see* John Carter.
Sermons, 1740, Feb. 17, Mar. 16; 1741, Mar. 15.
Servants, 1739, Aug. 11, 29; 1740, Nov. 9, 10, 11, 14, Dec. 26; 1741, Jan. 21, 23, 24, May 6, 7, July 5, 6, 29, Aug. 23.
Sheep, 1741, June 4.
Ships, 1739, Aug. 29; 1740, Feb. 24; 1741, Feb. 25, Mar. 31.
Shockoe, 1741, May 6.
Shoemaker, 1741, July 22.
Short, Thomas, 1739, Aug. 27, 29.
Slaves, 1739, Aug. 11. *See also* Negroes, Servants.
Smith, Mr., 1740, May 22.
Smith, the, 1739, Dec. 26.
Spalding, Alexander, 1739, Sept. 7; 1740, Feb. 24-26; 1741, Apr. 9, 10, 11.
Spotswood, Col. Alexander, 1740, Apr. 16, 18, June 14 (death).
Spotswood, Mrs. Alexander (Anne Brayne), 1740, June 29.
Spry, Capt. William, 1739, Aug. 23.
Stanton, Robert, 1740, Dec. 9.
Stegge, Thomas, 1739, Aug. 11.
Stevens, Mr., 1739, Dec. 26, 27, 28; 1740, Jan. 28, 29, May 21, June 23, 24; 1741, Feb. 27, 28, July 22, 23.
Stith, Miss, 1739, Dec. 23; 1740, Dec. 5; 1741, Aug. 2.
Stith, Anderson, 1739, Dec. 25; 1740, Dec. 25, 27; 1741, Apr. 5.
Stith, Drury, 1740, Apr. 9.

Stith, Elizabeth, **1740**, July 22, Dec. 4; **1741**, Mar. 11, Apr. 5, July 5.
Stith, Col. John, **1739**, Dec. 25; **1740**, Mar. 28, July 16, 27, Aug. 17, Dec. 4; **1741**, Mar. 15, 27, 28, Apr. 3, 6, May 10, 19, 21, July 26, 27.
Stith, Mrs. John (Elizabeth Anderson), **1739**, Dec. 25; **1740**, Mar. 28, July 16, 19, 27, Aug. 17, Sept. 17, Nov. 16, Dec. 4; **1741**, Mar. 15, 28, Apr. 6, July 26, 27.
Stith, Mary, **1740**, July 20, 21, Dec. 14; **1741**, May 10, 31, July 2.
Stith, The Rev. William, **1740**, June 15; **1741**, Mar. 17, June 1.
Store, **1741**, May 7, June 18.
Surveying, **1740**, Mar. 28.
Swineyards, **1741**, May 14.
Swiss settlers, **1739**, Aug. 10, Dec. 28.

T

Tailor, the, **1741**, Jan. 17, 18.
Talman, Capt. Henry, **1740**, July 11, 15, Sept. 10, 15, 17; **1741**, May 25, June 4, 5, July 3, 8, Aug. 7, 24.
Thornton, Mr., **1739**, Dec. 12; **1740**, Mar. 6.
Tobacco, **1741**, June 3, 15, 26, Aug. 5, 22.
Tschiffeley, Dr. Samuel, **1739**, Aug. 10, Dec. 18, 19; **1740**, Jan. 24, 25, Mar. 7, Apr. 7, 8; **1741**, May 28, June 14, Aug. 29, 30.
Turpin, Thomas, **1740**, Feb. 13.
Twelfth Night, **1740**, Jan. 7.

V

Vaulton, James, **1740**, Apr. 2.
Virginia Gazette, **1741**, Feb. 19, Mar. 22.

W

Wager, Sir Charles, **1740**, Mar. 30.
Walker, Charles, **1740**, June 17, Aug. 6.
Walthoe, Nathaniel, **1741**, Mar. 1, 3, 4, May 23.
Ward, Benjamin, **1740**, Nov. 15, 16, 17, Dec. 20, 21; **1741**, June 6, 14, 15, 16, 20, 27 (death).
—wife and child of, **1741**, June 14.
Warehouses, **1739**, Aug. 27; **1741**, June 15, 26.
Washington, Lawrence, **1740**, June 17, Aug. 6.
Wendy, Thomas, **1739**, Sept. 2, Dec. 16; **1740**, Jan. 27, Apr. 13, June 1, Aug. 31.
Westover, **1739**, Dec. 9; **1740**, Dec. 20, 22; **1741**, May 7, June 18.
Westover Church, **1740**, Nov. 24, Dec. 12; **1741**, Feb. 16.
Wetherburn's tavern, **1739**, Dec. 11; **1740**, Apr. 16, 17, 18, 21-25, 28-30; May 1, 2, June 9, 10, 11, 13, 16, 17, Aug. 6, 26, 28, Oct. 24, 27, 30, Nov. 3, Dec. 9; **1741**, Apr. 16, 20, 22-25, 27-30, May 1, 5, June 9, 10.
Wheat, **1739**, Dec. 30; **1740**, Jan. 2, 3, June 23; **1741**, June 29, 30, July 3, 4, Aug. 6.
Wilcox, Capt. John, **1740**, Apr. 25.
Wilkinson, cousin, **1740**, Mar. 4.
William and Mary College, **1740**, May 19; **1741**, Apr. 24.
Williams, John, **1740**, May 26.
Williamsburg, **1740**, Apr. 2, June 9-19, Aug. 5-7, 25-30, Oct. 21-Nov. 5, Dec. 8-12; **1741**, Feb. 24-26, Apr. 14-May 6, June 8-11.
Wilson, Capt., **1740**, May 18, June 1.
Wood, James, **1740**, Jan. 28, Mar. 27, 28, July 18, Dec. 15, 16; **1741**, Feb. 27, Mar. 10, 11, June 29, 30, Aug. 6, 7, 24.
W-l-s, Capt., **1741**, July 8, Aug. 24.
W-n, Capt., **1740**, Mar. 10; **1741**, Aug. 10.

Y

York, **1741**, May 2.

GENERAL INDEX

A

Abbington, 393.
Abercorn, Lord, 404.
Abram, Old, 341, 351.
Albin, Eleazar, xxiii.
"Altana," 211, 468.
"Altiero, Don," *see* Daniel Parke.
"Amasia," *see* Evelyn Byrd.
America, 424, 425, 440.
Argyle, John Campbell, 2d Duke ("Duke Dulchetti"), xxiii, xxviii, xli, 203, 368, 381.
Armiger, Mrs., 234, 334, 404.
Armistead, Henry, 193; *see Diary.*
Army, the English, 194-96, 205, 249, 277.
"Arroganti," *see* Alexander Spotswood.
Asgill, John, 192.
Auverquerque, Henry Nassau, Count, 239.

B

"Babbina," 197.
Bacon's Rebellion, xiv.
Balon, Monsieur, 266.
Banbury, 393.
Banister, John, xlii; *see Diary.*
Bartholomew Fair, 198.
Bassett, William, 370; *see Diary.*
Bath, xix, xxxv, 253, 461, 470.
Bathing, 222, 284.
Beaufort, Henry Somerset, Duke of, 253.
Beckford, Mr., xli.
"Belinda," 361.
"Bellamira," 242.
Bellenden, Margaret, xxiii.
Berkeley, xxviii.
Berkeley, Edmund, 296, 370.
Betterton, Thomas, 372.
Bible, 417, 418, 419.
Black Swan, 376.
Blackwater River, 219.
Blair, Dr. Archibald, 193.
Blair, The Rev. James, xxxi, xxxii, xli, xlv, 369, 370; *see Diary.*
Blakiston, Col. Nathaniel, 316, 359.
Blathwayt, William, 191.
Bleeding, 428, 438.
Blount, Patty, 213.
"Blouzina" (Lady Howard of Effingham), 201, 234, 267.
Board of Trade, 370.
"Bonboni, Cavaliero," 356, 368.
"Bonini, Cavaliero" (Sir John Huband), 208.
"Bordelio, Lord," 194.
Boundary survey, xxxix-xl.
Boyle, John, Lord, 381.
"Brandivia" (Annie Wilkinson), 361, 363, 364.
Brayne, Anne Butler, 317.
Brayne, John, xxvii.
Brayne, Susan, xxvii.
Brayne, William, xxvii.
Bridges, Charles, 382; *see Diary.*
Bridewell, 274.
"Brillante," 192.
Bruton churchyard, 360.
Buck, Lady Charles, xxvii, 406.
Buck, Sir Charles, 406.
Burgess, Dr. Daniel, 284.
Burnaby, William, xvi.
"Burrard, Mr." (William Byrd), xxvi-vii, 399.
Burrel, William, 407.
Burwell, Lucy, 296.
Burwell, Martha, 193.
Button's coffeehouse, 326, 470.
Byrd, Anne, xl; *see Diary.*
Byrd, Evelyn ("Amasia"), xxii, xxix, xxxiv-v, xl, 323, 381.
Byrd, Jane, xl; *see Diary.*
Byrd, Lucy Parke ("Fidelia"), xliv, 214-20, 290, 291-96.
Byrd, Maria, xl; *see Diary.*
Byrd, Maria Taylor, xxxv, xl, xliv, 386; *see* Mrs. William Byrd II, *in Diary.*
Byrd, Mary Horsmanden Filmer, xv, 195.
Byrd, Wilhelmina, xxii, xxix, xl, 323, 381; *see Diary.*
Byrd, William I, xiv-v, xviii.
Byrd, William II, character of ("Inamorato L'Oiseaux"), xxxvi, 203, 276, 379; diaries of, xiii, xvii, xxi, xxxix; portrait of, 279; tomb of, 206; writings of, xvii-ix, xxi, xxviii-x, xxxv-xl; *see* "Mr. Burrard," "Mr. Orris," *and* "Veramour."
Byrd, William III, xiv, xl, 382; *see Diary.*
Byrd family, 323-24.
B-r-n, Mrs., 298, 314, 316, 317, 319, 321, 339.
B-s, Mrs. ("Cleora"), 361, 362, 364, 367.

C

C——, Lady Betty, 238.
Calverley, Lady, 251, 267, 312.
Calverley, Mary, *see* Lady Sherard.
Caradoc of Llancarvan, *History of Wales,* 391, 393.
Caroline of Anspach, Princess of Wales, xxiii.
"Carotti, Seignour," 219.
Carter, Col. John, xxi; *see Diary.*
Carter, John, 369.
Carter, Robert, 370.
Carthagena, xlv; *see Diary.*
Carton, 393.
Chamberlayne, John, *Magnæ Britanniæ Notitia,* 391, 393.
Characters, writing of, xxxv-vii; *see also* Satires and Lampoons.
"Charmante" (Lady Elizabeth Lee), xxxii-iv, 379.
Cheyne, Dr. George, xliii.
"Clarinda," 236, 238, 240.
Clayton, John, 359, 369.
"Cleora" (Mrs. B-s), 361, 362, 364, 367.
Codrington, Christopher, 376.
Coffeehouses, London, xxiii, 201.
Congreve, William, xviii, xxiv, xxxvii, 202.
Cooke, Sir George, 243, 298.
"Cornelia," 379.
Cornish, Miss, xxvii, 399, 406.
Court, the royal, xxiii, 207, 277.
Coverly, Lady, 208.
Craggs, James, 371.
Crane Court, xxiv.
Creed, Major Richard, 230.
Cromwell, Lady Elizabeth ("Facetia"), xviii-ix, xxxvi, 191, 197, 200, 234, 236, 238, 284.
Cromwell, Oliver, 250, 372, 408.
Cromwell, Richard, 250.
Custis, Frances Parke, 290.
Custis, John, xxi, xxxi, xxxiv, 216, 290, 369; *see Diary.*

D

"De Booby, Chevalier," *see* Sir Edward Des Bouverie.
De Gols, Conrade, 321, 335.
Dennis, John, 269.
Des Bouverie, Sir Edward ("Chevalier de Booby"), xxv, 202, 298, 321, 346, 352, 354, 356.
Des Bouverie, Mary, Lady, 335; *see also* Mary Smith ("Sabina").
Discourse Concerning the Plague, xxviii-xxxi, 411-43.
Dover, Lady, 254.
Drawing, xxiii, 372, 373.
Dreams, 264, 381.
Drury Lane theatre, xxiii.
Dryden, John, 261, 372.
Drysdale, Hugh, xli, 453.
Duels, 356, 403.
"Dulchetti, Duke," *see* Duke of Argyle.
"Dunella," 290.
Dunkellen, Lady (Anne Smith Parker), xxv, 298, 315, 321, 326, 329, 335, 336, 339.
Dunkellen, Michael, Lord ("Tipperari"), xxv, 298, 315, 316, 318, 321, 324, 329, 340, 344, 346, 351, 353, 356, 358.
Dunn, Mrs. ("Incendia"), 290.
Dunn, Sir Patrick, 191.
Dutch Woman, the, 198, 456.

E

"Ebonia," 463.
Education, xv, 208, 253, 280, 286.
Ephesian Matron, the, 224, 235.
"Erranti," xxxiv, 381, 383.

F

"Facetia," *see* Lady Elizabeth Cromwell.
"Fanforoni, Seignor" (Daniel Parke), 220, 223.
Fast, 436.
Fear, 431-32, 437.
Female Creed, The, xxxvii-viii, 445-75.
"Fiddle Faddle, Lord," 201, 363, 365, 367.
"Fidelia," *see* Lucy Parke.
Filmer, Samuel, xv.
Finch, Mrs., 244, 470.
Fitz Herbert, Mrs., xxiv, 200, 341.
Flattery, 230, 239, 279.
"Florinda," 409.
Fontaine, The Rev. Peter, xxx, xli; *see Diary.*
Freind, Dr. John, 449.

G

G——, Lady, 259, 264.
Games, xxiv, xlii.
Gardens, 361.
Garraway's, xxiii.
Garth, Sir Samuel, xxx, xliii, 199, 209, 376.
Gavin, Anthony, xli.
George I, King of England, xxiii.
George, Prince of Wales, xxiii.

"Glysterio, Dr.", 209, 456.
Gooch, Governor William, xli, xlv; *see Diary.*
Green Spring, xxxi.
Gresham College, 191.
Groom porter's, 468.

H

H——, Mrs., 229.
Hackney, 269.
Hamilton, Lady Jane, 409.
Hammond, Mrs., 258.
Handel, Georg Friedrich, 365, 454.
Harbord, Philip, 234.
Hare, Francis, Bp. of Chichester, Psalms, 391, 393.
Harrison, Benjamin, 369; *see Diary.*
Harrison, Elizabeth Burwell, xxviii, xxx.
Harrison, Nathaniel, xxx, 249, 370.
Haymarket theatre, 365.
Heidigger, John James, 298, 365.
Hemp, 274.
Henry, Major John, xlv; *see Diary.*
Herbert, Sir Thomas, *A Relation of Some Yeares Travaile,* 391, 393.
Herbert family, 274.
Hill, Col. Edward, 219, 369.
Hilman, 391, 393; *see Diary.*
Hinchinbrook, Lady Elizabeth, xxvii, 403.
Hoare, Mrs. (Mary Buck), 406, 407.
Hogs Norton, 265.
Holland, 363, 367.
Horsmanden, Daniel, xxiv, 351, 356, 369.
Horsmanden, The Rev. Daniel, 195.
Horsmanden, Susanna, 406, 407.
Horsmanden, Ursula, 406, 407.
Horsmanden, Sir Warham, xv, 195.
Horsmanden family, xxiii, 195, 399, 406.
Howard, Henrietta, Countess of Suffolk, xxiii, xxvi, 381.
Howard of Effingham, Lady ("Blouzina"), 201, 234, 267.
Howard of Effingham, Francis, Baron, xv, 234.
Howe, Sophia, 230.
Huband, Sir John ("Cavaliero Bonini"), 208.
Hunter, Colonel, 219.
Hygiene, 436, 441.

I

"Inamorato L'Oiseaux" (William Byrd), xxxvi, 203, 276, 379.
"Incendia" (Mrs. Dunn), 290-96.
"Incognita, Seignora," 255.
"Indamira," 296.
Indians, xiv, 250.
Ireland, 201.
"Irene," 214, 217, 219, 220, 221.
Ireton, Mrs., 198.
Islay, Archibald Campbell, Lord, xxviii, xli, 261, 381.

J

Jamaica, xli.
James, the Old Pretender, 199.
Jefferson, Peter, 471.
Jeffreys, Molly, 372.
Jenner, Samuel, xxix.
"Jessamin, Sir Fragrant," 220.

K

Kecoughtan, 217.
Kensington Garden, 374.
Kielmansegge, Madame, xxiv.
Killigrew, Thomas, xxiv.
Kings, 287, 288.
Kinsale, 457.
Kneller, Godfrey, 279.

L

Land, 322, 324, 337.
Law, 210, 239, 243-44, 249, 277.
Lawson, Sir Wilfred, xxiv.
Lee, Lady Elizabeth ("Charmante"), xxxii-iv, 379.
Leeward Islands, 221, 376.
Le Grand, Helena (Southwell), xx, 274.
Lepel, Mary, xxiii.
Leprosy, 417.
Lethieullier, Mrs., xxvii, 407, 408.
Lethieullier family, 408.
Letter writing, xxxv, 263, 264, 266, 269, 282, 301-10, 339, 349.
Leveridge's coffeehouse, 316, 353.
Lewis, John, 370.
Lightfoot, Frank, 369.
Lincoln's Inn, 243, 298.
Lincoln's Inn theatre, xxiii, 314.
London life, xxiii-iv.
Lucrece, 376.
"Lucretia," 282, 286.
Ludwell, Philip, xxii, xxxi, 369, 370; *see Diary.*
"Lustabunda," 216.
Lyndseys, the, 399, 406, 407.

M

M——, Lady, 269.
Manners, xvi.
Maryland, xxii.

Masquerades, xxiv, 298, 365, 367, 461, 465.
Medicine, xvii, xxx, xliii, 205, 206, 209-11, 256, 417-43.
"Medusa" (Mrs. Taylor), xxxv, 386.
"Melantha," *see* Lady Sherard.
Messalina, 376.
"Methusalem," 362.
Middle Temple, xvi.
"Minionet," xxxiv, 207, 276, 371-80.
Monmouth, Duchess of, 211.
Montague, Lady Mary (Churchill), Duchess of, xxvii, 403.
"Monymia," 229, 232, 241.
Music, 246.

N

Naval stores, 322.
Negroes, xv, xxv, xliv, 284, 322, 324, 425.
Nevil, Rear-Admiral, 440.
Newton, Sir Isaac, 472.
Nicholson, Col. Francis, xv, 193, 234, 249, 316.
Nicolini, 265, 454.
Nightingale, Pliny's passage on, translated, 246.
Norfolk, Duchess of, 466.
Nott, Governor Edward, 219; epitaph of, 359.

O

Oldmixon, John, xxviii.
"Olibari," *see* John Orlebar.
Opera, 298, 332, 333, 365.
Orkney, Earl of, 359.
Orlebar, John ("Olibari"), 321, 326, 339, 348, 350.
"Ornis, Mr." (William Byrd), 386.
Orrery, Charles Boyle, Earl of, xix, xxiii, xxiv, xli, 207, 381.
Orrery, Roger Boyle, Earl of, 213, 330.
Otway, Mrs., 372.
Ozinda's coffeehouse, xxiii.

P

Page, Miss, 381.
Palms, Guy, 238, 263.
"Panthea," 196.
Parke, Col. Daniel ("Don Altiero," "Seignor Fanforoni"), xx, xxi, xxv, 214, 220, 223, 376.
Parke, Jane Ludwell, 215.
Parke, Frances, 193, 214, 216.
Parke, Lucy ("Fidelia"), xx-xxii, xxix, 193, 214-20; *see also* Lucy Parke Byrd.
Parr, Thomas, 458.
Parsons, Humphrey, 467.
"Parthenissa," 213.
"Pastorella," 253.
Pasquin and Morfario, 260.
"Peakamira," 219.
Percival, John, Earl of Edmont, xx, 207, 208, 324, 370, 399, 457.
Percival, Lady (Catherine Parker), xxvii, 399, 404.
Perry, Mrs., xxiii.
Perry, Micajah, xv, xxii, xxiii, xxv, xxix, xxx, 316, 322, 341, 342, 381.
Perry, Micajah, younger, xxiii, 322.
Perry, Philip, xxiii, 322.
Perry, Richard, xxiii, 322.
Peterborough, Earl of, xxiv, xxxiv-v, 332, 383, 449, 454.
Petkum, Monsieur, xxiii, 326.
Petronius, xvi, 224.
Pharaoh, 417.
Pierson, Mrs., xxv.
Plague, xxviii-xi, 411-43.
Pliny, on the Nightingale, 246.
Polhill, Mrs., xxvii, 408.
Pontack's, xxiv.
Pope, Alexander, 385, 454.
"Preciosa," 270.
"Prudella," 200, 202.
"Pulcherio," 198.
"Punchino, Seignor," 252.
P-t, Mr., 341.

Q

Quakers, 287, 288.
Quarantine, 436, 441.
Queen's theatre, 333.
"Quietissa," 200.

R

Radcliffee, Dr. John, xx, xliii, 253.
Ramillies, 455.
"Rampana," 193, 217, 222, 223.
Rand, uncle, 369.
Randolph, Edward, xlii; *see Diary.*
Randolph, Capt. Isham, xxii, 323; *see Diary.*
Randolph, Sir John, xli, 369.
Randolph, Lady Susannah, xli; *see Diary.*
Ranelagh, Lady Margaret, xxvii, 404.
Religion, xli, xliii, 280.
Richmond, 269.
Richmond Lodge, 310, 311.
Ridotti, 365.
Robinson, Anastasia, xxiv, 332, 384, 454.
Robinson, Margaret, 332.

Rollin, Charles, *Ancient History of the Egyptians,* 391, 393.
Roscow, James, 369.
Royal Society, xvii, xxiv, xxviii, 191, 192, 206, 459.
Russel, William, 211.

S

"Sabina," *see* Mary Smith.
St. Andrew's Parish, 349.
St. Clement Danes, 342, 344.
St. James's Park, xxiii.
St. Leger, Sir Warham, xv.
"Sapiente, Cavaliero," *see* Sir Robert Southwell.
Satires and lampoons, xvi, xix, xxvi, xxxv-viii, 244, 248, 268, 374-75, 399.
Sayer, Dr., 432-33, 435, 437.
Scarburgh, Sir Charles, 459.
Science, xvii, xlii.
Scott, Lady Charlotte, xxvii, 405.
Scott, Lady Isabella, xxvii, 405.
Sedley, Katherine, 212.
"Sempronia," 374, 375, 379.
Senesino, 406, 454.
Servants, xliv, 292.
Seymour, Francis, 404.
Sheppard, Jack, 447, 454.
Sherard, Bennet Sherard, Baron, 228, 251, 267.
Sherard, Lady Mary Calverley ("Melantha"), 228, 251, 257, 268, 312, 313.
Shipton, Mother, 299.
Shirley, xxi.
"Shrimponi, Seignor," 249.
Sloane, Sir Hans, xvii, xxx, xliii, 191, 207.
"Slovena, Cavaliero," 205, 378.
Smallpox, xxii, xxix, 343, 381, 423, 429.
Smith, Captain, 369.
Smith, Mrs. (a bawd), xxiv.
Smith, John, of Virginia, 370.
Smith, John ("Vigilante"), xxv, 298, 299, 316, 321, 335, 340, 344, 347, 349, 350, 351, 353, 356, 357, 358.
Smith, Joseph, 454.
Smith, Mary ("Sabina"), xxv, 202, 298-359, 391, 394.
Socrates, 426.
Somers, John, Lord, 192.
Somerset, Duke of, 254.
Southwell, Anne Blathwayt, 191, 339.
Southwell, Edward, xviii-xix, xxxii, 191, 324, 457.
Southwell, Sir Robert ("Cavaliero Sapiente"), xvi, xix, xxxvi, 191, 206, 376, 378.
Spanish Ambassador, 329, 330, 341, 356.
Spectator, the, 470.
Spencer, Mr., 243.
Spotswood, Alexander ("Arroganti"), xxi-ii, xxxi-ii, xlv, 201, 203, 317, 360, 368, 453; *see Diary.*
Stapleford, 267.
Stegge, Thomas, xiii-xiv.
Strafford, Lady, 465.
"Sufficiento, Count," 204, 256.
Suffolk, Lady, 258.
Swift, Dean, 384.
Sydenham, Dr., 433.

T

Taylor, Maria, xxxv, xl, lxiv, 386.
Taylor, Thomas, xxxv.
Taylor, Mrs. Thomas ("Medusa"), xxxv, 386.
Temperance, 426-27, 437.
Theatres, xvi, xxiii-iv, 198-99, 326.
"Tipparari, Lord," *see* Lord Dunkellen.
Titles, 237-41.
Tobacco, xv, xxi, xxx-xxxi, 274, 287, 322, 393, 424, 428, 436, 438-42.
Tofts, Madame Catherine, 454.
"Torismond," 221.
Treasury, Lords of, 369.
"Trolly," 305, 306.
Tunbridge, Poems on some ladies at, 248.
Tunbridge Wells, xix, xxvi-vii, xxxv, 248, 253, 267, 310, 312, 399, 456, 470.
Tunbrigalia, xxvi-vii, 229, 248, 361, 379, 397-409, 463.
"Turnover, Madame," 301, 309.
Twine, Captain, 393.
Tyburn, 447, 453, 454, 455, 456.

U

Upon a Fart, 245.
Upon a Sigh, 244.

V

Vaccination, 429.
Vanbrugh, Sir John, 333.
Vanity, 231, 255, 274.
"Vaporina," 272.
Venereal disease, 200, 205, 206, 256.
"Veramour" (William Byrd), xviii, xix, 214, 216, 301, 303, 306, 315, 318, 329.
"Vigilante," *see* John Smith.

Vinegar Yard, 210.
Virginia, xxv, xxxix, 287, 318, 322, 324, 337, 347, 359, 368-71, 440.
Virginia Council of State, xv, xx, xxi-ii, xxxi-ii, xl, xlv, 369; *see* Council of State *in Diary*.
Virginia, Governor of, xv, xli, 249, 250, 359, 453.
Virtue, 206, 229, 233-34, 258, 288.

W

Wager, Sir Charles, xxviii, 391, 393; *see Diary*.
Wallingford Castle, 432.
Wallis, Dr. John, 263, 269.
Walpole, Horace, xxiii.
"Wasperini" (—— Herbert), 274.
Weaver, 293.
Westminster Hall, 210.
Westover, xx, xxvii, xl, 290-96, 369, 391, 393.
Wharton, Philip, Duke of, xxxiii.
Whores, xxiv, 195, 199, 200, 205, 232, 256, 274, 280.
Wild, Jonathan, 453.
Wilkinson, Annie ("Brandivia"), 361, 363, 364.
William and Mary College, xlii; *see Diary*.
Williamsburg, xxxi, xl, 359, 369; *see Diary*.
Willis, Dr., 433.
Wills, 385.
Will's coffeehouse, xxiii, 326, 346, 353, 386, 387.
Winchelsea, Anne, Countess of, *see* Mrs. Finch.
Wit, 194, 212, 238, 242, 270.
Wray, Captain, 323.
W-n, Captain, 356.

Y

Young, Edward, xxxiii.

Z

"Zenobia," 259, 260, 261, 263, 264, 266; *see also* Mrs. Pierson.